# The ETS Test Collection Catalog

# The ETS Test Collection Catalog

## Volume 2: Vocational Tests and Measurement Devices
## Second Edition

Compiled by Test Collection,
Educational Testing Service

**Table of Contents**



ORYX PRESS
1995

*The rare Arabian Oryx is believed to have inspired the myth of the unicorn. This desert antelope became virtually extinct in the early 1960s. At that time several groups of international conservationists arranged to have 9 animals sent to the Phoenix Zoo to be the nucleus of a captive breeding herd. Today the Oryx population is over 1,000 and nearly 500 have been returned to reserves in the Middle East.*


4041 North Central at Indian School Road
Phoenix, Arizona 85012-3397



Published simultaneously in Canada
Printed and Bound in the United States of America

∞The paper used in this publication meets the minimum requirements of American National Standard for Information Science—Permanence of Paper for Printed Library Materials, ANSI Z39.48, 1984.

*Library of Congress Cataloging-in-Publication Data*

(Revised for vol. 2)

The ETS Test Collection catalog.

Includes indexes.
Contents: v. 1. Achievement tests and measurement devices—v. 2. Vocational tests and measurement devices.
1. Educational tests and measurements—United States Catalogs. 2. Achievement tests—United States—Catalogs. 3. Occupational aptitude tests—United States—Catalogs. 4. Educational Testing Service—Catalogs. I. Educational Testing Service. Test Collection.
LB3051.E79 1993 016.3712'6 92-36992
ISBN 0-89774-743-7 (v. 1: alk. paper)

# INTRODUCTION

The Test Collection, Educational Testing Service, is an extensive library of approximately 19,000 tests and other measurement devices. It was established to provide descriptive information on tests and assessment materials to those in research, advisory services, education, and related activities. As part of its function, the Test Collection acquires and disseminates information on hard-to-locate research instruments as well as on commercially available standardized tests. Because the Test Collection deals only with tests and evaluation tools, it has been able to provide a reasonable amount of bibliographic control over what has historically been a scattering of information among many and diverse sources.

This catalog describes approximately 1310 vocational measures, and the information is drawn from the Test Collection's database which is available on the Internet through the Gopher at Catholic University of America. The tests described cover all age and grade levels from elementary school through adults. A variety of tests are described: work sample tests, attitude measures, vocational interests, career planning aids, vocational aptitude instruments for particular types of occupations and for various populations, self-assessment measures, and evaluation instruments to use in assessing certain professionals, such as teachers, administrators, and nurses. Measures assessing such areas as organizational climate, managerial style, and interpersonal competence within an organizational setting are also included.

For each entry in the Main Entry section of this directory, the following information is always present: test title, author, descriptors and/or identifiers (subject indexing terms), availability source, and an abstract. Other information, which is provided when available, includes publication or copyright date, number of test items, and the time required for an individual to complete the test. The test descriptions are arranged sequentially by the Test Collection's identification number in the Main Entry section. Commonly used acronyms are referenced in the List of Acronyms on page vi.

There are three indexes that provide access to the main entry section: subject, author, and test title. The Subject Index uses ERIC descriptors from the *Thesaurus of ERIC Descriptors*, 13th edition. Each test title and its unique identification number are listed under the major descriptors assigned to the test, so that there are several subject access points. In addition, some tests may be indexed under major identifiers, which are additional subject indexing terms not found in the *Thesaurus of ERIC Descriptors* but which help in describing the content of the test. In the Author Index, tests and their corresponding identification numbers are listed under the author's name. The Title Index is an alphabetical list of all tests included in the directory and their identification numbers.

The following criteria were used to include a test description in this revised edition; a publication date of 1980 or later; earlier tests where test items are available as a part of a kit or in a book, journal article, or ERIC; and all pertinent tests in the Tests in Microfiche series produced by the Test Collection at Educational Testing Service. There are over 700 new or revised tests in this edition.

Some of the tests referred to in the abstracts are listed in this volume. Check the Title Index to locate these tests. For information about tests not included in this catalog, contact Test Collection at Educational Testing Service.

At the time the test catalog was compiled, all the tests included were still available from the test distributors indicated in the availability source. However, distribution of certain tests may be discontinued by test publishers or distributors, just as new tests may be developed and published.

The staff of the Test Collection will be happy to answer any questions about this catalog or other products and services. Inquires may be addressed to Test Collection, Educational Testing Service, Princeton, NJ 08541.

# LIST OF ACRONYMS

| | |
|---|---|
| **16PF** | Sixteen Personality Factor Questionnaire |
| **ACT** | American College Testing |
| **ACER** | Australian Council for Educational Research |
| **ASTD** | American Society for Training and Development |
| **BCSP** | Board of Certified Safety Professionals |
| **CETA** | Comprehensive Employment and Training Act (1973) |
| **COBOL** | Common Business Oriented Language |
| **DSM** | Diagnostic and Statistical Manual of Mental Disorders |
| **EEO** | Equal Employment Opportunity |
| **FHFMA** | Fellowship Healthcare Financial Management Association |
| **HRD** | Human Resources Development |
| **IPI** | Industrial Psychology International |
| **IPMA** | International Personnel Management Association |
| **NOCTI** | National Occupational Competency Testing Institute |
| **NTE** | National Teacher Examinations |
| **OD** | Organizational Development |
| **PSA** | Professional Self-Assessment |
| **PSI** | Psychological Services Incorporated |
| **TIM** | Tests In Microfiche |
| **USES** | United State Employment Service |

# SAMPLE ENTRY

ETS ACCESSION NO.

**18039**

TEST TITLE

**Common Business Oriented Language Test.** Science Research Associates, Inc., Rosemont, IL 1989.

INSTITUTIONAL AND/OR PERSONAL AUTHOR(S)

TEST PUBLICATION DATE

DESCRIPTORS (*=Indexed Subject Terms)

*Descriptors:* *Computer Assisted Testing; *Knowledge Level; *Occupational Tests; *Personnel Selection; *Programming Languages; *Screening Tests; Adults; Computers

*Identifiers:* *COBOL Programming Language

IDENTIFIERS (*=Indexed Subject Terms)

TEST AVAILABLE FROM

*Availability:* London House, SRA Product Group, 9701 W. Higgins Rd., Rosemont, IL 60018.

RELATED TESTS

*Notes:* See Thurstone Test of Mental Alertness (81035); SRA Verbal (18036); Supervisory Behavior Description Questionnaire (18037); and CRT Skills Test (1838) for related instruments.

TIME TO TAKE TEST AND/OR NO. OF TEST ITEMS

Time, 45. Items, 44.

ABSTRACT

A technical knowledge exam designed to measure the extent to which individuals are knowledgeable about Common Business Oriented Language (COBOL). Used as a preemployment screening device for COBOL programmers. Can also be used as a placement tool or to assess training needs by organizations. In some situations, applicants may request retesting. The test was developed according to equal employment opportunity and affirmative action guidelines. This is not a timed test.

# MAIN ENTRY SECTION

**3**
**Industrial Occupational Competency Tests, Journeyworker Level Two: Plumbing (010).** National Occupational Competency Testing Institute, Big Rapids, MI 1989.
*Descriptors:* *Occupational Tests; *Personnel Evaluation; *Personnel Selection; *Plumbing; Adults; Industrial Training; Job Skills; Knowledge Level; Multiple Choice Tests; Performance Tests; Promotion (Occupational); Skilled Workers; Work Sample Tests
*Identifiers:* IOCT; National Occupational Competency Testing Institute; NOCTI
*Availability:* National Occupational Competency Testing Institute, 409 Bishop Hall, Ferris State University, Big Rapids, MI 49307.
*Notes:* For the complete series of Industrial Occupational Competency Tests, Entry Level One, see 17778 through 17845. For the Industrial Occupational Competency Tests, Journeyworker Level Two, see 17721 through 17777. Time, 480. Items, 200.

Level Two assessments measure worker competency at the journeyworker level. These were designed for use in industry to measure journeyworker-level skills in prospective and current employees. Both written and performance components are included in the tests, and separate scores are reported. May be used for employee selection, upgrading, or advancement, and in planning training or retraining programs. The written assessment is multiple choice and covers factual knowledge, technical information, understanding of principles, and problem-solving skills related to the occupation. The performance component is administered in a shop and consists of manipulative tasks related to a particular occupation. The written test covers water supply and distribution; drainage, waste, and venting systems; installation and operation of storm water drainage; plumbing fixtures; industrial and special wastes; safety; inspection and tests; general trade information; plumbing math; and drawing interpretations. The performance test covers drawing interpretation and specifications, layout and rough-in, testing, identification of piping procedures, setting fixtures, and safety practices.

**4**
**Professional Accounting Testing Program.** American Institute of Certified Public Accountants, New York, NY 1980.
*Descriptors:* *Accounting; *Business Skills; *Certified Public Accountants; *Job Applicants; *Occupational Tests; *Undergraduate Students; *Vocational Aptitude; Achievement Tests; Adults; Education; Job Placement; Minimum Competencies; National Competency Tests; Office Occupations; Timed Tests; Vocational Education
*Identifiers:* AICPA Accounting Aptitude and Achievement Test; American Institute of Certified Public Accts; College Accounting Testing Program; Competency Tests; Proficiency Tests
*Availability:* The Psychological Corp., 555 Academic Ct., San Antonio, TX 78204.

To provide the accounting profession with effective measures for personnel evaluation by assessing both job aptitude and job knowledge. This timed battery of tests includes (1) Orientation Test (57-minute test of aptitude covering vocabulary, reading of business materials, and business arithmetic problems); (2) Level I Achievement Test (45 minutes for each form: Financial Accounting, Managerial Accounting, or Financial and Managerial Accounting); and Level II Achievement Test (50-minute and 2-hour version with problems in advanced accounting, cost, auditing, and managerial topics). Restricted distribution. Tests under continual revision. Used for employment of new staff accountants, retention of temporary staff, and training and promotion of present staff.

**404**
**Wonderlic Personnel Test.** Wonderlic, E.F.
*Descriptors:* *Cognitive Ability; *Employees; *Job Applicants; Abstract Reasoning; Adults; Cognitive Tests; French; Large Type Materials; Mathematical Concepts; Occupational Tests; Spanish
*Availability:* E.F. Wonderlic Personnel Test, Inc., 820 Frontage Rd., Northfield, IL 60093.
*Notes:* Time, 12. Items, 50.

Designed as objective measure of applicant potential for job success. Critical scores are established for each occupation by test administrator or corporation. Equivalent forms are available. Employers use forms A, B, I, II, IV, V, T-11, and T-21. Employment agencies use forms EM, APT, BPT, and CPT. Forms A and B are available in French and Spanish editions. A large-print version for use with people with vision impairments is now available.

**1751**
**Problem-Analysis Questionnaire.** Oshry, Barry; Harrison, Roger 1975.
*Descriptors:* *Attitude Measures; *Employees; *Human Relations; *Locus of Control; *Work Attitudes; Administrators; Adults; Interpersonal Relationship; Work Environment
*Availability:* Jones, John E., and Pfeiffer, J. William, eds., *The 1975 Annual Handbook for Group Facilitators.* San Diego: University Associates, 1975. Pfeiffer and Co., formerly University Associates, 8517 Production Ave., San Diego, CA 92121-2280.
*Notes:* Items, 48.

Designed to identify problem situations in organizational environment and analyze the causes. Failure to resolve problems may result from deficiencies in areas of rational-technical analysis and openness. These failures may be found in others, in the organization, and in oneself. Human relations training may cause individuals to accept more responsibility for their problems, rather than blaming external influences.

**1752**
**Decision-Style Inventory.** Roskin, Rick 1975.
*Descriptors:* *Administrators; *Decision Making Skills; Adults; Problem Solving; Rating Scales
*Availability:* Jones, John E., and Pfeiffer, J. William, eds., *The 1975 Annual Handbook for Group Facilitators.* San Diego: University Associates, 1975. Pfeiffer and Co., formerly University Associates, 8517 Production Ave., San Diego, CA 92121-2280.
*Notes:* Items, 10.

Developed to increase manager's awareness of importance of flexibility in decision style. Decision making focuses on quality, as in mathematical models, or acceptance, as in behavioral models. This instrument is used to illustrate that focus of decision should be influenced by the nature of the problem.

**1753**
**Diagnosing Organization Ideology.** Harrison, Roger 1975.
*Descriptors:* *Employees; *Ideology; *Organizational Climate; *Values; Adults; Attitude Measures; Employee Attitudes; Management Development; Work Attitudes
*Availability:* Jones, John E., and Pfeiffer, J. William, eds., *The 1975 Annual Handbook for Group Facilitators.* San Diego: University Associates, 1975. Pfeiffer and Co., formerly University Associates, 8517 Production Ave., San Diego, CA 92121-2280.
*Notes:* Items, 15.

Designed to help participants in management development training identify their organization's ideology. Items are responded to in terms of organization ideology and personal ideology.

**1788**
**Tuckman Teacher Feedback Form.** Tuckman, Bruce W. 1971.
*Descriptors:* *Classroom Observation Techniques; *Teacher Characteristics; *Teacher Evaluation; Adults; Rating Scales
*Identifiers:* TIM(B); TTFF
*Availability:* Tests in Microfiche, Test Collection, Educational Testing Service, Princeton, NJ 08541.
*Notes:* Time, 45 approx. Items, 28.

Designed to enable any classroom observer to describe a teacher's behavior over approximately a 45-minute time span. The form consists of 28 paired adjectives, each of which represents a personal construct that can be used to construe the teacher's behavior. The form yields 4 scale scores: creativity, dynamism (dominance and energy), organized demeanor (organization and control), and warmth and acceptance.

**2078**
**Miller Analogies Test.** Miller, W.S. 1981.
*Descriptors:* *Academic Aptitude; *Adults; *Aptitude Tests; *College Graduates; *Graduate Students; Admission Criteria; Graduate Study; Higher Education; Personnel Selection
*Identifiers:* Analogies; MAT
*Availability:* The Psychological Corp., 555 Academic Ct., San Antonio, TX 78204.
*Notes:* Time, 50. Items, 100.

Designed to measure scholastic aptitude at graduate school level. May be used in business and government for selection of high-level personnel. Analogy items are used to assess knowledge in vocabulary, literature, social sciences, chemistry, biology, physics, mathematics, and general information. May be administered to groups or individuals. Instrument is restricted for distribution only to authorized personnel. Test is not administered in New York State.

**3218**
**Jurgensen Classification Inventory.** Jurgensen, Clifford E. 1947.
*Descriptors:* *Job Applicants; *Personnel Selection; Adults; Industrial Personnel; Personality Measures; Predictive Measurement
*Identifiers:* TIM(A)
*Availability:* Tests in Microfiche, Test Collection, Educational Testing Service, Princeton, NJ 08541.
*Notes:* Time, 20 approx. Items, 108.

Designed to aid executives and supervisors in assessing an individual's personality. The test consists of items in triad or paired form. Subtests are Irritations, Reputation Preferences, Personal Likes and Dislikes, Personal Choices, and Type of Person Disliked. User develops own item validity and establishes test norms.

**3586**
**Fireman Entrance Aptitude Tests.** McCann Associates, Inc., Langhorne, PA
*Descriptors:* *Fire Fighters; *Job Applicants; *Occupational Tests; *Vocational Aptitude; Adults; Aptitude Tests
*Availability:* McCann Associates, Inc., 603 Corporate Dr. West, Langhorne, PA 19047.

Designed to assess applicant's aptitude for firefighting and ability to learn firefighting skills quickly. Form 62A consists of 100 questions. Form 70A consists of 130 questions. Form 70A is easier and intended for users who are legally required to use 70 percent as minimum passing score. Tests are restricted and may be purchased only by Civil Service Commissions or other responsible municipal offical.

**3589**
**Police Officer Examination.** McCann Associates, Inc., Langhorne, PA 1980.
*Descriptors:* *Job Applicants; *Occupational Tests; *Police; *Vocational Aptitude; Adults; Aptitude Tests
*Availability:* McCann Associates, 603 Corporate Dr. West, Langhorne, PA 19047.
*Notes:* See also Aptitude Tests for Policemen (11687).

Form 100 consists of 100 questions and requires 160 minutes. Areas assessed include observational ability, ability to exercise judgment and common sense, interest in police work, ability to exercise judgment in map reading and dealing with people, ability to read and comprehend police text material, and reasoning ability. Form 125 consists of 125 questions and requires 185 minutes. Areas assessed include observational ability, police aptitude, police public relations, and police judgment. Tests are restricted and are rented, not sold. User must return used and unused question booklets to publisher. Tests are available only to Civil Service Commissions and other responsible officials.

**4171**
**AMRA Accreditation Examination for Medical Record Technicians.** American Medical Record Association, Chicago, IL 1983.
*Descriptors:* *Certification; *Medical Record Technicians; Accreditation (Institutions); Accrediting Agencies; Adults
*Availability:* American Medical Record Association, 875 N. Michigan Ave., Ste. 1850, Chicago, IL 60611.
*Notes:* Time, 225 approx. Items, 200.

Designed to provide accreditation as a medical record technician to qualified applicants. Examination is administered twice per year by the AMRA at specified test centers. Items are updated annually.

**4172**
**AMRA Registration Examination for Medical Record Administrators.** American Medical Record Association, Chicago, IL 1983.
*Descriptors:* *Certification; *Medical Record Administrators; Accreditation (Institutions); Accrediting Agencies; Adults
*Availability:* American Medical Record Association, 875 N. Michigan Ave., Ste. 1850, Chicago, IL 60611.
*Notes:* Time, 255 approx. Items, 250.

Designed to provide certification as a medical record administrator to applicants who have qualified by completion of a baccalaureate degree or program of post-baccalaureate study. Examination is administered by the AMRA twice a year at specified test centers. Items are updated annually.

**4534**
**Qualification Examination for Registered Representatives.** National Association of Securities Dealers, Inc., Washington, DC 1980.
*Descriptors:* *Certification; *Employees; *Financial Services; *Investment; *Mastery Tests; *National Competency Tests; Adults; Finance Occupations; Money Management; Occupational Tests; Timed Tests
*Identifiers:* Examination for Qualification as a Reg Rep; NASD Qualification Exam for Registered Rep; Registered Representative Examination
*Availability:* National Association of Securities Dealers, Inc., 1735 K St., N.W., Washington, DC 20006.
*Notes:* Time, 120. Items, 125.

Exam to meet the registration requirements as NASD representative. Includes knowledge of the securities and exchange business, rules and policies of the NASD, and applicable federal and state laws.

**4998**
**Learning Focus Inventory.** Clasen, Robert E.; Bowman, William E. 1974.
*Descriptors:* *Secondary School Teachers; *Teaching Styles; Adults; Behavior Rating Scales; Junior High Schools; Middle Schools; Semantic Differential; Teacher Evaluation
*Availability:* *The Journal of Educational Research,* v68 nl p9-11, Sep 1974.
*Notes:* Items, 16.

Developed to assess teaching style of junior high and middle school teachers in terms of the relative student-centeredness of their approach. Useful in evaluating most effective style for teaching students in grades 6-9, either student-centered or subject-centered. Instrument is also available from the author, Robert E. Clasen, Department of Education, University of Wisconsin Extension, Madison, WI 53706.

**5124**
**Behavioral Objectives Writing Skills Test.** Lapp, Diane 1970.
*Descriptors:* *Behavioral Objectives; *Elementary School Teachers; *Work Sample Tests; Adults; Arithmetic; Reading; Sciences; Social Studies; Writing Skills
*Identifiers:* BOWST; TIM(A)
*Availability:* Tests in Microfiche, Test Collection, Educational Testing Service, Princeton, NJ 08541.
*Notes:* Time, 55. Items, 12.

Designed to provide an estimate of the elementary teacher's ability to write behavioral objectives. The test requires the teacher to write three behavioral objectives for each of four hypothetical classroom settings. Two forms of the test are available. Four subject areas are covered. Point values are allotted for the respondent's mention of external conditions, terminal behavior, and acceptable behavior in each objective written.

**5161**
**Job Diagnostic Survey.** Hackman, J. Richard; Oldham, Greg R. 1974.
*Descriptors:* *Employee Attitudes; *Employees; *Job Satisfaction; *Motivation; Adults; Affective Measures; Career Change; Rating Scales
*Identifiers:* JDS; TIM(E)
*Availability:* Tests in Microfiche, Test Collection, Educational Testing Service, Princeton, NJ 08541.
*Notes:* Time, 25 approx. Items, 203.

Designed to measure three classes of variables: (1) the objective characteristics of jobs, particularly the degree to which jobs are designed so that they enhance internal work motivation and job satisfaction; (2) the personal affective reactions of individuals to their jobs and to the broader work setting; and (3) the readiness of individuals for jobs which have high measured potential for generating internal work motivation. The survey is intended for two general types of use: (1) for diagnosing existing jobs to determine whether (and how) they might be redesigned to improve employee productivity and satisfaction; and (2) for evaluating the effect of job changes on employees.

**5267**
**Temperament Comparator.** Baehr, Melany E.; Pranis, Robert W. 1981.
*Descriptors:* *Adults; *Personality Traits; *Self Concept Measures; *Self Evaluation (Individuals); Administrators; Counseling Techniques; Personality Assessment; Personality Measures; Personnel Selection; Professional Occupations; Promotion (Occupational); Sales Occupations; Sales Workers
*Identifiers:* Comparability
*Availability:* London House, SRA Product Group, 9701 W. Higgins Rd., Rosemont, IL 60018.
*Notes:* Time, 20 approx. Items, 153.

Designed to assess relatively permanent temperament traits that are characteristic of an individual's behavior. Yields a profile of scores for 18 temperament traits and for 5 temperament factors composed of analytically determined combinations of these traits. May be used for individual or group administration. Classified as a Level C instrument in accordance with the American Psychological Association's recommendations. For selection, promotion, and counseling of sales, high-level professional, and management personnel.

**5436**
**Work Adjustment Rating Form.** Bitter, James A.; Bolanovich, D.J. 1969.
*Descriptors:* *Behavior Rating Scales; *Employment Potential; *Mental Retardation; Adults; Rehabilitation Programs; Vocational Rehabilitation
*Identifiers:* TIM(B); WARF
*Availability:* Tests in Microfiche, Test Collection, Educational Testing Service, Princeton, NJ 08541.
*Notes:* Time, 7 approx. Items, 40.

Developed to assess the job readiness behaviors of individuals involved in vocational rehabilitation programs. Designed for use with mentally retarded adults. The test includes 8 subscales: amount of supervision required, realism of job goals, teamwork, acceptance of rules/authority, work tolerance, perseverance in work, extent trainee seeks assistance, and importance attached to job training.

**5595**
**Student Perception of Teacher Style.** Tuckman, Bruce W. 1968.
*Descriptors:* *High School Students; *Student Evaluation of Teacher Performance; *Teaching Styles; *Vocational Education Teachers; Adolescents; Behavior Rating Scales; High Schools; Teacher Student Relationship
*Identifiers:* SPOTS; TIM(B)
*Availability:* Tests in Microfiche, Test Collection, Educational Testing Service, Princeton, NJ 08541.
*Notes:* Items, 32.

Behavior rating scale consists of 32 items each of which describes a facet of common classroom behavior. Students in grades 9 to 12 rate the intensity or frequency of particular teacher behaviors on 9-point scales.

**5599**
**Teacher Style Checklist.** Tuckman, Bruce W. 1968.
*Descriptors:* *Secondary School Teachers; *Teaching Styles; Adults; Behavior Rating Scales; Teacher Student Relationship; Teacher Effectiveness; Teacher Evaluation; Vocational Education Teachers
*Identifiers:* TSC
*Availability:* ERIC Document Reproduction Service, 7420 Fullerton Rd., Ste. 110, Springfield, VA 22153-2852 (ED208990, 119 pages).
*Notes:* See also Observer Rating Scale of Teacher Style: Revised (5601). Items, 20.

Designed to assess teacher's classroom behavior as directive or nondirective.

**5601**
**Observer Rating Scale of Teacher Style: Revised.** Tuckman, Bruce W. 1968.
*Descriptors:* *Secondary School Teachers; *Teacher Evaluation; *Teaching Styles; Adults; Behavior Rating Scales; Observation; Teacher Student Relationship; Vocational Education Teachers
*Availability:* ERIC Document Reproduction Service, 7420 Fullerton Rd., Ste. 110, Springfield, VA 22153-2852 (ED208990, 119 pages).
*Notes:* See also Teacher Style Checklist (5599). Items, 19.

An observer-rated, 9-point scale of teacher directiveness. Designed for use by trained raters.

**5856**
**Most Preferred Co-Worker Scale.** Fiedler, Fred E.

*Descriptors:* *Employees; *Peer Evaluation; Adults; Likert Scales; Rating Scales; Work Environment
*Identifiers:* MPC; TIM(E)
*Availability:* Tests in Microfiche, Test Collection, Educational Testing Service, Princeton, NJ 08541.
*Notes:* Items, 16.

Designed to elicit a description of a person with whom the respondent has been able to work best. The individual is described through the rating of 16 bipolar adjectives on an 8-point scale.

**5857**
**Least Preferred Co-Worker Scale.** Fiedler, Fred E.
*Descriptors:* *Employees; *Interaction; *Peer Evaluation; *Personality Measures; *Personality Traits; Adults; Human Relations; Rating Scales
*Identifiers:* LPC; TIM(E)
*Availability:* Tests in Microfiche, Test Collection, Educational Testing Service, Princeton, NJ 08541.
*Notes:* Items, 17.

An employee is asked to rate a person of his/her choice with whom the employee has had the most difficulty in getting a job done. Adjectives are used to describe this person on a scale of 1 to 8, e.g., pleasant to unpleasant, gloomy to cheerful.

**6105**
**Job Satisfaction Blank No. 5.** Hoppock, Robert 1970.
*Descriptors:* *Attitude Measures; *Job Satisfaction; Adults; Career Change; Questionnaires; Work Attitudes
*Identifiers:* TIM(A)
*Availability:* Tests in Microfiche, Test Collection, Educational Testing Service, Princeton, NJ 08541.
*Notes:* Items, 28.

Designed to assess respondents' feelings about their jobs, how much of the time they are satisfied, their feelings about changing jobs, and job-related attitudes as compared to those of other people. Percentiles are provided based on data obtained from 301 employed adults in 1933 in New Hope, PA, which was then a manufacturing village.

**6182**
**The Nature and Function of Social Work Questionnaire.** Taber, Merlin; Vattano, Anthony J. 1970.
*Descriptors:* *Attitude Measures; *Job Satisfaction; *Social Workers; *Work Attitudes; Adults; Attitudes; Rating Scales
*Identifiers:* TIM(B)
*Availability:* Tests in Microfiche, Test Collection, Educational Testing Service, Princeton, NJ 08541.
*Notes:* Items, 71.

Designed to assess the attitudes of social workers, and others who are well-oriented to social work, toward the profession. The test encompasses 5 professional orientations: psychodynamic-mindedness, social action, social-environment-mindedness, title-protection and training, and private practice. The instrument is recommended for group rather than individual analysis.

**6199**
**Reid Report, Revised Edition.** Reid Psychological Systems, Chicago, IL 1984.
*Descriptors:* *Job Applicants; *Predictive Measurement; *Stealing; Adults; Questionnaires
*Availability:* Psychological Surveys Corp., 900 Jorie Blvd., Ste. 130, Oak Brook, IL 60521.
*Notes:* Time, 40 approx.

Instrument designed to predict the likelihood that a job applicant will steal from an employer. Designed to predict only one kind of delinquent behavior, namely, theft. Its purpose should be transparent to subject completing the questionnaire. Consists of three parts: attitudes toward theft inventory, biographical data, and admissions list of past delinquencies. Does not discriminate based on age, sex, or race. Currently available in French, Spanish, Portuguese, Italian, and Polish.

**6271**
**Faculty Morale—Institutional Climate Scale.** Bowers, Orville E. 1968.
*Descriptors:* *Attitude Measures; *College Faculty; *Faculty College Relationship; *Morale; *Teacher Attitudes; Adults; Interprofessional Relationship; Personnel Policy; Teacher Student Relationship; Teacher Administrator Relationship; Work Environment
*Identifiers:* TIM(A)
*Availability:* Tests in Microfiche, Test Collection, Educational Testing Service, Princeton, NJ 08541.
*Notes:* Time, 35. Items, 50.

Designed to identify the elements that describe institutional climate and faculty morale prevailing on a college campus. The items are grouped in the following areas: working conditions and services, personnel policies and practices, faculty-administrator relationships, colleague relationships, and student relationships.

**6777**
**Dental Auxiliary Image Test.** Chambers, David W. 1971.
*Descriptors:* *Attitude Measures; *Attitudes; *Dental Assistants; *Dental Hygienists; *Patients; *Projective Measures; Adults
*Identifiers:* DAIT; TIM(B)
*Availability:* Tests in Microfiche, Test Collection, Educational Testing Service, Princeton, NJ 08541.
*Notes:* Time, 5. Items, 15.

Projective instrument designed to elicit perceptions of dental assistants and dental hygienists. Responses are scored according to 10 coding categories: tasks, human relations, significant contributions, competence and confidence, integrity, qualifications, health, job opportunity, work constraints, and negative image. Instrument may be administered to individuals or small groups. Suitable for dental patients, dental students and dental assisting students, as well as practicing dental professionals.

**6850**
**Pediatrics Review and Education Program.** American Academy of Pediatricians, Evanston, IL 1983.
*Descriptors:* *Pediatrics; *Physicians; *Professional Continuing Education; *Self Evaluation (Individuals); Adults; Educational Objectives; Multiple Choice Tests
*Identifiers:* PREP
*Availability:* American Academy of Pediatricians, Box 1034, Evanston, IL 60204.

A coordinated program designed for self-evaluation and continuing education of practicing pediatricians. PREP curriculum is based on educational objectives defined and published in advance for each curricular year. Test material is updated periodically using similar format.

**6892**
**Annual Otolaryngology—Head and Neck Surgery Examination.** American Academy of Otolaryngology, Washington, DC
*Descriptors:* *Multiple Choice Tests; *Physicians; *Professional Continuing Education; *Self Evaluation (Individuals); *Surgery; Adults
*Identifiers:* AOE; *Otolaryngology
*Availability:* American Academy of Otolaryngology, Head and Neck Surgery, Ste. 302, 1101 Vermont Ave., N.W., Washington, DC 20005.

This yearly, multiple-choice examination serves as a basis of self-evaluation for residents, practicing otolaryngologists, and other interested physicians. All participants receive feedback information that will enable them to compare their performance with that of others at the same level of training or experience. This examination is acceptable for 4 Category 1 credit hours by the Accreditation Council for Continuing Medical Education.

**7079**
**Critical Behavior Scales.** Muthard, John E.; Miller, Leonard A. 1966.
*Descriptors:* *Counselor Evaluation; *Rehabilitation Counseling; *Semantic Differential; Administrators; Adults; Rating Scales
*Identifiers:* CBS; TIM(A)
*Availability:* Tests in Microfiche, Test Collection, Educational Testing Service, Princeton, NJ 08541.
*Notes:* Time, 45 approx. Items, 18.

Designed to assess perceptions concerning the nature of effective rehabilitation counselor performance. The scales consist of 18 vignettes describing specific counselor behavior. Each vignette is responded to on 6 bipolar semantic-differential scales. Two scales for each vignette are relatively evaluative in character, 2 are relatively activity oriented, and 2 are of a relative potency nature.

**7255**
**Physician Assistant National Certifying Examination.** National Commission on Certification of Physician's Assistants, Inc., Atlanta, GA 1982.
*Descriptors:* *Certification; *National Competency Tests; *Physicians Assistants; Adults; Mastery Tests; Medical Case Histories; Multiple Choice Tests; Physical Examinations
*Availability:* National Commission on Certification of Physician's Assistants, Inc., 2845 Henderson Mill Rd., N.E., Ste. 560, Atlanta, GA 30341.

Designed to assess candidates' knowledge, and skill in applying knowledge, related to health care functions primary care physician's assistants must be able to perform. Examinations are updated periodically. Candidates must be graduates of AMA-accredited physician or surgeon assistant programs.

**7484**
**Child-Aide Evaluation Form.** Dorr, Darwin; Cowen, Emory L. 1972.
*Descriptors:* *Mental Health Programs; *Nonprofessional Personnel; *Personnel Evaluation; *School Aides; Adults; Behavior Rating Scales; Psychologists; Social Workers
*Identifiers:* Primary Mental Health Project
*Availability:* *American Journal of Community Psychology,* v1 n3 p258-65, 1973.
*Notes:* Items, 16.

An evaluation form for social workers and psychologists to use in assessing effectiveness of child aides (nonprofessional mental health workers). Instrument is also available from the author, Dr. Darwin Dorr, Highland Hospital, Asheville, NC 28802.

**7525**
**Questionnaire on the Occupational Status of Women.** Bingham, William C.; House, Elaine
*Descriptors:* *Attitude Measures; *Counselor Attitudes; *Equal Opportunities (Jobs); *Negative Attitudes; *Sex Role; *Sex Stereotypes; Adults; Career Counseling; Counselor Educators; School Counselors
*Identifiers:* TIM(A)
*Availability:* Tests in Microfiche, Test Collection, Educational Testing Service, Princeton, NJ 08541.
*Notes:* Items, 50.

Designed to assess knowledge of and attitudes toward the occupational status of women. The questionnaire was intended to investigate the extent to which misinformation and negative attitudes toward women and work prevail among counselors and counselor educators.

**7607**
**Group Leadership Questionnaire.** Wile, Daniel B. 1972.
*Descriptors:* *Leaders; *Leadership Styles; Adults; Group Dynamics; Human Relations; Situational Tests

*Identifiers:* Self Report Measures; Self Scoring Tests
*Availability:* Pfeiffer, J. William, and Jones, John E., eds., *The 1972 Annual Handbook for Group Facilitators.* San Diego: University Associates, 1972. Pfeiffer and Co., formerly University Associates, 8517 Production Ave., San Diego, CA 92121-2280.
*Notes:* Items, 21.

Designed to assess an individual's leadership style. Situations which may occur in human interaction groups are presented followed by 19 alternative responses. The responses are indicative of various leadership styles.

**7668**
**Educational Work Components Study.** Miskel, Cecil; Heller, Leonard 1973.
*Descriptors:* *Motivation; *Predictive Measurement; *School Administration; *Work Attitudes; Administrators; Adults; Likert Scales; Rating Scales
*Identifiers:* EWCS; TIM(A)
*Availability:* Tests in Microfiche, Test Collection, Educational Testing Service, Princeton, NJ 08541.
*Notes:* Items, 36.

Based on Borgatta's Work Components Study, this questionnaire is designed to measure work motivation in the educational organization. The test includes 6 factors: potential for personal challenge and development, competitiveness, desirability, tolerance for work pressure, conservative security, willingness to seek reward, and surround concern.

**7686**
**Revised Scale of Employability.** Bolton, Brian 1970.
*Descriptors:* *Disabilities; *Emotional Disturbances; *Employment Potential; Adults; Interpersonal Competence; Mental Retardation; Physical Disabilities; Rating Scales; Rehabilitation; Vocational Evaluation; Work Attitudes
*Identifiers:* TIM(A)
*Availability:* Tests in Microfiche, Test Collection, Educational Testing Service, Princeton, NJ 08541.
*Notes:* Items, 11.

Assesses the potential employability of adults with mental, physical, and emotional disabilities who are clients of rehabilitation workshops. The test consists of two parts. The Counseling Scale assesses 6 dimensions of vocational competence: adequacy of work history, appropriateness of job demands, interpersonal competence (vocational), interpersonal competence (social), language facility, and prominence of disability. The Workshop Scale assesses 5 dimensions of job competence: attitudinal conformity to work role, maintenance of quality, acceptance of work demands, interpersonal security, and speed of production.

**7719**
**Self and Role Concept Instrumentation.** Richardson, Mary Sue 1973.
*Descriptors:* *College Students; *Females; *Self Concept Measures; *Sex Role; Adults; Career Choice; Homemakers; Likert Scales; Rating Scales; Self Esteem
*Identifiers:* TIM(C)
*Availability:* Tests in Microfiche, Test Collection, Educational Testing Service, Princeton, NJ 08541.
*Notes:* Items, 58.

Developed to measure a woman's self-concept, ideal woman concept, career woman concept, and homemaker concept, and to assess the degree of similarity among the various concepts. The concepts are measured by means of a 58-item adjective rating scale. The respondent rates each adjective according to the degree to which it is descriptive of the way she perceives herself, the ideal woman, the career woman, and the homemaker.

**7721**
**Ramak Interest Inventory.** Meir, Elchanan I. 1970.
*Descriptors:* *Adults; *Career Counseling; *Hebrew; *Interest Inventories; *Vocational Interests; Adolescents; Secondary School Students
*Identifiers:* Israel; TIM(C)
*Availability:* Tests in Microfiche, Test Collection, Educational Testing Service, Princeton, NJ 08541.
*Notes:* Time, 10 approx. Items, 76.

Inventory of vocational interests is based on Roe's classifications of occupations by fields: service, business, organization, technology, outdoor, science, general cultural, and arts and entertainment. The inventory lists 76 occupational titles. Respondents are required to designate their interest in each occupational title on a 3-point scale. The inventory is in Hebrew; however, an English version of the manual is now available.

**7758**
**Trainee Rating Scale.** Adelman, Howard S.; Sperber, Zanwil 1969.
*Descriptors:* *Preschool Teachers; *Teacher Evaluation; Adults; Behavior Rating Scales; Emotional Disturbances; Job Performance; Professional Training
*Identifiers:* TIM(C)
*Availability:* Tests in Microfiche, Test Collection, Educational Testing Service, Princeton, NJ 08541.
*Notes:* See Stick Figure Rating Scale (7759); Q Sort Procedure for Describing Nursery School Children (7760); Nursery School Situations (7761); and Interview Summary and Outline (7762). Items, 31.

One of a battery of tests developed to evaluate therapeutic nursery school teacher trainees. The scale is designed to evaluate trainee performance directly under the pressure of working situations, such as actual interaction with children. The two-part test covers both the trainee's personal qualities and professional competencies. The ratings are made by training personnel.

**7759**
**Stick Figure Rating Scale.** Adelman, Howard S.; Sperber, Zanwil 1969.
*Descriptors:* *Comparative Testing; *Preschool Teachers; *Teacher Evaluation; Adults; Comparative Analysis; Emotional Disturbances; Professional Training
*Identifiers:* TIM(C)
*Availability:* Tests in Microfiche, Test Collection, Educational Testing Service, Princeton, NJ 08541.
*Notes:* See also Trainee Rating Scale (7758); Q Sort Procedure for Describing Nursery School Children (7760); Nursery School Situations (7761); and Interview Summary and Outline (7762).

One of a battery of tests developed to evaluate therapeutic nursery school teacher trainees, this scale is devised as a relativistic measure of overall performance. The scale consists of 50 stick figures placed in a vertical column ranging from best to worst. Raters are asked to compare each individual's performance to professional rather than trainee performance levels. Ratings are made by training personnel.

**7760**
**Q-Sort Procedure for Describing Nursery School Children.** Adelman, Howard S.; And Others 1966.
*Descriptors:* *Disability Identification; *Preschool Teachers; *Teacher Evaluation; Adults; Comparative Analysis; Emotional Disturbances; Professional Training; Q Methodology; Videotape Recordings
*Identifiers:* TIM(C)
*Availability:* Tests in Microfiche, Test Collection, Educational Testing Service, Princeton, NJ 08541.
*Notes:* See also Trainee Rating Scale (7758); Stick Figure Rating Scale (7759); Nursery School Situations (7761); and Interview Summary and Outline (7762). Items, 105.

Part of a battery of tests developed to evaluate therapeutic nursery school teacher trainees. The procedure is designed to tap trainees' performance in the area of patient diagnosis and to compare their perceptual-conceptual behavior before and after training with that of professionals in the field. The test consists of 2 decks of cards, one listing behaviors reflecting healthy or adaptive potential, and the other referring to behaviors with a pathological or negative potential. The trainee views a videotape of a child interacting in various situations and then sorts the cards according to the degree to which each is descriptive of the child.

**7761**
**Nursery School Situations.** Adelman, Howard S.; Sperber, Zanwil 1969.
*Descriptors:* *Preschool Teachers; *Situational Tests; *Teacher Evaluation; Adults; Emotional Disturbances; Professional Training; Teacher Response; Verbal Tests
*Identifiers:* TIM(C)
*Availability:* Tests in Microfiche, Test Collection, Educational Testing Service, Princeton, NJ 08541.
*Notes:* See also Trainee Rating Scale (7758); Stick Figure Rating Scale (7759); Q-Sort Procedure for Describing Nursery School Children (7760); and Interview Summary and Outline (7762). Items, 13.

Part of a battery of tests developed to evaluate the performance of therapeutic nursery school teacher trainees. The test is designed to assess the decisions, diagnoses, and plans of action which the trainees would employ in various hypothetical problem situations. The test consists of 4 detailed descriptions of children with particular symptoms interacting in a variety of nursery school situations. The trainee is asked to describe and explain his or her handling of each situation.

**7762**
**Interview Summary and Outline.** Adelman, Howard S.; Sperber, Zanwil 1969.
*Descriptors:* *Preschool Teachers; *Teacher Evaluation; *Videotape Recordings; Adults; Emotional Disturbances; Essay Tests; Interviews; Parent Child Relationship; Professional Training
*Identifiers:* TIM(C)
*Availability:* Tests in Microfiche, Test Collection, Educational Testing Service, Princeton, NJ 08541.
*Notes:* See also Trainee Rating Scale (7758); Stick Figure Rating Scale (7759); Q-Sort Procedure for Describing Nursery School Children (7760); and Nursery School Situations (7761). Items, 20.

Part of a battery of tests developed to evaluate therapeutic nursery school teacher trainees, this device is designed to assess the trainees' comprehension of the interview process and of parents of emotionally disturbed children. The trainees are shown a videotape in which a social worker does an intake interview with a mother. The interview includes a discussion of the child's symptoms, the mother's experiences with the child, and the family's reaction to the problems. After viewing the tape, the trainees are given a relatively open-ended task that includes discussing the interview.

**7776**
**The Perceived Equity Scale.** Spector, Paul E.; And Others 1975.
*Descriptors:* *Compensation (Remuneration); *Employee Attitudes; *Job Satisfaction; Adults; Employees; Likert Scales; Rating Scales; Work Attitudes
*Identifiers:* PES; TIM(C)
*Availability:* Tests in Microfiche, Test Collection, Educational Testing Service, Princeton, NJ 08541.
*Notes:* Items, 19.

Designed to measure whether or not an individual feels equitably compensated in his or her job. The items pertain to rewards or inducements that an employer or organization can give an employee. Respondents are required to compare the rewards they receive with the efforts they must make.

**7813**
**Conference Role Semantic Differential.** Hecht, Alfred R. 1975.
*Descriptors:* *Administrator Evaluation; *Leadership; *Semantic Differential; Administrators; Adults; Educational Administration; Interpersonal Relationship; Rating Scales
*Identifiers:* CRSD; TIM(C)
*Availability:* Tests in Microfiche, Test Collection, Educational Testing Service, Princeton, NJ 08541.
*Notes:* Items, 17.

Brief, diagnostic measure of administrative performance. The 15 bipolar adjective pairs sample task and interpersonal functions of educational leaders in individual conferences. Two free-response items ask evaluators to identify strengths and weaknesses in the conference roles performed by the person being evaluated.

**7883**
**Teacher Rating Form.** Knox, Alan B.; And Others 1973.
*Descriptors:* *Adult Basic Education; *Program Evaluation; *Teacher Evaluation; Adults; Records (Forms); Teachers
*Availability:* ERIC Document Reproduction Service, 7420 Fullerton Rd., Ste. 110, Springfield, VA 22153-2852 (ED091537, 160 pages).
*Notes:* For entire series, see 7873 through 7888. Items, 8.

A rating of overall performance of teachers instructing in an adult basic education program. Also records other pertinent data, such as class taught and background.

**7921**
**Medical Assistant Registry Examination.** American Medical Technologists, Park Ridge, IL 1981.
*Descriptors:* *Certification; *Medical Assistants; Adults; Anatomy; Business; Clinics; Ethics; Medical Vocabulary
*Availability:* American Medical Technologists, 710 Higgins Rd., Park Ridge, IL 60068.

A certification examination for medical assistants who aid a practicing physician in the office. Covers anatomy, medical terminology, law, ethics, business procedures, and clinical procedures. Updated 3 times a year.

**7935**
**Trouble Shooting Checklist—A.** Manning, Brad A. 1973.
*Descriptors:* *Administrators; *Change Strategies; *Educational Innovation; *Innovation; *Organizational Climate; Administrator Characteristics; Adoption (Ideas); Adults; Change Agents; College Environment; Higher Education; Predictive Measurement
*Identifiers:* TSCA
*Availability:* ERIC Document Reproduction Service, 7420 Fullerton Rd., Ste. 110, Springfield, VA 22153-2852 (ED103431, 154 pages).
*Notes:* Items, 315.

A predictive measure used to access an overall institutional profile. Designed to measure probable success of change agent at an institution. Form A is designed for use with institutions or organizations concerned with adopting modules to effect innovation.

**7936**
**Trouble Shooting Checklist—B.** Manning, Brad A. 1973.
*Descriptors:* *Administrators; *Change Strategies; *Educational Innovation; *Organizational Climate; Administrator Characteristics; Adoption (Ideas); Adults; Change Agents; College Environment; Higher Education; Predictive Measurement
*Identifiers:* TSCB
*Availability:* ERIC Document Reproduction Service, 7420 Fullerton Rd., Ste. 110, Springfield, VA 22153-2852 (ED103431, 154 pages).
*Notes:* Items, 348.

A predictive measure used to assess an overall institutional profile and measure probable success of a change agent at an institution. Form B is for use with institutions that have adopted a psychological assessment battery with a counseling orientation.

**8028**
**Leader Effectiveness and Adaptability Description (LEAD Profile).** Hersey, Paul; Blanchard, Kenneth H. 1973.
*Descriptors:* *Administrator Evaluation; *Leadership Styles; *Self Evaluation (Individuals); Adults; Peer Evaluation
*Identifiers:* LEAD
*Availability:* Learning Resources Corp., 8517 Production Ave., P.O. Box 26240, San Diego, CA 92126.
*Notes:* Items, 12.

Assists individuals in determining their tendency to rely on certain leadership styles and provides feedback on individual ability. Questionnaire is included in *The 1976 Annual Handbook for Group Facilitators,* edited by J. William Pfeiffer and John E. Jones.

**8029**
**Organization Behavior Describer Survey.** Harrison, Roger; Oshry, Barry 1976.
*Descriptors:* *Group Behavior; *Leadership Qualities; *Staff Meetings; Adults; Behavior Rating Scales; Peer Evaluation; Self Evaluation (Individuals)
*Identifiers:* OBDS; Self Scoring Tests
*Availability:* Pfeiffer, J. William, and Jones, John E., eds., *The 1976 Annual Handbook for Group Facilitators.* San Diego: University Associates, 1976. Pfeiffer and Co., formerly University Associates, 8517 Production Ave., San Diego, CA 92121-2280.
*Notes:* Items, 25.

Designed to describe an individual's behavior in staff and problem-solving meetings. Examinee may rate self, supervisor, subordinate, or someone at equivalent level. Four scales include rational-technical competence, verbal dominance, emotional expressiveness, and consideration.

**8115**
**Uni-Sex Interest Inventory.** Rayman, Jack
*Descriptors:* *Career Choice; *High School Seniors; *Interest Inventories; *Sex Fairness; *Vocational Interests; College Students; Grade 12; High Schools; Likert Scales
*Identifiers:* ACT Interest Inventory; TIM(D)
*Availability:* Tests in Microfiche, Test Collection, Educational Testing Service, Princeton, NJ 08541.
*Notes:* Time, 15. Items, 74.

The result of an effort to develop an interest measure consisting primarily of sex-balanced items, the inventory includes 6 scales. It is patterned after the ACT Interest Inventory and employs the same scoring procedures.

**8272**
**Trouble Shooting Checklist for School-Based Settings.** Manning, Brad A. 1976.
*Descriptors:* *Adoption (Ideas); *Change Agents; *Educational Innovation; *Elementary Schools; *School Attitudes; *Secondary Schools; Administrators; Adults; Attitude Measures; Educational Change; Likert Scales; Organizational Climate; Predictive Measurement; School Community Relationship
*Identifiers:* Concerns Based Adoption Model; TSC
*Availability:* ERIC Document Reproduction Service, 7420 Fullerton Rd., Ste. 110, Springfield, VA 22153-2852 (ED126095, 52 pages).
*Notes:* Time, 30 approx. Items, 100.

Designed to provide an overall predictive score that estimates the likelihood of a school adopting and implementing an innovation. Also provides a diagnostic profile focusing on school environment's strengths and weaknesses in relation to the adoption and implementation of innovations. Developed in conjunction with a project that had the Concerns-Based Adoption Model as its theoretical framework.

**8273**
**Trouble Shooting Checklist for Higher Educational Settings.** Manning, Brad A. 1976.
*Descriptors:* *Adoption (Ideas); *Change Agents; *Educational Innovation; Administrators; Adults; College Faculty; Educational Change; Higher Education; Organizational Climate; Predictive Measurement
*Identifiers:* Concerns Based Adoption Model; TSC
*Availability:* ERIC Document Reproduction Service, 7420 Fullerton Rd., Ste. 110, Springfield, VA 22153-2852 (ED126833, 47 pages).
*Notes:* Time, 30 approx. Items, 100.

Designed to measure an organization's potential for successfully adopting and implementing educational innovations. Provides a diagnostic profile indicating strengths and weaknesses with respect to the adoption process.

**8290**
**Employment Readiness Scale.** Alfano, Anthony M. 1973.
*Descriptors:* *Attitude Measures; *Work Attitudes; Adults; Unemployment
*Identifiers:* TIM(J)
*Availability:* Tests in Microfiche, Test Collection, Educational Testing Service, Princeton, NJ 08541.
*Notes:* Items, 43.

The scale was developed to measure attitudes toward work and to help determine the relation between length of unemployment time and work attitudes.

**8298**
**Scientific New Uses Test.** Gough, Harrison G. 1975.
*Descriptors:* *Creativity; *Engineers; *Scientists; Adults; Creative Thinking; Creativity Tests
*Availability:* *Journal of Creative Behavior,* v9 n4 p245-52, Fourth Quarter 1975.
*Notes:* Time, 30. Items, 20.

Designed to measure creativity of scientists and engineers. Examinees are asked to think of as many new scientific uses as possible for each of 20 items.

**8299**
**Scientific Word Association Test.** Gough, Harrison G. 1976.
*Descriptors:* *Association (Psychology); *Creativity; *Engineers; *Scientists; Adults; Divergent Thinking; Projective Measures
*Identifiers:* TIM(E)
*Availability:* Tests in Microfiche, Test Collection, Educational Testing Service, Princeton, NJ 08541.
*Notes:* Time, 10 approx. Items, 200.

Employs the word association technique to provide a measure of associational fluency and creative thinking in scientists.

**8336**
**Vocational Interest Inventory.** Lokan, Jan 1969.
*Descriptors:* *Disadvantaged; *High Risk Students; *Interest Inventories; *Job Training; *Noncollege Bound Students; *Vocational High Schools; *Vocational Interests; Foreign Countries; High Schools; Likert Scales; Low Achievement; Rating Scales; Semiskilled Occupations; Slow Learners; Trade and Industrial Education
*Identifiers:* Canada; Ottawa Board of Education (Ontario)
*Availability:* ERIC Document Reproduction Service, 7420 Fullerton Rd., Ste. 110, Springfield, VA 22153-2852 (ED078012, 53 pages).
*Notes:* Time, 15 approx. Items, 30.

Untimed instrument developed to identify suitable careers for vocational high school students with limited reading ability who are from disadvantaged backgrounds and who are low academic achievers. Measures vocational interest by having subjects indicate their preferred job tasks on a 4-point scale. Each task is represented pictorially and verbally at a 5th to 6th grade reading level. Used to place these students in the appropriate job training programs. Comes in 2 forms: a 30-item form for boys and a 28-item form for girls. Adapted from Freeberg's test booklet on assessment of disadvantaged adolescents.

**8437**
**Minnesota Job Description Questionnaire, Forms E and S.** Vocational Psychology Research, Minneapolis, MN 1980.
*Descriptors:* *Employees; *Job Satisfaction; *Occupational Information; *Supervisors; Adults; Job Analysis; Rating Scales
*Identifiers:* MJDQ
*Availability:* Vocational Psychology Research, N620 Elliott Hall, 75 E. River Rd., University of Minnesota, Minneapolis, MN 55455.

Designed to measure reinforcer characteristics of jobs along 21 dimensions. A group of raters, including supervisors, employees, and job analysts, is asked to rate a specific job. Composite scaling of results is called an Occupational Reinforcer Pattern (ORP). An ORP is the pattern of rated reinforcers or need-satisfiers on a given job. Form E is for employees and Form S for supervisors. Computer scoring is available.

**8519**
**Supervisory Attitudes: The X-Y Scale.** Ford, Robert N. 1972.
*Descriptors:* *Attitude Measures; *Self Evaluation (Individuals); *Supervisors; Administrator Attitudes; Adults; Behavior Rating Scales; Leadership Styles; Supervision
*Identifiers:* Theory X; Theory Y
*Availability:* Pfeiffer, J. William and Jones, John E., eds., *The 1972 Annual Handbook for Group Facilitators.* San Diego: University Associates, 1972. Pfeiffer and Co., formerly University Associates, 8517 Production Ave., San Diego, CA 92121-2280.

Designed to determine supervisory behavior in relation to subordinates. Assesses supervisor's attitudes toward subordinates in terms of McGregor's Theory X and Theory Y.

**8520**
**Intervention Style Survey.** Arbes, B.H. 1972.
*Descriptors:* *Administrators; *Intervention; *Leadership Styles; *Situational Tests; Adults; Problem Solving; Self Evaluation (Individuals)
*Identifiers:* Self Scoring Tests
*Availability:* Pfeiffer, J. William and Jones, John E., eds., *The 1972 Annual Handbook For Group Facilitators.* San Diego: University Associates, 1972. Pfeiffer and Co., formerly University Associates, 8517 Production Ave., San Diego, CA 92121-2280.
*Notes:* Items, 12.

Designed to assess intervention style. Examinee assumes position of chief student personnel administrator of a university, reporting directly to the president. Typical situations are described with 5 alternative responses. Examinee rates responses from most similar to least similar to his/her intervention style. Yields scores for 5 intervention styles: leadership-impoverished, task, country club, middle of the road, and team.

**8557**
**National Board of Podiatric Medical Examinations.** Educational Testing Service, Princeton, NJ 1982.
*Descriptors:* *Certification; *Mastery Tests; *National Competency Tests; *Podiatry; *Professional Education; *State Licensing Boards; Adults; Graduate Study; Higher Education; Multiple Choice Tests
*Identifiers:* NBPME
*Availability:* National Board of Podiatric Medical Examiners, P.O. Box 6516, Princeton, NJ 08541-6516.

A series of written qualifying tests recognized or utilized by legal agencies governing the practice of podiatric medicine. Part 1 is generally taken after candidates' second year of study. Measures knowledge in general anatomy, lower extremity anatomy, biochemistry, microbiology, pathology, pharmacology, and physiology. Part 2 is generally taken near the completion of candidates' final year of study. Measures knowledge of clinical areas of community health-jurisprudence, dermatology, medicine, orthopedics-biomechanics, podiatric medicine, radiology, surgery-anesthesia-hospital protocol. Part 1 tests in lower extremity anatomy, pathology, pharmacology, and physiology consists of 75 items and have a 60-minute time limit. Biochemistry, general anatomy, and microbiology tests consist of 100 items and have an 80-minute time limit. Each test in Part 2 consists of 75 items and has a time limit of 60 minutes. Tests are updated annually.

**8563**
**National Board for Respiratory Care Examinations.** National Board for Respiratory Care, Shawnee Mission, KS
*Descriptors:* *Certification; *Occupational Tests; *Respiratory Therapy; Adults; Allied Health Occupations; Knowledge Level
*Availability:* National Board for Respiratory Care, 11015 W. 75th Terrace, Shawnee Mission, KS 66214.

There are 2 levels of certification. The Certification Examination for Entry Level Respiratory Therapy Practitioners (CRTT) assesses the essential knowledge, skills, and abilities needed by entry-level respiratory therapy personnel. The Examination System for the Registered Respiratory Therapist (RRT) evaluates the essential knowledge, skills, and abilities required by experienced respiratory therapists. The Certification Examination for Entry Level Respiratory Therapy Practitioners is a 200-item test covering clinical data, equipment, and therapeutic procedures. Time alloted for the exam is three hours. The Examination System for the Registered Respiratory Therapist consists of a written portion and a clinical simulation portion. Both parts are administered on the same day. Candidates may elect to take one or both parts on the same day. The written test consists of 200 multiple-choice questions. The clinical simulation portion consists of 10 patient management problems designed to sample a broad area of competencies rather than the recall of isolated facts. The registry exam takes 6 hours. To take the Certification Examination for Entry Level Respiratory Therapy Practitioners, a candidate must be a graduate of an accredited respiratory therapy technician or respiratory therapist educational program. To take the Examination System for the Registered Respiratory Therapist, a candidate must meet one of the following requirements: be a graduate of an accredited respiratory therapy educational program with at least 62 semester hours from an accredited college or university and have 1 year of clinical experience, or be a certified respiratory therapist (CRTT) with 4 years of full-time clinical experience and 62 semester hours of college or university credit, or be a certified respiratory therapist (CRTT) with a bachelor's degree and 2 years of full-time clinical experience.

**8628**
**My Thoughts: A Self-Evaluation Instrument.** Richardson, Edward T. 1975.
*Descriptors:* *Self Evaluation (Individuals); *Teacher Characteristics; *Teacher Evaluation; *Teachers; Adults; Likert Scales; Personality Measures
*Identifiers:* TIM(D)
*Availability:* Tests in Microfiche, Test Collection, Educational Testing Service, Princeton, NJ 08541.
*Notes:* Items, 65.

Designed as a method by which teachers may rate themselves in each of 13 areas that are considered representative of the talented teacher. Includes a section for follow-up with 3 sentence completion exercises: (1) The talent I desire to improve is...; (2) The following materials or activities have helped me improve this talent...; and (3) As I look back through the year, I feel my improvement in this talent has been.... The main objective is for the teacher to perceive his or her own areas of weakness.

**8939**
**Foreign Medical Graduate Examination in the Medical Sciences and ECFMG English Test.** Educational Commission for Foreign Medical Graduates, Philadelphia, PA
*Descriptors:* *Certification; *English; *Foreign Medical Graduates; *Language Proficiency; *Medicine; *Physicians; Adults; Foreign Students; Gynecology; Higher Education; Internal Medicine; Obstetrics; Surgery
*Availability:* Educational Commission for Foreign Medical Graduates Examination, 3624 Market St., Philadelphia, PA 19104.
*Notes:* Time, 450 approx.

Assesses the readiness of graduates of foreign medical schools to enter residency or fellowship programs in the United States that are accredited by the Accreditation Council for Graduate Medical Education. There are 2 parts to the examination. Day 1 Basic Medical Science Component consists of basic medical science tests with about 500 items from the disciplines of anatomy, behavioral sciences, biochemistry, microbiology, pathology, pharmacology, and physiology. The Day 2 Clinical Science Component consists of about 450 items from the disciplines of internal medicine, obstetrics and gynecology, pediatrics, preventive medicine and public health, psychiatry, and surgery. Demonstration of competence in the English language is required for certification and to revalidate Standard ECFMG certificates. The ECFMG English language test is administered semiannually in January and July and is adapted from the validated Test of English as a Foreign Language (TOEFL).

**8970**
**Formal Lecture Observation Assessment Technique.** Love, Judith A.; And Others 1977.
*Descriptors:* *Classroom Observation Techniques; *College Faculty; *Teacher Effectiveness; *Teacher Evaluation; Behavior Rating Scales; College Instruction; Higher Education; Lecture Method; Student Evaluation of Teacher Performance; Teacher Behavior; Videotape Recordings
*Identifiers:* FLOAT
*Availability:* ERIC Document Reproduction Service, 7420 Fullerton Rd., Ste. 110, Springfield, VA 22153-2852 (ED135862, 21 pages).
*Notes:* Items, 21.

Designed to assess college teachers' instructional behaviors as recorded on videotape. Intended to structure the systematic observation and rating of college teaching. May also be used by students to rate instructors.

**9011**
**Reading Test for Vocational Education.** Weiss, Lucile 1976.
*Descriptors:* *Cloze Procedure; *High School Students; *Reading Comprehension; *Screening Tests; *Vocational Aptitude; Aptitude Tests; High Schools; Vocational Education
*Identifiers:* TIM(E)
*Availability:* Tests in Microfiche, Test Collection, Educational Testing Service, Princeton, NJ 08541.
*Notes:* Items, 300.

Designed to function as a screening procedure to identify students who lack academic skills but who, because of interest and knowledge in nonacademic areas, will succeed in vocational education programs. The test was developed to serve as an alternative to academically oriented tests used for screening purposes.

**9131**
**Auditory Automotive Mechanics Diagnostic Achievement Test.** Swanson, Richard Arthur 1968.
*Descriptors:* *Achievement Tests; *Auditory Perception; *Auto Mechanics; Adults; Audiotape Recordings; Auditory Tests; Listening Skills; Occupational Tests; Postsecondary Education; Trade and Industrial Education

*Identifiers:* AAMDAT
*Availability:* ERIC Document Reproduction Service, 7420 Fullerton Rd., Ste. 110, Springfield, VA 22153-2852 (ED154034, 125 pages).
*Notes:* Items, 44.

Designed to measure ability to diagnose malfunctions in automobiles using auditory clues.

9231
**Delta Nursing Survey.** Wilson, Barry J.; Packwood, Gene 1975.
*Descriptors:* *Job Performance; *Nurses; Adults; Nursing; Nursing Education; Peer Evaluation; Rating Scales
*Identifiers:* Delta Nursing Scales
*Availability:* ERIC Document Reproduction Service, 7420 Fullerton Rd., Ste. 110, Springfield, VA 22153-2852 (ED129879, 15 pages).
*Notes:* Items, 55.

Designed to assess job performance of graduate nurses. May be used to evaluate quality of nursing school curriculum.

9381
**Biology Teacher Behavior Inventory.** Evans, Thomas P. 1969.
*Descriptors:* *Biology; *Secondary School Teachers; Classroom Communication; Classroom Observation Techniques; Science Instruction; Secondary Education; Teacher Behavior; Teacher Evaluation; Teaching Styles; Videotape Recordings
*Identifiers:* BTBI
*Availability:* *Journal of Experimental Education,* v38 n1 p38-47, Fall 1969.

A category system for the systematic observation of biology teachers was developed. Teachers' verbal and nonverbal behaviors were assessed. Videotape recordings were made of biology teachers during regular classroom and laboratory presentations. These recordings were evaluated by observers.

9397
**Child Day Care Center Job Inventory.** Zaccaria, Michael A.; And Others 1976.
*Descriptors:* *Child Caregivers; *Child Care Occupations; *Day Care Centers; *Rating Scales; *Task Analysis; Adults; Day Care; Preschool Education
*Identifiers:* TIM(E)
*Availability:* Tests in Microfiche, Test Collection, Educational Testing Service, Princeton, NJ 08541.
*Notes:* Items, 167.

Developed as an occupational analysis of day care personnel. One hundred sixty-seven tasks performed by day care workers are listed. The items can be rated in terms of highest priority for training, time spent on each task, amount of training time necessary to perform each task, and consequences of inadequate performance of each task.

9474
**Change Scale.** Trumbo, Don A. 1961.
*Descriptors:* *Attitude Measures; *Change; *Employee Attitudes; *Employees; Adults; Organizational Change; Work Attitudes
*Availability:* *Journal of Applied Psychology,* v45 n5 p338-44, Oct 1961.
*Notes:* Items, 9.

Designed to assess employee attitudes toward work-related change.

9759
**Job Satisfaction Inventory.** Schmid, John Jr. 1958.
*Descriptors:* *Attitude Measures; *Job Satisfaction; *Military Personnel; *Work Attitudes; Adults; Employee Attitudes; Employer Employee Relationship; Peer Relationship
*Identifiers:* Air Force
*Availability:* *Educational and Psychological Measurement,* v58 n1 p189-202, 1958.
*Notes:* Items, 21.

Measures Air Force mechanics' expressed degree of satisfaction with their work. There are 7 classes of items related to higher organization of the Air Force, supervisors' technical competence, supervisors' leadership and social capacity, coworkers, job duties, living conditions on the base, and job in general.

9861
**Job Preferences (What Makes a Job Good or Bad?).** Jurgensen, Clifford E. 1945.
*Descriptors:* *Attitude Measures; *Job Applicants; *Work Attitudes; Adults; Fringe Benefits; Promotion (Occupational); Salaries; Work Environment
*Availability:* *Journal of Applied Psychology,* v63 n3 p267-76, Jun 1978.

Designed to assess applicants' priorities in work-related factors. Respondents are asked to rank 10 factors of a job in order of importance to themselves and again rank these factors as they believe others would.

10165
**STEP Observation Schedule.** Wallen, Norman E. 1969.
*Descriptors:* *Classroom Observation Techniques; *Classroom Techniques; *Elementary School Teachers; *Teacher Evaluation; *Teaching Styles; Adults; Teacher Behavior; Teacher Effectiveness
*Identifiers:* Sausalito Teacher Education Project; STEPOS; TIM(E)
*Availability:* Tests in Microfiche, Test Collection, Educational Testing Service, Princeton, NJ 08541.
*Notes:* Time, 40 approx.

Developed as part of the Sausalito Teacher Education Project, the test provides a method for systematically observing teacher classroom behavior within the framework of specific questions dealing with generally agreed upon requirements for effective teaching. The schedule consists of 10 areas plus 2 descriptive scales for teacher rating and class rating.

10171
**Short Form Measure of Self-Actualization.** Bonjean, Charles M.; Vance, Gary 1968.
*Descriptors:* *Employees; *Self Actualization; Adults; Occupational Tests; Personality Measures
*Availability:* *Journal of Applied Behavioral Science,* v4 n3 p299-312, 1968.
*Notes:* Time, 8. Items, 24.

A measure of self-actualization, which occurs in an occupational setting when members of a group believe that their occupation permits them to express themselves fully and expand their potential. The scale has 2 sections. Subjects first select from a list of conditions those important to an ideal job and then describe their present job.

10195
**Counselor Response Questionnaire.** Stokes, Joseph; Lautenschlager, Gary 1977.
*Descriptors:* *Counseling Techniques; *Counselor Training; *Microcounseling; Adults; Graduate Students; Paraprofessional Personnel; Questionnaires
*Identifiers:* CRQ; TIM(I)
*Availability:* Tests in Microfiche, Test Collection, Educational Testing Service, Princeton, NJ 08541.
*Notes:* Items, 15.

Paper and pencil instrument to measure beginning counseling skills. The CRQ is influenced by a reflective orientation to counseling and especially by microcounseling. Is intended for use with paraprofessional and beginning graduate student counselors and not to discriminate between skilled counselors. Model underlying development of CRQ assumes that counselor should remain nonjudgmental and should refrain from giving advice. Consists of 15 client statements, each followed by 3 counselor responses of varying quality.

10244
**Competency Based Teacher Evaluation Guide.** Johnson, Charles E.; Bauch, Jerold P. 1970.
*Descriptors:* *Behavior Rating Scales; *Elementary School Teachers; *Teacher Behavior; *Teacher Evaluation; Adults; Teacher Aides; Teacher Characteristics; Teacher Effectiveness
*Identifiers:* *Competency Based Assessment; TIM(E)
*Availability:* Tests in Microfiche, Test Collection, Educational Testing Service, Princeton, NJ 08541.
*Notes:* Items, 171.

Designed to evaluate the performance, behaviors, characteristic qualities, and competencies of teachers, assistant teachers, and aides. Contains one section that applies to all groups and separate sections relating specifically to each group.

10257
**Teaching Assistant Evaluator.** Meredith, Gerald R. 1979.
*Descriptors:* *Graduate Students; *Student Evaluation of Teacher Performance; *Teacher Evaluation; *Teaching Assistants; Class Organization; Higher Education; Outcomes of Education; Rating Scales; Teacher Student Relationship
*Availability:* *Psychological Reports,* v45 n1 p229-230, Aug 1979.
*Notes:* Items, 17.

Rating scale for appraising the performance of graduate-level teaching assistants. Three factors were identified: relational impact, classroom organization, and learning outcomes.

10294
**The Purdue Interest Questionnaire.** DeLauretis, Robert; And Others 1977.
*Descriptors:* *College Freshmen; *College Students; *Engineering Education; *Interest Inventories; *Predictive Measurement; *Vocational Interests; Career Counseling; Higher Education; Persistence; Specialization; Student Interests
*Identifiers:* PIQ
*Availability:* ERIC Document Reproduction Service, 7420 Fullerton Rd., Ste. 110, Springfield, VA 22153-2852 (ED170312, 9 pages).
*Notes:* Items, 264.

Designed for use in career planning for engineering students. Assists students in determining areas of interest in engineering specialties. May also be used to predict which students will remain in the engineering program and which are likely to transfer to other disciplines.

10683
**Career Planning Questionnaire.** Tennessee University, Office of Institutional Research, Knoxville, TN 1975.
*Descriptors:* *Career Planning; *College Students; Career Guidance; Counseling Objectives; Higher Education; Information Sources; Questionnaires
*Identifiers:* TIM(G); University of Tennessee Knoxville
*Availability:* Tests in Microfiche, Test Collection, Educational Testing Service, Princeton, NJ 08541.
*Notes:* Time, 15. Items, 12.

Used in research at the University of Tennessee to gain an accurate and thorough insight into students' needs for developing an awareness of careers and for planning their entry into the workforce following graduation.

10729
**ASTA Proficiency Program.** American Society of Travel Agents, Washington, DC 1982.
*Descriptors:* *Certification; *Job Skills; *Occupational Tests; *Travel; Adults; Minimum Competencies; Multiple Choice Tests; National Competency Tests; Timed Tests

*Identifiers:* American Society of Travel Agents; APP; ASTA Travel Agent Proficiency Program; Competence Test; National Certification Examinations; Proficiency Tests; *Travel Agents; Travel Agents Proficiency Test
*Availability:* American Society of Travel Agents, Education and Training Dept., 4400 MacArthur Blvd., N.W., Washington, DC 20007.

This examination is used to establish minimum standards within the travel agent industry for entry-level travel agents and to provide travel agents with the opportunity to demonstrate their competence so that it will be recognized by employers, clients, and peers. The examination covers land arrangements, cruise and ship transportation, domestic air transportation, and international air transportation. There are no eligibility requirements to take the examination. However, it is recommended that candidates for the examination have travel school experience, 4 years or 2 years of college, a vocational school experience, or 6 months' to 1 year's experience in a travel agency.

**10741**
**Consultant/Linker Knowledge and Skills Inventory.** Smink, Jay 1979.
*Descriptors:* *Competence; *Consultants; *Job Skills; *Self Evaluation (Individuals); Adults; Change Agents; Interpersonal Relationship; Knowledge Level; Rating Scales
*Availability:* ERIC Document Reproduction Service, 7420 Fullerton Rd., Ste. 110, Springfield, VA 22153-2852 (ED185080, 14 pages).
*Notes:* Time, 30 approx. Items, 72.

Self-administered inventory intended for educational consultants. Used to assess both existing and needed levels of knowledge and skills for consulting with school staff.

**10759**
**My Vocational Situation.** Holland, John L.; And Others 1980.
*Descriptors:* *Career Counseling; *Vocational Interests; Adults; Career Awareness; Diagnostic Tests
*Availability:* Consulting Psychologists Press, Inc., 3803 E. Bayshore Rd., Palo Alto, CA 94303.
*Notes:* Time, 10 approx. Items, 20.

Questionnaire developed to determine which of three possible difficulties - lack of vocational identity, lack of information or training, and environmental or personal barriers - may be troubling a client seeking help with career decisions.

**10770**
**The Six-Hour Search Toward Occupational Literacy.** Watkins, Ed 1980.
*Descriptors:* *Career Choice; *Career Counseling; *Job Skills; *Occupational Information; *Vocational Interests; College Students; Higher Education
*Availability:* National Institute for Career Development, Doane College, Crete, NE 68333.
*Notes:* Time, 360 approx. Items, 728.

Designed to help the respondents in selecting possible future occupations. Through research exercises individuals can identify 10-15 occupations that suit their skills and interests.

**10775**
**Job Awareness Inventory.** Makowski, Teen 1980.
*Descriptors:* *Career Awareness; *Career Education; *Occupational Information; Criterion Referenced Tests; Employment Interviews; High Schools
*Availability:* Academic Therapy Publications, 20 Commercial Blvd., Novato, CA 94947-6191.
*Notes:* Items, 100.

Group or individual criterion-referenced measure of knowledge about occupations, interviews, findings, jobs, and general work-related information. Designed for use with nondisabled or educable mentally retarded, learning disabled, and deaf students.

**10799**
**Course Faculty Evaluation Instrument.** Freedman, Richard D.; Stumpf, Stephen A. 1976.
*Descriptors:* *Business Administration Education; *Course Evaluation; *Graduate School Faculty; *Student Evaluation of Teacher Performance; Adults; Graduate Students; Higher Education
*Identifiers:* TIM(G)
*Availability:* Tests in Microfiche, Test Collection, Educational Testing Service, Princeton, NJ 08541.
*Notes:* Items, 60.

Developed for student evaluation of New York University Graduate Business Administration courses and faculty. This questionnaire provides descriptive feedback of the extent to which students perceive courses, instructors, and course elements as generating a high or low learning experience.

**10811**
**Checklist for Effectiveness, Efficiency, and Safety of Nursing Care.** Lindeman, Carol A.; Stetzer, Steven L.
*Descriptors:* *Medical Care Evaluation; *Nurses; *Nursing; *Patients; Adults; Check Lists; Efficiency
*Identifiers:* Nursing Care; Self Administered Tests; Surgical Nursing
*Availability:* ERIC Document Reproduction Service, 7420 Fullerton Rd., Ste. 110, Springfield, VA 22153-2852 (ED171763, 842 pages).
*Notes:* Items, 30.

This volume consists of a series of psychosocial and physiological clinical nursing instruments selected from the published literature in health care, education, psychology, and the social sciences. Instruments focus upon nursing practice and stress patient variables. The tests were designed to measure the combined aspects of effectiveness, efficiency, and safety of nursing care with respect to 30-item checklist.

**10973**
**Profiles of Teaching Competency.** Wassermann, Selma; Eggert, Wallace 1973.
*Descriptors:* *Student Teachers; *Teacher Behavior; *Teacher Evaluation; Adults; Classroom Techniques; Elementary Secondary Education; Informal Assessment; Rating Scales; Teacher Characteristics; Teacher Student Relationship; Teaching Methods
*Availability:* ERIC Document Reproduction Service, 7420 Fullerton Rd., Ste. 110, Springfield, VA 22153-2852 (ED194460, 25 pages).

Designed for use in rating student teachers. Contains 19 behavioral profiles related to competent performance in classroom teaching. Profiles concern characteristics and behaviors important in facilitating students' learning. Subjects are rated as having either the positive or negative version of the profile. Covers teacher behavior, outlook, attitudes and beliefs, and interaction with pupils.

**11012**
**Job Involvement Questionnaire.** Lodahl, Thomas M.; Kejner, Mathilde 1965.
*Descriptors:* *Attitude Measures; *Job Performance; *Self Esteem; *Work Attitudes; Adults; Questionnaires
*Availability:* *Journal of Applied Psychology,* v49 n1 p24-33, Feb 1965.
*Notes:* Items, 20.

A scale to measure job involvement, which is defined as the degree to which a person's job performance affects his or her self-esteem.

**11096**
**Ohio Vocational Interest Survey. Second Edition.** Psychological Corp., San Antonio, TX 1981.
*Descriptors:* *Career Planning; *Secondary School Students; *Vocational Interests; Career Choice; Interest Inventories; Job Training; Occupational Information; Postsecondary Education; School Surveys; Secondary Education; Secondary School Curriculum; Student Characteristics
*Identifiers:* OVIS
*Availability:* The Psychological Corp., 555 Academic Ct., San Antonio, TX 78204.
*Notes:* Time, 45. Items, 277.

Students select from statements describing job activities those they would like to perform, assuming they have the necessary training. An optional Career Planning Questionnaire concerned with school subjects and training may be included. Up to 18 questions may be added by the school to form a local survey.

**11106**
**Career Development Inventory: College and University Form.** Super, Donald E.; And Others 1981.
*Descriptors:* *Career Awareness; *Graduate Students; *Undergraduate Students; *Vocational Interests; *Vocational Maturity; Career Exploration; Career Planning; College Freshmen; Decision Making; Higher Education; Interest Inventories; Knowledge Level; Student Attitudes
*Identifiers:* CDI
*Availability:* Consulting Psychologists Press, Inc., 3803 E. Bayshore Rd., Palo Alto, CA 94303.
*Notes:* Time, 65. Items, 120.

Designed for use in assessing career development and vocational or career maturity. Resembles the school form of the test in structure to facilitate longitudinal studies. Content is relevant to the college and university context and occupations entered by college graduates. May be used to assess readiness of entering college and postgraduate students to make career decisions and to assist liberal arts majors in choosing a major field.

**11125**
**Work Relevant Attitudes Inventory.** Walther, Regis H. 1975.
*Descriptors:* *Attitude Measures; *Individual Needs; *Labor Force Development; *Program Effectiveness; *Work Attitudes; Adolescents; Adults; Disadvantaged
*Identifiers:* TIM (H); WRAI
*Availability:* Tests in Microfiche, Test Collection, Educational Testing Service, Princeton, NJ 08541.
*Notes:* Items, 26.

Used to diagnose individual needs and to evaluate effectiveness of manpower programs. Can be useful in counseling process involved in manpower training programs.

**11172**
**Gordon Occupational Check List II.** Gordon, Leonard V. 1981.
*Descriptors:* *Interest Inventories; *Vocational Interests; Adolescents; Adults; Career Counseling; Check Lists; Entry Workers; Job Training; Middle Aged Adults; Noncollege Bound Students; Occupations; Trainees
*Availability:* The Psychological Corp., 555 Academic Ct., San Antonio, TX 78204.
*Notes:* Time, 25. Items, 240.

Interest check list for use in counseling high school students who do not plan to enter college and others entering training programs or the work force. This revised edition is organized and coded for use with the *Dictionary of Occupational Titles* and other publications that use the Department of Labor coding system.

**11218**
**Vocational Adaptation Rating Scales.** Malgady, Robert G.; And Others 1980.

*Descriptors:* *Adjustment (to Environment); *Behavior Problems; *Mental Retardation; *Rating Scales; *Vocational Training Centers; Adolescents; Adults; Attendance Patterns; Communication Skills; Discipline Problems; Hygiene; Interpersonal Competence; Verbal Communication
*Identifiers:* VARS
*Availability:* Western Psychological Services, 12031 Wilshire Blvd., Los Angeles, CA 90025.
*Notes:* Time, 40 approx. Items, 133.

Measures mentally retarded individuals' maladaptive behavior likely to occur in a vocational setting, such as a sheltered workshop, job facility in the community, or vocational training classroom. Rater records the behaviors of each worker who has been observed during a specified observation period (typically, about one month).

**11243**
**Humanistic Leadership Questionnaire.** Eagleton, Cliff; Cogdell, Roy 1981.
*Descriptors:* *Human Relations; *Leadership Styles; *School Personnel; Adults; Questionnaires; Superintendents
*Availability:* *Educational Research Quarterly,* v5 n4, p51-70, Win 1980-81.
*Notes:* Items, 55.

Describes dimensions of leadership in terms of principles and practices related to a human relations model. Also assesses public school superintendents' perceptions of their own and their administrative staffs' leadership performance.

**11303**
**The Self-Expression Measure.** Bonjean, Charles M.; And Others 1980.
*Descriptors:* *Job Satisfaction; *Organizational Climate; *White Collar Occupations; *Work Environment; Adults; Rating Scales
*Availability:* *The Journal of Applied Behavioral Science,* v16 n2, p167-91, Apr-May-Jun 1980.
*Notes:* Time, 10 approx. Items, 31.

Theory-based instrument to measure congruence of organizational conditions with individual predispositions toward work. Instrument is grounded in personality and organization theory. Instrument can be used in organizational assessment and development.

**11315**
**Economy Police Promotion Tests.** McCann Associates, Inc., Langhorne, PA 1982.
*Descriptors:* *Police; *Promotion (Occupational); Administration; Adults; Crime; Criminal Law; Knowledge Level; Laws; Multiple Choice Tests; Supervision
*Identifiers:* Police Captains; Police Chiefs; Police Detectives; Police Lieutenants; Police Sergeants
*Availability:* McCann Associates, Inc., 603 Corporate Dr. West, Langhorne, PA 19047.
*Notes:* Items, 100.

Designed for use in cities under 100,000 in population. Covers legal knowledge and police knowledge typically involved in the duties of chief, captain, sergeant, detective, lieutenant, and assistant chief. Includes questions on patrol, crime investigation, supervision and administration.

**11316**
**Economy Fire Promotion Tests.** McCann Associates, Inc., Langhorne, PA 1982.
*Descriptors:* *Fire Fighters; *Promotion (Occupational); Administration; Adults; Fire Protection; Investigations; Knowledge Level; Multiple Choice Tests; Supervision
*Identifiers:* Fire Captain; Fire Chief; Fire Chief (Batallion); Fire Driver Engineer; Fire Lieutenant; Fires
*Availability:* McCann Associates, Inc., 603 Corporate Dr. West, Langhorne, PA 19047.
*Notes:* Items, 100.

Designed for use in cities under 100,000 in population. Covers knowledge and skills typically involved in the duties of chief, assistant chief, battalion chief, captain, lieutenant, and driver-engineer. Includes questions on circumstances before the fire, extinguishment, overhaul, salvage and rescue, fire prevention and investigation, supervision, and administration.

**11326**
**Energy Auditors Certification Program.** Educational Testing Service, Princeton, NJ; National Conference of States on Building Codes and Standards, Herndon, VA 1981.
*Descriptors:* *Certification; *Energy; *Energy Audits; *Energy Occupations; Adults; Competence; Energy Conservation; Knowledge Level; Multiple Choice Tests; Occupational Tests
*Identifiers:* EACP
*Availability:* Energy Auditors Certification Program, P.O. Box 2884, Educational Testing Service, Princeton, NJ 08541.
*Notes:* Items, 100.

Designed to allow those who work as energy auditors to demonstrate competence to warrant certification by the National Conference of States on Building Codes and Standards and states in which they practice. Items are job related and based on specific activities performed by energy auditors.

**11327**
**Electronic Data Processing Auditors Test.** Educational Testing Service, Princeton, NJ; EDP Auditors Foundation, Cold Stream, IL 1981.
*Descriptors:* *Certification; *Data Processing; Adults; Competence; Computer Software; Data Processing Occupations; Knowledge Level; Multiple Choice Tests; Occupational Tests; Systems Development
*Identifiers:* *Auditors; Certified Information Systems Auditors
*Availability:* Educational Testing Service, Princeton, NJ 08541.
*Notes:* Time, 360.

A certification examination for Certified Information Systems Auditors. Tests knowledge and skills in various fields of electronic data processing auditing.

**11330**
**Wolfe Programming Language Test: COBOL.** Walden Computer Aptitude Testing, Ltd., Oradell, NJ 1982.
*Descriptors:* *Data Processing Occupations; *Programmers; *Programming Languages; Adults; Job Applicants; Knowledge Level; Occupational Tests
*Identifiers:* *COBOL Programming Language; WCOBL
*Availability:* Walden Computer Aptitude Testing, Ltd., Box 319, Oradell, NJ 07649.

Designed for use in evaluating a job candidate's knowledge of COBOL. For use with COBOL programmers with all levels of experience.

**11331**
**Wolfe-Winrow OS JCL Proficiency Test.** Walden Computer Aptitude Testing, Ltd., Oradell, NJ 1982.
*Descriptors:* *Data Processing Occupations; *Programmers; *Programming Languages; Adults; Job Applicants; Knowledge Level; Occupational Tests; Coding
*Identifiers:* *Computer Operators; Error Detection; Job Control Language; OS JCL; Proficiency Tests; Programmer Analysts; WWJCL
*Availability:* Walden Computer Aptitude Testing, Ltd., Box 319, Oradell, NJ 07649.

Designed for evaluating job applicants for positions as computer operators, OS JCL analysts, and applications programmers at all levels of experience. For use in the following environments: MVS, OS/VS1, OS/MVT, PCP, SVS(OS/VS2), OS/MFT. Covers knowledge of JCL statements and parameters, understandings of same, catalogued procedures, symbolic parameters, and overriding JCL. Measures ability to code and identify errors in OSJCL.

**11332**
**Wolfe-Winrow CICS/VS Command Level Proficiency Test.** Walden Computer Aptitude Testing, Ltd., Oradell, NJ 1982.
*Descriptors:* *Computer Software; *Data Processing Occupations; *Programmers; *Programming Languages; Adults; Job Applicants; Knowledge Level; Occupational Tests; Coding
*Identifiers:* Basic Mapping Support; CICS(VS); Command Language; Debugging; Proficiency Tests; *Software Specialists; WWCICS
*Availability:* Walden Computer Aptitude Testing, Ltd., Box 319, Oradell, NJ 07649.

Designed for evaluating job applicants for positions as applications programmers and software specialists at all levels of experience. For use in DOS/VS and OS/VS installations. Covers general knowledge of commands, concepts, and facilities; coding CICS/VS commands; debugging; and testing. Optional section on Basic Mapping Support (BMS) and commands.

**11333**
**Wolfe-Winrow TSO/SPF Proficiency Test.** Walden Computer Aptitude Testing, Ltd., Oradell, NJ 1982.
*Descriptors:* *Computer Software; *Data Processing Occupations; *Programmers; *Programming Languages; Adults; Job Applicants; Knowledge Level; Occupational Tests
*Identifiers:* Command Language; Proficiency Tests; *Software Specialists; WWTSO
*Availability:* Walden Computer Aptitude Testing, Ltd., Box 319, Oradell, NJ 07649.

Designed for use in evaluating job applicants for positions as applications programmers and software specialists at all levels of experience. Covers knowledge of TSO/SPF features and commands.

**11342**
**Personal Reaction Index. Revised Edition.** Hall, Jay 1980.
*Descriptors:* *Decision Making; *Employee Attitudes; *Organizational Climate; *Participant Satisfaction; Rating Scales
*Availability:* Teleometrics International, 1755 Woodstead Ct., The Woodlands, TX 77380.
*Notes:* Items, 6.

Designed to give managerial-level employees feedback in the form of subordinate assessments regarding the decision structure that governs their work, i.e., the amount of influence subordinates feel they have in making work-related decisions and their consequent satisfaction with and commitment to those decisions.

**11363**
**The Harrington-O'Shea Career Decision-Making System.** Harrington, Thomas F.; O'Shea, Arthur J. 1982.
*Descriptors:* *Interest Inventories; *Secondary School Students; *Vocational Interests; Adults; Career Choice; Computer Assisted Testing; Computers; Decision Making; Microcomputers; Rating Scales; Secondary Education
*Identifiers:* CDM
*Availability:* American Guidance Service, Publishers' Bldg., Circle Pines, MN 55014.
*Notes:* Time, 40 approx. Items, 120.

A systemized approach to career decision making that integrates 4 major dimensions in choosing a career: abilities, values, interests, and information. The system is a simulation of a career counseling situation in which individuals learn about factors important in choosing a career and selecting a course of study or a job. The self-scored edition is available in English or Spanish. There is also a machine-scorable edition in English. Also available for use on a microcomputer. Program diskette and two data diskettes are available for use on an Apple II+ or IIe or on a TRS-80, model III or IV. Each diskette can be used for 25 administrations.

**11370**
**Correctional Officers' Interest Blank.** Gough, Harrison G.; Aumack, F.L. 1980.
*Descriptors:* *Correctional Institutions; *Institutional Personnel; *Interest Inventories; *Job Applicants; *Predictive Measurement; Adults; Attitudes; Interests
*Identifiers:* COIB
*Availability:* Consulting Psychologists Press, Inc., 3803 E. Bayshore Rd., Palo Alto, CA 94303.
*Notes:* Time, 10 approx. Items, 40.

Contains questions about personal interests and attitudes that have been found to have modest potential for predicting performance of correctional officers. May be administered to groups or individuals. Test is intended for use in evaluating correctional officers and job applicants. Scoring key is available only to qualified persons representing state, federal, or other bona fide law enforcement or judicial agencies.

**11377**
**Ohio Vocational Achievement Tests: Agricultural Education, Agricultural Business.** Ohio State Dept. of Education, Div. of Vocational Education, Columbus, OH 1980.
*Descriptors:* *Achievement Tests; *Agribusiness; *Agricultural Education; *High School Students; *Vocational Education; Advertising; Agricultural Occupations; Animal Husbandry; Data Analysis; Grade 11; Grade 12; High Schools; Knowledge Level; Merchandising; Money Management; Office Practice; Plant Growth; Problem Solving; Synthesis
*Availability:* Ohio State University, Instructional Materials Lab., 1885 Neil Ave., Columbus, OH 43210.
*Notes:* Time, 240. Items, 308.

For use in the evaluation and diagnosis of vocational achievement. Developed to measure skills and understanding in specific vocational areas. Items measure ability to solve problems, analyze data, recall facts, have a knowledge of principles, react to generalizations, use abstractions in specific situations, and form parts into complete structures. Administered with the California Short Form Test of Academic Aptitude (5919 through 5923).

**11378**
**Ohio Vocational Achievement Tests: Agricultural Education, Agricultural Mechanic.** Ohio State Dept. of Education, Div. of Vocational Education, Columbus, OH 1981.
*Descriptors:* *Achievement Tests; *Agricultural Education; *Agricultural Engineering; *Agricultural Machinery Occupations; *High School Students; *Vocational Education; Auto Mechanics; Data Analysis; Diesel Engines; Grade 11; Grade 12; High Schools; Individual Development; Knowledge Level; Problem Solving; Repair; Synthesis
*Availability:* Ohio State University, Instructional Materials Lab., 1885 Neil Ave., Columbus, OH 43210.
*Notes:* Time, 240. Items, 343.

For use in the evaluation and diagnosis of vocational achievement. Developed to measure skills and understanding in specific vocational areas. Items measure ability to solve problems, analyze data, recall facts, have a knowledge of principles, react to generalizations, use abstractions in specific situations, and form parts into complete structures. Administered with the California Short Form Test of Academic Aptitude (919 through 923).

**11379**
**Ohio Vocational Achievement Tests: Agricultural Education, Farm Management.** Ohio State Dept. of Education, Div. of Vocational Education, Columbus, OH 1981.
*Descriptors:* *Achievement Tests; *Agricultural Education; *Farm Management; *High School Students; *Vocational Education; Agricultural Machinery; Agricultural Production; Data Analysis; Employment Practices; Facility Inventory; Financial Policy; Grade 11; Grade 12; High Schools; Knowledge Level; Merchandising; Problem Solving; Recordkeeping; Supervision; Synthesis
*Availability:* Ohio State University, Instructional Materials Lab., 1885 Neil Ave., Columbus, OH 43210.
*Notes:* Time, 240. Items, 334.

For use in the evaluation and diagnosis of vocational achievement. Developed to measure skills and understanding in specific vocational areas. Items measure ability to solve problems, analyze data, recall facts, have a knowledge of principles, react to generalizations, use abstractions in specific situations, and form parts into complete structures. Administered with the California Short Form Test of Academic Aptitude (5919 through 5923).

**11381**
**Ohio Vocational Achievement Tests: Business and Office Education, Accounting/Computing Clerk.** Ohio State Dept. of Education, Div. of Vocational Education, Columbus, OH 1980.
*Descriptors:* *Accounting; *Achievement Tests; *Business Education; *Data Processing; *High School Students; *Vocational Education; Data Analysis; Employment Practices; Facility Inventory; Grade 11; Grade 12; High Schools; Knowledge Level; Payroll Records; Problem Solving; Recordkeeping; Synthesis
*Identifiers:* Accounts Receivable Clerks
*Availability:* Ohio State University, Instructional Materials Lab., 1885 Neil Ave., Columbus, OH 43210.
*Notes:* Time, 240. Items, 321.

For use in the evaluation and diagnosis of vocational achievement. Developed to measure skills and understanding in specific vocational areas. Items measure ability to solve problems, analyze data, recall facts, have a knowledge of principles, react to generalizations, use abstractions in specific situations, and form parts into complete structures. Administered with the California Short Form Test of Academic Aptitude (5919 through 5923).

**11382**
**Ohio Vocational Achievement Tests: Business and Office Education, Clerk-Stenographer.** Ohio State Dept. of Education, Div. of Vocational Education, Columbus, OH 1981.
*Descriptors:* *Achievement Tests; *Business Education; *Dictation; *High School Students; *Shorthand; *Vocational Education; Business Correspondence; Data Analysis; Grade 11; Grade 12; High Schools; Individual Development; Knowledge Level; Problem Solving; Recordkeeping; Reprography; Synthesis
*Identifiers:* Finance
*Availability:* Ohio State University, Instructional Materials Lab., 1885 Neil Ave., Columbus, OH 43210.
*Notes:* Time, 240. Items, 278.

For use in the evaluation and diagnosis of vocational achievement. Developed to measure skills and understanding in specific vocational areas. Items measure ability to solve problems, analyze data, recall facts, have a knowledge of principles, react to generalizations, use abstractions in specific situations, and form parts into complete structures. Administered with the California Short Form Test of Academic Aptitude (5919 through 5923).

**11383**
**Ohio Vocational Achievement Tests: Business and Office Education, Data Processing.** Ohio State Dept. of Education, Div. of Vocational Education, Columbus, OH 1981.
*Descriptors:* *Achievement Tests; *Business Education; *Data Processing; *High School Students; *Vocational Education; Accounting; Data Analysis; Employment Practices; Equipment; Flow Charts; Grade 11; Grade 12; High Schools; Human Relations; Knowledge Level; Mathematics; Office Practice; Problem Solving; Programming Languages; Synthesis
*Identifiers:* Computer Systems; Data Entry
*Availability:* Ohio State University, Instructional Materials Lab., 1885 Neil Ave., Columbus, OH 43210.
*Notes:* Time, 240. Items, 383.

For use in the evaluation and diagnosis of vocational achievement. Developed to measure skills and understanding in specific vocational areas. Items measure ability to solve problems, analyze data, recall facts, have a knowledge of principles, react to generalizations, use abstractions in specific situations, and form parts into complete structures. Administered with the California Short Form Test of Academic Aptitude (5919 through 5923).

**11384**
**Ohio Vocational Achievement Tests: Business and Office Education, General Office Clerk.** Ohio State Dept. of Education, Div. of Vocational Education, Columbus, OH 1980.
*Descriptors:* *Achievement Tests; *Business Education; *Clerical Workers; *High School Students; *Vocational Education; Accounting; Business Correspondence; Data Analysis; Editing; Grade 11; Grade 12; High Schools; Job Search Methods; Knowledge Level; Problem Solving; Receptionists; Recordkeeping; Reprography; Synthesis; Telephone Usage Instruction; Typewriting; Writing Skills; Word Processing
*Identifiers:* Finance
*Availability:* Ohio State University, Instructional Materials Lab., 1885 Neil Ave., Columbus, OH 43210.
*Notes:* Time, 240. Items, 285.

For use in the evaluation and diagnosis of vocational achievement. Developed to measure skills and understanding in specific vocational areas. Items measure ability to solve problems, analyze data, recall facts, have a knowledge of principles, react to generalizations, use abstractions in specific situations, and form parts into complete structures. Administered with the California Short Form Test of Academic Aptitude (5919 through 5923).

**11385**
**Ohio Vocational Achievement Tests: Construction Trades, Carpentry.** Ohio State Dept. of Education, Div. of Vocational Education, Columbus, OH 1981.
*Descriptors:* *Achievement Tests; *Building Trades; *Carpentry; *High School Students; *Trade and Industrial Education; *Vocational Education; Blueprints; Data Analysis; Estimation (Mathematics); Flooring; Grade 11; Grade 12; High Schools; Knowledge Level; Mathematical Applications; Problem Solving; Roofing; Surveys; Synthesis
*Identifiers:* Finishing (Building); Foundations (Building); Framing (Building); Insulation
*Availability:* Ohio State University, Instructional Materials Lab., 1885 Neil Ave., Columbus, OH 43210.
*Notes:* Time, 240. Items, 325.

For use in the evaluation and diagnosis of vocational achievement. Developed to measure skills and understanding in specific vocational areas. Items measure ability to solve problems, analyze data, recall facts, have a knowledge of principles, react to generalizations, use abstractions in specific situations, and form parts into complete structures. Administered with the California Short Form Test of Academic Aptitude (5919 through 5923).

**11388**
**Ohio Vocational Achievement Tests: Construction Trades, Masonry.** Ohio State Dept. of Education, Div. of Vocational Education, Columbus, OH 1981.

*Descriptors:* *Achievement Tests; *Building Trades; *High School Students; *Masonry; *Trade and Industrial Education; *Vocational Education; Blueprints; Bricklaying; Chimneys; Data Analysis; Grade 11; Grade 12; High Schools; Individual Development; Knowledge Level; Mathematical Applications; Problem Solving; Surveys; Synthesis
*Identifiers:* Arches; Concrete (Building); Fireplaces
*Availability:* Ohio State University, Instructional Materials Lab., 1885 Neil Ave., Columbus, OH 43210.
*Notes:* Time, 240. Items, 319.

For use in the evaluation and diagnosis of vocational achievement. Developed to measure skills and understanding in specific vocational areas. Items measure ability to solve problems, analyze data, recall facts, have a knowledge of principles, react to generalizations, use abstractions in specific situations, and form parts into complete structures. Administered with the California Short Form Test of Academic Aptitude (5919 through 5923).

**11390**
**Ohio Vocational Achievement Tests: Distributive Education, Food Service Personnel.** Ohio State Dept. of Education, Div. of Vocational Education, Columbus, OH 1981.
*Descriptors:* *Achievement Tests; *Distributive Education; *Food Service; *High School Students; *Vocational Education; Advertising; Business Communication; Data Analysis; Employment Practices; Facility Inventory; Grade 11; Grade 12; High Schools; Human Relations; Knowledge Level; Merchandise Information; Problem Solving; Purchasing; Safety; Synthesis
*Identifiers:* Business Principles; Cashier Checker Training; Selling Practices; Waiters Waitresses
*Availability:* Ohio State University, Instructional Materials Lab., 1885 Neil Ave., Columbus, OH 43210.
*Notes:* Time, 240. Items, 383.

For use in the evaluation and diagnosis of vocational achievement. Developed to measure skills and understanding in specific vocational areas. Items measure ability to solve problems, analyze data, recall facts, have a knowledge of principles, react to generalizations, use abstractions in specific situations, and form parts into complete structures. Administered with the California Short Form Test of Academic Aptitude (5919 through 5923).

**11391**
**Ohio Vocational Achievement Tests: Distributive Education, General Merchandising.** Ohio State Dept. of Education, Div. of Vocational Education, Columbus, OH 1980.
*Descriptors:* *Achievement Tests; *Distributive Education; *High School Students; *Merchandising; *Vocational Education; Advertising; Business Communication; Data Analysis; Employment Practices; Facility Inventory; Grade 11; Grade 12; High Schools; Human Relations; Knowledge Level; Marketing; Merchandise Information; Problem Solving; Services; Synthesis
*Identifiers:* Business Principles; Cashier Checker Training; Finance
*Availability:* Ohio State University, Instructional Materials Lab., 1885 Neil Ave., Columbus, OH 43210.
*Notes:* Time, 240. Items, 352.

For use in the evaluation and diagnosis of vocational achievement. Developed to measure skills and understanding in specific vocational areas. Items measure ability to solve problems, analyze data, recall facts, have a knowledge of principles, react to generalizations, use abstractions in specific situations, and form parts into complete structures. Administered with the California Short Form Test of Academic Aptitude (5919 through 5923).

**11394**
**Ohio Vocational Achievement Tests: Graphic Communications, Commercial Art.** Ohio State Dept. of Education, Div. of Vocational Education, Columbus, OH 1980.
*Descriptors:* *Achievement Tests; *Commercial Art; *Graphic Arts; *High School Students; *Vocational Education; Data Analysis; Design; Drafting; Engineering Drawing; Freehand Drawing; Grade 11; Grade 12; High Schools; Illustrations; Knowledge Level; Layout (Publications); Photography; Problem Solving; Synthesis
*Identifiers:* Typography
*Availability:* Ohio State University, Instructional Materials Lab., 1885 Neil Ave., Columbus, OH 43210.
*Notes:* Time, 240. Items, 311.

For use in the evaluation and diagnosis of vocational achievement. Developed to measure skills and understanding in specific vocational areas. Items measure ability to solve problems, analyze data, recall facts, have a knowledge of principles, react to generalizations, use abstractions in specific situations, and form parts into complete structures. Administered with the California Short Form Test of Academic Aptitude (5919 through 5923).

**11397**
**Ohio Vocational Achievement Tests: Health Occupations Education, Dental Assisting.** Ohio State Dept. of Education, Div. of Vocational Education, Columbus, OH 1981.
*Descriptors:* *Achievement Tests; *Dental Assistants; *Health Occupations; *High School Students; *Vocational Education; Anatomy; Data Analysis; Ethics; Grade 11; Grade 12; High Schools; Knowledge Level; Microbiology; Office Management; Pharmacology; Problem Solving; Radiology; Synthesis
*Identifiers:* Chairside Assisting (Dental); Dental Emergencies; Dental Laboratory Methods; Dental Materials; Preventive Dentistry
*Availability:* Ohio State University, Instructional Materials Lab., 1885 Neil Ave., Columbus, OH 43210.
*Notes:* Time, 240. Items, 396.

For use in the evaluation and diagnosis of vocational achievement. Developed to measure skills and understanding in specific vocational areas. Items measure ability to solve problems, analyze data, recall facts, have a knowledge of principles, react to generalizations, use abstractions in specific situations, and form parts into complete structures. Administered with the California Short Form Test of Academic Aptitude (5919 through 5923).

**11400**
**Ohio Vocational Achievement Tests: Home Economics Education, Community and Home Services.** Ohio State Dept. of Education, Div. of Vocational Education, Columbus, OH 1981.
*Descriptors:* *Achievement Tests; *Food Service; *High School Students; *Home Economics; *Medical Services; *Vocational Education; Child Caregivers; Cleaning; Data Analysis; Grade 11; Grade 12; High Schools; Knowledge Level; Problem Solving; Synthesis
*Identifiers:* Vital Signs
*Availability:* Ohio State University, Instructional Materials Lab., 1885 Neil Ave., Columbus, OH 43210.
*Notes:* Time, 240. Items, 380.

For use in the evaluation and diagnosis of vocational achievement. Developed to measure skills and understanding in specific vocational areas. Items measure ability to solve problems, analyze data, recall facts, have a knowledge of principles, react to generalizations, use abstractions in specific situations, and form parts into complete structures. Administered with the California Short Form Test of Academic Aptitude (5919 through 5923).

**11401**
**Ohio Vocational Achievement Tests: Home Economics Education, Fabric Services.** Ohio State Dept. of Education, Div. of Vocational Education, Columbus, OH 1981.
*Descriptors:* *Achievement Tests; *High School Students; *Home Economics; *Vocational Education; Career Awareness; Clothing; Data Analysis; Grade 11; Grade 12; High Schools; Interior Design; Knowledge Level; Laundry Drycleaning Occupations; Problem Solving; Sewing Machine Operators; Synthesis
*Identifiers:* Drapery Makers; *Fabric Services; Upholsterers
*Availability:* Ohio State University, Instructional Materials Lab., 1885 Neil Ave., Columbus, OH 43210.
*Notes:* Time, 240. Items, 371.

For use in the evaluation and diagnosis of vocational achievement. Developed to measure skills and understanding in specific vocational areas. Items measure ability to solve problems, analyze data, recall facts, have a knowledge of principles, react to generalizations, use abstractions in specific situations, and form parts into complete structures. Administered with the California Short Form Test of Academic Aptitude (5919 through 5923).

**11402**
**Ohio Vocational Achievement Tests: Home Economics Education, Food Services.** Ohio State Dept. of Education, Div. of Vocational Education, Columbus, OH 1981.
*Descriptors:* *Achievement Tests; *Dietetics; *Food Service; *High School Students; *Home Economics; *Vocational Education; Bakery Industry; Career Awareness; Cooks; Data Analysis; Dining Facilities; Grade 11; Grade 12; High Schools; Knowledge Level; Problem Solving; Synthesis
*Identifiers:* Catering
*Availability:* Ohio State University, Instructional Materials Lab., 1885 Neil Ave., Columbus, OH 43210.
*Notes:* Time, 240. Items, 376.

For use in the evaluation and diagnosis of vocational achievement. Developed to measure skills and understanding in specific vocational areas. Items measure ability to solve problems, analyze data, recall facts, have a knowledge of principles, react to generalizations, use abstractions in specific situations, and form parts into complete structures. Administered with the California Short Form Test of Academic Aptitude (5919 through 5923).

**11407**
**Ohio Vocational Achievement Tests: Personal Services, Cosmetology.** Ohio State Dept. of Education, Div. of Vocational Education, Columbus, OH 1980.
*Descriptors:* *Achievement Tests; *Cosmetology; *High School Students; *Service Occupations; *Vocational Education; Data Analysis; Grade 11; Grade 12; High Schools; Knowledge Level; Mathematical Applications; Problem Solving; Sanitation; Synthesis; Technology
*Identifiers:* Hairstyles; Permanent Waving; Scalp Care; Shop Management
*Availability:* Ohio State University, Instructional Materials Lab., 1885 Neil Ave., Columbus, OH 43210.
*Notes:* Time, 240. Items, 338.

For use in the evaluation and diagnosis of vocational achievement. Developed to measure skills and understanding in specific vocational areas. Items measure ability to solve problems, analyze data, recall facts, have a knowledge of principles, react to generalizations, use abstractions in specific situations, and form parts into complete structures. Administered with the California Short Form Test of Academic Aptitude (5919 through 5923).

**11410**
**Ohio Vocational Achievement Tests: Automotive, Diesel Mechanic.** Ohio State Dept. of Education, Div. of Vocational Education, Columbus, OH 1981.
*Descriptors:* *Achievement Tests; *Auto Mechanics; *Diesel Engines; *High School Students; *Vocational Education; Auto Body Repairers; Data Analysis; Equipment Maintenance; Grade 11; Grade 12; High Schools; Knowledge Level; Problem Solving; Synthesis
*Identifiers:* Automotive Service Management; Automotive Systems; Brake Services; Ignition Systems; Steering (Automotive)
*Availability:* Ohio State University, Instructional Materials Lab., 1885 Neil Ave., Columbus, OH 43210.
*Notes:* Time, 240. Items, 332.

For use in the evaluation and diagnosis of vocational achievement. Developed to measure skills and understanding in specific vocational areas. Items measure ability to solve problems, analyze data, recall facts, have a knowledge of principles, react to generalizations, use abstractions in specific situations, and form parts into complete structures. Administered with the California Short Form Test of Academic Aptitude (5919 through 5923).

**11415**
**Experience Exploration.** Ewens, William P. 1981.
*Descriptors:* *High School Students; *Interest Inventories; *Student Experience; *Undergraduate Students; *Vocational Interests; Higher Education; High Schools; Self Evaluation (Individuals)
*Availability:* Chronicle Guidance Publications, Aurora St. Extension, P.O. Box 1190, Moravia, NY 13118-1190.
*Notes:* Items, 200.

Self-scored and self-interpreted instrument that allows students to assess their experiences in relation to their interests, values, data-people-things, and school subjects. Interpretation process relates experiences to possible occupations from the job chart by considering the most satisfying school courses, interests from the exploration section, and perceived abilities.

**11429**
**Ohio Vocational Achievement Tests.** Ohio State Dept. of Education, Div. of Vocational Education, Columbus, OH 1980.
*Descriptors:* *Achievement Tests; *Agricultural Education; *Business Education; *Distributive Education; *Health Occupations; *High School Students; *Home Economics; *Trade and Industrial Education; *Vocational Education; Data Analysis; Grade 11; Grade 12; High Schools; Knowledge Level; Problem Solving; Synthesis
*Availability:* Ohio State University, Instructional Materials Lab., 1885 Neil Ave., Columbus, OH 43210.
*Notes:* Time, 240. Items, 300.

Thirty-four achievement tests for use in secondary schools offering vocational education. Tests cover Agricultural Education, Business and Office Education, Distributive Education, Health Occupations, Home Economics, and Trade and Industrial Education. Each has approximately 300 items. Developed to measure skills and understanding in specific vocational areas. Items measure ability to solve problems, analyze data, recall facts, have a knowledge of principles, react to generalizations, use abstractions in specific situations, and form parts into complete structures. Administered with the California Short Form Test of Academic Aptitude (5919 through 5923).

**11437**
**Differential Aptitude Tests. Forms V and W.** Bennett, George K.; And Others 1982.
*Descriptors:* *Aptitude Tests; *Career Guidance; *Educational Counseling; *Secondary School Students; Abstract Reasoning; Language Usage; Mathematical Applications; Mechanical Skills; Secondary Education; Spatial Ability; Spelling; Verbal Ability
*Identifiers:* Clerical Aptitude; DAT
*Availability:* The Psychological Corp., 555 Academic Ct., San Antonio, TX 78204.
*Notes:* Time, 171. Items, 605.

Integrated battery of aptitude tests designed for educational and vocational guidance in junior and senior high schools. Yields 9 scores including an index of scholastic ability.

**11471**
**The Self-Directed Search, New Zealand Revision.** Keeling, Brian; Tuck, Bryan F. 1982.
*Descriptors:* *Career Counseling; *Foreign Countries; *High School Students; *Self Evaluation (Individuals); *Vocational Interests; Adolescents
*Identifiers:* Holland (John L); New Zealand; Personality Types
*Availability:* New Zealand Council for Educational Research, Education House, P.O. Box 3237, Wellington, New Zealand.
*Notes:* Time, 50.

Self-administered, self-scored, and self-interpreted vocational counseling aid based on Holland's theory of vocational choice. Separate sections determine a person's resemblance to each of 6 personality types: realistic, investigative, artistic, social, enterprising and conventional. In this revision, the occupations finder includes those occupations peculiar to New Zealand.

**11522**
**Law Enforcement Assessment and Development Report.** Dee, Burnett R.; And Others 1981.
*Descriptors:* *Assertiveness; *Emotional Response; *Interpersonal Competence; *Personality Measures; *Personnel Selection; *Police; *Promotion (Occupational); Adults; Cooperation; Creativity; Group Testing; Individual Testing; Intelligence; Persistence
*Identifiers:* 16PF; Accident Proneness; LEADR; Sixteen Personality Factor Questionnaire
*Availability:* Institute for Personality and Ability Testing, P.O. Box 188, Champaign, IL 61820.
*Notes:* Time, 45. Items, 187.

A computer-based analysis of Cattell's 16 Personality Factor Questionnaire that provides information about how a person can be expected to function in law enforcement work. Based on the following personality characteristics: intelligence, shrewdness, creativity, accident/error-proneness, warmth, cooperation, assertiveness, sociability, venturesomeness, perseverance, and conscientiousness. Has 6th to 7th grade reading level. May be group or individually administered.

**11582**
**Leadership Scale.** Hersey, Paul; And Others 1980.
*Descriptors:* *Administrators; *Employer Employee Relationship; *Leadership Styles; Adults; Rating Scales; Self Evaluation (Individuals)
*Availability:* Pfeiffer and Co., formerly University Associates, 8517 Production Ave., San Diego, CA 92121-2280.
*Notes:* Items, 10.

Two forms are available: manager form and staff member form. Manager form allows supervisor to determine his or her leadership behavior with staff members. Staff member form helps employee determine his or her perception of manager's leadership style. Designed to be used in conjunction with the Maturity Scales (11580).

**11622**
**WPT Wolfe Screening Test for Programming Aptitude.** Wolfe Computer Aptitude Testing, Ltd., Oradell, NJ 1982.
*Descriptors:* *Aptitude Tests; *Career Guidance; *Computer Software; *Programming; *Screening Tests; *Simulation; Adolescents; Adults; Elementary Secondary Education; Job Placement; Mathematical Logic; Specifications
*Availability:* Wolfe Computer Aptitude Testing Ltd., Box 319, Oradell, NJ 07649.

Series of simulated on-the-job tasks evaluates documentation ability, logical ability, and interpretation of specifications. For use by schools, placement agencies, and vocational institutes.

**11673**
**Information Index: Health-Form 1.** Life Insurance Marketing and Research Association, Inc., Hartford, CT 1980.
*Descriptors:* *Achievement Tests; *Insurance; *Knowledge Level; Adults; Insurance Occupations
*Identifiers:* *Insurance Agents; Life Insurance Education
*Availability:* Life Insurance Marketing and Research Association, Inc., P.O. Box 208, Hartford, CT 06141-0208.
*Notes:* Time, 45. Items, 40.

Designed to assess insurance knowledge of individuals who have been trained or are actively engaged in selling insurance. Specific uses include identification of agents ready for more advanced training or those who require more time in basic training. May be used to determine knowledge obtained from a specific course. May also be used to draw comparisons among field offices or regions on insurance knowledge.

**11690**
**Bus Roadeo Test.** American Public Transit Association, Washington, DC 1982.
*Descriptors:* *Bus Transportation; *Item Banks; *Performance Tests; *Service Vehicles; *Traffic Safety; Adults; Inspection; Knowledge Level; Multiple Choice Tests; Signs
*Identifiers:* *Driver Performance
*Availability:* American Public Transit Association, 1225 Connecticut Ave., N.W., Washington, DC 20036.
*Notes:* Items, 153.

A competitive test of a bus driver's skill behind the wheel, knowledge of safety regulations, and knowledge of bus equipment. Sixty to 90 days are required to plan and complete the exercises. A written quiz is taken from a pool of 50 items and administered after the driving test. Actual bus handling in a variety of situations is required. New versions are available each year.

**11692**
**The Harvard Bank Teller Proficiency Test.** Harvard Personnel Testing, Oradell, NJ 1982.
*Descriptors:* *Banking; *Communication Skills; *Occupational Tests; *Screening Tests; Adults
*Identifiers:* Accuracy; *Bank Tellers; Customer Relations; Initiative; Judgment; Numerical Ability; Word Speed
*Availability:* Harvard Personnel Testing, Box 319, Oradell, NJ 07649.
*Notes:* Time, 30.

Pre-screening test used along with interviews and reference checks, to select candidates for teller positions. Designed to measure traits and skills identified as being required for successful performance: accuracy, speed, customer relations, judgment, numerical ability, initiative, and communication skills.

**11693**
**The Word Processing Operator Assessment Battery.** Harvard Personnel Testing, Oradell, NJ 1982.
*Descriptors:* *Occupational Tests; *Problem Solving; *Screening Tests; *Word Processing; Adults; Alphabetizing Skills; English; Filing; French; Coding
*Identifiers:* Manual Dexterity; Numerical Ability
*Availability:* Harvard Personnel Testing, Box 319, Oradell, NJ 07649.

Screening test for applicants to the position. Measures attention to detail, ability to solve problems, manual dexterity, numerical skills, alphabetizing, filing, and coding. Used along with interviews, reference checking, and machine tests. Available in English and French.

**11703**
**American Society of Clinical Pathologists Self-Assessment Program for Medical Laboratory Personnel: Series III—Chemistry.** American Society of Clinical Pathologists, Chicago, IL 1982.
*Descriptors:* *Allied Health Personnel; *Chemistry; *Laboratory Technology; *Pathology; *Physicians; *Self Evaluation (Individuals); Adults; Medical Laboratory Assistants; Medical Technologists; Objective Tests
*Identifiers:* ASCP; PSA
*Availability:* Staff Manager, PSA Program, American Society of Clinical Pathologists, 2100 W. Harrison, Chicago, IL 60612.

Designed to assess knowledge of basic fundamentals in clinical chemistry and proficiency in applying knowledge to specific technical and medical problems. Major areas include biochemical aspects of disease, diagnostic application of chemical tests, analytical methodology, instrumentation, quality control, and laboratory management. Devised for pathologists, pathology residents, clinical chemists, and medical technologists whose primary interests are in clinical chemistry. Designed to permit medical laboratory personnel to assess their strengths and weaknesses in scientific and technical areas. Examinations are updated biennially.

**11704**
**American Society of Clinical Pathologists Self-Assessment Program for Medical Laboratory Personnel: Series II—Cytology.** American Society of Clinical Pathologists, Chicago, IL 1982.
*Descriptors:* *Cytology; *Medical Technologists; *Pathology; *Physicians; *Self Evaluation (Individuals); Adults; Allied Health Personnel; Medical Laboratory Assistants; Objective Tests
*Identifiers:* ASCP; PSA
*Availability:* Staff Manager, PSA Program, American Society of Clinical Pathologists, 2100 W. Harrison, Chicago, IL 60612.

Designed to permit medical laboratory personnel to assess their strengths and weaknesses in scientific and technical areas. Examinations are updated biennially. Cytology examination is appropriate for cytopathologists and cytotechnologists engaged in interpretation of cytologic preparations from various body sites. Gynecologic and nongynecologic cases are examined through presentation of 53 color transparencies. Emphasis is on interpretation and diagnosis of cytologic specimens and follow-up of clinical cases. Questions on specimen preparation are included.

**11705**
**American Society of Clinical Pathologists Self-Assessment Program for Medical Laboratory Personnel: Series III—Forensic Pathology.** American Society of Clinical Pathologists, Chicago, IL 1982.
*Descriptors:* *Graduate Medical Students; *Pathology; *Physicians; *Self Evaluation (Individuals); Adults; Objective Tests
*Identifiers:* ASCP; PSA; *Forensic Science; Legal Medicine
*Availability:* Staff Manager, PSA Program, American Society of Clinical Pathologists, 2100 W. Harrison, Chicago, IL 60612.

Available only to physicians. Examination is updated biennially. Designed to increase awareness of cases which are or may become medicolegal and to assess proficiency in forensic pathology. Evaluates knowledge in clinical and anatomic pathology. Set of 48 color transparencies is an integral part of examination.

**11706**
**American Society of Clinical Pathologists Self-Assessment Program for Medical Laboratory Personnel: Series III—Hematology.** American Society of Clinical Pathologists, Chicago, IL 1982.
*Descriptors:* *Allied Health Personnel; *Medical Technologists; *Pathology; *Self Evaluation (Individuals); Adults; Objective Tests; Physicians
*Identifiers:* ASCP; PSA; *Hematology
*Availability:* Staff Manager, PSA Program, American Society of Clinical Pathologists, 2100 W. Harrison, Chicago, IL 60612.

Intended to permit medical laboratory personnel to assess their strengths and weaknesses in scientific and technical areas. Examinations are updated biennially. Designed to assess knowledge in areas including anemias, leukocyte disorders, instrumentation, examination of tissue and smears, and coagulation. Fifty-one color transparencies are used as part of examination.

**11707**
**American Society of Clinical Pathologists Self-Assessment Program for Medical Laboratory Personnel: Series III—Immunohematology.** American Society of Clinical Pathologists, Chicago, IL 1982.
*Descriptors:* *Medical Technologists; *Pathology; *Physicians; *Self Evaluation (Individuals); Adults; Allied Health Personnel; Objective Tests
*Identifiers:* ASCP; PSA; Hematology; *Immunology
*Availability:* Staff Manager, PSA Program, American Society of Clinical Pathologists, 2100 W. Harrison, Chicago, IL 60612.

Designed to permit medical laboratory personnel to assess their strengths and weaknesses in scientific and technical areas. Examinations are updated biennially. Areas emphasized include antibody systems, component therapy and preparation, adverse reactions of donors and recipients, hemolytic disease of the newborn, hepatitis testing, and aspects of serology.

**11708**
**American Society of Clinical Pathologists Self-Assessment Program for Medical Laboratory Personnel: Series III—Immunology.** American Society of Clinical Pathologists, Chicago, IL 1982.
*Descriptors:* *Medical Technologists; *Pathology; *Physicians; *Self Evaluation (Individuals); Adults; Allied Health Personnel; Objective Tests
*Identifiers:* ASCP; PSA; *Immunology
*Availability:* Staff Manager, PSA Program, American Society of Clinical Pathologists, 2100 W. Harrison, Chicago, IL 60612.

Intended to permit medical laboratory personnel to assess their strengths and weaknesses in scientific and technical areas. Examinations are updated biennially. Areas assessed include antigen-antibody reactions, immunoglobulins, cell-mediated immunity, immunoproliferative disorders, immunodeficiency states, tissue immunology, immune injury states, and serology. Designed for pathologists, clinical scientists, and technologists working in field of immunology. Simulation of clinical problems is stressed and 35 mm transparencies are used extensively.

**11709**
**American Society of Clinical Pathologists Self-Assessment Program for Medical Laboratory Personnel: Series III—Microbiology.** American Society of Clinical Pathologists, Chicago, IL 1982.
*Descriptors:* *Medical Technologists; *Microbiology; *Pathology; *Physicians; *Self Evaluation (Individuals); Adults; Objective Tests
*Identifiers:* ASCP; PSA
*Availability:* Staff Manager, PSA Program, American Society of Clinical Pathologists, 2100 W. Harrison, Chicago, IL 60612.

Designed to permit medical laboratory personnel to assess their strengths and weaknesses in scientific and technical areas. Examinations are updated biennially. Evaluates basic knowledge with emphasis on clinical consultation role of microbiology laboratory. Assesses knowledge in areas of identification of organisms from various culture media, tissue, exudates, and blood smears. Questions cover antibiotic therapy, basic epidemiology, and specimen handling. Thirty-five mm transparencies are used to illustrate questions covering areas of bacteriology, virology, parasitology, micology, serology, and rickettsiae.

**11710**
**American Society of Clinical Pathologists Self-Assessment Program for Medical Laboratory Personnel: Series III—Nuclear Medicine.** American Society of Clinical Pathologists, Chicago, IL 1982.
*Descriptors:* *Pathology; *Physicians; *Radiologic Technologists; *Radiology; *Self Evaluation (Individuals); Adults; Allied Health Personnel; Objective Tests
*Identifiers:* ASCP; PSA
*Availability:* Staff Manager, PSA Program, American Society of Clinical Pathologists, 2100 W. Harrison, Chicago, IL 60612.

Provides general assessment of in vitro uses of radionuclides in laboratory and examines topic areas such as types and sources of radioactivity used in clinical laboratory, appropriate methods of detection, radiation health physics, analysis and evaluation of raw test data, clinical relevance and decision making, and interpretation of several types of radionuclide test results. Designed to permit medical laboratory personnel to assess their strengths and weaknesses in scientific and technical areas. Examinations are updated biennially.

**11739**
**Profiles of Organizational Influence Strategies.** Kipnis, David; Schmidt, Stuart M. 1982.
*Descriptors:* *Administrators; *Employer Employee Relationship; *Organizational Communication; *Peer Influence; *Supervisory Methods; Adults; Behavior Patterns; Feedback; Organizations (Groups); Rating Scales
*Identifiers:* Communications Behavior; POIS; Self Administered Tests; Self Scoring Tests
*Availability:* Learning Resources Corp., 8517 Production Ave., P.O. Box 26240, San Diego, CA 92126.

Measures the way people influence one another upward, downward, and laterally in organizations. Three forms are available. Form M contains 27 statements which are used to determine how respondents attempt to influence their supervisors. Form C contains 27 statements used to provide a profile of how respondents attempt to influence their coworkers. Form S consists of 33 statements used to determine how respondents attempt to influence subordinates. May be used as organizational assessment tools, to obtain specific behavioral feedback for determining managerial training needs, to provide feedback on managers' influence, to aid in designing training programs, or to measure changes over time in the types of influence strategies used.

**11742**
**Sales Staff Selector.** Harvard Personnel Testing, Oradell, NJ 1982.
*Descriptors:* *French; *Motivation; *Occupational Tests; *Personnel Selection; *Salesmanship; *Sales Occupations; Adults; Cognitive Style; Interpersonal Competence; Job Skills; Reliability; Sales Workers
*Identifiers:* Drives (Personality); Initiative; Service Representatives; Stability (Occupational)
*Availability:* Harvard Personnel Testing, Box 319, Oradell, NJ 07649.

Designed for use as a predictor of performance in hiring sales professionals. Measures sales ability, motivation, social intelligence, drive, reliability, quick thinking, stability, and initiative. Selection kits are available for sales clerks, technical service representatives, technical sales representatives, sales representatives, sales engineers, and sales supervisors. Available in English and

French. This test is scored and evaluated by the publisher.

**11760**
**Wide Range Employability Sample Test.** Jastak, Joseph F.; Jastak, Sarah 1980.
*Descriptors:* *Adults; *Disabilities; *Employment Potential; *Job Skills; *Mental Retardation; *Work Sample Tests; Adolescents; Occupational Tests; Sheltered Workshops
*Identifiers:* WREST
*Availability:* Jastak Associates, P.O. Box 3410, Wilmington, DE 19806.
*Notes:* Time, 120 approx.

Designed to measure productivity in terms of quantity and quality. Measures "horizontal" achievement (capacity to do routine operations involved in all jobs). Measures ability to complete tasks that are carefully taught before testing. May also be useful in diagnosis of mental retardation.

**11762**
**Career Assessment Inventory, Revised Edition.** Johansson, Charles B. 1982.
*Descriptors:* *Adolescents; *Adults; *Career Guidance; *French; *Interest Inventories; *Spanish; *Vocational Education; *Vocational Interests; Community Colleges; Counseling Techniques
*Identifiers:* CAI; Self Administered Tests
*Availability:* National Computer Systems, Professional Assessment Services, P.O. Box 1416, Minneapolis, MN 55440.
*Notes:* Time, 40 approx. Items, 305.

Designed to assess career interests of individuals pursuing occupations that require a minimum of postsecondary training. Item content, reading level, and scale development are oriented toward "nonprofessional" end of the vocational spectrum. Items are written at a 6th grade reading level. Instrument is frequently used with adults who have poor reading skills. Six general theme scales include realistic, investigative, artistic, social, enterprising, and conventional. Forms available in Spanish and French.

**11763**
**Wolfe Data Entry Operator Test.** Walden Computer Aptitude Testing, Ltd., Oradell, NJ 1982.
*Descriptors:* *Data Processing; *Occupational Tests; Adults; Editing; Input Output Devices; Screening Tests
*Identifiers:* Coding (Data Processing); *Computer Operators; *Data Entry; Manual Dexterity; Numerical Ability; Work Speed
*Availability:* Walden Computer Aptitude Testing, Ltd., Box 319, Oradell, NJ 07649.
*Notes:* Time, 20.

Designed to screen out error-prone job candidates. Measures manual dexterity, coding, accuracy, work speed, editing, and numerical facility. For use with data entry and terminal operators and all types of data entry equipment.

**11766**
**Career Occupational Preference System Professional Level Interest Inventory: Form P.** Knapp-Lee, Lisa; And Others 1982.
*Descriptors:* *Career Guidance; *College Bound Students; *College Students; *High School Students; *Professional Occupations; *Professional Personnel; *Student Educational Objectives; Career Counseling; Career Planning; Higher Education; High Schools; Interest Inventories
*Identifiers:* COPS (P); Self Administered Tests; Self Scoring Tests; Test Batteries
*Availability:* Educational and Industrial Testing Service, P.O. Box 7234, San Diego, CA 92107.
*Notes:* See also Career Orientation Placement and Evaluation Survey (8882); California Occupational Preference System Interest Inventory (10727); and Career Ability Placement Survey (5834). Time, 30 approx. Items, 192.

Examinees should be familiar with COPSystem before administration of this instrument. Designed to assist in career decision-making process for professionally oriented individuals. Machine-scored and self-scoring forms are available.

**11774**
**IPI Hiring Manual and Job-Tests Program.** Industrial Psychology International, Ltd., Champaign, IL 1981.
*Descriptors:* *Employees; *Job Applicants; *Job Skills; Adults; Aptitude Tests; Biographical Inventories; Clerical Occupations; Employee Attitudes; Job Performance; Personality Measures; Professional Occupations; Semiskilled Workers; Skilled Workers; Supervisors
*Identifiers:* Test Batteries
*Availability:* Industrial Psychology International, Ltd., 111 N. Market St., Champaign, IL 61820.

Series of 23 test forms used in different combinations for 24 job-test fields. Lower-level jobs use 5 or 6 tests, whereas upper-level jobs use 10 to 12 tests. Tests A-N are aptitude-intelligence tests. Tests O, P, and R are personality or temperament tests. Tests T through X are biography or weighted application forms. Most job tests require about 5 minutes. Testing at lower-level jobs requires about 30 minutes. Testing at higher levels requires about 1 hour.

**11801**
**Management Inventory on Time Management.** Kirkpatrick, Donald L. 1980.
*Descriptors:* *Administrator Attitudes; *Attitude Measures; *Management Development; *Supervisors; *Time Management; Administrative Principles; Administrators; Adults
*Identifiers:* MITM
*Availability:* Dr. Donald L. Kirkpatrick, 1920 Hawthorne Dr., Elm Grove, WI 53122.
*Notes:* See also Management Inventory on Leadership and Motivation (7680) and Management Inventory on Managing Change (11800). Time, 15 approx. Items, 60.

Designed to assess opinions and attitudes toward effective time utilization and delegation techniques. May be used to plan and evaluate training courses on time management. Applicable to all levels of management with emphasis on middle- and top-level managers.

**11805**
**NTE Core Battery: Test of General Knowledge.** Educational Testing Service, Princeton, NJ 1982.
*Descriptors:* *Achievement Tests; *Fine Arts; *Literature; *Mathematics; *Sciences; *Social Studies; *Teacher Certification; *Teacher Education Programs; *Teachers; *Teacher Selection; College Students; Higher Education
*Identifiers:* National Teacher Examinations
*Availability:* NTE Programs, Educational Testing Service, CN 6051, Princeton, NJ 08541.
*Notes:* See also NTE Core Battery: Test of Professional Knowledge (11807); NTE Core Battery: Test of Communication Skills (11806); and NTE Specialty Area Tests (11834 through 11861). Time, 120.

Part of a standardized, secure measure of academic achievement for college students in, or completing, teacher education programs. Covers literature, fine arts, mathematics, science, and social studies. Used by associations, school systems, state agencies, and institutions for decisions about the certification and selection of teachers. Other measures include the Test of Communication Skills (11806) and Test of Professional Knowledge (11807). Twenty-seven tests in specialization areas are also available as part of the testing program.

**11806**
**NTE Core Battery: Test of Communication Skills.** Educational Testing Service, Princeton, NJ 1982.
*Descriptors:* *Achievement Tests; *Communication Skills; *Teacher Certification; *Teacher Education Programs; *Teachers; *Teacher Selection; College Students; Higher Education; Listening Skills; Reading Skills; Writing Skills
*Identifiers:* National Teacher Examinations; Writing Samples
*Availability:* NTE Programs, Educational Testing Service, CN 6051, Princeton, NJ 08541.
*Notes:* See also NTE Core Battery: Test of Professional Knowledge (11807); NTE Core Battery: Test of General Knowledge (11805); and NTE Specialty Area Tests (11834 through 11861). Time, 120.

Part of a standardized, secure measure of academic achievement for college students in, or completing, teacher education programs. Covers listening, reading, and writing skills. The writing skills subtest includes a short essay. Used by associations, school systems, state agencies, and institutions for decisions about the certification and selection of teachers. Other measures include the Test of Professional Knowledge (11807) and Test of General Knowledge (11805). Twenty-seven tests in specialization areas are also available as part of the testing program.

**11807**
**NTE Core Battery: Test of Professional Knowledge.** Educational Testing Service, Princeton, NJ 1982.
*Descriptors:* *Achievement Tests; *Educational Theories; *Teacher Certification; *Teacher Education Programs; *Teachers; *Teacher Selection; College Students; Cultural Influences; Curriculum; Higher Education; Learning Processes; Social Influences; Teaching Methods
*Identifiers:* National Teacher Examinations
*Availability:* NTE Programs, Educational Testing Service, CN 6051, Princeton, NJ 08541.
*Notes:* See also NTE Core Battery: Test of Communication Skills (11806); NTE Core Battery: Test of General Knowledge (11805); and NTE Specialty Area Tests (11834 through 11861). Time, 120.

Part of a standardized, secure measure of academic achievement for college students in, or completing, teacher education programs. Covers questions related to the social and cultural forces that influence curriculum and teaching, as well as questions dealing with general principles of learning and instruction. Used by associations, school systems, state agencies, and institutions for decisions about the certification and selection of teachers. Other measures include the Test of General Knowledge (11805) and the Test of Communication Skills (11806). Twenty-seven tests in specialization areas are also available as part of the testing program.

**11809**
**Occ-U-Sort. Second Edition.** Jones, Lawrence K. 1981.
*Descriptors:* *Career Choice; *Interest Inventories; *Vocational Interests; Adolescents; Adults; Career Guidance; Individual Testing
*Identifiers:* Card Sort; Self Administered Tests; Self Scoring
*Availability:* Publishers Test Service, 2500 Garden Rd., Monterey, CA 93940.
*Notes:* Items, 60.

Aids individuals in making an occupational choice, stimulates their thinking about motives and self-perceptions, broadens awareness of occupations, and encourages consideration of nontraditional occupations. Can be self-administered and self-scored, individually administered, administered to small groups, or used as part of a structured counseling interview. Appropriate for use by counselors, occupational-vocational educators, individuals in junior and senior high schools, Employment Security Commission offices, libraries, college counseling and career placement offices, and adult career development programs.

**11810**
**Supervisory Skills Inventory.** Lafferty, J. Clayton 1982.

*Descriptors:* *Administrator Evaluation; *Self Evaluation (Individuals); *Supervisors; *Supervisory Methods; Adults; Rating Scales
*Identifiers:* SSI; Supervisor Evaluation
*Availability:* Human Synergistics, 39819 Plymouth Rd., Plymouth, MI 48170.
*Notes:* Items, 90.

Developed to assess supervisors' on-the-job behavior as seen by themselves and collectively by 5 others. Focuses on day-to-day activities rather than on long-term objective setting and overall planning. Twelve skill areas crucial to effective supervision are assessed.

**11823**
**Reading-Free Vocational Interest Inventory. Revised.** Becker, Ralph L. 1981.
*Descriptors:* *Interest Inventories; *Learning Disabilities; *Mental Retardation; *Nonverbal Tests; *Vocational Interests; Forced Choice Technique; Pictorial Stimuli; Reading Difficulties
*Identifiers:* RFVII
*Availability:* Elbern Publications, P.O. Box 09497, Columbus, OH 43209.
*Notes:* Time, 20 approx. Items, 55.

A nonreading vocational preference test for use with mentally retarded and learning disabled individuals from age 13 to adult. Pictorial illustrations with occupational significance are presented in forced-choice format for selections. Devised to provide systematic information on the range of interest patterns of the exceptional male or female who is diagnosed as mentally retarded or learning disabled. Provides scores in 11 interest areas in which this population is productive and proficient.

**11824**
**Power Management Inventory.** Hall, Jay; Hawker, James 1981.
*Descriptors:* *Administrators; *Leadership Styles; *Self Evaluation (Individuals); Adults
*Identifiers:* PMI; *Power (Personal)
*Availability:* Telеometrics International, 1755 Woodstead Ct., The Woodlands, TX 77380.
*Notes:* See also Power Management Profile (11825). Items, 70.

Self-assessment instrument designed to give a manager information on his or her management of influence dynamics, i.e., how a given manager prefers to handle situations calling for the exercise of power and authority.

**11825**
**Power Management Profile.** Hall, Jay; Hawker, James 1981.
*Descriptors:* *Administrators; *Employee Attitudes; *Leadership Styles; Adults; Employer Employee Relationship; Rating Scales
*Identifiers:* PMP; *Power (Personal)
*Availability:* Telеometrics International, 1755 Woodstead Ct., The Woodlands, TX 77380.
*Notes:* See also Power Management Inventory (11824). Items, 76.

Used by subordinates to assess manager's characteristic management of influence dynamics and to allow for observation of how manager handles situations calling for the exercise of power and authority.

**11834**
**NTE Specialty Area Tests: Agriculture (California).** Educational Testing Service, Princeton, NJ 1982.
*Descriptors:* *Achievement Tests; *Agriculture; *Teacher Certification; *Teacher Education Programs; *Teachers; *Teacher Selection; Agricultural Engineering; Agronomy; Animal Husbandry; College Students; Higher Education; Soil Science
*Identifiers:* Agricultural Resources; California; National Teacher Examinations
*Availability:* NTE Programs, Educational Testing Service, CN 6051, Princeton, NJ 08541.
*Notes:* See also NTE Core Battery (11805 through 11807) and other NTE Specialty Area Tests (11835 through 11861). Time, 120.

Part of a standardized, secure measure of academic achievement for college students in, or completing, teacher education programs. Used by associations, school systems, state agencies, and institutions, for decisions about the certification and selection of teachers. One of 27 tests measuring understanding of the content and methods applicable to teaching in subject areas. This test covers agriculture and society, animal science, plant and soil science, agriculture mechanics, and agricultural resources management in the state of California.

**11835**
**NTE Specialty Area Tests: Art Education.** Educational Testing Service, Princeton, NJ 1982.
*Descriptors:* *Achievement Tests; *Art Education; *Art Teachers; *Teacher Certification; *Teacher Education Programs; *Teachers; *Teacher Selection; Art Activities; College Students; Higher Education
*Identifiers:* National Teacher Examinations
*Availability:* NTE Programs, Educational Testing Service, CN 6051, Princeton, NJ 08541.
*Notes:* See also NTE Core Battery (11805 through 11807) and other NTE Specialty Area Tests (11834 through 11861). Time, 120.

Part of a standardized, secure measure of academic achievement for college students in, or completing, teacher education programs. Used by associations, school systems, state agencies, and institutions, for decisions about the certification and selection of teachers. One of 27 tests measuring understanding of the content and methods applicable to teaching in subject areas. This test covers world art and art analysis, materials, tools, techniques and processes of art, and professional practices in the teaching of art.

**11836**
**NTE Specialty Area Tests: Biology and General Science.** Educational Testing Service, Princeton, NJ 1982.
*Descriptors:* *Achievement Tests; *Biology; *General Science; *Science Teachers; *Teacher Certification; *Teacher Education Programs; *Teachers; *Teacher Selection; Astronomy; Chemistry; College Students; Geology; Higher Education; Meteorology; Oceanography; Physics; Scientific Methodology; Space Sciences; Molecular Biology
*Identifiers:* Cells (Biology); National Teacher Examinations
*Availability:* NTE Programs, Educational Testing Service, CN 6051, Princeton, NJ 08541.
*Notes:* See also NTE Core Battery (11805 through 11807) and other NTE Specialty Area Tests (11834 through 11861). Time, 120.

Part of a standardized, secure measure of academic achievement for college students in, or completing, teacher education programs. Used by associations, school systems, state agencies, and institutions for decisions about the certification and selection of teachers. One of 27 tests measuring understanding of the content and methods applicable to teaching in subject areas. This test covers molecular and cellular biology, chemistry, physics, astronomy, space science, geology, oceanography and meteorology, and the history, philosophy, and methodology of science.

**11837**
**NTE Specialty Area Tests: Business Education.** Educational Testing Service, Princeton, NJ 1982.
*Descriptors:* *Achievement Tests; *Business Education; *Business Education Teachers; *Teacher Certification; *Teacher Education Programs; *Teacher Selection; Banking; Business Communication; College Students; Data Processing; Economics; Government Role; Higher Education; Marketing; Office Practice; Shorthand; Typewriting; Accounting
*Identifiers:* Business Law; Business Mathematics; Finance; Keyboarding; National Teacher Examinations; Transcription
*Availability:* NTE Programs, Educational Testing Service, CN 6051, Princeton, NJ 08541.
*Notes:* See also NTE Core Battery (11805 through 11807) and other NTE Specialty Area Tests (11834 through 11861). Time, 120.

Part of a standardized, secure measure of academic achievement for college students in, or completing, teacher education programs. Used by associations, school systems, state agencies, and institutions for decisions about the certification and selection of teachers. One of 27 tests measuring understanding of the content and methods applicable to teaching in subject areas. This test covers mathematics and communication for business, finance, government and banking, business law, economics, professional information related to business education in general, and areas of specialization within business education. These areas are typewriting and keyboarding, shorthand and transcription, office procedures, accounting, data processing, marketing, and distribution.

**11838**
**NTE Specialty Area Tests: Audiology.** Educational Testing Service, Princeton, NJ 1982.
*Descriptors:* *Achievement Tests; *Allied Health Personnel; *Audiology; *Teacher Certification; *Teacher Education Programs; *Teachers; *Teacher Selection; Acoustics; Anatomy; Auditory Evaluation; College Students; Hearing Conservation; Hearing Impairments; Higher Education; Rehabilitation; Speech; Psychoacoustics
*Identifiers:* Habilitation; National Teacher Examinations
*Availability:* NTE Programs, Educational Testing Service, CN 6051, Princeton, NJ 08541.
*Notes:* See also NTE Core Battery (11805 through 11807) and other NTE Specialty Area Tests (11834 through 11861). Time, 120.

Part of a standardized, secure measure of academic achievement for college students in, or completing, teacher education programs. Used by associations, school systems, state agencies, and institutions for decisions about the certification and selection of teachers. One of 27 tests measuring understanding of the content and methods applicable to teaching in subject areas. Covers basic science of audiology, including acoustics, psychoacoustics, and anatomy; evaluation of hearing impairment; habilitation and rehabilitation; hearing conservation; and speech.

**11839**
**NTE Specialty Area Tests: Chemistry, Physics and General Science.** Educational Testing Service, Princeton, NJ 1982.
*Descriptors:* *Achievement Tests; *Chemistry; *General Science; *Physics; *Science Teachers; *Teacher Certification; *Teacher Education Programs; *Teachers; *Teacher Selection; Astronomy; Biology; College Students; Geology; Higher Education; Meteorology
*Identifiers:* National Teacher Examinations
*Availability:* NTE Programs, Educational Testing Service, CN 6051, Princeton, NJ 08541.
*Notes:* See also NTE Core Battery (11805 through 11807) and other NTE Specialty Area Tests (11834 through 11861). Time, 120.

Part of a standardized, secure measure of academic achievement for college students in, or completing, teacher education programs. Used by associations, school systems, state agencies, and institutions for decisions about the certification and selection of teachers. One of 27 tests measuring understanding of the content and methods applicable to teaching in subject areas. This test covers chemistry, physics, astronomy, geology, meteorology, and biology.

**11840**
**NTE Specialty Area Tests: Early Childhood Education (Ages 3-8).** Educational Testing Service, Princeton, NJ 1982.

*Descriptors:* *Achievement Tests; *Early Childhood Education; *Elementary School Teachers; *Preschool Teachers; *Teacher Certification; *Teacher Education Programs; *Teachers; *Teacher Selection; Child Development; Class Organization; College Students; Curriculum; Higher Education; Learning; Teaching Methods; Teaching Styles
*Identifiers:* National Teacher Examinations
*Availability:* NTE Programs, Educational Testing Service, CN 6051, Princeton, NJ 08541.
*Notes:* See also NTE Core Battery (11805 through 11807), NTE Specialty Area Tests (11834 through 11861). Time, 120.

Part of a standardized, secure measure of academic achievement for college students in, or completing, teacher education programs. Used by associations, school systems, state agencies, and institutions for decisions about the certification and selection of teachers. One of 27 tests measuring understanding of the content and methods applicable to teaching in subject areas. This test covers the nature of the growth, development, and learning of young children and the appropriateness of teaching behaviors, curriculum organization, and activities for children ages 3-8 in relation to growth, development, and learning.

**11841**
**NTE Specialty Area Tests: Education in the Elementary School (Grades 1-8).** Educational Testing Service, Princeton, NJ 1982.
*Descriptors:* *Achievement Tests; *Elementary Education; *Elementary School Teachers; *Teacher Certification; *Teacher Education Programs; *Teachers; *Teacher Selection; Art; Child Development; College Students; Diagnostic Teaching; Higher Education; Instruction; Intellectual Disciplines; Language Arts; Mathematics; Music; Physical Education; Reading; Social Studies; Teaching Methods
*Identifiers:* National Teacher Examinations
*Availability:* NTE Programs, Educational Testing Service, CN 6051, Princeton, NJ 08541.
*Notes:* See also NTE Core Battery (11805 through 11807) and other NTE Specialty Area Tests (11834 through 11861). Time, 120.

Part of a standardized, secure measure of academic achievement for college students in, or completing, teacher education programs. Used by associations, school systems, state agencies, and institutions for decisions about the certification and selection of teachers. One of 27 tests measuring understanding of the content and methods applicable to teaching in subject areas. This test covers the child as the focus of teaching, the child's development, and the process of teaching, e.g., diagnostic and prescriptive teaching. Other questions concern teaching in subject areas: language arts, reading, mathematics, social studies, science, music, art, and physical education.

**11842**
**NTE Specialty Area Tests: Education of Mentally Retarded Students.** Educational Testing Service, Princeton, NJ 1982.
*Descriptors:* *Achievement Tests; *Mild Mental Retardation; *Moderate Mental Retardation; *Special Education; *Special Education Teachers; *Teacher Certification; *Teacher Education Programs; *Teachers; *Teacher Selection; Behavior Standards; College Students; Educational Assessment; Educational Needs; Higher Education; Instructional Materials; Learning Theories; Teacher Responsibility; Teaching Methods
*Identifiers:* Curriculum Models; National Teacher Examinations; Psychological Problems; Service Models
*Availability:* NTE Programs, Educational Testing Service, CN 6051, Princeton, NJ 08541.
*Notes:* See also NTE Core Battery (11805 through 11807) and other NTE Specialty Area Tests (11834 through 11861). Time, 120.

Part of a standardized, secure measure of academic achievement for college students in, or completing, teacher education programs. Used by associations, school systems, state agencies, and institutions for decisions about the certification and selection of teachers. One of 27 tests measuring understanding of the content and methods applicable to teaching in subject areas. This test covers psychological and educational problems of various disabled groups, learning theories, mental disabilities, use of assessment data, delivery of service models, curriculum models, methods and materials, and professional concerns, e.g., ethics, responsibilities. Questions focus on the general field of special education, and specifically on the trainable and educable mentally retarded.

**11843**
**NTE Specialty Area Tests: Educational Administration and Supervision.** Educational Testing Service, Princeton, NJ 1982.
*Descriptors:* *Achievement Tests; *Administrators; *Educational Administration; *School Supervision; *Teacher Certification; *Teacher Education Programs; *Teachers; *Teacher Selection; Curriculum Design; Graduate Students; Higher Education; Human Relations; Personnel Evaluation; Program Improvement
*Identifiers:* National Teacher Examinations
*Availability:* NTE Programs, Educational Testing Service, CN 6051, Princeton, NJ 08541.
*Notes:* See also NTE Core Battery (11805 through 11807) and other NTE Specialty Area Tests (11834 through 11861). Time, 120.

Part of a standardized, secure measure of academic achievement for college students in, or completing, teacher education programs. Used by associations, school systems, state agencies, and institutions for decisions about the certification and selection of teachers. One of 27 tests measuring understanding of the content and methods applicable to teaching in subject areas. This test covers program improvement, e.g., curriculum design, staff evaluation, program evaluation; management; and human relations. Intended for those who possess or are candidates for master's degrees.

**11844**
**NTE Specialty Area Tests: English Language and Literature.** Educational Testing Service, Princeton, NJ 1982.
*Descriptors:* *Achievement Tests; *English Literature; *Language Arts; *Teacher Certification; *Teacher Education Programs; *Teachers; *Teacher Selection; *United States Literature; College Students; Higher Education; Language Usage; Mass Media; Reference Materials; Rhetoric; Writing (Composition)
*Identifiers:* National Teacher Examinations
*Availability:* NTE Programs, Educational Testing Service, CN 6051, Princeton, NJ 08541.
*Notes:* See also NTE Core Battery (11805 through 11807) and other NTE Specialty Area Tests (11834 through 11861). Time, 120.

Part of a standardized, secure measure of academic achievement for college students in, or completing, teacher education programs. Used by associations, school systems, state agencies, and institutions for decisions about the certification and selection of teachers. One of 27 tests measuring understanding of the content and methods applicable to teaching in subject areas. Test covers English and American literature, composition, rhetoric and language, reference materials, and the media.

**11845**
**NTE Specialty Area Tests: French.** Educational Testing Service, Princeton, NJ 1982.
*Descriptors:* *Achievement Tests; *French; *Language Teachers; *Teacher Certification; *Teacher Education Programs; *Teachers; *Teacher Selection; College Students; Cultural Background; Higher Education; Listening Comprehension; Reading Comprehension; Second Language Learning; Written Language
*Identifiers:* National Teacher Examinations
*Availability:* NTE Programs, Educational Testing Service, CN 6051, Princeton, NJ 08541-6056.
*Notes:* See also NTE Core Battery (11805 through 11807) and other NTE Specialty Area Tests (11834 through 11861). Time, 120.

Part of a standardized, secure measure of academic achievement for college students in, or completing, teacher education programs. Used by associations, school systems, state agencies, and institutions for decisions about the certification and selection of teachers. One of 27 tests measuring understanding of the content and methods applicable to teaching in subject areas. This test covers listening comprehension, reading comprehension, written expression, language learning problems, and cultural background.

**11846**
**NTE Specialty Area Tests: German.** Educational Testing Service, Princeton, NJ 1982.
*Descriptors:* *Achievement Tests; *German; *Language Teachers; *Teacher Certification; *Teacher Education Programs; *Teachers; *Teacher Selection; College Students; Cultural Background; Higher Education; Listening Comprehension; Morphology (Languages); Phonemics; Reading Comprehension; Second Language Learning; Syntax; Written Language
*Identifiers:* National Teacher Examinations
*Availability:* NTE Programs, Educational Testing Service, CN 6051, Princeton, NJ 08541.
*Notes:* See also NTE Core Battery (11805 through 11807) and other NTE Specialty Area Tests (11834 through 11861). Time, 120.

Part of a standardized, secure measure of academic achievement for college students in, or completing, teacher education programs. Used by associations, school systems, state agencies, and institutions for decisions about the certification and selection of teachers. One of 27 tests measuring understanding of the content and methods applicable to teaching in subject areas. This test covers comprehension and specific language skills; listening, reading, structure, and written expression; phonemics, morphology, and syntax; and cultural background.

**11847**
**NTE Specialty Area Tests: School and Guidance Counseling.** Educational Testing Service, Princeton, NJ 1982.
*Descriptors:* *Achievement Tests; *School Counselors; *Teacher Certification; *Teacher Education Programs; *Teachers; *Teacher Selection; Codes of Ethics; Counselor Role; Graduate Students; Higher Education; Legal Responsibility; Mainstreaming; Program Administration
*Identifiers:* National Teacher Examinations
*Availability:* NTE Programs, Educational Testing Service, CN 6051, Princeton, NJ 08541.
*Notes:* See also NTE Core Battery (11805 through 11807) and other NTE Specialty Area Tests (11834 through 11861). Time, 120.

Part of a standardized, secure measure of academic achievement for college students in, or completing, teacher education programs. Used by associations, school systems, state agencies, and institutions for decisions about the certification and selection of teachers. One of 27 tests measuring understanding of the content and methods applicable to teaching in subject areas. This test covers counseling skills; the role of a consultant; administrative, management, and organizational skills; legal and ethical considerations; and how these skills are applied to helping students develop self-awareness, interpersonal skills, values, and knowledge about sexuality. Also focuses on concerns such as mainstreaming and the impact of federal law 94-142. Taped stimulus materials are utilized. Intended for those completing masters-level programs who expect to become counselors. Directed primarily at the secondary level.

**11848**
**NTE Specialty Area Tests: Home Economics Education.** Educational Testing Service, Princeton, NJ 1982.
*Descriptors:* *Achievement Tests; *Home Economics Education; *Home Economics Teachers; *Teacher Certification; *Teacher Education Programs; *Teachers; *Teacher Selection; Clothing Instruction; College Students; Consumer Economics; Family Environment; Higher Education; Home Management; Housing; Individual Development; Nutrition
*Identifiers:* National Teacher Examinations
*Availability:* NTE Programs, Educational Testing Service, CN 6051, Princeton, NJ 08541.
*Notes:* See also NTE Core Battery (11805 through 11807) and other NTE Specialty Area Tests (11834 through 11861). Time, 120.

Part of a standardized, secure measure of academic achievement for college students in, or completing, teacher education programs. Used by associations, school systems, state agencies, and institutions, for decisions about the certification and selection of teachers. One of 27 tests measuring understanding of the content and methods applicable to teaching in subject areas. This test covers family and human development, management, consumerism, nutrition and foods, clothing and textiles, housing, and home economics education.

**11849**
**NTE Specialty Area Tests: Industrial Arts Education.** Educational Testing Service, Princeton, NJ 1982.
*Descriptors:* *Achievement Tests; *Industrial Arts; *Industrial Arts Teachers; *Teacher Certification; *Teacher Education Programs; *Teachers; *Teacher Selection; Codes of Ethics; College Students; Construction (Process); Energy; Higher Education; Manufacturing; Power Technology; Professional Development; Program Administration; Teaching Methods; Transportation
*Identifiers:* Materials Technology; Metrology; National Teacher Examinations
*Availability:* NTE Programs, Educational Testing Service, CN 6051, Princeton, NJ 08541.
*Notes:* See also NTE Core Battery (11805 through 11807) and other NTE Specialty Area Tests (11834 through 11861). Time, 120.

Part of a standardized, secure measure of academic achievement for college students in, or completing, teacher education programs. Used by associations, school systems, state agencies, and institutions for decisions about the certification and selection of teachers. One of 27 tests measuring understanding of the content and methods applicable to teaching in subject areas. This test covers manufacturing, construction, communications, energy/power/transportation, metrology and material science, program management and teaching strategies, and professional growth and philosophy.

**11850**
**NTE Specialty Area Tests: Introduction to the Teaching of Reading.** Educational Testing Service, Princeton, NJ 1982.
*Descriptors:* *Achievement Tests; *Reading; *Reading Teachers; *Teacher Certification; *Teacher Education Programs; *Teachers; *Teacher Selection; College Students; Diagnostic Teaching; Educational Resources; Educational Theories; Higher Education; Reading Attitudes; Reading Instruction; Reading Processes; Reading Skills; School Organization; Teaching Methods
*Identifiers:* National Teacher Examinations
*Availability:* NTE Programs, Educational Testing Service, CN 6051, Princeton, NJ 08541.
*Notes:* See also NTE Core Battery (11805 through 11807) and other NTE Specialty Area Tests (11834 through 11861). Time, 120.

Part of a standardized, secure measure of academic achievement for college students in, or completing, teacher education programs. Used by associations, school systems, state agencies, and institutions for decisions about the certification and selection of teachers. One of 27 tests measuring understanding of the content and methods applicable to teaching in subject areas. This test covers nature of the reading process, reading skills and teaching methods, theories of and approaches to reading instruction, school organization for teaching reading, affective aspects of reading instruction, and teacher resources.

**11851**
**NTE Specialty Area Tests: Mathematics.** Educational Testing Service, Princeton, NJ 1982.
*Descriptors:* *Achievement Tests; *Mathematics; *Mathematics Teachers; *Teacher Certification; *Teacher Education Programs; *Teachers; *Teacher Selection; Algebra; Arithmetic; Calculus; College Students; Geometry; Higher Education; Measurement; Number Concepts; Number Systems; Probability; Statistics; Trigonometry
*Identifiers:* National Teacher Examinations
*Availability:* NTE Programs, Educational Testing Service, CN 6051, Princeton, NJ 08541.
*Notes:* See also NTE Core Battery (11805 through 11807) and other NTE Specialty Area Tests (11834 through 11861). Time, 120.

Part of a standardized, secure measure of academic achievement for college students in, or completing, teacher education programs. Used by associations, school systems, state agencies, and institutions for decisions about the certification and selection of teachers. One of 27 tests measuring understanding of the content and methods applicable to teaching in subject areas. This test covers numeration systems, concepts, and structures; algebra; arithmetic; measurement; geometry; trignometry; probability and statistics; and calculus.

**11852**
**NTE Specialty Area Tests: Library Media Specialist.** Educational Testing Service, Princeton, NJ 1982.
*Descriptors:* *Achievement Tests; *Audiovisual Coordinators; *Library Services; *Media Specialists; *Teacher Certification; *Teacher Education Programs; *Teachers; *Teacher Selection; College Students; Higher Education; Instructional Materials; Library Administration; Reference Services
*Identifiers:* National Teacher Examinations
*Availability:* NTE Programs, Educational Testing Service, CN 6051, Princeton, NJ 08541.
*Notes:* See also NTE Core Battery (11805 through 11807) and other NTE Specialty Area Tests (11834 through 11861). Time, 120.

Part of a standardized, secure measure of academic achievement for college students in, or completing, teacher education programs. Used by associations, school systems, state agencies, and institutions for decisions about the certification and selection of teachers. One of 27 tests measuring understanding of the content and methods applicable to teaching in subject areas. This test covers making materials available, providing reference services, producing educational materials, instructing in the use of media resources and services, providing consultive services, managing a library media program, and addressing professional concerns. For use with students in either bachelor or master degree programs.

**11853**
**NTE Specialty Area Tests: Music Education.** Educational Testing Service, Princeton, NJ 1982.
*Descriptors:* *Achievement Tests; *Music Education; *Music Teachers; *Teacher Certification; *Teacher Education Programs; *Teachers; *Teacher Selection; Applied Music; College Students; Higher Education
*Identifiers:* National Teacher Examinations
*Availability:* NTE Programs, Educational Testing Service, CN 6051, Princeton, NJ 08541.
*Notes:* See also NTE Core Battery (11805 through 11807) and other NTE Specialty Area Tests (11834 through 11861). Time, 120.

Part of a standardized, secure measure of academic achievement for college students in, or completing, teacher education programs. Used by associations, school systems, state agencies, and institutions for decisions about the certification and selection of teachers. One of 27 tests measuring understanding of the content and methods applicable to teaching in subject areas. This test covers basic musicianship, curriculum and instruction, and professional information. A taped musical excerpt is the basis for a number of questions concerned with characteristics of the excerpt.

**11854**
**NTE Specialty Area Tests: Physical Education.** Educational Testing Service, Princeton, NJ 1982.
*Descriptors:* *Achievement Tests; *Physical Education; *Physical Education Teachers; *Teacher Certification; *Teacher Education Programs; *Teachers; *Teacher Selection; College Students; Curriculum Development; Evaluation Methods; Higher Education; History; Program Administration; Teacher Responsibility
*Identifiers:* National Teacher Examinations
*Availability:* NTE Programs, Educational Testing Service, CN 6051, Princeton, NJ 08541.
*Notes:* See also NTE Core Battery (11805 through 11807) and other NTE Specialty Area Tests (11834 through 11861). Time, 120.

Part of a standardized, secure measure of academic achievement for college students in, or completing, teacher education programs. Used by associations, school systems, state agencies, and institutions for decisions about the certification and selection of teachers. One of 27 tests measuring understanding of the content and methods applicable to teaching in subject areas. This test covers history and philosophy of physical education, scientific foundations, curriculum development and planning, administration of a total physical education program, professional responsibilities, evaluation, and assessment.

**11855**
**NTE Specialty Area Tests: Reading Specialist.** Educational Testing Service, Princeton, NJ 1982.
*Descriptors:* *Achievement Tests; *Reading; *Reading Consultants; *Teacher Certification; *Teacher Education Programs; *Teachers; *Teacher Selection; Diagnostic Teaching; Graduate Students; Higher Education; Language Skills; Program Development; Program Improvement; Reading Comprehension; Word Study Skills
*Identifiers:* National Teacher Examinations
*Availability:* NTE Programs, Educational Testing Service, CN 6051, Princeton, NJ 08541.
*Notes:* See also NTE Core Battery (11805 through 11807) and other NTE Specialty Area Tests (11834 through 11861). Time, 120.

Part of a standardized, secure measure of academic achievement for college students in, or completing, teacher education programs. Used by associations, school systems, state agencies, and institutions for decisions about the certification and selection of teachers. One of 27 tests measuring understanding of the content and methods applicable to teaching in subject areas. This test covers language foundations for reading, comprehension, word analysis, enjoyment of reading, diagnostic teaching, and program planning and improvement. Most appropriate for candidates with a master's degree who expect to have special responsibilities related to reading or who are seeking positions with titles, such as reading consultant.

**11856**
**NTE Specialty Area Tests: Social Studies.** Educational Testing Service, Princeton, NJ 1982.
*Descriptors:* *Achievement Tests; *Social Studies; *Teacher Certification; *Teacher Education Programs; *Teachers; *Teacher Selection; Anthropology; College Students; Economics; Geography; Higher Education; Political Science; United States History; World History
*Identifiers:* National Teacher Examinations
*Availability:* NTE Programs, Educational Testing Service, CN 6051, Princeton, NJ 08541.
*Notes:* See also NTE Core Battery (11805 through 11807) and other NTE Specialty Area Tests (11834 through 11861). Time, 120.

Part of a standardized, secure measure of academic achievement for college students in, or completing, teacher education programs. Used by associations, school systems, state agencies, and institutions for decisions about the certification and selection of teachers. One of 27 tests measuring understanding of the content and methods applicable to teaching in subject areas. This test covers conceptual approaches to social studies, political science, economics, history, geography, and sociology/anthropology.

**11857**
**NTE Specialty Area Tests: Spanish.** Educational Testing Service, Princeton, NJ 1982.
*Descriptors:* *Achievement Tests; *Language Teachers; *Spanish; *Teacher Certification; *Teacher Education Programs; *Teachers; *Teacher Selection; College Students; Cultural Background; Higher Education; Listening Comprehension; Morphology (Languages); Phonemics; Reading Comprehension; Second Language Learning; Syntax; Written Language
*Identifiers:* National Teacher Examinations
*Availability:* NTE Programs, Educational Testing Service, CN 6051, Princeton, NJ 08541.
*Notes:* See also NTE Core Battery (11805 through 11807) and other NTE Specialty Area Tests (11834 through 11861). Time, 120.

Part of a standardized, secure measure of academic achievement for college students in, or completing, teacher education programs. Used by associations, school systems, state agencies, and institutions for decisions about the certification and selection of teachers. One of 27 tests measuring understanding of the content and methods applicable to teaching in subject areas. This test covers comprehension and specific language skills; listening, reading, structure, and written expression; phonemics, morphology, and syntax; and cultural background.

**11858**
**NTE Specialty Area Tests: Speech Communication.** Educational Testing Service, Princeton, NJ 1982.
*Descriptors:* *Achievement Tests; *Speech Communication; *Teacher Certification; *Teacher Education Programs; *Teachers; *Teacher Selection; College Students; Drama; Higher Education; Interpersonal Communication; Mass Media; Oral Interpretation; Persuasive Discourse; Public Speaking
*Identifiers:* National Teacher Examinations; Professionalism; Small Group Communication
*Availability:* NTE Programs, Educational Testing Service, CN 6051, Princeton, NJ 08541.
*Notes:* See also NTE Core Battery (11805 through 11807) and other NTE Specialty Area Tests (11834 through 11861). Time, 120. Items, 150.

Part of a standardized, secure measure of academic achievement for college students in, or completing, teacher education programs. Used by associations, school systems, state agencies, and institutions for decisions about the certification and selection of teachers. One of 27 tests measuring understanding of the content and methods applicable to teaching in subject areas. This test covers interpersonal communication, small group communication, public speaking, mass communication, play production, oral interpretation, forensics, and professional concerns.

**11860**
**NTE Specialty Area Tests: Speech-Language Pathology.** Educational Testing Service, Princeton, NJ 1982.
*Descriptors:* *Achievement Tests; *Speech Language Pathology; *Teacher Certification; *Teacher Education Programs; *Teachers; *Teacher Selection; Audiology; Codes of Ethics; College Students; Hearing Therapy; Higher Education; Language Impairments; Speech Communication; Student Evaluation
*Identifiers:* National Teacher Examinations
*Availability:* NTE Programs, Educational Testing Service, CN 6051, Princeton, NJ 08541.
*Notes:* See also NTE Core Battery (11805 through 11807) and other NTE Specialty Area Tests (11834 through 11861). Time, 120.

Part of a standardized, secure measure of academic achievement for college students in, or completing, teacher education programs. Used by associations, school systems, state agencies, and institutions for decisions about certification and selection of teachers. One of 27 tests measuring understanding of the content and methods applicable to teaching in subject areas. Recognized as the national examination in speech pathology. Required in some states for certification or licensing. Covers basic communication processes, specific disorders in speech and language pathology, audiology and aural rehabilitation, and related areas, such as assessment and ethics.

**11861**
**NTE Specialty Area Tests: Agriculture.** Educational Testing Service, Princeton, NJ 1982.
*Descriptors:* *Achievement Tests; *Agriculture; *Teacher Certification; *Teacher Education Programs; *Teachers; *Teacher Selection; Agricultural Engineering; Agronomy; Animal Husbandry; College Students; Higher Education; Knowledge Level; Soil Science
*Identifiers:* National Teacher Examinations
*Availability:* NTE Programs, Educational Testing Service, CN 6051, Princeton, NJ 08541.
*Notes:* See also NTE Core Battery (11805 through 11807) and other NTE Specialty Area Tests (11834 through 11861). Time, 120.

Part of a standardized, secure measure of academic achievement for college students in, or completing, teacher education programs. Used by associations, school systems, state agencies, and institutions for decisions about the certification and selection of teachers. One of 27 tests measuring understanding of the content and methods applicable to teaching in subject areas. Covers knowledge related to agricultural practices and information specifically related to the agricultural products grown and the farming conditions in those states. Administered only in participating states.

**11918**
**Occupational Aptitude Survey and Interest Schedule: Interest Schedule.** Parker, Randall M. 1983.
*Descriptors:* *Interest Inventories; *Secondary School Students; *Vocational Interests; Adolescents; Career Planning; Secondary Education
*Identifiers:* OASIS
*Availability:* PRO-ED, 8700 Shoal Creek Blvd., Austin, TX 78758.
*Notes:* See also Occupational Aptitude Survey and Interest Schedule: Aptitude Survey (11919). Time, 30 approx. Items, 240.

One of 2 separate instruments comprising the Occupational Aptitude Survey and Interest Schedule (OASIS). Developed to aid students in formulating educational and vocational goals and generally in career planning. Inventory measures 12 broad vocational areas, and scores are keyed directly to the *Dictionary of Occupational Titles, Guide for Occupational Explorations,* and the *Worker Trait Group Guide.* May be administered to individuals or to groups.

**11919**
**Occupational Aptitude Survey and Interest Schedule: Aptitude Survey.** Parker, Randall M. 1983.
*Descriptors:* *Aptitude Tests; *Secondary School Students; *Vocational Aptitude; Adolescents; Computation; Motor Reactions; Secondary Education; Spatial Ability; Visual Discrimination; Vocabulary
*Identifiers:* Manual Dexterity; OASIS
*Availability:* PRO-ED, 8700 Shoal Creek Blvd., Austin, TX 78758.
*Notes:* See also Occupational Aptitude Survey and Interest Schedule: Interest Schedule (11918). Time, 35 approx. Items, 185.

One of 2 separate instruments comprising the Occupational Aptitude Survey and Interest Schedule (OASIS). The aptitude test was developed to assist students in making career decisions by providing them with information regarding their relative strength in several aptitude areas related to the world of work. Scores are keyed directly to the *Dictionary of Occupational Titles, Guide for Occupational Exploration,* and the *Worker Trait Group Guide.* In addition to the 185 items of the first 4 subtests, the Making Marks subtest is a speeded task requiring the examinee to draw an asterisk-like figure in each of 160 boxes. May be administered to individuals or to groups.

**11923**
**Screening Form for District Manager Selection.** Newspaper Advertising Bureau, New York, NY 1982.
*Descriptors:* *Newspapers; *Occupational Tests; *Personnel Selection; *Screening Tests; Adults; Job Performance; Job Satisfaction; Personality Measures
*Identifiers:* District Managers; Newspaper Readership Project
*Availability:* Newspaper Advertising Bureau, 485 Lexington Ave., New York, NY 10017.
*Notes:* Items, 14.

Designed to assist newspapers in selecting the best candidates for district manager positions. Items are concerned with personality characteristics. Correlates with job performance and satisfaction.

**11939**
**Certified Dental Technician Program Comprehensive Examinations.** National Association of Dental Laboratories, Alexandria, VA 1982.
*Descriptors:* *Certification; *Dental Technicians; Adults; Anatomy; Dentistry; Equipment; Knowledge Level; Multiple Choice Tests
*Identifiers:* Bridges (Dental); Crowns (Dental); Dental Ceramics; Dentures; Orthodontics; Tooth Morphology
*Availability:* National Board for Certification in Dental Lab. Technology, 3801 Mt. Vernon Ave., Alexandria, VA 22305.
*Notes:* Time, 75.

Multiple-choice tests designed for use in certifying technicians who have not completed an accredited dental technology education program. Written tests cover basic dental laboratory knowledge, oral anatomy, tooth morphology, theory, materials, and equipment. Tests are updated periodically.

**11945**
**Missouri Occupational Preference Inventory.** Moore, Earl; And Others 1980.
*Descriptors:* *Interest Inventories; *Vocational Interests; Adolescents; Adults; Career Choice; Career Counseling; College Students; Higher Education; High Schools; High School Students
*Identifiers:* *Card Sort; MOPI

*Availability:* Human Systems Consultants, 110 N. Tenth St., Columbia, MO 65201.
*Notes:* Time, 60 approx.

Used to assist individuals in exploring career options, understanding reasons behind occupational choices, and identifying next steps to guide further exploration. Adaptable to many counseling and career exploration situations, a variety of work settings, and needs of various populations. There are 3 formats in which to use MOPI: self-guided approach, which involves using the cards as a resource file; self-directed card sort, in which individual assumes responsibility for career exploration; and counselor-directed card sort, which provides for in-depth career exploration and planning with help from a counselor.

**11954**
**Missouri Occupational Card Sort: College Form. Second Edition.** Hansen, Robert N.; Johnston, Joseph A. 1980.
*Descriptors:* *College Students; *Interest Inventories; *Vocational Interests; Adults; Career Counseling; Higher Education; High School Students
*Identifiers:* *Card Sort; MOCS
*Availability:* Missouri Occupational Card Sort, Career Planning and Placement Center, 100 Noyes Bldg., University of Missouri-Columbia, Columbia, MO 65211.
*Notes:* Items, 90.

Deck of 90 cards, each listing an occupational title on 1 side with descriptive information about the job on the reverse side. Goals of the card-sort process are to increase the amount and quality of information on specific careers, to formulate the range and appropriateness of occupations being considered, and to encourage more career exploration. Has also been used successfully with adults and high school-age individuals. Promotes interaction with a counselor and may result in greater clarification of values and interests.

**11958**
**National Business Competency Tests: Office Procedures.** National Business Education Association, Reston, VA 1981.
*Descriptors:* *Achievement Tests; *High School Students; *National Competency Tests; *Office Practice; *Undergraduate Students; Clerical Occupations; Higher Education; High Schools; Occupational Tests
*Identifiers:* Clerical Skills
*Availability:* National Business Education Association, 1914 Association Dr., Reston, VA 22091.
*Notes:* Time, 110 approx. Items, 21.

Administered to students in office procedures, secretarial practice, or cooperative office education, preferably the final course. May be used with high school and college students who are participating in a national project to help teachers and employers determine whether students as prospective employees are ready for entry-level office jobs, excluding typewriting. Test consists of 2 parts, which can be administered on 2 different days. Part 1, Office Services, consists of jobs typically found in the office and includes such things as checking, proofreading, telephoning, and mail services. Part 2 consists of 9 jobs involving computation and accounting services typically performed in offices.

**11977**
**Talent Assessment Program. Revised Edition.** Nighswonger, Wilton E. 1981.
*Descriptors:* *Aptitude Tests; *Performance Tests; *Secondary School Students; *Vocational Aptitude; Adolescents; Adults; Learning Disabilities; Secondary Education; Skilled Occupations; Spatial Ability; Tactual Perception; Unskilled Occupations; Visual Discrimination; Visualization
*Identifiers:* Manual Dexterity; TAP; Test Batteries
*Availability:* Talent Assessment, Inc., P.O. Box 5087, Jacksonville Beach, FL 32207.
*Notes:* Time, 150 approx.

Consists of 10 tests that require hands-on work by client. Used to measure innate vocational aptitudes of all types of individuals, including disabled, disadvantaged, and nondisabled vocational students. Tests measure skills applicable to work in trade, industrial, technical, and professional technical lines, including skilled and unskilled occupations. Measures aptitudes in the general categories of visualization and retention, visual discrimination, and manual dexterity.

**12004**
**Supervisory Inventory on Non-Union Relations.** Wyman, Earl J. 1980.
*Descriptors:* *Administrators; *Industrial Personnel; *Labor Relations; *Unions; Adults; Human Relations; Legal Responsibility; Objective Tests; Work Environment
*Identifiers:* SINR
*Availability:* Earl J. Wyman, Box 4778, Berkeley, CA 94704.
*Notes:* Time, 20 approx. Items, 80.

Used to assess knowledge of the first-level supervisor with respect to key areas of nonunion environment. Items are designed to identify specific areas where supervisory training needs exist in order for a particular organization to maintain a nonunion environment. Key areas of a nonunion environment include job security, compensation, benefits, supervision, discipline, performance appraisal, communcations, and the law. The SINR can be used to determine the need for supervisory training, as a tool for conference discussions, to evaluate the effectiveness of the supervisor training program, or to train the management team.

**12014**
**Nonreading Aptitude Test Battery, 1982 Edition.** U.S. Employment Service, Div. of Testing, Salem, OR 1982.
*Descriptors:* *Aptitude Tests; *Disadvantaged; *Occupational Tests; Adults; Career Guidance; Cognitive Ability; Personnel Selection; Psychomotor Skills; Spatial Ability; Verbal Ability; Visual Discrimination; Vocabulary
*Identifiers:* General Aptitude Test Battery; Manual Dexterity; NATB; Numerical Ability; Oral Tests; Perceptual Speed Finger Dexterity; United States Employment Service
*Availability:* State Employment Service Offices only.
*Notes:* Time, 107. Items, 468.

Developed for use with disadvantaged individuals. This revision is shorter than earlier versions and is purported to be easier to understand and administer, without loss of internal validity. Aptitudes measured are general learning ability, verbal ability, numerical ability, spatial aptitude, form perception, clerical perception, motor coordination, finger dexterity, and manual dexterity. Administered by offices of the U.S. Employment Service for vocational guidance and employee selection.

**12028**
**Survey of Organizations.** Rensis Likert Associates, Inc., Ann Arbor, MI 1980.
*Descriptors:* *Employee Attitudes; *Organizational Climate; Adults; Employees; Group Behavior; Job Satisfaction; Leadership; Occupational Information; Peer Relationship; Supervision; Surveys
*Identifiers:* SOO
*Availability:* Rensis Likert Associates, Inc., 3001 S. State St., Ste. 401, Ann Arbor, MI 48104.
*Notes:* Items, 125.

Designed to measure employee perceptions of organizational behavior, including organizational climate, supervisory leadership, peer relationships, group functioning, job characteristics, and job satisfaction. Two levels are available. Level A is used with work groups, and level B is used organization-wide.

**12037**
**NCEE Fundamentals of Engineering. Typical Questions.** National Council of Engineering Examiners, Clemson, SC 1982.
*Descriptors:* *Certification; *Engineering; Adults; Minimum Competencies
*Availability:* National Council of Examiners for Engineering and Surveying, P.O. Box 1686 (State Rd. 210), Clemson, SC 29633-1686.

Sample questions typical of those found in the Fundamentals of Engineering examination. Purpose is to determine whether candidates for professional engineering registration meet the minimum requirements for registration established by law.

**12038**
**NCEE Surveying: Fundamentals/Principles and Practice. Typical Questions.** National Council of Engineering Examiners, Clemson, SC 1983.
*Descriptors:* *Certification; *Engineering; Adults; Minimum Competencies
*Identifiers:* *Surveying (Engineering)
*Availability:* National Council of Examiners for Engineering and Surveying, P.O. Box 1686 (State Rd. 210), Clemson, SC 29633-1686.

Sample questions typical of those found in the certification exam. Fundamentals section is an 8-hour examination consisting of a closed-book 4-hour test and an open-book 4-hour test. The principles and practice section consists of 2 parts: a 4-hour open-book test and a 4-hour jurisdictional exam, administered and scored by individual state boards, designed to assess the competence of the candidate to deal with in-depth legal interpretations and professional decisions involved in everyday practice and unique to the particular state.

**12039**
**NCEE Principles and Practice of Engineering. Typical Questions.** National Council of Engineering Examiners, Clemson, SC 1983.
*Descriptors:* *Certification; *Engineering; Adults; Minimum Competencies
*Availability:* National Council of Examiners for Engineering and Surveying, P.O. Box 1686 (State Rd. 210), Clemson, SC 29633-1686.

Questions typical of those found on the 8-hour examination whose purpose is to determine whether the candidate has an adequate understanding of the basic and applicable engineering sciences and also to determine whether training and experience have taught examinee to apply skills to the solution of engineering problems in a minimally competent manner.

**12042**
**Vocational Exploration and Insight Kit.** Holland, John L.; And Others 1980.
*Descriptors:* *Career Exploration; *Interest Inventories; *Vocational Interests; Adolescents; Adults; Career Counseling; Self Evaluation (Individuals)
*Identifiers:* Self Directed Search; VEIK; Vocational Card Sort
*Availability:* Consulting Psychologists Press, Inc., 3803 E. Bayshore Rd., Palo Alto, CA 94303.
*Notes:* Time, 240 approx.

A 15-step treatment in which person begins with the Vocational Card Sort (VCS), uses the Self-Directed Search (SDS) and its interpretive booklet, and fills out an action plan developed to stimulate commitment to additional vocational exploration activities. VEIK should be completed over a period of several days. Was developed to encourage self-exploration and self-understanding, to resolve vocational indecision, to clarify advantages of one vocational choice over another, and to increase the range of vocational options considered. Can be used in vocational counseling and group work.

**12047**
**Work Attitudes Questionnaire. Version for Research.** Doty, M.S.; Betz, N.E. 1980.
*Descriptors:* *Attitude Measures; *Employee Attitudes; *Mental Health; *Work Attitudes; *Type A Behavior; Adults; Rating Scales
*Identifiers:* Commitment; WAQ; Workaholics; Work Habits
*Availability:* Marathon Consulting and Press, P.O. Box 09189, Columbus, OH 43209-0189.
*Notes:* Items, 45.

Designed to measure high degrees of work commitment and to distinguish 2 types of highly career-committed individuals: those whose commitment is positive and those whose commitment has an adverse impact on their psychological health (workaholics or Type A personality).

**12048**
**Occupational Environment Scales, Form E-2.** Osipow, Samuel H.; Spokane, Arnold R. 1981.
*Descriptors:* *Stress Variables; *Work Environment; Adults; Employee Responsibility; Physical Environment; Rating Scales; Role Conflict; Self Evaluation (Individuals)
*Identifiers:* OES
*Availability:* Psychological Assessment Resources, Inc., P.O. Box 998, Odessa, FL 33556.
*Notes:* For related tests, see Personal Strain Questionnaire (12049) and Personal Resources Questionnaire (12050). Items, 60.

Designed to measure different kinds of stress people experience in their work. Measures 6 aspects of the work environment that may cause stress. Designed to be used across occupational fields and levels and is not occupationally specific. Follows a "social roles" approach to work stress. Potential uses include as a screening instrument for assessment of stress, strain, and coping or assessment of organizational milieu; as a stimulus for family discussions at counseling; as a career counseling tool; and as a measure of the effects of stress management intervention.

**12050**
**Personal Resources Questionnaire, Form E-2.** Osipow, Samuel H.; Spokane, Arnold R. 1981.
*Descriptors:* *Coping; *Stress Variables; *Work Environment; Adults; Cognitive Style; Rating Scales; Recreation; Reference Groups; Self Care Skills; Self Evaluation (Individuals)
*Identifiers:* PRQ
*Availability:* Psychological Assessment Resources, Inc., P.O. Box 998, Odessa, FL 33556.
*Notes:* For related tests, see Occupational Environment Scales (12048) and Personal Strain Questionnaire (12049). Items, 40.

Measures the potential individuals have for dealing effectively with work stress to minimize the strains measured with the Personal Strain Questionnaire. Measures recreational, self-care, and rational/coping behaviors, along with social support system available to individual. Potential uses include as a screening instrument for assessment of stress, strain, and coping or assessment of organizational milieu; as a stimulus for family discussions at counseling; as a career counseling tool; and as a measure of the effects of stress management intervention.

**12053**
**Vocational Interest, Experience and Skill Assessment.** American College Testing Program, Iowa City, IA 1983.
*Descriptors:* *Career Guidance; *Vocational Evaluation; *Vocational Interests; Adolescents; Adults; Career Choice; Job Skills; Self Evaluation (Groups); Self Evaluation (Individuals); Sex Fairness; Values; Work Experience; Young Adults
*Identifiers:* Holland (John L); Self Scoring Tests; VIESA
*Availability:* American College Testing Program, Career Planning Services, Operations Div., P.O. Box 168, Iowa City, IA 52243.
*Notes:* Time, 45.

Self-administered, self-scored short form of the Career Planning Program (7582). Group or individually administered. Uses data-ideas and people-things dimensions underlying Holland and Roe typologies. The Unisex Act Interest Inventory is used to minimize sex restrictiveness. Separate levels are available for grades 8 to 10 and grade 11 to adults. For use by professionals. Has 7th grade reading level. Also assesses job values, skills, and experiences.

**12070**
**Team Development Inventory.** Jones, John E. 1982.
*Descriptors:* *Employees; *Interpersonal Relationship; *Peer Evaluation; *Teamwork; Adults
*Identifiers:* TDI
*Availability:* Learning Resources Corp., 8517 Production Ave., P.O. Box 26240, San Diego, CA 92126.
*Notes:* Time, 45 approx.

Used to help members of a work group clarify their perceptions of each other so they can improve their interpersonal relationship and their teamwork. Each individual ranks all members of group on 8 separate characteristics: participation, collaboration, flexibility, sensitivity, risk taking, commitment, facilitation, and openness. Most appropriate use is in team-building efforts within a group. Also useful for management training programs and career development programs, as pre-work for team development session, or with team members individually.

**12094**
**Level II: Life Styles Inventory (Description by Others).** Lafferty, J. Clayton 1981.
*Descriptors:* *Administrator Characteristics; *Administrator Evaluation; *Administrators; *Feedback; Adults; Behavior Patterns; Rating Scales
*Availability:* Human Synergistics, 39819 Plymouth Rd., Plymouth, MI 48170.
*Notes:* Items, 244.

Part of a multilevel diagnostic system whose purpose is to provide accurate, detailed feedback of manager's behavior as perceived by others. Peers, subordinates, and/or superiors complete questionnaires concerning manager's style. Provides information on how others see manager's concern for people, satisfaction, task, and security, as well as their perceptions of manager's thinking style, self-concept, and behavior in relation to others and to organization.

**12114**
**Career Profile.** Life Insurance Marketing and Research Association, Inc., Hartford, CT 1983.
*Descriptors:* *Insurance Companies; *Salesmanship; *Vocational Aptitude; Adults; Questionnaires
*Availability:* Life Insurance Marketing and Research Association, Inc., P.O. Box 208, Hartford, CT 06141-0208.

Helps determine which candidates have most potential for success as insurance sales representatives. There are 2 questionnaires. The Initial Career Profile, which consists of 183 questions, is for those who have had no previous full-time experience as an insurance sales representative or who have not had full-time experience in the past 5 years. The Advanced Career Profile, consisting of 158 questions, is for those who are currently full-time insurance sales representatives or who have been in the last 5 years. The Initial Career Profile covers feelings about present job; self-assessed skills and abilities; motivating goals; opinions, knowledge, and career expectations; potential market; and concerns. The Advanced Career Profile covers satisfaction with insurance sales career; clients; self-assessed sales activity; sales summary; sales result; insurance income, income needs, and income expectations; and managerial background.

**12121**
**USES Interest Inventory.** Employment and Training Administration (DOL), Washington, DC 1981.
*Descriptors:* *Interest Inventories; *Vocational Interests; Adults; Career Counseling; Computer Assisted Testing; High School Students; Microcomputers
*Identifiers:* Counselee Assessment Occupational Exploration; United States Employment Service
*Availability:* Superintendent of Documents, U.S. Government Printing Office, Washington, DC 20402.
*Notes:* Items, 162.

Designed to help individuals learn more about their occupational interests and how these interests relate to work. Meant primarily for use by employment service interviewers to assess applicants, but also useful for high school counselors, CETA organizations, rehabilitation agencies, and other services. This inventory is one component of a new counselee assessment/occupational exploration system developed by the U.S. Employment Service (USES). Other components include the General Aptitude Test Battery (1422) and the Interest Check List (10718). Organizations interested in using the inventory or other USES tests should contact the local office of their state employment service. There are 2 versions of the Interest Inventory, one available from the Government Printing Office and the other from Intran Corporation, P.O. Box 9479, Minneapolis, MN 55440. Also available for computer-administered testing from Integrated Professional Systems, 5211 Mahoning Avenue, Suite 135, Youngstown, OH 44515.

**12183**
**Orthopedic In-Training Examination.** American Academy of Orthopedic Surgeons, Chicago, IL 1982.
*Descriptors:* *Knowledge Level; *Physicians; *Self Evaluation (Individuals); Adults; Graduate Medical Students; Multiple Choice Tests; Occupational Tests; Pictorial Stimuli
*Identifiers:* *Orthopedics
*Availability:* American Academy of Orthopedic Surgeons, Committee on Examinations and Evaluation, 444 N. Michigan Ave., Ste. 1500, Chicago, IL 60611.
*Notes:* Items, 282.

An untimed self-assessment aid for the practicing orthopedic resident or physician. Items are multiple choice. Some items are based on photographs of x-rays and other exhibits.

**12198**
**Supervisory Profile Record.** Richardson, Bellows, Henry and Co., Inc., Washington, DC 1981.
*Descriptors:* *Administrator Evaluation; *Administrator Selection; Adults; Job Analysis; Job Skills; Predictive Measurement; Rating Scales
*Identifiers:* SPR
*Availability:* Richardson, Bellows, Henry and Co., Inc., 1140 Connecticut Ave., N.W., Ste. 610, Washington, DC 20036.

Used to identify potential supervisors. Described as an objective, standardized, and empirically designed autobiographical and judgment questionnaire system. Objective of system is to predict supervisory success within organizations that differ from each other. System consists of Job Requirements Questionnaire for Supervisory Classification (JRQ) and Supervisory Performance Evaluation Record (SPER). The JRQ permits respondents to rate job duties and job abilities considered necessary for successful performance of supervisory tasks. The SPER is a rating form that focuses on those supervisory duties and abilities that have been empirically determined though job analysis.

**12221**
**Certification for Dental Assistants.** Dental Assisting National Board, Chicago, IL 1983.
*Descriptors:* *Certification; *Dental Assistants; Adults; Dental Health; Knowledge Level; Occupational Tests
*Identifiers:* Certification Examination for Dental Assistants; Dental Assisting National Board Examinations
*Availability:* Dental Assisting National Board, Inc., 216 E. Ontario St., Chicago, IL 60611.
*Notes:* Time, 300 approx.

Designed to assess knowledge of dental assistants applying for certification. Areas assessed include collection and recording of clinical data; dental radiography; chairside dental procedures; chairside dental materials; lab materials and procedures; prevention of disease transmission; patient education and oral health management; prevention and management of emergencies; occupational safety; office management procedures; general anesthesia, sedation, and analgesia; and oral and maxillofacial procedures. Dental charting is required, as well as knowledge of the Universal tooth numbering system. Applicants may be certified in General Chairside Assisting, Oral and Maxillofacial Surgery Assisting, or Dental Practice Management Assisting. Certification must be renewed periodically. Administration of the test is conducted at testing centers in February, June, August, and October nationwide. Tests are updated periodically.

**12247**
**Business Skills Inventory.** Kampmeier Group, Columbus, OH 1982.
*Descriptors:* *Attitude Measures; *Personnel Selection; *Vocational Interests; Adults; Career Guidance; Interpersonal Competence; Leadership Qualities; Problem Solving; Questionnaires; Salesmanship; Self Concept; Self Concept Measures
*Identifiers:* Self Administered Tests; Self Report Measures
*Availability:* The Kampmeier Group, 3360 Tremont Rd., Columbus, OH 43221.
*Notes:* Time, 120 approx.

Designed to select and position higher-level employees for maximum efficiency. Assesses sales ability; interpersonal skills; growth potential; leadership, problem solving, delegating, and administrative ability; self-confidence; and entrepreneurship. Instrument is normally administered with a structured interview and background investigation. Useful with salespeople, office workers, managers, and entrepreneurs.

**12273**
**Styles of Career Management.** Carney, Tom 1983.
*Descriptors:* *Occupational Aspiration; *Organizational Climate; *Self Evaluation (Individuals); *Work Attitudes; Adults; Rating Scales; Vocational Maturity
*Availability:* Goodstein, Leonard D., and Pfeiffer, J. William, eds., *The 1983 Annual for Facilitators, Trainers, and Consultants.* San Diego: University Associates, 1983. Pfeiffer and Co., formerly University Associates, 8517 Production Ave., San Diego, CA 92121-2280.
*Notes:* Items, 10.

A self-assessment instrument that allows people to assess their style of career management or the way they pursue their career. The questionnaire consists of 10 theme statements, each followed by 4 possible responses, which the respondents rank. The 4 types of career managers are the careerist, who builds networks and finds mentors; the organizational entrepreneur or task-force manager, who reorganizes systems and puts together task forces to solve difficult problems; the organizational person, who identifies with the organization itself; and the specialist or expert, who sees the organization as providing opportunities to develop his or her capabilities.

**12275**
**Organizational Role Stress Scale.** Pareek, Udai 1983.
*Descriptors:* *Administrators; *Organizational Climate; *Role Perception; *Self Evaluation (Individuals); *Stress Variables; Adults; Likert Scales; Rating Scales
*Availability:* Goodstein, Leonard D., and Pfeiffer, J. William, eds., *The 1983 Annual for Facilitators, Trainers, and Consultants.* San Diego: University Associates, 1983. Pfeiffer and Co., formerly University Associates, 8517 Production Ave., San Diego, CA 92121-2280.
*Notes:* Items, 50.

Used to examine role stress of organizational executives. Role stress is one factor that may contribute to burnout. Scale is used to categorize role stress in terms of role space and role set. Role space conflict is defined in terms of conflict between one's organizational role and other roles; role stagnation caused by lack of opportunities for learning and growth; conflicting role expectations based on demands made by others in the organization; personal inadequacy consisting of lack of knowledge, skill, or preparation for a particular role; and self-role conflict, a conflict between one's personal values and job demands. Role set conflict is measured in terms of role erosion, which is a decrease in level of responsibility or underutilization; role overload, which consists of too much to do or too many responsibilities to do everything well; role isolation, not being part of what is happening; role ambiguity because of unclear feedback; and resource inadequacy in which lack of resources or information makes effective performance difficult.

**12276**
**The TEM Survey: An Assessment of Your Effectiveness in Managing Your Time, Energy, and Memory.** Petrello, George J. 1983.
*Descriptors:* *Professional Personnel; *Time Management; Adults; Memory; Motivation; Organizational Climate; Self Evaluation (Individuals); Work Environment
*Identifiers:* TEM
*Availability:* Goodstein, Leonard D., and Pfeiffer, J. William, eds., *The 1983 Annual for Facilitators, Trainers, and Consultants.* San Diego: University Associates, 1983. Pfeiffer and Co., formerly University Associates, 8517 Production Ave., San Diego, CA 92121-2280.
*Notes:* Time, 30 approx. Items, 50.

Used with knowledge workers, those workers Peter Drucker defines as usually college educated with expertise in some technical, professional, or administrative field. These are professionals who have control over their time in the work environment. Job success for these knowledge workers depends largely on how effectively they use their time. Survey has 50 sets of statements concerning attitudes or knowledge about time, energy, and memory management. Each set contains 2 statements and respondent chooses the statement he or she considers to be the better answer.

**12281**
**Explore the World of Work.** Cutler, Arthur; And Others 1980.
*Descriptors:* *Career Exploration; *Elementary School Students; *Reading Difficulties; *Special Education; Elementary Education; Grade 4; Intermediate Grades; Mild Mental Retardation; Occupational Clusters; Slow Learners
*Identifiers:* EWOW
*Availability:* CFKR Career Materials, Inc., 11860 Kemper Rd., Unit 7, Auburn, CA 95603.
*Notes:* Time, 60.

A career awareness and exploration tool for use with elementary students, special education students, and others who read at 4th grade level or above. Uses game-like format in which students color pictures of job activities preferred and not preferred. Intended to introduce students to concept of job clusters and to encourage job exploration.

**12301**
**Organization Renewal Inventory.** Lippitt, Gordon L. 1981.
*Descriptors:* *Morale; *Organizational Climate; *Organizational Effectiveness; Adults; Employee Attitudes; Rating Scales
*Availability:* Development Publications, 5605 Lamar Rd., Bethesda, MD 20816-1398.
*Notes:* Items, 17.

Used by managers concerned about organizational climate and level of employee involvement with organizational goals. Purposes are to analyze areas of effective and ineffective functioning of the organization; to identify underlying causes of low organization morale; to create a basis for analyzing loss of productivity, absence of motivation, and other impediments to organizational improvement; and to begin a process of data gathering for organizational renewal. May be used by executives, managers, supervisors, employees, volunteer groups, educators, intergenerational planning groups, and members of health care systems.

**12306**
**Work Motivation Checklist.** This, Leslie E.; Lippitt, Gordon L. 1981.
*Descriptors:* *Employees; *Motivation; Administrators; Adults; Employee Attitudes; Rating Scales; Work Attitudes
*Availability:* Development Publications, 5605 Lamar Rd., Bethesda, MD 20816-1398.

Most often used with employees and managerial groups concerned about motivation and willing to spend time examining the concept and planning more effective ways of coping with motivational situations. Used to assist participants in analyzing their primary work motivations; to examine those motivations in light of past, present, and future; and to plan personal and organizational strategies for coping with anticipated changes. Can be used by managers or supervisors; employee groups; task forces; and voluntary, educational, or health care groups.

**12310**
**Job Skills Test: Measurement.** Ramsay, Roland T. 1983.
*Descriptors:* *Industrial Personnel; *Job Applicants; *Mathematics Tests; Adults; Computation; Job Skills; Occupational Tests; Timed Tests
*Identifiers:* Measurement (Mathematics)
*Availability:* Ramsay Corp., 1050 Boyce Rd., Pittsburgh, PA 15241-3907.
*Notes:* Time, 15. Items, 20.

Designed to evaluate job applicants' and incumbents' ability to measure accurately with a ruler. Form 2, published in 1985, is similar and requires the measurement of bolts and round mechanical parts.

**12329**
**Specific Aptitude Test Battery S-473 R82. Gambling Dealer (amuse. and rec.) 343.467-018.** Employment and Training Administration (DOL), Washington, DC 1982.
*Descriptors:* *Aptitude Tests; *Culture Fair Tests; *Employment Potential; *Ethnic Groups; *Job Applicants; *Minority Groups; *Personnel Selection; *Vocational Aptitude; Adults; Career Guidance; Employment Qualifications; Job Skills; Job Training; Object Manipulation; Personnel Evaluation; Predictive Measurement; Spatial Ability; Timed Tests
*Identifiers:* *Gambling Dealer; GATB; General Aptitude Test Battery; Manual Dexterity; SATB; USES Specific Aptitude Test Battery
*Availability:* Local U.S. Employment Service Office.

A series of aptitude tests for specific job skills. Designed to select inexperienced, or untrained, personnel for training and to predict their job proficiency. Instruments were developed to be culture-fair for minorities and ethnic groups. Subtests were drawn from the General Aptitude Test Battery (1422). Use of these instruments is restricted to state employment agencies. Designed to assess individual's aptitude for training as a gambling dealer. Data from 4 different jobs were combined to form this test battery. The jobs were dealers for dice, roulette, baccarat, and 21. A report describing the development of this test can be found in the ERIC system, document ED223707.

**12330**
**Specific Aptitude Test Battery S-200R82. Ticket Agent (any ind.) 238.367-026.** Employment and Training Administration (DOL), Washington, DC 1982.
*Descriptors:* *Aptitude Tests; *Culture Fair Tests; *Employment Potential; *Ethnic Groups; *Job Applicants; *Minority Groups; *Personnel Selection; *Vocational Aptitude; Adults; Career Guidance; Employment Qualifications; Job Analysis; Job Skills; Job Training; Personnel Evaluation; Predictive Measurement; Spatial Ability; Timed Tests
*Identifiers:* GATB; General Aptitude Test Battery; SATB; *Ticket Agents; USES Specific Aptitude Test Battery
*Availability:* Local U.S. Employment Service Office.

A series of aptitude tests for specific job skills. Designed to select inexperienced, or untrained, personnel for training and to predict their job proficiency. Instruments were developed to be culture-fair for minorities and ethnic groups. Subtests were drawn from the General Aptitude Test Battery (1422). Use of these instruments is restricted to state employment agencies. Designed to assess individual's aptitude for training as a ticket agent. A report describing the development of this test can be found in the ERIC system, document ED223718.

12331
**Specific Aptitude Test Battery S-179 R82. Waiter/Waitress, Informal (hotel and rest.) 311.477-030.** Employment and Training Administration (DOL), Washington, DC 1982.
*Descriptors:* *Aptitude Tests; *Culture Fair Tests; *Employment Potential; *Ethnic Groups; *Job Applicants; *Minority Groups; *Personnel Selection; *Vocational Aptitude; Adults; Career Guidance; Employment Qualifications; Job Analysis; Job Skills; Job Training; Object Manipulation; Personnel Evaluation; Predictive Measurement; Psychomotor Skills; Timed Tests
*Identifiers:* GATB; General Aptitude Test Battery; Manual Dexterity; SATB; USES Specific Aptitude Test Battery; *Waiters Waitresses
*Availability:* Local U.S. Employment Service Office.

A series of aptitude tests for specific job skills. Designed to select inexperienced, or untrained, personnel for training and to predict their job proficiency. Instruments were developed to be culture-fair for minorities and ethnic groups. Subtests were drawn from the General Aptitude Test Battery (1422). Use of these instruments is restricted to state employment agencies. Instrument was designed to assess aptitude for employment as a waiter or waitress. A report describing the development of this test can be found in the ERIC system, document ED223714.

12332
**Specific Aptitude Test Battery S-11R82. Carpenter (const.) 860.381-022.** Employment and Training Administration (DOL), Washington, DC 1982.
*Descriptors:* *Aptitude Tests; *Carpentry; *Construction (Process); *Culture Fair Tests; *Employment Potential; *Ethnic Groups; *Job Applicants; *Minority Groups; *Personnel Selection; *Vocational Aptitude; Adults; Building Trades; Career Guidance; Employment Qualifications; Job Analysis; Job Skills; Job Training; Object Manipulation; Personnel Evaluation; Predictive Measurement; Timed Tests
*Identifiers:* GATB; General Aptitude Test Battery; Manual Dexterity; SATB; USES Specific Aptitude Test Battery
*Availability:* Local U.S. Employment Service Office.

A series of aptitude tests for specific job skills. Designed to select inexperienced, or untrained, personnel for training and to predict their job proficiency. Instruments were developed to be culture-fair for minorities and ethnic groups. Subtests were drawn from the General Aptitude Test Battery (1422). Use of these instruments is restricted to state employment agencies. Designed to assess individual's aptitude for training and employment as a carpenter. A report describing the development of this test can be found in the ERIC system, document ED223695.

12333
**Specific Aptitude Test Battery S-474R82. Customer-Service Representative (light, heat, & power; telephone & telegraph; waterworks) 239.367-010.** Employment and Training Administration (DOL), Washington, DC 1982.
*Descriptors:* *Aptitude Tests; *Culture Fair Tests; *Employment Potential; *Ethnic Groups; *Job Applicants; *Minority Groups; *Personnel Selection; *Utilities; *Vocational Aptitude; Adults; Career Guidance; Employment Qualifications; Job Analysis; Job Skills; Job Training; Personnel Evaluation; Predictive Measurement; Timed Tests
*Identifiers:* *Customer Services; GATB; General Aptitude Test Battery; SATB; USES Specific Aptitude Test Battery
*Availability:* Local U.S. Employment Service Office.

A series of aptitude tests for specific job skills. Designed to select inexperienced, or untrained, personnel for training and to predict their job proficiency. Instruments were developed to be culture-fair for minorities and ethnic groups. Subtests were drawn from the General Aptitude Test Battery (1422). Use of these instruments is restricted to state employment agencies. This instrument was designed to assess individual's aptitude for training and employment as a customer service representative. A report describing the development of this test can be found in the ERIC system, document ED223696.

12334
**Specific Aptitude Test Battery S-68R82. Refinery Operator (petrol. refin.) 549.260-010.** Employment and Training Administration (DOL), Washington, DC 1982.
*Descriptors:* *Aptitude Tests; *Culture Fair Tests; *Employment Potential; *Ethnic Groups; *Job Applicants; *Minority Groups; *Personnel Selection; *Vocational Aptitude; Adults; Career Guidance; Employment Qualifications; Job Analysis; Job Skills; Job Training; Personnel Evaluation; Predictive Measurement; Timed Tests
*Identifiers:* GATB; General Aptitude Test Battery; Manual Dexterity; *Refinery Operators; SATB; USES Specific Aptitude Test Battery
*Availability:* Local U.S. Employment Service Office.

A series of aptitude tests for specific job skills. Designed to select inexperienced, or untrained, personnel for training and to predict their job proficiency. Instruments were developed to be culture-fair for minorities and ethnic groups. Subtests were drawn from the General Aptitude Test Battery (1422). Use of these instruments is restricted to state employment agencies. Designed to assess aptitude for training and employment as a refinery operator. A report describing the development of this test can be found in the ERIC system, document ED223722.

12335
**Specific Aptitude Test Battery S-326R82. Respiratory Therapist (medical ser.) 079.361-010.** Employment and Training Administration (DOL), Washington, DC 1982.
*Descriptors:* *Aptitude Tests; *Culture Fair Tests; *Employment Potential; *Ethnic Groups; *Job Applicants; *Minority Groups; *Personnel Selection; *Respiratory Therapy; *Therapists; *Vocational Aptitude; Adults; Career Guidance; Employment Qualifications; Job Analysis; Job Skills; Job Training; Personnel Evaluation; Predictive Measurement; Psychomotor Skills; Timed Tests
*Identifiers:* GATB; General Aptitude Test Battery; SATB; USES Specific Aptitude Test Battery
*Availability:* Local U.S. Employment Service Office.

A series of aptitude tests for specific job skills. Designed to select inexperienced, or untrained, personnel for training and to predict their job proficiency. Instruments were developed to be culture-fair for minorities and ethnic groups. Subtests were drawn from the General Aptitude Test Battery (1422). Use of these instruments is restricted to state employment agencies. Designed to assess individual's aptitude for training and employment as a respiratory therapist. A report describing the development of this test can be found in the ERIC system, document ED223723.

12352
**Specific Aptitude Test Battery S-471R81 Semiconductor Occupations (electronics).** Employment and Training Administration (DOL), Washington, DC 1982.
*Descriptors:* *Aptitude Tests; *Culture Fair Tests; *Electronic Technicians; *Employment Potential; *Ethnic Groups; *Job Applicants; *Minority Groups; *Personnel Selection; *Vocational Aptitude; Adults; Career Guidance; Employment Qualifications; Job Analysis; Job Skills; Job Training; Personnel Evaluation; Predictive Measurement; Timed Tests
*Identifiers:* GATB; General Aptitude Test Battery; Manual Dexterity; SATB; USES Specific Aptitude Test Battery
*Availability:* Local U.S. Employment Service Office.

A series of aptitude tests for specific job skills. Designed to select inexperienced, or untrained, personnel for training and to predict their job proficiency. Instruments were developed to be culture-fair for minorities and ethnic groups. Subtests were drawn from the General Aptitude Test Battery (1422). Use of these instruments is restricted to state employment agencies. Designed to assess individual's aptitude for training or employment in electronics occupations. A report describing the development of this test can be found in the ERIC system, document ED224826.

12364
**Vocational Competency Measures: Electronic Technician.** American Institutes for Research, Palo Alto, CA 1983.
*Descriptors:* *Achievement Tests; *Competence; *Electronic Technicians; *Postsecondary Education; *Secondary School Students; *Student Evaluation; *Vocational Education; *Work Sample Tests; Adolescents; Adults; Knowledge Level; Personnel Selection; Rating Scales; Screening Tests; Secondary Education
*Identifiers:* Test Batteries; Work Habits
*Availability:* American Association for Vocational Instructional Materials, 120 Driftmier Engineering Center, Athens, GA 30602.

Used to help teachers and administrators at secondary and postsecondary levels assess and improve the competencies of vocational education students, identify program areas in need of improvement, and inform prospective employers of student competencies. May also be used by employers to screen and select new employees and to assess training needs of present employees. The test battery consists of 3 components. The Job Information Test is a multiple-choice test of job-relevant knowledge. It is divided into 2 parts, each of which takes about 45 minutes to complete. The performance test has 12 performance tasks that are similar to entry-level activities expected of an electronics technician. Examinees are not required to perform all 12 tasks. The Work Habits Inventory has 3 parts: one which students complete concerning their own traits, one in which students are asked to estimate the importance of job traits from the employer's point of view, and one which the teacher completes concerning students' work habits.

12384
**Career Assessment Inventories for the Learning Disabled.** Weller, Carol; Buchanan, Mary 1983.
*Descriptors:* *Learning Disabilities; *Vocational Evaluation; Adolescents; Adults; Elementary School Students; Personality Traits; Psychomotor Skills; Spatial Ability; Verbal Development; Visual Perception; Vocational Interests
*Identifiers:* CAI
*Availability:* Academic Therapy Publications, 20 Commercial Blvd., Novato, CA 94947-6191.
*Notes:* Time, 30 approx. Items, 198.

Designed specifically for use by vocational counselors, psychologists, educational diagnosticians, and special education teachers who work with learning disabled adults or children. The attributes and ability inventories are completed by the examiner after a period of observation. The interest inventory is completed by the individual being assessed. The instrument consists of 3 parts. The attributes inventory, based on John I. Holland's theories of careers, assesses the individual's dominant personality characteristics. The ability inventory provides a profile of the examinee's auditory, visual, and motor areas. The interest inventory can be used to determine whether the individual's interests coincide with his or her personality attributes and abilities. Suitable for use across a wide range of ages from elementary school students through adults.

**12403**
**Survey of Management Practices, Form JE.** Wilson, Clark L. 1982.
*Descriptors:* *Administration; *Occupational Tests; *Supervisory Methods; *Surveys; Administrative Principles; Administrators; Adults; Attitude Measures; Behavior Rating Scales
*Availability:* Clark L. Wilson, Box 471, New Canaan, CT 06840.
*Notes:* For a parallel form, see 12404. Items, 100.

Designed to measure managerial and supervisory practices and attitudes. Form is completed by the manager, the manager's own supervisor, a person who is supervised by the manager, and another manager who is a peer. Questions are concerned with communication and relationships. Each behavior is rated on a 7-point scale of frequency.

**12404**
**Survey of Management Practices, Form JQ.** Wilson, Clark L. 1981.
*Descriptors:* *Administration; *Occupational Tests; *Supervisory Methods; *Surveys; Administrative Principles; Administrators; Adults; Attitude Measures; Behavior Rating Scales
*Identifiers:* Self Scoring Tests
*Availability:* Clark L. Wilson, Box 471, New Canaan, CT 06840.
*Notes:* For a parallel form, see 12403. Items, 100.

Designed to measure managerial and supervisory practices and attitudes. Form is completed by the manager, the manager's own supervisor, a person who is supervised by the manager, and another manager who is a peer. Questions are concerned with communication and relationships. Each behavior is rated on a 7-point scale of frequency. A self-scoring, pressure-sensitive answer sheet is attached.

**12405**
**Survey of Peer Relations, Form DQ.** Wilson, Clark L. 1981.
*Descriptors:* *Administrators; *Employees; *Interpersonal Competence; *Occupational Tests; Adults; Communication Skills; Peer Relationship; Problem Solving; Rating Scales; Surveys
*Availability:* Clark L. Wilson, Box 471, New Canaan, CT 06840.
*Notes:* Items, 80.

Designed for use by employee, employee's supervisor, and peers. Each responds to questions about organization of work, problem-solving approach, communication, work style, and interpersonal skills. All statements are rated on a 7-point scale, indicating the extent to which the statement is true of the individual being rated.

**12410**
**Management Development Inventory.** Daniels, Philip B.; And Others 1981.
*Descriptors:* *Administrator Evaluation; *Administrators; *Management Development; Adults; Behavior Rating Scales; Communication Skills; Decision Making Skills; Feedback; Self Evaluation (Individuals)
*Identifiers:* MDI
*Availability:* Behavioral Science Resources, P.O. Box 411, Provo, UT 84603.
*Notes:* Items, 62.

A survey instrument for use in management development. Manager is evaluated by supervisor, peers, subordinates, and self. Inventory may be manually tabulated or publisher will produce a computerized profile printout.

**12420**
**Vocational Competency Measures: Diesel Mechanic.** American Institutes for Research, Palo Alto, CA 1983.
*Descriptors:* *Achievement Tests; *Auto Mechanics; *Diesel Engines; *Entry Workers; *Personnel Selection; *Postsecondary Education; *Repair; *Secondary School Students; *Vocational Education; *Work Sample Tests; Adolescents; Adults; Competence; Knowledge Level; Rating Scales; Screening Tests; Secondary Education; Student Evaluation
*Identifiers:* Test Batteries; Work Habits
*Availability:* American Association for Vocational Instructional Materials, 120 Driftmier Engineering Center, Athens, GA 30602.

Used to assess job readiness of examinees who have completed vocational training at the secondary or postsecondary level in diesel mechanics and are preparing to work as apprentice diesel mechanics in repair shops. Focuses on diesel engines and is most relevant to engines used in heavy trucks. Measures readiness for entry-level job. Suitable for application to other diesel engines, including automotive, marine, farm, and stationary power-generating. May be used by vocational educators as a competency test or to assess gains in proficiency. May also be used as a screening test for prospective employees. Test package consists of a 2-part multiple-choice test of job relevant information, each part taking about 45 minutes; a performance test consisting of samples of tasks comparable to those done on a job; and a work habits inventory for assessing nontechnical, work-related attitudes and habits. The knowledge test covers diesel theory, safety, and tool use; tests and inspections; engines; fuel systems; lubrication system; and cooling system.

**12421**
**Vocational Competency Measures: Computer Operator.** American Institutes for Research, Palo Alto, CA 1983.
*Descriptors:* *Achievement Tests; *Competence; *Computers; *Entry Workers; *Personnel Selection; *Postsecondary Education; *Secondary School Students; *Vocational Education; *Work Sample Tests; Adolescents; Adults; Data Processing; Knowledge Level; Rating Scales; Screening Tests; Secondary Education; Student Evaluation
*Identifiers:* Computer Operators; Test Batteries; Work Habits
*Availability:* American Association for Vocational Instructional Materials, 120 Driftmier Engineering Center, Athens, GA 30602.

Used to assess job readiness of those who have completed training at the secondary or postsecondary level as computer operators. Measures readiness for an entry-level job, including knowledge of how to set up and load equipment, how to run programs, and what to do when a problem arises, as well as a general understanding of the overall data processing operation. Vocational educators may use test as a competency measure, to assess gains in proficiency, or to screen for advanced standing in a computer operator training program. May also be used to screen prospective applicants or to compare competencies among applicants. Test package consists of a 2-part, multiple-choice job knowledge test, each part taking approximately 45 minutes and comprising 56 items; a performance test of tasks comparable to those on the job; and a work habits inventory for assessing nontechnical, work-related attitudes and habits. The job knowledge test covers general concepts, storage media, peripherals, routine operations, troubleshooting, auxiliary equipment, and the computer operator's job.

**12422**
**Vocational Competency Measures: Carpenter.** American Institutes for Research, Palo Alto, CA 1983.
*Descriptors:* *Achievement Tests; *Carpentry; *Competence; *Construction (Process); *Entry Workers; *Personnel Selection; *Postsecondary Education; *Secondary School Students; *Vocational Education; *Work Sample Tests; Adolescents; Adults; Knowledge Level; Rating Scales; Screening Tests; Secondary Education; Student Evaluation
*Identifiers:* Test Batteries; Work Habits
*Availability:* American Association for Vocational Instructional Materials, 120 Driftmier Engineering Center, Athens, GA 30602.

Designed for those completing training in carpentry or residential construction programs at a vocational or technical school. May be used in vocational programs as a competency test, to assess gains in proficiency, or to screen for advanced standing in a carpenter training program. May also be used by employers to screen prospective employees or to compare competencies among applicants. The test package consists of a 2-part, multiple-choice job information test, each part taking approximately 45 minutes; a performance test consisting of samples of tasks similar to those performed on a job; and a work habits inventory for assessing nontechnical, work-related attitudes and behavior. Knowledge-level test covers safety; terminology; knowledge of tools and materials; use of tools and equipment; measurement and computation; concrete work, foundation layout, and construction of forms; and layout, framing construction, and finishing.

**12423**
**Vocational Competency Measures: Word Processing Specialist.** American Institutes for Research, Palo Alto, CA 1983.
*Descriptors:* *Achievement Tests; *Competence; *Entry Workers; *Personnel Selection; *Postsecondary Education; *Secondary School Students; *Vocational Education; *Word Processing; *Work Sample Tests; Adolescents; Adults; Knowledge Level; Rating Scales; Screening Tests; Secondary Education; Student Evaluation
*Identifiers:* Test Batteries; Work Habits
*Availability:* American Association for Vocational Instructional Materials, 120 Driftmier Engineering Center, Athens, GA 30602.

Used to assess job readiness of examinees who have completed vocational training at the secondary or postsecondary level as a word processing specialist. Measures readiness for an entry-level job. Examinee is expected to know how to perform standard operations that can be done on most word processors and to have a general understanding of the nature of a word processing specialist's job. May be used by vocational educators as a competency test or to assess gains in proficiency. May be used by employers as a screening test for prospective employees. The test package consists of the following: a 2-part, multiple-choice test of relevant job knowledge, each part taking approximately 45 minutes; a performance test consisting of samples of tasks comparable to those performed on the job; and a work habits inventory for assessing nontechnical, work-related attitudes and habits. Two-part job knowledge test covers technical information, judgment, English usage, punctuation, spelling, word division, and capitalization.

**12438**
**Measuring Student Achievement in Home Health Assisting Health Occupations Education.** New York State Education Dept., Albany, NY 1982.
*Descriptors:* *Achievement Tests; *Home Health Aides; *Item Banks; *Performance Tests; *Visiting Homemakers; Adults; Knowledge Level
*Availability:* ERIC Document Reproduction Service, 7420 Fullerton Rd., Ste. 110, Springfield, VA 22153-2852 (ED222541, 83 pages).

Test items developed specifically for use by educational agencies that offer a program in Home Health Assisting upon approval of the New York State Education Department. Items may be useful to other agencies or institutions. The Home Health Assisting Program is designed to prepare adults to work in the home under supervision of a health care agency. Focus is on the roles of homemaker/personal care services provider and home health aide as members of an agency team in the care of a patient. Items selected may be used as a pretest or achievement test. Areas covered by items include concepts of the world of work, home health and personal care services, communications and interpersonal relationships, household housekeeping and management services, nutritional status of patient and family, personal care services, patient care services, specialized home health care services, and recognition of special patient disabilities.

12458
**ACT Interest Inventory—Unisex Edition.** American College Testing Program, Iowa City, IA 1981.
*Descriptors:* *Adults; *College Students; *Interest Inventories; *Secondary School Students; *Sex Fairness; *Vocational Interests; Adolescents; Career Planning; Higher Education; Secondary Education
*Identifiers:* ACT Assessment; UNIACT; Unisex ACT Interest Inventory; VIESA; Vocational Interest Experience Skill Assessment
*Availability:* American College Testing Program, Publications Dept., P.O. Box 168, Iowa City, IA 52243.
*Notes:* Items, 90.

Used in both the ACT Assessment Program and the Vocational Interest, Experience and Skill Assessment Program. Intended for those from junior high school students through adults who are in the early stages of career planning or reassessment. Primary purpose is to stimulate and facilitate career exploration and to help individuals identify relevant educational and vocational choices. UNIACT was designed so that the distributions of career options suggested to males and females would be similar. Inventory has eliminated sex differences at the item level and consists of sex-balanced items. In addition to the 6 basic types of vocational interests corresponding to Holland's typology and theory, scores are also provided on 2 30-item summary scales with dimensions of work-related activity preferences: a data-idea dimension and a things-people dimension. Also available as ERIC document, ED224814.

12459
**Assertive Job Seeking Behavior Rating Scale.** Cianni-Surridge, Mary; Horan, John J. 1983.
*Descriptors:* *Assertiveness; *Job Applicants; *Job Search Methods; Adults; Rating Scales
*Availability:* *Journal of Counseling Psychology,* v30 n2 p209-14, Apr 1983.
*Notes:* Items, 16.

Used in a study to ascertain how employers react to potential applicants' assertive job-seeking behaviors. Rating scale consisted of 16 items representing behaviors advocated in current job-search literature.

12478
**Vocational Training Screening Test, Second Edition, 1978. Addendum 1981.** Mid Nebraska Mental Retardation Services, Hastings, NE 1981.
*Descriptors:* *Adults; *Mental Retardation; *Screening Tests; *Vocational Evaluation; Behavior Rating Scales; Criterion Referenced Tests; Developmental Disabilities; Job Skills; Sheltered Workshops; Vocational Rehabilitation
*Identifiers:* VTST
*Availability:* Mid Nebraska Mental Retardation Services, 522 E. Side Blvd., P.O. Box 1146, Hastings, NE 68901.
*Notes:* See also Vocational Training Quick Screening Test (12479).

A revision of the Competitive Employment Screening Test, this instrument is designed for use in assessing clients' vocational skills. Results indicate which vocational skills need to be taught in a community-based mental retardation program. Behavioral skills in prevocational areas are assessed, as well as vocational skills useful in sheltered workshop situations.

12479
**Vocational Training Quick Screening Test.** Mid-Nebraska Mental Retardation Services, Hastings, NE 1981.
*Descriptors:* *Mental Retardation; *Screening Tests; *Vocational Evaluation; Adults; Behavior Rating Scales; Criterion Referenced Tests; Developmental Disabilities; Sheltered Workshops; Vocational Rehabilitation
*Identifiers:* VTQS
*Availability:* Mid-Nebraska Mental Retardation Services, 522 E. Side Blvd., P.O. Box 1146, Hastings, NE 68901.
*Notes:* See also Vocational Training Screening Test, 2d edition, 1978, Addendum 1981 (12478). Items, 163.

Designed to assess client competencies in prevocational and vocational skill areas. Used for clients with developmental disabilities to prepare them for competitive or sheltered workshop employment.

12516
**Vocational Competency Measures: Dental Assistant.** American Institutes for Research, Palo Alto, CA 1983.
*Descriptors:* *Achievement Tests; *Dental Assistants; *Entry Workers; *Personnel Selection; *Postsecondary Education; *Secondary School Students; *Vocational Education; *Work Sample Tests; Adolescents; Adults; Competence; Knowledge Level; Rating Scales; Screening Tests; Secondary Education; Student Evaluation
*Identifiers:* Test Batteries; Work Habits
*Availability:* American Association for Vocational Instructional Materials, 120 Driftmier Engineering Center, Athens, GA 30602.

Designed to help teachers and administrators at secondary and postsecondary levels assess and improve competencies of their students in vocational education, identify areas of program improvement, and inform prospective employers of students' vocational competencies. Also useful for employers to screen and select new employees and to assess training needs of present employees. Test package consists of a 2-part, multiple-choice job information test, each part consisting of 56 items and taking 45 minutes to complete; a performance test consisting of 12 tests which represent tasks similar to those performed on the job; and a work habits inventory for assessing nontechnical, work-related attitudes and behavior. The job information test for dental assistants covers general tasks, chairside assisting, sterilization and disinfection, laboratory tasks and radiographs, and office management.

12517
**Vocational Competency Measures: Farm Equipment Mechanics.** American Institutes for Research, Palo Alto, CA 1983.
*Descriptors:* *Achievement Tests; *Agricultural Machinery Occupations; *Competence; *Entry Workers; *Mechanical Skills; *Mechanics (Process); *Personnel Selection; *Postsecondary Education; *Secondary School Students; *Vocational Education; *Work Sample Tests; Adolescents; Adults; Knowledge Level; Rating Scales; Screening Tests; Secondary Education; Student Evaluation
*Identifiers:* Test Batteries; Work Habits
*Availability:* American Association for Vocational Instructional Materials, 120 Driftmier Engineering Center, Athens, GA 30602.

Intended to assess those enrolled in or completing vocational or technical school programs in farm-equipment set-up or repair, usually those preparing to work in either dealers' service shops or on farms where equipment maintenance tasks are to be performed. Designed as a competency test in vocational programs, to assess gains in proficiency, to identify areas for program improvement or to advise prospective employers about job-related competencies of students, or to screen students for advanced standing. May also be used by employers to screen prospective employees or to compare competencies among applicants. Test package consists of a 2-part, multiple-choice job information test, each part consisting of 54 items and requiring 45 minutes to complete; a performance section of 13 tests representative of actual on-the-job tasks; and a work habits inventory for assessing nontechnical, work-related attitudes and behavior. The job information test covers the following topics: engines and electrical; hydraulics; welding; assembly, adjustment, and repair of equipment.

12564
**The Sentence Completion Blank.** Gekoski, Norman; Geisinger, Karl 1982.
*Descriptors:* *Personnel Selection; *Sales Workers; Adults; Questionnaires; Sales Occupations
*Identifiers:* Sales Sentence Completion Blank; *Sentence Completion Tests
*Availability:* Martin M. Bruce, Publishers, 50 Larchwood Rd., P.O. Box 248, Larchmont, NY 10538.
*Notes:* Items, 40.

Sentence completion questionnaire designed to aid in the selection of competent sales personnel. Guidelines for scoring and interpretation are given in the manual.

12565
**Multistate Professional Responsibility Examination.** National Conference of Bar Examiners, Iowa City, IA 1984.
*Descriptors:* *Ethics; *Knowledge Level; *Lawyers; Adults; Certification
*Identifiers:* American Bar Association; MPRE
*Availability:* National Conference of Bar Examiners, Multistate Professional Responsibility Examination, P.O. Box 4001, Iowa City, IA 52243.
*Notes:* Time, 125. Items, 60.

Administered by the National Conference of Bar Examiners as partial fulfillment of the requirements for application for admission to practice law in jurisdictions that require this instrument. Examination is administered 3 times a year at established test centers. Designed to measure examinee's knowledge of the ethical standards of the legal profession. Assesses knowledge and understanding of established ethical standards. Fifty multiple-choice items concerning ethical standards are followed by 10 test center review questions that assess examinee's reactions to the testing conditions. Instrument is updated periodically.

12585
**Attitudes Toward Pharmacy as a Profession.** Nuessle, Noel O.; Levine, Daniel U. 1982.
*Descriptors:* *Attitude Measures; *College Students; *Pharmaceutical Education; *Pharmacists; *Pharmacy; Higher Education; Rating Scales
*Availability:* *American Journal of Pharmaceutical Education,* v46 n1 p60-67, Spr 1982.
*Notes:* Items, 66.

Developed to measure students' attitudes toward pharmacy as a profession, professional principles, and preparation for a pharmacy career.

12591
**Tilesetting Testbook.** Strazicich, Mirko 1981.
*Descriptors:* *Apprenticeships; *Construction (Process); *Job Skills; *Multiple Choice Tests; *Postsecondary Education; *Skilled Occupations; *Trade and Industrial Education; Construction Materials; Unions; Vocational Education
*Identifiers:* California; Tile Occupations
*Availability:* ERIC Reproduction Service, 3900 Wheeler Ave., Alexandria, VA 22304 (ED211847, microfiche only).
*Notes:* Items, 445.

This test book contains objective tests for each topic in the "Tilesetting Workbook." Tests are all multiple choice, and 44 topics are covered in the 5 units. An alternate source is California State Department of Education, Bureau of Publications, Sacramento, CA 95814.

12602
**Vocational Assessment of the Severely Handicapped.** Larson, Keith; And Others 1979.
*Descriptors:* *Daily Living Skills; *Self Care Skills; *Severe Disabilities; *Vocational Evaluation; Basic Skills; Check Lists; Communication Skills; Hygiene; Interpersonal Competence; Mobility; Psychomotor Skills

*Identifiers:* Vocational Careers Assessment Severely Handicapped
*Availability:* ERIC Document Reproduction Service, 7420 Fullerton Rd., Ste. 110, Springfield, VA 22153-2852 (ED198668, 92 pages).
*Notes:* Items, 176.

This document contains an instrument for the vocational assessment of individuals with severe disabilities. There is a list of characteristics/procedures for each of the 8 assessment areas along with a form for recording results.

**12611**
**Employment Barrier Identification Scale.** McKee, John M.; And Others 1982.
*Descriptors:* *Adolescents; *Adults; *Employment Potential; Interviews; Job Skills; Unemployment; Vocational Rehabilitation
*Identifiers:* EBIS
*Availability:* Behavior Science Press, P.O. Box BV, University, AL 35486.
*Notes:* Time, 30 approx. Items, 19.

Designed to assess factors important to employment success. Items include assessment of job skills, education, environmental support, and personal survival skills. Interviewer should be familiar with behavioral interviewing techniques. Instrument may pinpoint areas and skills in which job seeker needs training.

**12617**
**Vocational Competency Measures: Fabric Sales.** American Institutes for Research, Palo Alto, CA 1983.
*Descriptors:* *Achievement Tests; *Entry Workers; *Personnel Selection; *Postsecondary Education; *Sales Occupations; *Secondary School Students; *Vocational Education; *Work Sample Tests; Adolescents; Adults; Clothing; Competence; Fashion Industry; Knowledge Level; Merchandising; Rating Scales; Screening Tests; Secondary Education; Student Evaluation
*Identifiers:* *Fabrics; Test Batteries; Work Habits
*Availability:* American Association for Vocational Instructional Materials, 120 Driftmier Engineering Center, Athens, GA 30602.

Designed to help teachers and administrators at secondary and postsecondary levels assess and improve competencies of their students in vocational education, identify areas for program improvement, and inform prospective employers of students' vocational competencies. Also useful for employers to screen and select new employees and to assess training needs of present employees. Test package consists of a 2-part multiple-choice job information test, each part taking about 45 minutes to complete; a performance test consisting of tests which represent tasks similar to those performed on the job; and a work habits inventory for assessing nontechnical, work-related attitudes and behavior. Test is specifically designed for individuals interested in fabric sales that combine knowledge of clothing construction with merchandising. Intended for those in retail merchandising programs at the secondary or postsecondary level rather than for those completing 4-year fashion or textile marketing programs. The job information tests assess knowledge of general fashion, sales, and sewing. The performance test requires examinee to carry out the following: take body measurements, determine figure type and size, construct a double-pointed dart, sew seams, adjust a blouse pattern to increase bustline, insert a front fly zipper, complete an exchange/return, close out a cash register, complete a sale, and maintain a book inventory. The performance section takes approximately 245 minutes to complete.

**12620**
**Vocational Competency Measures: Water Treatment Technician.** American Institutes for Research, Palo Alto, CA 1983.
*Descriptors:* *Achievement Tests; *Entry Workers; *Personnel Selection; *Postsecondary Education; *Secondary School Students; *Technical Occupations; *Vocational Education; *Water Treatment; *Work Sample Tests; Adolescents; Adults; Competence; Knowledge Level; Rating Scales; Screening Tests; Secondary Education; Student Evaluation; Water Quality
*Identifiers:* Test Batteries; Work Habits
*Availability:* American Association for Vocational Instructional Materials, 120 Driftmier Engineering Center, Athens, GA 30602.

Designed to help teachers and administrators at secondary and postsecondary levels assess and improve competencies of their students in vocational education, identify areas for program improvement, and inform prospective employers of students' vocational competencies. Also useful for employers to screen and select new employees and to assess training needs of present employees. Test package consists of a 2-part multiple-choice job information test, each part taking about 45 minutes to complete; a performance test consisting of tests which represent tasks similar to those performed on the job; and a work habits inventory for assessing nontechnical, work-related attitudes and behavior. Test package is intended for those completing vocational programs in water treatment and preparing to work as technicians in water treatment laboratories or plants. The job information test assesses knowledge of plant and equipment operation, record keeping, sampling and testing, inspection and calibration, and plant and equipment maintenance. The following activities are carried out for the performance tests: using an air mask, repairing a leaking chlorine cylinder, changing chart in flow recorder, checking dosage of fluoridator, performing a jar test to estimate optimum alum dosage, and collecting grab sample of process control. It takes approximately 100 minutes to complete the performance tests.

**12621**
**Vocational Competency Measures: Wastewater Treatment Technician.** American Institutes for Research, Palo Alto, CA 1983.
*Descriptors:* *Achievement Tests; *Entry Workers; *Personnel Selection; *Postsecondary Education; *Secondary School Students; *Technical Occupations; *Vocational Education; *Waste Water; *Water Treatment; *Work Sample Tests; Adolescents; Adults; Competence; Knowledge Level; Rating Scales; Screening Tests; Secondary Education; Student Evaluation
*Identifiers:* Test Batteries; Work Habits
*Availability:* American Association for Vocational Instructional Materials, 120 Driftmier Engineering Center, Athens, GA 30602.

Designed to help teachers and administrators at secondary and postsecondary levels assess and improve competencies of their students in vocational education, identify areas for program improvement, and inform prospective employers of students' vocational competencies. Also useful for employers to screen and select new employees and to assess training needs of present employees. Test package consists of a 2-part multiple-choice job information test, each part taking about 45 minutes to complete; a performance test consisting of tests that represent tasks similar to those performed on the job; and a work habits inventory for assessing nontechnical, work-related attitudes and behavior. Test package is intended for those completing vocational programs in wastewater treatment and who are preparing to work as technicians in wastewater treatment laboratories or plants. The job information test assesses knowledge of plant and equipment operation, record keeping, sampling and testing, inspection and calibration, and plant and equipment maintenance. The tasks to be carried out on the performance test include using an air pack, measuring pH of plant influent, aligning pump coupling, performing most probable number (MPN) test to measure coliform bacteria, measuring dissolved oxygen (DO) of a sample, reading and recording thermometers and pressure gauges, and deragging primary sludge pump. The performance tests take approximately 100 minutes to complete.

**12622**
**Vocational Competency Measures: Apparel Sales.** American Institutes for Research, Palo Alto, CA 1983.
*Descriptors:* *Achievement Tests; *Clothing; *Entry Workers; *Personnel Selection; *Postsecondary Education; *Sales Occupations; *Secondary School Students; *Vocational Education; *Work Sample Tests; Adolescents; Adults; Competence; Fashion Industry; Knowledge Level; Merchandising; Rating Scales; Screening Tests; Secondary Education; Student Evaluation
*Identifiers:* Test Batteries; Work Habits
*Availability:* American Association for Vocational Instructional Materials, 120 Driftmier Engineering Center, Athens, GA 30602.

Designed to help teachers and administrators at secondary and postsecondary levels assess and improve competencies of their students in vocational education, identify areas for program improvement, and inform prospective employers of students' vocational competencies. Also useful for employers to screen and select new employees and to assess training needs of present employees. Test package consists of a 2-part multiple-choice job information test, each part taking about 45 minutes to complete; a performance test consisting of tests which represent tasks similar to those performed on the job; and a work habits inventory for assessing nontechnical, work-related attitudes and behavior. Test is intended for persons in fashion apparel merchandising at the secondary or postsecondary level. It is not intended for individuals completing 4-year fashion merchandising programs. The 2 parts of the job information test assess general fashion knowledge and sales knowledge. The performance test requires examinee to carry out following activities: take body measurements, determine figure type and size, complete layaway forms, close out a cash register, handle a customer complaint, complete an exchange or return, complete a sale, and maintain a book inventory. The performance test takes approximately 180 minutes to complete.

**12625**
**Rehabilitation Task Performance Evaluation Scale.** Rehabilitation Research Institute, University of Wisconsin, Madison 1976.
*Descriptors:* *Counselor Evaluation; *Job Performance; *Staff Utilization; *Vocational Rehabilitation; Adults; Counselor Qualifications; Personnel Evaluation; Rating Scales; Self Evaluation (Individuals)
*Availability:* ERIC Document Reproduction Service, 7420 Fullerton Rd., Ste. 110, Springfield, VA 22153-2852 (ED193253, 50 pages).
*Notes:* Items, 294.

This scale is intended for the training and use of State Divisions of Vocational Rehabilitation (DVR) line supervisors. Use of the scale for periodic evaluations of the quality and extent of staff members' task performance provides information that the line supervisors need for personnel action. To enable supervisors to evaluate a staff member's qualifications to perform a large variety of rehabilitation tasks, the scale requires the individual to estimate the percent of time spent on the task and to check the level of capability to perform the task. The areas covered are administration/supervision, evaluation, consultation, client counseling and planning, rehabilitation client assessment, job placement, referral and community relations, case management and special services, intake and eligibility determination, recording and reporting, incidental client assistance, and clerical.

**12643**
**Administrator Professional Leadership Scale.** Thompson, Bruce 1974.
*Descriptors:* *Administrator Evaluation; *Attitude Measures; *Leadership Qualities; *Principals; *Teacher Administrator Relationship; Adults; Program Implementation; Rating Scales; Teacher Attitudes
*Identifiers:* APLS
*Availability:* ERIC Document Reproduction Service, 7420 Fullerton Rd., Ste. 110, Springfield, VA 22153-2852 (ED175911, 15 pages).
*Notes:* See also Administrator Professional Leadership Scale (10463). Items, 18.

The Administrator Professional Leadership Scale (APLS) was developed to measure the perceived professional leadership quality of school principals and to provide principals with anonymous feedback on teachers' perceptions of their leadership. The scale was further refined to increase its reliability, to discover categories of administrator behavior considered by teachers when evaluating leadership, and to improve the evaluation of principals according to these dimensions of leadership. The revised instrument may be appropriate for use by school principals who wish to obtain information about how the faculty perceive them, or for program evaluation efforts when leadership provided by principals may produce variations in program implementation and these influences need to be quantified.

**12686**
**The SOCO Scale: A Measure of the Customer Orientation of Salespeople.** Saxe, Robert; Weitz, Barton A. 1982.
*Descriptors:* *Attitude Measures; *Salesmanship; *Sales Workers; Adults; Rating Scales
*Identifiers:* Customer Satisfaction; SOCO
*Availability:* Marketing Science Institute, Publications Dept., 1000 Massachusetts Ave., Cambridge, MA 02138.
*Notes:* Items, 24.

The SOCO (Selling Orientation-Customer Orientation) Scale was developed to measure the degree to which salespersons engage in customer-oriented selling. Customer-oriented selling is defined as helping customers make purchase decisions that will satisfy customer needs. Highly customer-oriented behavior aims at increasing long-term customer satisfaction. The use of customer-oriented selling is related to the ability of salespeople to help their customers and the quality of the customer-salesperson relationship.

**12707**
**Exit Interviews.** American Association of School Personnel Administrators, Seven Hills, OH 1977.
*Descriptors:* *Employer Employee Relationship; *Interviews; *Personnel Data; *Records (Forms); *Work Attitudes; Elementary Secondary Education; Questionnaires; School Districts; School Personnel
*Identifiers:* *Exit Interviews
*Availability:* ERIC Document Reproduction Service, 7420 Fullerton Rd., Ste. 110, Springfield, VA 22153-2852 (ED151945, 27 pages).

There are 8 sample forms used in different districts for exit interviews: Joint School District No. 1, West Bend, WI; Metropolitan Nashville Public School System; School District of the City of Berkeley; Santa Cruz City School Resignation Form; Kearsley Board of Education; Belmont, Massachusetts Exit Questionnaire; North Carolina Department of Public Instruction Interviewer's Exit Interview Summary and a Report by Employee; and Kenosha Unified School District No. 1 Exit Opinionnaire. These are examples of forms used when an employee leaves his or her position.

**12965**
**Employee Attitude Inventory.** London House, Rosemont, IL 1982.
*Descriptors:* *Antisocial Behavior; *Attitude Measures; *Employee Attitudes; *Employees; *Stealing; Adults; Burnout; Drug Use; Job Satisfaction; Predictive Measurement
*Identifiers:* Drug Attitudes; EAI; *Honesty
*Availability:* London House, SRA Product Group, 9701 W. Higgins Rd., Rosemont, IL 60018.
*Notes:* Time, 30 approx. Items, 179.

Designed to predict theft and other forms of counterproductivity of current employees. Assesses attitudes of employees concerning theft, drug use, job burnout, and job dissatisfaction. Validity scale assesses employees' tendencies to "fake good" on the instrument by answering items in a socially acceptable direction.

**12973**
**Organizational Norms Opinionnaire.** Alexander, Mark 1978.
*Descriptors:* *Employee Attitudes; *Employees; *Norms; *Organizations (Groups); Adults; Attitude Measures; Management Development; Rating Scales; Self Evaluation (Groups); Sensitivity Training
*Identifiers:* Facilitators
*Availability:* Pfeiffer, J. William, and Jones, John E., eds., *The 1978 Annual Handbook for Group Facilitators.* San Diego: University Associates, 1978. Pfeiffer and Co., formerly University Associates, 8517 Production Ave., San Diego, CA 92121-2280.
*Notes:* Items, 42.

Designed to identify positive and negative organizational norms of behavior that influence the effectiveness and job satisfaction of employees.

**12974**
**Critical Consulting Incidents Inventory.** Jones, John E.; Banet, Anthony G. 1978.
*Descriptors:* *Consultants; Administrator Attitudes; Administrators; Adults; Human Relations; Management Development; Self Evaluation (Individuals); Situational Tests
*Identifiers:* CCII
*Availability:* Pfeiffer, J. William, and Jones, John E., eds., *The 1978 Annual Handbook for Group Facilitators.* San Diego: University Associates, 1978. Pfeiffer and Co., formerly University Associates, 8517 Production Ave., San Diego, CA 92121-2280.
*Notes:* Items, 20.

Designed to assist human relations consultants in assessing their style of response to critical incidents. Major options available to consultants in response to critical situations are support, direction, and problem solving.

**12981**
**Role Efficacy Scale.** Pareek, Udai 1980.
*Descriptors:* *Administrators; *Role Perception; Adults; Management Development; Management Teams; Self Concept Measures
*Identifiers:* Self Report Measures
*Availability:* Pfeiffer, J. William, and Jones, John E., eds., *The 1980 Annual Handbook for Group Facilitators.* San Diego: University Associates, 1980. Pfeiffer and Co., formerly University Associates, 8517 Production Ave., San Diego, CA 92121-2280.
*Notes:* Items, 20.

Designed to assess effectiveness of individual members of an organizational team. Role efficacy is defined as the psychological factor underlying role effectiveness.

**12982**
**Increasing Employee Self-Control.** Harvey, Barron H. 1977.
*Descriptors:* *Administrator Attitudes; *Administrators; *Attitude Measures; *Employee Responsibility; *Power Structure; Adults; Employees; Management by Objectives
*Identifiers:* IESC
*Availability:* Pfeiffer, J. William, and Jones, John E., eds., *The 1980 Annual Handbook for Group Facilitators.* San Diego: University Associates, 1980. Pfeiffer and Co., formerly University Associates, 8517 Production Ave., San Diego, CA 92121-2280.
*Notes:* Time, 20 approx. Items, 16.

Designed to assess manager's receptiveness toward increasing employees' self-control in organizations.

**12983**
**Organizational Diagnosis Questionnaire.** Preziosi, Robert C. 1980.
*Descriptors:* *Attitude Measures; *Employee Attitudes; *Employees; *Organizational Climate; *Organizational Development; *Self Evaluation (Groups); Adults; Organizations (Groups); Rating Scales
*Identifiers:* ODQ
*Availability:* Pfeiffer, J. William, and Jones, John E., eds., *The 1980 Annual Handbook for Group Facilitators.* San Diego: University Associates, 1980. Pfeiffer and Co., formerly University Associates, 8517 Production Ave., San Diego, CA 92121-2280.
*Notes:* Items, 35.

Designed to enable employees to assess the functioning of their organization. Measures attitudes on Weisbord's six box organizational model.

**12987**
**Organizational-Process Survey.** Burns, Frank; Gragg, Robert L. 1981.
*Descriptors:* *Administrators; *Management Development; *Organizational Effectiveness; Administrator Attitudes; Adults; Attitude Measures; Management Teams; Rating Scales
*Availability:* Jones, John E., and Pfeiffer, J. William, eds., *The 1981 Annual Handbook for Group Facilitators.* San Diego: University Associates, 1981. Pfeiffer and Co., formerly University Associates, 8517 Production Ave., San Diego, CA 92121-2280.
*Notes:* Items, 10.

Designed for use in organization survey, team building with executives, and management development.

**12989**
**Supervisory Behavior Questionnaire.** Sims, Henry P. Jr. 1981.
*Descriptors:* *Leadership Styles; *Leadership Training; *Supervisors; Adults; Behavior Patterns; Behavior Rating Scales; Employees; Leaders
*Availability:* Jones, John E., and Pfeiffer, J. William, eds., *The 1981 Annual Handbook for Group Facilitators.* San Diego: University Associates, 1981. Pfeiffer and Co., formerly University Associates, 8517 Production Ave., San Diego, CA 92121-2280.
*Notes:* Items, 9.

Developed for use in leadership training to direct participant's attention to 3 types of leader behavior: goal specification, positive reward, and punitive reward.

**12994**
**Managerial Attitude Questionnaire.** Roskin, Rick 1982.
*Descriptors:* *Administrator Attitudes; *Ambiguity; *Attitude Measures; *Leadership Styles; Administrators; Adults; Management Development; Situational Tests
*Identifiers:* Self Administered Tests; Self Scoring Tests
*Availability:* Pfeiffer, J. William, and Goodstein, Leonard D., eds., *The 1982 Annual Handbook for Group Facilitators.* San Diego: University Associates, 1982. Pfeiffer and Co., formerly University Associates, 8517 Production Ave., San Diego, CA 92121-2280.
*Notes:* Time, 40 approx. Items, 10.

Designed to assess a manager's ability to cope with ambiguous work situations. Respondent is asked to distribute 100 points over 6 responses for each of 10 situations.

**12997**
**Communication Climate Inventory.** Costigan, James I.; Schmeidler, Martha A. 1984.
*Descriptors:* *Employees; *Organizational Communication; Adults; Interpersonal Communication; Rating Scales; Supervisors; Supervisory Methods; Work Environment
*Identifiers:* Defensiveness; Subordinates (Employees); Supportive Supervision
*Availability:* Pfeiffer, J. William, and Goodstein, Leonard D., eds., *The 1984 Annual Handbook for Group Facilitators.* San Diego: University Associates, 1984. Pfeiffer and Co., formerly University Associates, 8517 Production Ave., San Diego, CA 92121-2280.
*Notes:* Items, 36.

Designed to measure an organization's communication environment. Employees are asked to rate supervisor's communication methods on a Likert scale.

**12998**
**Styles Profile of Interaction Roles in Organizations.** Pareek, Udai 1984.
*Descriptors:* *Interaction; *Leadership Styles; *Management Development; *Self Evaluation (Individuals); *Supervisors; Administrators; Adults; Interpersonal Communication; Organizational Communication; Rating Scales; Transactional Analysis
*Identifiers:* Self Administered Tests; SPIRO; Subordinates (Employees)
*Availability:* Pfeiffer, J. William, and Goodstein, Leonard D., eds., *The 1984 Annual Handbook for Group Facilitators.* San Diego: University Associates, 1984. Pfeiffer and Co., formerly University Associates, 8517 Production Ave., San Diego, CA 92121-2280.
*Notes:* Items, 36.

Designed for use in management training programs. A manager can examine the operating effectiveness scores for each of his or her transactional analysis ego states. The ego states are supportive, normative, problem solving, innovating, confronting, and resilient.

**12999**
**Quality of Work Life—Conditions/Feelings.** Sashkin, Marshall; Lengermann, Joseph J. 1984.
*Descriptors:* *Attitude Measures; *Employees; *Job Satisfaction; *Work Attitudes; *Work Environment; Adults; Job Analysis
*Identifiers:* QWL (C F)
*Availability:* Pfeiffer, J. William, and Goodstein, Leonard D., eds., *The 1984 Annual Handbook for Group Facilitators.* San Diego: University Associates, 1984. Pfeiffer and Co., formerly University Associates, 8517 Production Ave., San Diego, CA 92121-2280.
*Notes:* Time, 15 approx. Items, 35.

A 2-part instrument designed to measure objective conditions of one's work setting and one's personal reactions to those conditions. The QWL-C consists of 25 items and the QWL-F consists of 10 items.

**13007**
**Vocational Competency Measures: Physical Therapist Assistant.** American Institutes for Research, Palo Alto, CA 1983.
*Descriptors:* *Achievement Tests; *Entry Workers; *Personnel Selection; *Physical Therapists; *Postsecondary Education; *Secondary School Students; *Two Year Colleges; *Vocational Education; *Work Sample Tests; Adolescents; Adults; Competence; Knowledge Level; Physical Therapy; Rating Scales; Screening Tests; Secondary Education; Student Evaluation
*Identifiers:* Test Batteries; Work Habits
*Availability:* American Association for Vocational Instructional Materials, 120 Driftmier Engineering Center, Athens, GA 30602.

Designed to help teachers and administrators at secondary and postsecondary levels assess and improve competencies of their students in vocational education, identify areas for program improvement, and inform prospective employers of students' vocational competencies. Also useful for employers to screen and select new employees and to assess training needs of present employees. Test package consists of a 2-part multiple-choice job information test, each part taking about 45 minutes to complete; a performance test consisting of tests which represent tasks similar to those performed on the job; and a work habits inventory for assessing nontechnical, work-related attitudes and behavior. Intended for persons enrolled in or completing a 2-year, postsecondary-level training program to become physical therapist assistants. In states requiring board certification or licensing, test is generally applicable for those preparing for state board examinations. Not intended for those in physical therapist programs or for those in physical therapy aide programs. Job information test has 108 items and covers general activities, massage and exercise, physical modalities, gait training, and patient assistance and instruction. The 10 performance tests include administering ultrasound treatment, cervical traction, hot packs, tilt table treatment, range of motion exercise, whirlpool treatment, paraffin bath treatment, massage, instructing patient on Williams' flexion exercises, and providing gait training.

**13008**
**Vocational Competency Measures: Grocery Clerk.** American Institutes for Research, Palo Alto, CA 1983.
*Descriptors:* *Achievement Tests; *Entry Workers; *Food Stores; *Personnel Selection; *Postsecondary Education; *Secondary School Students; *Vocational Education; *Work Sample Tests; Adolescents; Adults; Competence; Knowledge Level; Rating Scales; Screening Tests; Secondary Education; Student Evaluation
*Identifiers:* Grocery Checkers; *Grocery Clerks; Test Batteries; Work Habits
*Availability:* American Association for Vocational Instructional Materials, 120 Driftmier Engineering Center, Athens, GA 30602.

Designed to help teachers and administrators at secondary and postsecondary levels assess and improve competencies of their students in vocational education, identify areas for program improvement, and inform prospective employers of students' vocational competencies. Also useful for employers to screen and select new employees and to assess training needs of present employees. Test package consists of a 2-part multiple-choice job information test, each part taking about 45 minutes to complete; a performance test consisting of tests that represent tasks similar to those performed on the job; and a work habits inventory for assessing nontechnical, work-related attitudes and behavior. Intended for people completing programs in food marketing and distribution who are preparing to work in grocery stores as clerks, checkers, baggers, or stockers. Applies to workers in both small retail businesses or large supermarket chains. Job information test consists of 108 items and covers general policies and procedures, checking, stocking, customers, and coworkers. Six performance tests require examinee to set up and close out a checkstand, check and bag merchandise, stock and price merchandise, take inventory, process a delivery, and organize a stockroom.

**13009**
**Vocational Competency Measures: Restaurant Service (Waiter, Waitress, Cashier).** American Institutes for Research, Palo Alto, CA 1983.
*Descriptors:* *Achievement Tests; *Dining Facilities; *Entry Workers; *Personnel Selection; *Postsecondary Education; *Secondary School Students; *Vocational Education; *Work Sample Tests; Adolescents; Adults; Competence; Food Service; Knowledge Level; Rating Scales; Screening Tests; Secondary Education; Student Evaluation
*Identifiers:* *Cashiers; Test Batteries; *Waiters Waitresses; Work Habits
*Availability:* American Association for Vocational Instructional Materials, 120 Driftmier Engineering Center, Athens, GA 30602.

Designed to help teachers and administrators at secondary and postsecondary levels assess and improve competencies of their students in vocational education, identify areas for program improvement, and inform prospective employers of students' vocational competencies. Also useful for employers to screen and select new employees and to assess training needs of present employees. Test package consists of a 2-part multiple-choice job information test, each part taking about 45 minutes to complete; a performance test consisting of tests that represent tasks similar to those performed on the job; and a work habits inventory for assessing nontechnical, work-related attitudes and behavior. Intended to assess job readiness of those who have been trained for front-of-the-house positions in restaurants, hotel dining rooms, and other eating facilities. The job information test consists of 122 items and covers routine dining room activities, nonroutine and problem situations, cashier activities, sanitation and safety, kitchen and sidestand activities, vocabulary, and restaurant operation. The 8 performance activities require examinee to handle cashier duties, change tablecloth, carry loaded tray, set dinner table, seat customer, serve dinner to customer, handle difficult customers, and handle a waiter-customer dispute.

**13010**
**Vocational Competency Measures: Custom Sewing.** American Institutes for Research, Palo Alto, CA 1983.
*Descriptors:* *Achievement Tests; *Entry Workers; *Needle Trades; *Personnel Selection; *Postsecondary Education; *Secondary School Students; *Sewing Machine Operators; *Vocational Education; *Work Sample Tests; Adolescents; Adults; Competence; Knowledge Level; Rating Scales; Screening Tests; Secondary Education; Student Evaluation
*Identifiers:* Test Batteries; Work Habits
*Availability:* American Association for Vocational Instructional Materials, 120 Driftmier Engineering Center, Athens, GA 30602.

Designed to help teachers and administrators at secondary and postsecondary levels assess and improve competencies of their students in vocational education, identify areas for program improvement, and inform prospective employers of students' vocational competencies. Also useful for employers to screen and select new employees and to assess training needs of present employees. Test package consists of a 2-part multiple-choice job information test, each part taking about 45 minutes to complete; a performance test consisting of tests that represent tasks similar to those performed on the job; and a work habits inventory for assessing nontechnical, work-related attitudes and behavior. Intended for persons in nonindustrial sewing programs at secondary or postsecondary level. Test is not designed for those completing 4-year fashion design or industrial sewing programs. Job information test consists of 101 items and covers general fashion knowledge and sewing. The 6 performance tests require examinee to take body measurements, determine figure type and size, construct a double-pointed dart, sew seams, adjust a blouse pattern to increase bustline, and insert a front fly zipper.

**13011**
**Vocational Competency Measures: Agricultural Chemicals Applications Technician.** American Institutes for Research, Palo Alto, CA 1983.
*Descriptors:* *Achievement Tests; *Agricultural Chemical Occupations; *Entry Workers; *Personnel Selection; *Postsecondary Education; *Secondary School Students; *Vocational Education; *Work Sample Tests; Adolescents; Adults; Agricultural Occupations; Competence; Knowledge Level; Rating Scales; Screening Tests; Secondary Education; Student Evaluation
*Identifiers:* Test Batteries; Work Habits
*Availability:* American Association for Vocational Instructional Materials, 120 Driftmier Engineering Center, Athens, GA 30602.

Designed to help teachers and administrators at secondary and postsecondary levels assess and improve competencies of their students in vocational education, identify areas for program improvement, and inform prospective employers of students' vocational competencies. Also useful for employers to screen and select new employees and to assess training needs of present employees. Test package consists of a 2-part multiple-choice job information test, each part taking about 45 minutes to complete; a performance test consisting of tests that represent tasks similar to those performed on the job; and a work habits inventory for assessing nontechnical, work-related attitudes and behavior. Intended for people completing vocational training in the field of agriculture and preparing to work in the more specialized area of agricultural chemicals, either in the marketing and distribution of such chemicals or in the actual application of the chemicals on the farm. The job information test consists of 106 items and covers safety, consulting and problem recognition, chemical mixing and disposal, equipment setup and operation, and clerical-customer service. The 9 performance tests require examinee to select and use protective clothing, identify broadleaf and narrowleaf weeds, calculate amount of pesticide to apply, prepare a billing form, calibrate a liquid spray applicator, operate a liquid spray application, clean it for storage, store chemicals safely, and rinse and empty pesticide containers.

**13069**
**Fine Finger Dexterity Work Task Unit: Electromechanical Vocational Assessment.** Mississippi State University, Rehabilitation Research and Training Center 1983.
*Descriptors:* *Blindness; *Kinesthetic Perception; *Performance Tests; *Visual Impairments; *Vocational Evaluation; Adults; Individual Testing; Psychomotor Skills
*Identifiers:* Bilateral Dexterity; Electromechanical Vocational Assessment; *Finger Dexterity; Frustration; Mississippi State University
*Availability:* Rehabilitation Research and Training Center, P.O. Box 5365, Mississippi State, MS 39762.
*Notes:* Time, 50.

Designed to provide a flexible system for evaluating a variety of work abilities including kinesthetic memory, bimanual coordination, finger dexterity, and tolerance for frustration tolerance. Purpose is to assist National Industries for the Blind and vocational evaluators to improve assessment of the vocational potential of blind and severely visually impaired persons, particularly blind persons with multiple disabilities. Subject is taught the task, then works for a 50-minute period and receives feedback on the rate and accuracy of work. Used to compare visually impaired person's performance with the sighted standard. The Methods - Time Measurement Procedure was used to develop the average sighted standard for this work task.

**13070**
**Foot Operated Hinged Box Work Task Unit: Electromechanical Vocational Assessment.** Mississippi State University, Rehabilitation Research and Training Center 1983.
*Descriptors:* *Blindness; *Individual Testing; *Performance Tests; *Visual Impairments; *Vocational Evaluation; Adults; Psychomotor Skills
*Identifiers:* Bilateral Dexterity; Electromechanical Vocational Assessment; Finger Dexterity; Hand Foot Coordination; Mississippi State University
*Availability:* Rehabilitation Research and Training Center, P.O. Box 5365, Mississippi State, MS 39762.
*Notes:* Time, 50.

Designed to provide a flexible system for evaluating a variety of work abilities including hand-foot coordination, bimanual coordination, and finger dexterity. Purpose is to assist National Industries for the Blind and vocational evaluators to improve assessment of the vocational potential of blind and severely visually impaired persons, particularly blind persons with mutliple disabilities. Subject is taught the task, then works for a 50-minute period and receives feedback on the rate and accuracy of work. Provides an objective method of comparing a blind or visually impaired person's performance in these work abilities against the performance expected from an average sighted worker. The Methods - Time Measurement Procedure was used to develop the average sighted standard for this work task.

**13071**
**Hinged Box Work Task Unit: Electromechanical Vocational Assessment.** Mississippi State University, Rehabilitation Research and Training Center 1983.
*Descriptors:* *Blindness; *Performance Tests; *Tactual Perception; *Visual Impairments; *Vocational Evaluation; Adults; Individual Testing; Psychomotor Skills
*Identifiers:* Bilateral Dexterity; Electromechanical Vocational Assessment; Frustration; Mississippi State University
*Availability:* Rehabilitation Research and Training Center, P.O. Box 5365, Mississippi State, MS 39762.
*Notes:* Time, 50.

Designed to provide a flexible system for evaluating a variety of work abilities including tactual perception, material control, bimanual coordination, and frustration tolerance. Purpose is to assist National Industries for the Blind and vocational evaluators to improve assessment of the vocational potential of blind and severely visually impaired persons, particularly blind persons with multiple disabilities. Subject is taught the task, then works for a 50-minute period and receives feedback on the rate and accuracy of work. Used to compare visually impaired person's performance with the sighted standard. The Methods - Time Measurement Procedure was used to develop the average sighted standard for this task.

**13072**
**Index Card Work Task Unit: Electromechanical Vocational Assessment.** Mississippi State University, Rehabilitation Research and Training Center 1983.
*Descriptors:* *Blindness; *Memory; *Performance Tests; *Visual Impairments; *Vocational Evaluation; Adults; Individual Testing; Psychomotor Skills
*Identifiers:* Bilateral Dexterity; Electromechanical Vocational Assessment; Finger Dexterity; Frustration; Mississippi State University
*Availability:* Rehabilitation Research and Training Center, P.O. Box 5365, Mississippi State, MS 39762.
*Notes:* Time, 50.

Designed to provide a flexible system for evaluating a variety of work abilities including bimanual coordination, finger dexterity, frustration tolerance, and memory for sequence of operations. Purpose is to assist National Industries for the Blind and vocational evaluators to improve assessment of the vocational potential of blind and severely visually impaired persons, particularly blind persons with multiple disabilities. Subject is taught the task, then works for a 50-minute period and receives feedback on the rate and accuracy of work. An objective method of comparing visually impaired person's performance with the sighted standard. The Methods - Time Measurement Procedure was used to develop the average sighted standard for this task.

**13073**
**Multifunctional Work Task Unit: Electromechanical Vocational Assessment.** Mississippi State University, Rehabilitation Research and Training Center 1983.
*Descriptors:* *Blindness; *Kinesthetic Perception; *Performance Tests; *Visual Impairments; *Vocational Evaluation; Adults; Assembly (Manufacturing); Individual Testing; Psychomotor Skills
*Identifiers:* Bilateral Dexterity; Electromechanical Vocational Assessment; Mississippi State University
*Availability:* Rehabilitation Research and Training Center, P.O. Box 5365, Mississippi State, MS 39762.
*Notes:* Time, 50.

Designed to provide a flexible system for evaluating a variety of work abilities including bimanual coordination, material control, and kinesthetic memory. Purpose is to assist National Industries for the Blind and vocational evaluators to improve assessment of the vocational potential of blind and severely visually impaired persons, particularly blind persons with multiple disabilities. Subject is taught the task, then works for a 50-minute period and receives feedback on the rate and accuracy of work. Used to compare visually impaired person's performance with the sighted standard. The Methods - Time Measurement Procedure was used to develop the average sighted standard for this task.

**13074**
**Revolving Assembly Table Work Task Unit: Electromechanical Vocational Assessment.** Mississippi State University, Rehabilitation Research and Training Center 1983.
*Descriptors:* *Blindness; *Individual Testing; *Kinesthetic Perception; *Performance Tests; *Visual Impairments; *Vocational Evaluation; Adults; Interpersonal Competence; Psychomotor Skills
*Identifiers:* Bilateral Dexterity; Electromechanical Vocational Assessment; Finger Dexterity; Mississippi State University
*Availability:* Rehabilitation Research and Training Center, P.O. Box 5365, Mississippi State, MS 39762.
*Notes:* Time, 50.

Designed to provide a flexible system for evaluating a variety of work abilities including bimanual coordination, finger dexterity, kinesthetic memory, and ability to work with others. Purpose is to assist National Industries for the Blind and vocational evaluators to improve assessment of the vocational potential of blind and severely visually impaired persons, particularly blind persons with multiple disabilities. Subject is taught the task, then works for a 50-minute period and receives feedback on the rate and accuracy of work. Used to compare performance of visually impaired persons with the sighted standard.

**13080**
**The Morale Index for Supervisors/Managers.** Bedell, Ralph; Lippitt, Gordon L. 1981.
*Descriptors:* *Administrator Attitudes; *Administrators; *Attitude Measures; *Morale; *Self Evaluation (Individuals); *Supervisors; *Supervisory Training; Adults; Job Satisfaction; Work Attitudes
*Identifiers:* Self Report Measures
*Availability:* Development Publications, 5605 Lamar Rd., Bethesda, MD 20816-1398.
*Notes:* See also Productivity Index for Supervisors/Managers (13081). Items, 25.

Designed to enable supervisors and managers to record feelings toward important aspects of their organizational life or supervisory work. Useful for self-evaluation in training programs.

**13081**
**Productivity Index for Supervisors/Managers.** Ericson, Richard F.; Lippitt, Gordon L. 1981.
*Descriptors:* *Administrator Attitudes; *Attitude Measures; *Organizational Effectiveness; *Productivity; *Supervisory Training; Administrators; Adults; Efficiency; Self Evaluation (Individuals); Supervisors
*Identifiers:* Self Report Measures
*Availability:* Development Publications, 5605 Lamar Rd., Bethesda, MD 20816-1398.
*Notes:* See also The Morale Index for Supervisors/Managers (13080). Items, 25.

Designed to enable supervisory personnel to record their feelings or attitudes toward elements affecting the efficiency of their own and their organization's operations. A stimulus for self-examination and group discussion.

**13165**
**Test of Sales Aptitude, Form A Revised.** Bruce, Martin M. 1983.
*Descriptors:* *Aptitude Tests; *Job Applicants; *Salesmanship; *Sales Occupations; Adults; Career Guidance; Multiple Choice Tests; Sales Workers
*Identifiers:* Self Administered Tests
*Availability:* Martin M. Bruce, Publishers, 50 Larchwood Rd., P.O. Box 248, Larchmont, NY 10538.
*Notes:* Time, 30 approx. Items, 50.

Designed to aid in the appraisal of sales aptitude. Provides an objective measure of one important aspect of sales aptitude, namely knowledge and understanding of basic principles of selling. Sales fields include selling to retailers, wholesalers, and consumers. Test can aid in appraising sales ability and potential in selecting sales personnel and for use in vocational guidance. Should be used as an aid only, and other important factors must be taken into account.

**13246**
**Wolfe-Winrow Structured COBOL Proficiency Test.** Walden Computer Aptitude Testing, Ltd., Oradell, NJ 1983.

*Descriptors:* *Achievement Tests; *Data Processing; *Programming Languages; Adults; Knowledge Level; On the Job Training; Personnel Selection; Promotion (Occupational)
*Identifiers:* COBOL Programming Language; *Structured COBOL; WWSCBL
*Availability:* Walden Computer Aptitude Testing Ltd., Box 319, Oradell, NJ 07649.
*Notes:* Time, 30. Items, 5.

Designed to measure a programmer's knowledge of Structured COBOL. For use in the evaluation of intermediate and senior programmers in advanced COBOL concepts and to determine proficiency when hiring or upgrading, evaluating training, or for needs assessment. Covers identification of structured programming constructs and other structured tools, defining storage attributes and code-acceptable picture clauses, table look-up and debugging aids, coding from specs, understanding arithmetic operations, and recognition of programming efficiencies.

**13247**
**Wolfe-Winrow DOS/VS and DOS/VSE Proficiency Test.** Walden Computer Aptitude Testing, Ltd., Oradell, NJ 1983.
*Descriptors:* *Achievement Tests; *Data Processing; Adults; Knowledge Level; On the Job Training; Personnel Selection; Programmers; Programming Languages; Promotion (Occupational)
*Identifiers:* Computer Operators; DOS; DOS VS; DOS VSE; JCL; WWDOS
*Availability:* Walden Computer Aptitude Testing Ltd., Box 319, Oradell, NJ 07649.
*Notes:* Time, 30. Items, 5.

Designed to assess applicants' Job Control Language (JCL) proficiency in a DOS, DOS/VS, or DOS/VSE environment. Used with job candidates for applications programmer, computer operators, and JCL specialists at all levels. For use in hiring experienced programmers, evaluating training needs or effectiveness, and identifying candidates for promotion. Covers ability to identify and define statements, identify errors, code from specifications, overwrite cataloged procedures, and other general and specific knowledge.

**13248**
**Wolfe-Winrow Structured Analysis and Design Concepts Proficiency Test.** Walden Computer Aptitude Testing, Ltd., Oradell, NJ 1983.
*Descriptors:* *Achievement Tests; *Data Processing; Adults; Design; Knowledge Level; On the Job Training; Personnel Selection; Programmers; Promotion (Occupational)
*Identifiers:* Programer Analysts; Structured Analysis
*Availability:* Walden Computer Aptitude Testing Ltd., Box 319, Oradell, NJ 07649.
*Notes:* Time, 30. Items, 4.

Designed to assess proficiency in structured analysis and design for experienced analysts, designers, or programmer analysts. For use in hiring, evaluating training effectiveness, determining training needs, and identifying promotable employees. Covers use of data flow diagrams; knowledge of systems development methodology, structured analysis process and tools, and structure charts; and knowledge of concepts, such as coupling, cohesion, control, and packaging.

**13340**
**Certification Examination for Occupational Therapist, Registered.** American Occupational Therapy Association, Rockville, MD 1984.
*Descriptors:* *Achievement Tests; *Certification; *Licensing Examinations (Professions); *Occupational Therapists; Adults; Cognitive Ability; Knowledge Level; Life Style; Multiple Choice Tests; Patients; Professional Development; Psychomotor Skills
*Identifiers:* American Occupational Therapy Association; AOTA; Sensory Motor Skills
*Availability:* The Psychological Corp., 555 Academic Ct., San Antonio, TX 78204.
*Notes:* Time, 240. Items, 250.

Open to those who have completed academic and field work requirements of an accredited program in occupational therapy. The test is multiple choice and administered several times per year at testing centers. Used for licensing in a number of states.

**13367**
**Computer Aptitude, Literacy, and Interest Profile.** Poplin, Mary S.; And Others 1984.
*Descriptors:* *Achievement Tests; *Adolescents; *Adults; *Aptitude Tests; *College Students; *Computer Literacy; *Computers; *Interest Inventories; *Programming; *Secondary School Students; Career Counseling; Higher Education; Knowledge Level; Secondary Education
*Identifiers:* CALIP
*Availability:* PRO-ED, 8700 Shoal Creek Blvd., Austin, TX 78758.
*Notes:* Time, 45 approx. Items, 138.

Comprehensive, standardized test battery designed to assess computer-related abilities. Can be administered individually or in groups. Measures aptitudes relevant to computer programming to a wide variety of computer-related uses, e.g., graphics, systems analysis, and repair. Also assesses computer literacy, interest, and experience. In addition to educational settings, may be used in business and industry for personnel decisions. Designed to accomplish 4 main purposes: identify talented minorities, women, individuals with reading disabilities, and disadvantaged persons; to broaden range of realistic career options; to provide an empirical basis for administrators, business, managers, and teachers to allocate organizational resources; and to document person's progress as a result of training.

**13372**
**Vocational Competency Measures: Hotel (Motel) Front Office.** American Institutes for Research, Palo Alto, CA 1983.
*Descriptors:* *Achievement Tests; *Entry Workers; *Hospitality Occupations; *Hotels; *Personnel Selection; *Postsecondary Education; *Secondary School Students; *Vocational Education; *Work Sample Tests; Adolescents; Adults; Competence; Knowledge Level; Office Occupations; Rating Scales; Screening Tests; Secondary Education; Student Evaluation
*Identifiers:* Test Batteries; Work Habits
*Availability:* American Association for Vocational Instructional Materials, 120 Driftmier Engineering Center, Athens, GA 30602.

Designed to help teachers and administrators at secondary and postsecondary levels assess and improve competencies of their students in vocational education, identify areas for program improvement, and inform prospective employers of student vocational competencies. Also useful for employers to screen and select new employees and to assess training needs of present employees. Test package consists of a 2-part multiple-choice job information test, each part taking about 45 minutes to complete; a performance test consisting of tests that represent tasks similar to those performed on the job; and a work habits inventory for assessing nontechnical, work-related attitudes and behavior. Intended for persons completing secondary or postsecondary level programs to train them for entry-level, front office jobs in motels or hotels. Not designed for those completing 4-year college programs for direct entry into management positions. Job information test section covers general front office duties, processing guests, cashier-accounting duties. The 4 tasks in the performance test include completing a hand transcript, checking guests in and out, completing an occupancy forecast sheet, and collecting problem accounts.

**13373**
**Four Self Assessment Questionnaires for Liberal Arts Majors: English, Political Science, Psychology, and Sociology.** Turner, Carol J. 1982.
*Descriptors:* *Career Choice; *College Students; *Liberal Arts; *Majors (Students); *Vocational Interests; Higher Education; Job Skills; Occupations; Political Science; Psychology; Questionnaires; Sociology; Work Attitudes
*Identifiers:* English Majors; TIM(J)
*Availability:* Tests in Microfiche, Test Collection, Educational Testing Service, Princeton, NJ 08541.
*Notes:* Items, 114.

Designed to help college students identify occupations consistent with a major field of study. Each form consists of items from 12 worker trait groups cited in the *Dictionary of Occupational Titles* and rated on 6 scales: appeal, realism, past experience, skills, attitudes, and preferences.

**13400**
**General Mental Ability Test, Test 1-A, Revised 1983.** Hadley, S. Trevor; Stouffer, George A.W. Jr. 1983.
*Descriptors:* *Aptitude Tests; *Cognitive Ability; *Cognitive Tests; *Employees; *Job Applicants; Abstract Reasoning; Adults; Multiple Choice Tests; Vocational Aptitude
*Identifiers:* ETSA Tests
*Availability:* Employers' Tests and Services Associates, 341 Garfield St., Chambersburg, PA 17201.
*Notes:* For complete series of ETSA tests, see 13400 through 13405 and 3471 through 3472. Time, 45 approx. Items, 75.

Part of the ETSA series of occupational aptitude tests, Test 1-A is designed to assess those mental abilities important in almost any type of learning and thinking. Emphasizes concepts and experiences familiar to examinees. Requires careful reasoning and the ability to comprehend and draw conclusions. Includes computational and nonverbal items so examinees with good reasoning ability but poor reading skills or verbal development also receive consideration. Test 1-A is not timed. ETSA tests are a series of aptitude tests and a personality inventory, designed to be administered, scored, and interpreted in one's own business, industry, organization, or institution. Tests emphasize power rather than speed. Each test has a time limit long enough to permit examinees to attempt all items. For a complete profile of an applicant, it is recommended that the General Mental Ability Test 1-A and the Personal Adjustment Index, Test 8-A (13405) be administered with the additional ETSA test designed for the particular job under consideration.

**13401**
**Office Arithmetic Test, Test 2-A, Revised 1984.** Hadley, S. Trevor; Stouffer, George A.W. Jr. 1984.
*Descriptors:* *Aptitude Tests; *Arithmetic; *Employees; *Job Applicants; *Mathematical Applications; *Office Occupations; Adults; Clerical Workers; Mathematics Tests; Occupational Tests; Timed Tests; Vocational Aptitude
*Identifiers:* ETSA Tests
*Availability:* Employers' Tests and Services Associates, 341 Garfield St., Chambersburg, PA 17201.
*Notes:* For complete series of ETSA tests, see 13400 through 13405 and 3471 through 3472. Time, 60. Items, 50.

Part of the ETSA series of occupational aptitude tests, Test 2-A measures the ability to use arithmetic in solving numerical problems encountered in most offices. Measures skills with addition, subtraction, multiplication, division, fractions, and percentages. Ability to read, comprehend, and extract needed information from tables and graphs is involved. Helps hire, place, and promote qualified person to a job requiring average or better mathematical ability or skills. This test is a timed test. ETSA tests are a series of aptitude tests and a personality inventory, designed to be administered, scored, and interpreted in one's own business, industry, organization, or institution. Tests emphasize power rather than speed. Each test has a time limit long enough to permit examinees to attempt all items. For a complete profile of an applicant, it is recommended that the General Mental Ability Tests Test 1-A (13400) and the Personal Adjustment Index, Test 8-A (13405) be administered with the additional ETSA test designed for the particular job under consideration.

13402
**General Clerical Ability Test, Test 3-A, Revised 1984.** Hadley, S. Trevor; Stouffer, George A.W. Jr. 1984.
*Descriptors:* *Aptitude Tests; *Clerical Occupations; *Clerical Workers; *Employees; *Job Applicants; Adults; Occupational Tests; Office Occupations; Screening Tests; Timed Tests; Vocational Aptitude
*Identifiers:* Clerical Aptitude; ETSA Tests
*Availability:* Employers' Tests and Services Associates, 341 Garfield St., Chambersburg, PA 17201.
*Notes:* For complete series of ETSA tests, see 13400 through 13405 and 3471 through 3472. Time, 30. Items, 131.

Part of the ETSA series of occupational aptitude tests. Measures the general skills required of clerical personnel in the performance of routine office work. Abilities assessed include alphabetizing, matching numbers, checking names, spelling,and using office vocabulary. Knowledge of mailing procedures and practices is tested also. This is a timed test. ETSA tests are a series of aptitude tests and a personality inventory, designed to be administered, scored, and interpreted in one's own business, industry, organization, or institution. Tests emphasize power rather than speed. Each test has a time limit long enough to permit examinees to attempt all items. For a complete profile of an applicant, it is recommended that the General Mental Ability Test, Test 1-A (13400) and the Personal Adjustment Index, Test 8-A (13405) be administered with the additional ETSA test designed for the particular job under consideration.

13403
**Stenographic Skills Test, Test 4-A, Revised 1984.** Hadley, S. Trevor; Stouffer, George A.W. Jr. 1984.
*Descriptors:* *Aptitude Tests; *Employees; *Job Applicants; *Secretaries; *Shorthand; *Typewriting; Adults; Clerical Occupations; Clerical Workers; Occupational Tests; Office Occupations; Screening Tests; Vocational Aptitude
*Identifiers:* ETSA Tests
*Availability:* Employers' Tests and Services Associates, 341 Garfield St., Chambersburg, PA 17201.
*Notes:* For complete series of ETSA tests, see 13400 through 13405 and 3471 through 3472. Time, 45 approx. Items, 120.

Part of the ETSA series of occupational aptitude tests. Measures typing and/or shorthand and general skills required of secretaries and stenographers. Spelling, grammar, filing, and general information needed by secretaries and stenographers are evaluated. Included as an optional supplement is a prepared letter to be dictated to, and then typed, by the examinee. For the typing test, the examinee is allowed 5 minutes. For taking a letter in shorthand and transcribing it, examinee is allowed a maximum of 18 minutes. ETSA tests are a series of aptitude tests and a personality inventory, designed to be administered, scored, and interpreted in one's own business, industry, organization, or institution. Tests emphasize power rather than speed. Each test has a time limit long enough to permit examinees to attempt all items. For a complete profile of an applicant, it is recommended that the General Mental Ability Test, Test 1-A (13400) and the Personal Adjustment Index, Test 8-A (13405) be administered with the additional ETSA test designed for the particular job under consideration.

13404
**Sales Aptitude Test, Test 7-A, Revised 1983.** Hadley, S. Trevor; Stouffer, George A.W. Jr. 1983.
*Descriptors:* *Aptitude Tests; *Employees; *Job Applicants; *Salesmanship; *Sales Occupations; Adults; Occupational Tests; Screening Tests; Vocational Aptitude
*Identifiers:* ETSA Tests; *Sales Aptitude
*Availability:* Employers' Tests and Services Associates, 341 Garfield St., Chambersburg, PA 17201.
*Notes:* For complete series of ETSA tests, see 13400 through 13405 and 3471 through 3472. Time, 60 approx. Items, 100.

Part of the ETSA series of occupational aptitude tests. Measures abilities and skills required in effective selling. Designed to aid in appraisal of sales aptitude and potential. Attempts to assess knowledge of basic principles of selling. Covers selling to wholesalers, retailers, and consumers and the sale of a wide variety of products. Test samples areas of sales judgment, interest in selling, personality factors involved in selling, identification with sales occupation, level of aspiration, insight into human nature, and awareness of sales approach. ETSA tests are a series of aptitude tests and a personality inventory, designed to be administered, scored, and interpreted in one's own business, industry, organization, or institution. Tests emphasize power rather than speed. Each test has a time limit long enough to permit examinees to attempt all items. For a complete profile of an applicant, it is recommended that the General Mental Ability Test, Test 1-A (13400) and the Personal Adjustment Index, Test 8-A (13405) be administered with the additional ETSA test designed for the particular job under consideration.

13405
**Personal Adjustment Index: A Vocational Adjustment Index, Test 8-A.** Hadley, S. Trevor; Stouffer, George A.W. Jr. 1984.
*Descriptors:* *Adjustment (to Environment); *Attitude Measures; *Employee Attitudes; *Job Applicants; *Personality Measures; *Screening Tests; Adults; Employees; Self Evaluation (Individuals); Work Attitudes
*Identifiers:* ETSA Tests
*Availability:* Employers' Tests and Services Associates, 341 Garfield St., Chambersburg, PA 17201.
*Notes:* For complete series of ETSA tests, see 13400 through 13405 and 3471 through 3472. Time, 45 approx. Items, 105.

Part of the ETSA series of occupational aptitude tests. Essentially a vocational adjustment inventory that measures certain aspects of the examinee's characteristic mode of adjustment to the environment. A self-report measure which yields a sampling of examinee's attitudes and feelings in relation to certain factors significant in the world of work. Findings may also be useful in counseling present employees. ETSA tests are a series of aptitude tests and a personality inventory, designed to be administered, scored, and interpreted in one's own business, industry, organization, or institution. Tests emphasize power rather than speed. Each test has a time limit long enough to permit examinees to attempt all items. For a complete profile of an applicant, it is recommended that the General Mental Ability Test, Test 1-A (13400) and the Personal Adjustment Index, Test 8-A (13405) be administered with the additional ETSA test designed for the particular job under consideration.

13414
**Harvard Manager/Supervisor Staff Selector.** Harvard Personnel Testing, Oradell, NJ 1984.
*Descriptors:* *Administrators; *Occupational Tests; *Personnel Selection; *Supervisors; Adults; Communication Skills; Emotional Adjustment; Intelligence; Interpersonal Competence; Problem Solving; Supervisory Methods
*Identifiers:* Judgment
*Availability:* Harvard Personnel Testing, Box 319, Oradell, NJ 07649.
*Notes:* Time, 45 approx.

Screening test for job applicants. Available in English and French. Provides an overall rating from excellent to unacceptable and a rating of "Likelihood for Success" ranging from far above average to far below average. Includes a narrative report and a plot of the applicants' performance against ideal performance in all 6 subtest areas. Norms are based on a population of supervisory trainees.

13420
**Harvard Learning Ability Profile.** Harvard Personnel Testing, Oradell, NJ 1984.
*Descriptors:* *Aptitude Tests; *Occupational Tests; *Vocational Aptitude; Adults; Decision Making Skills; Problem Solving
*Identifiers:* Flexibility (Cognitive); Frustration; Learning Ability
*Availability:* Harvard Personnel Testing, Box 319, Oradell, NJ 07649.
*Notes:* Time, 90.

Designed to measure the ability to learn a job. Measures ability to learn, flexibility, frustration level, problem-solving ability, and decisiveness. Norms provided by race, sex, age, and education. Said to be compatible with EEO requirements and useful with any position. Hand-scored by administrator.

13421
**Harvard Accounting Staff Selector.** Harvard Personnel Testing, Oradell, NJ 1984.
*Descriptors:* *Accountants; *Occupational Tests; *Personnel Selection; Adults; Emotional Adjustment; French; Intelligence; Interpersonal Competence; Mathematics Skills; Memory; Office Practice; Problem Solving; Psychological Needs; Reliability
*Identifiers:* Initiative; Organizational Skills; Self Sufficiency; Tough Mindedness
*Availability:* Harvard Personnel Testing, Box 319, Oradell, NJ 07649.

For use in hiring accounting or financial staff. Designed to predict success on the job. Covers general intelligence, attention to detail, memory, problem-solving ability, numerical skills, knowledge of office terms, layout and organization, emotional stability, people contact desired, consistency, self-sufficiency, initiative, and toughmindedness. Available in English or French. A narrative report and graphical summary are prepared by the publisher.

13422
**Harvard Sales Staff Selector.** Harvard Personnel Testing, Oradell, NJ 1984.
*Descriptors:* *Occupational Tests; *Personnel Selection; *Salesmanship; *Sales Workers; Adults; Communication Skills; Emotional Adjustment; French; Intelligence; Interpersonal Competence; Motivation; Psychological Needs
*Availability:* Harvard Personnel Testing, Box 319, Oradell, NJ 07649.

Designed for use in predicting performance of sales staff, including sales clerks, technical services and sales representatives, sales engineers, and sales supervisors. Available in English and French. Scored by publisher.

13423
**Harvard Secretarial Staff Selector.** Harvard Personnel Testing, Oradell, NJ 1984.
*Descriptors:* *Clerical Workers; *Occupational Tests; *Personnel Selection; *Secretaries; Adults; Emotional Adjustment; French; Intelligence; Mathematics Skills; Problem Solving
*Availability:* Harvard Personnel Testing, Box 319, Oradell, NJ 07649.

Designed for use in the selection of secretarial staff. Available in English and French. Test is scored by publisher.

13424
**Harvard Business Systems Analyst Staff Selector.** Harvard Personnel Testing, Oradell, NJ 1984.
*Descriptors:* *Occupational Tests; *Personnel Selection; *Systems Analysts; Adults; Communication Skills; Empathy; French; Interpersonal Competence; Leadership; Problem Solving
*Identifiers:* Business Judgment; Organizational Skills
*Availability:* Harvard Personnel Testing, Box 319, Oradell, NJ 07649.

Designed for use in employee selection. Covers problem solving, leadership, communication skills, people contact skills, user empathy, social intelligence, layout and organization, and business judgment. Available in English and French. Scored by publisher.

**13425**
**Mosby RT Assess Test.** Mosby Co., C.V., Saint Louis, MO 1984.
*Descriptors:* *Certification; Higher Education; Vocational Schools
*Identifiers:* Practice Tests; *Respiratory Therapists
*Availability:* C.V. Mosby Co., 11830 Westline Industrial Dr., Saint Louis, MO 63146.
*Notes:* Time, 240. Items, 240.

A practice exam taken before the National Board for Respiratory Care Entry Level Certification Examination. Can be group or individually administered. Covers 16 content areas, including clinical diagnostic and communication skills, oxygen administration, medical gases, airway and ventilation maintenance, pharmacology, and infection control. Measures ability, application of knowledge, and analytical skills. Scoring reports rationale behind students' answers.

**13426**
**Mosby Rad Tech Assess Test.** Mosby Co., C.V., Saint Louis, MO 1982.
*Descriptors:* *Radiologic Technologists; *Certification; Anatomy; Higher Education; Physiology; Vocational Schools
*Identifiers:* Practice Tests; Radiography
*Availability:* C.V. Mosby Co., 11830 Westline Industrial Dr., Saint Louis, MO 63146.
*Notes:* Time, 240. Items, 250.

A practice exam taken before the American Registry of Radiologic Technologists certification examination. Purchased by schools with radiography programs for administration to their students. Tests knowledge of radiography, comprehension, application, and analysis. Scoring reports the rationale behind students' answers.

**13427**
**Mosby Assess Test.** Mosby Co., C.V., Saint Louis, MO 1984.
*Descriptors:* *Nurses; *Licensing Examinations (Professions); Behavior Patterns; College Students; Decision Making; Higher Education; Knowledge Level; Nursing Education
*Identifiers:* Obstetrical Nurses; Pediatric Nurses; Practice Tests; Psychiatric Nurses; Surgical Nurses
*Availability:* C.V. Mosby Co., 11830 Westline Industrial Dr., Saint Louis, MO 63146.
*Notes:* Time, 480. Items, 480.

A practice exam taken before testing for licensure as a registered nurse. Purchased by schools with nursing programs and administered by them. A secure version is available for group testing. Measures student nurses' knowledge, strengths, and weaknesses. Scoring reports the rationale behind students' answers. Clinical areas covered are medical, surgical, obstetrical, psychiatric, and pediatric nursing.

**13432**
**IPI Aptitude Series: Junior Clerk.** Industrial Psychology, Inc., New York, NY 1981.
*Descriptors:* *Adults; *Aptitude Tests; *Clerical Workers; *Job Applicants; *Occupational Tests; Clerical Occupations; Extraversion Introversion; File Clerks; Filing; Job Performance; Job Skills; Personality Measures; Profiles
*Identifiers:* Test Batteries
*Availability:* Industrial Psychology International, Ltd., 111 N. Market St., Champaign, IL 61820.
*Notes:* See also IPI Hiring Manual and Job-Tests Program (11774) and CPF (3736). Time, 25 approx.

This instrument is a battery of tests designed to assess examinee's aptitude for the position of junior clerk on a lower clerical level. Assignments are minor, simple, routine, unskilled, repetitive, detailed, and require no decision making. Typical duties include filing, sorting, copying, classifying, compiling, checking, verifying, identifying, routing, distributing, posting, coding, recording, receiving, and shipping. This battery is suitable for use with applicants or employees for the position of checker, coder, mail clerk, shipper, sorter, or stock clerk. Consists of the following tests: Perception, Office Terms, CPF (Contact Personality Factor), Numbers, and Biography-Clerical.

**13433**
**IPI Aptitude Series: Numbers Clerk.** Industrial Psychology, Inc., New York, NY 1981.
*Descriptors:* *Adults; *Aptitude Tests; *Clerical Workers; *Job Applicants; *Mathematics Tests; *Occupational Tests; Accounting; Bookkeeping; Clerical Occupations; Extraversion Introversion; Insurance Occupations; Job Performance; Job Skills; Personality Measures; Profiles
*Identifiers:* Test Batteries
*Availability:* Industrial Psychology International, Ltd., 111 N. Market St., Champaign, IL 61820.
*Notes:* See also IPI Hiring Manual and Job-Tests Program (11774); CPF (3736); NPF. Time, 30 approx.

This instrument is a battery of tests designed to assess examinee's aptitude for the position of numbers clerk, a field that includes jobs involving systems. Numbers clerks need a mathematical-quantitative outlook, such as that involved in accounting, bookkeeping, billing, statistical, and inventory fields. This battery is suitable for evaluating applicants for the position of accounting, billing, insurance, inventory, payroll, or statistical clerk. The following tests make up this battery: Numbers, Perception, Office Terms, Judgment, Biography-Clerical, NPF (Neurotic Personality Factor), and CPF (Contact Personality Factor).

**13434**
**IPI Aptitude Series: Office Machine Operator.** Industrial Psychology, Inc., New York, NY 1981.
*Descriptors:* *Adults; *Aptitude Tests; *Job Applicants; *Occupational Tests; *Office Machines; *Spatial Ability; Accounting; Clerical Occupations; Clerical Workers; Job Performance; Job Skills; Personality Measures; Profiles; Typewriting
*Identifiers:* Keypunch Operators; Manual Dexterity; Test Batteries
*Availability:* Industrial Psychology International, Ltd., 111 N. Market St., Champaign, IL 61820.
*Notes:* See also IPI Hiring Manual and Job-Tests Program (11774); CPF (3736); NPF. Time, 30 approx.

This instrument is a battery of tests designed to assess examinee's aptitude for the position of office machine operator. This job field includes jobs involving set-up, operation, and minor adjustment of various types of office machines for such uses as typing, duplicating, recording, calculating, checking, billing, and sorting. Applicant needs manual dexterity and spatial relations aptitudes for machine operations. This battery is suitable for evaluating applicants for positions of accounting or billing clerk, keypunch operator, or typist. The battery consists of Dexterity, Parts, Perception, Office Terms, Biography-Clerical, NPF (Neurotic Personality Factor), and CPF (Contact Personality Factor).

**13435**
**IPI Aptitude Series: Contact Clerk.** Industrial Psychology, Inc., New York, NY 1981.
*Descriptors:* *Adults; *Aptitude Tests; *Communication Skills; *Job Applicants; *Occupational Tests; *Receptionists; Clerical Workers; Job Performance; Job Skills; Language Fluency; Memory; Personality Measures; Profiles
*Identifiers:* Test Batteries
*Availability:* Industrial Psychology International, Ltd., 111 N. Market St., Champaign, IL 61820.
*Notes:* See also IPI Hiring Manual and Job-Tests Program (11774); CPF (3736). Time, 30 approx.

This instrument is a battery of tests designed to assess examinee's aptitude for the position of contact clerk, a job field that includes jobs of contact with the public, along with clerical duties. Contact clerk is in fairly continuous contact with people and needs contact aptitude of memory and fluency, extraverted personality, and good appearance. This battery is useful in evaluation of applicants for positions of receptionist and complaint, information, or reservation clerk. The battery consists of CPF (Contact Personality Factor), Memory, Fluency, Perception, Sales Terms, and Biography-Clerical.

**13436**
**IPI Aptitude Series: Senior Clerk.** Industrial Psychology, Inc., New York, NY 1981.
*Descriptors:* *Adults; *Aptitude Tests; *Clerical Workers; *Job Applicants; *Occupational Tests; Bookkeeping; Clerical Occupations; Decision Making Skills; Job Performance; Job Skills; Memory; Personality Measures; Profiles
*Identifiers:* Test Batteries
*Availability:* Industrial Psychology International, Ltd., 111 N. Market St., Champaign, IL 61820.
*Notes:* See also IPI Hiring Manual and Job-Tests Program (11774); CPF (3736); 16 PF (2313). Time, 30 approx.

This instrument is a battery of tests designed to assess examinee's aptitude for the position of senior clerk, a job field which includes higher-level clerical jobs. Assignments are fairly complex, difficult, nonroutine, and nonrepetitive. Tasks require good intelligence and some amount of judgment and decision making. This battery is useful in evaluation of applicants for the position of administrative, correspondence, cost, or production clerks, and bookkeepers. The battery consists of Office Terms, Perception, CPF (Contact Personality Factor), Numbers, Judgment, 16 PF (16 Personality Factors), Fluency, and Biography-Clerical.

**13437**
**IPI Aptitude Series: Secretary.** Industrial Psychology, Inc., New York, NY 1981.
*Descriptors:* *Adults; *Aptitude Tests; *Job Applicants; *Occupational Tests; *Secretaries; Clerical Occupations; Clerical Workers; Job Performance; Job Skills; Memory; Personality Measures; Shorthand
*Identifiers:* Test Batteries
*Availability:* Industrial Psychology International, Ltd., 111 N. Market St., Champaign, IL 61820.
*Notes:* See also IPI Hiring Manual and Job-Tests Program (11774); CPF (3736); 16 PF (2313); NPF. Time, 30 approx.

This instrument is a battery of tests designed to assess examinee's aptitude for the position of secretary. Assignments are complex and difficult. Tasks involve public relations, clerical duties, screening appointments, typing, shorthand, handling correspondence, and relieving executive of minor administrative details. Applicants should have an extroverted personality and a good appearance. This battery consists of Judgment, Parts, Perception, Sales Terms, Fluency, Memory, 16 PF (16 Personality Factors), Biography-Clerical, NPF (Neurotic Personality Factor), and CPF (Contact Personality Factor).

**13438**
**IPI Aptitude Series: Unskilled Worker.** Industrial Psychology, Inc., New York, NY 1981.
*Descriptors:* *Adults; *Aptitude Tests; *Job Applicants; *Occupational Tests; *Unskilled Workers; Biographical Inventories; Hand Tools; Job Performance; Job Skills; Laborers; Mechanical Skills; Personality Measures; Psychomotor Skills
*Identifiers:* Test Batteries
*Availability:* Industrial Psychology International, Ltd., 111 N. Market St., Champaign, IL 61820.

*Notes:* See also IPI Hiring Manual and Job-Tests Program (11774); NPF. Time, 30 approx.

This instrument is a battery of tests designed to assess examinee's aptitude for the position of unskilled worker. The test battery includes Motor, Precision, Tools, NPF (Neurotic Personality Factor), and Biography-Mechanical. The battery is suitable for applicants to positions of janitor, laborer, loader, material handler, packer, and trucker.

**13439**
**IPI Aptitude Series: Semi-Skilled Worker.** Industrial Psychology, Inc., New York, NY 1981.
*Descriptors:* *Adults; *Aptitude Tests; *Job Applicants; *Mechanical Skills; *Occupational Tests; *Semiskilled Occupations; *Semiskilled Workers; Assembly (Manufacturing); Biographical Inventories; Building Trades; Hand Tools; Job Performance; Job Skills; Machine Tools; Personality Measures; Production Technicians; Psychomotor Skills
*Identifiers:* Test Batteries
*Availability:* Industrial Psychology International, Ltd., 111 N. Market St., Champaign, IL 61820.
*Notes:* See also IPI Hiring Manual and Job-Tests Program (11774); CPF (3736). Time, 30 approx.

This instrument is a battery of tests designed to assess examinee's aptitude for the position of semiskilled worker in mechanical occupations. The test battery includes Precision, Motor, NPF (Neurotic Personality Factor), Blocks, Tools, CPF (Contact Personality Factor), and Biography-Mechanical. The battery is suitable for evaluating applicants for positions as assembler, helper, or production or construction worker.

**13440**
**IPI Aptitude Series: Factory Machine Operator.** Industrial Psychology, Inc., New York, NY 1981.
*Descriptors:* *Adults; *Aptitude Tests; *Job Applicants; *Machine Tool Operators; *Machine Tools; *Mechanical Skills; *Occupational Tests; *Sewing Machine Operators; Biographical Inventories; Dental Technicians; Job Performance; Job Skills; Machinists; Personality Measures; Psychomotor Skills; Welding
*Identifiers:* Manual Dexterity; Test Batteries
*Availability:* Industrial Psychology International, Ltd., 111 N. Market St., Champaign, IL 61820.
*Notes:* See also IPI Hiring Manual and Job-Tests Program (11774); CPF (3736). Time, 30 approx.

This instrument is a battery of tests designed to assess examinee's aptitude for the position of factory machine operator. The test battery includes Motor, Precision, Tools, NPF (Neurotic Personality Factor), Blocks, CPF (Contact Personality Factor), Dexterity, and Biography-Mechanical. The battery is appropriate for evaluation of applicants for positions as cutters, dental lab technicians, lathe operators, sewing machine operators, pressers, or welders.

**13441**
**IPI Aptitude Series: Vehicle Operator.** Industrial Psychology, Inc., New York, NY 1981.
*Descriptors:* *Adults; *Aptitude Tests; *Job Applicants; *Motor Vehicles; *Occupational Tests; *Service Vehicles; Biographical Inventories; Job Performance; Job Skills; Mechanical Skills; Personality Measures; Psychomotor Skills
*Identifiers:* Manual Dexterity; Test Batteries
*Availability:* Industrial Psychology International, Ltd., 111 N. Market St., Champaign, IL 61820.
*Notes:* See also IPI Hiring Manual and Job-Tests Program (11774); CPF (3736). Time, 30 approx.

This instrument is a battery of tests designed to assess examinee's aptitude for the position of vehicle operator. The test battery includes Motor, Dimension, NPF (Neurotic Personality Factor), Precision, CPF (Contact Personality Factor), Tools, Dexterity, and Biography-Mechanical. The battery is appropriate for evaluation of applicants for positions as crane, elevator, motor, taxi, teamster, tractor, or truck operator.

**13442**
**IPI Aptitude Series: Inspector.** Industrial Psychology, Inc., New York, NY 1981.
*Descriptors:* *Adults; *Aptitude Tests; *Classification; *Job Applicants; *Mechanical Skills; *Occupational Tests; Biographical Inventories; Hand Tools; Inspection; Job Performance; Job Skills; Machine Tools; Personality Measures; Psychomotor Skills
*Identifiers:* *Inspectors; Test Batteries
*Availability:* Industrial Psychology International, Ltd., 111 N. Market St., Champaign, IL 61820.
*Notes:* See also IPI Hiring Manual and Job-Tests Program (11774); CPF (3736). Time, 30 approx.

This instrument is a battery of tests designed to assess examinee's aptitude for the position of inspector. The test battery includes Precision, Dimension, CPF (Contact Personality Factor), Parts, NPF (Neurotic Personality Factor), Tools, Blocks, and Biography-Mechanical. The battery is appropriate for evaluation of applicants for positions as checker, classifier, examiner, grader, pairer, scaler, or sorter.

**13443**
**IPI Aptitude Series: Skilled Worker.** Industrial Psychology, Inc., New York, NY 1981.
*Descriptors:* *Adults; *Aptitude Tests; *Job Applicants; *Machinists; *Occupational Tests; *Skilled Workers; *Tool and Die Makers; Biographical Inventories; Job Performance; Job Skills; Machine Tools; Mechanical Skills; Mechanics (Process); Personality Measures; Psychomotor Skills
*Identifiers:* Test Batteries
*Availability:* Industrial Psychology International, Ltd., 111 N. Market St., Champaign, IL 61820.
*Notes:* See also IPI Hiring Manual and Job-Tests Program (11774); 16 PF (2313). Time, 60 approx.

This instrument is a battery of tests designed to assess examinee's aptitude for the position of skilled worker. The test battery includes Blocks, Factory Terms, NPF (Neurotic Personality Factor), Numbers, Motor, 16 PF (16 Personality Factors), Office Terms, Tools, Precision, and Biography-Mechanical. The battery is appropriate for evaluation of applicants for positions as lineman, machinist, maintenance, mechanic, or tool maker.

**13444**
**IPI Aptitude Series: Sales Clerk.** Industrial Psychology, Inc., New York, NY 1981.
*Descriptors:* *Adults; *Aptitude Tests; *Job Applicants; *Occupational Tests; *Sales Occupations; *Sales Workers; Job Performance; Job Skills; Language Fluency; Memory; Personality Measures; Extraversion Introversion
*Identifiers:* Test Batteries
*Availability:* Industrial Psychology International, Ltd., 111 N. Market St., Champaign, IL 61820.
*Notes:* See also IPI Hiring Manual and Job-Tests Program (11774); CPF (3736). Time, 30 approx.

This instrument is a battery of tests designed to assess examinee's aptitude for the position of sales clerk. Tests in battery include CPF (Contact Personality Factor), Numbers, Perception, Memory, Sales Terms, Fluency, and Biography-Clerical. The battery is suitable for use in the evaluation of applicants for positions as department store sales clerk, post office clerk, teller, ticket clerk, waiter, or waitress. This test may be purchased by businesses that hire salespersons. The test is scored by the purchaser.

**13445**
**IPI Aptitude Series: Sales Person.** Industrial Psychology, Inc., New York, NY 1981.
*Descriptors:* *Adults; *Aptitude Tests; *Job Applicants; *Occupational Tests; *Salesmanship; *Sales Workers; Insurance Occupations; Job Performance; Job Skills; Language Fluency; Memory; Personality Measures; Sales Occupations; Extraversion Introversion
*Identifiers:* Test Batteries
*Availability:* Industrial Psychology International, Ltd., 111 N. Market St., Champaign, IL 61820.
*Notes:* See also IPI Hiring Manual and Job-Tests Program (11774); CPF (3736); 16 PF (2313). Time, 45 approx.

This instrument is a battery of tests designed to assess examinee's aptitude for the position of salesman/saleswoman. Tests in the battery include 16 PF (16 Personality Factors), Numbers, Sales Terms, Fluency, Memory, CPF (Contact Personality Factor), Perception, and Biography-Sales. The battery is useful in the evaluation of applicants for positions as agent; demonstrator; or insurance, retail, route, or wholesale salesperson. This test may be purchased by businesses that hire salespersons. The test is scored by the purchaser.

**13446**
**IPI Aptitude Series: Sales Engineer.** Industrial Psychology, Inc., New York, NY 1981.
*Descriptors:* *Adults; *Aptitude Tests; *Job Applicants; *Occupational Tests; *Sales Occupations; Job Performance; Job Skills; Language Fluency; Memory; Personality Measures; Salesmanship; Extraversion Introversion
*Identifiers:* Test Batteries
*Availability:* Industrial Psychology International, Ltd., 111 N. Market St., Champaign, IL 61820.
*Notes:* See also IPI Hiring Manual and Job-Tests Program (11774); CPF (3736); 16 PF (2313).

This instrument is a battery of tests designed to assess examinee's aptitude for the position of sales engineer. Tests in the battery include Sales Terms, 16 PF (16 Personality Factors), Parts, Judgment, Numbers, Fluency, Memory, CPF (Contact Personality Factors), NPF (Neurotic Personality Factors), and Biography-Sales. This battery may be used in the evaluation of applicants for positions as claims adjuster, purchasing agent, technical salesperson, or underwriter. This test may be purchased by businesses that hire salespersons. Scoring is done by the purchaser.

**13447**
**IPI Aptitude Series: Scientist.** Industrial Psychology, Inc., New York, NY 1981.
*Descriptors:* *Abstract Reasoning; *Adults; *Aptitude Tests; *Job Applicants; *Occupational Tests; *Scientists; Job Performance; Job Skills; Logical Thinking; Personality Measures; Professional Occupations; Spatial Ability; Extraversion Introversion
*Identifiers:* Manual Dexterity; Test Batteries
*Availability:* Industrial Psychology International, Ltd., 111 N. Market St., Champaign, IL 61820.
*Notes:* See also IPI Hiring Manual and Job-Tests Program (11774); CPF (3736); 16 PF (2313). Time, 60 approx.

This instrument is a battery of tests designed to assess examinee's aptitude for the position of scientist. Tests in the battery include Judgment, Dimension, CPF (Contact Personality Factor), NPF (Neurotic Personality Factor), Factory Terms, Precision, Office Terms, 16 PF (16 Personality Factors), Numbers, Dexterity, and Biography-Technical. This battery may be used in the evaluation of applicants for positions as biologist, chemist, economist, inventor, physicist, or research scientist.

**13448**
**IPI Aptitude Series: Engineer.** Industrial Psychology, Inc., New York, NY 1981.

*Descriptors:* *Abstract Reasoning; *Adults; *Aptitude Tests; *Engineers; *Job Applicants; *Occupational Tests; *Spatial Ability; Emotional Adjustment; Extraversion Introversion; Hand Tools; Job Performance; Job Skills; Logical Thinking; Machine Tools; Mathematical Concepts; Personality Measures; Professional Occupations
*Identifiers:* Test Batteries
*Availability:* Industrial Psychology International, Ltd., 111 N. Market St., Champaign, IL 61820.
*Notes:* See also IPI Hiring Manual and Job-Tests Program (11774); CPF (3736); 16 PF (2313). Time, 60 approx.

This instrument is a battery of tests designed to assess examinee's aptitude for the position of engineer. The tests in the battery include Factory Terms, Dimension, CPF (Contact Personality Factor), NPF (Neurotic Personality Factor), Judgment, Office Terms, Numbers, 16 PF (16 Personality Factors), Precision, Tools, and Biography-Technical. The battery is suitable for evaluation of applicants for positions as automotive, chemical, electrical, mechanical, or production engineer.

**13449**
**IPI Aptitude Series: Office Technical.** Industrial Psychology, Inc., New York, NY 1981.
*Descriptors:* *Accountants; *Adults; *Aptitude Tests; *Job Applicants; *Logical Thinking; *Memory; *Occupational Tests; Abstract Reasoning; Emotional Adjustment; Extraversion Introversion; Job Performance; Job Skills; Mathematical Concepts; Personality Measures; Professional Occupations
*Identifiers:* Test Batteries
*Availability:* Industrial Psychology International, Ltd., 111 N. Market St., Champaign, IL 61820.
*Notes:* See also IPI Hiring Manual and Job-Tests Program (11774); CPF (3736); 16 PF (2313). Time, 60 approx.

This instrument is a battery of tests designed to assess examinee's aptitude for the position of office technical personnel. The battery includes Office Terms, Perception, CPF (Contact Personality Factor), NPF (Neurotic Personality Factor), Judgment, Numbers, 16 PF (16 Personality Factors), Parts, Memory, and Biography-Technical. Battery is suitable for evaluation of applicants to positions as accountant, estimator, methods clerks, statistician, or time-study person.

**13450**
**IPI Aptitude Series: Writer.** Industrial Psychology, Inc., New York, NY 1981.
*Descriptors:* *Adults; *Aptitude Tests; *Job Applicants; *Language Fluency; *Occupational Tests; *Writing Skills; Abstract Reasoning; Advertising; Emotional Adjustment; Job Performance; Job Skills; Journalism; Logical Thinking; Memory; Personality Measures; Professional Occupations; Publicity
*Identifiers:* Test Batteries
*Availability:* Industrial Psychology International, Ltd., 111 N. Market St., Champaign, IL 61820.
*Notes:* See also IPI Hiring Manual and Job-Tests Program (11774); CPF (3736); 16 PF (2313). Time, 60 approx.

This instrument is a battery of tests designed to assess examinee's aptitude for the position of writer. The battery includes Fluency, Sales Terms, CPF (Contact Personality Factor), NPF (Neurotic Personality Factor), Memory, Judgment, 16 PF (16 Personality Factors), Perception, Parts, and Biography-Technical. Battery is suitable for the evaluation of applicants in the areas of advertising and publicity, as well as the positions of author, copywriter, critic, editor, or journalist.

**13451**
**IPI Aptitude Series: Designer.** Industrial Psychology, Inc., New York, NY 1981.
*Descriptors:* *Adults; *Aptitude Tests; *Architects; *Artists; *Drafting; *Job Applicants; *Layout (Publications); *Occupational Tests; *Photography; *Spatial Ability; Emotional Adjustment; Extraversion Introversion; Job Performance; Job Skills; Mathematical Concepts; Personality Measures; Professional Occupations
*Identifiers:* Manual Dexterity; Test Batteries
*Availability:* Industrial Psychology International, Ltd., 111 N. Market St., Champaign, IL 61820.
*Notes:* See also IPI Hiring Manual and Job-Tests Program (11774); CPF (3736); 16 PF (2313). Time, 60 approx.

This instrument is a battery of tests designed to assess examinee's aptitude for the position of designer. Tests in the battery include Dimension, Precision, NPF (Neurotic Personality Factor), CPF (Contact Personality Factor), Blocks, Dexterity, Sales Terms, 16 PF (16 Personality Factors), Parts, and Biography-Technical. Battery is suitable for the evaluation of applicants for positions as artist, architect, drafter, layout person, or photographer.

**13452**
**IPI Aptitude Series: Instructor.** Industrial Psychology, Inc., New York, NY 1981.
*Descriptors:* *Adults; *Aptitude Tests; *Counselors; *Job Applicants; *Language Fluency; *Occupational Tests; *Teachers; Emotional Adjustment; Extraversion Introversion; Job Performance; Job Skills; Logical Thinking; Mathematical Concepts; Memory; Personality Measures; Professional Occupations; Spatial Ability
*Identifiers:* Test Batteries
*Availability:* Industrial Psychology International, Ltd., 111 N. Market St., Champaign, IL 61820.
*Notes:* See also IPI Hiring Manual and Job-Tests Program (11774); CPF (3736); 16 PF (2313). Time, 60 approx.

This instrument is a battery of tests designed to assess examinee's aptitude for the position of instructor. Tests in the battery include Fluency, 16 PF (16 Personality Factors), Sales Terms, Parts, Memory, Judgment, CPF (Contact Personality Factor), NPF (Neurotic Personality Factor), Perception, and Biography-Technical. The battery is suitable for the evaluation of applicants for positions as counselor, instructor, safety director, teacher, or training director.

**13453**
**IPI Aptitude Series: Office Supervisor.** Industrial Psychology, Inc., New York, NY 1981.
*Descriptors:* *Administrators; *Adults; *Aptitude Tests; *Job Applicants; *Language Fluency; *Occupational Tests; *Supervisors; Emotional Adjustment; Extraversion Introversion; Job Performance; Job Skills; Managerial Occupations; Mathematical Concepts; Memory; Middle Management; Personality Measures
*Identifiers:* Test Batteries
*Availability:* Industrial Psychology International, Ltd., 111 N. Market St., Champaign, IL 61820.
*Notes:* See also IPI Hiring Manual and Job-Tests Program (11774); CPF (3736); 16 PF (2313). Time, 60 approx.

This instrument is a battery of tests designed to assess examinee's aptitude for the position of office supervisor. The tests in the battery include 16 PF (16 Personality Factors), Judgment, Parts, Fluency, Office Terms, Numbers, NPF (Neurotic Personality Factors), CPF (Contact Personality Factors), Perception, Memory, and Biography-Supervisor. Battery is suitable for evaluation of applicants to positions as administrator, controller, department head, or vice president.

**13454**
**IPI Aptitude Series: Sales Supervisor.** Industrial Psychology, Inc., New York, NY 1981.
*Descriptors:* *Adults; *Aptitude Tests; *Job Applicants; *Marketing; *Occupational Tests; *Supervisors; Emotional Adjustment; Extraversion Introversion; Job Performance; Job Skills; Language Fluency; Managerial Occupations; Memory; Merchandising; Personality Measures; Professional Occupations; Sales Occupations
*Identifiers:* Test Batteries
*Availability:* Industrial Psychology International, Ltd., 111 N. Market St., Champaign, IL 61820.
*Notes:* See also IPI Hiring Manual and Job-Tests Program (11774); (3736); 16 PF (2313). Time, 60 approx.

This instrument is a battery of tests designed to assess examinee's aptitude for the position of sales supervisor. Tests in the battery include 16 PF (16 Personality Factors), Fluency, Sales Terms, Memory, Judgment, CPF (Contact Personality Factors), and Biography-Supervisor. The battery is suitable for evaluation of applicants for the position of advertising, credit, merchandise, service, or store sales supervisor. This test may be purchased by businesses that hire salespersons. Scoring is done by the purchaser.

**13455**
**IPI Aptitude Series: Factory Supervisor.** Industrial Psychology, Inc., New York, NY 1981.
*Descriptors:* *Administrators; *Adults; *Aptitude Tests; *Job Applicants; *Occupational Tests; *Superintendents; *Supervisors; Emotional Adjustment; Extraversion Introversion; Hand Tools; Job Performance; Job Skills; Language Fluency; Logical Thinking; Machine Tools; Mathematical Concepts; Memory; Personality Measures; Spatial Ability
*Identifiers:* Test Batteries
*Availability:* Industrial Psychology International, Ltd., 111 N. Market St., Champaign, IL 61820.
*Notes:* See also IPI Hiring Manual and Job-Tests Program (11774); CPF (3736); 16 PF (2313). Time, 60 approx.

This instrument is a battery of tests designed to assess examinee's aptitude for the position of factory supervisor. The tests in the battery include 16 PF (16 Personality Factors), Factory Terms, Parts, NPF (Neurotic Personality Factors), Office Terms, Tools, Numbers, Judgment, CPF (Contact Personality Factors), Fluency, Memory, and Biography-Supervisor. The battery is suitable for the evaluation of applicants for the position of foreperson, maintenance or production supervisor, or superintendent.

**13459**
**Dartnell's Personnel Selection and Evaluation Forms Kit.** McMurry, Robert N. 1983.
*Descriptors:* *Job Applicants; *Personnel Evaluation; *Personnel Selection; *Records (Forms); Adults; Employment Interviews; Job Analysis; Job Application
*Availability:* The Dartnell Corp., 4660 Ravenswood Ave., Chicago, IL 60640.

This kit contains a series of application and evaluation forms for applicants to positions as industrial personnel or executives. Appraisal, rating, and development forms for employees are also included. A vacation chart and planning calendar are also included.

**13471**
**Automobile Mechanic Assistant Work Sample.** Shawsheen Valley Regional Vocational Technical High School, Billerica, MA 1979.
*Descriptors:* *Aptitude Tests; *Auto Mechanics; *Disabilities; *Vocational Aptitude; *Vocational Evaluation; *Work Sample Tests; High Schools; High School Students; Job Performance; Job Skills; Occupational Tests; Prevocational Education; Trade and Industrial Education; Vocational Interests
*Availability:* ERIC Document Reproduction Service, 7420 Fullerton Rd., Ste. 110, Springfield, VA 22153-2852 (ED236421, 40 pages).

*Notes:* See other Shawsheen Valley Regional Vocational-Technical High School Work Sample Tests (13472 through 13482).

The Automobile Mechanic Assistant Work Sample is intended to assess a disabled student's interest in and potential to successfully pass a training program in automotive mechanics or in a similar automotive job. On this work sample, the student is to look over and inspect the thermostat housing to intake manifold set-up and then remove the thermostat housing, gasket, and thermostat in order to place a new thermostat in the intake manifold. The sample involves physical demands and must be done by a 2-armed person standing in front of the work sample. The work sample is timed from the moment the student signifies the student is ready to begin until the last tool needed is put down and he or she indicates completion.

**13472**
**Automotive Work Sample.** Shawsheen Valley Regional Vocational Technical High School, Billerica, MA 1979.
*Descriptors:* *Aptitude Tests; *Auto Mechanics; *Disabilities; *High School Students; *Vocational Aptitude; *Vocational Evaluation; *Work Sample Tests; High Schools; Job Performance; Job Skills; Occupational Tests; Prevocational Education; Trade and Industrial Education; Vocational Interests
*Availability:* ERIC Document Reproduction Service, 7420 Fullerton Rd., Ste. 110, Springfield, VA 22153-2852 (ED236422, 34 pages).
*Notes:* See other Shawsheen Valley Regional Vocational-Technical High School Work Sample Tests (13471 through 13482).

The Automotive Work Sample is intended to assess a disabled student's interest in and potential to successfully pass a training program in automotive mechanics or in a similar automotive job. The work sample is timed from the moment the student signifies that he or she understands the instructions, picks up the first tool or piece of equipment, and indicates that he or she is ready to begin the removal phase until the last tool or piece of equipment needed for the replacement phase is put down and the student indicates completion. On this work sample the student is to replace an old oil filter with a new one. The sample involves physical demands and must be done by a 2-armed person standing in front of the work sample.

**13473**
**Bagger Work Sample.** Shawsheen Valley Regional Vocational Technical High School, Billerica, MA 1979.
*Descriptors:* *Aptitude Tests; *Disabilities; *Distributive Education; *Vocational Aptitude; *Vocational Evaluation; *Work Sample Tests; High School Students; Job Performance; Job Skills; Occupational Tests; Prevocational Education; Service Occupations; Vocational Interests
*Identifiers:* *Baggers
*Availability:* ERIC Document Reproduction Service, 7420 Fullerton Rd., Ste. 110, Springfield, VA 22153-2852 (ED236423, 25 pages).
*Notes:* See other Shawsheen Valley Regional Vocational-Technical High School Work Sample Tests (13471 through 13482).

The Bagger Work Sample is intended to assess a disabled student's interest in and potential to successfully complete a training program in Distributive Education I in the Shawsheen Valley Regional Vocational-Technical High School. The course is based upon the entry level of a bagger job. The sample involves medium work and must be performed by a person with both hands or one who has equivalent manual and finger dexterity from a chair or wheelchair. The work sample is timed from the moment the student signifies he or she understands the instructions and is ready to begin until the student has placed the last grocery bag in the basket and indicates that he or she is finished.

**13474**
**Clerical Machine Operator Work Sample.** Shawsheen Valley Regional Vocational Technical High School, Billerica, MA 1979.
*Descriptors:* *Aptitude Tests; *Clerical Occupations; *Disabilities; *High School Students; *Office Machines; *Typewriting; *Vocational Aptitude; *Vocational Evaluation; *Work Sample Tests; Clerical Workers; High Schools; Job Performance; Job Skills; Occupational Tests; Office Occupations Education; Prevocational Education; Vocational Interests
*Availability:* ERIC Document Reproduction Service, 7420 Fullerton Rd., Ste. 110, Springfield, VA 22153-2852 (ED236424, 42 pages).
*Notes:* See other Shawsheen Valley Regional Vocational-Technical High School Work Sample Tests (13471 through 13482).

The Clerical Machine Operator Work Sample is intended to assess a disabled student's interest in and potential to successfully pass a clerical business machine course (typing) in a comprehensive or vocational high school. This test can be done by a 2-armed person sitting in a wheelchair. The sample is designed to simulate the functions and methods of a typist in the clerical area as it may exist in a training program or a comprehensive or technical school. The work sample is timed from the moment the student signifies he or she understands the instructions and is ready to begin until the student indicates completion.

**13475**
**Color Discrimination Work Sample.** Shawsheen Valley Regional Vocational Technical High School, Billerica, MA 1979.
*Descriptors:* *Aptitude Tests; *Color; *Disabilities; *High School Students; *Visual Perception; *Vocational Aptitude; *Vocational Evaluation; *Work Sample Tests; High Schools; Industrial Arts; Job Performance; Job Skills; Occupational Tests; Painting (Industrial Arts); Prevocational Education; Vocational Interests
*Identifiers:* *Color Discrimination
*Availability:* ERIC Document Reproduction Service, 7420 Fullerton Rd., Ste. 110, Springfield, VA 22153-2852 (ED236425, 21 pages).
*Notes:* See other Shawsheen Valley Regional Vocational-Technical High School Work Sample Tests (13471 through 13482).

The Color Discrimination Work Sample is intended to assess a disabled student's ability to see likenesses or differences in colors or shades, by requiring test takers to identify or match certain colors and select colors that go together. The sample can be done by a 1- or 2-armed person from a chair or wheelchair. The sample is timed from the moment the student signifies that the instructions are understood and begins until the student signifies that the sample is completed.

**13476**
**Drafting Work Sample.** Shawsheen Valley Regional Vocational Technical High School, Billerica, MA 1979.
*Descriptors:* *Aptitude Tests; *Disabilities; *Drafting; *High School Students; *Vocational Aptitude; *Vocational Evaluation; *Work Sample Tests; Engineering Drawing; High Schools; Industrial Arts; Job Performance; Job Skills; Occupational Tests; Prevocational Education; Vocational Interests
*Availability:* ERIC Document Reproduction Service, 7420 Fullerton Rd., Ste. 110, Springfield, VA 22153-2852 (ED236426, 31 pages).
*Notes:* See other Shawsheen Valley Regional Vocational-Technical High School Work Sample Tests (13471 through 13482).

The Drafting Work Sample is intended to assess a disabled student's interest in and potential to successfully complete a training program in basic mechanical drawing. The sample involves sedentary work and must be performed by a person with both hands or one who has equivalent manual and finger dexterity from a chair or wheelchair. This sample is limited to a right-handed student; a left-handed drafting machine must be substituted if the student is left-handed. The work sample is timed from the moment the student signifies he or she understands the instructions until the student indicates that he or she is finished.

**13477**
**Drill Press Work Sample.** Shawsheen Valley Regional Vocational Technical High School, Billerica, MA 1979.
*Descriptors:* *Aptitude Tests; *Disabilities; *High School Students; *Machine Tool Operators; *Machine Tools; *Vocational Aptitude; *Vocational Evaluation; *Work Sample Tests; High Schools; Job Performance; Job Skills; Machinists; Occupational Tests; Prevocational Education; Trade and Industrial Education; Vocational Interests
*Availability:* ERIC Document Reproduction Service, 7420 Fullerton Rd., Ste. 110, Springfield, VA 22153-2852 (ED236427, 27 pages).
*Notes:* See other Shawsheen Valley Regional Vocational-Technical High School Work Sample Tests (13471 through 13482).

The Drill Press Work Sample is intended to assess a student's interest in and potential to successfully complete a training program in Basic Machine Shop I. The sample involves light work and must be performed by a person with both hands or one who has equivalent manual and finger dexterity from a chair or wheelchair. The sample is timed from the moment the student signifies he or she is ready to begin until the subject indicates that he or she is finished.

**13478**
**Electrical Wiring Work Sample.** Shawsheen Valley Regional Vocational Technical High School, Billerica, MA 1979.
*Descriptors:* *Aptitude Tests; *Disabilities; *Electricians; *Electricity; *High School Students; *Vocational Aptitude; *Vocational Evaluation; *Work Sample Tests; High Schools; Industrial Arts; Job Performance; Job Skills; Occupational Tests; Prevocational Education; Trade and Industrial Education; Vocational Interests
*Identifiers:* *Electrical Wiring
*Availability:* ERIC Document Reproduction Service, 7420 Fullerton Rd., Ste. 110, Springfield, VA 22153-2852 (ED236428, 27 pages).
*Notes:* See other Shawsheen Valley Regional Vocational-Technical High School Work Sample Tests (13471 through 13482).

The Electrical Work Sample is intended to assess a disabled student's interest in and potential to successfully complete a training program in basic electricity. The work sample involves light work and must be performed by a person with both hands or one who has equivalent manual and finger dexterity from a chair or wheelchair. The work sample is timed from the moment the student is ready to begin until he or she indicates that the sample is completed. The test is to wire an electrical duplex outlet.

**13479**
**Electronics Assembly Work Sample.** Shawsheen Valley Regional Vocational Technical High School, Billerica, MA 1979.
*Descriptors:* *Aptitude Tests; *Assembly (Manufacturing); *Disabilities; *Electronics; *High School Students; *Vocational Aptitude; *Vocational Evaluation; *Work Sample Tests; High Schools; Industrial Arts; Job Performance; Job Skills; Occupational Tests; Prevocational Education; Vocational Interests
*Identifiers:* *Electronics Assemblers
*Availability:* ERIC Document Reproduction Service, 7420 Fullerton Rd., Ste. 110, Springfield, VA 22153-2852 (ED236429, 26 pages).
*Notes:* See other Shawsheen Valley Regional Vocational-Technical High School Work Sample Tests (13471 through 13482).

The Electronics Assembly Work Sample is intended to assess a disabled student's interest in and potential to enter a training program in electronics assembly or a similar program. The sample involves sedentary work and can be done by a 2-armed person from a chair or wheelchair. Time is not a factor in this work sample.

**13480**
**Finger Dexterity Work Sample.** Shawsheen Valley Regional Vocational Technical High School, Billerica, MA 1979.
*Descriptors:* *Aptitude Tests; *Disabilities; *High School Students; *Motor Development; *Object Manipulation; *Vocational Aptitude; *Vocational Evaluation; *Work Sample Tests; High Schools; Job Performance; Job Skills; Occupational Tests; Prevocational Education; Vocational Interests
*Availability:* ERIC Document Reproduction Service, 7420 Fullerton Rd., Ste. 110, Springfield, VA 22153-2852 (ED236430, 22 pages).
*Notes:* See other Shawsheen Valley Regional Vocational-Technical High School Work Sample Tests (13471 through 13482).

The Finger Dexterity Work Sample is intended to assess a disabled student's ability to move the fingers and to manipulate small objects with fingers rapidly and accurately. The sample can be done by a 1- or 2-armed person from a chair or wheelchair. The sample is timed from the moment the student signifies readiness to completion of the task.

**13481**
**Manual Dexterity Work Sample.** Shawsheen Valley Regional Vocational Technical High School, Billerica, MA 1979.
*Descriptors:* *Aptitude Tests; *Disabilities; *High School Students; *Motor Development; *Object Manipulation; *Vocational Aptitude; *Vocational Evaluation; *Work Sample Tests; High Schools; Job Performance; Job Skills; Occupational Tests; Prevocational Education; Vocational Interests
*Identifiers:* Manual Dexterity
*Availability:* ERIC Document Reproduction Service, 7420 Fullerton Rd., Ste. 110, Springfield, VA 22153-2852 (ED236431, 21 pages).
*Notes:* See other Shawsheen Valley Regional Vocational-Technical High School Work Sample Tests (13471 through 13482).

The Manual Dexterity Work Sample is intended to assess a disabled student's ability to move the hands easily and skillfully and the ability to move the hands in placing and turning motions. The sample can be done by a 2-armed person from a chair or wheelchair. Time is not a factor in this work sample.

**13482**
**Small Parts Assembler Work Sample.** Shawsheen Valley Regional Vocational Technical High School, Billerica, MA 1979.
*Descriptors:* *Aptitude Tests; *Assembly (Manufacturing); *Disabilities; *High School Students; *Vocational Aptitude; *Vocational Evaluation; *Work Sample Tests; High Schools; Job Performance; Job Skills; Occupational Tests; Prevocational Education; Secondary Education; Secondary School Students; Trade and Industrial Education; Vocational Interests
*Identifiers:* *Assemblers
*Availability:* ERIC Document Reproduction Service, 7420 Fullerton Rd., Ste. 110, Springfield, VA 22153-2852 (ED236432, 29 pages).
*Notes:* See other Shawsheen Valley Regional Vocational-Technical High School Work Sample Tests (13471 through 13481).

The Small Parts Assembler Work Sample is intended to assess a disabled student's interest in and potential to enter a training program in small parts assembly or in a similar job. The sample involves light to medium work and can be done by a 2-armed person with good eyesight from a chair or wheelchair. Time is not a factor in scoring this work sample but is kept for informational purposes only.

**13504**
**Word Processor Assessment Battery.** Stanard, Steven J. 1984.
*Descriptors:* *Occupational Tests; *Word Processing; *Work Sample Tests; Achievement Tests; Adults; Aptitude Tests; Business Correspondence; Dictation; Personnel Evaluation; Personnel Selection; Typewriting; Vocational Aptitude
*Identifiers:* Transcription; WPAB
*Availability:* London House, SRA Product Group, 9701 W. Higgins Rd., Rosemont, IL 60018.
*Notes:* Time, 55.

A test consisting of 3 parts designed to measure specific skills and abilities necessary for success in word processing. Can be used to evaluate experienced and inexperienced persons for promotion, transfer, or hire, regardless of the type of equipment available for use in the evaluation. Part 1 is predictive of training success and job performance for word processors. Part 2 measures a person's ability to type quickly and accurately. Part 3 measures a person's ability to transcribe dictated material accurately and to produce a mailable letter.

**13545**
**Staff Burnout Scale for Health Professionals.** Jones, John W. 1980.
*Descriptors:* *Attitude Measures; *Burnout; *Health Personnel; Adults; Hospital Personnel; Job Satisfaction; Nurses; Self Concept
*Identifiers:* SBSHP; Self Report Measures
*Availability:* London House, SRA Product Group, 9701 W. Higgins Rd., Rosemont, IL 60018.
*Notes:* Time, 15 approx. Items, 30.

This inventory of attitudes is designed to assess staff burnout among health professionals. It measures degree of work stress experienced by hospital-related personnel.

**13546**
**Staff Burnout Scale for Police and Security Personnel.** Jones, John W. 1980.
*Descriptors:* *Attitude Measures; *Burnout; *Police; *Security Personnel; Adults; Job Satisfaction; Self Concept
*Identifiers:* SBSPS; Self Report Measures
*Availability:* London House, SRA Product Group, 9701 W. Higgins Rd., Rosemont, IL 60018.
*Notes:* Time, 15 approx. Items, 30.

An inventory of attitudes designed to assess staff burnout among police and security officers. Measures acute stress reactions of examinees and how they currently feel.

**13547**
**Rahim Organizational Conflict Inventory II.** Rahim, M. Afzalur 1983.
*Descriptors:* *Conflict Resolution; *Organizations (Groups); *Self Concept Measures; Adults; Employer Employee Relationship; Peer Relationship
*Identifiers:* ROC(II); Self Administered Tests; Self Report Measures
*Availability:* Consulting Psychologists Press, Inc., 3803 E. Bayshore Rd., Palo Alto, CA 94303.
*Notes:* Time, 8 approx. Items, 84.

Designed to measure styles of handling interpersonal conflict in an organizational setting. Forms A, B, and C each consist of 28 items. Form A assesses one's relationship with his or her boss. Form B assesses one's relationship with subordinates. Form C assesses conflict resolution style with peers.

**13555**
**The Management Burnout Scale.** Jones, John W.; Moretti, Donald 1980.
*Descriptors:* *Administrators; *Burnout; *Job Satisfaction; *Managerial Occupations; *Rating Scales; *Supervisors; Emotional Adjustment; Work Attitudes
*Identifiers:* MBS
*Availability:* London House, SRA Product Group, 9701 W. Higgins Rd., Rosemont, IL 60018.
*Notes:* Time, 5-15. Items, 35.

The MBS was designed to measure adverse cognitive, affective, behavioral, and psychophysiological reactions of managers to burnout, which is defined as "a syndrome of physical and emotional exhaustion involving the development of negative job attitudes, a poor professional self concept, and a loss of concern for employees and customers." Only one major validation study in the MBS has been completed.

**13561**
**Profile of Occupational Interests.** Dunne, Faith 1978.
*Descriptors:* *Attitude Measures; *Career Development; *Females; *High School Students; *Needs Assessment; *Rural Youth; *Vocational Interests; Academic Aspiration; High Schools; Marriage; Occupational Aspiration; Profiles; Questionnaires; School Attitudes; Sex Role; Surveys; Womens Education; Work Attitudes
*Identifiers:* Options Project; POI; TIM(J)
*Availability:* Tests in Microfiche, Test Collection, Educational Testing Service, Princeton, NJ 08541.
*Notes:* Items, 61.

A needs assessment questionnaire designed for use in a career development project for rural high school students, especially women. The profile covers career and educational aspirations, perceptions of school and work, attitudes about marriage and the division of labor, responsibility within the home, and suitability of various jobs for men and women. Has separate forms for males and females.

**13577**
**Nuclear Screening Services.** Institute for Personality and Ability Testing, Champaign, IL 1982.
*Descriptors:* *Emotional Adjustment; *Nuclear Power Plant Technicians; *Occupational Tests; *Personality Measures; *Screening Tests; *Stress Management; Adults; Nuclear Power Plants
*Availability:* Institute for Personality and Ability Testing, P.O. Box 188, Champaign, IL 61820.

A psychological screening service for personnel who need authorized, unescorted access to protected areas of a nuclear facility. Two programs are available. One is for regular employees and is used to determine emotional stability and personal reliability. The "extended assessment program" used with key personnel measures personality characteristics and ability to cope with stress. Uses 16 PF (2313), Clinical Analysis Questionnaire (6921), Motivation Analysis Test (7899), and the Stress Evaluation Inventory.

**13593**
**Minnesota Multiphasic Personality Inventory: Group Form, The Minnesota Report: Personnel Selection System.** Hathaway, S.R.; McKinley, J.C. 1982.
*Descriptors:* *Industrial Personnel; *Personality Assessment; *Personality Measures; *Personnel Selection; Adolescents; Adults; Personality Traits
*Identifiers:* MMPI
*Availability:* National Computer Systems, Professional Assessment Services, P.O. Box 1416, Minneapolis, MN 55440.
*Notes:* Items, 566.

The MMPI is used to generate 2 personnel reports that make up the Personnel Selection system. Reports provide qualified psychologists with results of job applicants in industrial settings. The interpretive report provides information relevant to personnel selection and a narrative describing pertinent personality characteristics and potential work-related problems. A personnel screening report provides information relevant to personnel selection and summary ratings of an applicant's MMPI profile over several areas found valuable in making personnel decisions. The reports are tailored for different occupational groups: nuclear power plant operator, police officer or other law enforcement officer, airline flight or noncombat military flight crew members, graduate mental health program or medical school or other health professions, firefighter, air traffic controller, seminary, and other.

**13596**
**Armed Services Civilian Vocational Interest Survey.** Kauk, Robert 1983.
*Descriptors:* *High School Students; *Interest Inventories; *Vocational Interests; *Young Adults; High Schools
*Identifiers:* ASCVIS; Self Administered Tests
*Availability:* CFKR Career Materials, Inc., 11860 Kemper Rd., Unit 7, Auburn, CA 95603.

A 4-step career interest survey that allows individuals to rate their occupational interests with 8 major groups of job activities, find armed services and related civilian jobs to match those interests, develop a career profile to use as a basis for career decisions, and organize educational plans for the careers they select. Focus is on careers that do not require traditional college degrees.

**13597**
**IPI Aptitude Series: Dental Office Assistant.** Industrial Psychology, Inc., New York, NY 1981.
*Descriptors:* *Adults; *Aptitude Tests; *Dental Assistants; *Job Applicants; *Occupational Tests; Abstract Reasoning; Emotional Adjustment; Extraversion Introversion; Job Performance; Job Skills; Mathematical Concepts; Neurosis; Personality Measures; Visual Perception; Vocabulary
*Identifiers:* Test Batteries
*Availability:* Industrial Psychology International, Ltd., 111 N. Market St., Champaign, IL 61820.
*Notes:* See also IPI Hiring Manual and Job-Tests Program (11774); CPF (3736); NPF (13601).

This is a battery of tests designed to assess examinee's aptitude for the position of dental assistant. Duties would include chairside work, light secretarial tasks, and working with patients and the dentist.

**13598**
**IPI Aptitude Series: Dental Technician.** Industrial Psychology, Inc., New York, NY 1981.
*Descriptors:* *Adults; *Aptitude Tests; *Dental Technicians; *Job Applicants; *Occupational Tests; Emotional Adjustment; Extraversion Introversion; Job Performance; Job Skills; Neurosis; Perceptual Motor Coordination; Personality Measures; Spatial Ability
*Identifiers:* Test Batteries
*Availability:* Industrial Psychology International, Ltd., 111 N. Market St., Champaign, IL 61820.
*Notes:* See also IPI Hiring Manual and Job-Tests Program (11774); CPF (3736); NPF (13601).

This is a battery of tests designed to assess examinee's aptitude for the position of dental technician. Duties would include laboratory work at 4 classification levels: cast metal, denture, crown and bridge, and porcelain and acrylic.

**13599**
**IPI Aptitude Series: Optometric Assistant.** Industrial Psychology, Inc., New York, NY 1981.
*Descriptors:* *Adults; *Aptitude Tests; *Job Applicants; *Occupational Tests; *Optometry; *Paraprofessional Personnel; Abstract Reasoning; Emotional Adjustment; Extraversion Introversion; Job Performance; Job Skills; Language Fluency; Mathematical Concepts; Neurosis; Personality Measures; Visual Perception; Vocabulary
*Identifiers:* Test Batteries
*Availability:* Industrial Psychology International, Ltd., 111 N. Market St., Champaign, IL 61820.
*Notes:* See also IPI Hiring Manual and Job-Tests Program (11774); CPF (3736); NPF (13601).

This is a battery of tests designed to assess examinee's aptitude for the position of optometric assistant. Duties include working as support person for optometrist, working with optometrist and patients, reception duties, and light secretarial work.

**13600**
**IPI Aptitude Series: General Clerk.** Industrial Psychology, Inc., New York, NY 1981.
*Descriptors:* *Adults; *Aptitude Tests; *Clerical Occupations; *Clerical Workers; *Job Applicants; *Occupational Tests; Abstract Reasoning; Job Performance; Job Skills; Language Fluency; Mathematical Concepts; Memory; Personality Measures; Spatial Ability; Visual Perception; Vocabulary
*Identifiers:* Test Batteries
*Availability:* Industrial Psychology International, Ltd., 111 N. Market St., Champaign, IL 61820.
*Notes:* See also IPI Hiring Manual and Job-Tests Program (11774).

This is a battery of tests designed to assess examinee's aptitude for the position of a general clerk who would perform a number of routine clerical tasks, such as typing, filing, billing, coding, verifying, transcribing, writing, sorting, and answering telephones. Battery is suitable to evaluate applicants for an office with a small staff in which employee might perform a number of the functions listed above or in a large office where clerk might circulate among various departments.

**13605**
**Behavioral Interviewing Skill Analyzer.** Green, Paul C.; Horgan, Dianne D. 1984.
*Descriptors:* *Employment Interviews; *Personnel Selection; Adults; Job Skills; Questionnaires; Work Attitudes
*Availability:* Behavioral Technologies, 6260 Poplar Ave., Memphis, TN 38119.

Used to aid managers in designing behaviorally based and structured interviews to evaluate candidates' skills for a particular position. Divides needed skills into 2 groups: technical job skills and performance skills. Technical job skills are the specific skills necessary for minimum performance of the job and are determined by the tasks performed on the job. Performance skills are those work habits and general skills transferable from job to job and reflect attitudes about the nature of work and how work should be done. A training program is required before any materials will be sold to purchasers.

**13620**
**IPI Aptitude Series: Computer Programmers.** Industrial Psychology, Inc., New York, NY 1984.
*Descriptors:* *Adults; *Aptitude Tests; *Job Applicants; *Occupational Tests; *Programmers; Job Performance; Job Skills
*Identifiers:* Test Batteries
*Availability:* Industrial Psychology International, Ltd., 111 N. Market St., Champaign, IL 61820.

A battery of tests designed to assist in the screening and selection of those applicants most likely to succeed in the programming area at an entry-level position. May also be used to identify employees in clerical positions who might possess the necessary skills to succeed in computer-related positions and are possible candidates for training programs.

**13652**
**Ohio Vocational Achievement Tests: Production Agriculture.** Ohio State Dept. of Education, Div. of Vocational Education, Columbus, OH 1982.
*Descriptors:* *Achievement Tests; *Agricultural Education; *Agricultural Occupations; *Agricultural Production; *High School Students; *Vocational Education; Abstract Reasoning; Data Analysis; Grade 11; Grade 12; High Schools; Knowledge Level; Problem Solving
*Availability:* Ohio State University, Instructional Materials Lab., 1885 Neil Ave., Columbus, OH 43210.
*Notes:* Time, 240 approx. Items, 393.

For use in the evaluation and diagnosis of vocational achievement. Developed to measure skills and understanding in specific vocational areas. Items measure ability to solve problems, analyze data, recall facts, have a knowledge of principles, react to generalizations, use abstractions in specific situations, and form parts into complete structures. Administered with the California Short Form Test of Academic Aptitude (5919 through 5923).

**13653**
**Ohio Vocational Achievement Tests: Clerk-Typist.** Ohio State Dept. of Education, Div. of Vocational Education, Columbus, OH 1982.
*Descriptors:* *Achievement Tests; *Clerical Occupations; *Clerical Workers; *High School Students; *Typewriting; *Vocational Education; Grade 11; Grade 12; High Schools; Office Occupations Education
*Identifiers:* Clerical Skills
*Availability:* Ohio State University, Instructional Materials Lab., 1885 Neil Ave., Columbus, OH 43210.
*Notes:* Time, 240 approx. Items, 355.

For use in the evaluation and diagnosis of vocational achievement. Developed to measure skills and understanding in specific vocational areas. Items measure ability to solve problems, analyze data, recall facts, have a knowledge of principles, react to generalizations, use abstractions in specific situations, and form parts into complete structures. Administered with the California Short Form Test of Academic Aptitude (5919 through 5923).

**13654**
**Ohio Vocational Achievement Tests: Word Processing.** Ohio State Dept. of Education, Div. of Vocational Education, Columbus, OH 1982.
*Descriptors:* *Achievement Tests; *Clerical Occupations; *High School Students; *Vocational Education; *Word Processing; Grade 11; Grade 12; High Schools; Office Occupations Education
*Identifiers:* Clerical Skills
*Availability:* Ohio State University, Instructional Materials Lab., 1885 Neil Ave., Columbus, OH 43210.
*Notes:* Time, 240 approx. Items, 373.

For use in the evaluation and diagnosis of vocational achievement. Developed to measure skills and understanding in specific vocational areas. Items measure ability to solve problems, analyze data, recall facts, have a knowledge of principles, react to generalizations, use abstractions in specific situations, and form parts into complete structures. Administered with the California Short Form Test of Academic Aptitude (5919 through 5923).

**13655**
**Ohio Vocational Achievement Tests: Apparel and Accessories.** Ohio State Dept. of Education, Div. of Vocational Education, Columbus, OH 1982.
*Descriptors:* *Achievement Tests; *Distributive Education; *Fashion Industry; *High School Students; *Vocational Education; Grade 11; Grade 12; High Schools; Retailing
*Availability:* Ohio State University, Instructional Materials Lab., 1885 Neil Ave., Columbus, OH 43210.
*Notes:* Time, 240 approx. Items, 386.

For use in the evaluation and diagnosis of vocational achievement. Developed to measure skills and understanding in specific vocational areas. Items measure ability to solve problems, analyze data, recall facts, have a knowledge of principles, react to generalizations, use abstractions in specific situations, and form parts into complete structures. Administered with the California Short Form Test of Academic Aptitude (5919 through 5923).

**13656**
**Ohio Vocational Achievement Tests: Small Engine Repair.** Ohio State Dept. of Education, Div. of Vocational Education, Columbus, OH 1983.
*Descriptors:* *Achievement Tests; *High School Students; *Small Engine Mechanics; *Vocational Education; Grade 11; Grade 12; High Schools

*Availability:* Ohio State University, Instructional Materials Lab., 1885 Neil Ave., Columbus, OH 43210.
*Notes:* Time, 240 approx. Items, 369.

For use in the evaluation and diagnosis of vocational achievement. Developed to measure skills and understanding in specific vocational areas. Items measure ability to solve problems, analyze data, recall facts, have a knowledge of principles, react to generalizations, use abstractions in specific situations, and form parts into complete structures. Administered with the California Short Form Test of Academic Aptitude (5919 through 5923).

**13673**
**APTICOM.** Vocational Research Institute, Philadelphia, PA 1984.
*Descriptors:* *Aptitude Tests; *Career Counseling; *Computer Assisted Testing; *Interest Inventories; *Vocational Aptitude; *Vocational Interests; Adolescents; Adults; Disabilities; Employment Potential; Job Training; Profiles; Vocational Education; Vocational Rehabilitation
*Identifiers:* Department of Labor; OAP
*Availability:* Vocational Research Institute, 1528 Walnut St., Ste. 1502, Philadelphia, PA 19102.
*Notes:* Time, 90.

APTICOM, developed by the Vocational Research Institute, is a computerized, desktop console designed specifically for assessing aptitudes and job interests. It is intended for use in the vocational guidance and counseling process and in employment and training selection and placement. The tests were designed to measure aptitude constructs that have been related to occupational success using the Department of Labor's defined aptitudes. They are intelligence, general learning ability, verbal aptitude, numerical aptitude, spatial aptitude, form perception, clerical perception, motor coordination, finger dexterity, manual dexterity, and eye-hand-foot coordination. APTICOM is computerized, self-scoring and self-timing, portable, and can be administered individually or to up to 12 people at one time. The APTICOM Occupational Interest Inventory provides schools, rehabilitation, industry, and job training programs with an interest measure that stimulates examinees' enthusiasm, minimizes time requirements, and is computerized. When both the aptitude and interest inventories are administered, the results are a means of initiating occupational exploration with information refined to the level of the Department of Labor Work Groups. The APTICOM Report gives aptitude scores and Occupational Aptitude Patterns (OAPs) based on these scores. It also gives interest scores and the interest areas related to these scores. The Occupational Interest Inventory Report reveals the degree of interest indicated by the test taker and an individual profile is generated showing the interest in various work tasks as compared to the normative sample. The final portion of the report lists those areas of employment in which the applicant has shown both the required aptitude and high interest. The accompanying Educational Skills Development Battery measures achieved math and language skills levels.

**13689**
**Employment Interview Analysis.** Selectform, Inc., Freeport, NY 1982.
*Descriptors:* *Employment Interviews; *Evaluation Methods; *Occupational Tests; Adults; Employees; Personality Traits; Rating Scales; Records (Forms)
*Availability:* Selectform, Inc., Box 3045, Freeport, NY 11520.
*Notes:* Items, 14.

A rating scale used to organize the information collected during an interview with a job applicant. A series of traits is rated on a 5-point scale from "unsatisfactory" to "clearly outstanding." Examples of traits are motivation to succeed, appearance, poise, and personality.

**13690**
**Employee Performance Evaluation.** Selectform, Inc., Freeport, NY 1981.
*Descriptors:* *Job Performance; *Occupational Tests; *Personnel Evaluation; *Vocational Evaluation; Adults; Employees; Personality Traits; Rating Scales
*Availability:* Selectform, Inc., Box 3045, Freeport, NY 11520.
*Notes:* Items, 19.

A form consisting of ratings of 15 personal traits of workers on a 5-point scale from unsatisfactory to clearly outstanding. A portion of the form is blank for written comments about strengths and weaknesses. Traits include knowledge, work quantity, initiative, stability, and alertness.

**13691**
**Selectform Employee Records.** Selectform, Inc., Freeport, NY 1984.
*Descriptors:* *Business; *Records (Forms); Adults; Attendance Records; Background; Discipline; Employees; Employment Qualifications; Job Performance; Payroll Records
*Availability:* Selectform, Inc., Box 3045, Freeport, NY 11520.

A series of forms and records for use in business applications. Includes an employment records jacket with space for personal information, an employee reprimand notice, attendance history, absence report, payroll status change, and an application for employment.

**13716**
**Sheltered Employment Work Experience Program, Second Revised Edition.** Gertrude A. Barber Center, Erie, PA 1982.
*Descriptors:* *Adolescents; *Adults; *Mental Retardation; *Sheltered Workshops; *Vocational Evaluation; Rating Scales
*Identifiers:* SEWEP
*Availability:* The Barber Center Press, 136 E. Ave., Erie, PA 16507.

Designed to assess and program the development of vocational capabilities of mentally retarded adolescents and adults. Focuses on subject who has achieved a minimal development in vocational independence and adequate independence in personal and social skills. Vocational skills assessed are those designed to facilitate success in traditional programs, such as sheltered workshops. SEWEP identifies 10 major vocational competency areas: factory work, carpentry, print shop, laundry, building maintenance, general and outdoor maintenance, transportation aide, library aide, food service, and housekeeping. The vocational competency areas are divided into 50 specific skill areas, which are subdivided into 504 specific skills. Two other competency areas are also assessed: personal-social development and general vocational development.

**13746**
**Attitudes Toward Women as Managers.** Yost, Edward B.; Herbert, Theodore T. 1977.
*Descriptors:* *Administrators; *Attitude Measures; *Females; *Managerial Occupations; *Sex Role; Adults
*Identifiers:* ATWAM
*Availability:* Goodstein, Leonard D., and Pfeiffer, J. William, eds., *The 1985 Annual Handbook for Group Facilitators.* San Diego: University Associates, 1985. Pfeiffer and Co., formerly University Associates, 8517 Production Ave., San Diego, CA 92121-2280.
*Notes:* Time, 15 approx. Items, 12.

Developed to measure subjects' attitudes toward women in managerial positions. A paper and pencil instrument that can be administered in a group or as a take-home questionnaire. Can be used as a practical tool or as a research instrument in management training situations, as a pretest and posttest, to increase self-awareness, or as the basis for discussions of biased or discriminatory behavior.

**13760**
**Multiple Management Instrument, Third Edition.** Smith, August William 1982.
*Descriptors:* *Administrator Attitudes; *Administrators; *Attitude Measures; *Supervisory Methods; Adults; Self Evaluation (Individuals)
*Availability:* August William Smith, Texas A & M University, College of Business Administration, College Station, TX 77843-4221.
*Notes:* Items, 24.

Instrument intended to help administrators, managers, supervisors, and executives find out more about their attitudes and practices. Instrument assesses how managers relate to particular dimensions and approaches to management. Subjects read 24 short work-situation scenarios and then select 1 of 4 response choices as being most characteristic of how they would act in that situation. Analysis of responses shows individual to have 1 of 4 supervisory styles: integrator, independent, intervenor, or investigator.

**13761**
**Managerial Diagnostic Instrument, Revised.** Smith, August William 1981.
*Descriptors:* *Administrator Attitudes; *Administrators; *Attitude Measures; *Self Evaluation (Individuals); *Supervisory Methods; Adults; Rating Scales
*Availability:* August William Smith, Texas A & M University, College of Business Administration, College Station, TX 77843-4221.
*Notes:* Items, 10.

A self-rating scale in which managers rank 4 methods of dealing with each of 10 managerial functions. Analysis of results indicates the individual's managerial style as being one of the following: integrator, intervenor, independent, or investigator.

**13762**
**Individual Motives Instrument.** Smith, August William 1981.
*Descriptors:* *Administrators; *Motivation; Achievement Need; Adults; Affiliation Need; Individual Power; Rating Scales; Self Evaluation (Individuals)
*Availability:* August William Smith, Texas A & M University, College of Business Administration, College Station, TX 77843-4221.
*Notes:* Items, 30.

A self-rating scale for individuals to determine their basic motives as an individual and as a manager. Analysis of results indicates individuals' need for achievement, affiliation, or power.

**13763**
**Stress Management Instrument.** Smith, August William 1982.
*Descriptors:* *Administrators; *Stress Management; Adults; Rating Scales; Self Evaluation (Individuals)
*Availability:* August William Smith, Texas A & M University, College of Business Administration, College Station, TX 77843-4221.
*Notes:* Items, 20.

A rating scale in which managers indicate how they would most often handle group differences in opinion and conflicting points of view. Responses and analysis of responses indicate 1 of 4 managerial styles in handling stress: intervenor, integrator, independent, or investigator.

**13764**
**Time Management Instrument.** Smith, August William 1981.
*Descriptors:* *Administrators; *Time Management; Adults; Rating Scales; Self Evaluation (Individuals)
*Availability:* August William Smith, Texas A & M University, College of Business Administration, College Station, TX 77843-4221.
*Notes:* Items, 16.

A self-rating scale in which manager evaluates his or her managerial style in terms of time allocations for various tasks or functions. Managerial styles in relation to time management are integrator, intervenor, independent, or investigator.

**13768**
**Organizational Culture Inventory, Federal Aviation Administration, Eastern Region.** Cooke, Robert A. 1983.

*Descriptors:* *Organizational Climate; *Organizations (Groups); Adults; Profiles; Rating Scales; Self Evaluation (Groups); Work Environment
*Identifiers:* Federal Aviation Administration
*Availability:* Human Synergistics, 39819 Plymouth Rd., Plymouth, MI 48170.
*Notes:* Items, 120.

This inventory presents a list of 120 statements that describe some of the behaviors and "personal styles" that might be expected or implicitly required of members of organizations. The examinee is to indicate the extent to which the behavior described helps people to "fit in" and meet expectations in the organization. The statements refer to the way people within the organization are expected to deal with one another rather than with people external to the organization. The responses are on a 5-point scale and range from not at all to a very great extent. The individual's scores are added to those of others in the organization to generate an aggregate cultural profile of the organization. There are 12 cultural styles in the profile: humanistic-helpful, affiliative, approval, conventional, dependent, avoidance, oppositional, power, competitive, competence, achievement, and self-actualization.

**13769**
**Educational Administrator Effectiveness Profile.** Human Synergistics, Plymouth, MI 1984.
*Descriptors:* *Administrator Evaluation; *Administrator Responsibility; *Administrators; *Formative Evaluation; *Management Development; *Professional Development; *School Administration; *Self Evaluation (Individuals); Administrator Role; Decision Making Skills; Interpersonal Communication; Planning; Problem Solving; Rating Scales
*Identifiers:* Danforth Foundation; EAEP
*Availability:* Human Synergistics, 39819 Plymouth Rd., Plymouth, MI 48170.
*Notes:* Time, 30 approx. Items, 120.

The Educational Administrator Effectiveness Profile (EAEP) is a self-diagnostic instrument designed to assist elementary, secondary, and central office public school administrators in assessing 11 key skill/behavior areas which are essential to their effectiveness. The 11 areas are setting goals and objectives, planning, making decisions and solving problems, managing business and fiscal affairs, assessing progress, delegating responsibilities, communicating, building and maintaining relationships, demonstrating professional commitment, improving instruction, and developing staff. In addition to the questionnaire for the administrator, there are 5 instruments which assess the same skill/behavior areas to be completed by individuals chosen by the administrator who know his or her administrative role. Based on the feedback, a self-improvement program can be designed to strengthen weak areas. A 7-point rating scale is used, ranging from almost never to always. The development of this instrument was sponsored by the Danforth Foundation.

**13770**
**Management Effectiveness Profile System.** Human Synergistics, Plymouth, MI 1983.
*Descriptors:* *Administrator Evaluation; *Formative Evaluation; *Interpersonal Communication; *Self Evaluation (Individuals); *Administrator Effectiveness; Adults; Business Administration; Conflict Resolution; Decision Making Skills; Problem Solving; Profiles; Questionnaires; Rating Scales; Stress Management
*Identifiers:* MEPS
*Availability:* Human Synergistics, 39819 Plymouth Rd., Plymouth, MI 48170.
*Notes:* Items, 95.

The Management Effectiveness Profile System (MEPS) is part of a multilevel diagnostic system. The purpose of the battery of instruments is to provide accurate, detailed information about healthy human behavior and to identify possible problem areas. This instrument focuses on managerial behavior and measures 15 management skill areas as reported by the subject and by 4 or 5 people who work with the subject. The self-description portion is done by the manager. There are 95 items; each has 2 different descriptions of how the manager might behave in different situations. The subject chooses on a 7-point scale which is the better answer, from react almost exactly like A to react almost exactly like B. Two sets of scores are produced. The first will be from the items the person filled out about himself or herself and the second will be the average scores of the questionnaires other people were asked to fill out by the manager. There must be at least 3 other questionnaires filled out to protect the anonymity of those who did respond.

**13797**
**COPSystem Intermediate Inventory.** Knapp, Robert R.; Knapp, Lila 1981.
*Descriptors:* *Career Awareness; *Career Development; *Career Exploration; *Career Guidance; *Career Planning; *Prevocational Education; *Self Evaluation (Individuals); *Vocational Interests; Attitude Measures; Elementary School Students; Interest Inventories; Intermediate Grades; Junior High Schools; Junior High School Students; Occupational Clusters; Occupational Information
*Identifiers:* California Occupational Preference System; COPSII
*Availability:* Educational and Industrial Testing Service, P.O. Box 7234, San Diego, CA 92107.
*Notes:* Time, 30 approx.

This inventory is designed for use with elementary grade students and those at higher grade levels for whom reading or language presents difficulties to help them make career decisions. It is essentially a self-administered test which can be given by the teacher and is scored by the student. There are 2 sections: the Inventory Section and the Self-Interpretation Section. The Inventory Section has 8 categories, including educational plans, preferred school subjects, selection of leisure time activities, and qualities preferred in a job and the work environment. The remaining categories present items more specifically related to the occupational family clusters. The Self-Interpretation Section provides a listing of the occupational clusters with sample occupations and suggested activities, such as clubs, part-time jobs, and community activities. There are also lists of some abilities needed and courses appropriate to jobs in the various clusters. The purpose of the COPSystem is to introduce students to families of related occupations for purposes of career exploration.

**13805**
**Micro W-Apt Programming Aptitude Test.** Wolfe Personnel Testing Systems, Oradell, NJ 1984.
*Descriptors:* *Aptitude Tests; *Occupational Tests; *Personnel Selection; *Programming; *Vocational Aptitude; Adults; Microcomputers
*Availability:* Wolfe Personnel Testing Systems, Box 319, Oradell, NJ 07649.
*Notes:* Items, 5.

Consists of 5 questions on a microcomputer diskette which candidate works on and solves interactively on a microcomputer. Currently, test can be administered on an IBM-PC or compatible.

**13806**
**Data Entry Operator Aptitude Test.** Wolfe Personnel Testing Systems, Oradell, NJ 1982.
*Descriptors:* *Occupational Tests; *Personnel Selection; *Vocational Aptitude; Adults; Aptitude Tests; French; Input Output Devices
*Identifiers:* *Data Entry; DEOAT
*Availability:* Walden Personnel Testing and Training Systems, Box 319, Oradell, NJ 07649.
*Notes:* Time, 20.

An aptitude test used to evaluate job candidate's aptitude as a data entry operator. Designed to evaluate coding ability, numerical facility, manual dexterity, clerical accuracy, detail, and editing. Test may be used for following purposes: to hire experienced data entry operators, to assess expertise of existing staff, to determine training needs and training effectiveness, to identify error-prone candidates, and to do a skills inventory analysis. Test is suitable for candidates for data entry operator or terminal operator. Available in English and French.

**13836**
**Ball Aptitude Battery.** Ball Foundation, Glen Ellyn, IL 1983.
*Descriptors:* *Ability Identification; *Aptitude Tests; *Career Counseling; *Career Guidance; *Cognitive Processes; *Object Manipulation; *Vocational Aptitude; *Vocational Interests; Adults; Employment Opportunities; High Schools; High School Students; Induction; Language Acquisition; Motor Development; Performance Tests; Personnel Selection; Vocational Evaluation; Writing Skills
*Identifiers:* BAB; Pitch (Music); Test Batteries
*Availability:* The Ball Foundation, 800 Roosevelt Rd., Bldg. C, Ste. 120, Glen Ellyn, IL 60137.
*Notes:* Time, 180 approx.

The Ball Aptitude Battery (BAB) is a multiple ability test battery designed to measure various aptitudes needed for successful performance in a variety of jobs. The BAB can be used to help determine the most appropriate occupations for an individual, as well as the most appropriate individuals for an occupation. The battery is also useful for individual career decision making and vocational guidance. The BAB was developed for the senior high school population and for the general adult population. It can also be used in organizational decision making, specifically for personnel selection and placement.

**13846**
**PSI Basic Skills Tests: Language Skills.** Ruch, William W.; And Others 1981.
*Descriptors:* *Clerical Occupations; *Occupational Tests; *Office Occupations; *Personnel Selection; *Written Language; Adults; Capitalization (Alphabetic); Culture Fair Tests; Grammar; Language Usage; Punctuation; Spelling
*Availability:* Psychological Services, Inc., 100 W. Broadway, Ste. 1100, Glendale, CA 91210.
*Notes:* For all the tests in the series, see 13846 through 13865. Time, 5.

One of a series of 20 practical, brief personnel selection tests. Designed to aid personnel managers in business, industry, and government in the selection and placement of employees. Test content was constructed to be bias-free. Validated against job performance in a nationwide survey. Language skills test measures ability to recognize correct spelling, punctuation, capitalization, grammar, and usage.

**13847**
**PSI Basic Skills Tests: Reading Comprehension.** Ruch, William W.; And Others 1981.
*Descriptors:* *Clerical Occupations; *Occupational Tests; *Office Occupations; *Personnel Selection; *Reading Comprehension; Adults; Culture Fair Tests
*Availability:* Psychological Services, Inc., 100 W. Broadway, Ste. 1100, Glendale, CA 91210.
*Notes:* For all the tests in the series, see 13846 through 13865. Time, 10.

One of a series of 20 practical, brief personnel selection tests. Designed to aid personnel managers in business, industry, and government in the selection and placement of employees. Test content was constructed to be bias-free. Validated against job performance in a nationwide survey. Measures the ability to read a passage and answer literal and inferential questions about it.

**13848**
**PSI Basic Skills Tests: Vocabulary.** Ruch, William W.; And Others 1981.
*Descriptors:* *Clerical Occupations; *Occupational Tests; *Office Occupations; *Personnel Selection; *Vocabulary; Adults; Culture Fair Tests

*Availability:* Psychological Services, Inc., 100 W. Broadway, Ste. 1100, Glendale, CA 91210.
*Notes:* For all the tests in the series, see 13846 through 13865. Time, 5.

One of a series of 20 practical, brief personnel selection tests. Designed to aid personnel managers in business, industry, and government in the selection and placement of employees. Test content was constructed to be bias-free. Validated against job performance in a nationwide survey. Measures the ability to recognize the correct meaning of words.

13849
**PSI Basic Skills Tests: Computation.** Ruch, William W.; And Others 1981.
*Descriptors:* *Clerical Occupations; *Computation; *Occupational Tests; *Office Occupations; *Personnel Selection; Adults; Culture Fair Tests
*Availability:* Psychological Services, Inc., 100 W. Broadway, Ste. 1100, Glendale, CA 91210.
*Notes:* For all the tests in the series, see 13846 through 13865. Time, 5.

One of a series of 20 practical, brief personnel selection tests. Designed to aid personnel managers in business, industry, and government in the selection and placement of employees. Test content was constructed to be bias-free. Validated against job performance in a nationwide survey. Measures the ability to solve arithmetic problems involving operations with whole numbers, decimals, percents, and simple fractions.

13850
**PSI Basic Skills Tests: Problem Solving.** Ruch, William W.; And Others 1981.
*Descriptors:* *Clerical Occupations; *Mathematical Applications; *Occupational Tests; *Office Occupations; *Personnel Selection; *Problem Solving; Adults; Culture Fair Tests
*Availability:* Psychological Services, Inc., 100 W. Broadway, Ste. 1100, Glendale, CA 91210.
*Notes:* For all the tests in the series, see 13846 through 13865. Time, 10.

One of a series of 20 practical, brief personnel selection tests. Designed to aid personnel managers in business, industry, and government in the selection and placement of employees. Test content was constructed to be bias-free. Validated against job performance in a nationwide survey. Measures the ability to solve story problems requiring the application of mathematical operations.

13851
**PSI Basic Skills Tests: Decision Making.** Ruch, William W.; And Others 1981.
*Descriptors:* *Clerical Occupations; *Decision Making; *Occupational Tests; *Office Occupations; *Personnel Selection; Adults; Culture Fair Tests
*Availability:* Psychological Services, Inc., 100 W. Broadway, Ste. 1100, Glendale, CA 91210.
*Notes:* For all the tests in the series, see 13846 through 13865. Time, 5.

One of a series of 20 practical, brief personnel selection tests. Designed to aid personnel managers in business, industry, and government in the selection and placement of employees. Test content was constructed to be bias-free. Validated against job performance in a nationwide survey. Measures the ability to read a set of procedures and apply them to new situations.

13852
**PSI Basic Skills Tests: Following Oral Directions.** Ruch, William W.; And Others 1981.
*Descriptors:* *Clerical Occupations; *Listening Comprehension; *Occupational Tests; *Office Occupations; *Personnel Selection; Adults; Culture Fair Tests
*Availability:* Psychological Services, Inc., 100 W. Broadway, Ste. 1100, Glendale, CA 91210.
*Notes:* For all the tests in the series, see 13846 through 13865. Time, 5.

One of a series of 20 practical, brief personnel selection tests. Designed to aid personnel managers in business, industry, and government in the selection and placement of employees. Test content was constructed to be bias-free. Validated against job performance in a nationwide survey. Measures the ability to listen to information and instructions presented orally, to take notes if desired, and to answer questions about the content.

13853
**PSI Basic Skills Tests: Following Written Directions.** Ruch, William W.; And Others 1981.
*Descriptors:* *Clerical Occupations; *Occupational Tests; *Office Occupations; *Personnel Selection; *Reading Comprehension; Adults; Culture Fair Tests
*Availability:* Psychological Services, Inc., 100 W. Broadway, Ste. 1100, Glendale, CA 91210.
*Notes:* For all the tests in the series, see 13846 through 13865. Time, 5.

One of a series of 20 practical, brief personnel selection tests. Designed to aid personnel managers in business, industry, and government in the selection and placement of employees. Test content was constructed to be bias-free. Validated against job performance in a nationwide survey. Measures the ability to read and follow a set of rules.

13854
**PSI Basic Skills Tests: Forms Checking.** Ruch, William W.; And Others 1981.
*Descriptors:* *Clerical Occupations; *Occupational Tests; *Office Occupations; *Personnel Selection; Adults; Culture Fair Tests
*Identifiers:* Accuracy; *Forms Checking
*Availability:* Psychological Services, Inc., 100 W. Broadway, Ste. 1100, Glendale, CA 91210.
*Notes:* For all the tests in the series, see 13846 through 13865. Time, 5.

One of a series of 20 practical, brief personnel selection tests. Designed to aid personnel managers in business, industry, and government in the selection and placement of employees. Test content was constructed to be bias-free. Validated against job performance in a nationwide survey. Measures the ability to verify the accuracy of completed forms by comparison to written information.

13855
**PSI Basic Skills Tests: Reasoning.** Ruch, William W.; And Others 1981.
*Descriptors:* *Abstract Reasoning; *Clerical Occupations; *Occupational Tests; *Office Occupations; *Personnel Selection; Adults; Culture Fair Tests
*Availability:* Psychological Services, Inc., 100 W. Broadway, Ste. 1100, Glendale, CA 91210.
*Notes:* For all the tests in the series, see 13846 through 13865. Time, 5.

One of a series of 20 practical, brief personnel selection tests. Designed to aid personnel managers in business, industry, and government in the selection and placement of employees. Test content was constructed to be bias-free. Validated against job performance in a nationwide survey. Measures the ability to analyze facts and to make valid judgments on the basis of the logical implications of such facts.

13856
**PSI Basic Skills Tests: Classifying.** Ruch, William W.; And Others 1981.
*Descriptors:* *Classification; *Clerical Occupations; *Occupational Tests; *Office Occupations; *Personnel Selection; Adults; Culture Fair Tests
*Availability:* Psychological Services, Inc., 100 W. Broadway, Ste. 1100, Glendale, CA 91210.
*Notes:* For all the tests in the series, see 13846 through 13865. Time, 5.

One of a series of 20 practical, brief personnel selection tests. Designed to aid personnel managers in business, industry, and government in the selection and placement of employees. Test content was constructed to be bias-free. Validated against job performance in a nationwide survey. Measures the ability to place information into predetermined categories.

13857
**PSI Basic Skills Tests: Coding.** Ruch, William W.; And Others 1981.
*Descriptors:* *Classification; *Clerical Occupations; *Coding; *Occupational Tests; *Office Occupations; *Personnel Selection; Adults; Culture Fair Tests
*Availability:* Psychological Services, Inc., 100 W. Broadway, Ste. 1100, Glendale, CA 91210.
*Notes:* For all the tests in the series, see 13846 through 13865. Time, 5.

One of a series of 20 practical, brief personnel selection tests. Designed to aid personnel managers in business, industry, and government in the selection and placement of employees. Test content was constructed to be bias-free. Validated against job performance in a nationwide survey. Measures the ability to code information according to a prescribed system.

13858
**PSI Basic Skills Tests: Filing Names.** Ruch, William W.; And Others 1981.
*Descriptors:* *Clerical Occupations; *Filing; *Occupational Tests; *Office Occupations; *Personnel Selection; Adults; Culture Fair Tests
*Availability:* Psychological Services, Inc., 100 W. Broadway, Ste. 1100, Glendale, CA 91210.
*Notes:* For all the tests in the series, see 13846 through 13865. Time, 2 approx.

One of a series of 20 practical, brief personnel selection tests. Designed to aid personnel managers in business, industry, and government in the selection and placement of employees. Test content was constructed to be bias-free. Validated against job performance in a nationwide survey. Measures the ability to insert names in a list in alphabetical order.

13859
**PSI Basic Skills Tests: Filing Numbers.** Ruch, William W.; And Others 1981.
*Descriptors:* *Clerical Occupations; *Filing; *Occupational Tests; *Office Occupations; *Personnel Selection; Adults; Culture Fair Tests
*Availability:* Psychological Services, Inc., 100 W. Broadway, Ste. 1100, Glendale, CA 91210.
*Notes:* For all the tests in the series, see 13846 through 13865. Time, 2.

One of a series of 20 practical, brief personnel selection tests. Designed to aid personnel managers in business, industry, and government in the selection and placement of employees. Test content was constructed to be bias-free. Validated against job performance in a nationwide survey. Measures the ability to insert numbers in a list in numerical order.

13860
**PSI Basic Skills Tests: Visual Speed and Accuracy.** Ruch, William W.; And Others 1981.
*Descriptors:* *Clerical Occupations; *Occupational Tests; *Office Occupations; *Personnel Selection; *Visual Acuity; Adults; Culture Fair Tests
*Availability:* Psychological Services, Inc., 100 W. Broadway, Ste. 1100, Glendale, CA 91210.
*Notes:* For all the tests in the series, see 13846 through 13865. Time, 5.

One of a series of 20 practical, brief personnel selection tests. Designed to aid personnel managers in business, industry, and government in the selection and placement of employees. Test content was constructed to be bias-free. Validated against job performance in a nationwide survey. Measures the ability to see differences in small details.

**13861**
**PSI Basic Skills Tests: Memory.** Ruch, William W.; And Others 1981.
*Descriptors:* *Clerical Occupations; *Occupational Tests; *Office Occupations; *Personnel Selection; *Short Term Memory; Adults; Culture Fair Tests
*Availability:* Psychological Services, Inc., 100 W. Broadway, Ste. 1100, Glendale, CA 91210.
*Notes:* For all the tests in the series, see 13846 through 13865. Time, 10.

One of a series of 20 practical, brief personnel selection tests. Designed to aid personnel managers in business, industry, and government in the selection and placement of employees. Test content was constructed to be bias-free. Validated against job performance in a nationwide survey. Measures the ability to recall information after having a chance to study it.

**13862**
**PSI Basic Skills Tests: Typing, Practice Copy.** Ruch, William W.; And Others 1981.
*Descriptors:* *Clerical Occupations; *Occupational Tests; *Office Occupations; *Personnel Selection; *Typewriting; Adults; Culture Fair Tests
*Availability:* Psychological Services, Inc., 100 W. Broadway, Ste. 1100, Glendale, CA 91210.
*Notes:* For all the tests in the series, see 13846 through 13865. Time, 2.

One of a series of 20 practical, brief personnel selection tests. Designed to aid personnel managers in business, industry, and government in the selection and placement of employees. Test content was constructed to be bias-free. Validated against job performance in a nationwide survey. Unscored exercise designed as a warm-up and to familiarize examinees with the typewriter. Must be administered before any of the 3 typing tests.

**13863**
**PSI Basic Skills Tests: Typing, Straight Copy.** Ruch, William W.; And Others 1981.
*Descriptors:* *Clerical Occupations; *Occupational Tests; *Office Occupations; *Personnel Selection; *Typewriting; Adults; Culture Fair Tests
*Availability:* Psychological Services, Inc., 100 W. Broadway, Ste. 1100, Glendale, CA 91210.
*Notes:* For all the tests in the series, see 13846 through 13865. Time, 5.

One of a series of 20 practical, brief personnel selection tests. Designed to aid personnel managers in business, industry, and government in the selection and placement of employees. Test content was constructed to be bias-free. Validated against job performance in a nationwide survey. Measures the ability to type straight copy, word-for-word, with no revisions.

**13864**
**PSI Basic Skills Tests: Typing, Revised Copy.** Ruch, William W.; And Others 1981.
*Descriptors:* *Clerical Occupations; *Occupational Tests; *Office Occupations; *Personnel Selection; *Typewriting; Adults; Culture Fair Tests
*Availability:* Psychological Services, Inc., 100 W. Broadway, Ste. 1100, Glendale, CA 91210.
*Notes:* For all the tests in the series, see 13846 through 13865. Time, 5.

One of a series of 20 practical, brief personnel selection tests. Designed to aid personnel managers in business, industry, and government in the selection and placement of employees. Test content was constructed to be bias-free. Validated against job performance in a nationwide survey. Measures the ability to type copy with handwritten corrections and changes.

**13865**
**PSI Basic Skills Tests: Typing, Tables.** Ruch, William W.; And Others 1981.
*Descriptors:* *Clerical Occupations; *Occupational Tests; *Office Occupations; *Personnel Selection; *Typewriting; Adults; Culture Fair Tests
*Availability:* Psychological Services, Inc., 100 W. Broadway, Ste. 1100, Glendale, CA 91210.
*Notes:* For all the tests in the series, see 13846 through 13865. Time, 7.

One of a series of 20 practical, brief personnel selection tests. Designed to aid personnel managers in business, industry, and government in the selection and placement of employees. Test content was constructed to be bias-free. Validated against job performance in a nationwide survey. Measures the ability to set up and type tables according to specific directions.

**13895**
**American Institute of Certified Planners Comprehensive Planning Examination.** American Institute of Certified Planners, Washington, DC 1982.
*Descriptors:* *Administration; *Certification; *Occupational Tests; *Planning; Adults; Knowledge Level; Urban Planning
*Identifiers:* *Planners
*Availability:* American Institute of Certified Planners, 1776 Massachusetts Ave., N.W., Washington, DC 20036.
*Notes:* Time, 180.

This examination is designed for certifying the applicant's knowledge and skills in planning as a measure of membership eligibility. The test covers history and theory of human settlement; planning theory and practice; interrelationships among components of planning; ability to formulate goals, identify needs, and develop and implement strategies and plans; sensitivity to political and social constraints; analytical methods; logic abilities; and management skills. To qualify for certification, the candidate must be a member of the American Planning Association, must currently engage in professional planning as defined by AICP, and must have had specified education and/or professional planning experience.

**13922**
**American Society of Plumbing Engineers Certified in Plumbing Engineering Program.** American Society of Plumbing Engineers, Sherman Oaks, CA 1982.
*Descriptors:* *Certification; *Occupational Tests; *Plumbing; Administration; Adults; Building Trades; Construction Industry; Design; Engineering; Knowledge Level
*Availability:* ASPE Certification Program, Educational Testing Service, P.O. Box 2890, Princeton, NJ 08541.
*Notes:* Time, 210. Items, 100.

The Certified in Plumbing Engineering Program was developed to provide professional recognition to qualified individuals who design plumbing systems. The examination is a multiple-choice test that covers gathering information, administration, design, specifications, and construction services. The test measures the knowledge and skills essential to performing the job of plumbing engineer.

**13939**
**Job Characteristics Index.** Sims, Henry P. Jr. 1976.
*Descriptors:* *Job Satisfaction; *Occupational Information; Adults; Feedback; Interpersonal Relationship; Personal Autonomy; Rating Scales; Work Environment
*Availability:* *Academy of Management Journal,* v19 n2 p195-211, Jun 1976.
*Notes:* Items, 37.

A 5-point frequency scale designed to investigate 6 job characteristics related to job satisfaction: variety, autonomy, task identity, feedback, dealing with others, and friendship opportunities. Respondents indicate the degree to which each characteristic is present in their job.

**13953**
**Career Motivation Achievement Planning.** Farmer, Helen; And Others 1981.
*Descriptors:* *Attitude Measures; *Career Choice; *Career Planning; *High School Students; Achievement Need; Attribution Theory; Employed Women; High Schools; Individual Characteristics; Motivation; Occupational Aspiration; Persistence; Personality Traits; Secondary Education; Self Concept; Socioeconomic Status
*Identifiers:* CMAP; Independent Behavior
*Availability:* ERIC Document Reproduction Service, 7420 Fullerton Rd., Ste. 110, Springfield, VA 22153-2852 (ED236388, 275 pages).
*Notes:* Time, 40. Items, 109.

A paper and pencil career planning instrument that considers motivational, background, environmental, and personality factors. Students indicate level of agreement/disagreement with given statements and estimate their own level of verbal and mathematical ability. There are 19 subscale scores. Many of the scales are adaptations of instruments by Spence and Helmreich, Bem, and Super. C-MAP is designed to measure long-range commitment to an occupational life role, short-range motivation to achieve at a particular task, and level of aspiration and education.

**14006**
**Supervisory Practices Inventory, Form A.** Canfield, Judith S.; Canfield, Albert A. 1981.
*Descriptors:* *Supervisory Methods; Administrator Attitudes; Adults; Business Administration; Occupational Tests; Supervision
*Availability:* Humanics Media, 5457 Pine Cone Rd., La Crescenta, CA 92124.
*Notes:* Items, 20.

Designed to measure the emphasis that administrators place on people, the task, or achieving results when supervising and whether a laissez-faire, democratic, or autocratic style is predominant. A "dissonance score" also shows whether administrators see themselves as functioning in a way they prefer or far from their own ideal of an administrator.

**14023**
**American Electrolysis Association Certification Examination.** American Electrolysis Association, East Providence, RI 1985.
*Descriptors:* *Certification; Adults; Occupational Tests
*Identifiers:* *Electrolysis
*Availability:* Educational Testing Service, Center for Occupational and Professional Assessment, Princeton, NJ 08541.

A national program for certifying electrologists, administered at testing centers. Covers knowledge and skills important for an entry-level electrologist.

**14033**
**School Board Development Questionnaire.** Neubauer, Antonia; National School Boards Association, Alexandria, VA 1980.
*Descriptors:* *Boards of Education; *Inservice Education; *Professional Development; Adults; Elementary Secondary Education; Job Skills; Questionnaires; Rating Scales
*Availability:* ERIC Document Reproduction Service, 7420 Fullerton Rd., Ste. 110, Springfield, VA 22153-2852 (ED193789, 20 pages).
*Notes:* Items, 36.

A questionnaire designed to elicit information on the kinds of activities school board members participate in to learn more about skills and knowledge important for effective service on a school board. The respondents also rate their level of skill in 15 areas said to be vital for effective board service.

**14041**
**The Self-Directed Search, Revised.** Holland, John L. 1985.

*Descriptors:* *Adolescents; *Adults; *Interest Inventories; *Reading Difficulties; *Vocational Interests; Career Counseling; Computer Assisted Testing; Computer Software; Majors (Students); Microcomputers; Self Evaluation (Individuals)
*Identifiers:* SDS; Self Administered Tests
*Availability:* Psychological Assessment Resources, Inc., P.O. Box 998, Odessa, FL 33556.
*Notes:* Time, 50 approx. Items, 228.

Self-administered, self-scored, and self-interpreted vocational interest inventory based on Holland's theory of careers. Developed for 2 major purposes: to increase the number of people a counselor can serve and to provide vocational counseling to those who need minimum counseling or do not have access to a counselor. Individual completes the assessment booklet and obtains a 3-letter occupational code. Code is then used to locate suitable occupations in the Occupations Finder booklet. May also be computer-administered using an Apple II+ or IIe or an IBM/PC. A new booklet is available that compares Holland summary codes to college majors.

**14042**
**The Self-Directed Search, Revised, Form E.** Holland, John L. 1985.
*Descriptors:* *Adolescents; *Adults; *Interest Inventories; *Reading Difficulties; *Vocational Interests; Career Counseling; Self Evaluation (Individuals)
*Identifiers:* SDS
*Availability:* Psychological Assessment Resources, Inc., P.O. Box 998, Odessa, FL 33556.

Self-administered, self-scored, and self-interpreted vocational counseling tool. Form E is for the benefit of those with limited reading ability, and the vocabulary employed is at the 4th grade reading level. This is a vocational interest inventory based on Holland's theory of careers. Individual completes the assessment booklet and obtains a 2-letter occupational code. Code is then used to locate suitable occupations in the Jobs Finder booklet.

**14054**
**Fogel Word Processing Operator Test.** Fogel, Max 1983.
*Descriptors:* *Occupational Tests; *Personnel Selection; *Word Processing; Adults; Individual Testing; Screening Tests
*Availability:* Association of Information Systems Professionals, 1015 N. York Rd., Willow Grove, PA 19090.
*Notes:* Time, 45 approx.

A paper and pencil test used to screen candidates who may be successful word processors. Useful for employee selection and placement. Includes sections on problem solving, regrouping, vocabulary, proofreading, figural transformations, mechanical spatial relationships, and personality. Author claims test satisfies all current employment laws and equal opportunity regulations.

**14058**
**System of Interactive Guidance Information, Plus.** Educational Testing Service, Princeton, NJ 1984.
*Descriptors:* *Career Exploration; *Career Guidance; *Career Planning; *Computer Assisted Testing; Adolescents; Adults; Job Skills; Microcomputers; Minicomputers; Vocational Interests
*Identifiers:* SIGI Plus; Work Values
*Availability:* Educational Testing Service, Princeton, NJ 08541.

An interactive software program for career guidance and information. Evaluates and integrates user's work-related values, interests, and skills to generate a list of suitable occupations based on these factors and level of education. Useful for those planning, entering, reentering, or changing occupations. Can be customized to include local information. Occupational information is updated annually. Also provides information, such as income and skills required, on selected occupations. For use with IBM-PC, IBM-PC-XT, PC/AT, highly compatible microcomputers, TRS-80, and VAX 11/780. Leased to users on an annual basis.

**14062**
**Power Base Inventory.** Thomas, Kenneth W. 1985.
*Descriptors:* *Supervisors; *Supervisory Methods; Administrators; Adults; Authoritarianism; Discipline; Managerial Occupations; Measures (Individuals); Rewards
*Identifiers:* *Power; Power Base
*Availability:* XICOM, Inc., Sterling Forest, Woods Rd., Tuxedo, NY 10987.
*Notes:* Items, 30.

This inventory is a measure of managerial power styles: information giving, expertise, goodwill, authority, reward, or discipline. Power is defined as the ability to influence people, either by "personal power" or "position power." Validated with 300 managers to provide norms. Respondents select whichever of 2 statements is more descriptive of the reasons why subordinates might comply with their wishes or beliefs.

**14071**
**Oliver Organization Description Questionnaire.** Oliver, John E. 1981.
*Descriptors:* *Organizational Theories; Adults; Horizontal Organization; Participative Decision Making; Professional Occupations; Questionnaires; Vertical Organization
*Identifiers:* Miner (John B); OODQ
*Availability:* Organizational Measurement Systems Press, P.O. Box 1656, Buffalo, NY 14221.
*Notes:* Items, 43.

A questionnaire that describes an organization or work group as hierarchical, professional, task oriented, or group oriented according to the theories of John B. Miner. Used to assess the extent to which each of the 4 organizational styles is present in the organization.

**14073**
**Miner Sentence Completion Scale, Form P.** Miner, John B. 1981.
*Descriptors:* *Employee Attitudes; *Motivation; *Projective Measures; Adults; College Faculty; Counseling; Employees; Occupational Tests; Professional Occupations; Work Attitudes
*Availability:* Organizational Measurement Systems Press, P.O. Box 1656, Buffalo, NY 14221.
*Notes:* Items, 40.

A measure of an individual's professional motivation. Used for employee counseling and organizational development. Normative data derive from a sample of professors in business schools involved in teaching, writing, and consulting.

**14085**
**Occupational Interest Check List.** Esdata and Associates 1984.
*Descriptors:* *Adults; *Computer Assisted Testing; *High School Students; *Interest Inventories; *Vocational Interests; Career Choice; High Schools; Rating Scales
*Identifiers:* OICL
*Availability:* Integrated Professional Systems, 5211 Mahoning Ave., Ste. 135, Youngstown, OH 44515.
*Notes:* Items, 198.

Vocational interest inventory designed to assist adolescents and adults in making career and vocational decisions. Computer program generates a profile of 12 interest areas together with a description of those interest areas recommended for further exploration. Also provides common occupations in work groups designated for further exploration. Computer-assisted test which may be used for either online or offline administration. The software is available to qualified professionals on a lease basis for either Apple or OSI computers.

**14086**
**Career and Vocational Interest Inventory.** Esdata and Associates 1984.
*Descriptors:* *Career Guidance; *Computer Assisted Testing; *Educational Counseling; *High School Students; *Interest Inventories; *Vocational Interests; Adolescents; Adults; High Schools
*Identifiers:* CVII
*Availability:* Integrated Professional Systems, 5211 Mahoning Ave., Ste. 135, Youngstown, OH 44515.
*Notes:* Items, 162.

Educational and career guidance instrument to assist high school students and adults in making educational and/or career decisions. Scores are provided on the 6 Holland theme scales, 12 interest areas, and several other scales. Computer-assisted test that uses the Integrated Professional Systems (IPS) program for either online or offline administration. The computer program is available to qualified professionals on a lease basis for OSI and Apple computers. Users must also have IN-PROS, the IPS disk operating system, and pay an initial fee.

**14102**
**NTE Specialty Area Tests: Special Education.** Educational Testing Service, Princeton, NJ 1985.
*Descriptors:* *Achievement Tests; *Special Education; *Special Education Teachers; *Teacher Certification; *Teacher Education Programs; *Teacher Selection; College Students; Graduate Students; Higher Education; Instruction; Learning Processes; Student Needs; Teachers; Teaching Methods
*Availability:* NTE Programs, Educational Testing Service, CN 6051, Princeton, NJ 08541-6051.
*Notes:* Time, 120.

Part of a standardized, secure measure of academic achievement for college students in, or completing, teacher education programs. Used by associations, school systems, state agencies, and institutions for decisions about the certification and selection of teachers. One of 28 tests measuring understanding of the content and methods applicable to teaching in subject areas. The test is intended for those students in teacher education programs in special education at elementary, middle, and high school levels. The test focuses on the examinee's understanding of the processes of teaching and learning and the specific neeeds of special education students in general. A specialty area test in education for mentally retarded students is also available (11842).

**14136**
**PSI Management Selection System.** Psychological Services International, Westborough, MA 1985.
*Descriptors:* *Managerial Occupations; *Personnel Selection; Adults; Background; Employment; Occupational Tests; Personality Measures
*Identifiers:* Test Batteries
*Availability:* Psychological Services International, 2000 W. Park Dr., P.O. Box 5000, Westborough, MA 01581-5000.
*Notes:* Items, 500.

Designed to select employees for management positions. Includes a personal history summary, a mental ability test, a management history test, and a personality measure to provide data on integrity, maturity, motivation, insight, and interpersonal style. The Wonderlic Personnel Test (404) is used to measure mental ability.

**14138**
**Pre-Professional Skills Test.** Educational Testing Service, Princeton, NJ 1984.
*Descriptors:* *Achievement Tests; *Basic Skills; *Mathematics; *Reading Tests; *Writing Skills; Admission (School); Adults; Certification; College Students; Higher Education; Multiple Choice Tests; Personnel Selection; Professional Occupations; Teachers
*Identifiers:* PPST; Writing Samples

*Availability:* PPST Program, Educational Testing Service, CN-6057, Princeton, NJ 08541-6057.
*Notes:* Time, 150. Items, 126.

Three separate tests designed to measure basic proficiency of those preparing to be teachers. May be used for selection, admissions, evaluation, and certification. Each test is multiple choice except the writing test, which also has one essay item (30 minutes). Each test provides only a total score ranging from 150 to 190. For use by school districts, colleges, state agencies, licensing boards, and employers. The test is administered on a date specified by the user and is scored by ETS.

**14141**
**The Stanton Inventory.** Stanton Corp., Chicago, IL 1985.
*Descriptors:* *Employee Responsibility; *Employees; *Stealing; Adults; Questionnaires; Work Environment
*Availability:* Stanton Corp., 417 Dearborn St., Chicago, IL 60605.

A questionnaire completed by employees to help identify company problems and those responsible for problems. Used also to detect theft and employee dishonesty. Covers employee's personal history, attitudes toward other employees, supervision and morale, personal attitude, social history, and company information.

**14142**
**Stanton Case Review.** Stanton Corp., Chicago, IL 1985.
*Descriptors:* *Case Studies; *Employee Responsibility; *Employees; Adults; Work Environment
*Availability:* Stanton Corp., 417 Dearborn St., Chicago, IL 60605.

Each booklet is prepared in response to a particular incident that occurred in an organization. A criminologist asks employees questions about the incident and then describes the incident in a few sentences. Employees then fill out a questionnaire based on the particular incident in order to try to pinpoint people responsible.

**14148**
**Inventory of Career Attitudes.** Pinkney, James W.; Ramirez, Marty 1985.
*Descriptors:* *Attitude Measures; *Career Planning; *Cultural Traits; *High School Students; *Mexican Americans; *Student Attitudes; High Schools; Rating Scales
*Identifiers:* *Chicanos; ICA
*Availability:* *Journal of College Student Personnel,* v26 n4 p300-05, Jul 1985.
*Notes:* Items, 28.

Developed to study the career-planning assumptions and beliefs of Chicano high school students and the cultural influences that affect their career-planning process. Findings from using the inventory in a research study indicated Chicano students were less realistic in their career-planning attitudes than were white students.

**14311**
**Assessment of Career Decision Making.** Buck, Jacqueline N.; Daniels, M. Harry 1985.
*Descriptors:* *Adults; *Career Choice; *College Students; *Decision Making; *Secondary School Students; Adolescents; Higher Education; Objective Tests; Questionnaires; Secondary Education
*Identifiers:* ACDM; Self Report Measures
*Availability:* Western Psychological Services, 12031 Wilshire Blvd., Los Angeles, CA 90025.
*Notes:* Items, 94.

A self-report measure that measures a student's career decision-making style and progress on 3 decision-making tasks. The decision-making style scales assess the strategy or combination of strategies a student uses in making decisions. The decision-making tasks scales assess a student's degree of overall satisfaction with his or her school, level of peer involvement, and degree of interaction with instructors, as well as degree of commitment or certainty the student feels toward a choice of future occupation choice of a major or field of study. This inventory is intended to assess a student's current stage in the career decision-making process. It does not provide information on an individual's vocational interests or abilities. Inventory is based on Harren's model of career decision making.

**14329**
**E.S. Survey: Emotional Status Survey.** Cormack, Robert W.; Strand, Alan L. 1983.
*Descriptors:* *Attitude Measures; *Job Applicants; *Mental Health; *Personality Traits; *Personnel Selection; Adults; Police; Psychological Evaluation; Security Personnel
*Identifiers:* PASS; Personnel Assessment Selection System
*Availability:* Psychological Surveys Corp., 900 Jorie Blvd., Ste. 130, Oak Brook, IL 60521.
*Notes:* For related documents, see also T.A. Survey: Trustworthiness Attitude Survey (14328) and A.I. Survey: Alienation Index Survey (14330). Time, 10 approx. Items, 101.

A self-report psychological survey to evaluate the emotional stability of job applicants. Designed specifically for applicants for sensitive positions. Can be administered, scored, and interpreted in-house by personnel or human resource specialists licensed by test publisher. Test was determined to be highly job-related for police and security positions. May be used in combination with A.I. Survey and T.A. Survey in the Personnel Assessment Selection System (PASS).

**14330**
**A.I. Survey: Alienation Index Survey.** Cormack, Robert W.; Strand, Alan L. 1982.
*Descriptors:* *Alienation; *Attitude Measures; *Job Applicants; *Personality Traits; *Personnel Selection; Adults; Psychological Evaluation
*Identifiers:* PASS; Personnel Assessment Selection System
*Availability:* Psychological Surveys Corp., 900 Jorie Blvd., Ste. 130, Oak Brook, IL 60521.
*Notes:* For related instruments, see also T.A. Survey: Trustworthiness Attitude Survey (14328) and E.S. Survey: Emotional Status Survey (14329). Items, 52.

Designed to identify alienated attitudes of job applicants toward employers, supervisors, coworkers, work conditions, and benefits and salary. A pre-employment survey designed to be administered, scored, and interpreted by personnel or human resources staff licensed by the test publisher. May be used in combination with T.A. Survey and E.S. Survey in the Personnel Assessment Selection System (PASS). Or may be used with T.A. Survey in the Personnel Assessment Selection System II (PASS II). There is also a Personnel Assessment Selection System III with youth norms that consists of a no-template, instant, graded 100-question digest of the T.A. Survey, A.I. Survey, and additional D.A. (Drug Attitude) questions designed as a projective attitude trust-risk screening instrument for part-time/hourly candidates.

**14341**
**Kilmann-Saxton Culture-Gap Survey.** Kilmann, Ralph H.; Saxton, Mary J. 1983.
*Descriptors:* *Cultural Influences; *Group Dynamics; *Work Attitudes; Adults; Attitude Measures; Group Behavior; Social Values
*Availability:* XICOM, Inc., Sterling Forest, Woods Rd., Tuxedo, NY 10987.
*Notes:* Items, 28.

A measure of the social and motivational factors present in the environment of a work group. Items cover intergroup communication, socializing within the group, peer pressure to conform, receptivity to change, fair division of work tasks, and competition. Used to identify forces outside of policies and rules that affect work group morale and performance.

**14361**
**Small Business Assessment.** Rensis Likert Associates, Inc., Ann Arbor, MI 1984.
*Descriptors:* *Attitude Measures; *Organizational Climate; *Small Businesses; Adults; Employee Attitudes; Group Dynamics; Job Satisfaction; Supervisory Methods
*Availability:* Rensis Likert Associates, Inc., 3001 S. State St., Ste. 401, Ann Arbor, MI 48104.
*Notes:* Items, 60.

An inventory derived from Likert's Survey of Organizations (12028), designed to measure organizational climate, including group functioning, supervisory leadership, and job satisfaction. Items are general and could be applied to many types of businesses.

**14408**
**Teacher Stress Inventory.** Fimian, Michael J. 1985.
*Descriptors:* *Special Education Teachers; *Stress Variables; Adults; Special Education; Teachers
*Identifiers:* Occupational Stress
*Availability:* *Techniques,* v1 n4 p270-85, Apr 1985.
*Notes:* Items, 30.

Developed to assess occupational stress in teachers of exceptional students. Consists of 6 subscale stress factors for each of 2 measures, strength and frequency. Subscales are categorized as either sources or manifestations of stress. Items were generated from a review of the literature and rated for relevancy by stress workshop presenters, researchers, and authors.

**14425**
**The Major-Minor Finder (1986-1996), Revised.** Cutler, Arthur; And Others 1986.
*Descriptors:* *College Bound Students; *Interest Inventories; *Majors (Students); *Student Interests; Adolescents; Adults; College Students; Higher Education; Self Evaluation (Individuals); Two Year College Students; Undergraduate Students; Vocational Interests
*Availability:* CFKR Career Materials, Inc., 11860 Kemper Rd., Unit 7, Auburn, CA 95603.
*Notes:* Time, 40 approx.

Designed to take student or subject through a decision-making process that includes self-assessment of basic interests and aptitudes, matching of majors with those interests and aptitudes, exploration of career opportunities closely related to college majors, and a choice of the most suitable major. This revision is designed to meet the needs of 4-year and 2-year college students and career planning offices. It has also been replicated for microcomputer use.

**14426**
**Job-O (1985-1995), Revised.** Cutler, Arthur; And Others 1985.
*Descriptors:* *Interest Inventories; *Self Evaluation (Individuals); *Spanish; *Vocational Interests; Adolescents; Adults; Career Awareness; Career Exploration
*Identifiers:* Judgment of Occupational Behavior Orientation
*Availability:* CFKR Career Materials, Inc., 11860 Kemper Rd., Unit 7, Auburn, CA 95603.
*Notes:* Time, 65 approx.

Exploratory instrument whose primary purpose is to facilitate self-awareness, career awareness, and career exploration. Updated biennially. Can be used on all educational levels and can be administered in classes, as a group activity, or individually. May be used to enhance self-awareness and career awareness at the intermediate school level or to make final job decisions at the secondary, college, and adult levels. Also available in Spanish.

**14432**
**Hogan Personnel Selection Series: Sales Potential Inventory.** Hogan, Robert; Hogan, Joyce 1985.

*Descriptors:* *Career Counseling; *Personnel Selection; *Salesmanship; *Sales Occupations; *Screening Tests; Adults; Interpersonal Competence; Job Applicants; Motivation; Objective Tests; Values
*Availability:* National Computer Systems, Professional Assessment Services, P.O. Box 1416, Minneapolis, MN 55440.
*Notes:* Items, 218.

Used to assist psychologists and personnel professionals in personnel screening and vocational counseling settings. Assesses interpersonal attitudes, values, and motivations to help predict and identify types of people who will perform well in various roles in an organization. Vocational counselors can use the inventory to evaluate the effectiveness of training in specialized areas and to help an individual's vocational development in specific occupational areas. The Sales Potential subtest aids in identifying individuals who are persistent, persuasive, socially skilled, and self-starting.

**14433**
**Hogan Personnel Selection Series: Managerial Potential Inventory.** Hogan, Robert; Hogan, Joyce 1985.
*Descriptors:* *Career Counseling; *Managerial Occupations; *Personnel Selection; *Screening Tests; Adults; Decision Making Skills; Interpersonal Competence; Job Applicants; Leadership Qualities; Motivation; Objective Tests; Values
*Identifiers:* HPSS
*Availability:* National Computer Systems, Professional Assessment Services, P.O. Box 1416, Minneapolis, MN 55440.
*Notes:* Items, 223.

Used to assist psychologists and personnel professionals in personnel screening and vocational counseling settings. Assesses interpersonal attitudes, values, and motivations to help predict and identify types of people who will perform well in various roles in an organization. Vocational counselors can use the inventory to evaluate the effectiveness of training in specialized areas and to help an individual's vocational development in specific occupational areas. Managerial Potential subtest identifies individuals with leadership ability, planning, and decision-making skills.

**14434**
**Hogan Personnel Selection Series: Clerical Potential Inventory.** Hogan, Robert; Hogan, Joyce 1985.
*Descriptors:* *Career Counseling; *Clerical Occupations; *Personnel Selection; *Screening Tests; Adults; Interpersonal Competence; Job Applicants; Motivation; Objective Tests; Values
*Identifiers:* HPSS
*Availability:* National Computer Systems, Professional Assessment Services, P.O. Box 1416, Minneapolis, MN 55440.
*Notes:* Items, 215.

Used to assist psychologists and personnel professionals in personnel screening and vocational counseling settings. Assesses interpersonal attitudes, values, and motivations to help predict and identify types of people who will perform well in various roles in an organization. Vocational counselors can use the inventory to evaluate the effectiveness of training in specialized areas and to help an individual's vocational development in specific occupational areas. The Clerical Potential subtest identifies individuals willing to follow directions, pay attention to details, and communicate accurately and well. This scale is associated with overall rated performance in clerical jobs and reflects individuals who show compliance, maturity, and industriousness.

**14435**
**Hogan Personnel Selection Series: Prospective Employee Potential Inventory.** Hogan, Robert; Hogan, Joyce 1985.
*Descriptors:* *Career Counseling; *Personnel Selection; *Screening Tests; Adults; Interpersonal Competence; Job Applicants; Motivation; Objective Tests; Values
*Identifiers:* HPSS
*Availability:* National Computer Systems, Professional Assessment Services, P.O. Box 1416, Minneapolis, MN 55440.
*Notes:* Items, 198.

Used to assist psychologists and personnel professionals in personnel screening and vocational counseling settings. Assesses interpersonal attitudes, values, and motivations to help predict and identify types of people who will perform well in various roles in an organization. Vocational counselors can use the inventory to evaluate the effectiveness of training in specialized areas and to help an individual's vocational development in specific occupational areas.

**14443**
**Trainer Type Inventory.** Wheeler, Mardy; Marshall, Jeanie
*Descriptors:* *Trainers; *Training Methods; Adults; Professional Development; Rating Scales
*Identifiers:* TTI
*Availability:* Pfeiffer, J. William, Goodstein, Leonard D., eds., *The 1986 Annual: Developing Human Resources.* San Diego: University Associates, 1986. Pfeiffer and Co., formerly University Associates, 8517 Production Ave., San Diego, CA 92121-2280.
*Notes:* Items, 12.

Designed to help trainers determine their preferred training methods in order to identify areas in which they have the greatest skill and expertise to share with other trainers and areas in which they need to increase their skills. Inventory describes 4 training approaches, categorized as listener, director, interpreter, or coach. This inventory is intended for professional development work and not for in-depth personal growth, psychodiagnostic, or therapeutic work. The instrument is contained in *The 1986 Annual: Developing Human Resources.*

**14445**
**Supervisory and Leadership Beliefs Questionnaire.** Rao, T. Venkateswara
*Descriptors:* *Administrator Attitudes; *Attitude Measures; *Leadership Styles; *Self Evaluation (Individuals); *Supervisory Methods; Adults; Professional Development; Rating Scales
*Availability:* Pfeiffer, J. William, and Goodstein, Leonard D., eds., *The 1986 Annual: Developing Human Resources.* San Diego: University Associates, 1986. Pfeiffer and Co., formerly University Associates, 8517 Production Ave., San Diego, CA 92121-2280.
*Notes:* Items, 9.

A rating scale used to determine a supervisor's style of supervising and interacting with subordinates. Scores are indicative of the strength of the beliefs or orientations underlying each of 3 styles: benevolent, critical, or self-dispensing. This inventory is intended for professional development work and not for in-depth personal growth, psychodiagnostic, or therapeutic work. The instrument is contained in *The 1986 Annual: Developing Human Resources.*

**14446**
**Motivational Analysis of Organizations—Behavior.** Pareek, Udai
*Descriptors:* *Administrator Characteristics; *Attitude Measures; *Employee Attitudes; *Interprofessional Relationship; *Work Environment; Adults; Professional Development; Rating Scales
*Identifiers:* MAOB
*Availability:* Pfeiffer, J. William, and Goodstein, Leonard D., eds., *The 1986 Annual: Developing Human Resources.* San Diego: University Associates, 1986. Pfeiffer and Co., formerly University Associates, 8517 Production Ave., San Diego, CA 92121-2280.
*Notes:* Items, 60.

Enables respondents to identify which of 6 primary factors motivates their behavior in their organizational settings. Instrument can be used in managerial and supervisory training, as part of a human resource development or team-building program, and for personal growth and development. It is not intended for in-depth personal awareness, psychodiagnostic, or therapeutic work. Can also be used in organization development and consulting work to obtain group profiles, to search for organizational factors to explain the profiles, to develop organizational strategies to improve the profiles, and to develop individual strategies to increase employees' effectiveness. The instrument is contained in *The 1986 Annual: Developing Human Resources.*

**14450**
**Responsibility for Student Achievement Questionnaire.** Guskey, Thomas R. 1981.
*Descriptors:* *Academic Achievement; *Locus of Control; *Teacher Responsibility; Adults; Questionnaires; Student Behavior; Student Responsibility; Teachers
*Identifiers:* RSA
*Availability:* *Journal of Teacher Education,* v32 n3 p44-51, May-Jun 1981.
*Notes:* Items, 30.

A measure of teachers' beliefs concerning the level of responsibility they have for grades that children achieve. Measures beliefs in internal vs external responsibility, for academic achievement and school-related situations. An equal number of positive and negative situations are sampled and separate scores are obtained for beliefs in internal responsibility for classroom success and for classroom failures.

**14461**
**Adult Career Concerns Inventory.** Super, Donald E.; And Others 1985.
*Descriptors:* *Attitude Change; *Career Development; *Interest Inventories; *Vocational Interests; Adults; Midlife Transitions; Self Evaluation (Individuals)
*Identifiers:* ACCI
*Availability:* Consulting Psychologists Press, Inc., 3803 E. Bayshore Rd., Palo Alto, CA 94303.
*Notes:* Items, 61.

Consists of 61 statements of career concerns based on Donald Super's theory of life stages. The stages are exploration, establishment, maintenance, and disengagement. Contains a special scale on career change status. Inventory can be self-scored to yield a profile based on the clusters of career development tasks of most importance to the individual. Inventory may be valuable for counselors in measuring subject's career stage and growth. Researchers may use it to examine the impact of an individual's life stage on such factors as productivity, creativity, and turnover.

**14480**
**Industrial Occupational Competency Testing: Locksmithing.** National Occupational Competency Testing Institute, Big Rapids, MI 1985.
*Descriptors:* *Occupational Tests; *Performance Tests; *Personnel Evaluation; Adults; Job Skills; Knowledge Level; Multiple Choice Tests; Promotion (Occupational); Skilled Workers
*Identifiers:* IOCT; *Locksmiths
*Availability:* National Occupational Competency Testing Institute, 409 Bishop Hall, Ferris State University, Big Rapids, MI 49307.
*Notes:* Time, 300. Items, 125.

A series of tests, customized to fit particular needs, designed to measure occupational competence. For use in industry to test current or prospective employees. There are 2 parts: written and performance. The written section is multiple choice covering keys, cores, and combinations; latching devices; and door closers. The performance test covers installation of the same items.

**14481**
**Industrial Occupational Competency Testing: Glazing.** National Occupational Competency Testing Institute, Big Rapids, MI 1985.
*Descriptors:* *Glaziers; *Occupational Tests; *Performance Tests; *Personnel Evaluation; Adults; Glass; Job Skills; Knowledge Level; Multiple Choice Tests; Promotion (Occupational); Skilled Workers
*Identifiers:* IOCT

*Availability:* National Occupational Competency Testing Institute, 409 Bishop Hall, Ferris State University, Big Rapids, MI 49307.
*Notes:* Time, 310. Items, 126.

A series of tests, customized to fit particular needs, designed to measure occupational competence. For use in industry to test current or prospective employees. There are 2 parts: written and performance. The written section is multiple choice covering preparation of glass, installation, furniture tops, tools, materials, and equipment. The performance test requires the use of tools to remove and replace damaged glass, operation of movable glass partitions, and specialty glass.

**14482**
**Industrial Occupational Competency Testing: Building Trades Maintenance.** National Occupational Competency Testing Institute, Big Rapids, MI 1985.
*Descriptors:* *Building Trades; *Maintenance; *Occupational Tests; *Performance Tests; *Personnel Evaluation; Adults; Job Skills; Knowledge Level; Multiple Choice Tests; Promotion (Occupational)
*Identifiers:* IOCT
*Availability:* National Occupational Competency Testing Institute, 409 Bishop Hall, Ferris State University, Big Rapids, MI 49307.
*Notes:* Time, 360. Items, 106.

A series of tests, customized to fit particular needs, designed to measure occupational competence. For use in industry to test current or prospective employees. There are 2 parts: written and performance. The written section is multiple choice covering steam, excavating, water piping, and sewer piping. The performance test requires demonstration of knowledge of steam traps, valves, construction of a trench, valve repair, and caulking of soil pipe.

**14496**
**International Dance-Exercise Association Foundation Certification Examination.** Educational Testing Service, Princeton, NJ 1986.
*Descriptors:* *Aerobics; *Certification; *Dance; *Occupational Tests; Adults; Knowledge Level; Teachers
*Identifiers:* IDEA
*Availability:* IDEA Foundation, 4501 Mission Bay Dr., Ste. 3A, San Diego, CA 92109.

Designed to test the minimum level of proficiency and knowledge essential for a dance instructor to design a safe and effective class, lead and instruct others in dance exercise, and respond to questions and problems that arise. This certification is for instructors of healthy individuals with no disabilities only. A certificate of proof of knowledge of cardiopulmonary resuscitation is required before the test can be taken.

**14509**
**La Serie de Pruebas de Aptitud Hay.** Hay, Edward N. 1984.
*Descriptors:* *Aptitude Tests; *Clerical Occupations; *Occupational Tests; *Spanish; *Vocational Aptitude; Adults
*Identifiers:* Clerical Skills; Hay Aptitude Test Battery; Numerical Ability; Test Batteries
*Availability:* E.F. Wonderlic Personnel Test, Inc., 820 Frontage Rd., Northfield, IL 60093.
*Notes:* Time, 13.

Spanish version of the Hay Aptitude Test Battery. Battery originally developed to use in selecting applicants for clerical work. Has proved effective in selecting employees in banks, utility firms, and insurance companies. Also proven valid for plant jobs and operating positions. Battery consists of 4 tests: a warm-up test, number perception test, name finding test, and number series completion test.

**14527**
**Strong-Campbell Interest Inventory, Form T325 of the Strong Vocational Interest Blank, Revised.** Hansen, Jo Ida C. 1985.
*Descriptors:* *Adolescents; *Adults; *Interest Inventories; *Vocational Interests; Activities; Career Guidance; Occupations; Recreational Activities; Self Evaluation (Individuals)
*Identifiers:* SCII; Strong Vocational Interest Blank
*Availability:* Consulting Psychologists Press, Inc., 3803 E. Bayshore Rd., Palo Alto, CA 94303.
*Notes:* Time, 35 approx. Items, 325.

Latest edition of the Strong Vocational Interest Blank. Compares a person's interests with the interests of people happily employed in a wide variety of occupations. The test is a measure of interests used chiefly as an aid in making curricular or career decisions. Respondents are scored on 6 general occupational themes, 23 basic interest scales, and 207 occupational scales. The general occupational themes are based on the 6 general occupational personalities proposed by John L. Holland. The basic interest scales measure the strength and consistency of the respondent's interest in specific areas, such as artistic activities. The occupational scales reflect the degree of similarity between the respondent's interests and those of people in particular occupations. There are also scores on 2 special scales that measure introversion-extraversion and degree of comfort in an academic environment, plus 26 administrative indexes that help identify invalid or unusual profiles.

**14530**
**Career Interest and Ability Inventory.** Gonyea, James C. 1983.
*Descriptors:* *Interest Inventories; *Vocational Interests; Adults; Career Guidance; Rating Scales
*Identifiers:* Career Appraisal Service
*Availability:* Chronicle Guidance Publications, Aurora St. Extension, P.O. Box 1190, Moravia, NY 13118-1190.
*Notes:* Items, 256.

Inventory is part of the Chronicle Career Appraisal Service designed to help individuals select a career suited to their interests, abilities, and personalities. Individuals rate both their interest and skills in relation to 256 work statements. Chronical Guidance scores and interprets the answer sheet and sends respondents a 20-page computer analysis outlining the strength of their interests and abilities in 16 major career fields comprising more than 650 of the most popular occupations. In addition, respondents receive recommendations on specific occupations which Chronicle Guidance believes best match their interests and abilities.

**14552**
**Food Protection Certification Test.** Educational Testing Service, Princeton, NJ 1985.
*Descriptors:* *Certification; *Food Service; *Food Standards; *Occupational Tests; Adults; Knowledge Level
*Availability:* Food Protection Certification Program, Educational Testing Service, CN6515, Princeton, NJ 08541-6515.
*Notes:* Items, 60.

A certification exam designed to evaluate the basic knowledge of individuals who have ongoing on-site responsibility for protecting the public from foodborne illness in food preparation, serving, or dispensing establishments. The test emphasizes generally recognized standards, procedures, and practices necessary to protect the public health, safety, and welfare. The multiple-choice test consists of 60 items and covers 3 broad subject areas: purchasing, receiving, and storing food; processing, serving, and dispensing food; and employees, facilities, and equipment.

**14554**
**InnerView Health Assessment.** Irons, John 1985.
*Descriptors:* *Employees; *Needs Assessment; *Physical Health; Adults; Costs; Health Conditions; Health Needs; Hygiene; Insurance; Life Style; Medical Services; Questionnaires
*Availability:* National Computer Systems, Health Assessment Services, P.O. Box 1416, Minneapolis, MN 55440.
*Notes:* Time, 30. Items, 150.

Designed to assess employee behaviors related to health and potential health risks related to their lifestyle. For use by industrial psychologists, human resource professionals, physicians, social workers and other health care professionals to help employers manage rising health care costs by locating employees who are at risk and who are in need of health education programs. There are 3 assessment areas: health risk analysis, lifestyle, and symptoms and health problems. Computer scoring produces a personal health report for the respondent, a health summary for clinical professionals, and a report concerning potential group health needs.

**14577**
**Certified Picture Framer Examination.** Professional Picture Framers Association, Richmond, VA 1986.
*Descriptors:* *Certification; *Occupational Tests; Adults; Knowledge Level
*Identifiers:* *Picture Frames
*Availability:* Professional Picture Framers Association, 4305 Sarellen Rd., Richmond, VA 23231.
*Notes:* Items, 150.

Developed to provide professional recognition to competent individuals engaged in the business of picture framing. Content of examination covers determining customer needs and assessing values, caring for customer property, selecting the nature and quality of materials to be used, and preparing and assembling materials.

**14583**
**Job Activity Preference Questionnaire.** Mecham, Robert C.; And Others 1980.
*Descriptors:* *Interest Inventories; *Vocational Interests; Adolescents; Adults; Career Guidance; Career Planning
*Identifiers:* JAPQ
*Availability:* PAQ Services, Inc., 1625 N. 1000 East, Logan, UT 84321.

Instrument for measuring job interests or preferences. Useful as an aid in career planning and guidance. May be used in counseling and guidance centers in colleges and universities and secondary schools, in personnel departments in business and industry, by administrators of rehabilitation organizations, and others involved in career counseling of older adults, veterans, and others. Inventory is based on a method of work measurement that involves using a standardized questionnaire to rate a position or job in terms of the requirements it makes on the individual. The work-oriented job analysis falls into broad categories of sensory, mental, and/or psychomotor behaviors and tolerances to work contexts. The contexts include the physical, social, and organizational environment in which the job is found.

**14587**
**Problem Management Survey, Revised.** Kolb, David A.; Baker, Richard J. 1984.
*Descriptors:* *Administrator Evaluation; *Supervisory Methods; Adults; Organizational Objectives; Participative Decision Making; Problem Solving; Rating Scales; Self Evaluation (Individuals)
*Identifiers:* PMS
*Availability:* McBer and Co., 137 Newbury St., Boston, MA 02116.
*Notes:* Items, 48.

Measures manager's self-perception and coworkers' perceptions of how the administrator manages the problems and opportunities that arise in his or her job. Survey focuses primarily on 2 complementary modes of effective management: analytic management and intuitive/participative management. Also assesses manager's skills and priorities in 4 stages of the problem-management process: situation analysis, problem analysis, solution analysis, and implementation analysis.

**14589**
**Managerial Style Questionnaire.** McBer and Co., Boston, MA 1981.
*Descriptors:* *Administrators; *Managerial Occupations; *Supervisory Methods; Adults; Human Services; Management Development; Occupational Tests; Self Evaluation (Individuals)

*Identifiers:* *Managerial Style
*Availability:* McBer and Co., 137 Newbury St., Boston, MA 02116.
*Notes:* Time, 20. Items, 36.

A self-report measure that gives the respondents a profile of their perceived managerial style on 6 dimensions: coercive, authoritative, affiliative, democratic, pacesetting, and coaching. The instrument is self-scored and said to be applicable to all levels of managers, from supervisors to upper-level executives. Can be used with human service workers (e.g., social workers) who supervise or influence clients. Used to gather information for management training programs.

**14600**
**Hogan Personality Inventory.** Hogan, Robert 1985.
*Descriptors:* *Personality Measures; *Personality Traits; Adolescents; Adults; Counseling; Personnel Selection; Research Projects
*Identifiers:* Self Administered Tests
*Availability:* National Computer Systems, Professional Assessment Services, P.O. Box 1416, Minneapolis, MN 55440.
*Notes:* Items, 310.

A true-false, self-report inventory that assesses 6 dimensions important for personal and social effectiveness. The 6 primary scales are "intellectance", adjustment, prudence, ambition, sociability, and likeability. Each primary scale is composed of homogeneous item composites, short scales that reflect facets or aspects of the primary scales. The inventory may be used in counseling, research, and personnel selection.

**14601**
**Navy Officer Recruiter Experimental Test Battery.** Borman, Walter C.; And Others 1984.
*Descriptors:* *Military Personnel; *Recruitment; *Screening Tests; Adults; Biographical Inventories; Personality Assessment; Self Evaluation (Individuals); Vocational Interests
*Identifiers:* *Navy; Recruiter Role; Test Batteries
*Availability:* National Technical Information Service, 5285 Port Royal Rd., Springfield, VA 22161 (Document AD-A149243).
*Notes:* Time, 60 approx.

Developed to help identify officers with the personal characteristics necessary for successful recruiting of naval personnel and to assess the effectiveness of incumbent officer recruiters. The test battery consists of 5 parts: a biographical survey, a vocational interests inventory, a personality test, and 2 self-description checklists.

**14614**
**Organizational Change Readiness Scale.** Conner, Daryl R. 1983.
*Descriptors:* *Change Agents; *Employee Attitudes; *Organizational Change; Adults; Diagnostic Tests; Occupational Tests; Readiness
*Identifiers:* OCRS
*Availability:* Pfeiffer and Co., formerly University Associates, 8517 Production Ave., San Diego, CA 92121-2280.
*Notes:* Items, 23.

Designed as an aid in dealing with the human aspects of an organization's adaptation to change. Can be used as a diagnostic tool to determine the overall acceptance level of an organizational change and to identify the resistance factors present that should be addressed when developing an implementation strategy.

**14615**
**Change Agent Skill Evaluation.** Conner, Daryl R.; DeBow, Rita T. 1984.
*Descriptors:* *Change Agents; *Self Evaluation (Individuals); Adults; Competence; Occupational Tests; Organizational Change; Rating Scales; Training
*Availability:* Pfeiffer and Co., formerly University Associates, 8517 Production Ave., San Diego, CA 92121-2280.
*Notes:* Items, 11.

Designed as a self-evaluation tool for change agents, as an assessment method for those who manage the agents' activities, and/or as a means of measuring skill development for those responsible for training agents in the skills necessary to implement change. Eleven factors indicative of change agent competency are rated on a 10-point scale from high to low competency.

**14616**
**Influence Style Survey.** Conner, Daryl R. 1983.
*Descriptors:* *Change Agents; Adults; Leadership Styles; Occupational Tests; Organizational Change; Stress Variables
*Identifiers:* ISS
*Availability:* Pfeiffer and Co., formerly University Associates, 8517 Production Ave., San Diego, CA 92121-2280.
*Notes:* Items, 16.

A measure of a change agent's style of handling or bringing about change in an organization under stressful and nonstressful conditions. Also contains a profile form to identify the target's capacity level for change. Influence styles include directing, coaching, supporting, and delegating.

**14617**
**Problems Encountered When Implementing Management Directives.** Conner, Daryl R. 1985.
*Descriptors:* *Change Agents; *Organizational Change; Adults; Occupational Tests; Problems; Questionnaires
*Availability:* Pfeiffer and Co., formerly University Associates, 8517 Production Ave., San Diego, CA 92121-2280.
*Notes:* Items, 33.

A questionnaire designed to identify symptoms of resistance to change in an organization, including the extent to which people in the organization perceive implementation problems to be a hindering factor in accomplishing assigned tasks and what the specific barriers are that contribute to the problem. The respondent indicates which of a list of barriers represent high, medium, or low problems.

**14618**
**Synergistic Change Survey.** Conner, Daryl R. 1983.
*Descriptors:* *Change Agents; *Interpersonal Competence; *Organizational Change; Adults; Occupational Tests; Surveys
*Availability:* Pfeiffer and Co., formerly University Associates, 8517 Production Ave., San Diego, CA 92121-2280.
*Notes:* Items, 16.

Provides the respondent with information concerning his or her capacity to work with others when implementing an organizational change. The questions are to be answered based on the relationship of the respondent with the individual or group members who are also working toward implementing change on an actual change project.

**14666**
**Career Survey.** American Testronics, Iowa City, IA 1984.
*Descriptors:* *Cognitive Ability; *Interest Inventories; *Secondary School Students; *Vocational Interests; Adults; Career Guidance; Nonverbal Ability; Secondary Education; Verbal Ability
*Availability:* American Testronics, P.O. Box 2270, Iowa City, IA 52244.
*Notes:* Time, 45 approx.

Consists of 2 major parts: the Ohio Career Interest Survey and the Career Ability Survey. The Ohio Career Interest Survey has 12 scales: accommodating/entertaining, humanitarian/caretaking, plant/animal/caretaking, mechanical, business detail, sales, numerical, communications/promotion, science/technology, artistic expression, educational/social, and medical. The ability survey consists of 2 subtests: verbal reasoning (verbal analogies) and nonverbal reasoning (number series and concept relationships). The interest scales were developed by the Ohio State Department of Education and consists of 132 items. The ability scale has 40 items.

**14668**
**Special Educator's Job Satisfaction.** Abelson, A. Geoffrey 1986.
*Descriptors:* *Job Satisfaction; *Special Education Teachers; *Teacher Burnout; Adults; Classroom Techniques; Questionnaires; Student Behavior; Teacher Administrator Relationship; Teachers; Work Environment
*Availability: Educational and Psychological Measurement,* v46 n1 p37-43, Spr 1986.
*Notes:* Items, 73.

This inventory was used with teachers of students who are mentally retarded, learning disabled, emotionally disturbed, and students who have severe disabilities. It was designed to investigate job satisfaction and its relationship to burnout. The inventory covers behavior management skills, administrative relationship and feedback, positive feelings, working conditions, leadership opportunities, authority and control, and relations with the total school.

**14809**
**The OD Kit.** Training House, Inc., Princeton, NJ 1984.
*Descriptors:* *Industrial Training; *Management Development; *Occupational Tests; *Organizational Development; Administrators; Adults; Business Communication; Career Planning; Job Performance; Leadership; Motivation; Needs Assessment; Organizational Climate; Organizational Communication; Personnel Management; Planning; Productivity; Self Evaluation (Groups); Time Management; Vocational Evaluation; Work Attitudes
*Availability:* Training House, Inc., 100 Bear Brook Rd., P.O. Box 3090, Princeton, NJ 08543.

This kit includes assessments, surveys, and self-inventory exercises for use in training sessions; to identify strengths and weaknesses of a work group during the needs analysis that precedes a management development program; and for personnel management and career planning. Instruments cover organizational climate, time management, motivation, leadership, management style, work attitudes, productivity, communication, performance review, job orientation, and career planning goals.

**14810**
**The I.Q. Kit.** Training House, Inc., Princeton, NJ 1984.
*Descriptors:* *Management Development; *Occupational Tests; *Teacher Evaluation; *Trainers; Administrators; Adults; Course Evaluation; Course Organization; Staff Development; Training Methods; Workshops
*Availability:* Training House, Inc., 100 Bear Brook Rd., P.O. Box 3090, Princeton, NJ 08543.

This kit is a collection of exercises, assessments, and forms that can be used in conducting workshops for trainers. Five aspects of training are evaluated: performance of participants on the job, tests in class, effectiveness of course design, effectiveness of instructor, and how well participants like the course. Separate exercises are specifically for trainers of supervisors and managers, both for evaluation of the trainers themselves and for use in training sessions with managers, including measures dealing with sex bias, self-awareness, and communication.

**14812**
**Assessment of Competencies for Instructor Development.** Training House, Inc., Princeton, NJ 1986.
*Descriptors:* *Occupational Tests; *Teacher Effectiveness; *Teachers; *Trainers; Adults; Educational Strategies; Instructional Development; Knowledge Level; Teacher Education; Teaching Methods; Teaching Skills
*Identifiers:* ACID
*Availability:* Training House, Inc., 100 Bear Brook Rd., P.O. Box 3090, Princeton, NJ 08543.

*Notes:* Items, 30.

This inventory is designed to measure 6 competencies important to effectiveness as an instructor: analyzing needs of the learner, specifying outcomes, designing instruction and materials, teaching in the inductive and deductive modes, maintaining an adult-to-adult tone, and remaining learner centered rather than information centered. The test is used with trainers in industrial settings.

**14878**
**Tests for Hiring Office Personnel: Clerical Test.** Healey, Mary 1986.
*Descriptors:* *Clerical Occupations; *Occupational Tests; *Office Occupations; *Personnel Selection; Adults; Arithmetic; Codification; Spelling; Vocabulary
*Availability:* Asher-Gallant Press, 201 Montrose Rd., Westbury, NY 11590.
*Notes:* For complete series, see 14878 through 14891. Items, 85.

This test is part of a series. It measures ability to understand basic words and identify synonyms, perform simple arithmetic, spell everyday words and recognize misspellings, use codes, and proofread words and numbers. The tests are not validated. Suggestions are given for setting up validation procedures to comply with Equal Employment Opportunity (EEO) guidelines.

**14879**
**Tests for Hiring Office Personnel: File Clerk Test.** Healey, Mary 1986.
*Descriptors:* *Clerical Occupations; *Filing; *Occupational Tests; *Office Occupations; *Personnel Selection; Adults; Knowledge Level; Office Practice; Spelling
*Identifiers:* Checking
*Availability:* Asher-Gallant Press, 201 Montrose Rd., Westbury, NY 11590.
*Notes:* For complete series, see 14878 through 14891. Time, 19. Items, 55.

This test is part of a series. It measures familiarity with office procedures and filing systems, as well as the ability to spell everyday words; recognize misspellings; put words, phrases, and names in alphabetic order; and check names and numbers for accuracy. The tests are not validated. Suggestions are given for setting up validation procedures to comply with Equal Employment Oppourtnity (EEO) guidelines.

**14880**
**Tests for Hiring Office Personnel: Typist Test.** Healey, Mary 1986.
*Descriptors:* *Clerical Occupations; *Occupational Tests; *Office Occupations; *Personnel Selection; *Typewriting; Adults; Capitalization (Alphabetic); Punctuation; Spelling
*Availability:* Asher-Gallant Press, 201 Montrose Rd., Westbury, NY 11590.
*Notes:* For complete series, see 14878 through 14891. Time, 25.

This test is part of a series. It consists of exercises requiring typing in a timed situation, typing from a marked manuscript, typing a table, spelling, punctuation, and capitalization. The tests are not validated. Suggestions are given for setting up validation procedures to comply with Equal Employment Opportunity (EEO) guidelines.

**14881**
**Tests for Hiring Office Personnel: Secretarial Test.** Healey, Mary 1986.
*Descriptors:* *Clerical Occupations; *Occupational Tests; *Office Occupations; *Personnel Selection; *Secretaries; *Typewriting; Adults; Business Correspondence; Letters (Correspondence); Spelling; Vocabulary; Writing (Composition)
*Availability:* Asher-Gallant Press, 201 Montrose Rd., Westbury, NY 11590.
*Notes:* For complete series, see 14878 through 14891. Items, 47.

This test is part of a series. It consists of exercises in typing a written letter, typing columns of numbers, selecting a vocabulary word to fill a space in a sentence, and selecting a misspelled word from a group of words. These tests are not validated. Suggestions are given for setting up validation procedures to comply with Equal Employment Opportunity (EEO) guidelines.

**14882**
**Tests for Hiring Office Personnel: Stenographer Test.** Healey, Mary 1986.
*Descriptors:* *Clerical Occupations; *Dictation; *Occupational Tests; *Office Occupations; *Personnel Selection; *Secretaries; *Shorthand; Adults; Business Correspondence; Letters (Correspondence)
*Availability:* Asher-Gallant Press, 201 Montrose Rd., Westbury, NY 11590.
*Notes:* For complete series, see 14878 through 14891. Time, 30.

This test is part of a series. It consists of an exercise in straight typing from dictation and typing of a business letter from dictation. These tests are not validated. Suggestions are given for setting up validation procedures to comply with Equal Employment Opportunity (EEO) guidelines.

**14883**
**Tests for Hiring Office Personnel: Legal Stenographer Test.** Healey, Mary 1986.
*Descriptors:* *Clerical Occupations; *Occupational Tests; *Office Occupations; *Personnel Selection; *Secretaries; Adults; Dictation; Spelling; Vocabulary
*Identifiers:* *Legal Secretaries
*Availability:* Asher-Gallant Press, 201 Montrose Rd., Westbury, NY 11590.
*Notes:* For complete series, see 14878 through 14891. Time, 21. Items, 25.

This test is part of a series. It consists of exercises in selecting correct spellings of legal terms and selecting words to fit given definitions, as well as an actual dictation and typing exercise. These tests are not validated. Suggestions are given for setting up validation procedures to comply with Equal Employment Opportunity (EEO) guidelines.

**14884**
**Tests for Hiring Office Personnel: Accounting Clerk/Bookkeeping Test.** Healey, Mary 1986.
*Descriptors:* *Accounting; *Bookkeeping; *Clerical Occupations; *Occupational Tests; *Office Occupations; *Personnel Selection; Adults; Arithmetic; Problem Solving; Vocabulary
*Availability:* Asher-Gallant Press, 201 Montrose Rd., Westbury, NY 11590.
*Notes:* For complete series, see 14878 through 14891. Time, 34. Items, 84.

This test is part of a series. It consists of exercises in simple math, word problems in arithmetic, multiple-choice questions concerning accounting vocabulary, and problems involving bookkeeping principles. Tests are not validated. Suggestions are given for setting up validation procedures to comply with Equal Employment Opportunity (EEO) guidelines.

**14885**
**Tests for Hiring Office Personnel: Administrative Assistant/Office Manager Test.** Healey, Mary 1986.
*Descriptors:* *Occupational Tests; *Office Management; *Office Occupations; *Personnel Selection; Adults; Arithmetic; Grammar; Language Usage; Vocabulary; Work Sample Tests
*Identifiers:* *Administrative Assistants
*Availability:* Asher-Gallant Press, 201 Montrose Rd., Westbury, NY 11590.
*Notes:* For complete series, see 14878 through 14891. Time, 48. Items, 56.

This test is part of a series. It consists of exercises in simple arithmetic, abbreviations used in a business context, grammar, and a written response to a typical work-related problem. Tests are not validated. Suggestions are given for setting up validation procedures to comply with Equal Employment Opportunity (EEO) guidelines.

**14886**
**Tests for Hiring Office Personnel: Word Processing/Data Entry Test.** Healey, Mary 1986.
*Descriptors:* *Clerical Occupations; *Occupational Tests; *Office Occupations; *Personnel Selection; *Word Processing; Adults; Computers; Data Analysis; Knowledge Level
*Availability:* Asher-Gallant Press, 201 Montrose Rd., Westbury, NY 11590.
*Notes:* For complete series, see 14878 through 14891. Time, 15. Items, 35.

This test is part of a series. Exercises cover knowledge of computer terminology and word processing procedures. Test takers analyze a chart with blank spaces and select data from a list for insertion. These tests are not validated. Suggestions are given for setting up validation procedures to comply with Equal Employment Opportunity (EEO) guidelines.

**14887**
**Tests for Hiring Office Personnel: Telemarketing and Credit Collection Positions.** Healey, Mary 1986.
*Descriptors:* *Occupational Tests; *Office Occupations; *Personnel Selection; *Sales Workers; Adults; Credit (Finance); Work Sample Tests
*Identifiers:* *Credit Collection; *Telemarketing
*Availability:* Asher-Gallant Press, 201 Montrose Rd., Westbury, NY 11590.
*Notes:* For complete series, see 14878 through 14891. Time, 25. Items, 16.

This test is part of a series. It consists of exercises covering sales ability using a prepared script and knowledge about credit and collection procedures. These tests are not validated. Suggestions are given for setting up validation procedures to comply with Equal Employment Opportunity (EEO) guidelines.

**14888**
**Tests for Hiring Office Personnel: Receptionist and Customer Relations Positions.** Healey, Mary 1986.
*Descriptors:* *Occupational Tests; *Office Occupations; *Personnel Selection; *Receptionists; Adults; Business; Knowledge Level; Problem Solving; Work Sample Tests
*Availability:* Asher-Gallant Press, 201 Montrose Rd., Westbury, NY 11590.
*Notes:* For complete series, see 14878 through 14891. Time, 20. Items, 11.

This test is part of a series. It consists of exercises in knowledge of business forms and procedures and resolving problems concerning an unhappy customer and a demanding visitor. These tests are not validated. Suggestions are given for setting up validation procedures to comply with Employment Opportunity (EEO) guidelines.

**14889**
**Tests for Hiring Office Personnel: Editorial Test.** Healey, Mary 1986.
*Descriptors:* *Editing; *Occupational Tests; *Office Occupations; *Personnel Selection; *Proofreading; *Writing (Composition); Adults
*Availability:* Asher-Gallant Press, 201 Montrose Rd., Westbury, NY 11590.
*Notes:* For complete series, see 14878 through 14891. Time, 60.

This test is part of a series. It consists of exercises in handling a creative writing assignment, using editorial skills, and proofreading a typeset document quickly and accurately. These tests are not validated. Suggestions are given for setting up validation procedures to comply with Equal Employment Opportunity (EEO) guidelines.

**14890**
**Tests for Hiring Office Personnel: Job Description Form.** Healey, Mary 1986.
*Descriptors:* *Occupational Information; *Office Occupations; *Personnel Selection; *Records (Forms); Adults; Clerical Occupations
*Identifiers:* *Job Descriptions

*Availability:* Asher-Gallant Press, 201 Montrose Rd., Westbury, NY 11590.
*Notes:* For complete series, see 14878 through 14891.

This form is used as part of a job analysis to describe the duties, skills, and experiences needed. The form should be completed before preparation of a job description and selection of tests for job applicants. It is part of a series of instruments for hiring personnel.

**14891**
**Tests for Hiring Office Personnel: Applicant Evaluation Form.** Healey, Mary 1986.
*Descriptors:* *Clerical Occupations; *Occupational Tests; *Office Occupations; *Personnel Evaluation; *Personnel Selection; *Records (Forms); Adults
*Availability:* Asher-Gallant Press, 201 Montrose Rd., Westbury, NY 11590.
*Notes:* For complete series, see 14878 through 14891.

This form, which allows for summarization of job position requirements and applicant qualifications on one form, is used during an initial interview for hiring. It is part of a series of instruments designed to evaluate applicants' knowledge and skills.

**14892**
**Human Resource Development Report.** Institute for Personality and Ability Testing, Champaign, IL 1986.
*Descriptors:* *Administrator Characteristics; *Administrators; *Personality Assessment; *Personality Measures; Adults; Management Development; Middle Management; Supervisors
*Identifiers:* 16PF; HRDR; IPAT; Stoplight Model
*Availability:* Institute for Personality and Ability Testing, P.O. Box 188, Champaign, IL 61820.
*Notes:* Time, 45 approx. Items, 187.

A 5- to 6-page computer-based analysis of Cattell's Sixteen Personality Factor Questionnaire (an instrument used to measure normal personality traits). The HRDR uses the person's responses to the 16PF to determine how he or she might be expected to function in a managerial position. It focuses on the 5 personality dimensions that have been proven to have the highest potential for yielding job-relevant information: leadership, interaction with others, decision making, initiative, and personal adjustment. Can also be used as personnel development tool by providing insights for guiding individual growth. The HRDR is not intended to establish "ideal" management style characteristics but to find a match between the personal characteristics of the individual and the needs of the position and organization.

**14930**
**American Board of Industrial Hygiene Examination.** American Board of Industrial Hygiene, Lansing, MI
*Descriptors:* *Certification; *Occupational Tests; *Technical Occupations; Adults; Air Pollution; Industrial Personnel; Knowledge Level; Occupational Safety and Health; Radiation; Safety; Toxicology
*Identifiers:* Industrial Hygiene; *Industrial Hygienists
*Availability:* American Board of Industrial Hygienists, 4600 W. Saginaw, Ste. 101, Lansing, MI 48917.
*Notes:* Time, 480.

This testing was designed as part of a voluntary certification program for qualified industrial hygienists, people who already possess college degrees and who have acquired competence in industrial hygiene. Nondegree applicants can be certified under special longevity requirements. The exam is offered at changing locations each spring and each fall. Deadline for application is approximately 4 months prior to exam date. Content may cover air pollution, industrial toxicology, chemistry, physics, protective equipment, radiation, and various topics related to industrial hygiene.

**14931**
**Career Suitability Profile.** Aldershof, Kent L. 1986.
*Descriptors:* *Career Planning; *Personality Measures; *Personality Traits; *Stress Variables; Adults; Employee Attitudes; Entrepreneurship; Occupational Tests; Personnel Selection; Sales Occupations; Vocational Interests; Work Attitudes
*Identifiers:* Honesty
*Availability:* Management Strategies, Inc., 170 Chestnut St., Ste. 2, Ridgewood, NJ 07450.
*Notes:* Items, 70.

This instrument is a personality test designed to determine an employee's potential for performance and suitability for career fields, as well as the type of business in which the individual will function best. A 30-page computer-generated report is provided for the individual. The profile indicates any qualities present or absent to extreme degrees and how the individual deals with stress. It is said to be valid and to correlate with work performance and career suitability.

**14966**
**Certified Occupational Health and Safety Technologist Examination.** American Board of Industrial Hygiene, Lansing, MI 1986.
*Descriptors:* *Certification; *Occupational Safety and Health; *Occupational Tests; *Technical Occupations; Adults; Data Collection; Industrial Training; Inspection; Knowledge Level; Laws; Sciences
*Availability:* American Board of Industrial Hygiene/BCSP Joint Committee, 208 Burwash Ave., Savoy, IL 61874.
*Notes:* Time, 420. Items, 200.

A measure designed for certification of technologists employed in all sectors of the economy and engaged in safety inspections, industrial hygiene monitoring, health and safety training, and occupational accident and illness record keeping functions. Applicants must have 5 years of experience in the field or have an associates degree and 2 years of experience. The exam is given at 25 locations nationwide in the spring and fall. The test is multiple choice.

**15012**
**Individual-Team-Organization Survey.** Anderson, Will 1987.
*Descriptors:* *Attitude Measures; *Employee Attitudes; *Occupational Tests; *Organizational Climate; *Work Environment; Adults; Behavior Patterns; Business Communication; Conflict Resolution; Employee Assistance Programs; Industrial Structure; Interpersonal Communication; Leadership; Planning; Problem Solving; Productivity; Staff Meetings; Stress Variables; Teamwork; Time Management; Work Attitudes
*Identifiers:* ITO; Risk Taking
*Availability:* Pfeiffer, J. William, ed., *The 1987 Annual: Developing Human Resources.* San Diego: University Associates, 1987. Pfeiffer and Co., formerly University Associates, 8517 Production Ave., San Diego, CA 92121-2280.
*Notes:* Items, 56.

Designed to create an awareness of differences in perceptions of employees concerning how various parts of the organization work together through hidden agreements. Items relate to the individual, the team, and the organization. Each respondent indicates the frequency of behaviors related to role clarity, job satisfaction, rewards, communication, collaboration, time management, risk taking, employee assistance, influence, purpose, leadership, meeting effectiveness, conflict management, problem solving, productivity, planning, structure, procedures, climate, and stress.

**15028**
**Oncology Nursing Certification Corporation Examination.** Educational Testing Service, Princeton, NJ
*Descriptors:* *Certification; *Nurses; *Occupational Tests; *Oncology; Adults; Knowledge Level
*Identifiers:* ONCC
*Availability:* Oncology Nursing Certification Corp. Examination, Educational Testing Service, CN-6501, Princeton, NJ 08541-6501.

A multiple-choice test covering 9 subject areas. Designed to measure the general oncology nursing knowledge base of the professional nurse. Items are based on the Oncology Nursing Core Curriculum Task Force of the Oncology Nursing Society. Exam administered each year at the Oncology Nursing Society's Annual Congress.

**15076**
**Dual Employed Coping Scales.** Skinner, Denise A.; McCubbin, Hamilton 1981.
*Descriptors:* *Coping; *Dual Career Family; *Spouses; Adults; Family Relationship; Family Structure; Home Management; Interpersonal Competence; Life Satisfaction; Social Support Groups
*Identifiers:* DECS
*Availability:* McCubbin, Hamilton, Thompson, Anne. *Family Inventories for Research and Practice.* Madison: University of Wisconsin, 1987. Family Stress Coping and Health Project, 1300 Linden Dr., University of Wisconsin, Madison, WI 53706.

Developed to identify coping behaviors that spouses find helpful in managing work and family roles when both spouses are employed outside the home. Five coping patterns covered are maintaining, strengthening, and restructuring the family system; modifying conditions of work/family interface; managing psychological tensions and strains; perceptually controlling the meaning of the lifestyle; and developing interpersonal relationships and support outside the family.

**15083**
**Management Inventory on Modern Management.** Kirkpatrick, Donald L. 1984.
*Descriptors:* *Administrators; *Aptitude Tests; *Attitude Measures; *Job Skills; *Management Development; Adults; Managerial Occupations; Personnel Selection
*Availability:* Dr. Donald L. Kirkpatrick, 1920 Hawthorne Dr., Elm Grove, WI 53122.
*Notes:* Time, 20 approx. Items, 80.

Covers 8 different topics of importance to managers: leadership styles; selecting and training; communicating; motivating; managing change; delegating; decision making; and managing time. There are 10 items for each topic. They cover philosophy, principles, and approaches related to the effective performance of managers. Can be used to determine the need for training, as a tool for conference discussions, to evaluate the effectiveness of a training course, to provide information for on-the-job coaching, and to assist in the selection of managers.

**15096**
**Multiple Management Styles Inventory.** Smith, August William 1987.
*Descriptors:* *Administrators; *Behavior Patterns; *Managerial Occupations; *Supervisory Methods; Administration; Adults; Management Development
*Identifiers:* M2SI; *Management Styles; TIM(M)
*Availability:* Tests in Microfiche, Test Collection, Educational Testing Service, Princeton, NJ 08541.
*Notes:* Items, 50.

Designed to measure the way individual managers relate to various dimensions and approaches to management. The inventory covers managerial style in a particular position, situation, organization, and environment. The manager is assigned to 1 of 5 styles: intervenor (manages by impulse and intervention); implementor (uses order and objectives); initiator (manages by diversity and discontinuity); investigator (uses preparation and prediction); and integrator, one who bridges the other managerial styles in varying degrees and is systemic, strategic, and synergistic, permitting new insights and solutions to emerge.

**15097**
**Personality Profile Inventory.** Smith, August William 1986.
*Descriptors:* *Administrators; *Managerial Occupations; *Personality Measures; *Personality Traits; Adults; Rating Scales
*Identifiers:* Jung (Carl G); Management Styles; P2; TIM(M)
*Availability:* Tests in Microfiche, Test Collection, Educational Testing Service, Princeton, NJ 08541.
*Notes:* Items, 40.

Used to assess the way people relate to various dimensions and approaches to management. Relates dimensions and management styles to Jungian personality characteristics and concepts: introvert-extravert, feeling-thinking, intuitive-sensing, and perceptive-judging.

**15098**
**Responsible Risk-Taking Inventory.** Smith, August William 1986.
*Descriptors:* *Administrators; *Managerial Occupations; *Risk; Administrator Responsibility; Adults; Rating Scales
*Identifiers:* Management Styles; R2I; TIM(M)
*Availability:* Tests in Microfiche, Test Collection, Educational Testing Service, Princeton, NJ 08541.
*Notes:* Items, 40.

Used to assess the way individuals relate to various dimensions and approaches to management. Designed to help people identify some characteristics that affect how they perform and contribute to their organizations. Questionnaire examines the relative risks related to position requirements and personal relationships that affect overall productive results.

**15100**
**Examination for the Certified Management Accountant.** Institute of Certified Management Accountants, Montvale, NJ 1987.
*Descriptors:* *Accountants; *Certification; *Occupational Tests; Achievement Tests; Adults; Behavior Patterns; Decision Making; Economics; Ethics; Finance Occupations; Financial Audits; Knowledge Level; Management Information Systems; Money Management; Organizations (Groups)
*Identifiers:* CMA
*Availability:* Institute of Certified Management Accountants, 10 Paragon Dr., Montvale, NJ 07645-1759.
*Notes:* Time, 1050.

The examination consists of 5 parts scheduled consecutively over 2 1/2-day period. Each part requires 3 1/2 hours. Candidates for CMA must be employed in management accounting and should possess a baccalaureate degree or achieve a satisfactory score on either the Graduate Record Examination or Graduate Management Admissions tests published by Educational Testing Service. The test is designed to provide evidence of exposure to and proficiency in various areas of financial practice. Tests are administered in June and December. Examinations are updated periodically. The released booklets of prior examinations can be purchased from ICMA at the address given in the availability section. New forms are developed regularly.

**15101**
**mCircle Instrument.** Brain Technologies Corp., Fort Collins, CO 1986.
*Descriptors:* *Decision Making; Adults; Behavior Patterns; Decision Making Skills; Organizations (Groups); Personality; Problem Solving
*Availability:* Brain Technologies Corp., 414 Buckeye St., Fort Collins, CO 80525.
*Notes:* Items, 20.

Designed to identify the typical way an individual responds to others when confronted with a choice between 2 difficult alternatives, the kind of circumstance found in high-stress, rapid-change business or organizational environments. Said to be different from other conflict resolution measures in that it uses mental "reframing" abilities to turn problems into opportunities. Explores the use of 5 strategies: get out, give in, take over, trade off, and breakthrough.

**15103**
**Business Skills Inventory, Form Seven.** Kampmeier Group, Columbus, OH 1990.
*Descriptors:* *Administrators; *Business Skills; *Occupational Tests; *Personnel Selection; *Professional Personnel; *Sales Workers; Academic Ability; Adults; Cognitive Ability; Decision Making; Entrepreneurship; Leadership; Personality; Public Relations
*Availability:* The Kampmeier Group, 3360 Tremont Rd., Columbus, OH 43221.

Designed for use in hiring managers, sales staff, administrators, and customer service and professional personnel. This instrument measures interpersonal skills, ability to learn, leadership, persuasiveness, decision making, delegating, administrative skills, organizational skills, and entrepreneurship. Completed by prospective or current employee and scored and interpreted by the publisher.

**15104**
**Mindmaker 6.** Brain Technologies Corp., Fort Collins, CO 1987.
*Descriptors:* *Beliefs; *Brain Hemisphere Functions; *Values; Adults; Behavior Patterns; Change Agents; Interpersonal Competence; Personality; Self Concept; Social Behavior; Work Attitudes
*Availability:* Brain Technologies Corp., 2290 E. Prospect, Ste. 2, Fort Collins, CO 80525.
*Notes:* Items, 25.

Uses hemispheric dominance theories to identify group members' values and beliefs in 6 areas. Said to be useful for management, employees, markets, regulators, and critics to determine coinciding viewpoints and as an information gathering tool for change agents. Assists in matching employees with available positions.

**15113**
**Stress Processing Report.** Human Synergistics, Plymouth, MI 1984.
*Descriptors:* *Administrators; *Stress Variables; Adults; Behavior Patterns; Cognitive Processes; Occupational Tests; Self Esteem; Social Behavior; Time Management
*Availability:* Human Synergistics, 39819 Plymouth Rd., Plymouth, MI 48170.
*Notes:* Items, 160.

This inventory identifies factors that contribute to psychological stress. It is a self-report and self-evaluation designed to help improve thought patterns to reduce stress. The respondent answers questions that reveal 19 different thinking styles said to be related to stress, strain, and medical problems. Responses are plotted on a circular graph. Items are concerned with self-perceptions, belief systems, goal directedness, relationships with others, and effectiveness. Suggestions are given regarding causes and improvement of stress-producing thinking styles.

**15114**
**Nonverbal Sensitivity Indicator.** Glaser, Rollin 1983.
*Descriptors:* *Emotional Response; *Nonverbal Communication; Administrators; Adults; Communication Skills; Interpersonal Competence; Personality; Supervisors
*Availability:* Organization Design and Development, Inc., 2002 Renaissance Blvd., Ste. 100, King of Prussia, PA 19406-2746.
*Notes:* Items, 50.

Designed to help individuals assess their awareness of nonverbal communication, such as body movements, gestures, facial expressions, space and territory, etc. The respondents write a short description of the probable meaning of a statement describing a nonverbal behavior and then describe their response to it.

**15115**
**Dealing with Feelings.** Sashkin, Marshall 1987.
*Descriptors:* *Affective Behavior; *Emotional Problems; *Emotional Response; Adults; Communication Skills; Interpersonal Competence; Management Teams; Occupational Tests; Personality
*Availability:* Organization Design and Development, Inc., 2002 Renaissance Blvd., Ste. 100, King of Prussia, PA 19406-2746.
*Notes:* Time, 20. Items, 40.

A self-assessment tool that helps individuals determine how they handle their feelings. Based on a model of how people receive information from the environment, reflect on the information, and respond to information. Four scores are developed: effectiveness, receiving, reflecting, and responding. Useful for communication skills training, self-study, counseling, team building, interpersonal skills development, and career development.

**15116**
**Participative Management Profile: Optimizing Your Decision-Making Style.** Jones, John E.; Bearley, William L. 1986.
*Descriptors:* *Administrators; *Decision Making; *Participative Decision Making; *Supervisors; Adults; Occupational Tests; Supervisory Methods
*Availability:* Organization Design and Development, Inc., 2002 Renaissance Blvd., Ste. 100, King of Prussia, PA 19406-2746.
*Notes:* Items, 20.

Twenty decision situations are presented, requiring the respondent to select 1 of 4 decision formats: consultation, command, consensus, or convenience. Scoring provides information on the effectiveness of the respondent's decision selection, preferred and backup styles, and types of decisions needing further study and practice.

**15117**
**Managerial Values Profile, Japanese Version.** Sashkin, Marshall 1986.
*Descriptors:* *Administrators; *Ethics; *Japanese; Administrator Attitudes; Adults; Beliefs; Business; Occupational Tests; Values
*Availability:* Organization Design and Development, Inc., 2002 Renaissance Blvd., Ste. 100, King of Prussia, PA 19406-2746.
*Notes:* Time, 10. Items, 24.

Japanese-language version of a survey designed for use in determining a respondent's beliefs and values relating to business ethics. Three ethical positions are presented: utilitarian (the greatest good for the greatest number); moral rights (personal rights are inviolable); and justice (benefits and burdens must be allocated fairly). For use in stimulating discussions during training sessions.

**15120**
**Performance Management Strategies Inventory—Associate.** Glaser, Rollin; Sashkin, Marshall 1986.
*Descriptors:* *Administration; *Employees; *Personnel Evaluation; *Supervisors; *Vocational Evaluation; Adults; Job Performance; Occupational Tests
*Availability:* Organization Design and Development, Inc., 2002 Renaissance Blvd., Ste. 100, King of Prussia, PA 19406-2746.
*Notes:* Time, 20. Items, 25.

Designed to measure, from the employee's perspective, the extent to which managers use opportunities for improving employee performance by defining expectations, setting goals, delegating, training, coaching and counseling, and appraising performance. This form is completed by the employee. Another form is completed by the manager.

**15123**
**Test Your Intuitive Powers.** Agor, Weston H. 1985.
*Descriptors:* *Intuition; Adults; Cognitive Style; Decision Making; Occupational Tests; Surveys

*Identifiers:* AIM Survey
*Availability:* Organization Design and Development, Inc., 2002 Renaissance Blvd., Ste. 100, King of Prussia, PA 19406-2746.
*Notes:* Items, 10.

This survey is a measure of underlying or potential intuitive ability and whether or not intuitive powers are actually being used to help guide decision making in situations where uncertainty is high; there is little precedent; variables are less scientifically predictable; facts are limited; there are several plausible solutions with good arguments; time is limited; and there is pressure to be right.

**15152**
**Career/Personality Compatibility Inventory.** Brewer, James H. 1985.
*Descriptors:* *Personality; *Work Environment; Adults; Job Skills; Occupational Information; Occupational Tests; Self Evaluation (Individuals); Work Attitudes
*Availability:* Organization Design and Development, Inc., 2002 Renaissance Blvd., Ste. 100, King of Prussia, PA 19406-2746.
*Notes:* Time, 20. Items, 48.

This inventory is designed to indicate personal style or personality type and give a description of present or desired career characteristics. A profile form allows for an interpretation of the compatibility between personality and career type. May be used for planning, placement, training, and development. Does not require professional assistance for administration.

**15153**
**Inventory of Ghosts.** Laus, Michael; Champagne, David W. 1986.
*Descriptors:* *Cognitive Style; Adults; Behavior Patterns; Learning Strategies; Management Development; Occupational Tests; Self Evaluation (Individuals)
*Identifiers:* Learning Style
*Availability:* Organization Design and Development, Inc., 2002 Renaissance Blvd., Ste. 100, King of Prussia, PA 19406-2746.
*Notes:* Time, 20. Items, 50.

Designed to identify behaviors, styles, and needs that have become internalized from prior learning situations and may adversely affect learning in management development situations or facilitate learning. Scores are developed in ghosts of classroom history, work history, time/life demands, and personal needs. The test is self-scored, and an interpretive guide is included.

**15154**
**Group Development Assessment Questionnaire.** Jones, John E.; Bearley, William L. 1986.
*Descriptors:* *Group Behavior; *Management Teams; *Teamwork; Adults; Behavior Patterns; Group Dynamics; Interpersonal Relationship; Problem Solving; Profiles
*Availability:* Organization Design and Development, Inc., 2002 Renaissance Blvd., Ste. 100, King of Prussia, PA 19406-2746.
*Notes:* Items, 40.

Designed to determine the level of development of functioning within a group. The questionnaire is based on a theory that groups go through phases of development when becoming a team. Two dimensions of behavior are covered. The task behaviors dimension has 4 phases: orientation, organization, open data flow, and problem solving. Process behaviors include dependency, conflict, cohesion, and interdependence. The results are used in training and development.

**15155**
**Personal Style Inventory.** Hogan, R. Craig; Champagne, David W. 1985.
*Descriptors:* *Management Teams; *Personality Measures; *Teamwork; Administrators; Adults; Management Development; Occupational Tests; Supervisors
*Identifiers:* Jungian Typology
*Availability:* Organization Design and Development, Inc., 2002 Renaissance Blvd., Ste. 100, King of Prussia, PA 19406-2746.
*Notes:* Time, 10. Items, 32.

For use in industrial settings prior to development activities related to how personal style affects teamwork. Uses Carl Jung's theories. Determines personality makeup as a combination of 2 ways of perceiving (sensing and intuition), 2 ways of judging (thinking and feeling), preferred mental process (perceiving or judging), and preferred orientation to the world (extraversion or introversion).

**15156**
**Team-Work and Team-Roles Inventory.** Mummo, Frederick S. 1984.
*Descriptors:* *Administrators; *Management Teams; *Supervisors; *Teamwork; Adults; Management Development; Occupational Tests; Role Conflict; Role Perception
*Availability:* Organization Design and Development, Inc., 2002 Renaissance Blvd., Ste. 100, King of Prussia, PA 19406-2746.
*Notes:* Items, 18.

This inventory helps participants in team-building or training sessions to determine which phase of team building interests them and what roles in team building they regularly play or disregard. Team roles include leader, moderator, creator, innovator, manager, organizer, evaluator, and finisher. The inventory provides a model that shows the relationship between phases of teamwork, from initiation through completion, and necessary team member roles.

**15157**
**Phases of Integrated Problem Solving, Revised Edition.** Morris, William C.; Sashkin, Marshall 1985.
*Descriptors:* *Group Behavior; *Problem Solving; Adults; Behavior Patterns; Occupational Tests; Rating Scales
*Identifiers:* PIPS
*Availability:* Organization Design and Development, Inc., 2002 Renaissance Blvd., Ste. 100, King of Prussia, PA 19406-2746.
*Notes:* Items, 36.

Designed for use during a group problem-solving discussion. Six problem-solving phases are identified: problem definition, problem solution generation, ideas to actions, solution-action planning, solution-evaluation planning, and evaluation of the product and process. The group evaluates its behavior in each phase via a 36 item, 5-point scale rating the problem-solving behaviors they exhibited.

**15158**
**Team Effectiveness Profile, Second Edition.** Glaser, Rollin; Glaser, Christine 1984.
*Descriptors:* *Interpersonal Relationship; *Teamwork; Adults; Group Behavior; Group Dynamics; Management Teams; Objectives; Occupational Tests; Planning; Self Evaluation (Groups)
*Identifiers:* TEP
*Availability:* Organization Design and Development, Inc., 2002 Renaissance Blvd., Ste. 100, King of Prussia, PA 19406-2746.
*Notes:* Items, 60.

Designed to determine issues that are blocking effective teamwork in an organization. Items relate to 5 areas of team activity: group mission, planning, and goal setting; group organization; group operating processes; group interpersonal relationships; and intergroup relations. Yields an overall score and part score to pinpoint blockages. May be used before and after team-building activities.

**15160**
**Problem Solving Style Inventory.** Phillips, Kenneth R. 1986.
*Descriptors:* *Administrators; *Participative Decision Making; *Supervisors; Adults; Behavior Patterns; Measures (Individuals); Occupational Tests; Problem Solving
*Availability:* Organization Design and Development, Inc., 2002 Renaissance Blvd., Ste. 100, King of Prussia, PA 19406-2746.
*Notes:* Time, 20. Items, 30.

Designed to help managers who resist using participative approaches to problem solving confront and consider their habits. Measures ego-centered and other-centered problem-solving behavior and 5 problem-solving styles related to these behaviors. Styles include: ego-oriented, deferred, other-oriented, I-we-oriented, and we-oriented.

**15161**
**Timestyle.** Brewer, James H. 1985.
*Descriptors:* *Management Development; *Time Management; Administrators; Adults; Interpersonal Relationship; Occupational Tests; Supervisors; Teamwork
*Availability:* Organization Design and Development, Inc., 2002 Renaissance Blvd., Ste. 100, King of Prussia, PA 19406-2746.
*Notes:* Items, 1-16.

Designed to measure individuals' time management style by measuring their awareness of deadlines or people. Four time styles are identified. The Road Runner does not waste words or time. The Race Horse is conscious of time and teamwork. The New Pup believes people are more important than time. The Tom Cat has a low awareness of both time and people. May be used as part of a supervisory skills/management development training program.

**15162**
**Performance Appraisal Skills Inventory.** Phillips, Kenneth R. 1987.
*Descriptors:* *Interviews; *Personnel Evaluation; Administrators; Adults; Communication Skills; Interpersonal Competence; Meetings; Occupational Tests; Supervisors
*Availability:* Organization Design and Development, Inc., 2002 Renaissance Blvd., Ste. 100, King of Prussia, PA 19406-2746.
*Notes:* Time, 20. Items, 18.

This instrument provides 18 performance appraisal situations. Respondent selects from 4 possible solutions. These indicate the respondent's overall effectiveness in handling performance appraisal interviews and point out specific skills. Situations are set up to help a manager view the meeting as a 6-step process to conducting meetings more effectively.

**15163**
**Communication Style.** Brewer, James H. 1984.
*Descriptors:* *Administrators; *Communication Skills; *Supervisors; Adults; Interpersonal Communication; Leaders; Management Development; Occupational Tests
*Availability:* Organization Design and Development, Inc., 2002 Renaissance Blvd., Ste. 100, King of Prussia, PA 19406-2746.
*Notes:* Time, 20. Items, 18.

Designed to assess the communication style of those in leadership positions. Four major styles are identified: directive, talkative, sincere, and organized. Designed for use by counselors or training personnel prior to management development sessions.

**15164**
**Organizational Change Orientation Scale.** Jones, John E.; Bearley, William L. 1986.
*Descriptors:* *Organizational Change; Adults; Behavior Patterns; Employee Attitudes; Occupational Tests
*Identifiers:* OCOS
*Availability:* Organization Design and Development, Inc., 2002 Renaissance Blvd., Ste. 100, King of Prussia, PA 19406-2746.
*Notes:* Time, 20. Items, 36.

Designed to assess the tendencies of individuals to behave in predictable ways in response to change. Used to identify employees' behaviors so that they can be made conscious of their response styles and make changes. Responses vary from embracing change to neutrality to resistance and are classified as functional, nonfunctional, or dysfunctional. Interpretive materials are included.

**15165**
**Organizational Change Readiness Survey.** Jones, John E.; Bearley, William L. 1986.
*Descriptors:* *Organizational Change; *Readiness; Administrators; Adults; Employee Attitudes; Industrial Structure; Occupational Tests; Organizational Climate; Self Evaluation (Groups); Supervisors; Surveys
*Identifiers:* OCRS
*Availability:* Organization Design and Development, Inc., 2002 Renaissance Blvd., Ste. 100, King of Prussia, PA 19406-2746.
*Notes:* Time, 20. Items, 76.

A survey designed to determine the total organizational system's readiness for change. It is designed for use by managers, trainers, and consultants to analyze their organization's ability to manage change effectively. Items are classified into 5 categories: structural readiness, technological readiness, climatic readiness, systemic readiness, and people readiness.

**15168**
**Negotiating Style.** Brewer, James H. 1984.
*Descriptors:* *Administrators; *Negotiation Agreements; *Supervisors; *Supervisory Training; Adults; Communication Skills; Occupational Tests; Work Environment
*Availability:* Organization Design and Development, Inc., 2002 Renaissance Blvd., Ste. 100, King of Prussia, PA 19406-2746.
*Notes:* Items, 16.

Designed to determine the respondent's negotiating style for use in training. Styles consist of "pushy," "stand pat," "buddy," "check all." Self-scored and self-interpreted. Each person selects items that reflect his or her behavior patterns.

**15169**
**Conflict Style Inventory.** Sashkin, Marshall 1986.
*Descriptors:* *Administrators; *Conflict Resolution; *Management Development; *Supervisors; Adults; Interpersonal Competence; Occupational Tests; Supervisory Training; Work Environment
*Availability:* Organization Design and Development, Inc., 2002 Renaissance Blvd., Ste. 100, King of Prussia, PA 19406-2746.
*Notes:* Time, 25. Items, 10.

Ten cases of typical work-related conflict situations are described. Each is followed by 5 alternative actions. Respondents allocate 10 points among the alternatives. Norms are provided. This inventory was designed to help people discover their typical reactions to conflict at work in order to develop more productive means of conflict resolution. Five conflict styles are used: avoiding/withdrawing, smoothing, forcing, bargaining, and problem-solving. Used in management development and training activities.

**15170**
**BEST Behavior Profile.** Brewer, James H. 1984.
*Descriptors:* *Administrators; *Management Development; *Personality Measures; *Supervisors; Adults; Occupational Tests; Personality; Self Evaluation (Individuals)
*Availability:* Organization Design and Development, Inc., 2002 Renaissance Blvd., Ste. 100, King of Prussia, PA 19406-2746.
*Notes:* Time, 15. Items, 32.

This personality measure is designed for use in training and management development, to determine the respondent's personality type. Possible types are bold, expressive, sympathetic, or technical. Contains 2 types of items: word association and situational analysis. The test is self-scored and interpretive materials are included.

**15171**
**MbM Questionnaire.** Sashkin, Marshall 1986.
*Descriptors:* *Administrators; *Employees; *Industrial Training; *Management Development; *Motivation; *Supervisors; Adults; Individual Needs; Motivation Techniques; Needs Assessment; Occupational Tests; Self Evaluation (Individuals)
*Identifiers:* Maslow (Abraham); Needs Hierarchy
*Availability:* Organization Design and Development, Inc., 2002 Renaissance Blvd., Ste. 100, King of Prussia, PA 19406-2746.
*Notes:* Time, 10. Items, 20.

This questionnaire, based on 4 of the 5 needs in Maslow's needs hierarchy, is designed to identify motivations for work in order to improve job performance. It is useful in training sessions for managers to introduce and develop the concept of motivation. Needs assessed are security, social, self-esteem, and self-actualization.

**15180**
**Supervisory Behavior Description Questionnaire.** Sistrunk, Walter E. 1981.
*Descriptors:* *School Administration; *Supervisory Methods; Adults; Questionnaires; Self Evaluation (Individuals); Teacher Response
*Identifiers:* SBDQ; TIM(M)
*Availability:* Tests in Microfiche, Test Collection, Educational Testing Service, Princeton, NJ 08541.
*Notes:* Time, 40 approx. Items, 159.

Designed to provide investigators with a measure of perceived and/or preferred supervisory methods of supervisors of instruction in schools. If respondents are supervisors, they choose the statements that best describe their most frequent practices. If respondents are teachers, they choose the statements that come closest to their perceptions or their preferences for supervisory style of the individual they are rating. There are 2 forms of the questionnaire. Form 1 is an ordinal scale composed of 8 tasks and 53 triads of items. Each triad is composed of a directive description, a collaborative description, and a nondirective description of a supervisory behavior. Form 2 is a semantic differential in which respondents are asked to choose 1 adjective descriptor from each of 3 pairs of dichotomous adjectives. This form also yields data about the supervisor's approach to supervision as directive, collaborative, or nondirective.

**15186**
**Employee Assessment Tool for Nurses.** Lee, Pat Chikamoto; Shorr, Judy
*Descriptors:* *Job Satisfaction; *Nurses; Adults; Job Performance; Labor Turnover; Productivity; Quality of Working Life; Questionnaires; Rating Scales
*Identifiers:* Absenteeism
*Availability:* *Journal of Nursing Administration,* p31-38, Jan 1984.
*Notes:* Items, 138.

Assessment instrument used to measure the job satisfaction of nurses. Subjects rate the importance of various aspects of their jobs and indicate how satisfied they are with their jobs and the changes they would like to see take place. Initial uses of the instrument indicated that the subject's job expectation and the job components deemed to be important were predictors of job satisfaction. May be used to commence changes in the workplace to help alleviate staff turnover.

**15193**
**Conflict Management Appraisal.** Hall, Jay 1986.
*Descriptors:* *Behavior Rating Scales; *Conflict; *Conflict Resolution; Adults
*Availability:* Telemetrics International, 1755 Woodstead Ct., The Woodlands, TX 77380.
*Notes:* Items, 60.

An assessment of an associate's reaction to, and management of, conflict. (Associate is defined as a coworker, personal or social acquaintance, or family member). Meant to help the subject gain greater self-understanding. This questionnaire is divided into 4 major categories ranging from interpersonal to intergroup relations. Under each category, 3 conflict situations are described, and 5 alternative ways of behaving are presented for each situation. The total score is determined by assessing the subject's preference for using each of the 5 alternatives.

**15194**
**Teamwork Appraisal Survey.** Hall, Jay 1987.
*Descriptors:* *Behavior Rating Scales; *Interpersonal Competence; *Teamwork; Adults; Conflict Resolution; Leadership Qualities
*Availability:* Teleometrics International, 1755 Woodstead Ct., The Woodlands, TX 77380.
*Notes:* Items, 80.

An assessment of associates' feelings about working in teams and the behaviors they employ in work-team situations. The survey contains 80 items, which represent a variety of responses to situations common in a work-team setting. For each situation, the assessor must choose from 5 alternatives the ones which are most and least characteristic of the subject. Intended to provide meaningful feedback to the associate regarding his or her functioning as a team member.

**15195**
**Survey of Management Practices.** Hall, Jay 1987.
*Descriptors:* *Administrators; *Rating Scales; *Supervisory Methods; Administration; Adults; Behavior; Employee Attitudes; Job Performance; Productivity
*Identifiers:* Management Skills
*Availability:* Teleometrics International, 1755 Woodstead Ct., The Woodlands, TX 77380.
*Notes:* Items, 72.

A survey of a manager's practices regarding 9 component areas of management. Made up of 72 independent statements concerning management behavior. The respondent is asked to assess how often his or her manager engages in this particular behavior; and then, how often the respondent would like his or her boss to use this practice in order for the employee to be most productive. Designed to identify some of the managerial practices which may affect productivity of those being managed.

**15196**
**Productive Practices Survey.** Hall, Jay 1987.
*Descriptors:* *Administrator Characteristics; *Administrators; *Self Evaluation (Individuals); *Supervisory Methods; Adults; Norm Referenced Tests; Problem Solving; Productivity; Rating Scales; Social Environment; Work Environment
*Identifiers:* PPS
*Availability:* Teleometrics International, 1755 Woodstead Ct., The Woodlands, TX 77380.
*Notes:* Items, 72.

Self-evaluation instrument to be used by managers to determine whether their managerial practices are productive. Using a 9-point scale, managers rate themselves in areas of management style. Feedback from the survey may help managers find the management practices that affect employee productivity and change their methods accordingly. Instrument has been tested for reliability and validity and is norm referenced. May be used in conjunction with Survey of Management Practices (15195), which assesses others' ratings of the manager.

**15234**
**Wolfe Microcomputer User Aptitude Test—W-Micro.** Walden Computer Aptitude Testing, Ltd., Oradell, NJ
*Descriptors:* *Adults; *Aptitude Tests; *Microcomputers; *Occupational Tests; *Personnel Selection; French; Personnel Evaluation
*Identifiers:* WMICRO
*Availability:* Walden Computer Aptitude Testing, Ltd., Box 319, Oradell, NJ 07649.
*Notes:* Time, 75.

Evaluates a candidate's practical and analytical skills required for effective use of the microcomputer. (Does not include programming skills.) Traits measured include understanding supplier manuals, problem-solving skills, ability to understand and use common spreadsheet and database packages, ability to work accurately and rapidly, and ability to sustain concentration and solve in-depth problems. Also available in French. Test scoring done by Wolfe.

**15246**
**Berger Tests of Programming Proficiency: IBM 360/370 Assembler.** Psychometrics, Inc., Sherman Oaks, CA 1984.
*Descriptors:* *Data Processing Occupations; *Occupational Tests; *Programming Languages; Adults; Computers; Job Training; Personnel Evaluation; Personnel Selection; Promotion (Occupational)
*Identifiers:* Assemblers; Assembler 360 370; BTOPP; IBM
*Availability:* Psychometrics, Inc., 4730 Woodman Ave., Sherman Oaks, CA 91423.

A job-related proficiency test designed for programmers skilled in the Assembler instruction set who have expertise in understanding the relationship between Assembler language, machine language, and data representation. Test items emphasize machine instructions (arithmetic, data manipulation, condition code setters, flow of control, instruction formats, and PSW); Assembler instructions (storage and data definitions, assembler arithmetic, CSECT, DSECT, base displacement, Boolean logic, and Assembler attributes); and logic routines (indexing, table matchups, branching/looping, comparing, bit manipulation, scanning, translation, and editing). Test is multiple choice. Can be used for personnel selection, evaluation of individual programmers, and determination of training needs.

**15248**
**Berger Tests of Programming Proficiency: Structured COBOL.** Psychometrics, Inc., Sherman Oaks, CA 1984.
*Descriptors:* *Data Processing Occupations; *Occupational Tests; *Programming Languages; Adults; Computers; Job Training; Personnel Evaluation; Personnel Selection; Promotion (Occupational)
*Identifiers:* BTOPP; *COBOL Programming Language
*Availability:* Psychometrics, Inc., 4730 Woodman Ave., Sherman Oaks, CA 91423.

Designed to supplement the Berger Test of Programming Proficiency: COBOL (11720). It covers module design (module development, top down considerations, module complexity, and general principles); program structures (IF/THEN/ELSE, CASE, DOUNTIL, DOWHILE); structured programming (logic, coding, and testing). Scoring is done by the publisher. This is a multiple-choice test. Can be used to select personnel, to evaluate staff, or to determine training needs.

**15249**
**Berger Tests of Programming Proficiency: Ada.** Psychometrics, Inc., Sherman Oaks, CA 1984.
*Descriptors:* *Data Processing Occupations; *Occupational Tests; *Programming Languages; Adults; Computers; Job Training; Personnel Evaluation; Personnel Selection; Promotion (Occupational)
*Identifiers:* Ada; BTOPP; Department of Defense
*Availability:* Psychometrics, Inc., 4730 Woodman Ave., Sherman Oaks, CA 91423.

Designed to measure proficiency in Ada, the programming language developed by the Department of Defense (DOD) for critical missions applications. Test items reflect the technical standards established by the DOD/Ada Joint Program Office. Measures knowledge in declarations and types, names and extensions, statements, subprograms, packages, visibility rules, tasks, program structure and compilation issues, exceptions, and generic units. Can be used to select personnel, to evaluate staff, or to determine training needs.

**15267**
**Berger Tests of Programming Proficiency: Basics of Programming II.** Psychometrics, Inc., Sherman Oaks, CA 1986.
*Descriptors:* *Data Processing Occupations; *Occupational Tests; *Programming; *Programming Languages; Adults; Computers; Computer Software; Job Training; Logic; Personnel Evaluation; Personnel Selection; Program Design; Program Development; Promotion (Occupational)
*Identifiers:* BOPII; Debugging
*Availability:* Psychometrics, Inc., 4730 Woodman Ave., Sherman Oaks, CA 91423.
*Notes:* Time, 60. Items, 30.

Contains items designed to measure the proficiency of experienced programmers and assist in decisions related to hiring, promotion, and advanced training. BOP-II is used to measure overall programming logic and design. Uses multiple-choice format and can be administered by data processing or personnel staff. Scoring is done by the publisher. National norms are available. In some cases, industry or company norms can be given. This test emphasizes program design, methods, logic, testing, debugging, data structure, and manipulation.

**15268**
**Berger Tests of Programming Proficiency: C Language.** Psychometrics, Inc., Sherman Oaks, CA 1986.
*Descriptors:* *Data Processing Occupations; *Occupational Tests; *Programming Languages; Adults; Computers; Job Training; Personnel Evaluation; Personnel Selection; Promotion (Occupational)
*Identifiers:* BTOPP; *C Language
*Availability:* Psychometrics, Inc., 4730 Woodman Ave., Sherman Oaks, CA 91423.
*Notes:* Time, 60. Items, 25.

Designed to measure proficiency in order to assess training effectiveness or for personnel selection. Covers arrays and pointers, declarations, expressions, functions, standard "C" environment, input and output, statements, preprocessor, structures, and unions. For use in decisions related to hiring and promotion. Test is scored by publisher. Items are in multiple-choice format.

**15269**
**Berger Tests of Programming Proficiency: Systems Programmer Proficiency Test.** Psychometrics, Inc., Sherman Oaks, CA 1986.
*Descriptors:* *Data Processing Occupations; *Occupational Tests; *Programmers; Adults; Computers; Job Training; Personnel Evaluation; Personnel Selection; Promotion (Occupational)
*Identifiers:* SYSPRO
*Availability:* Psychometrics, Inc., 4730 Woodman Ave., Sherman Oaks, CA 91423.

Designed for systems programmers who are experienced with the MVS Operating System. Includes questions on DASD management, capacity planning, database, online systems, application support, and program products. Scores are provided in each area, along with a total score. Content includes software installation and maintenance; operating and fine-tuning the system; problem analysis related to installation, maintenance and systems services, and utilities; and debugging techniques. Scoring is done by the publisher. Can be used to assist in hiring, promotion, and advanced training decisions. Can be administered by data processing or personnel staff.

**15270**
**Berger Tests of Programming Proficiency: UNIX.** Psychometrics, Inc., Sherman Oaks, CA 1986.
*Descriptors:* *Data Processing Occupations; *Occupational Tests; *Programming Languages; Adults; Computers; Job Training; Personnel Evaluation; Personnel Selection; Program Design; Promotion (Occupational)
*Identifiers:* *UNIX
*Availability:* Psychometrics, Inc., 4730 Woodman Ave., Sherman Oaks, CA 91423.
*Notes:* Time, 60. Items, 25.

Designed to measure proficiency in order to assess training effectiveness or for personnel selection. Covers specialized commands, general commands, shell syntax, meta characters and quoting, environmental variables, shell variables, process, I/O system, and file system. For use in decisions related to hiring and promotion. Test is scored by the publisher. Can be administered by data processing or personnel staff.

**15271**
**Berger Tests of Programming Proficiency: C and UNIX Interface.** Psychometrics, Inc., Sherman Oaks, CA 1986.
*Descriptors:* *Data Processing Occupations; *Occupational Tests; *Programming Languages; Adults; Computers; Job Training; Personnel Evaluation; Personnel Selection; Promotion (Occupational)
*Identifiers:* *C Language; *UNIX
*Availability:* Psychometrics, Inc., 4730 Woodman Ave., Sherman Oaks, CA 91423.
*Notes:* Time, 30. Items, 15.

This test covers I/O functions, process control, file protection, signal handling, and system call. Both the UNIX (see 15270) and the C and UNIX Interface tests are in one book but are administered separately. For use in assessing training effectiveness and in decisions related to hiring and promotion. Test is scored by the publisher. Can be administered by data processing or personnel staff.

**15272**
**Berger Tests of Programming Proficiency: CICS.** Psychometrics, Inc., Sherman Oaks, CA 1986.
*Descriptors:* *Data Processing Occupations; *Occupational Tests; *Programming; *Programming Languages; Adults; Computers; Job Training; Personnel Evaluation; Personnel Selection; Promotion (Occupational)
*Identifiers:* *CICS; IBM DOS; IBM OS; IBM OS2
*Availability:* Psychometrics, Inc., 4730 Woodman Ave., Sherman Oaks, CA 91423.
*Notes:* Time, 60. Items, 30.

Designed to measure knowledge of command level CICS (Customer Information Control Systems) in either IBM DOS or IBM OS programming environments. Questions cover CICS system resources (table relationships, recovery/restart, design); BMS mapping; task initiation/task control, coding (general, base level locator linkage, program control, temporary storage); debugging; and services (file services, transient data, destination queues, terminal services, dump services, exception services). For use in hiring decisions, personnel selection, or evaluation training. Can be administered by data processing or personnel staff.

**15273**
**Berger Tests of Programming Proficiency: B-Word Aptitude.** Psychometrics, Inc., Sherman Oaks, CA 1986.
*Descriptors:* *Aptitude Tests; *Occupational Tests; *Personnel Selection; *Proofreading; *Word Processing; Adults; Clerical Occupations; Computer Assisted Testing; Data Processing Occupations
*Availability:* Psychometrics, Inc., 4730 Woodman Ave., Sherman Oaks, CA 91423.
*Notes:* Time, 105.

Designed to select word processor trainees who have a high potential for operating any word processing system. No prior experience or training is required. The test consists of 2 parts. Proofreading takes 15 minutes and requires correction of 40 errors. The word processor subtest requires 75 minutes to answer 25 multiple-choice questions. Examinees are expected to correct errors in spelling, punctuation, and formatting consistency in the proofreading section and then read about and apply information about word processors. A paper and pencil version and an online version are available. Scored by publisher.

**15274**
**B-Word Speed and Accuracy Typing Test.** Psychometrics, Inc., Sherman Oaks, CA 1986.
*Descriptors:* *Clerical Occupations; *Occupational Tests; *Personnel Selection; *Typewriting; Adults

*Availability:* Psychometrics, Inc., 4730 Woodman Ave., Sherman Oaks, CA 91423.

This is a measure of standard typing speed. A scoring key is provided to calculate words per minute and net words per minute. Any company using the test can set its own standard for speed and accuracy as needed.

**15277**
**Leadership Personality Compatibility Inventory.** Brewer, James H. 1983.
*Descriptors:* *Administrators; *Leadership Styles; *Personality Measures; *Supervisors; Adults; Behavior Patterns; Leadership Qualities; Occupational Tests; Personality Traits
*Identifiers:* LPCI
*Availability:* Organization Design and Development, Inc., 2002 Renaissance Blvd., Ste. 100, King of Prussia, PA 19406-2746.

Designed to assist managers in determining and understanding factors that affect their leadership: basic personality style, present or desired leadership role, and compatibility between personality and leadership role. A personality inventory and a leadership role inventory are included. Personality types can be bold, expressive, sympathetic, or technical. Leadership role characteristics can be active/competitive, persuasive/interactive, precise/systematic, and willing/steady. Data from both inventories are plotted on a compatibility graph. Respondents can then decide whether there is a need to adjust their personalities to their positions or vice-versa.

**15279**
**Career Development Assessment.** Pollard, Harry V. 1987.
*Descriptors:* *Career Development; *Employees; *Individual Development; *Job Performance; *Personnel Evaluation; Adults; Affective Behavior; Career Counseling; Employee Responsibility; Job Skills; Occupational Tests; Work Attitudes
*Availability:* Organization Design and Development, Inc., 2002 Renaissance Blvd., Ste. 100, King of Prussia, PA 19406-2746.
*Notes:* Time, 20. Items, 40.

Designed for use with employees and employers for career planning, career counseling, individual assessment and planning, and as part of a performance appraisal interview. Each item is rated in terms of performance expectancy (expected, no longer expected, or not yet expected), and in terms of the associate's current position and likely future position. The score shows the level of development of the examinee and information about the achievement of each competency at each level.

**15281**
**Training Needs Assessment Tool.** McCann, Travis A.; Tashima, James 1981.
*Descriptors:* *Job Training; *Needs Assessment; *Personnel Evaluation; Adults; Employees; Job Performance; Job Skills; Occupational Information; Occupational Tests; Profiles
*Availability:* Organization Design and Development, Inc., 2002 Renaissance Blvd., Ste. 100, King of Prussia, PA 19406-2746.
*Notes:* Items, 12.

Designed to identify skills and knowledge required in a particular job so that the job incumbent's current ability can be compared to the job requirements. Results are plotted on a grid, and a training plan is constructed based on information provided by the instrument. Said to be useful for individual or group training, career development, and training needs assessment.

**15282**
**Organizational Survival and Success: Do You Have What It Takes?** Simonetti, Jack L. 1981.
*Descriptors:* *Individual Characteristics; *Organizational Climate; *Success; *Work Environment; Adjustment (to Environment); Adults; Behavior Patterns; Group Activities; Occupational Tests
*Availability:* Organization Design and Development, Inc., 2002 Renaissance Blvd., Ste. 100, King of Prussia, PA 19406-2746.
*Notes:* Time, 60. Items, 20.

Designed for use as a teaching tool or an individual exercise in organizational culture and personal behaviors that will help an individual to succeed within an organization. Covers factors such as appearance, performance, and personality. May be used as a group exercise by developing a consensus of the ranking of the importance of each attribute to a specific organization. About one hour is suggested for the group exercise.

**15283**
**Berger Tests of Programming Proficiency: B-SAGE, Form C.** Psychometrics, Inc., Sherman Oaks, CA 1986.
*Descriptors:* *Data Processing Occupations; *Occupational Tests; *Systems Analysis; Adults; Computers; Personnel Evaluation; Personnel Selection; Promotion (Occupational); Systems Analysts
*Identifiers:* BTOPP
*Availability:* Psychometrics, Inc., 4730 Woodman Ave., Sherman Oaks, CA 91423.
*Notes:* Time, 60. Items, 30.

Designed to measure systems analysis "life cycle" functions, techniques, and management. Test combines questions from other Psychometrics tests: Systems Analysis (11727); Systems Design and Development (11728); Systems Management (11730); and Systems Testing, Operations, and Maintenance (11729). Can be administered by data processing or personnel staff.

**15284**
**Sales Style.** Brewer, James H.
*Descriptors:* *Salesmanship; *Sales Workers; Adults; Behavior Patterns; Occupational Tests
*Availability:* Organization Design and Development, Inc., 2002 Renaissance Blvd., Ste. 100, King of Prussia, PA 19406-2746.
*Notes:* Time, 15. Items, 18.

Designed to determine which of 4 sales styles an individual may use in selling a product. Styles consist of quick sell, talkative sell, persistent sell, or precise sell. Does not require professional assistance for administration, scoring, or interpretation.

**15285**
**Burnout Assessment Inventory.** Jones, John E.; Bearley, William L. 1986.
*Descriptors:* *Burnout; Adults; Alienation; Hostility; Occupational Tests; Self Concept; Self Evaluation (Individuals); Withdrawal (Psychology)
*Availability:* Organization Design and Development, Inc., 2002 Renaissance Blvd., Ste. 100, King of Prussia, PA 19406-2746.
*Notes:* Time, 30. Items, 60.

Designed to assess symptoms of burnout, described as a generalized mental and physical state characterized by depletion of energy and significantly lessened personal effectiveness. Respondents use a 10-point scale to assess their behavior in terms of common burnout symptoms and signs. The inventory is self-scoring and yields an overall burnout level score and 4 subscales measuring negative self-concept, alienation, antagonism, and withdrawal.

**15294**
**Job Stress Questionnaire.** Hamel, Karin; Bracken, Duane 1986.
*Descriptors:* *Stress Variables; *Work Environment; Adults; Likert Scales; Rating Scales; Role Conflict
*Identifiers:* *Job Stress; JSQ
*Availability:* *Educational and Psychological Measurement,* v46 n3 p777-86, Aut 1986.
*Notes:* Items, 13.

Scale used to determine the factors that may cause job stress. Scale is divided into 4 subscales that relate to causes of job stress: work load, role conflict, role ambiguity, and utilization of skills. Factor analysis, internal consistency, and factorial composition have been analyzed. Scale may be used to determine the difference in job stress causes among blue collar, white collar, and professional workers.

**15296**
**Bank Personnel Selection Inventory—3 and 7.** London House, Rosemont, IL 1988.
*Descriptors:* *Banking; *Occupational Tests; *Personality Measures; *Personnel Selection; Adults; Behavior Patterns; Computers; Drug Use; Employee Attitudes; Employment Potential; Interpersonal Competence; Scoring; Social Desirability; Supervision; Values; Violence; Work Attitudes
*Identifiers:* BPSI; Honesty
*Availability:* London House, SRA Product Group, 9701 W. Higgins Rd., Rosemont, IL 60018.
*Notes:* Time, 40.

Designed to assist banks in selecting employees. This instrument was developed in conjunction with the Bank Administration Institute. A 3-scale version can be used that features the honesty, drug avoidance, and nonviolence scales. On both the 3- and 7-scale versions validity is also measured. Can be administered in-house as no training is required. Scored by publisher or via IBM-compatible software in-house.

**15312**
**Managerial and Professional Job Functions Inventory.** Baehr, Melany E.; And Others; London House, Rosemont, IL 1988.
*Descriptors:* *Industrial Training; *Occupational Information; *Occupational Tests; *Personnel Evaluation; *Supervisors; Adults; Job Skills; Needs Assessment; Professional Occupations; Self Evaluation (Individuals)
*Identifiers:* MP(JFI)
*Availability:* London House, SRA Product Group, 9701 W. Higgins Rd., Rosemont, IL 60018.
*Notes:* Time, 60.

Designed to assess the importance of 16 job functions for performance in a higher-level position, based on information provided by a job incumbent. Also measures the incumbent's perceived ability to perform those functions. This is a self-report and may be used to diagnose individual and group training needs. Job functions include setting organizational objectives, financial planning and review, improving work procedures and practices, interdepartmental coordination, developing and implementing technical ideas, judgment and decision making, developing teamwork, coping with difficulties and emergencies, promoting safety attitudes and practices, communications, developing employee potential, supervisory practices, self-development and improvement, personnel practices, promoting community/organization relations, handling outside contacts.

**15313**
**Observational Assessments of Temperament.** Baehr, Melany E. 1988.
*Descriptors:* *Personnel Selection; *Personality Measures; *Affective Behavior; *Emotional Adjustment; *Supervisors; Adults; Occupational Tests; Predictive Measurement; Behavior Patterns
*Identifiers:* *Professional Position; Independence (Psychology); Temperament Comparator
*Availability:* London House, SRA Product Group, 9701 W. Higgins Rd., Rosemont, IL 60018.

The assessment was designed to measure 3 behavioral factors derived from another instrument, the Temperament Comparator (5267). These factors are reserved/cautious versus extroversive/impulsive, emotionally controlled versus emotionally responsive, and dependent/group-oriented versus self-reliant/individually oriented. These factors have been shown to be effective in predicting performance in higher-level specialized and managerial personnel. The instruments are hand-scored on site and may be used with the Temperament Comparator to determine how individuals present themselves to others in interviews.

**15314**
**Experience and Background Inventory.** Baehr, Melany E.; Froemel, Ernest C.; London House, Rosemont, IL 1988.

*Descriptors:* *Background; *Occupational Tests; *Personnel Selection; *Professional Personnel; *Supervisors; Academic Achievement; Adults; Aspiration; Career Counseling; Employment Experience; Job Performance; Job Satisfaction; Leadership; Predictive Measurement; Responsibility
*Identifiers:* EBI
*Availability:* London House, SRA Product Group, 9701 W. Higgins Rd., Rosemont, IL 60018.
*Notes:* Time, 20.

Designed to assess an individual's past achievements and behavior in developmental areas to assist in predicting successful job performance or career counseling of high-level professionals and executives. Covers school achievement, aspiration level, leadership, vocational satisfaction, financial and family responsibility, parental family adjustment, and leisure pursuits. Scored in-house by hand, or machine-scored by publisher.

**15315**
**Experience and Background Questionnaire.** Baehr, Melany E.
*Descriptors:* *Background; *Biographical Inventories; *Job Performance; *Predictive Measurement; Achievement; Adjustment (to Environment); Adults; Health; Questionnaires; Responsibility; Self Evaluation (Individuals)
*Identifiers:* EBQ
*Availability:* London House, SRA Product Group, 9701 W. Higgins Rd., Rosemont, IL 60018.
*Notes:* Time, 10 approx.

Designed to assess past achievement and development of individuals in 8 developmental areas. Items cover the areas of school achievement, drive, mobility, financial experience and responsibility, family responsibility, parental family adjustment, job and personal stability, and health. May be used to predict performance in entry-level positions in industrial organizations that carry some responsibility or performance in positions, such as municipal and state police in government organizations. May also be used to structure and direct background and employment interviews. May be administered to individuals or groups.

**15318**
**Station Employee Applicant Inventory.** London House, Rosemont, IL 1988.
*Descriptors:* *Attitude Measures; *Occupational Tests; *Personnel Selection; *Sales Workers; Adults; Arithmetic; Computer Software; Cooperation; Drug Use; Interpersonal Competence; Job Skills; Personality; Predictive Measurement; Scoring
*Identifiers:* *Cashiers; *Gas Station Employees; Honesty; SEAI
*Availability:* London House, SRA Product Group, 9701 W. Higgins Rd., Rosemont, IL 60018.
*Notes:* Time, 45. Items, 144.

Designed to predict on-the-job attitudes and behaviors of prospective gas station or convenience store cashiers. Said to select those who will be less often late or absent; safeguard money; be accurate and honest with cash or change; use safe work habits; perform well when rushed and distracted; and give the company a positive image. A lie scale is included to detect faked responses. Administered on-site by company personnel with no special training. Scoring is by mail, via phone, or via IBM-compatible PC. Said to be highly valid, that is, correlates with future performance evaluation.

**15319**
**Attitude Survey Program for Business and Industry.** London House, Rosemont, IL 1988.
*Descriptors:* *Attitude Measures; *Job Satisfaction; *Occupational Tests; *Organizations (Groups); *Professional Personnel; *Sales Occupations; *Supervisors; Adults; Business Communication; Job Performance; Leadership; Salaries; Supervisory Methods
*Identifiers:* Coworkers
*Availability:* London House, SRA Product Group, 9701 W. Higgins Rd., Rosemont, IL 60018.

Designed to measure attitudes of employee groups: hourly employees, managers above first line, staff, and field sales personnel. Said to be useful in measuring causes for low morale and productivity, predicting employee acceptance of change; and determining training needs for managers. Consists of organization survey, managerial survey, professional survey, and sales survey. Modifications and customized versions can be made to specifications. Profiles compare results to a national norm. Scoring is done by the publisher. Covers organization identification, job satisfaction, material rewards, leadership, supervision, work efficiency, communication, and sales-related factors for that survey.

**15320**
**Attitude Survey Program for Health Care.** London House, Rosemont, IL 1988.
*Descriptors:* *Allied Health Occupations; *Attitude Measures; *Job Satisfaction; *Nurses; *Occupational Tests; *Physicians; Adults; Business Communication; Job Performance; Leadership; Organizations (Groups); Paraprofessional Personnel; Salaries; Supervisory Methods
*Availability:* London House, SRA Product Group, 9701 W. Higgins Rd., Rosemont, IL 60018.

Designed to measure attitudes of staff members in hospitals, health maintenance organizations (HMOs), clinics, and nursing care facilities. Surveys focus on organizational efficiency, harmony, and factors that influence patient care. Said to uncover attitudes that could result in absenteeism, excessive lateness, and high turnover. The following surveys are available: Nursing Staff, Physicians, Paraprofessionals, Nonmedical Professionals, and Health Care Employees. Some areas covered are organization identification, job satisfaction, salaries and benefits, supervisory practices, work efficiency, communication, and other matters directly related to concerns of medical staff.

**15321**
**Employment Productivity Index.** London House, Rosemont, IL
*Descriptors:* *Job Applicants; *Job Performance; *Personality Measures; *Personnel Evaluation; *Personnel Selection; *Predictive Measurement; Adults; Drug Use; Interpersonal Competence; Productivity; Rating Scales; Reliability; Safety; Self Evaluation (Individuals); Validity
*Identifiers:* EPI
*Availability:* London House, SRA Product Group, 9701 W. Higgins Rd., Rosemont, IL 60018.
*Notes:* Time, 30 approx.

Assesses an individual's personality traits that have been determined to lead to productive and responsible work behavior. Measures are made in the areas of dependability, interpersonal cooperation, and drug avoidance. A validity scale, which assists test givers in determining whether the applicant understood the test and was accurate, is included. A second version of this test includes an optional safety scale to assess the safety consciousness of individuals who are being considered for jobs that involve safety. May be administered to individuals or groups.

**15322**
**Personnel Selection Inventory.** London House, Rosemont, IL
*Descriptors:* *Employee Attitudes; *Job Applicants; *Job Performance; *Personnel Selection; *Predictive Measurement; *Work Attitudes; Adults; Background; Drug Use; Emotional Problems; Interpersonal Competence; Personnel Evaluation; Productivity; Questionnaires; Self Evaluation (Individuals); Validity
*Identifiers:* Honesty; PSI
*Availability:* London House, SRA Product Group, 9701 W. Higgins Rd., Rosemont, IL 60018.

Designed to screen out job applicants who fall into the high-risk employee categories of dishonesty, neglect of duties, and disruptive behavior. Items cover the areas of honesty, drug avoidance, nonviolence, employee-customer relations, emotional stability, safety, work values, supervision attitudes, and applicant employability. Includes 2 scales that measure the validity of job applicants' answers. There are 8 versions of the inventory. Employers may choose the version that best suits their needs. Another 2 versions are available for selection of bank employees.

**15325**
**Occupational Stress Inventory.** Osipow, Samuel H.; Spokane, Arnold R. 1987.
*Descriptors:* *Coping; *Emotional Adjustment; *Stress Variables; *Work Environment; Adults; Interpersonal Relationship; Occupational Tests; Physical Environment; Physical Health; Research Tools; Role Conflict
*Identifiers:* Job Stress
*Availability:* Psychological Assessment Resources, Inc., P.O. Box 998, Odessa, FL 33556.
*Notes:* Time, 40.

Designed to measure 3 domains of occupational adjustment: occupational stress, psychological strain, and coping resources. The test was developed as a generic measure of occupational stressors that could be used at different occupational levels and in various work environments. It is also meant to provide a measure of a theoretical model that links work stress sources, individual strain, and coping resources. Fourteen scales measure the 3 domains. The scale is divided into an Occupational Roles Questionnaire, a Personal Strain Questionnaire, and a Personal Resources Questionnaire. At this writing there is limited normative information in the form of percentiles and T-scores.

**15327**
**Audit of Principal Effectiveness.** Valentine, Jerry W.; Bowman, Michael L. 1986.
*Descriptors:* *Administrator Evaluation; *Attitude Measures; *Organizational Climate; *Principals; *Teacher Attitudes; Elementary Secondary Education; Feedback; Instructional Leadership
*Availability:* ERIC Document Reproduction Service, 7420 Fullerton Rd., Ste. 110, Springfield, VA 22153-2852 (ED281319, 21 pages).
*Notes:* Items, 80.

Designed to determine teachers' perceptions of principal effectiveness, to allow principals to obtain feedback from teachers regarding strengths and weaknesses, and to provide a useful tool for teachers studying principals. Focuses on 3 broad domains of administration: organizational development, organizational environment, and educational reform. In addition, each of these domains is broken down into its respective discrete factors. Statistical reliability for factors is indicated.

**15329**
**Sales Personnel Tests: Business Comprehension Test (Experienced Applicant).** Rosenthal, Walter 1987.
*Descriptors:* *Business; *Occupational Tests; *Personnel Selection; *Sales Occupations; Adults; Knowledge Level; Multiple Choice Tests; Sales Workers; Work Experience
*Availability:* Caddylak Systems, Inc., 131 Heartland Blvd., P.O. Box W, Brentwood, NY 11717-0698.
*Notes:* For complete series of tests, see 15329 through 15351. Time, 15. Items, 31.

Designed to measure knowledge of business terms and concepts for people who are being considered for sales positions. The test is multiple choice. It is part of a series of tests to screen candidates for hiring or advancement or evaluate current sales personnel. Tests in the series may be reproduced as necessary and are scored by the employer. These tests are sold as part of a portfolio guide to recruiting, screening, selecting, or evaluating sales personnel. Tests must be validated by the user.

**15330**
**Sales Personnel Tests: Business Comprehension Tests (Sales Manager).** Rosenthal, Walter 1987.
*Descriptors:* *Business; *Managerial Occupations; *Occupational Tests; *Personnel Selection; *Sales Occupations; Adults; Knowledge Level; Multiple Choice Tests; Sales Workers; Work Experience
*Identifiers:* *Sales Managers
*Availability:* Caddylak Systems, Inc., 131 Heartland Blvd., P.O. Box W, Brentwood, NY 11717-0698.
*Notes:* For complete series of tests, see 15329 through 15351. Time, 15. Items, 11.

Designed to measure knowledge of business terms and concepts for people who are being considered for positions as sales managers. The test is multiple choice. It is part of a series of tests to screen candidates for hiring or advancement or evaluate current sales personnel. Tests in the series may be reproduced as necessary and are scored by the employer. These tests are sold as part of a portfolio guide to recruiting, screening, selecting or evaluating sales personnel. Tests must be validated by the user.

**15331**
**Sales Personnel Tests: Business Comprehension Test (Sales Trainee).** Rosenthal, Walter 1987.
*Descriptors:* *Business; *Occupational Tests; *Personnel Selection; *Sales Occupations; *Trainees; Adults; Knowledge Level; Multiple Choice Tests; Sales Workers
*Availability:* Caddylak Systems, Inc., 131 Heartland Blvd., P.O. Box W, Brentwood, NY 11717-0698.
*Notes:* For complete series of tests, see 15329 through 15351. Items, 11.

Designed to measure knowledge of very basic business terms and practices for people who are being considered for positions as sales trainees. The test is multiple choice. It is part of a series of tests to screen candidates for hiring or advancement or to evaluate current sales personnel. Tests in the series may be reproduced as necessary and are scored by the employer. These tests are sold as part of a portfolio guide to recruiting, screening, selecting, or evaluating sales personnel. Tests must be validated by the user.

**15332**
**Sales Personnel Tests: Checklist of Environmental Factors in a Job Analysis.** Rosenthal, Walter 1987.
*Descriptors:* *Job Analysis; *Occupational Tests; *Personnel Selection; *Sales Occupations; Adults; Sales Workers
*Availability:* Caddylak Systems, Inc., 131 Heartland Blvd., P.O. Box W, Brentwood, NY 11717-0698.
*Notes:* For complete series of tests, see 15329 through 15351. Items, 11.

Designed for use in describing the market environment in which a company is operating prior to designing a job description. The test is part of a series of tests to screen candidates for hiring or advancement or evaluate current sales personnel. Tests in the series may be reproduced as necessary and are scored by the employer. These tests are sold as part of a portfolio guide to recruiting, screening, selecting, or evaluating sales personnel. Tests must be validated by the user.

**15333**
**Sales Personnel Tests: Checklist of Performance Factors in a Job Analysis.** Rosenthal, Walter 1987.
*Descriptors:* *Job Analysis; *Occupational Tests; *Personnel Selection; *Sales Occupations; Adults; Job Performance; Sales Workers
*Availability:* Caddylak Systems, Inc., 131 Heartland Blvd., P.O. Box W, Brentwood, NY 11717-0698.
*Notes:* For complete series of tests, see 15329 through 15351. Items, 11.

Designed for use in describing percentages of time spent on tasks related to selling prior to developing a job description. The test is part of a series of tests to screen candidates for hiring or advancement or evaluate current sales personnel. Tests in the series may be reproduced as necessary and are scored by the employer. These tests are sold as part of a portfolio guide to recruiting, screening, selecting, or evaluating sales personnel. Tests must be validated by the user.

**15334**
**Sales Personnel Tests: Communications Skills Test (Sales Manager).** Rosenthal, Walter 1987.
*Descriptors:* *Managerial Occupations; *Mathematics; *Occupational Tests; *Personnel Selection; *Sales Occupations; *Writing Skills; Adults; Communication Skills; Sales Workers
*Identifiers:* *Sales Managers
*Availability:* Caddylak Systems, Inc., 131 Heartland Blvd., P.O. Box W, Brentwood, NY 11717-0698.
*Notes:* For complete series of tests, see 15329 through 15351. Items, 3.

Designed to measure written communication skills of the job candidate. Several questions consist of statements about human relations to which the candidate responds. Responses are evaluated only as to the effectiveness of the writing. The test is part of a series of tests to screen candidates for hiring or advancement or to evaluate current sales personnel. Tests in the series may be reproduced as necessary and are scored by the employer. These tests are sold as part of a portfolio guide to recruiting, screening, selecting, or evaluating sales personnel. Tests must be validated by the user.

**15335**
**Sales Personnel Tests: In-Depth Interview Questions (Sales Manager).** Rosenthal, Walter 1987.
*Descriptors:* *Managerial Occupations; *Occupational Tests; *Personnel Selection; *Sales Occupations; Adults; Background; Interviews; Sales Workers; Work Experience
*Identifiers:* *Sales Managers
*Availability:* Caddylak Systems, Inc., 131 Heartland Blvd., P.O. Box W, Brentwood, NY 11717-0698.
*Notes:* For complete series of tests, see 15329 through 15351. Items, 7.

Designed for use in collecting information about the sales history of sales managers prior to hiring. The candidate answers questions, in writing, about sales and selling. The test is part of a series of tests to screen candidates for hiring or advancement or evaluate current sales personnel. Tests in the series may be reproduced as necessary and are scored by the employer. These tests are sold as part of a portfolio guide to recruiting, screening, selecting, or evaluating sales personnel. Responses are evaluated by the interviewer. Test must be validated by the user.

**15336**
**Sales Personnel Tests: Language Skills Test (Experienced Applicant).** Rosenthal, Walter 1987.
*Descriptors:* *Language Usage; *Occupational Tests; *Personnel Selection; *Sales Occupations; Adults; Multiple Choice Tests; Sales Workers; Work Experience
*Availability:* Caddylak Systems, Inc., 131 Heartland Blvd., P.O. Box W, Brentwood, NY 11717-0698.
*Notes:* For complete series of tests, see 15329 through 15351. Time, 10. Items, 12.

Designed to measure knowledge of correct English usage for people who are being considered for positions as sales workers. The test is multiple choice and has the test taker select, from 4 choices, the sentence that is in correct English. The test is part of a series of tests to screen candidates for hiring or advancement or evaluate current sales personnel. Tests in the series may be reproduced as necessary and are scored by the employer. These tests are sold as part of a portfolio guide to recruiting, screening, selecting, or evaluating sales personnel. Tests must be validated by the user.

**15337**
**Sales Personnel Tests: Language Skills Test (Sales Manager).** Rosenthal, Walter 1987.
*Descriptors:* *Language Usage; *Managerial Occupations; *Occupational Tests; *Personnel Selection; *Sales Occupations; Adults; Multiple Choice Tests; Sales Workers
*Identifiers:* *Sales Managers
*Availability:* Caddylak Systems, Inc., 131 Heartland Blvd., P.O. Box W, Brentwood, NY 11717-0698.
*Notes:* For complete series of tests, see 15329 through 15351. Time, 10. Items, 11.

Designed to measure knowledge of correct English usage for people who are being considered for positions as sales managers. The test is multiple choice and requires the test taker to select, from 4 choices, the sentence that is in correct English. The test is part of a series of tests to screen candidates for hiring or advancement or evaluate current employees. Tests in the series may be reproduced as necessary and are scored by the employer. These tests are sold as part of a portfolio guide to recruiting, screening, selecting, or evaluating sales personnel. Tests must be validated by the user.

**15338**
**Sales Personnel Tests: Language Skills Test (Sales Trainee).** Rosenthal, Walter 1987.
*Descriptors:* *Language Usage; *Occupational Tests; *Personnel Selection; *Sales Occupations; *Trainees; Adults; Multiple Choice Tests; Sales Workers
*Availability:* Caddylak Systems, Inc., 131 Heartland Blvd., P.O. Box W, Brentwood, NY 11717-0698.
*Notes:* For complete series of tests, see 15329 through 15351. Time, 10. Items, 12.

Designed to measure knowledge of correct English usage for people who are being considered for positions as sales trainees. The test is multiple choice and has the test taker select, from 4 choices, the sentence that is in correct English. It is part of a series of tests to screen candidates for hiring or advancement or evaluate current sales personnel. Tests in the series may be reproduced as necessary and are scored by the employer. These tests are sold as part of a portfolio guide to recruiting, screening, selecting, or evaluating sales personnel. Tests must be validated by the user.

**15339**
**Sales Personnel Tests: Math Skills Test (Experienced Applicant).** Rosenthal, Walter 1987.
*Descriptors:* *Mathematics; *Occupational Tests; *Personnel Selection; *Sales Occupations; Adults; Arithmetic; Multiple Choice Tests; Percentage; Sales Workers; Work Experience
*Availability:* Caddylak Systems, Inc., 131 Heartland Blvd., P.O. Box W, Brentwood, NY 11717-0698.
*Notes:* For complete series of tests, see 15329 through 15351. Time, 15. Items, 12.

Designed to measure the knowledge of simple mathematics of experienced sales workers who are being considered for sales positions. This brief, multiple-choice test covers fractions, percents, and working with dollar amounts. It is part of a series of tests to screen candidates for hiring or advancement or evaluate current sales personnel. Tests in the series may be reproduced as necessary and are scored by the employer. These tests are sold as part of a portfolio guide to recruiting, screening, selecting, or evaluating sales personnel. Tests must be validated by the user.

**15340**
**Sales Personnel Tests: Math Skills Test (Sales Manager).** Rosenthal, Walter 1987.
*Descriptors:* *Managerial Occupations; *Mathematics; *Occupational Tests; *Personnel Selection; *Sales Occupations; Adults; Arithmetic; Multiple Choice Tests; Percentage; Sales Workers
*Identifiers:* *Sales Managers
*Availability:* Caddylak Systems, Inc., 131 Heartland Blvd., P.O. Box W, Brentwood, NY 11717-0698.

*Notes:* For complete series of tests, see 15329 through 15351. Time, 15. Items, 10.

Designed to measure the knowledge of simple mathematics of people who are being considered for positions as sales managers. This brief, multiple-choice test covers fractions, percents, and working with dollar amounts. It is part of a series of tests to screen candidates for hiring or advancement or to evaluate current sales personnel. Tests in the series may be reproduced as necessary and are scored by the employer. These tests are sold as part of a portfolio guide to recruiting, screening, selecting, or evaluating sales personnel. Tests must be validated by the user.

**15341**
**Sales Personnel Tests: Math Skills Test (Sales Trainee).** Rosenthal, Walter 1987.
*Descriptors:* *Mathematics; *Occupational Tests; *Personnel Selection; *Sales Occupations; *Trainees; Adults; Arithmetic; Multiple Choice Tests; Percentage; Sales Workers
*Availability:* Caddylak Systems, Inc., 131 Heartland Blvd., P.O. Box W, Brentwood, NY 11717-0698.
*Notes:* For complete series of tests, see 15329 through 15351. Items, 13.

Designed to measure the knowledge of simple mathematics of people who are being considered for positions as sales trainees. This brief, multiple-choice test covers fractions, percents, and working with dollar amounts. It is part of a series of tests, used in conjunction with an in-depth interview to screen candidates. The test is scored by the employer. It is sold as part of a portfolio guide to recruiting, screening, selecting, and evaluating sales personnel and may be reproduced as needed. Tests must be validated by the user.

**15342**
**Sales Personnel Tests: Personal Qualifications Checklist.** Rosenthal, Walter 1987.
*Descriptors:* *Employment Qualifications; *Occupational Tests; *Personnel Selection; *Sales Occupations; Adults; Check Lists; Individual Characteristics; Records (Forms); Sales Workers
*Availability:* Caddylak Systems, Inc., 131 Heartland Blvd., P.O. Box W, Brentwood, NY 11717-0698.
*Notes:* For complete series of tests, see 15329 through 15351. Items, 12.

Designed for use in determining personal qualifications needed to fill a sales position. Employer checks off those thought to be important for each category of sales position. The test is part of a series of tests to screen candidates for hiring or advancement or to evaluate current sales personnel. Tests in the series may be reproduced as necessary and are scored by the employer. These tests are sold as part of a portfolio guide to recruiting, screening, selecting, or evaluating sales personnel. Tests must be validated by the user.

**15343**
**Sales Personnel Tests: Reading Comprehension Test (Experienced Applicant).** Rosenthal, Walter 1987.
*Descriptors:* *Occupational Tests; *Personnel Selection; *Reading Comprehension; *Sales Occupations; Adults; Sales Workers; Work Experience
*Availability:* Caddylak Systems, Inc., 131 Heartland Blvd., P.O. Box W, Brentwood, NY 11717-0698.
*Notes:* For complete series of tests, see 15329 through 15351. Items, 9.

Designed to measure the reading comprehension of persons who are being considered for positions as sales workers. This brief test requires the test taker to read a short paragraph and answer questions about the content, which is concerned with selling. The test is part of a series of tests to screen candidates for hiring or advancement or to evaluate current sales personnel. Tests in the series may be reproduced as necessary and are scored by the employer. These tests are sold as part of a portfolio guide to recruiting, screening, selecting, or evaluating sales personnel. Tests must be validated by the user.

**15344**
**Sales Personnel Tests: Reading Comprehension Test (Sales Managers).** Rosenthal, Walter 1987.
*Descriptors:* *Managerial Occupations; *Occupational Tests; *Personnel Selection; *Reading Comprehension; *Sales Occupations; Adults; Sales Workers
*Identifiers:* *Sales Managers
*Availability:* Caddylak Systems, Inc., 131 Heartland Blvd., P.O. Box W, Brentwood, NY 11717-0698.
*Notes:* For complete series of tests, see 15329 through 15351. Time, 10. Items, 10.

Designed to measure the reading comprehension of people who are being considered for positions as sales managers. This brief multiple-choice test requires the test taker to read a short paragraph and answer questions about the content. It is part of a series of tests to screen candidates for hiring or advancement or to evaluate current sales personnel. Tests in the series may be reproduced as necessary and are scored by the employer. These tests are sold as part of a portfolio guide to recruiting, screening, selecting, or evaluating sales personnel. Tests must be validated by the user.

**15345**
**Sales Personnel Test: Reading Comprehension Tests (Sales Trainee).** Rosenthal, Walter 1987.
*Descriptors:* *Occupational Tests; *Personnel Selection; *Reading Comprehension; *Sales Occupations; *Trainees; Adults; Sales Workers
*Availability:* Caddylak Systems, Inc., 131 Heartland Blvd., P.O. Box W, Brentwood, NY 11717-0698.
*Notes:* For complete series of tests, see 15329 through 15351. Items, 9.

Designed to measure the reading comprehension of people who are being considered for positions as sales trainees. This brief true/false test requires the test taker to read a short paragraph and answer questions about the content. It is part of a series of tests, used in conjunction with an in-depth interview, to screen candidates. The test is sold as part of a portfolio guide to recruiting, screening, selecting, and evaluating sales personnel and may be reproduced as needed. Content of the paragraphs is concerned with selling. Tests must be validated by the user.

**15346**
**Sales Personnel Tests: Role Playing and Simulation (Experienced Applicant).** Rosenthal, Walter 1987.
*Descriptors:* *Occupational Tests; *Personnel Selection; *Role Playing; *Salesmanship; *Sales Occupations; *Simulation; Adults; Sales Workers; Work Experience
*Availability:* Caddylak Systems, Inc., 131 Heartland Blvd., P.O. Box W, Brentwood, NY 11717-0698.
*Notes:* For complete series of tests, see 15329 through 15351. Time, 30. Items, 6.

Designed to measure an interviewee's behavior in situations that may be experienced by trained sales workers. The candidate can write responses to each situation or participate in a role play or simulation. The test is part of a series of tests to screen candidates for hiring or advancement or to evaluate current sales personnel. Tests in the series may be reproduced as necessary and are scored by the employer. These tests are sold as part of a portfolio guide to recruiting, screening, selecting, or evaluating sales personnel. Tests must be validated by the user.

**15347**
**Sales Personnel Tests: Role Playing and Simulation (Sales Managers).** Rosenthal, Walter 1987.
*Descriptors:* *Managerial Occupations; *Occupational Tests; *Personnel Selection; *Role Playing; *Salesmanship; *Sales Occupations; *Simulation; Adults; Sales Workers
*Identifiers:* *Sales Managers
*Availability:* Caddylak Systems, Inc., 131 Heartland Blvd., P.O. Box W, Brentwood, NY 11717-0698.
*Notes:* For complete series of tests, see 15329 through 15351. Time, 30. Items, 6.

Designed to measure an interviewee's behavior in situations that may be experienced by trained sales managers. The candidate can write responses to each situation or participate in a role play or simulation. The test is part of a series of tests to screen candidates for hiring or advancement or to evaluate current sales personnel. Tests in the series may be reproduced as necessary and are scored by the employer. These tests are sold as part of a portfolio guide to recruiting, screening, selecting, or evaluating sales personnel. The responses are evaluated by the employer. Tests may be validated by the user.

**15348**
**Sales Personnel Tests: Role Playing and Simulation (Sales Trainee).** Rosenthal, Walter 1987.
*Descriptors:* *Occupational Tests; *Personnel Selection; *Role Playing; *Salesmanship; *Sales Occupations; *Simulation; *Trainees; Adults; Sales Workers
*Availability:* Caddylak Systems, Inc., 131 Heartland Blvd., P.O. Box W, Brentwood, NY 11717-0698.
*Notes:* For complete series of tests, see 15329 through 15351. Time, 30. Items, 6.

Designed to measure an interviewee's behavior in situations that may be experienced by sales workers. The applicant can write responses to each situation or participate in a role play or simulation. The test is part of a series of tests to screen candidates for hiring or advancement or to evaluate current sales personnel. Tests in the series may be reproduced as necessary and are scored by the employer. These tests are sold as part of a portfolio guide to recruiting, screening, selecting, or evaluating sales personnel. Tests must be validated by the user.

**15349**
**Sales Personnel Tests: Written Response Form for Experienced Sales Representatives.** Rosenthal, Walter 1987.
*Descriptors:* *Occupational Tests; *Personnel Selection; *Salesmanship; *Sales Occupations; Adults; Background; Records (Forms); Sales Workers; Work Experience
*Availability:* Caddylak Systems, Inc., 131 Heartland Blvd., P.O. Box W, Brentwood, NY 11717-0698.
*Notes:* For complete series of tests, see 15329 through 15351. Items, 8.

Designed for use in collecting information about the sales history of experienced sales personnel before hiring. Candidate answers questions in writing about sales and selling. The test is part of a series of tests to screen candidates for hiring or advancement or to evaluate current sales personnel. Tests in the series may be reproduced as necessary and are scored by the employer. These tests are sold as part of a portfolio guide to recruiting, screening, selecting, or evaluating sales personnel. The data are interpreted by the employer. Tests must be validated by the user.

**15350**
**Sales Personnel Tests: Written Response Form for Sales Managers.** Rosenthal, Walter 1987.
*Descriptors:* *Managerial Occupations; *Occupational Tests; *Personnel Selection; *Salesmanship; *Sales Occupations; Adults; Background; Records (Forms); Sales Workers
*Identifiers:* *Sales Managers
*Availability:* Caddylak Systems, Inc., 131 Heartland Blvd., P.O. Box W, Brentwood, NY 11717-0698.
*Notes:* For complete series of tests, see 15329 through 15351. Items, 4.

Designed for use in collecting information about the sales history of experienced sales personnel before hiring. The candidate answers questions, in writing, about sales and selling. The test is part of a series of tests to screen candidates for hiring or advancement or to evaluate current employees who are sales personnel. Tests in the series may be reproduced as necessary and are scored by the employer. These tests are sold as part of a portfolio guide to recruiting, screening, selecting, or evaluating sales personnel. Responses are evaluated by the employer. Tests must be validated by the user.

**15351**
**Sales Personnel Tests: Written Response Form for Sales Trainees.** Rosenthal, Walter 1987.
*Descriptors:* *Occupational Tests; *Personnel Selection; *Salesmanship; *Sales Occupations; *Trainees; Adults; Background; Records (Forms); Sales Workers
*Availability:* Caddylak Systems, Inc., 131 Heartland Blvd., P.O. Box W, Brentwood, NY 11717-0698.
*Notes:* For complete series of tests, see 15329 through 15351. Items, 5.

Designed for use in collecting information about the work history of potential sales personnel before hiring as trainees. The candidate answers questions about background. The test is part of a series of tests to screen candidates for hiring or advancement or to evaluate current employees who are sales personnel. Tests in the series may be reproduced as necessary and are scored by the employer. These tests are sold as part of a portfolio guide to recruiting, screening, selecting, or evaluating sales personnel. Tests must be validated by the user.

**15363**
**University Associates Instrumentation Kit.** University Associates, San Diego, CA 1988.
*Descriptors:* *Human Resources; *Industrial Training; *Labor Force Development; *Management Development; Adults; Group Counseling; Group Discussion; Interpersonal Relationship; Occupational Tests; Organizational Communication; Personnel Evaluation
*Identifiers:* Group Facilitation
*Availability:* Pfeiffer and Co., formerly University Associates, 8517 Production Ave., San Diego, CA 92121-2280.

This series of instruments has been selected from other University Associates publications and formatted so that the materials may be reproduced as needed by human resources development professionals for educational and training activities. Large-scale distribution (over 100 copies) requires further permission before reproduction. Instruments cover 7 major categories: communication; consulting/facilitation; groups/teams; interpersonal; management/leadership; organizations; and personal issues. Subtopics include: values, stress, organizational culture, employee attitudes, leadership, and learning style.

**15364**
**Assertion-Rights Questionnaire.** Woodcock, Mike; Francis, Dave 1981.
*Descriptors:* *Assertiveness; *Attitude Measures; *Human Resources; *Industrial Training; *Labor Force Development; Adults; Behavior Patterns; Group Counseling; Occupational Tests; Personnel Evaluation; Rating Scales
*Identifiers:* ARQ
*Availability:* Pfeiffer and Co., formerly University Associates, 8517 Production Ave., San Diego, CA 92121-2280.
*Notes:* Contained in University Associates Instrumentation Kit (15363). Items, 12.

Designed to assist participants in evaluating their own attitudes about personal assertion. Part of a kit of instruments that may be reproduced as needed without permission (up to 100 copies) by human resources development personnel for educational and training activities. This 5-point agree/disagree scale elicits the participants' perceptions of their rights and how their perceptions are translated into behavior.

**15365**
**Blockage Questionnaire.** Woodcock, Mike; Francis, Dave 1979.
*Descriptors:* *Administrators; *Human Resources; *Industrial Training; *Management Development; *Organizational Climate; *Problems; Adults; Creativity; Industrial Structure; Labor Force Development; Motivation; Occupational Tests; Organizational Objectives; Personnel Management; Questionnaires; Supervisors; Teamwork
*Identifiers:* BQ
*Availability:* Pfeiffer and Co., formerly University Associates, 8517 Production Ave., San Diego, CA 92121-2280.
*Notes:* Contained in University Associates Instrumentation Kit (15363). Items, 120.

Designed to collect information on "blockages," weaknesses in an organization that retard the effective use of personnel. The questionnaire, to be completed by managers, may be used to describe part of an organization or the entire organization. It covers inadequate recruitment and selection, confused organizational structure, inadequate control, poor training, low motivation, low creativity, poor teamwork, inappropriate management philosophy, lack of succession planning and management development, unclear aims, unfair rewards, and personal stagnation. Part of a kit of instruments that may be reproduced as needed without permission (up to 100 copies) by human resources development personnel for educational and training activities. Other blockage instruments are Blockages Survey (Other) (15368); Blockages Survey (Job) (15367); and Blockages Survey (Self) (15366).

**15366**
**Blockages Survey (Self).** Francis, Dave; Woodcock, Mike 1980.
*Descriptors:* *Administrators; *Human Resources; *Industrial Training; *Management Development; Adults; Behavior Problems; Creativity; Individual Development; Intuition; Job Skills; Labor Force Development; Objectives; Occupational Tests; Problem Solving; Self Evaluation (Individuals); Supervision; Supervisors; Teamwork; Values
*Identifiers:* BSS; Personal Influence; Team Building
*Availability:* Pfeiffer and Co., formerly University Associates, 8517 Production Ave., San Diego, CA 92121-2280.
*Notes:* Contained in University Associates Instrumentation Kit (15363). Time, 20. Items, 110.

Designed for use by human resources development personnel for educational and training activities. Part of a kit of instruments that may be reproduced as needed (up to 100 copies) without permission. Identifies strengths and "blockages," or weaknesses, of managers. Is self-administered by managers. Items cover self-management competence, personal values, personal goals, personal development, adequate problem-solving skills, creativity, influence, managerial insight, supervisory skills, trainer capability, and team-building capacity. Other blockage instruments are: Blockage Questionnaire (15365); Blockages Survey (Job) (15367); and Blockages Survey (Other) (15368).

**15367**
**Blockages Survey (Job).** Francis, Dave; Woodcock, Mike 1981.
*Descriptors:* *Administrators; *Human Resources; *Industrial Training; *Management Development; *Occupational Information; *Supervisors; Adults; Behavior Patterns; Creativity; Individual Development; Intuition; Job Skills; Labor Force Development; Objectives; Occupational Tests; Problem Solving; Supervision; Values
*Identifiers:* BSJ
*Availability:* Pfeiffer and Co., formerly University Associates, 8517 Production Ave., San Diego, CA 92121-2280.
*Notes:* Contained in University Associates Instrumentation Kit (15363). Items, 110.

Part of a series of surveys for use in management development training by human resources personnel. This survey measures strengths and weaknesses in managerial ability that match the particular demands of the job, and determines which abilities need further development through comparison of scores with the Blockages Survey (Self) (15366). Both instruments are part of a kit that may be reproduced as needed (up to 100 copies) without permission. Other blockage instruments are Blockages Survey (Other) (15368) and Blockage Questionnaire (15365). Covers recruitment and selection, organizational structure, control, training, motivation, creativity, teamwork, inappropriate management philosophy, unclear aims, and personal stagnation.

**15368**
**Blockages Survey (Other).** Francis, Dave; Woodcock, Mike 1981.
*Descriptors:* *Administrator Evaluation; *Administrators; *Human Resources; *Industrial Training; *Management Development; *Supervisors; Adults; Behavior Patterns; Creativity; Individual Development; Intuition; Labor Force Development; Objectives; Occupational Tests; Peer Evaluation; Problem Solving; Rating Scales; Values
*Identifiers:* BSO
*Availability:* Pfeiffer and Co., formerly University Associates, 8517 Production Ave., San Diego, CA 92121-2280.
*Notes:* Contained in University Associates Instrumentation Kit (15363). Items, 110.

Part of a series of surveys designed for use in management development training by human resources personnel. This survey measures strengths and weaknesses in managerial ability as perceived by others in a position to view overall managerial performance: bosses, peers, subordinates. Other instruments concerned with "blockages" are Blockage Questionnaire (15365); Blockages Survey (Self) (15366); and Blockages Survey (Job) (15367). All instruments are part of a large kit and may be reproduced as needed (up to 100 copies) without permission. Covers recruitment and selection, organizational structure, control, training, motivation, creativity, teamwork, inappropriate management philosophy, unclear aims, and personal stagnation.

**15369**
**Central West Virginia Cultural-Awareness Quiz.** Morgan, James P. Jr.; Beeler, Kent D.
*Descriptors:* *Administrators; *Culture Conflict; *Human Resources; *Industrial Training; *Management Development; *Regional Dialects; *Supervisors; *Testing; Adults; Cultural Differences; Ethnic Groups; Knowledge Level; Labor Force Development; Occupational Tests
*Identifiers:* CWVCAQ; Nonstandard English; West Virginia
*Availability:* Pfeiffer and Co., formerly University Associates, 8517 Production Ave., San Diego, CA 92121-2280.
*Notes:* Contained in University Associates Instrumentation Kit (15363). Time, 50.

Designed to help supervisors, managers, and others who may use test results to experience the frustration and confusion that a culturally different person may experience during a testing situation. Said to help others understand the lifestyles of those from other cultures. Items consist of colloquial expressions or local names for common items. Respondent selects the meaning from a choice of 4 or selects the standard English equivalent. Part of a large kit of instruments that may be reproduced as needed (up to 100 copies) without permission.

**15370**
**Client-Consultant Questionnaire: Checking for Client Involvement in OD.** University Associates, San Diego, CA 1986.
*Descriptors:* *Consultants; *Counselor Client Relationship; *Human Resources; *Industrial Training; *Management Development; *Organizational Development; Administrators; Adults; Occupational Tests; Organizational Change; Questionnaires; Supervisors; Values
*Identifiers:* CCQ
*Availability:* Pfeiffer and Co., formerly University Associates, 8517 Production Ave., San Diego, CA 92121-2280.

*Notes:* Contained in University Associates Instrumentation Kit (15363). Time, 10. Items, 10.

Designed to measure organizational development (OD) of consultants' involvement with their clients. Covers types of client involvement in the OD process, the quick fix without change, common values, as well as the possibility that consultants will become involved in the client's political process, rather than in the diagnosis of central issues more relevant to organizational development. Part of a large kit of instruments that may be reproduced as needed (up to 100 copies) without permission.

**15371**
**Disclosure/Feedback Instrument.** Cinnamon, Kenneth M.; Matulef, Norman J. 1979.
*Descriptors:* *Feedback; *Human Resources; *Industrial Training; *Management Development; *Self Disclosure (Individuals); Administrators; Adults; Occupational Tests; Supervisors
*Identifiers:* DFI
*Availability:* Pfeiffer and Co., formerly University Associates, 8517 Production Ave., San Diego, CA 92121-2280.
*Notes:* Contained in University Associates Instrumentation Kit (15363). Items, 20.

Designed to provide information on the amount of self-disclosure one is willing to make and the degree to which feedback is willingly received from boss, subordinate, or coworker. Respondents rate their willingness on a 5-point scale with each category of person. Part of a large kit of instruments that may be reproduced as needed (up to 100 copies) without permission.

**15373**
**Feedback Rating Scales.** University Associates, San Diego, CA 1974.
*Descriptors:* *Feedback; *Human Resources; *Industrial Training; *Management Development; Adults; Occupational Tests; Rating Scales
*Identifiers:* FRS
*Availability:* Pfeiffer and Co., formerly University Associates, 8517 Production Ave., San Diego, CA 92121-2280.
*Notes:* Contained in University Associates Instrumentation Kit (15363). Items, 8.

This instrument is designed to evaluate the quality of feedback one is receiving. For its purposes, this instrument defines feedback as "communication which gives (a) person information about how he or she affects others." Uses a 6-point biplоar adjective scale. Qualities of feedback that are rated include descriptive-evaluative, specific-general, etc. Part of a large kit of instruments that may be reproduced as needed (up to 100 copies) without permission. For use by human resources development professionals in educational and training activities.

**15374**
**Gap Identification: The Form-Substance Check List.** Bell, Chip R. 1982.
*Descriptors:* *Human Resources; *Industrial Structure; *Industrial Training; *Management Development; Adults; Check Lists; Occupational Tests; Organizational Effectiveness; Pyramid Organization; Rating Scales
*Identifiers:* FSCL
*Availability:* Pfeiffer and Co., formerly University Associates, 8517 Production Ave., San Diego, CA 92121-2280.
*Notes:* Contained in University Associates Instrumentation Kit (15363). Items, 14.

A checklist and rating scale designed to determine the disparity between the size, character, and complexity of an organization and its form, e.g., plan, infrastructure, tasks, objectives, performance standards, etc. Respondents indicate which conditions exist and rate their effectiveness. Part of a large kit of instruments that may be reproduced as needed (up to 100 copies) without permission. For use by human resources development professionals in educational and training activities.

**15375**
**General Evaluation Survey.** Cinnamon, Kenneth M.; Matulef, Norman J. 1979.
*Descriptors:* *Human Resources; *Industrial Training; *Program Evaluation; Adults; Management Development; Occupational Tests; Surveys
*Identifiers:* GES
*Availability:* Pfeiffer and Co., formerly University Associates, 8517 Production Ave., San Diego, CA 92121-2280.
*Notes:* Contained in University Associates Instrumentation Kit (15363). Items, 12.

A brief measure of a training participant's satisfaction with the content of a training program, the process, and the general experience. Part of a large kit of instruments that may be reproduced as needed (up to 100 copies) without permission. For use by human resources development professionals in educational and training activities.

**15376**
**Group Climate Inventory.** University Associates, San Diego, CA 1974.
*Descriptors:* *Group Behavior; *Human Resources; *Industrial Training; *Management Development; *Peer Groups; Adults; Occupational Tests; Peer Acceptance; Peer Relationship
*Identifiers:* GCI
*Availability:* Pfeiffer and Co., formerly University Associates, 8517 Production Ave., San Diego, CA 92121-2280.
*Notes:* Contained in University Associates Instrumentation Kit (15363). Items, 16.

A measure of behaviors expected of a peer group by a group member. Various behaviors of the group toward the member are rated on a 6-point frequency scale from "always be counted on" to "never expected." Part of a large kit of instruments that may be reproduced as needed (up to 100 copies) without permission. For use by human resources development professionals in educational and training activities.

**15378**
**Group Leadership Functions Scale.** University Associates, San Diego, CA 1975.
*Descriptors:* *Counselor Role; *Group Counseling; *Human Resources; *Industrial Training; *Interpersonal Competence; Adults; Behavior; Leadership; Occupational Tests
*Identifiers:* GLFS; *Group Facilitators
*Availability:* Pfeiffer and Co., formerly University Associates, 8517 Production Ave., San Diego, CA 92121-2280.
*Notes:* Contained in University Associates Instrumentation Kit (15363). Items, 28.

Designed for use by group facilitators in describing their interpersonal behavior as a facilitator. Behaviors are categorized as emotional stimulation, caring, meaning attribution, and executive function. Part of a large kit of instruments that may be reproduced as needed (up to 100 copies) without permission. For use by human resources development professionals in educational and training activities.

**15379**
**Identity Issues Work Sheet: Clarifying One's Position.** Mosel, Doug 1981.
*Descriptors:* *Industrial Training; *Self Concept; Adults; Group Counseling; Human Resources; Management Development; Occupational Tests; Sexual Identity
*Identifiers:* IIWS
*Availability:* Pfeiffer and Co., formerly University Associates, 8517 Production Ave., San Diego, CA 92121-2280.
*Notes:* Contained in University Associates Instrumentation Kit (15363). Items, 9.

Designed to identify the respondent's self-perceptions of identity prior to group discussion. Covers identity in terms of self-confidence, work, authority, and other aspects of the environment. For use by human resources development professionals in educational and training activities. Part of a large kit of instruments that may be reproduced as needed (up to 100 copies) without permission.

**15380**
**Interpersonal Check List.** LaForge, Rolfe 1977.
*Descriptors:* *Human Resources; *Industrial Training; *Interpersonal Relationship; *Management Development; *Personality; Adults; Group Discussion; Occupational Tests; Self Evaluation (Individuals)
*Identifiers:* ICL
*Availability:* Pfeiffer and Co., formerly University Associates, 8517 Production Ave., San Diego, CA 92121-2280.
*Notes:* Contained in University Associates Instrumentation Kit (15363). Time, 15. Items, 134.

Designed for use in obtaining a self-description of personality as it relates to a small group environment. The checklist is not to be used as a personality test, but only to stimulate group discussion. Part of a large kit of instruments that may be reproduced as needed (up to 100 copies) without permission. For use by human resources development professionals in educational and training activities. The instrument is in nontechnical language, and no training is necessary for use. Scales are dominant, submissive, hostile, and loving.

**15381**
**Interpersonal Communication Inventory.** University Associates, San Diego, CA 1974.
*Descriptors:* *Human Resources; *Industrial Training; *Interpersonal Communication; *Management Development; Adults; Behavior Patterns; Communication Skills; Listening Skills; Occupational Tests; Self Disclosure (Individuals)
*Identifiers:* ICI
*Availability:* Pfeiffer and Co., formerly University Associates, 8517 Production Ave., San Diego, CA 92121-2280.
*Notes:* Contained in University Associates Instrumentation Kit (15363). Items, 40.

Designed to help individuals determine behavior patterns they use in communications with others, not family members or relatives. Respondent selects those behaviors performed that relate to listening, interpersonal communications, openness, sensitivity to feelings expressed, trust, and conversing. Part of a large kit of instruments that may be reproduced as needed (up to 100 copies) without permission. For use by human resources development professionals in educational and training activities.

**15383**
**Job Suitability Analysis.** Adams, John D. 1980.
*Descriptors:* *Human Resources; *Industrial Training; *Management Development; *Occupational Information; *Stress Management; Adults; Employee Responsibility; Interpersonal Relationship; Occupational Tests; Peer Relationship; Work Attitudes; Work Environment
*Identifiers:* JSA; Role Ambiguity; Workload
*Availability:* Pfeiffer and Co., formerly University Associates, 8517 Production Ave., San Diego, CA 92121-2280.
*Notes:* Contained in University Associates Instrumentation Kit (15363). Items, 20.

A measure of real versus ideal job responsibility, difficulty, and work load, designed to determine whether the respondent is overstressed or understressed by a job. Respondent indicates degree of presence of various job responsibilities on a 5-point scale from "very little" to "very great," and the degree of responsibility desired. Dimensions are work load, qualitative; work load, quantitative; people responsibility; thing responsibility; role ambiguity; participation; supervisor relationship; peer relationship; and subordinate relationship. Part of a large kit of instruments that may be reproduced as needed (up to 100 copies) without permission. For use by human resources development professionals in educational and training activities.

**15384**
**Leadership Style Profile.** Francis, Dave; Young, Don 1979.
*Descriptors:* *Human Resources; *Industrial Training; *Leadership Styles; *Management Development; Administrators; Adults; Behavior Patterns; Managerial Occupations; Occupational Tests; Rating Scales
*Identifiers:* LSP
*Availability:* Pfeiffer and Co., formerly University Associates, 8517 Production Ave., San Diego, CA 92121-2280.
*Notes:* Contained in University Associates Instrumentation Kit (15363). Items, 15.

Designed to aid a team in understanding and defining the manager's style. Also used for providing feedback to the manager. Uses a 7-point scale anchored by contrasting behaviors. Part of a large kit of instruments that may be reproduced as needed (up to 100 copies) without permission. For use by human resources development professionals in educational and training activities.

**15385**
**Life-Style Preference Evaluation.** Adams, John D. 1980.
*Descriptors:* *Human Resources; *Industrial Training; *Life Style; *Management Development; *Values; Adults; Locus of Control; Needs; Occupational Tests; Stress Management
*Identifiers:* LSPE
*Availability:* Pfeiffer and Co., formerly University Associates, 8517 Production Ave., San Diego, CA 92121-2280.
*Notes:* Contained in University Associates Instrumentation Kit (15363). Items, 24.

Designed to measure an individual's lifestyle preference and whether it conforms to 1 of 3 different approaches: personalistic, sociocentric, or formalistic. Personalistic individuals like to have responsibility and be a motivating force. Sociocentric people reference others as important. Formalistic individuals refer to society as a whole and established procedures and policies. Part of a large kit of instruments that may be reproduced as needed (up to 100 copies) without permission. For use by human resources development professionals in educational and training activities.

**15387**
**Male-Female Role Questionnaire.** Carney, Clark G.; McMahon, Sarah Lynne 1977.
*Descriptors:* *Human Resources; *Industrial Training; *Management Development; *Sensitivity Training; *Sex Bias; *Sex Discrimination; *Sex Role; Adults; Attitude Measures; Occupational Tests; Sex Differences
*Identifiers:* MFRQ
*Availability:* Pfeiffer and Co., formerly University Associates, 8517 Production Ave., San Diego, CA 92121-2280.
*Notes:* Contained in University Associates Instrumentation Kit (15363). Items, 50.

A measure of the perception of the roles, characteristics, and issues involving the sexes in our society. Four separate scales require the respondent to describe the opposite sex and oneself, rate various traits as common to one sex and either cultural or biological, agree/disagree with statements about differences and similarities in the treatment of the sexes in society, and approve/disapprove of equality issues. Part of a large kit of instruments that may be reproduced as needed (up to 100 copies) without permission. For use by human resources development professionals in educational and training activities.

**15388**
**Management Skills Inventory: Assessing Personal Performance.** Levin, Carol J. 1983.
*Descriptors:* *Human Resources; *Industrial Training; *Job Skills; *Management Development; *Managerial Occupations; Administrators; Adults; Business Communication; Decision Making Skills; Group Dynamics; Interpersonal Competence; Occupational Tests; Planning; Problem Solving; Staff Utilization; Supervisors; Morale
*Identifiers:* MSI; Organizing Skills
*Availability:* Pfeiffer and Co., formerly University Associates, 8517 Production Ave., San Diego, CA 92121-2280.
*Notes:* Contained in University Associates Instrumentation Kit (15363). Time, 85. Items, 73.

A measure designed to elicit managers' perceptions of their performance of management-related behaviors and whether these behaviors need to be increased or decreased. These include communicating, problem solving and decision making, planning, staffing, organizing, group dynamics, morale building, and personal relationship skills. Part of a large kit of instruments that may be reproduced as needed (up to 100 copies) without permission. For use by human resources development professionals in educational and training activities.

**15389**
**Manager's Dilemma Work Sheet.** Glaser, Rollin; Glaser, Christine 1983.
*Descriptors:* *Administrators; *Attitude Measures; *Human Resources; *Industrial Training; *Management Development; *Supervisors; Administration; Adults; Employees; Employer Attitudes; Job Performance; Managerial Occupations; Occupational Tests; Theories
*Identifiers:* McGregor (Douglas); MDWS; Theory X; Theory Y
*Availability:* Pfeiffer and Co., formerly University Associates, 8517 Production Ave., San Diego, CA 92121-2280.
*Notes:* Contained in University Associates Instrumentation Kit (15363). Items, 11.

Designed to measure a manager's agreement with McGregor's Theory X and Theory Y, which deal with a supervisor's perceptions of employees as capable, achieving, and responsible (Theory Y) or avoiding, incapable, and indifferent (Theory X). Part of a large kit of instruments that may be reproduced as needed (up to 100 copies) without permission. For use by human resources development professionals in educational and training activities.

**15390**
**Meetings Review Questionnaire.** Woodcock, Mike; Francis, Dave 1981.
*Descriptors:* *Human Resources; *Industrial Training; *Management Development; *Meetings; Administrators; Adults; Occupational Tests; Rating Scales; Supervisors
*Identifiers:* MRQ
*Availability:* Pfeiffer and Co., formerly University Associates, 8517 Production Ave., San Diego, CA 92121-2280.
*Notes:* Contained in University Associates Instrumentation Kit (15363). Items, 8.

A rating scale for evaluating a meeting or a series of meetings according to 8 criteria: importance, membership, task, climate, openness, procedures, energy, and outside relationships. Part of a large kit of instruments that may be reproduced as needed (up to 100 copies) without permission. For use by human resources development professionals in educational and training activities.

**15391**
**Motivation Blockages Questionnaire.** Woodcock, Mike; Francis, Dave 1981.
*Descriptors:* *Employees; *Human Resources; *Industrial Training; *Management Development; *Motivation; *Work Environment; Adults; Job Layoff; Job Satisfaction; Occupational Tests; Questionnaires; Salaries; Self Actualization
*Identifiers:* Job Security; MBQ
*Availability:* Pfeiffer and Co., formerly University Associates, 8517 Production Ave., San Diego, CA 92121-2280.
*Notes:* Contained in University Associates Instrumentation Kit (15363). Items, 36.

Designed to identify conditions in the work environment that inhibit motivation or human energy in an organization or unit. Factors are working conditions, remuneration, security, personal development, involvement, interest, and challenge. Part of a large kit of instruments that may be reproduced as needed (up to 100 copies) without permission. For use by human resources development professionals in educational and training activities.

**15392**
**Nutrition Evaluation.** Adams, John D. 1980.
*Descriptors:* *Human Resources; *Industrial Training; *Management Development; *Nutrition; Administrators; Adults; Employees; Health; Supervisors
*Identifiers:* NE
*Availability:* Pfeiffer and Co., formerly University Associates, 8517 Production Ave., San Diego, CA 92121-2280.
*Notes:* Contained in University Associates Instrumentation Kit (15363). Items, 18.

Designed to measure the frequency of a variety of health-related nutritional behaviors, such as chewing one's food thoroughly. Part of a large kit of instruments that may be reproduced as needed (up to 100 copies) without permission. For use by human resources development professionals in educational and training activities.

**15393**
**OD Readiness Check List.** Pfeiffer, J. William; Jones, John E. 1978.
*Descriptors:* *Human Resources; *Industrial Training; *Needs Assessment; *Occupational Tests; *Organizational Development; Adults; Check Lists; Management Development; Organizational Change
*Identifiers:* ODRCL
*Availability:* Pfeiffer and Co., formerly University Associates, 8517 Production Ave., San Diego, CA 92121-2280.
*Notes:* Contained in University Associates Instrumentation Kit (15363). Items, 15.

Designed to quantify the need of an organization for organizational development (OD) procedures, including training, small-scale projects, and crisis intervention; management development and preliminary OD activities; and the willingness of an organization to commit itself to planned change. Part of a large kit of instruments that may be reproduced as needed (up to 100 copies) without permission. For use by human resources development professionals in educational and training activities.

**15394**
**Organizational Performance-Appraisal Questionnaire Evaluation.** Sashkin, Marshall 1981.
*Descriptors:* *Attitude Measures; *Employee Attitudes; *Human Resources; *Industrial Training; *Occupational Tests; *Personnel Evaluation; Adults; Employer Attitudes; Organizational Development; Supervisors
*Identifiers:* OPAQUE; *Performance Appraisal
*Availability:* Pfeiffer and Co., formerly University Associates, 8517 Production Ave., San Diego, CA 92121-2280.
*Notes:* Contained in University Associates Instrumentation Kit (15363). Items, 6.

A measure of the respondent's perception of performance appraisal in an organization. Some items refer to the experience of appraising others and some to the experience of being appraised. Uses an agree/disagree response format. Part of a large kit of instruments that may be reproduced as needed (up to 100 copies) without permission. For use by human resources development professionals in educational and training activities.

**15395**
**Performance Appraisal System Evaluation.** Sashkin, Marshall 1981.
*Descriptors:* *Attitude Measures; *Employer Attitudes; *Human Resources; *Industrial Training; *Occupational Tests; *Personnel Evaluation; Adults; Organizational Development
*Identifiers:* PASE; *Performance Appraisal
*Availability:* Pfeiffer and Co., formerly University Associates, 8517 Production Ave., San Diego, CA 92121-2280.
*Notes:* Contained in University Associates Instrumentation Kit (15363). Items, 15.

Designed to elicit respondent's perceptions about the general practices in an organization that are related to the performance-appraisal system. Uses a 5-point agree/disagree response format. Part of a large kit of instruments that may be reproduced as needed (up to 100 copies) without permission. For use by human resources development professionals in educational and training activities.

**15396**
**Personal Power and Confidence Inventory.** Robert, Marc 1982.
*Descriptors:* *Human Resources; *Individual Power; *Industrial Training; *Management Development; *Occupational Tests; *Self Esteem; Administration; Adults; Conflict Resolution; Organizations (Groups); Self Evaluation (Individuals)
*Identifiers:* PPCI
*Availability:* Pfeiffer and Co., formerly University Associates, 8517 Production Ave., San Diego, CA 92121-2280.
*Notes:* Contained in University Associates Instrumentation Kit (15363). Items, 10.

Designed to measure self-confidence and personal power in the context of an organization. Used to measure self-confidence of those who manage conflict. Self-confidence is said to be important in conflict management because its opposite, insecurity, causes destructive behavior and animosity. Part of a large kit of instruments that may be reproduced as needed (up to 100 copies) without permission. For use by human resources development professionals in educational and training activities.

**15397**
**Postmeeting Reactions Form.** University Associates, San Diego, CA 1974.
*Descriptors:* *Administrators; *Human Resources; *Industrial Training; *Management Development; *Meetings; *Occupational Tests; Adults; Behavior Patterns; Group Behavior; Rating Scales
*Identifiers:* PRF
*Availability:* Pfeiffer and Co., formerly University Associates, 8517 Production Ave., San Diego, CA 92121-2280.
*Notes:* Contained in University Associates Instrumentation Kit (15363). Items, 10.

A simple rating scale describing conditions during a meeting and the respondent's own behavior in that meeting. Descriptive statements are ranked from 1 to 10. No further descriptive information about the scale is provided. Part of a large kit of instruments that may be reproduced as needed (up to 100 copies) without permission. For use by human resources development professionals in educational and training activities.

**15398**
**Risk-Taking Behavior in Groups Questionnaire.** Kurtz, Robert 1974.
*Descriptors:* *Human Resources; *Industrial Training; *Occupational Tests; *Risk; Adults; Behavior Patterns; Groups; Questionnaires; Self Evaluation (Individuals)
*Identifiers:* RTBGQ
*Availability:* Pfeiffer and Co., formerly University Associates, 8517 Production Ave., San Diego, CA 92121-2280.
*Notes:* Contained in University Associates Instrumentation Kit (15363). Items, 28.

Designed to determine which of a set of behaviors constitutes a risk for the respondent within a group situation because it is either new behavior or engenders a sense of danger. Respondent indicates the degree of risk taken, from "no risk" to "high risk" on a 5-point scale. Part of a large kit of instruments that may be reproduced as needed (up to 100 copies) without permission. For use by human resources development professionals in educational and training activities.

**15399**
**Self-Assessment Inventory: Behavior in Groups.** Thayer, Louis 1976.
*Descriptors:* *Attitude Measures; *Group Dynamics; *Human Resources; *Industrial Training; *Occupational Tests; Adults; Behavior Patterns; Groups; Self Evaluation (Individuals)
*Identifiers:* SAI
*Availability:* Pfeiffer and Co., formerly University Associates, 8517 Production Ave., San Diego, CA 92121-2280.
*Notes:* Contained in University Associates Instrumentation Kit (15363). Time, 30. Items, 25.

Designed to assist members of a training group in assessing their attitudes and behavior during the sessions. Attitudes are concerned with the learning process, expression of feelings, and behaviors occurring within the group. Part of a large kit of instruments that may be reproduced as needed (up to 100 copies) without permission. For use by human resources development professionals in educational and training activities.

**15400**
**Stress Evaluation.** Adams, John D. 1980.
*Descriptors:* *Human Resources; *Industrial Training; *Occupational Tests; *Stress Variables; Administrators; Adults; Self Evaluation (Individuals)
*Identifiers:* SE
*Availability:* Pfeiffer and Co., formerly University Associates, 8517 Production Ave., San Diego, CA 92121-2280.
*Notes:* Contained in University Associates Instrumentation Kit (15363). Items, 30.

Measures the frequency and intensity of stress caused by events occurring in the environment that directly affect the respondent. Numerical values are attached to each event, and the respondent indicates the numerical value of that event to herself or himself. Ratings are summed. Separate forms cover work-related and non-work-related episodic stress; work-related and non-work-related chronic stress. Percentiles are provided based on data gathered from 570 administrators, managers, and educators. Part of a large kit of instruments that may be reproduced as needed (up to 100 copies) without permission. For use by human resources development professionals in educational and training activities.

**15401**
**Team-Review Questionnaire.** Francis, Dave; Young, Don 1979.
*Descriptors:* *Group Behavior; *Human Resources; *Industrial Training; *Management Teams; *Occupational Tests; *Teamwork; Adults; Climate; Creativity; Goal Orientation; Group Dynamics; Individual Development; Leadership; Peer Relationship
*Identifiers:* TRQ
*Availability:* Pfeiffer and Co., formerly University Associates, 8517 Production Ave., San Diego, CA 92121-2280.
*Notes:* Contained in University Associates Instrumentation Kit (15363). Time, 120. Items, 108.

Designed to determine whether a work team has the motivation to begin a team-building program, determine its strengths and weaknesses, and understand the characteristics of effective teamwork. Team members indicate truth or falsity of statements about their team. The statements concern leadership, membership, group commitment, climate, achievement orientation, corporate role, work methods, team organization, criticism, individual development, creative capacity, and negative intergroup relationships. Part of a large kit of instruments that may be reproduced as needed (up to 100 copies) without permission. For use by human resources development professionals in educational and training activities.

**15402**
**T.P. Leadership Questionnaire: An Assessment of Style.** University Associates, San Diego, CA 1974.
*Descriptors:* *Human Resources; *Industrial Training; *Leadership Styles; *Occupational Tests; *Supervisory Methods; Administrators; Adults; Behavior Patterns; Participative Decision Making; Self Evaluation (Individuals); Supervisors
*Identifiers:* Autocratic Leadership; Group Oriented Behavior; Laissez Faire Leadership; Task Oriented Behavior; TPLQ
*Availability:* Pfeiffer and Co., formerly University Associates, 8517 Production Ave., San Diego, CA 92121-2280.
*Notes:* Contained in University Associates Instrumentation Kit (15363). Time, 45. Items, 35.

A self-evaluation tool for managers designed to determine position in regard to either a task orientation or a people orientation. Respondent indicates the frequency of particular behaviors on a 5-point scale from "frequently" to "never." Behaviors are concerned with autocratic, shared, or laissez-faire leadership. Part of a large kit of instruments that may be reproduced as needed (up to 100 copies) without permission. For use by human resources development professionals in educational and training activities.

**15403**
**Training Philosophies Profile.** Beamish, G.E.H. 1983.
*Descriptors:* *Attitude Measures; *Human Resources; *Industrial Training; *Occupational Tests; *Philosophy; *Trainers; Adults; Behavior Patterns; Self Concept; Self Evaluation (Individuals)
*Identifiers:* TPP
*Availability:* Pfeiffer and Co., formerly University Associates, 8517 Production Ave., San Diego, CA 92121-2280.
*Notes:* Contained in University Associates Instrumentation Kit (15363). Time, 60. Items, 36.

Designed to determine the philosophies of participants in management training about the training itself and to help participants clarify their perceptions about the relationship between training and management. Uses a pair comparison format. Respondent allocates 3 points between statements in each pair. Scored to reveal the trainers' behaviors, self-images, and underlying attitudes. Part of a large kit of instruments that may be reproduced as needed (up to 100 copies) without permission. For use by human resources development professionals in educational and training activities.

**15404**
**Type A/Type B Habits Questionnaire.** Mill, Cyril R. 1980.
*Descriptors:* *Human Resources; *Industrial Training; *Occupational Tests; *Stress Variables; *Type A Behavior; *Type B Behavior; Adults; Behavior Patterns
*Identifiers:* Coronary Prone Behavior; TATBHQ
*Availability:* Pfeiffer and Co., formerly University Associates, 8517 Production Ave., San Diego, CA 92121-2280.
*Notes:* Contained in University Associates Instrumentation Kit (15363). Items, 32.

Designed to help individuals identify Type A and Type B behaviors in their own pattern of living. Also promotes recognition of these behavior patterns and their significance in coronary heart disease. Part of a large kit of instruments that may be reproduced as needed (up to 100 copies) without permission. For use by human resources development professionals in educational and training activities.

**15405**
**Views about People Survey: Theory X and Theory Y.** Woodcock, Mike; Francis, Dave 1981.
*Descriptors:* *Human Resources; *Industrial Training; *Management Development; *Occupational Tests; *Supervisory Methods; Adults; Theories
*Identifiers:* McGregor (Douglas); *Theory X; *Theory Y; VAPS
*Availability:* Pfeiffer and Co., formerly University Associates, 8517 Production Ave., San Diego, CA 92121-2280.
*Notes:* Contained in University Associates Instrumentation Kit (15363). Items, 9.

Places McGregor's Theory X and Theory Y on a 5-point rating scale as opposite poles. The respondents mark their positions on the scale to compare their own beliefs about people with McGregor's model. Part of a large kit of instruments that may be reproduced as needed (up to 100 copies) without permission. For use by human resources development professionals in educational and training activities.

**15406**
**Work-Needs Assessment Inventory: Achievement, Affiliation and Power.** Doyle, Patrick 1985.
*Descriptors:* *Human Resources; *Industrial Training; *Needs; *Needs Assessment; *Occupational Tests; Achievement Need; Adults; Affiliation Need; Employee Attitudes; Management Development; Work Attitudes
*Identifiers:* Power Need; WNAI
*Availability:* Pfeiffer and Co., formerly University Associates, 8517 Production Ave., San Diego, CA 92121-2280.
*Notes:* Contained in University Associates Instrumentation Kit (15363). Items, 18.

Designed to identify the needs in the workplace that motivate people, as well as the respondents' own needs. Statements are ranked. The ordering reveals whether the respondents desire achievement, affiliation, or power as first, second, or third priorities. Part of a large kit of instruments that may be reproduced as needed (up to 100 copies) without permission. For use by human resources development professionals in educational and training activities.

**15419**
**Job Effectiveness Prediction System.** Life Office Management Association, Atlanta, GA 1981.
*Descriptors:* *Aptitude Tests; *Entry Workers; *Insurance Companies; *Personnel Selection; Adults; Job Applicants
*Identifiers:* JEPS
*Availability:* Life Office Management Association, 5770 Powers Ferry Rd., Atlanta, GA 30327.

A series of tests used to assess skills required for entry-level positions in life and casualty-property insurance companies. The tests are used to assess numerical ability, mathematical skills, spelling, language usage, reading comprehension, verbal comprehension, filing, coding and converting, comparing, and checking. Tests are used for job applicants for clerical, technical, and professional positions.

**15420**
**PSI Professional Employment Test.** Psychological Services, Glendale, CA 1987.
*Descriptors:* *Managerial Occupations; *Occupational Tests; *Personnel Selection; *Professional Occupations; Administrators; Adults; Data Analysis; Interpretive Skills; Logical Thinking; Mathematics; Problem Solving; Reading Comprehension; Technical Occupations
*Availability:* Psychological Services, Inc., 100 W. Broadway, Ste. 1100, Glendale, CA 91210.
*Notes:* Time, 80. Items, 40.

A paper and pencil test of cognitive abilities designed to predict performance in professional, administrative, and managerial jobs. Covers quantitative problem solving, reading comprehension, data interpretation, and reasoning. Reading level is at grade 16 or below as measured by the SMOG Index of Readability. Criterion-related validity studies were conducted with 3 major occupational groups. Said to be free of bias toward minority groups. Test is hand-scored. Norms are provided. Alternate forms are available. Occupational groups studied include facilitative (those who determine need for services/supplies); research and investigative (those who do research and provide information); and technical/administrative (those who apply procedures to organize information and solve problems).

**15426**
**PSI Firefighter Selection Test.** Psychological Services, Glendale, CA 1987.
*Descriptors:* *Fire Fighters; *Occupational Tests; *Personnel Selection; *Screening Tests; Adults; Court Litigation; Culture Fair Tests; Interpretive Skills; Job Performance; Job Training; Knowledge Level; Mechanical Skills; Predictive Validity; Reading Comprehension
*Availability:* Psychological Services, Inc., 100 W. Broadway, Ste. 1100, Glendale, CA 91210.
*Notes:* Time, 150. Items, 100.

An entry-level selection test said to be job-related and conforming to legal and professional requirements. Can be used to rank applicants for firefighter positions according to their probability of success in training and on the job. Used as a screening test to reduce number of applicants prior to physical or oral screening. Said to be valid for African American, Hispanic, and nonminority groups. Said to be court approved in a consent decree in a large city. Has been validated. Items cover mechanical comprehension, reading comprehension, and report interpretation. Said to be valid as a predictor of job and task performance, fire academy performance, and dropout rate.

**15437**
**Microcomputer Evaluation and Screening Assessment.** Valpar International Corp., Tucson, AZ 1986.
*Descriptors:* *Career Exploration; *Computer Assisted Testing; *Job Placement; *Job Training; *Screening Tests; Academic Ability; Adolescents; Adults; Career Awareness; Eye Hand Coordination; Language Skills; Physical Fitness; Problem Solving; Spatial Ability; Tactual Perception; Vision Tests; Vocational Interests
*Identifiers:* Manual Dexterity; MESA
*Availability:* Valpar International Corp., P.O. Box 5767, Tuscon, AZ 85703-5767.
*Notes:* See also Microcomputer Evaluation and Screening Assessment—Short Form 2 (MESA SF2) (15438). Time, 270 approx.

Assesses individual's job-related knowledge, skills, and aptitudes for use in career exploration and job or training placement. This comprehensive, computerized screening instrument gathers large quantities of information in short periods of time. Although it is meant to interface with other assessment programs, the test can also be used alone. The subject's performance is measured against the Worker Qualifications Profile of the *Dictionary of Occupational Titles.* During the computer exercises, a large number of factors are measured in approximately 30 minutes. These factors include shape discrimination, problem solving, and academics. Subjects begin with a brief vision-screening test and a hand-eye coordination component. Other components include a hardware exercise, which assesses tool use, assembly skills, dexterity, manipulation, and ability to follow instructions; independent perceptual screening to measure tactile sensitivity and spatial aptitude; talking/persuasive screening related to language development; physical capacity and mobility to provide nonmedical screening before training or job placement; screening of vocational interests and awareness used to analyze vocational interests and to assess subject's basic understanding of the world of work; and an access profile, which allows comparison of evaluee's performance to specific requirements for success in a job, training, or classroom setting. Available for use on IBM PC or XT or Apple IIe.

**15438**
**Microcomputer Evaluation and Screening Assessment—Short Form 2.** Valpar International Corp., Tucson, AZ 1986.
*Descriptors:* *Career Exploration; *Computer Assisted Testing; *Job Placement; *Job Training; *Screening Tests; Academic Ability; Adolescents; Adults; Memory; Problem Solving; Psychomotor Skills; Visual Perception
*Identifiers:* MESA SF2
*Availability:* Valpar International Corp., P.O. Box 5767, Tuscon, AZ 85703-5767.
*Notes:* See also Microcomputer Evaluation and Screening Assessment (MESA) (15437). Time, 75 approx.

Computerized screening instrument used to assess an individual's job-related knowledge, skills, and aptitudes for use in career exploration and job training or placement. Uses game-like exercises to measure motor coordination, academics, problem solving, size and shape discrimination, and memory. Computer exercises are self-administered and automatically scored. There is also a paper and pencil survey, which is self-administered. This is a shorter version of the Microcomputer Evaluation and Screening Assessment (15437). Available for use on IBM PC or XT or Apple IIe.

**15439**
**Job Search Assessment.** PREP, Inc., Trenton, NJ
*Descriptors:* *Audiovisual Aids; *Diagnostic Tests; *Employment Qualifications; *Job Applicants; *Job Search Methods; *Job Skills; *Outcomes of Education; *Program Evaluation; Adults; Employment Programs; Employment Services
*Availability:* PREP, Inc., 1007 Whitehead Rd. Extension, Trenton, NJ 08638.
*Notes:* Items, 80.

An audiovisual assessment of 20 content areas which identifies the skills that job seekers lack in preparing for new employment. Designed to be part of an entire job search program covering the following applications: determining the needs of each program participant, evaluating the program content, determining further needs of the participants at the end of a job search program, and demonstrating measurable gains. Available in filmstrip/cassette or Labelle cartridge formats.

**15440**
**American Nurses Association: Adult Nurse Practitioner.** American Nurses Association, Kansas City, MO
*Descriptors:* *Certification; *Nurse Practitioners; *Occupational Tests; Adults; Knowledge Level
*Identifiers:* ANA
*Availability:* American Nurses Association, 2420 Pershing Rd., Kansas City, MO 64108.
*Notes:* See also American Nurses Association (15440 through 15458).

The certification examinations sponsored by the American Nurses' Association (ANA) are objective tests that assess knowledge, understanding, and application of professional nursing theory and practice. Certification is valid for 5 years. The examinations are offered on specific dates at various locations. To apply for certification as an adult nurse practitioner, the applicant must (1) be currently licensed as a registered nurse in the U.S. or its territories; (2) have been prepared as an adult nurse practitioner in either a master's degree program or hold a baccalaureate in nursing or a higher degree in any field of nursing and have completed an approved certificate program. The examination covers such topics as assessment, interpretation and management, evaluation of patient care, health policies, adolescent care, care of the adult, care of the aging adult, and family systems.

**15441**
**American Nurses Association: Clinical Specialist in Adult Psychiatric and Mental Health Nursing.** American Nurses Association, Kansas City, MO

*Descriptors:* *Certification; *Nurses; *Occupational Tests; *Psychiatric Services; Adults; Knowledge Level
*Identifiers:* ANA
*Availability:* American Nurses Association, 2420 Pershing Rd., Kansas City, MO 64108.
*Notes:* See also American Nurses Association (15440 through 15458).

The certification examinations sponsored by the American Nurses' Association (ANA) are objective tests that assess knowledge, understanding, and application of professional nursing theory and practice. Certification is valid for 5 years. The examinations are offered on specific dates at various locations. To apply for certification as a clinical specialist in adult psychiatric and mental health nursing, an individual must be currently licensed as a registered nurse in the U.S., be currently involved in the field, and meet various minimum standards for psychiatric and mental health education and length of practice in the field. Examination covers such topics as treatment, education, research, management, and consultation.

**15442**
**American Nurses Association: Clinical Specialist in Child and Adolescent Psychiatric and Mental Health Nursing.** American Nurses Association, Kansas City, MO
*Descriptors:* *Certification; *Nurses; *Occupational Tests; Adolescents; Adults; Children; Knowledge Level; Mental Health; Nursing; Psychiatry; Specialists
*Identifiers:* ANA; *Psychiatric Nursing
*Availability:* American Nurses Association, 2420 Pershing Rd., Kansas City, MO 64108.
*Notes:* See also American Nurses Association (15440 through 15458).

One of a series of American Nurses Association certification exams that assesses the knowledge, understanding, and application of professional nursing theory and practice in defined functional or clinical areas in nursing. Currently, to apply for certification in child and adolescent psychiatric and mental health nursing, one must (1) be currently licensed as a registered nurse in the U.S.; (2) be currently involved in direct psychiatric and mental health nursing practice at least 4 hours per week; (3) hold a master's degree or higher with a specialization in psychiatric and mental health nursing; and (4) since completing the educational requirements, have practiced in the speciality either 8 hours/week for 2 years or 4 hours/week for 4 years. Covers such topics as treatment, education of others and self, research, management, and consultation.

**15443**
**American Nurses Association: Clinical Specialist in Medical-Surgical Nursing.** American Nurses Association, Kansas City, MO
*Descriptors:* *Certification; *Nurses; *Occupational Tests; Adults; Knowledge Level; Nursing; Physiology; Specialists; Surgery
*Identifiers:* ANA
*Availability:* American Nurses Association, 2420 Pershing Rd., Kansas City, MO 64108.
*Notes:* See also American Nurses Association (15440 through 15458).

One of a series of American Nurses Association certification exams that assesses the knowledge, understanding, and application of professional nursing theory and practice in defined functional or clinical areas in nursing. Currently, to apply for certification in medical-surgical nursing, one must (1) be currently licensed as a registered nurse in the U.S.; (2) hold a master's degree with an area of concentration in nursing; and (3) have provided direct patient care in medical surgical nursing a minimum of 800 hours for 12 of the last 24 months. Covers such topics as independent client care issues, interdependent client care issues, and professional and practice issues.

**15444**
**American Nurses Association: Community Health Nurse.** American Nurses Association, Kansas City, MO
*Descriptors:* *Certification; *Nurses; *Occupational Tests; *Public Health; Adults; Community Health Services; Knowledge Level; Nursing; Specialists
*Identifiers:* ANA
*Availability:* American Nurses Association, 2420 Pershing Rd., Kansas City, MO 64108.
*Notes:* See also American Nurses Association (15440 through 15458).

One of a series of American Nurses Association certification exams that assesses the knowledge, understanding, and application of professional nursing theory and practice in defined functional or clinical areas in nursing. Currently, to apply for certification in community health nursing, one must (1) be currently licensed as a registered nurse in the U.S.; (2) hold a baccalaureate or higher degree; and (3) by the time of application, have practiced as a registered nurse 1,600 hours in community health nursing within 24 of the last 48 months. Covers such topics as assessment of health characteristics, planning for health promotion and disease prevention, implementation/intervention, evaluation of services provided, and knowledge of trends and issues.

**15445**
**American Nurses Association: Family Nurse Practitioner.** American Nurses Association, Kansas City, MO
*Descriptors:* *Certification; *Family Health; *Nurse Practitioners; *Occupational Tests; Adults; Knowledge Level; Nursing; Specialists
*Identifiers:* ANA
*Availability:* American Nurses Association, 2420 Pershing Rd., Kansas City, MO 64108.
*Notes:* See also American Nurses Association (15440 through 15458).

One of a series of American Nurses Association certification exams that assesses the knowledge, understanding, and application of professional nursing theory and practice in defined functional or clinical areas in nursing. Currently, to apply for certification as a family nurse practitioner, one must (1) be a registered nurse in the U.S.; (2) have been prepared as a family nurse practitioner in either a master's degree program or hold a baccalaureate in nursing or a higher degree in any field of nursing and have completed a certificate program which was at least 9 months or 1 academic year of full-time study. Covers such topics as assessment, interpretation and management, evaluation of patient care, health policies, care of the child (pediatrics), adolescent care, care of the adult, care of the aging adult, obstetrics, and family systems.

**15446**
**American Nurses Association: General Nursing Practice.** American Nurses Association, Kansas City, MO
*Descriptors:* *Certification; *Nurses; *Occupational Tests; Adults; Knowledge Level
*Identifiers:* ANA
*Availability:* American Nurses Association, 2420 Pershing Rd., Kansas City, MO 64108.
*Notes:* See also American Nurses Association (15440 through 15458).

One of a series of American Nurses Association certification exams that assesses the knowledge, understanding, and application of professional nursing theory and practice in defined functional or clinical areas in nursing. The examination for certification in general nursing practice covers such topics as physiological alterations; psychological disturbance; human sexuality and parenting; health promotion, disease prevention and control; adaptation to illness; psychological responses to illness and change; and professional issues. Although the test reflects all steps of the nursing process, the greatest emphasis is placed on the assessment phase. Currently, to apply for this certification one must be licensed as a registered nurse in the U.S. or its territories and have had a minimum of 4,000 hours experience as a registered nurse in general nursing practice, 1,000 hours of which must have been within the last 3 years.

**15447**
**American Nurses Association: Gerontological Nurse.** American Nurses Association, Kansas City, MO
*Descriptors:* *Certification; *Geriatrics; *Nurses; *Occupational Tests; Adults; Knowledge Level
*Identifiers:* ANA
*Availability:* American Nurses Association, 2420 Pershing Rd., Kansas City, MO 64108.
*Notes:* See also American Nurses Association (15440 through 15458).

One of a series of American Nurses Association certification exams that assesses the knowledge, understanding, and application of professional nursing theory and practice in defined functional or clinical areas in nursing. Currently, to apply for certification as a gerontological nurse one must be licensed as a registered nurse in the U.S. or its territories, and have practiced as a registered nurse in gerontological nursing in the 2 years preceding application. The examination covers such topics as nursing process; nursing practice and policy issues; management (administration); and education and advocacy.

**15448**
**American Nurses Association: Gerontological Nurse Practitioner.** American Nurses Association, Kansas City, MO
*Descriptors:* *Certification; *Geriatrics; *Nurse Practitioners; *Occupational Tests; Adults; Knowledge Level
*Identifiers:* ANA
*Availability:* American Nurses Association, 2420 Pershing Rd., Kansas City, MO 64108.
*Notes:* See also American Nurses Association (15440 through 15458).

One of a series of American Nurses Association certification exams that assesses the knowledge, understanding, and application of professional nursing theory and practice in defined functional or clinical areas in nursing. Currently, to apply for certification as a gerontological nurse practitioner one must be licensed as a registered nurse in the U.S. or its territories and have been prepared as a gerontological practitioner in either (1) a master's in nursing program or (2) a certificate program, which was at least 9 months or 1 academic year of full-time study, or the equivalent, as defined by the sponsoring institution. The examination for certification as a gerontological nurse practitioner covers such topics as assessment diagnosis, planning treatment, evaluation, and practice issues.

**15449**
**American Nurses Association: High Risk Perinatal Nurse.** American Nurses Association, Kansas City, MO
*Descriptors:* *Certification; *Neonates; *Nurses; *Occupational Tests; Adults; Knowledge Level
*Identifiers:* ANA
*Availability:* American Nurses Association, 2420 Pershing Rd., Kansas City, MO 64108.
*Notes:* See also American Nurses Association (15440 through 15458).

One of a series of American Nurses Association certification exams that assesses the knowledge, understanding, and application of professional nursing theory and practice in defined functional or clinical areas in nursing. Currently, to apply for certification as a high-risk perinatal nurse one must (1) be licensed as a registered nurse in the U.S. or its territories; (2) by the time of application, have provided as a registered nurse 1,500 hours of direct nursing care to a client/family in an area of maternal and child health nursing practice; and, in addition, have provided direct nursing care to a client/family in the specialty area of high-risk perinatal nursing for a minimum of 600 hours within the last 3 years; and (3) have had 30 contact hours of continuing education applicable to the specialty area within the last 3 years. The examination for certification covers such topics as assessment; planning; interventions; and evaluation of patient care.

**15450**
**American Nurses Association: Maternal-Child Nurse.** American Nurses Association, Kansas City, MO
*Descriptors:* *Certification; *Nurses; *Occupational Tests; Adults; Knowledge Level
*Identifiers:* ANA
*Availability:* American Nurses Association, 2420 Pershing Rd., Kansas City, MO 64108.
*Notes:* See also American Nurses Association (15440 through 15458).

One of a series of American Nurses Association certification exams that assesses the knowledge, understanding, and application of professional nursing theory and practice in defined functional or clinical areas in nursing. Currently, to apply for certification as a maternal-child nurse one must (1) be licensed as a registered nurse in the U.S. or its territories; (2) by the time of application, have provided as a registered nurse 2,100 hours of direct nursing care to a client/family in an area of maternal-child health, 600 hours of which must have been provided within the last 3 years; and (3) have had 30 contact hours of continuing education applicable to the specialty area within the last 3 years. The examination for certification covers such topics as: nursing diagnosis, provider/manager relations, evaluation, and professional practice.

**15451**
**American Nurses Association: Medical-Surgical Nurse.** American Nurses Association, Kansas City, MO
*Descriptors:* *Certification; *Nurses; *Occupational Tests; *Surgery; Adults; Knowledge Level
*Identifiers:* ANA
*Availability:* American Nurses Association, 2420 Pershing Rd., Kansas City, MO 64108.
*Notes:* See also American Nurses Association (15440 through 15458).

One of a series of American Nurses Association certification exams that assesses the knowledge, understanding, and application of professional nursing theory and practice in defined functional or clinical areas in nursing. Currently, to apply for certification as a medical-surgical nurse one must (1) be licensed as a registered nurse in the U.S. or its territories; (2) by the time of application, have practiced as a registered nurse 2 of the last 5 years in medical-surgical nursing with an average of 16 hours per week; and (3) currently practice medical-surgical nursing a minimum of 16 hours per week. The examination for certification covers such topics as independent client care issues; interdependent client care issues; and professional and practice issues.

**15452**
**American Nurses Association: Nursing Administration.** American Nurses Association, Kansas City, MO
*Descriptors:* *Administrators; *Certification; *Nurses; *Occupational Tests; Adults; Knowledge Level
*Identifiers:* ANA
*Availability:* American Nurses Association, 2420 Pershing Rd., Kansas City, MO 64108.
*Notes:* See also American Nurses Association (15440 through 15458).

One of a series of American Nurses Association certification exams that assesses the knowledge, understanding, and application of professional nursing theory and practice in defined functional or clinical areas in nursing. Currently, to apply for certification as a nursing administrator one must (1) be licensed as a registered nurse in the U.S. or its territories; (2) hold a baccalaureate or higher degree or expect to receive one in 90 days; and (3) by the time of application, have held a middle or executive level nursing administrative position at least 24 months within the past 5 years. The examination for certification covers such topics as nursing organization, nursing service delivery systems, resources, and issues.

**15453**
**American Nurses Association: Nursing Administration, Advanced.** American Nurses Association, Kansas City, MO
*Descriptors:* *Administrators; *Certification; *Nurses; *Occupational Tests; Adults; Knowledge Level
*Identifiers:* ANA
*Availability:* American Nurses Association, 2420 Pershing Rd., Kansas City, MO 64108.
*Notes:* See also American Nurses Association (15440 through 15458).

One of a series of American Nurses Association certification exams that assesses the knowledge, understanding, and application of professional nursing theory and practice in defined functional or clinical areas in nursing. Currently, to apply for certification in advanced nursing administration, one must (1) be licensed as a registered nurse in the U.S. or its territories; (2) hold a master's or higher degree or expect to receive one within 90 days; and (3) by the time of application, have held an executive level nursing administrative position at least 36 months within the past 5 years. The examination covers such topics as nursing organization, nursing service delivery systems, resources, issues, personnel management, planning and evaluation, total health care organizations, and professional and societal concerns.

**15454**
**American Nurses Association: Pediatric Nurse (Child and Adolescent Nurse).** American Nurses Association, Kansas City, MO
*Descriptors:* *Certification; *Nurses; *Occupational Tests; *Pediatrics; Adults; Knowledge Level
*Identifiers:* ANA
*Availability:* American Nurses Association, 2420 Pershing Rd., Kansas City, MO 64108.
*Notes:* See also American Nurses Association (15440 through 15458).

One of a series of American Nurses Association certification exams that assesses the knowledge, understanding, and application of professional nursing theory and practice in defined functional or clinical areas in nursing. Currently, to apply for certification as a pediatric nurse (child and adolescent nurse) one must (1) be licensed as a registered nurse in the U.S. or its territories; (2) by the time of application, have provided as a registered nurse 1,500 hours of direct nursing care to a client/family in an area of maternal and child health nursing practice; and, in addition, have provided direct nursing care to a client/family in this specialty area for a minimum of 600 hours within the last 3 years, and (3) have had 30 contact hours of continuing education applicable to this specialty area within the last 3 years. The examination for certification covers such topics as: principles of growth and development; principles of family dynamics and development; issues affecting practice; illnesses that require short-term care; illnesses that might require long-term care; and common nursing problems and interventions.

**15455**
**American Nurses Association: Pediatric Nurse Practitioner.** American Nurses Association, Kansas City, MO
*Descriptors:* *Certification; *Nurse Practitioners; *Occupational Tests; *Pediatrics; Adults; Knowledge Level
*Identifiers:* ANA
*Availability:* American Nurses Association, 2420 Pershing Rd., Kansas City, MO 64108.
*Notes:* See also American Nurses Association (15440 through 15458).

One of a series of American Nurses Association certification exams that assesses the knowledge, understanding, and application of professional nursing theory and practice in defined functional or clinical areas in nursing. Currently, to apply for certification as a pediatric nurse practitioner, one must (1) be licensed as a registered nurse in the U.S. or its territories; (2) have been prepared as a pediatric nurse practitioner in either a master's in nursing program or a certificate program; and (3) within the last 3 years must have practiced as a pediatric nurse practitioner for a minimum of 600 hours. The examination for certification covers such topics as health assessment and diagnosis, planning, intervention, evaluation, and professional issues.

**15456**
**American Nurses Association: Psychiatric and Mental Health Nurse.** American Nurses Association, Kansas City, MO
*Descriptors:* *Certification; *Mental Health; *Nurses; *Occupational Tests; Adults; Knowledge Level
*Identifiers:* ANA
*Availability:* American Nurses Association, 2420 Pershing Rd., Kansas City, MO 64108.
*Notes:* See also American Nurses Association (15440 through 15458).

One of a series of American Nurses Association certification exams that assesses the knowledge, understanding, and application of professional nursing theory and practice in defined functional or clinical areas in nursing. Currently, to apply for certification as a psychiatric and mental health nurse, one must (1) be licensed as a registered nurse in the U.S. or its territories; (2) by the time of application, have practiced as a registered nurse in direct psychiatric and mental health nursing practice a minimum of 1,600 hours within 24 of the last 48 months; (3) be currently involved in direct psychiatric and mental health nursing practice for a minimum of 8 hours per week; and (4) currently have access to consultation or clinical supervision by a qualified member of one of several mental health disciplines. The examination for certification covers such topics as assessment, problem identification and planning, intervention, evaluation, and professional issues.

**15457**
**American Nurses Association: School Nurse.** American Nurses Association, Kansas City, MO 1988.
*Descriptors:* *Certification; *Occupational Tests; *School Nurses; Adults; Knowledge Level
*Identifiers:* ANA
*Availability:* American Nurses Association, 2420 Pershing Rd., Kansas City, MO 64108.
*Notes:* See also American Nurses Association (15440 through 15458).

One of a series of American Nurses Association certification exams that assesses the knowledge, understanding, and application of professional nursing theory and practice in defined functional or clinical areas in nursing. Currently, to apply for certification as a school nurse, one must (1) be licensed as a registered nurse in the U.S. or its territories; (2) have successfully completed a minimum of 15 semester hours of related coursework; and (3) have completed a minimum of 200 hours in a supervised university/college sponsored internship or practicum; or have completed a minimum of 3,600 hours in school nursing practice within the last 3 years. The examination for certification covers such topics as professional issues in school nursing; school and community health; growth and development; health assessment; exceptional children; special health conditions; safety, accident prevention, and emergency care; and health counseling, education, and promotion.

**15458**
**American Nurses Association: School Nurse Practitioner.** American Nurses Association, Kansas City, MO
*Descriptors:* *Certification; *Nurse Practitioners; *Occupational Tests; *School Nurses; Adults; Knowledge Level
*Identifiers:* ANA
*Availability:* American Nurses Association, 2420 Pershing Rd., Kansas City, MO 64108.
*Notes:* See also American Nurses Association (15440 through 15457).

One of a series of American Nurses Association certification exams that assesses the knowledge, understanding, and application of professional nursing theory and practice in defined functional or clinical areas in nursing. Currently, to apply for certification as a school nurse practitioner, one must (1) be licensed as a registered nurse in the U.S. or its territories; and (2) have been prepared as a school nurse practitioner in a master's nursing program or hold a baccalaureate in nursing or a higher degree in any field of nursing and have completed an approved certificate program. The examination for certification covers such topics as assessment, interpretation and management, evaluation of patient care, health economics, care of the school-age child, health education, family, and issues affecting practice.

**15472**
**Chartered Life Underwriter Examination.** The American College, Bryn Mawr, PA
*Descriptors:* *Certification; *Insurance Occupations; *Occupational Tests; Adults; Computer Assisted Testing; Estate Planning; Financial Services; Insurance; Knowledge Level; Professional Occupations; Retirement Benefits; Taxes
*Identifiers:* Chartered Life Underwriters; CLU
*Availability:* The American College, 270 Bryn Mawr Ave., Bryn Mawr, PA 19010-2196.
*Notes:* Time, 120. Items, 100.

This examination awards a designation of Chartered Life Underwriter (CLU) to insurance professionals who have completed coursework independently or in classes sponsored by the American College, and achieved a passing score. Designations are available for those specializing in the areas of life insurance and personal insurance. Content of the examination may vary by course of study. Paper and pencil administrations of the examinations are given at designated times and test sites. A computerized administration, on demand, is available. Examinations are updated regularly.

**15473**
**Chartered Financial Consultant.** The American College, Bryn Mawr, PA
*Descriptors:* *Certification; *Finance Occupations; *Occupational Tests; Adults; Computer Assisted Testing; Estate Planning; Financial Services; Fringe Benefits; Investment; Knowledge Level; Taxes
*Identifiers:* Chartered Financial Consultant; ChFC
*Availability:* The American College, 270 Bryn Mawr Ave., Bryn Mawr, PA 19010-2196.
*Notes:* Time, 120. Items, 100.

This examination awards a designation of Chartered Financial Consultant (ChFC) to financial services professionals: accountants, attorneys, bankers, insurance agents and brokers, and securities representatives, who have completed coursework independently or in classes sponsored by the American College, and achieved a passing score. Content of the examination may vary by course of study elected. Paper and pencil administrations of the examinations are given at designated times and test sites. A computerized administration, on demand, is available. Examinations are updated regularly.

**15498**
**Job Matching Survey II.** PREP Inc., Trenton, NJ 1982.
*Descriptors:* *Job Placement; *Job Skills; *Occupational Tests; Adults; Professional Occupations; Profiles; Questionnaires; Semiskilled Occupations; Skilled Occupations; Technical Occupations; Vocational Interests
*Identifiers:* JMS II
*Availability:* PREP, Inc., 1007 Whitehead Rd. Extension, Trenton, NJ 08638.
*Notes:* Time, 60 approx. Items, 200.

To help adults make career decisions and to overcome the problem of mismatching between individuals and jobs or training programs in the workplace at the semiskilled, skilled, technical, and professional levels. Scores are generated for individuals and jobs and training programs across 20 dimensions of work. The scores for the 20 dimensions form a profile of the individual's activity preferences and experiences; the job's activity requirements; and the activities required in a training program. These profiles are compared to identify the most appropriate matches between the individual and the jobs or training programs. The 20 dimensions fall into 3 categories: information or data-oriented activities, social or people-oriented activities, and concrete or things-oriented activities.

**15569**
**Professional Development Inventory: Feedback from Associates.** Daniels, Philip B.; Dyer, William G. 1986.
*Descriptors:* *Occupational Tests; *Personnel Evaluation; *Staff Development; Adults; Business Communication; Decision Making; Innovation; Interpersonal Competence; Organizational Change; Peer Evaluation; Self Evaluation (Individuals); Teamwork; Time Management
*Availability:* Behavioral Science Resources, P.O. Box 411, Provo, UT 84603.
*Notes:* See also Supervisory Development Inventory (15570). Items, 44.

Designed to provide feedback on performance to individuals within an organization who are key staff members but not supervisors or managers. Evaluation is performed by supervisors and coworkers. Ratings are made twice for each statement of behavior on 2 7-point scales. The first rating is made of the staff member's degree of effectiveness from ineffective to extremely effective. The second rating is made of that behavior's importance to the staff member's overall effectiveness on the job. Scoring is done by the publisher via computer to produce a profile of areas needing improvement and areas that are most important to improve.

**15570**
**Supervisory Development Inventory: Feedback from Associates.** Daniels, Philip B.; And Others 1986.
*Descriptors:* *Adults; *Occupational Tests; *Personnel Evaluation; *Staff Development; *Supervisory Methods; Business Communication; Conflict Resolution; Decision Making; Motivation; Organizational Change; Peer Evaluation; Safety; Teamwork
*Availability:* Behavioral Science Resources, P.O. Box 411, Provo, UT 84603.
*Notes:* See also Professional Development Inventory (15569). Items, 52.

Designed to provide information on job performance of first-line supervisors. Feedback is gathered from supervisor, peers, and subordinates. Scoring is done by the publisher. The resulting printout gives suggestions for improvement and a list of the test taker's strengths and weaknesses. Ratings are made twice for each statement of behavior on 2 7-point scales. The first rating is made of the supervisor's degree of effectiveness from ineffective to extremely effective. The second rating is made of that behavior's importance to the staff member's overall effectiveness on the job.

**15587**
**Work Skill Development Package.** Bastian, Donald
*Descriptors:* *Adolescents; *Adults; *Assembly (Manufacturing); *Disabilities; *Physical Disabilities; *Severe Mental Retardation; *Vocational Rehabilitation; *Work Sample Tests; Job Skills; Psychomotor Skills; Skill Development; Special Education; Visual Discrimination; Vocational Evaluation
*Identifiers:* WSD
*Availability:* Attainment Co., P.O. Box 103, Oregon, WI 53575.

Designed to develop prevocational, basic work skills in severely mentally retarded, mentally ill, and/or physically disabled persons in special education and vocational rehabilitation facilities. The WSD assesses a baseline for performance and subsequent progress, encourages acquisition of skills, production or refinement of skills and speed, and development of acceptable work behaviors and habits. Covers 3 basic vocational skills: ability to discriminate between objects; ability to manipulate objects; and ability to apply basic concepts. Used primarily for training and, on a limited basis, as an evaluation system.

**15621**
**Technician Electrical Test.** Ramsay, Roland T. 1987.
*Descriptors:* *Achievement Tests; *Electrical Systems; *Electronic Technicians; Adults; Knowledge Level
*Availability:* Ramsay Corp., 1050 Boyce Rd., Pittsburgh, PA 15241-3907.
*Notes:* Time, 120 approx. Items, 132.

Measures knowledge and skills in the following electrical areas: motors, digital electronics, analog electronics, schematics and print reading, control circuits, power supplies, basic AC and DC theory, power distribution, test instruments, mechanical, computers and PLC, hand and power tools, electrical maintenance, and construction and installation.

**15622**
**Technician Mechanical Test.** Ramsay, Roland T. 1987.
*Descriptors:* *Achievement Tests; *Mechanical Skills; *Paraprofessional Personnel; Adults; Knowledge Level
*Availability:* Ramsay Corp., 1050 Boyce Rd., Pittsburgh, PA 15241-3907.
*Notes:* Time, 120 approx. Items, 124.

Designed to measure knowledge and skills in the following mechanical areas: hydraulics, pneumatics, print reading, welding, power transmission, lubrication, pumps, piping, rigging, mechanical maintenance, shop machines, tools, and equipment.

**15623**
**Job Skills Test, Arithmetic, Form A.** Ramsay, Roland T. 1983.
*Descriptors:* *Arithmetic; *Occupational Tests; *Personnel Selection; Adults; Employment; Personnel Evaluation; Screening Tests
*Availability:* Ramsay Corp., 1050 Boyce Rd., Pittsburgh, PA 15241-3907.
*Notes:* Time, 20. Items, 24.

This brief test is used to measure the basic arithmetic skills of addition, subtraction, multiplication, and division for hiring and screening of applicants for employment. Applicant supplies answers to 24 examples. Also includes examples using arithmetic operations with fractions.

**15625**
**Career Values Card Sort.** Career Research and Testing, San Jose, CA 1981.
*Descriptors:* *Career Planning; *Occupational Tests; *Values; *Vocational Evaluation; Adults; Classification; Job Satisfaction; Work Environment
*Identifiers:* *Card Sort; *Work Values
*Availability:* Career Research and Testing, 2005 Hamilton Ave., Ste. 250, San Jose, CA 95125.
*Notes:* Items, 41.

This card sorting procedure is designed to assist the vocational evaluee in clarifying the most important desires in a career. Statements about career values are sorted into five categories ranging from "always valued" to "never valued". Values include work on frontiers of knowledge, creativity, time, freedom, etc.

**15626**
**Motivated Skills Card Sort.** Career Research and Testing, San Jose, CA 1981.
*Descriptors:* *Job Skills; *Occupational Tests; *Vocational Evaluation; Adults; Career Planning; Job Satisfaction
*Identifiers:* *Card Sort
*Availability:* Career Research and Testing, 2005 Hamilton Ave., Ste. 250, San Jose, CA 95125.
*Notes:* Items, 56.

This card sorting procedure is designed to assist the vocational evaluee in identifying skills that lead to career satisfaction and success. A series of cards containing work activities, such as "tend animals," are arranged according to the subject's interest in them and proficiency level.

**15627**
**Florida Teacher Certification Examination, Sample Items.** Florida State Dept. of Education, Tallahassee, FL 1980.
*Descriptors:* *Certification; *Occupational Tests; *Teacher Qualifications; *Teachers; Adults; Knowledge Level; State Licensing Boards
*Identifiers:* Florida

*Availability:* ERIC Document Reproduction Service, 7420 Fullerton Rd., Ste. 110, Springfield, VA 22153-2852 (ED193172, 132 pages).
*Notes:* Items, 30.

Assesses mastery of the 22 generic competencies adopted by the state of Florida in 1978 as necessary for teacher certification. These competencies and their related skills include reading, writing, mathematics, and professional education.

**15659**
**Clerical Series Tests: Clerical Skills Series, 361.1.** International Personnel Management Association, Alexandria, VA
*Descriptors:* *Clerical Workers; *Occupational Tests; *Public Service Occupations; Adults; Filing; Grammar; Punctuation; Reading; Spelling; Vocabulary
*Identifiers:* IPMA
*Availability:* International Personnel Management Association, 1617 Duke St., Alexandria, VA 22314.
*Notes:* See also Clerical Series Tests (15660 through 15664). Time, 54. Items, 150.

Assesses language and filing abilities related to clerical positions. Available on a rental basis only. Developed from an extensive job analysis of public service positions. All material is drawn directly from work samples. Series is designed in modular form and the Job Test Content Matching and Weighing Tool allows user agencies to assemble job-relevant examinations for their own purposes. IMPA test services are available to civil service commissions, personnel boards, personnel departments, and other similar centralized public personnel agencies upon completion and return of a standard test security agreement.

**15660**
**Clerical Series Tests: Clerical Skills Series, 362.1.** International Personnel Management Association, Alexandria, VA
*Descriptors:* *Clerical Workers; *Occupational Tests; *Public Service Occupations; Adults; Arithmetic; Reading; Vocabulary; Coding
*Identifiers:* Checking (Mathematics); IPMA
*Availability:* International Personnel Management Association, 1617 Duke St., Alexandria, VA 22314.
*Notes:* See also Clerical Series Tests (15659 through 15664). Time, 57. Items, 130.

Assesses the language, coding, and numerical skills related to clerical positions. Available on a rental basis only. Developed from an extensive job analysis of public service positions. All material is drawn directly from work samples. Series is designed in modular form and the Job Test Content Matching and Weighing Tool allows user agencies to assemble job-relevant examinations for their own purposes. IMPA test services are available to civil service commissions, personnel boards, personnel departments, and other similar centralized public personnel agencies upon completion and return of a standard test security agreement.

**15661**
**Clerical Series Tests: Clerical Skills Series, 363.1.** International Personnel Management Association, Alexandria, VA
*Descriptors:* *Clerical Workers; *Occupational Tests; *Public Service Occupations; Adults; Filing; Vocabulary; Coding
*Identifiers:* Checking (Mathematics); IPMA
*Availability:* International Personnel Management Association, 1617 Duke St., Alexandria, VA 22314.
*Notes:* See also Clerical Series Tests (15659 through 15664). Time, 42. Items, 130.

Assesses language, filing and coding skills related to clerical positions. Available on a rental basis only. Developed from an extensive job analysis of public service positions. All material is drawn directly from work samples. Series is designed in modular form and the Job Test Content Matching and Weighing Tool allows user agencies to assemble job-relevant examinations for their own purposes. IPMA test services are available to civil service commissions, personnel boards, personnel departments, and other similar centralized public personnel agencies upon completion and return of a standard test security agreement.

**15662**
**Clerical Series Tests: Dictation/Transcription Test, 367.1.** International Personnel Management Association, Alexandria, VA
*Descriptors:* *Clerical Workers; *Dictation; *Occupational Tests; *Public Service Occupations; Adults; Vocabulary
*Identifiers:* IPMA
*Availability:* International Personnel Management Association, 1617 Duke St., Alexandria, VA 22314.
*Notes:* See also Clerical Series Tests (15659 through 15664). Time, 6.

Assesses the stenographic ability of candidates for clerical positions. Available on a rental basis. Developed from an extensive job analysis of public service positions. All material is drawn directly from work samples. Series is designed in modular form and the Job Test Content Matching and Weighing Tool allows user agencies to assemble job relevant examinations for their own purposes. IPMA test services are available to civil service commissions, personnel boards, personnel departments, and other similar centralized public personnel agencies upon completion and return of a standard test security agreement.

**15663**
**Clerical Series Tests: Oral Instruction and Forms Completion, 364.1.** International Personnel Management Association, Alexandria, VA
*Descriptors:* *Clerical Workers; *Occupational Tests; *Public Service Occupations; Adults; Oral Language; Records (Forms)
*Identifiers:* IPMA
*Availability:* International Personnel Management Association, 1617 Duke St., Alexandria, VA 22314.
*Notes:* See also Clerical Series Tests (15659 through 15664). Time, 12. Items, 20.

Assesses the ability to follow directions. Used with applicants for clerical positions. Available on a rental basis only. Developed from an extensive job analysis of public service positions. All material is drawn directly from work samples. Series is designed in modular form and the Job Test Content Matching and Weighing Tool allows user agencies to assemble job-relevant examinations for their own purposes. IPMA test services are available to civil service commissions, personnel boards, personnel departments, and other similar centralized public personnel agencies upon completion and return of a standard test security agreement.

**15664**
**Clerical Series Tests: Typing Test, 365.1.** International Personnel Management Association, Alexandria, VA
*Descriptors:* *Clerical Workers; *Occupational Tests; *Public Service Occupations; *Typewriting; Adults
*Identifiers:* IPMA
*Availability:* International Personnel Management Association, 1617 Duke St., Alexandria, VA 22314.
*Notes:* See also Clerical Series Tests (15659 through 15663). Time, 5.

Assesses the typing ability and speed of candidates for clerical positions. Available on a rental basis only. Developed from an extensive job analysis of public service positions. All material is drawn directly from work samples. Series is designed in modular form and the Job Test Content Matching and Weighing Tool allows user agencies to assemble job-relevant examinations for their own purposes. IPMA test services are available to civil service commissions, personnel boards, personnel departments, and other similar centralized public personnel agencies upon completion and return of a standard test security agreement.

**15665**
**Entry-Level Fire Service Tests: B-3 Firefighter.** Advanced Research Resources Organization, Bethesda, MD
*Descriptors:* *Entry Workers; *Fire Fighters; *Occupational Tests; Adults
*Identifiers:* IPMA
*Availability:* International Personnel Management Association, 1617 Duke St., Alexandria, VA 22314.
*Notes:* See also Entry-Level Fire Service Test: B-4 Firefighter (15666).

Assesses the following performance dimensions for entry-level firefighter positions: responding to alarms; firefighting and extinguishing operations; postfire operations; emergency and rescue operations; first aid and assistance; fire prevention; inspection and code enforcing activities; apparatus and equipment maintenance; fire/arson investigation; training activities; general firehouse duties; management, administration, and housewatch; and public relations and community activities. Supported by predictive criterion-related validity evidence. Available on a rental basis only.

**15666**
**Entry-Level Fire Service Tests: B-4 Firefighter.** Advanced Research Resources Organization, Bethesda, MD
*Descriptors:* *Entry Workers; *Fire Fighters; *Occupational Tests; Adults
*Identifiers:* IPMA
*Availability:* International Personnel Management Association, 1617 Duke St., Alexandria, VA 22314.
*Notes:* See also Entry-Level Fire Service Test: B-3 Firefighter (15665). Time, 120. Items, 85.

Assesses the following performance dimensions for entry-level firefighter positions. responding to alarms; firefighting and extinguishing operations; postfire operations; emergency and rescue operations; first aid and assistance; fire prevention; inspection and code enforcing activities; apparatus and equipment maintenance; fire/arson investigation; training activities; general firehouse duties; management, administration, and housewatch; and public relations and community activities. Supported by predictive criterion-related validity evidence. Available on a rental basis only.

**15667**
**Promotional Fire Service Tests: Supervisory Level, Fire Service Supervisor (Sergeant, Lieutenant), 573.** Advanced Research Resources Organization, Bethesda, MD
*Descriptors:* *Fire Fighters; *Occupational Tests; *Promotion (Occupational); *Supervisors; Adults
*Identifiers:* IPMA; *Lieutenant; *Sergeant
*Availability:* International Personnel Management Association, 1617 Duke St., Alexandria, VA 22314.
*Notes:* For other tests in the Promotional Fire Service Tests, see 15668 through 15676. Time, 150. Items, 150.

Available on a rental basis only. Documentation is available in event of challenge. Content validation. Assesses the knowledge, skills, and abilities of candidates for positions of fire service sergeant or lieutenant.

**15668**
**Promotional Fire Service Tests: Specialized Positions, Fire Engineer, 577.** Williams and Associates
*Descriptors:* *Fire Fighters; *Occupational Tests; *Promotion (Occupational); *Specialists; Adults
*Identifiers:* *Fire Engineers; IPMA
*Availability:* International Personnel Management Association, 1617 Duke St., Alexandria, VA 22314.
*Notes:* For other tests in the Promotional Fire Service Tests, see 15667 through 15676. Time, 120. Items, 109.

Assesses the knowledge, skills, and abilities of candidates for the position of fire engineer. Available on a rental basis only. Content validation.

15669
**Promotional Fire Service Tests: Specialized Positions, Fire Inspector, 530.** Williams and Associates
*Descriptors:* *Fire Fighters; *Occupational Tests; *Promotion (Occupational); *Specialists; Adults
*Identifiers:* *Fire Inspectors; IPMA
*Availability:* International Personnel Management Association, 1617 Duke St., Alexandria, VA 22314.
*Notes:* For other tests in the Promotional Fire Service Tests, see 15667 through 15676.

Assesses the knowledge, skills, and abilities of candidates for the position of fire inspector. Available on a rental basis only. Content validation.

15670
**Promotional Fire Service Tests: Specialized Positions, Radio Operator, 307.** Williams and Associates
*Descriptors:* *Fire Fighters; *Occupational Tests; *Promotion (Occupational); *Specialists; Adults
*Identifiers:* IPMA; *Radio Operators
*Availability:* International Personnel Management Association, 1617 Duke St., Alexandria, VA 22314.
*Notes:* For other tests in the Promotional Fire Service Tests, see 15667 through 15676. Time, 120. Items, 100.

Assesses the knowledge, skills, and abilities of candidates for the position of fire service radio operator. Available on a rental basis only. Content validation.

15671
**Promotional Fire Service Tests: Specialized Positions, Senior Fire Inspector, 530.** Williams and Associates
*Descriptors:* *Fire Fighters; *Occupational Tests; *Promotion (Occupational); *Specialists; Adults
*Identifiers:* *Fire Inspectors; IPMA
*Availability:* International Personnel Management Association, 1617 Duke St., Alexandria, VA 22314.
*Notes:* For other tests in the Promotional Fire Service Tests, see 15667 through 15676. Time, 180. Items, 159.

Assesses the knowledge, skills, and abilities of candidates for the position of senior fire inspector. Available on a rental basis. Content validation.

15672
**Promotional Fire Service Tests: Specialized Positions, Senior Radio Operator, 307.** Williams and Associates
*Descriptors:* *Fire Fighters; *Occupational Tests; *Promotion (Occupational); *Specialists; Adults
*Identifiers:* IPMA; *Radio Operators
*Availability:* International Personnel Management Association, 1617 Duke St., Alexandria, VA 22314.
*Notes:* For other tests in the Promotional Fire Service Tests, see 15667 through 15676.

Assesses the knowledge, skills, and abilities of candidates for the position of fire service senior radio operator. Available on a rental basis only. Content validation.

15673
**Promotional Fire Service Tests: Command Level, Fire Service Administrator (Battalion Chief), 575.** Advanced Research Resources Organization, Bethesda, MD
*Descriptors:* *Fire Fighters; *Occupational Tests; *Promotion (Occupational); *Supervisors; Adults
*Identifiers:* *Fire Chiefs; IPMA
*Availability:* International Personnel Management Association, 1617 Duke St., Alexandria, VA 22314.
*Notes:* For other tests in the Promotional Fire Service Tests, see 15667 through 15676. Time, 180. Items, 175.

Assesses the knowledge, skills, and abilities of candidates for the position of battalion fire chief. Available on a rental basis only. Documentation is available in event of challenge. Content validation.

15674
**Promotional Fire Service Tests: Command Level, Fire Service Administrator (Captain), 574.** Advanced Research Resources Organization, Bethesda, MD
*Descriptors:* *Fire Fighters; *Occupational Tests; *Promotion (Occupational); *Supervisors; Adults
*Identifiers:* *Captain; IPMA
*Availability:* International Personnel Management Association, 1617 Duke St., Alexandria, VA 22314.
*Notes:* For other tests in the Promotional Fire Service Tests, see 15667 through 15676. Time, 150. Items, 150.

Assesses the knowledge, skills, and abilities of candidates for the position of fire captain. Available on a rental basis. Documentation is available in event of challenge. Content validation.

15675
**Promotional Fire Service Tests: Command Level, Fire Service Administrator (Chief), 578.** Advanced Research Resources Organization, Bethesda, MD
*Descriptors:* *Fire Fighters; *Occupational Tests; *Promotion (Occupational); *Supervisors; Adults
*Identifiers:* *Fire Chiefs; IPMA
*Availability:* International Personnel Management Association, 1617 Duke St., Alexandria, VA 22314.
*Notes:* For other tests in the Promotional Fire Service Tests, see 15667 through 15676. Time, 150. Items, 150.

Assesses the knowledge, skills, and abilities of candidates for the position of fire chief. Available on a rental basis only. Documentation is available in event of challenge. Content validation.

15676
**Promotional Fire Service Tests: Command Level, Fire Service Administrator (Deputy Chief), 576.** Advanced Research Resources Organization, Bethesda, MD
*Descriptors:* *Fire Fighters; *Occupational Tests; *Promotion (Occupational); *Supervisors; Adults
*Identifiers:* *Fire Chiefs; IPMA
*Availability:* International Personnel Management Association, 1617 Duke St., Alexandria, VA 22314.
*Notes:* For other tests in the Promotional Fire Service Tests, see 15667 through 15675. Time, 180. Items, 175.

Assesses the knowledge, skills, and abilities of candidates for the position of deputy fire chief. Available on a rental basis only. Documentation is available in event of challenge. Content validation.

15678
**Entry-Level Police Service Tests: Police Officer Examination, 175.1 and 175.2.** Advanced Research Resources Organization, Bethesda, MD
*Descriptors:* *Entry Workers; *Occupational Tests; *Police; Adults
*Identifiers:* IPMA; POE
*Availability:* International Personnel Management Association, 1617 Duke St., Alexandria, VA 22314.
*Notes:* See Entry-Level Police Service Tests: Police Officer Examination, 375.1 and 375.2 (18169), and Entry-Level Police Officer Background Data Questionnaire (18170) for related instruments. Time, 150. Items, 140.

Two alternate forms of the Police Officer Examination. The 175.1 and the 175.2 are available for rental. Assesses the following performance dimensions: preparing for duty; patrol activities; response to call for assistance; arrest and detention procedures; search and seizure; traffic control and traffic investigation; public relations; investigation; court activities; and administrative duties. Tests are supported by predictive, criterion-related validity evidence. Inspection copies for the POE are not available. POE study guides are available for review. The guide gives an indication of the types of items contained within the examinations.

15679
**Promotional Police Service Tests: Supervisory Level, Police Corporal/Sergeant, 562.** Advanced Research Resources Organization, Bethesda, MD
*Descriptors:* *Occupational Tests; *Police; *Promotion (Occupational); *Supervisors; Adults
*Identifiers:* *Corporal; IPMA; *Sergeant
*Availability:* International Personnel Management Association, 1617 Duke St., Alexandria, VA 22314.
*Notes:* Time, 150. Items, 145.

Available on a rental basis only. Documentation available in event of challenge. Content validation. Assesses the knowledge, skills, and abilities of candidates for supervisory-level police officer positions of corporal and sergeant.

15684
**Teacher Evaluation Rating Scales.** Ysseldyke, James E.; And Others 1988.
*Descriptors:* *Instructional Development; *Instructional Improvement; *Teacher Evaluation; *Teacher Improvement; Adults; Rating Scales; Self Evaluation (Individuals); Teacher Administrator Relationship
*Availability:* PRO-ED, 8700 Shoal Creek Blvd., Austin, TX 78758.

Comprehensive system for instructional improvement. Represents results of research on effective schools and instructional excellence that includes a collaboration between administrative-supervisory staff and teaching staff. This system involves input and feedback from supervisors and teachers and consists of 3 major components. Supervisor's scale allows an observer to evaluate a teacher on 6 critical elements of teaching and professional development: instructional planning, instructional management, teaching procedures, monitoring procedures, personal qualities, and professionalism. The teacher's self-assessment scale allows self-ratings on the same dimensions as on the supervisor's scale. The instructional improvement plan is completed after collaboration between the teacher and observer and includes a plan of action for the teacher to improve aspects of instruction and professionalism.

15687
**Supervisor Behavior Observation Scale.** Cherniss, Cary 1983.
*Descriptors:* *Administrators; *Employer Employee Relationship; *Leadership Styles; *Observation; *Special Schools; *Supervisory Methods; Adults; Behavior Patterns; Coding; Interpersonal Communication; Mental Retardation; Objectives; School Personnel; Supervision
*Identifiers:* TIM(P)
*Availability:* Tests in Microfiche, Test Collection, Educational Testing Service, Princeton, NJ 08541.
*Notes:* Additional information can be found in *American Journal of Mental Deficiency;* v91 n1 p18-21, 1986. Time, 30.

An observation and coding method for use in describing frequency and types of behaviors of supervisors or administrators of schools for mentally retarded children. Data were gathered based on 2,500 observations of 5 female administrators. Observation categories are based on the path goal theory of leadership which suggests that supervisors assist subordinates in achieving at high levels by setting clear goals and helping subordinates overcome obstacles to attain these goals. Categories include 6 dimensions of behavior and several subcategories, e.g.: mode (listening); function (guiding); content (administrative); tone (neutral); location (office); and target (ancillary staff). Norms are available as means and ranges of counts. Reliability data are available.

**15695**
**Reid Survey.** Reid Psychological Systems, Chicago, IL 1985.
*Descriptors:* *Attitude Measures; *Employee Attitudes; *Values; Adults; Questionnaires
*Identifiers:* Honesty
*Availability:* Psychological Surveys Corp., 900 Jorie Blvd., Ste. 130, Oak Brook, IL 60521.
*Notes:* Time, 40 approx. Items, 90.

Designed to be used only with employees who have worked in their positions for at least 2 years. Questionnaire yields the following assessments of current employees: their attitudes toward honesty; information on any wrongdoing by the employee; employees' knowledge and views of coworkers' honesty and performance; employees' propensity to use drugs and alcohol; employees' contentment or unhappiness in the job; and the employees' degree of cooperativeness related to the job and the company.

**15714**
**Visibility/Credibility Inventory: Measuring Power and Influence.** Reddy, W. Brendan; Williams, Gil
*Descriptors:* *Group Dynamics; *Organizational Effectiveness; *Power Structure; Adults; Peer Influence; Rating Scales; Training Methods
*Availability:* Pfeiffer, J. William, ed., *The 1988 Annual: Developing Human Resources.* San Diego: University Associates, 1988. Pfeiffer and Co., formerly University Associates, 8517 Production Ave., San Diego, CA 92121-2280.
*Notes:* Time, 10 approx. Items, 50.

Instrument to assist group members to understand their own and others' functioning with regard to power within a group. Instrument is based on 2 components of power: visibility and credibility. The 2 components are interactive. Can be used for: activities related to team building; training involving groups, such as work teams; power-related laboratories and activities; influence exercises; multicultural laboratory work; training involving male-female dynamics; racism/ethnism workshops; training trainers; and management work conferences. Instrument is generally administered in a group setting. The test is designed to serve as a guide and aid in exploring, understanding, and discussing power and influence in a group. Used most effectively in conjunction with other data, instruments, activities, and feedback.

**15715**
**Organizational-Learning Diagnostics (OLD).** Pareek, Udai
*Descriptors:* *Administrators; *Organizational Effectiveness; Adults; Organizational Change; Rating Scales
*Identifiers:* OLD
*Availability:* Pfeiffer, J. William, ed., *The 1988 Annual: Developing Human Resources.* San Diego: University Associates, 1988. Pfeiffer and Co., formerly University Associates, 8517 Production Ave., San Diego, CA 92121-2280.
*Notes:* Items, 23.

The author defines organizational learning as "the process by which an organization acquires, retains, and uses inputs for its development, and the process results in an enhanced capacity for continued self learning and self renewal." This instrument was developed to help organizations know about the level of their learning potential and discover which dimensions are strong or weak. The instrument assesses 2 dimensions of organizational learning: organizational learning subsystems or phases and organizational learning mechanisms. The instrument should be administered to a fairly large number of managers in an organization.

**15736**
**Electronics Test.** Ramsay, Roland T. 1987.
*Descriptors:* *Achievement Tests; *Electronics; *Knowledge Level; *Occupational Tests; *Personnel Evaluation; *Personnel Selection; Adults; Electronics Industry
*Availability:* Ramsay Corp., 1050 Boyce Rd., Pittsburgh, PA 15241-3907.
*Notes:* Time, 120 approx. Items, 125.

Developed for use with applicants and incumbents for jobs where electronics knowledge and skills are necessary parts of job activities. There are 2 forms of the test. Knowledge areas assessed include motors, digital electronics, analog electronics, schematics and print reading, radio control, power supplies, basic AC/DC theory, test instruments, mechanics, computer and PLC, regulators, electronic equipment, and power distribution.

**15737**
**Security Aptitude Fitness Evaluation.** Taccarino, John R.
*Descriptors:* *Job Skills; *Personality Traits; *Personnel Selection; *Screening Tests; Adults; Attitude Measures; Language Skills; Mathematics; Microcomputers
*Identifiers:* *Honesty; SAFE
*Availability:* SAFE, Inc., 141 Briarwood North, Oak Brook, IL 60521.
*Notes:* See also Security Aptitude Fitness Evaluation—Resistance (15738). Time, 30 approx. Items, 130.

Identifies theft-prone job applicants and measures an individual's capability and suitability to do the job. Assesses individuals' attitudes about work and theft and tests their basic math and language skills. Provides an evaluation of an applicant's total potential job suitability and performance. Scored and interpreted automatically through the SAFE hand-held computer or using special software on an IBM PC.

**15738**
**Security Aptitude Fitness Evaluation—Resistance.** Taccarino, John R.
*Descriptors:* *Job Skills; *Personality Traits; *Personnel Selection; *Screening Tests; Adults; Attitude Measures; Language Skills; Mathematics; Microcomputers
*Identifiers:* *Honesty; SAFE(R)
*Availability:* SAFE, Inc., 141 Briarwood North, Oak Brook, IL 60521.
*Notes:* See also Security Aptitude Fitness Evaluation (15737). Time, 30 approx. Items, 164.

Assesses individuals' attitudes about work and theft, their psychological and personality characteristics, and their life experiences relating to substance abuse potential. Also tests basic math and language skills. Provides information for the employer in hiring suitable, honest, and drug-free employees. May be scored using a SAFE hand-held computer or using special software on an IBM PC.

**15759**
**Ethical Standards for School Counselors: Test Your Knowledge.** Huey, Wayne C. 1987.
*Descriptors:* *Adults; *Ethics; *School Counselors; *Self Evaluation (Individuals); Codes of Ethics; Decision Making; Elementary Secondary Education
*Availability:* *School Counselor,* v34 n5 p331-35, May 1987.
*Notes:* Items, 25.

Presents 25 situations that address ethical issues involving school counselors. Respondents indicate whether they agree or disagree with the action taken by the counselor in the situation presented. Correctness of the answers is based on the code of ethics set down in the American School Counselor Association's (ASCA) publication *Ethical Standards for School Counselors* (1984). Each test item contains the section and item number of the ASCA publication where ethical standards for the situation in question are described. May be used to indicate areas in which counselors need more training.

**15760**
**Teacher Stress Inventory.** Blase, Joseph J. 1986.
*Descriptors:* *Stress Variables; *Teachers; Adults; Elementary Secondary Education; Questionnaires
*Availability:* *American Educational Research Journal,* v23 n1 p13-40, Spr 1986.
*Notes:* Items, 12.

A questionnaire designed to collect qualitative data reflecting teachers' perceptions of stress. Items are open-ended. Teachers are asked for detailed descriptions of what they consider to be 3 important sources of stress. Used with a sample of teachers enrolled in graduate courses. Teachers represent all levels except postsecondary and all geographical areas except the Northeast. Mean number of years of experience was 10.

**15794**
**Employee Reliability Inventory.** Borofsky, Gerald L.; And Others 1986.
*Descriptors:* *Job Performance; *Occupational Tests; *Personnel Selection; Adults; Alcoholism; Computer Software; Drug Abuse; Drug Use; Employee Responsibility; Persistence; Scoring
*Identifiers:* ERI; Honesty
*Availability:* E.F. Wonderlic Personnel Test, 820 Frontage Rd., Northfield, IL 60093.
*Notes:* Time, 15. Items, 81.

This pre-interview questionnaire is designed to help employers identify reliable and productive employees prior to making a hiring decision. Suggests areas that may be further explored during a job interview. The subscores measure likelihood of job disruption due to substance abuse; vandalism and theft; job commitment for at least 30 days; and likelihood that the employee will not be fired for 30 days. Questions require a true/false response. Handscored and interpreted by publisher via phone. May also be scored and interpreted via IBM compatible software. Validated using employees that demonstrated unreliable behavior on the job.

**15795**
**Army Battalion Unit Morale Measure.** Kimmel, Melvin J.; And Others 1984.
*Descriptors:* *Attitude Measures; *Military Organizations; *Military Service; *Morale; *Organizational Climate; Adults; Job Satisfaction; Occupational Tests
*Availability:* National Technical Information Service, 5285 Port Royal Rd., Springfield, VA 22161 (Document AD-A168311).
*Notes:* Items, 73.

Designed for use as a measure of organizational morale for military personnel within battalions. Was administered to a sample of service personnel, noncommissioned officers, and other officers. A general satisfaction score is calculated. To develop a morale score, all individual scores are averaged. Items cover organizational climate in 4 domains: unit, supervisor, coworker, and job domain.

**15800**
**Basic Bank Skills Battery.** London House, Rosemont, IL 1988.
*Descriptors:* *Banking; *Occupational Tests; *Personnel Selection; Adults; Computer Software; Interpersonal Competence; Leadership; Mathematics; Personality Measures; Scoring
*Identifiers:* BBSB
*Availability:* London House, SRA Product Group, 9701 W. Higgins Rd., Rosemont, IL 60018.
*Notes:* Time, 45.

Developed to aid in the selection of bank tellers and customer service personnel. Covers background information examining drive and school achievement. Measures of job-related abilities cover arithmetic computation, error recognition, name comparison, and number comparison. Personality measures assess interpersonal skills, cognitive skills, self-discipline, and leadership. A single "Potential Estimate" score is provided by the publisher or through PC-based software.

**15801**
**Insurance Selection Inventory.** London House, Rosemont, IL 1988.
*Descriptors:* *Insurance; *Insurance Occupations; *Occupational Tests; *Personnel Selection; Adults; Computer Software; Interpersonal Competence; Mathematics; Personality Measures; Writing Skills
*Identifiers:* ISI
*Availability:* London House, SRA Product Group, 9701 W. Higgins Rd., Rosemont, IL 60018.
*Notes:* Time, 26.

Designed to select claims examiners/adjusters, customer service representatives, and correspondence representatives. Based on job analysis, this test measures skill in number comparsion, verbal reasoning, arithmetic computation, error recognition, applied arithmetic, drive, interpersonal skills, cognitive skills, self-discipline, writing skills, and work preference. Scored by publisher or PC-based software. Provides a single "Potential Estimate" score.

**15802**
**Station Manager Applicant Inventory.** London House, Rosemont, IL 1988.
*Descriptors:* *Fuels; *Occupational Tests; *Personnel Selection; *Service Occupations; Administrators; Adults; Arithmetic; Background; Computer Software; Drug Use; Interpersonal Competence; Mathematics; Personality Measures; Work Experience
*Identifiers:* Gas Stations; Honesty; SMAI
*Availability:* London House, SRA Product Group, 9701 W. Higgins Rd., Rosemont, IL 60018.
*Notes:* Time, 45. Items, 144.

Designed to hire productive service station managers. A managerial potential index is calculated. The test is scored by the publisher or by the purchaser via PC-based software. Said to select managers who hire good employees and motivate them, encourage team spirit, and keep up competitive spirit.

**15807**
**Berger Tests of Programming Proficiency: COBOL II.** Berger, Francis; Berger, Raymond M.
*Descriptors:* *Data Processing Occupations; *Job Training; *Occupational Tests; *Personnel Selection; *Programming; *Programming Languages; *Promotion (Occupational); Adults; Computers
*Identifiers:* COBOL
*Availability:* Psychometrics, Inc., 4730 Woodman Ave., Sherman Oaks, CA 91423.
*Notes:* Time, 60. Items, 30.

An updated version of the original with a more structured approach. Measures knowledge of data descriptions and file handling, tables and sorting (sort, search, subscripting, and indexing), statements and operations (move, go to, perform), arithmetic statements and operations, conditional statements, and logic, structured programming, and program organization. Designed to measure proficiency of experienced programmers and to assist in hiring, promotion, and advanced training decisions.

**15809**
**Berger Tests of Programming Proficiency: BASIC Language.** Berger, Francis; Berger, Raymond M.
*Descriptors:* *Data Processing Occupations; *Job Training; *Occupational Tests; *Personnel Selection; *Programming; *Programming Languages; *Promotion (Occupational); Adults; Computers
*Identifiers:* BASIC
*Availability:* Psychometrics, Inc., 4730 Woodman Ave., Sherman Oaks, CA 91423.
*Notes:* Time, 35. Items, 30.

Measures an examinee's knowledge of BASIC in the following areas: general programming, (programming fundamentals, debugging, error handling, merge/replace); structure (program logic, looping, and branching); variables and expressions (variables, arithmetic and logic expressions); and I/O and character manipulation (input/output, string manipulation, ASCII conversion). Designed to measure proficiency of experienced programmers and to assist in hiring, promotion, and advanced training decisions.

**15814**
**Multimethod Job Design Questionnaire.** Campion, Michael A. 1982.
*Descriptors:* *Job Analysis; *Job Development; *Job Satisfaction; *Job Skills; *Occupational Tests; Adults; Observation; Rating Scales; Work Environment
*Identifiers:* MJDQ
*Availability:* Select Press, P.O. Box 9838, San Rafael, CA 94912.
*Notes:* When ordering, request Ms. No. 2695. Time, 30. Items, 70.

An interdisciplinary measure that combines over 700 specific job design rules into 4 sets of principles, each constituting a job design approach: motivational approach; mechanistic approach; biological approach; and classical-experimental approach. Each approach is related to job outcomes of satisfaction, efficiency, comfort, and reliability (safety). Uses observational method and 5-point rating scales anchored by descriptive definitions. Scores are summed within each approach. Assists in determining if organizational problems are a result of job design. For assisting in redesign of jobs and as a guide during system development.

**15834**
**EASY: Employee Attitude Study.** Walden Computer Aptitude Testing, Ltd., Oradell, NJ 1988.
*Descriptors:* *Attitude Measures; *Computer Assisted Testing; *Employee Attitudes; *Work Attitudes; *Work Environment; Adults; Computers; Computer Software
*Identifiers:* EASY
*Availability:* Walden Computer Aptitude Testing, Ltd., Box 319, Oradell, NJ 07649.
*Notes:* Time, 60. Items, 84.

Assesses employee attitudes toward actual work environment using true/false format. The employee then responds to the same statements with respect to an ideal work environment. A group's manager completes the same scale. The instrument is offered as a PC-based system for corporatewide use only. IBM compatible. Can be generalized to work groups at various levels to allow comparsion. A report is produced for each group to integrate all input.

**15841**
**Job Interactions Inventory, Revised.** Porter, Elias H. 1987.
*Descriptors:* *Employees; *Interaction; *Interpersonal Relationship; Adults; Career Planning; Forced Choice Technique; Job Satisfaction; Rating Scales; Self Evaluation (Individuals)
*Identifiers:* JII
*Availability:* Personal Strengths Publishing, P.O. Box 397, Pacific Palisades, CA 90272-0397.
*Notes:* See also Strength Deployment Inventory (12349). Items, 10.

Helps to clarify how compatible a person's style of interaction is with the demands of that person's job. Job situation or environment influences interaction with others. This inventory is designed to assess the pattern of interactions that a particular job or situation demands. Inventory is helpful in the areas of career planning and development, job compatibility, job stress, conflict resolution, burnout prevention, motivation, and rewards.

**15843**
**Teacher Occupational Competency Testing: Auto Body Repair (083).** National Occupational Competency Testing Institute, Big Rapids, MI
*Descriptors:* *Achievement Tests; *Auto Body Repairers; *Certification; *Equivalency Tests; *Vocational Education Teachers; *Work Sample Tests; Adults; College Credits; Credentials; Multiple Choice Tests; Occupational Tests; Performance Tests
*Identifiers:* NOCTI; TOCT
*Availability:* National Occupational Competency Testing Institute, 409 Bishop Hall, Ferris State University, Big Rapids, MI 49307.
*Notes:* Time, 420. Items, 190.

One of a series of tests designed to determine a level of occupational competence for vocational education teachers. A written test covers theoretical concepts of the occupation and a performance test examines selected manipulative skills. The tests may be used for credit-by-examination and also for teacher certification. The written test covers welding; filling operations and plastics; repairing sheet metal; refinishing; panel replacement, frame (unitized body repair); front-end alignment; electrical and accessory systems; glass, trim, and hardware; estimating; tools and equipment; and safety. The performance test covers metal forming, welding, diagnosing structural damage, refinishing, and electrical troubleshooting.

**15844**
**Teacher Occupational Competency Testing: Building and Home Maintenance Services (067).** National Occupational Competency Testing Institute, Big Rapids, MI
*Descriptors:* *Achievement Tests; *Certification; *Construction Industry; *Equivalency Tests; *Maintenance; *Vocational Education Teachers; *Work Sample Tests; Adults; College Credits; Credentials; Multiple Choice Tests; Occupational Tests; Performance Tests
*Identifiers:* NOCTI; TOCT
*Availability:* National Occupational Competency Testing Institute, 409 Bishop Hall, Ferris State University, Big Rapids, MI 49307.
*Notes:* Time, 480. Items, 162.

One of a series of tests designed to determine a level of occupational competence for vocational education teachers. A written test covers theoretical concepts of the occupation. The performance test examines selected manipulative skills. The tests may be used for credit-by-examination and also for teacher certification. The written test covers: floor stripping, refinishing and buffing, carpet care, general electricity and repair, building security, fire prevention, records, general cleaning, plumbing, employee/staff relations, heating, and painting. The performance test covers general cleaning of office or classroom and a restroom or shower/locker room area; floor stripping, refinishing and buffing; carpet care; welding or soldering; electrical repair; small hand/power tools; and interior/exterior painting.

**15845**
**Teacher Occupational Competency Testing: Child Care and Guidance (081).** National Occupational Competency Testing Institute, Big Rapids, MI 1988.
*Descriptors:* *Achievement Tests; *Certification; *Child Care Occupations; *Day Care; *Equivalency Tests; *Vocational Education Teachers; *Work Sample Tests; Adults; College Credits; Credentials; Multiple Choice Tests; Occupational Tests; Performance Tests
*Identifiers:* NOCTI; TOCT
*Availability:* National Occupational Competency Testing Institute, 409 Bishop Hall, Ferris State University, Big Rapids, MI 49307.
*Notes:* Time, 480. Items, 200.

One of a series of tests designed to determine a level of occupational competence for vocational education teachers. A written test covers theoretical concepts of the occupation and a performance test examines selected manipulative skills. The tests may be used for credit-by-examination and also for teacher certification. The written test covers infant-toddler development and learning, preschool and young child development and learning, guiding behavior, health and safety, center management, and special needs children. The performance test covers infant diapering, toddler observation, large group teaching, small group teaching, daily program plans, role play (parent/staff interaction), and role play (child discipline situation).

15846
**Teacher Occupational Competency Testing: Computer Science for Secondary Teachers (080).** National Occupational Competency Testing Institute, Big Rapids, MI
*Descriptors:* *Achievement Tests; *Certification; *Computer Science; *Equivalency Tests; *Programming Languages; *Secondary School Teachers; *Vocational Education Teachers; *Work Sample Tests; Adults; College Credits; Credentials; Multiple Choice Tests; Occupational Tests; Performance Tests
*Identifiers:* NOCTI; TOCT
*Availability:* National Occupational Competency Testing Institute, 409 Bishop Hall, Ferris State University, Big Rapids, MI 49307.
*Notes:* Time, 540. Items, 158.

One of a series of tests designed to determine a level of occupational competence for vocational education teachers. A written test covers theoretical concepts of the occupation and a performance test examines selected manipulative skills. The tests may be used for credit-by-examination and also for teacher certification. The written test covers general concepts, program design, microcomputers, on-line communications, including magnetic files and data communications. The performance test covers use of microcomputers for word processing and spreadsheets, systems analysis, program design, BASIC programming, PASCAL programming, FORTRAN programming, and COBOL programming.

15847
**Teacher Occupational Competency Testing: Electrical Construction and Maintenance (061).** National Occupational Competency Testing Institute, Big Rapids, MI
*Descriptors:* *Achievement Tests; *Certification; *Electrical Occupations; *Equivalency Tests; *Vocational Education Teachers; *Work Sample Tests; Adults; College Credits; Construction (Process); Credentials; Equipment Maintenance; Multiple Choice Tests; Occupational Tests; Performance Tests
*Identifiers:* NOCTI; TOCT
*Availability:* National Occupational Competency Testing Institute, 409 Bishop Hall, Ferris State University, Big Rapids, MI 49307.
*Notes:* Time, 420. Items, 180.

One of a series of tests designed to determine a level of occupational competence for vocational education teachers. A written test covers theoretical concepts of the occupation, and a performance test examines selected manipulative skills. The tests may be used for credit-by-examination and also for teacher certification. The written test covers electron theory and basic circuit calculations, A.C. theory and conductors, motor control circuits and motors, wiring methods, transformers and lighting, and basic electricity. The performance test covers motors and motor circuits, troubleshooting, transformer layout and connectors, component identification and testing, and raceways and lighting.

15848
**Teacher Occupational Competency Testing: Heavy Equipment Mechanics (069).** National Occupational Competency Testing Institute, Big Rapids, MI
*Descriptors:* *Achievement Tests; *Certification; *Equipment; *Equivalency Tests; *Vocational Education Teachers; *Work Sample Tests; Adults; College Credits; Credentials; Mechanics (Process); Multiple Choice Tests; Occupational Tests; Performance Tests
*Identifiers:* NOCTI; TOCT
*Availability:* National Occupational Competency Testing Institute, 409 Bishop Hall, Ferris State University, Big Rapids, MI 49307.
*Notes:* Time, 480. Items, 200.

One of a series of tests designed to determine a level of occupational competence for vocational education teachers. A written test covers theoretical concepts of the occupation and a performance test examines selected manipulative skills. The tests may be used for credit-by-examination and also for teacher certification. The written test covers diesel fuel injection system and engine troubleshooting, diesel and gasoline engine tune-up and overhaul, power trains, steering and suspension, welding and cutting, brakes, cooling and exhaust systems, electrical systems, hydraulic systems, and general, including air conditioning. The performance test covers engine tune-up, hydraulic troubleshooting and repair, power trains (differentials), basic engine measurements, welding and cutting, gasoline engines, electrical system, undercarriage inspection, and operation of tracked equipment (road grader, dump truck, or road tractor).

15849
**Teacher Occupational Competency Testing: Scientific Data Processing (084).** National Occupational Competency Testing Institute, Big Rapids, MI
*Descriptors:* *Achievement Tests; *Certification; *Data Processing; *Equivalency Tests; *Programming Languages; *Vocational Education Teachers; *Work Sample Tests; Adults; College Credits; Credentials; Multiple Choice Tests; Occupational Tests; Performance Tests
*Identifiers:* NOCTI; TOCT
*Availability:* National Occupational Competency Testing Institute, 409 Bishop Hall, Ferris State University, Big Rapids, MI 49307.
*Notes:* Time, 540. Items, 167.

One of a series of tests designed to determine a level of occupational competence for vocational education teachers. A written test covers theoretical concepts of the occupation and a performance test examines selected manipulative skills. The tests may be used for credit-by-examination and also for teacher certification. The written test covers understanding computer fundamentals, performing equipment operations, using software packages, generating documentation, using programming languages (BASIC, FORTRAN, PASCAL, C), and applying numerical analysis. The performance test covers comprehension of computer fundamentals by generating documentation demonstrating an understanding of numerical analysis; performing equipment operations using operating systems and software packages with a programming language; and developing a program using a programming language to apply numerical analysis and generate a solution.

15850
**Teacher Occupational Competency Testing: Welding (041).** National Occupational Competency Testing Institute, Big Rapids, MI
*Descriptors:* *Achievement Tests; *Certification; *Equivalency Tests; *Vocational Education Teachers; *Welding; *Work Sample Tests; Adults; College Credits; Credentials; Multiple Choice Tests; Occupational Tests; Performance Tests
*Identifiers:* NOCTI; TOCT
*Availability:* National Occupational Competency Testing Institute, 409 Bishop Hall, Ferris State University, Big Rapids, MI 49307.
*Notes:* Time, 420. Items, 174.

One of a series of tests designed to determine a level of occupational competence for vocational education teachers. A written test covers theoretical concepts of the occupation and a performance test examines selected manipulative skills. The tests may be used for credit-by-examination and also for teacher certification. The written test covers safety; oxyfuel welding; torch brazing and oxyfuel cutting; shielded metal arc welding; gas tungsten arc welding; welding symbols and joint design; gas metal arc welding; flux-cored arc welding; other industrial welding and cutting processes; inspection, testing, and welding codes; and welding metallurgy. The performance test covers shielded metal arc welding, oxyfuel welding, oxyfuel torch brazing, flux-cored arc welding, gas metal arc welding, gas tungsten arc welding, airarc cutting, and oxyfuel cutting.

15893
**Self-Assessment Exam: Blood Banking.** American Society of Clinical Pathologists, Chicago, IL 1983.
*Descriptors:* *Allied Health Occupations; *Knowledge Level; *Medical Technologists; *Self Evaluation (Individuals); Adults
*Identifiers:* *Blood Banks; *Immunohematology
*Availability:* American Society of Clinical Pathologists, P.O. Box 12075, Chicago, IL 60612-0075.
*Notes:* For the complete series of self-assessment exams, see 15894 through 15909.

Self-assessment exam that helps individuals measure their strengths and potential weaknesses in specific laboratory specialties. Self-assessment programs are available to meet the needs of all clinical laboratory personnel - pathologists, residents, clinical scientists, and technologists. Each exam consists of 70 to 200 multiple-choice questions and takes between 1 to 4 hours to complete. This immunohematology test is designed for blood bankers who have at least 3 years of experience in the field. Exam covers all areas of blood banking, including immunology, genetics, transfusion and antibody-related problems, pre- and perinatal situations, donor collection and processing, apheresis, HLA studies, and quality control.

15894
**Self-Assessment Exam: Chemistry.** American Society of Clinical Pathologists, Chicago, IL 1983.
*Descriptors:* *Allied Health Occupations; *Chemistry; *Knowledge Level; *Medical Technologists; *Self Evaluation (Individuals); Adults
*Availability:* American Society of Clinical Pathologists, P.O. Box 12075, Chicago, IL 60612-0075.
*Notes:* For the complete series of self-assessment exams, see 15893 through 15909.

Self-assessment exam that helps individuals measure their strengths and potential weaknesses in specific laboratory specialties. Self-assessment programs are available to meet the needs of all clinical laboratory personnel - pathologists, residents, clinical scientists, and technologists. Each exam consists of 70 to 200 multiple-choice questions and takes between 1 to 4 hours to complete. Designed for medical technologists with several years of experience and who have a broad base in clinical laboratory procedures. Covers electrolyte and acid-base balance, carbohydrate metabolism, lipids, endocrine function, statistics and quality control, proteins, immunology, therapeutic drug monitoring and toxicology, and liver function and enzymes.

15896
**Self-Assessment Exam: Fine Needle Aspiration.** American Society of Clinical Pathologists, Chicago, IL 1984.
*Descriptors:* *Allied Health Occupations; *Culturing Techniques; *Cytology; *Graduate Medical Students; *Knowledge Level; *Pathology; *Self Evaluation (Individuals); Adults
*Availability:* American Society of Clinical Pathologists, P.O. Box 12075, Chicago, IL 60612-0075.
*Notes:* For the complete series of self-assessment exams, see 15893 through 15909. Items, 40.

Self-assessment exam that helps individuals measure their strengths and potential weaknesses in specific laboratory specialties. Self-assessment programs are available to meet the needs of all clinical laboratory personnel - pathologists, residents, clinical scientists, and technologists. Each exam consists of 70 to 200 multiple-choice questions and takes between 1 to 4 hours to complete. There are 40 35-mm slide-related questions used to assess the ability to interpret fine-needle aspiration smears, including benign and malignant lesions of lung, breast, head, and neck (including thyroid), and abdominal organs. Test is suitable for pathologists practicing cytology, pathology residents, and cytotechnologists.

15898
**Self-Assessment Exam: Fundamentals of Blood Banking.** American Society of Clinical Pathologists, Chicago, IL 1987.

*Descriptors:* *Allied Health Occupations; *Knowledge Level; *Self Evaluation (Individuals); Adults
*Identifiers:* *Blood Banks
*Availability:* American Society of Clinical Pathologists, P.O. Box 12075, Chicago, IL 60612-0075.
*Notes:* For the complete series of self-assessment exams, see 15893 through 15909. Items, 70.

Self-assessment exam that helps individuals measure their strengths and potential weaknesses in specific laboratory specialties. Self-assessment programs are available to meet the needs of all clinical laboratory personnel - pathologists, residents, clinical scientists, and technologists. Each exam consists of 70 to 200 multiple-choice questions and takes between 1 to 4 hours to complete. Multiple-choice test that covers immunoserology and genetics, transfusion practices, blood group systems, basic blood banking and blood products, and laboratory management and operation. Published in association with the American Association of Blood Banks.

**15899**
**Self-Assessment Exam: Generalist II.** American Society of Clinical Pathologists, Chicago, IL 1986.
*Descriptors:* *Allied Health Occupations; *Entry Workers; *Knowledge Level; *Medical Technologists; *Self Evaluation (Individuals); Adults
*Availability:* American Society of Clinical Pathologists, P.O. Box 12075, Chicago, IL 60612-0075.
*Notes:* For the complete series of self-assessment exams, see 15893 through 15909. Items, 200.

Self-assessment exam that helps individuals measure their strengths and potential weaknesses in specific laboratory specialties. Self-assessment programs are available to meet the needs of all clinical laboratory personnel - pathologists, residents, clinical scientists, and technologists. Each exam consists of 70 to 200 multiple-choice questions and takes between 1 to 4 hours to complete. Used to assess mastery of full range of laboratory medicine, including hematology, chemistry, body fluids, immunology, blood banking and transfusion practices, microbiology, and management. Intended for entry-level technologists.

**15900**
**Self-Assessment Exam: Gynecologic Cytopathology.** American Society of Clinical Pathologists, Chicago, IL 1984.
*Descriptors:* *Allied Health Occupations; *Cytology; *Graduate Medical Students; *Gynecology; *Knowledge Level; *Self Evaluation (Individuals); Adults
*Availability:* American Society of Clinical Pathologists, P.O. Box 12075, Chicago, IL 60612-0075.
*Notes:* For the complete series of self-assessment exams, see 15893 through 15909. Items, 40.

Self-assessment exam that helps individuals measure their strengths and potential weaknesses in specific laboratory specialties. Self-assessment programs are available to meet the needs of all clinical laboratory personnel - pathologists, residents, clinical scientists, and technologists. Each exam consists of 70 to 200 multiple-choice questions and takes between 1 to 4 hours to complete. Consists of 40 35-mm slide-related questions dealing primarily with cytologic evaluation of the vagina, uterus, cervix, and endometrium. Included are questions on benign processes, infections, premalignant cellular changes, diagnostic pitfalls, and malignancies. Suitable for self-evaluation by pathologists practicing cytology, experienced pathology residents, and cytotechnologists.

**15901**
**Self-Assessment Exam: Hematology.** American Society of Clinical Pathologists, Chicago, IL 1983.
*Descriptors:* *Allied Health Occupations; *Knowledge Level; *Self Evaluation (Individuals); Adults
*Identifiers:* *Hematology
*Availability:* American Society of Clinical Pathologists, P.O. Box 12075, Chicago, IL 60612-0075.
*Notes:* For the complete series of self-assessment exams, see 15893 through 15909.

Self-assessment exam that helps individuals measure their strengths and potential weaknesses in specific laboratory specialties. Self-assessment programs are available to meet the needs of all clinical laboratory personnel - pathologists, residents, clinical scientists, and technologists. Each exam consists of 70 to 200 multiple-choice questions and takes between 1 to 4 hours to complete. Appropriate for those with several years of experience in a hematology laboratory and for those who want to improve their understanding of hematology. Directed toward general hematologists and covers normal function and production of hematopoietic cells, leukemias, reactive states, myeloproliferative conditiions, anemias, coagulation, automation, and quality control.

**15904**
**Self-Assessment Exam: Laboratory Management.** American Society of Clinical Pathologists, Chicago, IL 1985.
*Descriptors:* *Administrators; *Allied Health Occupations; *Knowledge Level; *Laboratories; *Self Evaluation (Individuals)
*Availability:* American Society of Clinical Pathologists, P.O. Box 12075, Chicago, IL 60612-0075.
*Notes:* For the complete series of self-assessment exams, see 15893 through 15909. Items, 100.

Self-assessment exam that helps individuals measure their strengths and potential weaknesses in specific laboratory specialties. Self-assessment programs are available to meet the needs of all clinical laboratory personnel - pathologists, residents, clinical scientists, and technologists. Each exam consists of 70 to 200 multiple-choice questions and takes between 1 to 4 hours to complete. Designed for self-evaluation by technologists with several years of experience and who have a broad base of administrative and managerial responsiblities. Multiple-choice questions cover management theory, techniques, and methods that relate to the introduction of diagnostic related groups; and current medical laboratory economics, forecasting and statistics, laboratory safety, personnel management, data processing, accreditation, regulations, inspections, materials management, and research and development.

**15905**
**Self-Assessment Exam: Microbiology.** American Society of Clinical Pathologists, Chicago, IL 1983.
*Descriptors:* *Allied Health Occupations; *Knowledge Level; *Microbiology; *Self Evaluation (Individuals); Adults
*Availability:* American Society of Clinical Pathologists, P.O. Box 12075, Chicago, IL 60612-0075.
*Notes:* For the complete series of self-assessment exams, see 15893 through 15909.

Self-assessment exam that helps individuals measure their strengths and potential weaknesses in specific laboratory specialties. Self-assessment programs are available to meet the needs of all clinical laboratory personnel - pathologists, residents, clinical scientists, and technologists. Each exam consists of 70 to 200 multiple-choice questions and takes between 1 to 4 hours to complete. Designed for self-evaluation by microbiologists who have worked in a clinical microbiology laboratory for at least 3 years.

**15907**
**Problem Solving in Immunohematology (Third Edition).** Silver, Herbert; And Others 1987.
*Descriptors:* *Allied Health Occupations; *Knowledge Level; *Self Evaluation (Individuals); Adults
*Identifiers:* *Immunohematology
*Availability:* American Society of Clinical Pathologists, P.O. Box 12075, Chicago, IL 60612-0075.

Self-assessment workbook with exercises and problems that simulate situations faced by laboratory personnel, including the area of blood banking. Recommended for self-evaluation by pathologists, residents, and technologists.

**15908**
**Self-Assessment Exam: Pulmonary Cytopathology.** American Society of Clinical Pathologists, Chicago, IL 1986.
*Descriptors:* *Allied Health Occupations; *Cytology; *Graduate Medical Students; *Knowledge Level; *Medical Technologists; *Self Evaluation (Individuals); Adults
*Identifiers:* *Lung Diseases
*Availability:* American Society of Clinical Pathologists, P.O. Box 12075, Chicago, IL 60612-0075.
*Notes:* For the complete series of self-assessment exams, see 15893 through 15909. Items, 60.

Self-assessment exam that helps individuals measure their strengths and potential weaknesses in specific laboratory specialities. Self-assessment programs are available to meet the needs of all clinical laboratory personnel - pathologists, residents, clinical scientists, and technologists. Each exam consists of 70 to 200 multiple-choice questions and takes between 1 to 4 hours to complete. Consists of 60 35-mm slide-related questions covering neoplastic and non-neoplastic lung diseases. Test covers collection and preparation techniques; interpretation of conventional specimens taken from sputum; bronchial washings and bronchial brushings; and the role of special techniques, such as tracheal aspirates and bronchoalveolar lavages. Suitable for pathologists practicing cytology, cytopathology residents, and cytotechnologists.

**15926**
**Store Management Effectiveness Inventory.** Human Synergistics, Plymouth, MI 1986.
*Descriptors:* *Administrator Evaluation; *Retailing; *Self Evaluation (Individuals); Adults; Job Skills; Organizational Climate; Personality Traits; Rating Scales; Recognition (Achievement); Supervisory Methods; Supervisory Training
*Identifiers:* SMEI; *Store Managers
*Availability:* Human Synergistics, 39819 Plymouth Rd., Plymouth, MI 48170.
*Notes:* Items, 230.

Developed under a grant from the Coca-Cola Retailing Research Council to assess store and department managers' on-the-job skills and behavior. There are 2 forms: the first is for self-evaluation and the other is used by 5 other people to rate the manager. Most effective when used in a training situation or by training, organizational development, or personnel and human resources personnel for professional development purposes. Part A measures manager's thinking style and self-concept. Part B assesses management skills in 9 areas. Part C deals with areas that are specific to managing a store, including customer-community relations, sales and marketing strategy, information adequacy, and maintenance. Part D investigates how the manager rewards the employees. Part E measures the culture of the store, based on the values, traditions, and expectations for employees.

**15928**
**Hilson Personnel Profile/Success Quotient.** Inwald, Robin E.; Brobst, Karen E. 1988.
*Descriptors:* *Job Performance; *Personnel Selection; *Promotion (Occupational); *Success; Academic Ability; Adults; Goal Orientation; Interpersonal Competence; Questionnaires; Self Esteem; Self Evaluation (Individuals)
*Identifiers:* HPP(SQ); Success Quotient Theory
*Availability:* Hilson Research, Inc., 82-28 Abingdon Rd., P.O. Box 239, Kew Gardens, NY 11415.
*Notes:* Items, 150.

Conceived as a measure of success in a majority of workplaces and to identify productive, winning behavior and characteristics necessary for achievement in the working world. Designed to aid personnel administrators and others who make hiring and promotion decisions by providing them with information on job applicants. This scale is based on the Success Quotient Theory of Inwald, which assumes that success in the workplace can be predicted by certain measurable and consistent factors, including academic ability, social ability, self-confidence and competitive spirit, and initiative or drive or follow-through. Can be administered individually or in group settings.

**15948**
**Situation Diagnosis Questionnaire.** Michalak, Don 1983.
*Descriptors:* *Administrators; *Work Environment; Adults; Questionnaires
*Identifiers:* Management Styles; Managerial Grid
*Availability:* Michalak Training Associates, 875 Pinto Pl. South, Tucson, AZ 85748-7921.
*Notes:* Items, 21.

Diagnoses a manager's work situation to identify which management style is most appropriate. Does not measure a person's management style. Identifies the management style most likely to be effective based on the nature of the job being managed. Two questionnaires to be completed by managers and employees so responses can be compared.

**16000**
**Self-Assessment Examination for the Dietary Manager.** Dietary Managers Association, Hillside, IL 1985.
*Descriptors:* *Dietitians; *Self Evaluation (Individuals); Adults
*Availability:* Dietary Managers Association, 4410 W. Roosevelt Rd., Hillside, IL 60162-2077.

A self-study instrument designed to help dietary managers prepare for their credentialing examination. Each item represents a critical incident scenario with a selection of responses from which to choose. Test book, answer book, and answer sheet included.

**16037**
**NTE Specialty Area Tests: School Psychologist Examination.** Educational Testing Service, Princeton, NJ 1988.
*Descriptors:* *Achievement Tests; *Certification; *Graduate Students; *School Psychologists; Educational Assessment; Educational Psychology; Higher Education; Knowledge Level; Masters Programs; Professional Occupations; Social Psychology; Student Evaluation
*Identifiers:* NTE
*Availability:* NTE Programs, Educational Testing Service, CN 6051, Princeton, NJ 08541-6051.
*Notes:* Time, 120.

This test is designed to measure examinees' knowledge of underlying principles and generally accepted practices of school psychologists in order to provide assistance to educational institutions in preparing students for certification. It is intended for use with master's degree level students who have had a supervised practicum. Covers assessment, intervention, evaluation, professional practice, psychological foundations, and educational foundations. Questions focus on both content and process issues that are relevant to the school setting.

**16043**
**Personal Expectations Inventory.** Forisha Kovach, Barbara; And Others 1980.
*Descriptors:* *Employee Attitudes; *Occupational Tests; *Work Attitudes; Adults; Behavior Patterns; Group Behavior; Interpersonal Relationship; Personality Measures; Productivity; Social Integration
*Identifiers:* PXI
*Availability:* Organization Design and Development, Inc., 2002 Renaissance Blvd., Ste. 100, King of Prussia, PA 19406-2746.
*Notes:* Items, 72.

Designed to measure individual employees' expectations and perceptions which are the framework of their behaviors. Identifies employees who are: producers (those who get things done), processors (those who affiliate with others), and integrators (those who make all the parts fit). Said to assist in determining who is "in synchrony" with the employee group, which may lead to increased productivity, depending on the norms of the group.

**16045**
**Selling Skills Inventory.** Phillips, Kenneth R. 1987.
*Descriptors:* *Salesmanship; *Sales Occupations; Adults; Questionnaires; Self Evaluation (Individuals)
*Availability:* Organization Design and Development, Inc., 2002 Renaissance Blvd., Ste. 100, King of Prussia, PA 19406-2746.
*Notes:* Items, 18.

Designed to assess the ability of a sales representative to recognize when and how to use the skills necessary to conduct successful sales calls. Successful sales calls are defined as those that lead to a close and establish the sales representative as a partner with the customer. The successful selling approach is viewed as a process consisting of 7 steps: building rapport, establishing a reason to meet, identifying needs and problems, considering possible options, agreeing on a solution, overcoming resistance, and pledging to act. This inventory covers all the processes, except building rapport. The inventory consists of 18 situations, each of which has 4 possible actions that a salesperson might initiate.

**16047**
**Group Process Questionnaire.** Hill, Richard; And Others 1988.
*Descriptors:* *Feedback; *Group Dynamics; *Interaction; Adults; Rating Scales
*Availability:* Organization Design and Development, Inc., 2002 Renaissance Blvd., Ste. 100, King of Prussia, PA 19406-2746.
*Notes:* Time, 15 approx. Items, 53.

Developed to encourage groups who have been engaged in problem-solving activities to continue learning activities based on the group's interactions. Can be used by individual and groups to analyze their task and maintenance behaviors during a previous discussion. Task behaviors include initiating, seeking information or opinions, giving information or opinions, clarifying and elaborating, summarizing, and consensus-taking. Maintenance behaviors include listening, harmonizing, gatekeeping, encouraging, compromising, and standard setting. Participants first rank the group on these behaviors and then reach a consensus through discussion. This succeeds in moving the focus away from content to how the group interacted and worked together. Each participant also rates herself or himself on these behaviors. Also small feedback cards can be completed and given by each member of the group to every other member of the group. These methods encourage the occurrence of learning from the interactions.

**16048**
**Managerial Interest Audit.** Nowack, Kenneth M. 1986.
*Descriptors:* *Administrators; *Interests; *Job Satisfaction; *Managerial Occupations; *Occupational Tests; *Personnel Selection; *Work Attitudes; Adults; Affiliation Need; Computer Assisted Testing; Interpersonal Competence; Leadership; Management Development; Values
*Identifiers:* MIA
*Availability:* Organization Design and Development, Inc., 2002 Renaissance Blvd., Ste. 100, King of Prussia, PA 19406-2746.
*Notes:* See also Employee Interest Audit (16049). Items, 150.

Designed to measure an employee's interest in 15 job relevant areas: autonomy, variety, innovation, achievement, self-assessment, persuasion, affiliation, people perception, group communication, leading, negotiation, problem analysis, planning and organizing, coaching, and delegation. May be used for employee selection, placement, training and development, presupervisory development and succession planning. This instrument is said to be predictive of job satisfaction. May be administered and scored via a software package.

**16049**
**Employee Interest Audit.** Nowack, Kenneth M. 1986.
*Descriptors:* *Computer Assisted Testing; *Employees; *Interests; *Job Satisfaction; *Occupational Tests; *Work Attitudes; Adults; Affiliation Need; Interpersonal Competence; Personnel Selection; Problem Solving; Values
*Identifiers:* EIA
*Availability:* Organization Design and Development, Inc., 2002 Renaissance Blvd., Ste. 100, King of Prussia, PA 19406-2746.
*Notes:* See also Managerial Interest Audit (16048). Items, 130.

Measures an employee's interests in 13 job relevant areas: variety, autonomy, achievement, persuasion, affiliation, poeple perception, group communication, leading, negotiating, problem solving, planning and organizing, coaching, and administering. This instrument is said to be predictive of job satisfaction. May be administered and scored via a software package.

**16051**
**Leadership Report, Second Edition.** W. Warner Burke Associates, Pelham, NY 1988.
*Descriptors:* *Leadership Styles; *Managerial Occupations; Adults; Middle Management; Rating Scales; Self Evaluation (Individuals)
*Identifiers:* Senior Management
*Availability:* Organization Design and Development, Inc., 2002 Renaissance Blvd., Ste. 100, King of Prussia, PA 19406-2746.
*Notes:* Time, 25 approx. Items, 18.

Based on the work of James MacGregor Burns. Helps individuals make distinctions between transformational leadership and transactional leadership. Transformational leaders are concerned primarily with change. Transactional leaders primarily view the leader-follower relationship as a process of exchange. Organizations need a balance between the two types of leaders. The instrument and discussion manual are suitable for senior- and middle-level managers. Consultants and trainers interested in current approaches to leadership will also be interested in this material.

**16052**
**Corporate Culture Survey.** Glaser, Rollin 1983.
*Descriptors:* *Occupational Tests; *Organizational Climate; *Work Environment; Adults; Cultural Context; Surveys
*Identifiers:* Organizational Culture
*Availability:* Organization Design and Development, Inc., 2002 Renaissance Blvd., Ste. 100, King of Prussia, PA 19406-2746.
*Notes:* Time, 20. Items, 50.

This survey is designed to measure type and strength of organizational culture, those values and beliefs that contribute to an organizational persona. Uses the classification system described by Terrance Deal and Alan Kennedy in the book *Corporate Cultures* (Addison-Wesley, 1984). Said to be useful in introducing the concept of culture and its impact on profits, in analyzing culture for change, and for developing the team. Covers rituals and ceremonies, corporate heroines/heroes, presence of culture communicators, etc.

**16054**
**Coaching Skills Inventory.** Phillips, Kenneth R. 1987.
*Descriptors:* *Administrators; *Change Strategies; *Employer Employee Relationship; Adults; Employee Attitudes; Questionnaires
*Identifiers:* *Coaching
*Availability:* Organization Design and Development, Inc., 2002 Renaissance Blvd., Ste. 100, King of Prussia, PA 19406-2746.
*Notes:* Items, 18.

Designed to assess the ability of a manager or supervisor to recognize when and how to use the skills necessary to conduct effective coaching meetings. Primary purpose of a coaching meeting is to help redirect an employee's behavior to improve future performance. Coaching can be viewed as a 6-step process: opening the meeting, getting agreement, exploring alternatives, getting a commitment to act, handling excuses, and closing the meeting. Inventory consists of 18 coaching meeting situations, each of which has 4 alternative actions a manager might initiate.

**16055**
**Management Orientation Inventory.** Pollard, Harry V. 1988.
*Descriptors:* *Administrators; *Leadership Styles; Adults; Supervisory Methods
*Identifiers:* MOI
*Availability:* Organization Design and Development, Inc., 2002 Renaissance Blvd., Ste. 100, King of Prussia, PA 19406-2746.
*Notes:* Items, 8.

Used to examine the philosophies of managers about people in their organizations. Inventory identifies 3 primary managerial orientations: traditional, enlightened, and emergent. The traditional and enlightened philosophies correlate with the Theory X and Theory Y of Douglas McGregor. The emergent philosophy (Theory Z) places a premium on peoples' competence and requires leaders who use information and expertise as their primary source of power.

**16057**
**Management of Differences Inventory.** Kindler, Herbert S. 1981.
*Descriptors:* *Administrators; *Conflict Resolution; *Leadership Styles; *Managerial Occupations; *Occupational Tests; Adults; Behavior Patterns; Peer Evaluation; Self Evaluation (Individuals)
*Identifiers:* MODI
*Availability:* Organization Design and Development, Inc., 2002 Renaissance Blvd., Ste. 100, King of Prussia, PA 19406-2746.
*Notes:* Time, 20. Items, 36.

Designed to determine how a manager handles differences or conflict. Questions are stated as behaviors rather than attitudes about situations. Styles measured include: domination, smoothing, maintenance, bargaining, coexistence, decision rule, collaboration, supportive release, and nonresistance. Viewpoint firmness and flexibility are considered, as well as intensity of interaction from "impersonal and uninvolved" to "highly personal." One form is for self-evaluation and another for evaluation by others.

**16058**
**Decision Process Inventory.** Kindler, Herbert S. 1983.
*Descriptors:* *Administrators; *Decision Making; *Occupational Tests; Adults; Situational Tests
*Identifiers:* DPI
*Availability:* Organization Design and Development, Inc., 2002 Renaissance Blvd., Ste. 100, King of Prussia, PA 19406-2746.
*Notes:* Time, 20. Items, 12.

This situational test requires the respondent to select 1 of 4 decision processes that should be applied in the situation described. These processes are: unilateral or sole judgment; bargaining or mutual adjustment; collaboration; and decision rule by majority, coin flip, or arbitration. Designed to determine the respondent's preferred decision process style and the effectiveness of the decision process choices.

**16059**
**AIM: Agor Intuitive Management Survey.** Agor, Weston H. 1985.
*Descriptors:* *Administrators; *Decision Making; *Intuition; *Occupational Tests; Adults; Brain Hemisphere Functions; Management Development; Managerial Occupations; Personnel Selection
*Identifiers:* AIM
*Availability:* Organization Design and Development, Inc., 2002 Renaissance Blvd., Ste. 100, King of Prussia, PA 19406-2746.
*Notes:* Time, 20. Items, 26.

This instrument is based on the work of Dr. Weston H. Agor and his book, *Intuitive Management: Integrating Left and Right Brain Management Skills.* (Prentice-Hall, 1984). It measures underlying intuitive ability and is designed to measure how managers use intuitive ability to make critical decisions. For use in management selection, development, or identification of human capital resources, including employees who can generate ideas for increasing productivity. Norms are available for public and private sector managers.

**16060**
**Measuring Your Leadership Skills.** Mackenzie, Alec 1988.
*Descriptors:* *Leadership Styles; *Managerial Occupations; Adults; Management Development; Rating Scales; Self Evaluation (Individuals)
*Identifiers:* Mackenzie Memo 50
*Availability:* Organization Design and Development, Inc., 2002 Renaissance Blvd., Ste. 100, King of Prussia, PA 19406-2746.
*Notes:* Items, 78.

A self-audit used to assess individuals' leadership skills in the following areas: decision making, planning, organizing, staffing, leading, controlling, and communicating. Useful for helping new and experienced managers understand the management process and chart a development plan. Package includes a 4-color chart of the management process and a series of audits participants can take to determine how well they perform each of the leadership skills.

**16068**
**Foreign Service Officer Examination, Written Assessment.** Board of Examiners for the Foreign Service, Arlington, VA
*Descriptors:* *English; *Foreign Workers; *Government Employees; *Occupational Tests; *Personnel Selection; *Written Language; Administration; Adults; Art Activities; Geography; Grammar; International Relations; Language Skills; Multiple Choice Tests; North American Culture; Occupational Information; Scientific Principles
*Availability:* Dept. of State, Recruitment Div., Box 9317, Rosslyn Station, Arlington, VA 22209.
*Notes:* For a description of the oral assessment, see 16069. Time, 180.

This test is designed to measure knowledge and skills found to be necessary for successful functioning as a foreign service officer. Applicants must be U.S. citizens, 20 years of age, and available for assignment worldwide. No specific educational background is required. The test is given once yearly on the first Saturday in December. The exam covers U.S.-related institutions and concepts, trends in the arts, scientific and management principles, knowledge and skills required to perform effectively in specific functional areas of the Departments of State and Commerce and the U.S. Information Agency. Candidate must pass only 1 function area subtest. The English Expression test measures skill in written English. The test is in multiple-choice format.

**16069**
**Foreign Service Officer Examination, Oral Assessment.** Board of Examiners for the Foreign Service, Arlington, VA
*Descriptors:* *Foreign Workers; *Government Employees; *Interpersonal Competence; *Occupational Tests; *Personnel Selection; *Speech Communication; Adults; Cultural Awareness; Interpersonal Communication; Leadership; Performance Tests; Problem Solving; Simulation; Writing (Composition)
*Identifiers:* In Basket Test; *Oral Tests
*Availability:* Dept. of State, Recruitment Div., Box 9317, Rosslyn Station, Arlington, VA 22209.
*Notes:* For a description of the written assessment, see 16068. Time, 305.

This test is designed to measure knowledge and skills found to be necessary for successful functioning as a foreign service officer. Applicants must be U.S. citizens, 20 years of age, and pass a written exam (16068). The oral exam assesses problem-solving skills, communication skills, leadership, interpersonal skills, cultural awareness, sensitivity, stability, and resourcefulness. It consists of the oral exam, a written essay, a written summary, an oral presentation to a group, and an in-basket exercise measuring problem solving that involves sorting and prioritizing the contents of a sample in-basket.

**16070**
**Pennsylvania Dental Auxiliary Radiography Examination.** Dental Assisting National Board, Chicago, IL
*Descriptors:* *Dentistry; *Licensing Examinations (Professions); *Occupational Tests; *Radiographers; Adults; Dental Evaluation; Dental Technicians; Knowledge Level; State Licensing Boards
*Availability:* Dental Assisting National Board, Inc., 216 E. Ontario St., Chicago, IL 60611.
*Notes:* Time, 120. Items, 100.

Designed for use as part of a licensing requirement in the state of Pennsylvania for persons who will be working as auxiliaries to professional staff and who will be performing radiologic procedures. The test is multiple choice and covers radiographic exposure and processing techniques, mounting and labeling of radiographics, application of patient, and operator safety procedures.

**16072**
**Account Clerk I, II.** International Personnel Management Association, Alexandria, VA
*Descriptors:* *Accounting; *Clerical Occupations; *Occupational Tests; *Personnel Selection; Adults
*Identifiers:* IPMA
*Availability:* IPMA Test Publications, 1617 Duke St., Alexandria, VA 22314.
*Notes:* Time, 69 approx. Items, 150.

Consists of a combination of IPMA Clerical Series Tests: Clerical Skills Series, 362.1 (15660); Oral Instruction and Forms Completion, 364.1 (15663); and Oral Instruction Cassette 366.1. All IPMA test materials are available on a rental basis only. Developed from a job analysis of public service positions. Used for the selection of entry-level and intermediate clerical staff.

**16073**
**Library Assistant I, II.** International Personnel Management Association, Alexandria, VA
*Descriptors:* *Clerical Occupations; *Library Technicians; *Occupational Tests; *Personnel Selection; Adults
*Identifiers:* IPMA
*Availability:* IPMA Test Publications, 1617 Duke St., Alexandria, VA 22314.
*Notes:* Time, 70. Items, 170.

Consists of a combination of IPMA Clerical Series Tests: Clerical Skills Series, 361.1 (15659); Oral Instruction and Forms Completion, 364.1 (15663); and Oral Instruction Cassette 366.1. All IPMA test materials are available on a rental basis only. Developed from a job analysis of public service positions. Used for the selection of entry level and intermediate clerical staff.

**16074**
**Stenographer I, II.** International Personnel Management Association, Alexandria, VA
*Descriptors:* *Clerical Occupations; *Occupational Tests; *Personnel Selection; *Shorthand; Adults
*Identifiers:* IPMA
*Availability:* IPMA Test Publications, 1617 Duke St., Alexandria, VA 22314.
*Notes:* Time, 105 approx. Items, 151.

Consists of a combination of IPMA Clerical Series Tests: Clerical Skills Series, 361.1 (15659) Oral Instruction and Forms Completion, 364.1 (15663); Oral Instruction Cassette, 366.1; and Dictation/Transcription Test 367.1 (15662). All IPMA test materials are available on a rental basis only. Developed from a job analysis of public service positions. Used for selection of entry-level and intermediate clerical staff.

**16075**
**Typist I, II.** International Personnel Management Association, Alexandria, VA

*Descriptors:* *Clerical Occupations; *Occupational Tests; *Personnel Selection; *Typewriting; Adults
*Identifiers:* IPMA
*Availability:* IPMA Test Publications, 1617 Duke St., Alexandria, VA 22314.
*Notes:* Time, 76. Items, 170.

Consists of a combination of IPMA Clerical Series Tests: Clerical Skills Series, 361.1 (15659); Oral Instruction and Forms Completion, 364.1 (15663); Typing Test, 365.1 (15664); and Oral Instruction Cassette 366.1. All IPMA test materials are available on a rental basis only. Developed from a job analysis of public service positions. Used for the selection of entry-level and intermediate clerical staff.

**16078**
**Organizational Competence Index.** Hall, Jay 1987.
*Descriptors:* *Organizational Climate; *Organizational Effectiveness; *Productivity; Administrators; Adults; Cooperation; Creativity; Employee Attitudes; Job Performance; Management Development; Needs Assessment; Occupational Tests; Program Evaluation; Work Attitudes; Work Environment
*Identifiers:* Competence Theory; OCI
*Availability:* Telemetrics International, 1755 Woodstead Ct., The Woodlands, TX 77380.
*Notes:* Items, 40.

This validated survey is based on a model of organizational functioning called competence theory, which states that an organization can create rather than inhibit individual competence and the result will be a state of organized or collective competence. The OCI differentiates between high- and low-performing groups in an organization. Measures amount of employee collaboration, commitment, and creativity allowed that supports organizational productivity. Also measures actual versus desired conditions. Used to demonstrate competence theory for feedback and analysis by managers, training needs analysis, comparison of groups, as a pre- and post-test to determine effectiveness of management or organizational development activities.

**16091**
**Custometrics: Customer Satisfaction Survey System.** Shamrock Press, San Diego, CA 1988.
*Descriptors:* *Computer Software; *Microcomputers; *Surveys; *Test Construction; Adults
*Identifiers:* Customer Satisfaction; Opinionnaires
*Availability:* Shamrock Press, 1277 Garnet Ave., P.O. Box 90699, San Diego, CA 92109.
*Notes:* Former title was People Facts.

A personal computer software package for use on any IBM or true compatible MS-DOS computer with 512K of memory and 1 disk drive. Used to create questionnaires for conducting customer satisfaction surveys. A menu-driven software program that allows users to enter up to 200 questions and derive a variety of statistical results.

**16114**
**Voc-Tech Quick Screener.** Kauk, Robert; Robinett, Robert 1988.
*Descriptors:* *Computer Assisted Testing; *Interest Inventories; *Technical Occupations; *Two Year Colleges; *Vocational Education; *Vocational Interests; *Vocational Schools; Adults; Postsecondary Education; Vocational Rehabilitation; Vocational Training Centers
*Identifiers:* VTQS
*Availability:* CFKR Career Materials, Inc., 11860 Kemper Rd., Unit 7, Auburn, CA 95603.
*Notes:* Time, 10. Items, 20.

This interest inventory was designed to assist the portion of the work force that does not attend college to explore careers that do not require college degrees. Useful with those who will attend rehabilitation programs, vocational courses, apprenticeship training, private vocational and technical schools, community and junior college programs, and military training programs. The VTQS matches occupational interests with vocational/technical occupational clusters. A computerized version is available for Apple II, IBM and compatibles, and TRS-80.

**16118**
**Cognitive-Style Inventory.** Martin, Lorna P.
*Descriptors:* *Cognitive Processes; *Cognitive Style; *Decision Making; *Learning; *Organizational Climate; *Organizational Development; *Problem Solving; Adults; Rating Scales
*Availability:* Pfeiffer, J. William, ed., *The 1989 Annual: Developing Human Resources.* San Diego: University Associates, 1989. Pfeiffer and Co., formerly University Associates, 8517 Production Ave., San Diego, CA 92121-2280.
*Notes:* Items, 40.

This inventory identifies and characterizes respondents' approaches to the cognitive behaviors of thinking, learning, problem solving, and decision making. Systematic, intuitive, integrated, undifferentiated, and split individual cognitive styles are identified. The quantity and quality of these cognitive behaviors have an impact on the organization's productivity, performance, and potential for growth. The results gathered also assist in determining whether an organization, as an entity, practices or prefers a particular cognitive style. This instrument is included in *The 1989 Annual: Developing Human Resources.*

**16119**
**Organizational-Health Survey.** Phillips, Will
*Descriptors:* *Organizational Climate; *Organizational Development; *Organizational Effectiveness; *Organizational Objectives; Adults; Individual Development; Job Performance; Rating Scales; Staff Development
*Identifiers:* Organizational Health
*Availability:* Pfeiffer, J. William, ed., *The 1989 Annual: Developing Human Resources.* San Diego: University Associates, 1989. Pfeiffer and Co., formerly University Associates, 8517 Production Ave., San Diego, CA 92121-2280.

The Organizational-Health Survey (short form) and The Organizational-Health Survey (Long Form) both measure the organization's health in terms of the following dimensions: strategic position, purpose, alignment, stretching versus coasting, control versus responsiveness, growth versus profit, and individual versus organization. The short form, which consists of 7 scales, is scored subjectively by the participants. The 45-item long form consists of questions relating to each of the 7 dimensions of organizational health. Use of the data can help to define more clearly the goal of organizational and invididual development efforts in an organization.

**16120**
**Motivational Analysis of Organizations—Climate.** Pareek, Udai
*Descriptors:* *Motivation; *Organizational Climate; *Organizational Development; Adults; Decision Making; Job Performance; Rating Scales
*Identifiers:* MAO(C)
*Availability:* Pfeiffer, J. William, ed., *The 1989 Annual: Developing Human Resources.* San Diego: University Associates, 1989. Pfeiffer and Co., formerly University Associates, 8517 Production Ave., San Diego, CA 92121-2280.
*Notes:* Items, 72.

This inventory analyzes the connection between organizational climate and motivation. The instrument can focus on the perception of the overall organizational climate or individual units or departments within the organization. The instrument employs the 12 dimensions of organizational climate: orientation; interpersonal relationships; supervision; problem management; management of mistakes; conflict management; communication; decision making; trust; management of rewards; risk taking; and innovation and change. It also uses 6 motivators: achievement; affiliation; expert influence; control; extension; and dependency. Where these 12 dimensions intersect the the 6 motivators form the matrix or profile connecting organizational climate and motivation. This instrument is in *The 1989 Annual: Developing Human Resources.*

**16131**
**Survey of Organizational Climate.** Training House, Inc., Princeton, NJ 1984.
*Descriptors:* *Organizational Climate; *Surveys; *Work Environment; Adults
*Availability:* Training House, Inc., 100 Bear Brook Rd., P.O. Box 3090, Princeton, NJ 08540.
*Notes:* Contained in The OD Kit (14809). Items, 60.

Survey of the work environment as an employee believes the organization is rather than what a person thinks it should be. Enables supervisors to examine the strengths and weaknesses of their work group "climate" based on 12 factors affecting productivity and morale.

**16133**
**Self-Awareness Profile.** Training House, Inc., Princeton, NJ 1980.
*Descriptors:* *Self Concept Measures; *Self Evaluation (Individuals); *Work Attitudes; Adults; Employment
*Availability:* Training House, Inc., 100 Bear Brook Rd., P.O. Box 3090, Princeton, NJ 08540.
*Notes:* Contained in The OD Kit (14809). Time, 90. Items, 16.

Enables people to collect and analyze information about the way they think, feel, and act at work. Provides insight into the basic personality attributes that influence the way people behave. Gives a better understanding of how respondees respond to situations and people and how this relates to their effectiveness at work.

**16134**
**Personal Inventory of Needs.** Training House, Inc., Princeton, NJ 1984.
*Descriptors:* *Achievement Need; *Affiliation Need; *Individual Needs; *Individual Power; Adults; Employee Attitudes; Measures (Individuals); Rating Scales
*Identifiers:* Power
*Availability:* Training House, Inc., 100 Bear Brook Rd., P.O. Box 3090, Princeton, NJ 08540.
*Notes:* Contained in The OD Kit (14809). Items, 30.

Shows a person's relative strength regarding 3 needs: achievement, affiliation, and power. Different types of jobs, assignments, and organizations draw on an individual's different needs. Can be used in business sessions dealing with motivation, management style, personality, and recruitment.

**16135**
**Leadership and Team Building.** Training House, Inc., Princeton, NJ 1980.
*Descriptors:* *Leadership; *Self Evaluation (Individuals); *Teamwork; Adults; Rating Scales
*Availability:* Training House, Inc., 100 Bear Brook Rd., P.O. Box 3090, Princeton, NJ 08540.
*Notes:* Contained in The OD Kit (14809). Items, 60.

A self-assessment tool that enables the members of a work group or team and their leader to identify the group's strengths and weaknesses on 10 dimensions that are important to the team-building process. Enables a team and its leader to review overall effectiveness by focusing on a number of factors that are important to the success of work groups.

**16136**
**Personal Style Assessment.** Training House, Inc., Princeton, NJ 1980.
*Descriptors:* *Interpersonal Relationship; *Interprofessional Relationship; Adults; Personality Traits; Self Evaluation (Individuals)
*Availability:* Training House, Inc., 100 Bear Brook Rd., P.O. Box 3090, Princeton, NJ 08540.

*Notes:* Contained in The OD Kit (14809). Time, 20. Items, 10.

Designed to give people insight into their style in dealing with others and in learning new things in the workplace.

**16138**
**Survey of Supervisory Style (X-Y).** Training House, Inc., Princeton, NJ 1980.
*Descriptors:* *Administrator Attitudes; *Self Evaluation (Individuals); *Supervisory Methods; Adults
*Availability:* Training House, Inc., 100 Bear Brook Rd., P.O. Box 3090, Princeton, NJ 08540.
*Notes:* Contained in The OD Kit (14809). Items, 30.

Designed to determine a person's predominant managerial style. Based on 2 sets of assumptions, Theory X and Y. Theory X managers believe the average employee dislikes work and will avoid it if possible. Theory Y managers believe average employee wants a challenging job and opportunities for work.

**16139**
**Survey of Attitudes Toward Work.** Training House, Inc., Princeton, NJ 1984.
*Descriptors:* *Administrator Attitudes; *Attitude Measures; *Employee Attitudes; Adults; Employer Employee Relationship; Rating Scales
*Availability:* Training House, Inc., 100 Bear Brook Rd., P.O. Box 3090, Princeton, NJ 08540.
*Notes:* Contained in The OD Kit (14809). Items, 24.

Designed to determine participants' atttitudes toward manager-employee relationship. Based on "parent-child" and "adult-adult" view of work. Useful in courses dealing with interpersonal communications, motivation and organizational climate, and transactional analysis.

**16140**
**PAR Proficiency Assessment Report.** Training House, Inc., Princeton, NJ 1984.
*Descriptors:* *Administrator Evaluation; *Administrator Qualifications; Adults; Personnel Evaluation; Rating Scales
*Identifiers:* PAR
*Availability:* Training House, Inc., 100 Bear Brook Rd., P.O. Box 3090, Princeton, NJ 08540.
*Notes:* Contained in The OD Kit (14809). Items, 22.

Designed to help supervisors and managers determine their proficiency on a series of abilities commonly associated with effective management. A supervisor can rate and compare these ratings with those assigned by the boss. Information can be used as a basis for training and development and as a benchmark against which future growth can be compared.

**16141**
**Productivity Profile.** Training House, Inc., Princeton, NJ 1981.
*Descriptors:* *Productivity; Administrators; Adults; Employees; Rating Scales; Self Evaluation (Individuals)
*Availability:* Training House, Inc., 100 Bear Brook Rd., P.O. Box 3090, Princeton, NJ 08540.
*Notes:* Contained in The OD Kit (14809). Items, 60.

Enables supervisors and members of their work group to assess the degree of opportunity for improved productivity. Can focus on a number of factors that contribute to improved productivity.

**16142**
**Communication Audit.** Training House, Inc., Princeton, NJ 1981.
*Descriptors:* *Administrators; *Business Communication; *Communication Skills; *Employees; Adults; Rating Scales
*Availability:* Training House, Inc., 100 Bear Brook Rd., P.O. Box 3090, Princeton, NJ 08540.
*Notes:* Contained in The OD Kit (14809). Items, 20.

Three-part survey. Respondents score themselves, their boss, and top management on statements describing the nature of communications that each initiates. They then identify the person with whom they most frequently communicate and describe that person's communication using a rating scale with adjectives. Finally, respondents answer 4 questions that help them analyze the nature of communication barriers they most often face.

**16143**
**Communication Response Style Assessment.** Training House, Inc., Princeton, NJ 1981.
*Descriptors:* *Business Communication; *Communication Skills; *Self Evaluation (Individuals); Adults; Communications
*Availability:* Training House, Inc., 100 Bear Brook Rd., P.O. Box 3090, Princeton, NJ 08540.
*Notes:* Contained in The OD Kit (14809). Items, 20.

Enables respondents to determine the nature of their "response style", how they are likely to respond to a statement or a question made by another person. Our effectiveness in communicating with others depends on the degree to which we are aware and in control of our responses to the information we receive from others.

**16144**
**Needs Inventory.** Training House, Inc., Princeton, NJ
*Descriptors:* *Administrators; *Management Development; *Needs Assessment; Adults; Labor Needs; Rating Scales
*Availability:* Training House, Inc., 100 Bear Brook Rd., P.O. Box 3090, Princeton, NJ 08540.
*Notes:* Contained in The OD Kit (14809). Items, 17.

Designed to obtain input from supervisors and managers on their needs. Used to select topics and skills areas to be included in a management development program.

**16145**
**Management Style Inventory.** Training House, Inc., Princeton, NJ 1982.
*Descriptors:* *Adults; *Management Development; *Rating Scales; *Supervisory Methods; Administration
*Availability:* Training House, Inc., 100 Bear Brook Rd., P.O. Box 3090, Princeton, NJ 08540.
*Notes:* Contained in The OD Kit (14809). Items, 50.

Designed to give people some insights into their management style and how it affects others. Assesses the values and styles of managers/supervisors and yields a score on each of the 5 positions on the managerial grid: soft, hard, team builder, middle of the road, and ineffective.

**16147**
**Inventory of Work-Related Feelings.** Training House, Inc., Princeton, NJ
*Descriptors:* *Attitude Measures; *Employee Attitudes; *Work Attitudes; Adults; Measures (Individuals); Self Evaluation (Individuals)
*Availability:* Training House, Inc., 100 Bear Brook Rd., P.O. Box 3090, Princeton, NJ 08540.
*Notes:* Contained in The OD Kit (14809). Items, 20.

Instrument to assist employees in gaining a clearer sense of their own personal feelings toward their jobs.

**16156**
**Leader Behavior Analysis II: Self and Other.** Blanchard, Kenneth H.; And Others 1985.
*Descriptors:* *Attitude Measures; *Employee Attitudes; *Job Performance; *Leadership; *Leadership Styles; *Management Development; *Self Evaluation (Individuals); *Supervisory Methods; Adults; Feedback
*Identifiers:* LBAII
*Availability:* Blanchard Training and Development, 125 State Pl., Escondido, CA 92025.
*Notes:* Items, 20.

The LBA II provides leaders with information about their perception of their own leadership style and the perception of one or more staff members about that style. Both the leader and staff member(s) are presented with 20 typical job situations in which they may be involved together. The respondents are asked to select from 4 leader decisions that would best describe the leader's behavior in that situation. The data reflect whether there is a "match" or "mismatch" between the leaders' perception of their style and the perceptions of others.

**16166**
**Teacher Occupational Competency Testing: Microcomputer Repair (085).** National Occupational Competency Testing Institute, Big Rapids, MI
*Descriptors:* *Achievement Tests; *Certification; *Machine Repairers; *Microcomputers; *Vocational Education Teachers; *Work Sample Tests; Adults; College Credits; Credentials; Equivalency Tests; Multiple Choice Tests; Occupational Tests; Performance Tests
*Identifiers:* NOCTI; TOCT
*Availability:* National Occupational Competency Testing Institute, 409 Bishop Hall, Ferris State University, Big Rapids, MI 49307.
*Notes:* Time, 360. Items, 200.

One of a series of tests designed to determine a level of occupational competence for vocational education teachers. A written test covers theoretical concepts of the occupation and a performance test examines selected manipulative skills. The tests may be used for credit-by-examination and also for teacher certification. The written test covers safety, hand tools, D.C. theory, A.C. theory, semiconductors, digital logic, flip flops and registers, encoders and decoders, counters, multiplexer and demultiplexer, A/D and D/A converters, computer maintenance, fundamentals and peripherals, and microprocessors. The performance test covers troubleshooting solid state circuit devices, computer malfunctions, and peripherals; constructing/analyzing digital circuits; and constructing a full-wave bridge rectifier and analyzing the power supply.

**16170**
**Becker Work Adjustment Profile.** Becker, Ralph L. 1989.
*Descriptors:* *Emotional Disturbances; *Learning Disabilities; *Mental Retardation; *Physical Disabilities; *Poverty; *Vocational Adjustment; *Vocational Evaluation; Adolescents; Adults; Norm Referenced Tests; Rating Scales; Rehabilitation Centers; Sheltered Workshops; Work Experience Programs
*Identifiers:* BWAP
*Availability:* Elbern Publications, P.O. Box 09497, Columbus, OH 43209.
*Notes:* Items, 63.

Provides a method for vocational evaluators, work adjustment specialists, and other professionals to acquire information about the work habits, attitudes, and skills of individuals in sheltered and competitive work. Designed to assess the vocational competency of mentally retarded, emotionally disturbed, learning disabled, economically disadvantaged, and physically disabled persons. For use in a wide range of vocational facilities and for various types of placements for individuals with disabilities, in either part-time or full-time job situations. There is also a 32-item short form of the scale.

**16174**
**Developmental Task Analysis II.** Blanchard, Kenneth H.; And Others 1985.

*Descriptors:* *Improvement Programs; *Job Performance; *Leadership Styles; *Supervisory Methods; *Training Methods; Adults; Evaluation Methods; Motivation; Transfer of Training
*Identifiers:* DTA II
*Availability:* Blanchard Training and Development, 125 State Pl., Escondido, CA 92025.
*Notes:* Items, 43.

This tool evaluates job performance in terms of selected tasks for which the target person (self, associate, subordinate) is accountable. The tasks are viewed based on the development level that the target person displays in performing these tasks. The tool assists in identifying the leadership style appropriate for the development level of each task. The results are used to create an action plan and coaching and counseling strategy to improve the supervision of the individual on tasks where there is a need for a change in leadership style.

**16175**
**Supervisor Behavior Analysis II.** Blanchard, Kenneth H.; And Others 1985.
*Descriptors:* *Attitude Measures; *Employee Attitudes; *Job Performance; *Management Development; *Self Evaluation (Individuals); *Supervisory Methods; Feedback; Leadership; Profiles
*Identifiers:* SBA II
*Availability:* Blanchard Training and Development, 125 State Pl., Escondido, CA 92025.
*Notes:* Items, 20.

The purpose of the SBA II is to provide a supervisor with perceptions of that individual's supervisory style through feedback from those who are being supervised. A self-administered set of 20 typical job situations that involve 1 or more staff employees provides the individual with personal insights about supervisory behavior. Both the supervisor and those being supervised react to the same set of job situations. An important outcome of the data gathered is whether there is a "match" or "mismatch" between the perceptions of others about the supervisor's supervisory style and the supervisor's own perception.

**16177**
**One-Minute Manager Goal Setting: Self and Others.** Zigarmi, Drea; Tyson, Kelsey 1984.
*Descriptors:* *Administrators; *Job Performance; *Objectives; Adults
*Availability:* Blanchard Training and Development, 125 State Pl., Escondido, CA 92025.

The One-Minute Manager Goal Setting consists of worksheets for managers to write down goals for themselves and others.

**16178**
**Personal Style Survey.** Performax Systems International, Inc., Minneapolis, MN 1987.
*Descriptors:* *Behavior Patterns; *Employees; *Personality Traits; *Work Attitudes; Administrators; Adults; Job Performance; Occupational Tests; Personnel Evaluation; Personnel Selection; Profiles; Supervisors
*Availability:* Blanchard Training and Development, 125 State Pl., Escondido, CA 92025.
*Notes:* Items, 48.

This instrument is designed for use in business and industry to identify an employee's or applicant's personal work behavior style. Respondents select from a group of 48 adjectives, descriptive of personal traits that are most and least like themselves. There are 4 behavioral styles: dominance, influencing, steadiness, and caution.

**16179**
**Values Analysis Profile, Revised.** Performax Systems International, Inc., Minneapolis, MN 1986.
*Descriptors:* *Administrators; *Beliefs; *Employees; *Values; Adults; Personality; Personnel Evaluation; Profiles; Work Attitudes
*Availability:* Blanchard Training and Development, 125 State Pl., Escondido, CA 92025.
*Notes:* Items, 40.

This instrument uses common phrases or "old sayings" to determine individuals' values or belief systems. Respondents indicate level of agreement with or importance of 40 of these statements as they felt about them in the first 10-20 years of their life and how they feel about them now. A profile is prepared and compared to others to determine a "value profile pattern." Designed to assist in the development of strategies for "managing values conflicts involving people, products, issues, and events."

**16186**
**Desert and Desert II Survival Situations.** Human Synergistics, Plymouth, MI
*Descriptors:* *Group Dynamics; *Simulation; *Situational Tests; Adults; Group Unity; Logical Thinking; Objectives; Participation; Problem Solving; Productivity
*Availability:* Human Synergistics, 39819 Plymouth Rd., Plymouth, MI 48170.

Simulations that provide interactive experiences to help groups improve the way they handle problems and reach decisions in group settings. Provides facilitators with the opportunity to observe the ways individuals interact and perform within the group. The survival simulations offer a neutral setting, which does not include tactics that might emerge in a business environment. Simulations are useful for building problem-solving skills, improving planning and goal setting, developing skills to elicit group consensus, encouraging work teams and increasing individual participation in work groups, developing logical thinking, and increasing productivity through effective use of human resources.

**16187**
**Subarctic Survival Situation.** Lafferty, J. Clayton 1987.
*Descriptors:* *Group Dynamics; *Problem Solving; Adults; Group Discussion; Interpersonal Competence; Interpersonal Relationship; Logical Thinking; Occupational Tests; Participative Decision Making; Simulation
*Availability:* Human Synergistics, 39819 Plymouth Rd., Plymouth, MI 48170.
*Notes:* Time, 120. Items, 15.

This group problem-solving simulation requires the rank ordering of 15 items according to their importance for survival in an isolated region of Canada. Scores for individuals are compared to a team score and the score of a survival expert. The decision-making process requires interpersonal skills and rational thinking skills. The difference between individual and team scores indicates level of interpersonal competence for individuals. The difference between individual and team scores and survival experts' scores indicate rational thinking ability.

**16189**
**Project Planning Situation.** Human Synergistics, Plymouth, MI 1985.
*Descriptors:* *Decision Making Skills; *Simulation; *Work Environment; Adults; Managerial Occupations
*Availability:* Human Synergistics, 39819 Plymouth Rd., Plymouth, MI 48170.

A hypothetical work situation designed to test decision-making skills in a work group situation.

**16190**
**Turnaround.** Lafferty, J. Clayton 1983.
*Descriptors:* *Administrators; *Decision Making Skills; *Management Development; *Management Games; *Simulation; *Training Methods; Adults
*Availability:* Human Synergistics, 39819 Plymouth Rd., Plymouth, MI 48170.

Turnaround (formerly the Grindtown Plant Project) is a simulation for management training. Equipped with fiscal and personnel data, managers are assigned the job of rescuing a troubled manufacturing plant. The plant's survival is determined by key management decisions made by the group.

**16200**
**High School Career-Course Planner.** CFKR Career Materials, Meadow Vista, CA 1988.
*Descriptors:* *Career Awareness; *Career Exploration; *Course Selection (Students); *High School Students; *Interest Inventories; *Vocational Interests; High Schools
*Identifiers:* HSCCP
*Availability:* CFKR Career Materials, Inc., 11860 Kemper Rd., Unit 7, Auburn, CA 95603.
*Notes:* Time, 50 approx.

Designed to help high school students develop a course plan that will be consistent with their career goals. Conceived as a counseling and teaching tool to combine career awareness, career exploration, and high school course planning. Can be used with any existing high school curriculum.

**16201**
**Career Exploration Series, AG-O, 1988 Revision.** Cutler, Arthur; And Others 1986.
*Descriptors:* *Agricultural Occupations; *Career Exploration; *Conservation (Environment); *Forestry; *Interest Inventories; *Vocational Interests; Adolescents; Adults; Computer Software; Self Evaluation (Individuals); Vocational Education
*Identifiers:* CES
*Availability:* CFKR Career Materials, Inc., 11860 Kemper Rd., Unit 7, Auburn, CA 95603.
*Notes:* Time, 50 approx.

One of a series of job interest inventories that focus on specific occupational fields. Useful in vocational education programs. Is designed as a career guidance tool and takes subject through the following steps: self assessment, job exploration, job matching, and decision making. Computer versions are also available. AG-O covers agricultural, forestry, and conservation occupations.

**16202**
**Career Exploration Series, BIZ-O, 1988 Revision.** Cutler, Arthur; And Others 1988.
*Descriptors:* *Business; *Career Exploration; *Interest Inventories; *Vocational Interests; Adolescents; Adults; Clerical Occupations; Computers; Computer Software; Consultants; Creative Activities; Managerial Occupations; Office Machines; Sales Occupations; Self Evaluation (Individuals); Vocational Education
*Identifiers:* CES
*Availability:* CFKR Career Materials, Inc., 11860 Kemper Rd., Unit 7, Auburn, CA 95603.
*Notes:* Time, 50 approx.

One of a series of job interest inventories that focus on specific occupational fields. Useful in vocational education programs. Is designed as a career guidance tool and takes subject through the following steps: self assessment, job exploration, job matching, and decision making. Computer versions are also available. BIZ-O covers sales, clerical, management/administrative/personnel, computers and office machines, consultant/educational, and creative work.

**16203**
**Career Exploration Series, CER-O, 1988 Revision.** Cutler, Arthur; And Others 1988.
*Descriptors:* *Career Exploration; *Consumer Economics; *Interest Inventories; *Vocational Interests; Adolescents; Adults; Computer Software; Self Evaluation (Individuals); Vocational Education
*Identifiers:* CES
*Availability:* CFKR Career Materials, Inc., 11860 Kemper Rd., Unit 7, Auburn, CA 95603.
*Notes:* Time, 50 approx.

One of a series of job interest inventories that focus on specific occupational fields. Useful in vocational education programs. Is designed as a career guidance tool and takes subject through the following steps: self assessment, job exploration, job matching, and decision making. Computer versions are also available. CER-O covers consumer economics and related occupations.

**16204**
**Career Exploration Series, DAC-O, 1988 Revision.** Cutler, Arthur; And Others 1988.
*Descriptors:* *Career Exploration; *Craft Workers; *Design Crafts; *Interest Inventories; *Vocational Interests; Adolescents; Adults; Art; Communications; Computer Software; Self Evaluation (Individuals); Vocational Education
*Identifiers:* CES
*Availability:* CFKR Career Materials, Inc., 11860 Kemper Rd., Unit 7, Auburn, CA 95603.
*Notes:* Time, 50 approx.

One of a series of job interest inventories that focus on specific occupational fields. Useful in vocational education programs. Is designed as a career guidance tool and takes subject through the following steps: self assessment, job exploration, job matching, and decision making. Computer versions are also available. DAC-O covers design, art, and communications occupations.

**16205**
**Career Exploration Series, IND-O, 1988 Revision.** Cutler, Arthur; And Others 1988.
*Descriptors:* *Career Exploration; *Construction Industry; *Engineering Technicians; *Industrial Personnel; *Interest Inventories; *Mechanical Skills; *Transportation; *Vocational Interests; Adolescents; Adults; Computer Software; Self Evaluation (Individuals); Vocational Education
*Identifiers:* CES
*Availability:* CFKR Career Materials, Inc., 11860 Kemper Rd., Unit 7, Auburn, CA 95603.

One of a series of job interest inventories that focus on specific occupational fields. Useful in vocational education programs. Is designed as a career guidance tool and takes subject through the following steps: self assessment, job exploration, job matching, and decision making. Computer versions are also available. IND-O covers the following areas: industrial/production; construction; transportation; machine operations; engineering and design; and mechanics-repair.

**16206**
**Career Exploration Series, SCI-O, 1988 Revision.** Cutler, Arthur; And Others 1986.
*Descriptors:* *Career Exploration; *Health Personnel; *Interest Inventories; *Mathematics; *Scientific Personnel; *Vocational Interests; Adolescents; Adults; Computer Software; Self Evaluation (Individuals); Vocational Education
*Identifiers:* CES
*Availability:* CFKR Career Materials, Inc., 11860 Kemper Rd., Unit 7, Auburn, CA 95603.

One of a series of job interest inventories that focus on specific occupational fields. Useful in vocational education programs. Is designed as a career guidance tool and takes subject through the following steps: self assessment, job exploration, job matching, and decision making. Computer versions are also available. SCI-O covers scientific, mathematical, and health occupations.

**16208**
**Reading Prints and Drawings, Form A.** Ramsay, Roland T. 1988.
*Descriptors:* *Achievement Tests; *Blueprints; *Occupational Tests; *Personnel; *Technical Occupations; Adults; Selection
*Availability:* Ramsay Corp., 1050 Boyce Rd., Pittsburgh, PA 15241-3907.
*Notes:* Time, 30. Items, 33.

Developed to evaluate the skills required to learn and perform jobs that involve reading prints and drawings. Used in employee selection. Covers views and surfaces; dimensions in single drawings; dimensions in intermediate drawings; and dimensions and finishes in complex drawings.

**16209**
**Office Reading, Form G.** Ramsay, Roland T. 1988.
*Descriptors:* *Achievement Tests; *Clerical Occupations; *Clerical Workers; *Occupational Tests; *Personnel Selection; *Reading Comprehension; *Reading Tests; Adults
*Availability:* Ramsay Corp., 1050 Boyce Rd., Pittsburgh, PA 15241-3907.
*Notes:* Time, 30. Items, 40.

Developed to measure the reading skills required for office or clerical workers. Is a test of reading comprehension intended for use with job applicants and incumbents for jobs where reading is a necessary part of training for job activities.

**16210**
**Office Arithmetic, Form CA.** Ramsay, Roland T. 1988.
*Descriptors:* *Achievement Tests; *Arithmetic; *Clerical Occupations; *Clerical Workers; *Occupational Tests; *Personnel Selection; Adults
*Availability:* Ramsay Corp., 1050 Boyce Rd., Pittsburgh, PA 15241-3907.
*Notes:* Time, 30. Items, 40.

Used to evaluate the ability of office and clerical workers to perform arithmetic operations. Covers operations using whole numbers and decimals.

**16212**
**Fellowship in the Healthcare Financial Management Association Examination.** Healthcare Financial Management Association, Westchester, IL
*Descriptors:* *Certification; *Finance Occupations; *Health Occupations; *Managerial Occupations; *Money Management; *Occupational Tests; Accounting; Administration; Administrators; Adults; Health Facilities; Information Systems; Knowledge Level
*Identifiers:* Chief Financial Officers; FHFMA; Healthcare Financial Management Association; HFMA
*Availability:* Healthcare Financial Management Association, 2 Westbrook Corporate Center, Ste. 700, Westchester, IL 60154.
*Notes:* Time, 480.

This is a mastery-level examination for those who are, or aspire to be, chief financial officers. It measure the ability of the candidate to exercise sound judgment in this area and assesses understanding of the principles of financial management and application of this knowledge. The test covers financial management, accounting theory and practice, management process, information systems, and the healthcare industry. To be eligible for the examination, candidates must hold regular or advanced membership in the Healthcare Financial Management Association for at least 2 years. There is a study guide available.

**16228**
**Performance Analysis Inventory.** Vineberg, Robert; Taylor, Elaine N. 1976.
*Descriptors:* *Job Performance; *Military Personnel; *Performance Tests; *Personnel Evaluation; Adults; Cognitive Ability; Likert Scales; Performance Factors; Rating Scales
*Identifiers:* Navy; PAI
*Availability:* ERIC Document Reproduction Service, 7420 Fullerton Rd., Ste. 110, Springfield, VA 22153-2852 (ED133467, 138 pages).
*Notes:* Time, 20 approx.

Rating instrument for evaluating the performance of people in Navy jobs. Evaluations are made by supervisors. Measures how effectively people of varying ability perform different tasks. Analyzes performance in terms of worker-oriented variables. Instrument is based upon job analyses using a modification of the Position Analysis Questionnaire (7523). Activities assessed are: use of tools and equipment; hand-arm manipulation; coordination; work habits and processes; and obtaining and observing job relevant information. There are several versions of this instrument, with questions slightly varied, which are administered according to the job title of the person being evaluated.

**16229**
**Task Proficiency Inventory.** Vineberg, Robert; Taylor, Elaine N. 1976.
*Descriptors:* *Job Performance; *Military Personnel; *Performance Tests; *Personnel Evaluation; Adults; Cognitive Ability; Likert Scales; Performance Factors; Rating Scales
*Identifiers:* Navy; TPI
*Availability:* ERIC Document Reproduction Service, 7420 Fullerton Rd., Ste. 110, Springfield, VA 22153-2852 (ED133467, 138 pages).
*Notes:* Time, 20 approx.

Rating instrument for evaluating the performance of people in Navy jobs. Evaluations are made by supervisors. Measures how effectively people of varying abilities perform different tasks. Analyzes performance in terms of job-oriented variables. There are several versions of this instrument that are to be administered according to the job of the person being evaluated.

**16240**
**Valpar B-Kit Series.** Valpar International Corp., Tucson, AZ
*Descriptors:* *Visual Impairments; *Work Sample Tests; Adults; Behavior Patterns; Diagnostic Tests; Performance Tests; Predictive Measurement
*Identifiers:* VCWS
*Availability:* Valpar International Corp., P.O. Box 5767, Tucson, AZ 85703-5767.
*Notes:* See also Valpar Component Work Samples (14391), 2 (14392), 4 (14394), 8 (14398), 9 (14399), 10 (14400).

Adaptations of the Valpar Component Work Samples 1, 2, 4, 8, 9 and 10 for use with visually handicapped individuals. Designed to measure the ability of the visually handicapped individuals to perform in jobs compatible with skills and interests as measured by the respective Valpar Component Work Sample. Modifications are tactile and audio. Emphasizes two kinds of assessment: behavioral and performance. A predictive and diagnostic measure.

**16261**
**Communications Profile Questionnaire for Managers/Supervisors in the Health Care Industry.** Michalak, Don 1984.
*Descriptors:* *Health Occupations; *Interpersonal Communication; *Managerial Occupations; *Self Evaluation (Individuals); *Spanish Speaking; *Supervisory Training; Adults; Health Personnel; Rating Scales; Spanish
*Availability:* Michalak Training Associates, 875 Pinto Pl. South, Tucson, AZ 85748-7921.
*Notes:* Time, 10 approx. Items, 20.

Designed for use with administrators, managers, and supervisors in health care facilities, such as hospitals and clinics. Used to identify individuals' communication style, assess strengths and weaknesses, and suggest ways of improving. Used mainly in training workshops in management, supervisory, and communication skills. Also available in Spanish. Forms are available for participants and companions (subordinates or coworkers).

**16262**
**Communications Profile Questionnaire for Sales Managers/Supervisors.** Michalak, Don 1984.
*Descriptors:* *Interpersonal Communication; *Managerial Occupations; *Sales Occupations; *Self Evaluation (Individuals); *Spanish Speaking; *Supervisory Training; Adults; Rating Scales; Spanish
*Availability:* Michalak Training Associates, 875 Pinto Pl. South, Tucson, AZ 85748-7921.
*Notes:* Time, 10 approx. Items, 20.

Instrument designed for use with managers and supervisors in retail and wholesale organizations to help identify their communication style, assess their strengths and weaknesses, and indicate means of improvement. Used in training workshops in management, supervisory, and communications skills. Available in Spanish. Includes participant form and companion form for coworkers or subordinates.

**16263**
**Communications Profile Questionnaire, Non-Managers.** Michalak, Don 1986.
*Descriptors:* *Interpersonal Communication; *Spanish Speaking; *Training; Adults; Rating Scales; Self Evaluation (Individuals); Spanish
*Identifiers:* *Nonmanagerial Occupations
*Availability:* Michalak Training Associates, 875 Pinto Pl. South, Tucson, AZ 85748-7921.
*Notes:* Time, 10 approx. Items, 20.

For use with nonmanagerial employees to identify their communication style, assess their strengths and weaknesses, and indicate means of improvement. Used in training workshops. Also available in Spanish. There are participant forms and companion forms for coworkers or subordinates.

**16264**
**Interaction Index, Revised.** Michalak, Don 1980.
*Descriptors:* *Employees; *Interpersonal Competence; *Managerial Occupations; *Supervisory Training; *Training; Adults; Rating Scales; Self Evaluation (Individuals)
*Availability:* Michalak Training Associates, 875 Pinto Pl. South, Tucson, AZ 85748-7921.
*Notes:* Time, 10 approx. Items, 24.

Developed to identify causes of poor on-the-job relationships and to prescribe methods of improvement. For use in interpersonal skills training workshops for managers, supervisors, and employees in all job functions.

**16265**
**Styles of Training Index, Revised.** Michalak, Don 1983.
*Descriptors:* *Trainers; *Training Methods; Adults; Self Evaluation (Individuals)
*Availability:* Michalak Training Associates, 875 Pinto Pl. South, Tucson, AZ 85748-7921.
*Notes:* Time, 15 approx. Items, 41.

Developed to identify a trainer's classroom style and to indicate what a trainer can do in specific areas needing change. Used in train-the-trainer workshops.

**16267**
**Basic Academic Skills for Employment.** Educational Technologies, Trenton, NJ 1987.
*Descriptors:* *Basic Skills; *Computer Assisted Testing; *Diagnostic Tests; *Disadvantaged Youth; *Item Banks; *Job Training; *Occupational Tests; Adults; Computer Software; Diagnostic Teaching; Language Skills; Mathematics; Pretests Posttests; Reading; Writing Skills
*Identifiers:* BASE
*Availability:* Educational Technologies, Inc., 1007 Whitehead Rd. Extension, Trenton, NJ 08638.
*Notes:* Items, 3000.

BASE is a computerized diagnostic and remediation system designed to measure and teach the reading, writing, language, and mathematics skills needed to get and hold a job. Relates basic skills to the requirements of jobs. Contains a bank of 3,000 test items measuring 250 basic skill competencies. Said to automatically create diagnostic tests of skills needed for 12,000 jobs and to be useful in youth job training programs. Supplies computer-assisted instruction for all prescriptions. Supplies posttesting to show gains in job-specific basic skills knowledge.

**16268**
**Management Styles Questionnaire.** Michalak, Don 1984.
*Descriptors:* *Managerial Occupations; *Supervisory Methods; *Supervisory Training; Adults; Leadership Styles; Rating Scales; Self Evaluation (Individuals)
*Availability:* Michalak Training Associates, 875 Pinto Pl. South, Tucson, AZ 85748-7921.
*Notes:* Time, 15 approx. Items, 31.

Developed to identify individuals' management style, assess strengths and weaknesses, and locate areas where changes can be made. This is a generic version for use with managers and supervisors participating in training workshops in management and supervisory skills. There are 2 forms: a participant form and a companion form for supervisor's subordinates.

**16269**
**Management Styles Questionnaire for Managers/Supervisors of Professionals.** Michalak, Don 1984.
*Descriptors:* *Managerial Occupations; *Professional Personnel; *Supervisory Methods; *Supervisory Training; Adults; Leadership Styles; Rating Scales; Self Evaluation (Individuals)
*Availability:* Michalak Training Associates, 875 Pinto Pl. South, Tucson, AZ 85748-7921.
*Notes:* Time, 15 approx. Items, 33.

Developed to identify individuals' management style, assess strengths and weaknesses, and locate areas where changes can be made. For use with managers and supervisors of professional staff and in such professional firms as accounting and law. Used in training workshops in management and supervisory skills. There are 2 forms: a participant form and a companion form for staff being supervised.

**16270**
**Management Styles Questionnaire for Managers/Supervisors in the Health Care Industry.** Michalak, Don 1984.
*Descriptors:* *Health Occupations; *Managerial Occupations; *Supervisory Methods; *Supervisory Training; Adults; Health Personnel; Leadership Styles; Rating Scales; Self Evaluation (Individuals)
*Availability:* Michalak Training Associates, 875 Pinto Pl. South, Tucson, AZ 85748-7921.
*Notes:* Time, 15 approx. Items, 33.

Developed to identify individuals' management style, assess strengths and weaknesses, and locate areas where changes can be made. Used in training workshops in management and supervisory skills for administrators, managers, and supervisors in health care facilities, such as hospitals and clinics. There are 2 forms: a participant form and a companion form for supervisor's subordinates.

**16271**
**Management Styles Questionnaire for Sales Managers/Supervisors.** Michalak, Don 1984.
*Descriptors:* *Managerial Occupations; *Sales Occupations; *Supervisory Methods; *Supervisory Training; Adults; Leadership Styles; Rating Scales; Self Evaluation (Individuals)
*Availability:* Michalak Training Associates, 875 Pinto Pl. South, Tucson, AZ 85748-7921.
*Notes:* Time, 15 approx. Items, 33.

Developed to identify individuals' management style, assess strengths and weaknesses, and locate areas where changes can be made. Used in training workshops in managerial and supervisory skills for managers and supervisors in retail and wholesale organizations. There are 2 forms: a participant form and a companion form for supervisor's subordinates.

**16276**
**Career Guidance Inventory.** Oliver, James E. 1989.
*Descriptors:* *Career Guidance; *Community Colleges; *Computer Assisted Testing; *Course Selection (Students); *Educational Counseling; *High School Students; *Interest Inventories; *Majors (Students); *Student Educational Objectives; *Technical Institutes; *Trade and Industrial Education; *Two Year College Students; *Vocational Interests; High Schools; Two Year Colleges
*Identifiers:* CEP; CGI
*Availability:* Orchard House, 112 Balls Hill Rd., Concord, MA 01742.
*Notes:* See also Educational Interest Inventory (16275). Items, 235.

For use by students planning an instructional program in a trade, vocational, or technical school or a community college. Provides measures of interest in career activities associated with programs most often completed in these schools. Intended for use in a total educational and career guidance program. Can be of benefit to students and counselors in determining students' instructional needs and areas of study. Allows for assessment of personal preferences for activities associated with 47 instructional programs. Also available in a software program, Computerized Educational Planning Program, that incorporates all components of the Educational Interest Inventory and the Career Guidance Inventory.

**16283**
**My Approach to Handling Conflict.** George Truell Associates, Williamsville, NY 1983.
*Descriptors:* *Conflict Resolution; *Self Evaluation (Individuals); *Training; Adults; Employer Employee Relationship; Peer Relationship; Rating Scales
*Availability:* PAT Publications, P.O. Box 681, Buffalo, NY 14221.
*Notes:* See also Your Approach to Handling Conflict (16284). Items, 24.

Learning instrument designed to help individuals gain insight into various approaches they use when interacting with others in conflict situations. Focuses on conflict under 3 sets of conditions: with people in high-level positions, with peers, and with subordinates or others in lower-level positions.

**16284**
**Your Approach to Handling Conflict.** George Truell Associates, Williamsville, NY 1983.
*Descriptors:* *Conflict Resolution; *Training; Adults; Employees; Peer Evaluation; Rating Scales; Supervisors
*Availability:* PAT Publications, P.O. Box 681, Buffalo, NY 14221.
*Notes:* See also My Approach to Handling Conflict (16283). Items, 8.

Learning instrument designed to help individuals gain insight into various approaches they use when interacting with others in conflict situations. Three instruments provide feedback from supervisor, peers, and subordinates.

**16285**
**Boss-Analysis.** George Truell Associates, Williamsville, NY 1980.
*Descriptors:* *Employer Employee Relationship; *Training; Adults; Questionnaires
*Availability:* PAT Publications, P.O. Box 681, Buffalo, NY 14221.

Designed to help people improve their working relationships with their boss or supervisor. The instrument has 3 parts. Part 1 lets individuals think about themselves and their work patterns. Part 2 allows them to analyze their supervisor as a person and as a boss and to analyze the supervisor's work patterns. Part 3 analyzes the present degree of compatibility between boss and subordinate.

**16287**
**Our Organizational Norms.** George Truell Associates, Williamsville, NY 1980.
*Descriptors:* *Organizational Climate; *Supervisory Training; Adults; Employer Employee Relationship; Rating Scales; Self Evaluation (Groups)
*Availability:* PAT Publications, P.O. Box 681, Buffalo, NY 14221.
*Notes:* Items, 10.

Learning instrument designed to help people identify the norms or unwritten codes of conduct that exist in their own organization. Norms are defined as the result of the values, attitudes, and beliefs of individuals in an organization that interact with the requirements of the organization. This checklist assesses the extent to which 10 different norms exist in an organization.

**16288**
**Organizational Excellence-How We Rate.** George Truell Associates, Williamsville, NY 1984.
*Descriptors:* *Organizational Climate; *Organizational Effectiveness; *Supervisory Training; *Work Environment; Adults; Rating Scales; Self Evaluation (Groups)
*Availability:* PAT Publications, P.O. Box 681, Buffalo, NY 14221.
*Notes:* Items, 36.

Designed to help people evaluate their work environment in terms of characteristics found in highly effective organizations. Identifies 12 categories or areas for analysis. Enables managers to isolate specific areas which need attention in order to improve operating effectiveness.

**16289**
**Assessing Organizational Readiness.** George Truell Associates, Williamsville, NY 1985.
*Descriptors:* *Employer Employee Relationship; *Organizational Climate; *Supervisory Training; *Work Environment; Adults; Rating Scales; Self Evaluation (Individuals)
*Availability:* PAT Publications, P.O. Box 681, Buffalo, NY 14221.
*Notes:* Items, 32.

Designed to help managers evaluate their work environment to determine to what extent their organizations can support greater employee involvement. Identifies the organization's overall degree of readiness plus 4 key areas that can be strengthened: organizational characteristics, employee characteristics, supervisory characteristics, and managerial characteristics.

**16290**
**Personnel Policies/Operating Systems.** George Truell Associates, Williamsville, NY 1985.
*Descriptors:* *Administrative Organization; *Employee Attitudes; *Organizational Climate; *Personnel Policy; *Supervisory Training; Adults; Rating Scales
*Availability:* PAT Publications, P.O. Box 681, Buffalo, NY 14221.
*Notes:* Items, 50.

Designed to help managers evaluate some important aspects of their organization's climate - its personnel policies and operating systems - to determine organizational compatibility and ways to increase employee involvement. Enables managers to determine which specific organizational attitudes, values, beliefs, policies, and practices need revision in order to have successful employee involvement.

**16291**
**Assessing the Key Elements in a Union-Free Operation.** George Truell Associates, Williamsville, NY 1985.
*Descriptors:* *Organizational Climate; *Quality of Working Life; *Supervisory Training; *Unions; Adults; Rating Scales
*Availability:* PAT Publications, P.O. Box 681, Buffalo, NY 14221.
*Notes:* Items, 32.

Used to measure an organization's degree of potential vulnerability to union organizing efforts. Examines 32 factors found to cause employee discontent and decreased operating effectiveness.

**16299**
**Comprehensive Occupational Exams: Apparel and Accessories Marketing, Master Employee Level.** Marketing Education Resource Center, Columbus, OH 1989.
*Descriptors:* *Clothing; *Fashion Industry; *Item Banks; *Marketing; *Occupational Tests; Adults; Criterion Referenced Tests
*Availability:* Marketing Education Resource Center, 1375 King Ave., P.O. Box 12226, Columbus, OH 43212-0226.
*Notes:* Items, 100.

Designed to assess the marketing skills of mid-level employees involved in apparel and accessories marketing. Examples include salespersons, copywriters, buyers, or manufacturers' representatives. One of a series of competency-based instruments based on the curriculum developed by the Marketing Education Resource Center. Each instrument tests a different level, facet, or industry-specific knowledge of marketing principles. Descriptive test keys included with the test provide a rationale for each answer and are useful for review and remediation. Items used in this test have been randomly selected from the resource center test item bank.

**16300**
**Comprehensive Occupational Exams: Apparel and Accessories Marketing, Supervisory Level.** Marketing Education Resource Center, Columbus, OH 1989.
*Descriptors:* *Clothing; *Fashion Industry; *Item Banks; *Marketing; *Occupational Tests; *Supervisors; Adults; Criterion Referenced Tests
*Availability:* Marketing Education Resource Center, 1375 King Ave., P.O. Box 12226, Columbus, OH 43212-0226.
*Notes:* Items, 100.

Designed to assess the skills of supervisors in apparel and accessories marketing whose responsibilities include planning, coordinating, and supervising people and/or marketing-related activities. One of a series of competency-based instruments modeled on the curriculum developed by the Marketing Education Resource Center. Each instrument tests a different level, facet, or industry-specific knowledge of marketing principles. Descriptive test keys included with the test provide a rationale for each answer and are useful for review and remediation. Items used in this test have been randomly selected from the resource center test item bank.

**16301**
**Comprehensive Occupational Exams: Advertising and Display Services.** Marketing Education Resource Center, Columbus, OH 1989.
*Descriptors:* *Advertising; *Item Banks; *Marketing; *Occupational Tests; Adults; Criterion Referenced Tests; Merchandising
*Availability:* Marketing Education Resource Center, 1375 King Ave., P.O. Box 12226, Columbus, OH 43212-0226.
*Notes:* Items, 100.

Designed to assess the marketing skills of employees involved in advertising and display services. Examples include salespersons, copywriters, buyers, or manufacturers' representatives. One of a series of competency-based instruments modeled on the curriculum developed by the Marketing Education Resource Center. Each instrument tests a different level, facet, or industry-specific knowledge of marketing principles. Descriptive test keys included with the test provide a rationale for each answer and are useful for review and remediation. Items used in this test have been randomly selected from the resource center test item bank.

**16302**
**Comprehensive Occupational Exams: Finance and Credit Services.** Marketing Education Resource Center, Columbus, OH 1989.
*Descriptors:* *Finance Occupations; *Item Banks; *Marketing; *Occupational Tests; Adults; Criterion Referenced Tests
*Availability:* Marketing Education Resource Center, 1375 King Ave., P.O. Box 12226, Columbus, OH 43212-0226.
*Notes:* Items, 100.

Designed to assess the marketing skills of employees involved in finance and credit services. Examples include salespersons, copywriters, buyers, or manufacturers' representatives. One of a series of competency-based instruments modeled on the curriculum developed by the Marketing Education Resource Center. Each instrument tests a different level, facet, or industry-specific knowledge of marketing principles. Descriptive test keys included with the test provide a rationale for each answer and are useful for review and remediation. Items used in this test have been randomly selected from the resource center test item bank.

**16303**
**Comprehensive Occupational Exams: Food Marketing, Master Employee Level.** Marketing Education Resource Center, Columbus, OH 1989.
*Descriptors:* *Food Service; *Item Banks; *Marketing; *Occupational Tests; Adults; Criterion Referenced Tests; Food Stores
*Availability:* Marketing Education Resource Center, 1375 King Ave., P.O. Box 12226, Columbus, OH 43212-0226.
*Notes:* Items, 100.

Designed to assess the marketing skills of mid-level employees involved in food marketing. Examples include salespersons, copywriters, buyers, or manufacturers' representatives. One of a series of competency-based instruments modeled on the curriculum developed by the Marketing Education Resource Center. Each instrument tests a different level, facet, or industry-specific knowledge of marketing principles. Descriptive test keys included with the test provide a rationale for each answer and are useful for review and remediation. Items used in this test have been randomly selected from the resource center test item bank.

**16305**
**Comprehensive Occupational Exams: Free Enterprise Economics.** Marketing Education Resource Center, Columbus, OH 1989.
*Descriptors:* *Economics; *Item Banks; *Marketing; *Occupational Tests; Adults; Capitalism; Criterion Referenced Tests
*Availability:* Marketing Education Resource Center, 1375 King Ave., P.O. Box 12226, Columbus, OH 43212-0226.
*Notes:* Items, 100.

Designed to assess students' knowledge of free enterprise economics. One of a series of competency-based instruments keyed to the curriculum developed by the Marketing Education Resource Center. Each instrument tests a different level, facet, or industry-specific knowledge of marketing principles. Descriptive test keys included with the test provide a rationale for each answer and are useful for review and remediation. Items used in this test have been randomly selected from the resource center test item bank.

**16306**
**Comprehensive Occupational Exams: General Marketing, Master Employee Level.** Marketing Education Resource Center, Columbus, OH 1989.
*Descriptors:* *Item Banks; *Marketing; *Occupational Tests; Adults; Criterion Referenced Tests
*Availability:* Marketing Education Resource Center, 1375 King Ave., P.O. Box 12226, Columbus, OH 43212-0226.
*Notes:* Items, 100.

Designed to assess the general marketing skills of mid-level employees involved in one or more aspects of marketing. Examples include salespersons, copywriters, buyers, or manufacturers' representatives. One of a series of competency-based instruments modeled on the curriculum developed by the Marketing Education Resource Center. Each instrument tests a different level, facet, or industry-specific knowledge of marketing principles. Descriptive test keys included with the test provide a rationale for each answer and are useful for review and remediation. Items used in this test have been randomly selected from the resource center test item bank.

**16307**
**Comprehensive Occupational Exams: General Marketing, Supervisory Level.** Marketing Education Resource Center, Columbus, OH 1989.
*Descriptors:* *Item Banks; *Marketing; *Occupational Tests; *Supervisors; Adults; Criterion Referenced Tests
*Availability:* Marketing Education Resource Center, 1375 King Ave., P.O. Box 12226, Columbus, OH 43212-0226.
*Notes:* Items, 100.

Designed to assess the general marketing skills of supervisors whose responsibilities include planning, coordinating, and supervising people and/or marketing-related activities. One of a series of competency-based instruments based on the curriculum developed by the Marketing Education Resource Center. Each instrument tests a different level, facet, or industry-specific knowledge of marketing principles. Descriptive test keys included with the test provide a rationale for each answer and are useful for review and remediation. Items used in this test have been randomly selected from the resource center test item bank.

**16308**
**Comprehensive Occupational Exams: General Merchandise Retailing, Master Employee Level.** Marketing Education Resource Center, Columbus, OH 1989.
*Descriptors:* *Item Banks; *Marketing; *Occupational Tests; *Retailing; Adults; Criterion Referenced Tests
*Availability:* Marketing Education Resource Center, 1375 King Ave., P.O. Box 12226, Columbus, OH 43212-0226.
*Notes:* Items, 100.

Designed to assess the marketing skills of mid-level employees involved in general merchandise retailing. Examples include salespersons or manufacturers' representatives. One of a series of competency-based instruments modeled on the curriculum developed by the Marketing Education Resource Center. Each instrument tests a different level, facet, or industry-specific knowledge of marketing principles. Descriptive test keys included with the test provide a rationale for each answer and are useful for review and remediation. Items used in this test have been randomly selected from the resource center test item bank.

**16309**
**Comprehensive Occupational Exams: General Merchandise Retailing, Supervisory Level.** Marketing Education Resource Center, Columbus, OH 1989.
*Descriptors:* *Item Banks; *Marketing; *Occupational Tests; *Retailing; *Supervisors; Adults; Criterion Referenced Tests
*Availability:* Marketing Education Resource Center, 1375 King Ave., P.O. Box 12226, Columbus, OH 43212-0226.
*Notes:* Items, 100.

Designed to assess the skills of marketing supervisors in general merchandise retailing, whose responsibilities include planning, coordinating, and supervising people and/or marketing-related activities. One of a series of competency-based instruments modeled on the curriculum developed by the Marketing Education Resource Center. Each instrument tests a different level, facet, or industry-specific knowledge of marketing principles. Descriptive test keys included with the test provide a rationale for each answer and are useful for review and remediation. Items used in this test have been randomly selected from the Resource Center test item bank.

**16310**
**Comprehensive Occupational Exams: Marketing Math.** Marketing Education Resource Center, Columbus, OH 1989.
*Descriptors:* *Item Banks; *Marketing; *Mathematics; *Mathematics Tests; *Occupational Tests; Adults; Criterion Referenced Tests
*Availability:* Marketing Education Resource Center, 1375 King Ave., P.O. Box 12226, Columbus, OH 43212-0226.
*Notes:* Items, 100.

Designed to assess the basic math computational and conceptual skills necessary for those entering the marketing profession. One of a series of competency-based instruments modeled on the curriculum developed by the Marketing Education Resource Center. Each instrument tests a different level, facet, or industry-specific knowledge of marketing principles. Descriptive test keys included with the test provide a rationale for each answer and are useful for review and remediation. Items used in this test have been randomly selected from the resource center test item bank.

**16311**
**Comprehensive Occupational Exams: Full-Service Restaurant Management.** Marketing Education Resource Center, Columbus, OH 1989.
*Descriptors:* *Administrators; *Dining Facilities; *Food Service; *Item Banks; *Marketing; *Occupational Tests; Adults; Criterion Referenced Tests
*Availability:* Marketing Education Resource Center, 1375 King Ave., P.O. Box 12226, Columbus, OH 43212-0226.
*Notes:* Items, 100.

Designed to assess the marketing skills of employees involved in the full-service restaurant industry. Examples include salespersons, copywriters, buyers, or manufacturers' representatives. One of a series of competency-based instruments modeled on the curriculum developed by the Marketing Education Resource Center. Each instrument tests a different level, facet, or industry-specific knowledge of marketing principles. Descriptive test keys included with the test provide a rationale for each answer and are useful for review and remediation. Items used in this test have been randomly selected from the resource center test item bank.

**16312**
**Comprehensive Occupational Exams: Quick-Serve Restaurant Management.** Marketing Education Resource Center, Columbus, OH 1989.
*Descriptors:* *Administrators; *Dining Facilities; *Food Service; *Item Banks; *Marketing; *Occupational Tests; Adults; Criterion Referenced Tests
*Identifiers:* Fast Foods
*Availability:* Marketing Education Resource Center, 1375 King Ave., P.O. Box 12226, Columbus, OH 43212-0226.
*Notes:* Items, 100.

Designed to assess the skills of employees in the fast-food restaurant industry. One of a series of competency-based instruments modeled on the curriculum developed by the Marketing Education Resource Center. Each instrument tests a different level, facet, or industry-specific knowledge of marketing principles. Descriptive test keys included with the test provide a rationale for each answer and are useful for review and remediation. Items used in this test have been randomly selected from the resource center test item bank.

**16313**
**Comprehensive Occupational Exams: Vehicles and Petroleum Marketing.** Marketing Education Resource Center, Columbus, OH 1989.
*Descriptors:* *Fuels; *Item Banks; *Marketing; *Motor Vehicles; *Occupational Tests; *Retailing; Adults; Criterion Referenced Tests
*Availability:* Marketing Education Resource Center, 1375 King Ave., P.O. Box 12226, Columbus, OH 43212-0226.
*Notes:* Items, 100.

Designed to assess the skills of employees in vehicles and petroleum marketing whose responsibilities include planning, coordinating, and supervising people and/or marketing-related activities. One of a series of competency-based instruments based on the curriculum developed by the Marketing Education Resource Center. Each instrument tests a different level, facet, or industry-specific knowledge of marketing principles. Descriptive test keys included with the test provide a rationale for each answer and are useful for review and remediation. Items used in this test have been randomly selected from the resource center test item bank.

**16314**
**Comprehensive Occupational Exams: Hotel-Motel Management.** Marketing Education Resource Center, Columbus, OH 1989.
*Descriptors:* *Administrators; *Hotels; *Item Banks; *Marketing; *Occupational Tests; Adults; Criterion Referenced Tests
*Identifiers:* Motels
*Availability:* Marketing Education Resource Center, 1375 King Ave., P.O. Box 12226, Columbus, OH 43212-0226.
*Notes:* Items, 100.

Designed to assess knowledge of hotel-motel management. One of a series of competency-based instruments keyed to the curriculum developed by the Marketing Education Resource Center. Each instrument tests a different level, facet, or industry-specific knowledge of marketing principles. Descriptive test keys included with the test provide a rationale for each answer and are useful for review and remediation. Items used in this test have been randomly selected from the resource center test item bank.

**16316**
**National Business Competency Tests: Word Processing.** National Business Education Association, Reston, VA 1986.
*Descriptors:* *Business Education; *High School Students; *Occupational Tests; *Two Year College Students; *Word Processing; Adults; Clerical Occupations; Postsecondary Education; Secondary Education
*Availability:* National Business Education Association, 1914 Association Dr., Reston, VA 22091.
*Notes:* Time, 45. Items, 62.

This test is designed for use with students in business education. It consists of 60 multiple-choice questions testing knowledge and understanding of word processing theory, principles, terminology, equipment, and procedures. Includes a business letter to be processed; a 2-page manuscript to be processed, filed, printed, then revised and reprinted; and a table to be processed. Test is for secondary and postsecondary students and adults.

**16317**
**Aptitude-Based Career Decision Test.** PREP, Inc., Trenton, NJ 1986.
*Descriptors:* *Aptitude Tests; *Career Choice; *Career Counseling; *Vocational Aptitude; Adolescents; Adults; Cognitive Ability; Computation; Personnel Selection; Profiles; Spatial Ability; Vocabulary
*Identifiers:* ABCD; Dictionary of Occupational Titles; Guide for Occupational Exploration; IBCD; Occupational Outlook Handbook
*Availability:* PREP, Inc., 1007 Whitehead Rd. Extension, Trenton, NJ 08638.
*Notes:* Time, 104. Items, 414.

This battery of 7 aptitude tests is designed to assist in career selection. Used for career counseling and employee selection, training, and development. Said to correlate with General Aptitude Test Battery (GATB), Differential Aptitude Test (DAT) and Comprehensive Ability Battery (CAB). The individual's profile is matched to 66 occupational families of the *Guide for Occupational Exploration*. Uses the *Dictionary of Occupational Titles* and *Occupational Outlook Handbook*. Can be scored by user via scanner and other hardware. Profile indicates high, medium, and low potential for 66 occupational families and produces a graphic report using standard scores and percentiles. A recommendation form indicates specific occupations.

**16318**
**Employability Attitudes Assessment.** PREP, Inc., Trenton, NJ 1986.
*Descriptors:* *Attitude Measures; *Audiovisual Aids; *Occupational Tests; *Work Attitudes; Adults; Behavior Problems; Employment Potential; Industrial Training; Job Applicants; Job Search Methods; Multiple Choice Tests; Pictorial Stimuli
*Availability:* PREP, Inc., 1007 Whitehead Rd. Extension, Trenton, NJ 08638.
*Notes:* Items, 360.

This audiovisual program and paper and pencil test are designed to assess individuals' employability-related attitudes. Uses a self-paced system. Uses an instrument with 36 behavior categories, 13 job seeking and 23 job keeping, based on a survey of hiring, firing, and promotion-inspiring behaviors seen in industry. The assessment is presented on audiovisual cartridges for individual or small group administration. For each attitude assessed there are 10 behavioral incidents portrayed followed by a multiple-choice test item. Respondent chooses from among 7 behavioral solutions to the incident. Prescriptive and training materials included.

**16320**
**Universal Skills Survey.** PREP, Inc., Trenton, NJ 1987.
*Descriptors:* *Industrial Training; *Job Analysis; *Occupational Tests; *Personnel Selection; Adults; Job Skills; Occupational Information; Personnel Evaluation; Surveys
*Availability:* PREP, Inc., 1007 Whitehead Rd. Extension, Trenton, NJ 08638.

This employee selection survey is designed to identify the skills a job requires, those possessed by job applicants and others taught by corporate training programs. Said to be useful in recruitment by creating workable job descriptions, setting wage guidelines, and facilitating worker transfers. Reports include job descriptions, profiles of applicants' work skills, lists of training skills, and skills required by a specific job. Surveys are completed by the user. Computer analysis is provided by the availability source listed.

**16321**
**Entry-Level Police/Fire/Deputy Sheriff Candidates: Fire Fighter Examination.** Biddle and Associates, Sacramento, CA 1980.
*Descriptors:* *Fire Fighters; *Occupational Tests; *Personnel Selection; *Work Sample Tests; Adults; Job Skills; Knowledge Level; Multiple Choice Tests; Occupational Information; Physical Fitness; Screening Tests
*Availability:* Biddle and Associates, Inc., 903 Enterprise Dr., Ste. 1, Sacramento, CA 95825.
*Notes:* Items, 120.

This validated employee selection test is designed to screen candidates for firefighter positions. Includes a written test and a physical capability demonstration consisting of a series of work-related drills with descriptions and diagrams. Said to reduce Equal Employment Opportunity (EEO) liability and adverse impact. A test preparation manual is available for each candidate prior to the test. A pool of 360 test questions exists so that 3 forms of the test can be developed.

**16322**
**Entry-Level Police/Fire/Deputy Sheriff Candidates: Police Officer/Deputy Sheriff Exam.** Biddle and Associates, Sacramento, CA 1980.
*Descriptors:* *Occupational Tests; *Personnel Selection; *Police; *Work Sample Tests; Adults; Job Skills; Knowledge Level; Multiple Choice Tests; Occupational Information; Physical Fitness; Screening Tests
*Identifiers:* Deputy Sheriff
*Availability:* Biddle and Associates, Inc., 903 Enterprise Dr., Ste. 1, Sacramento, CA 95825.
*Notes:* Items, 120.

This validated employee selection test is designed to screen candidates for law enforcement positions. Includes a written test and a physical capability demonstration. Said to reduce Equal Employment Opportunity (EEO) liability and adverse impact. A test preparation manual is available for each candidate prior to the test. A pool of 360 test questions exists so that 3 forms of the test can be developed.

**16323**
**Survey of California State University (CSU) Librarians: Professional Staff Participation in Decision-Making.** Gerry, Ellen; Klingberg, Susan 1984.
*Descriptors:* *Administration; *Librarians; *Libraries; *Participative Decision Making; Adults; Library Administration; Pyramid Organization; Surveys
*Identifiers:* California; California State University (CSU); TIM(O)
*Availability:* Tests in Microfiche, Test Collection, Educational Testing Service, Princeton, NJ 08541.
*Notes:* Items, 53.

Thirty-nine items from this survey elicit information about librarians' participation in work-related decision making within a library and the organizational structure. An additional 14 items elicit information about the background and characteristics of the respondent with reference to librarianship. Uses several versions of Likert-type, agree/disagree, and frequency scales, that vary by response, wording, and number of response choices. There is opportunity for a paragraph-length written response. No psychometric data are published.

**16349**
**Force Field Analysis Inventory.** Harris, Philip R. 1984.
*Descriptors:* *Change Agents; *Change Strategies; *Force Field Analysis; *Group Dynamics; *Management Development; *Managerial Occupations; *Organizational Change; *Organizational Development; Adults; Self Evaluation (Individuals)
*Identifiers:* Lewin (Kurt)
*Availability:* Talico, Inc., 2320 S. Third St., Ste. 5, Jacksonville Beach, FL 32250.
*Notes:* See organization development instruments (16348 to 16361). Time, 180 approx. Items, 18.

Based on Kurt Lewin's research on the management of change, this instrument provides an 18-step procedure for the analysis of organizational benefits, identification of driving and restraining factors, and strategies for gaining acceptance of change. Self-administered or facilitator-administered, this instrument assists managers in planning and implementing change. Depending on the group size and complexity of the planned change, the inventory may take from 30 minutes to 2-3 hours. This instrument may be used in organizational development, preparation for planned change, and management development.

**16351**
**Individual Behavior Analysis (Team Member).** Harris, Philip R. 1984.
*Descriptors:* *Group Dynamics; *Interpersonal Communication; *Staff Meetings; *Teamwork; Adults; Organizational Communication; Rating Scales; Self Evaluation (Individuals)
*Identifiers:* Team Member; Work Groups
*Availability:* Talico, Inc., 2320 S. Third St., Ste. 5, Jacksonville Beach, FL 32250.
*Notes:* See organization development instruments (16348 to 16361). Time, 20 approx. Items, 36.

This tool presents 36 descriptions of ways in which people participate in group meetings. The respondent marks the alternative that best expresses his or her feelings or perceptions about another's behavior or his or her own behavior during group meetings. Completing the analysis again 6-12 months after initially taking it offers the opportunity to compare progress in behavior patterns in a group's life cycle. This instrument may be used in team building and group development.

**16352**
**Intercultural Relations Inventory.** Harris, Philip R. 1984.
*Descriptors:* *Cultural Background; *Cultural Interrelationships; *Intercultural Communication; *Managerial Occupations; *Organizational Development; Adults; Interpersonal Communication; Nonverbal Communication; Verbal Communication
*Identifiers:* IRI
*Availability:* Talico, Inc., 2320 S. Third St., Ste. 5, Jacksonville Beach, FL 32250.
*Notes:* See organization development instruments (16348 to 16361). Items, 39.

This 2-part resource instrument considers intercultural business and worker relationships between the manager or supervisor and worker. The respondent is presented, on Form A, with a short, realistic situation related to international commerce to which the individual is asked to respond using a common set of characteristics. These include: verbal and nonverbal communication, diet, clothing, business values and ethics, and work habits and practices. Also included are: work and family customs and beliefs and traditions. Form A helps individuals to assess perceived cultural differences between the American culture and the culture of a foreign country of their choice. The second part, Form B, narrows the focus of the perceived cultural differences between an American manager or supervisor from an ethnic minority or young worker under 21 years old. The manager or supervisor considers his or her own cultural background and that of the worker according to the same common set of characteristics used in Form A.

**16353**
**Inventory of Transformational Management Skills.** Harris, Philip R. 1984.
*Descriptors:* *Change Strategies; *Interpersonal Competence; *Leadership Styles; *Managerial Occupations; Adults; Motivation; Supervisory Methods
*Identifiers:* *Management Skills; Management Styles
*Availability:* Talico, Inc., 2320 S. Third St., Ste. 5, Jacksonville Beach, FL 32250.
*Notes:* See organization development instruments (16348 to 16361). Items, 25.

This instrument is designed to measure the effectiveness of managers and supervisors in critical knowledge and skill dimensions. It assesses managers' ability to energize themselves and others, to inspire others to achieve beyond the status quo, and to assist others to actualize their potential.

**16354**
**Managing People Skills Inventory.** Harris, Philip R. 1987.
*Descriptors:* *Human Relations; *Interpersonal Communication; *Leadership Qualities; *Leadership Styles; *Managerial Occupations; Adults; Interpersonal Competence; Rating Scales
*Identifiers:* Management Practices; Management Styles; Managerial Communication; MPSI
*Availability:* Talico, Inc., 2320 S. Third St., Ste. 5, Jacksonville Beach, FL 32250.
*Notes:* See organization development instruments (16348 to 16361). Items, 24.

This instrument is designed to measure the effectiveness of managers and supervisors in critical knowledge and skill dimensions. It is used for those in management who are concerned about the human side of the enterprise and its impact on productivity. This tool assesses people skills - behavioral science management techniques that complement managers' technical proficiency. It also covers behaviors and innovative management practices related to human relations and communication. This instrument can be self-administered or administered by another colleague or subordinate.

**16355**
**Meetings Management Planning Inventory.** Harris, Philip R. 1987.
*Descriptors:* *Managerial Occupations; *Meetings; *Planning; *Supervisors; Adults; Coordination; Needs Assessment; Questionnaires; Rating Scales
*Identifiers:* MMPI
*Availability:* Talico, Inc., 2320 S. Third St., Ste. 5, Jacksonville Beach, FL 32250.
*Notes:* See organization development instruments (16348 to 16361). Items, 30.

This instrument is designed to measure the effectiveness of managers and supervisors in critical knowledge and skill dimensions. It assesses how effectively managers and supervisors plan meetings, conferences, or seminars. This tool includes intercultural factors if the meetings are cross-cultural or international in scope. A wide range of planning activities are measured in this tool. It takes into account meeting content input, objectives, site, budget, site visitation, international protocol, detail preparations, and arrangements.

**16356**
**Organization Communication Analysis.** Harris, Philip R. 1984.

*Descriptors:* *Interpersonal Communication; *Organizational Climate; *Organizational Communication; *Organizational Development; *Organizational Effectiveness; *Public Relations; Adults; Human Relations; Questionnaires; Self Evaluation (Groups)
*Identifiers:* Work Groups
*Availability:* Talico, Inc., 2320 S. Third St., Ste. 5, Jacksonville Beach, FL 32250.
*Notes:* See organization development instruments (16348 to 16361). Time, 15 approx.

This checklist enhances management's awareness of the organization's communication systems. It is geared to aid in developing strategies to improve internal and external organizational communication. Employees describe their perceptions of the organization's formal and informal, internal and external communications systems through a checklist. The respondent's perceptions of organizational image and strategies for self-improvement are included. The checklist can be self-administered or facilitator-administered. It may be used for communication, assessment/improvement, human relations training, and organizational analysis.

**16358**
**Organizational Roles and Relationships Inventory.** Harris, Philip R. 1984.
*Descriptors:* *Job Analysis; *Managerial Occupations; *Organizational Climate; *Organizational Development; *Professional Occupations; Adults; Group Behavior; Questionnaires; Teamwork
*Identifiers:* Work Groups
*Availability:* Talico, Inc., 2320 S. Third St., Ste. 5, Jacksonville Beach, FL 32250.
*Notes:* See organization development instruments (16348 to 16361). Time, 90 approx.

This series of questions and a worksheet are designed to clarify roles, responsibilities, and relationships within a triad of organizational peers or work group members at all management and professional levels. Also identified are barriers to effective group performance. Using this data in group discussion as part of the inventory process assists in developing strategies for improvement. This inventory may be used in team building, communication improvement, and organizational development.

**16359**
**Quality of Life Index.** Harris, Philip R. 1984.
*Descriptors:* *Adjustment (to Environment); *Life Style; *Management Development; *Managerial Occupations; *Organizational Climate; *Organizational Development; *Professional Occupations; *Quality of Life; *Well Being; Adults; Self Evaluation (Individuals)
*Availability:* Talico, Inc., 2320 S. Third St., Ste. 5, Jacksonville Beach, FL 32250.
*Notes:* See organization development instruments (16348 to 16361). Time, 20 approx. Items, 30.

This assessment tool measures an individual's quality of life by measuring the respondent's perception of his or her effectiveness in the areas of self-care; psychological, philosophical, and social well-being; and life style. A discussion of the rationale for managing all aspects of one's own wellness is included. The index is self- or facilitator-administered and is suitable for managers and other professionals. It may be used for wellness and health management, as well as for stress management.

**16361**
**Team Synergy Analysis Inventory.** Harris, Philip R. 1984.
*Descriptors:* *Cooperation; *Group Dynamics; *Managerial Occupations; *Supervisory Methods; *Teamwork; Adults; Cooperative Planning; Organizational Communication; Questionnaires; Self Evaluation (Individuals); Sharing Behavior
*Identifiers:* TSAI
*Availability:* Talico, Inc., 2320 S. Third St., Ste. 5, Jacksonville Beach, FL 32250.
*Notes:* See organization development instruments (16348 to 16361). Time, 15 approx. Items, 16.

This instrument is designed to measure the effectiveness of managers and supervisors in critical knowledge and skill dimensions. It assesses synergistic skills within a work group. This tool is self-administered or facilitator-administered, and is used in team building sessions to sensitize participants to key concerns for group effectiveness. It is suitable for ongoing work groups of managers and professionals. There is no scoring involved. Respondents rate their own performance.

**16362**
**Employee Opinion Survey.** Talico, Inc., Jacksonville Beach, FL 1987.
*Descriptors:* *Attitude Measures; *Employee Attitudes; *Feedback; *Organizational Climate; *Organizational Development; *Quality of Working Life; *Work Environment; Adults; Job Satisfaction
*Availability:* Talico, Inc., 2320 S. Third St., Ste. 5, Jacksonville Beach, FL 32250.
*Notes:* See team building and group process instruments (16362 to 16373). Time, 35 approx. Items, 46.

This instrument measures and evaluates employees' attitudes, perceptions, and beliefs about their jobs, their organization, and other work-related issues. Items dealing with 12 key organization impact areas are included. They are: management effectiveness, supervisory practices, communication effectiveness, nondiscrimination, pay and benefits, interpersonal relations, policies and work rules, job interest, work performance, and general level of job satisfaction. The test includes 3 items calling for written comments or suggestions. The test may be used for employee opinion surveys, employee attitude studies, and organization climate surveys.

**16363**
**Group Communication Assessment.** Talico, Inc., Jacksonville Beach, FL 1988.
*Descriptors:* *Employee Attitudes; *Group Dynamics; *Interpersonal Communication; *Organizational Communication; *Organizational Development; *Self Evaluation (Individuals); *Staff Development; Adults; Rating Scales; Teamwork
*Identifiers:* GCA
*Availability:* Talico, Inc., 2320 S. Third St., Ste. 5, Jacksonville Beach, FL 32250.
*Notes:* See team building and group process instruments (16362 to 16373). Time, 20 approx. Items, 30.

GCA is designed to help group or team members to improve the quality and effectiveness of their communication within their group. This 2-part, 30-item self-administered instrument with a Likert-type response scale measures employees' perceptions about the quality of communication within a group with respect to timeliness, accuracy, openness, honesty, candor, relevancy, meaningfulness, and trustfulness, as well as group process behaviors. This tool may be used for team building, communication training, quality circles, task team improvements, and supervisory training.

**16364**
**Group Creativity Index.** Talico, Inc., Jacksonville Beach, FL 1988.
*Descriptors:* *Creativity; *Group Behavior; *Group Dynamics; *Innovation; *Organizational Climate; *Organizational Development; *Teamwork; Adults; Feedback; Informal Organization; Self Evaluation (Individuals)
*Identifiers:* GCI
*Availability:* Talico, Inc., 2320 S. Third St., Ste. 5, Jacksonville Beach, FL 32250.
*Notes:* See team building and group process instruments (16362 to 16373). Time, 20 approx. Items, 30.

The GCI is a diagnostic tool that measures perceptions about conditions within or external to a group that can affect group creativity and innovativeness. The test measures perceptions about the creative characteristics of group members, the extent to which group members use the creative process, freedom from barriers to creativity, and the extent to which the organizational climate encourages creativity and innovation. The GCI can be self-administered or administered by a facilitator. This index may be used in team building, productivity task teams, quality circles, strategic planning, technical problem solving, and management and supervisory training.

**16365**
**Group Participation Analysis.** Talico, Inc., Jacksonville Beach, FL 1988.
*Descriptors:* *Group Behavior; *Group Dynamics; *Observation; *Organizational Development; *Teamwork; Adults; Decision Making; Informal Organization; Leadership Styles; Rating Scales
*Identifiers:* GPA; Team Leader; Work Groups
*Availability:* Talico, Inc., 2320 S. Third St., Ste. 5, Jacksonville Beach, FL 32250.
*Notes:* See team building and group process instruments (16362 to 16373). Items, 34.

GPA is a guide designed to help facilitators observe and critique the group process, including problem-solving process skills of a team whose members are working on a group task. This 2-part tool consists of 24 items that facilitators can use as an observational guide regarding such specific issues as initiating, information sharing, candor, mutual support and encouragement, harmonizing, conflict, task interest, goal setting, task process, superficiality, rationality, and conflict. An additional 10 items in a separate section examine the team leader's behavior in conducting the team meeting and how well the leader fosters team climate. This tool may be used in team building, management and supervisory training, and employee participation programs.

**16367**
**Human Resource Survey.** Talico, Inc., Jacksonville Beach, FL 1988.
*Descriptors:* *Attitude Measures; *Employee Attitudes; *Employer Employee Relationship; *Organizational Climate; *Quality of Working Life; *Work Environment; Adults; Equal Opportunities (Jobs); Fringe Benefits; Rating Scales
*Identifiers:* HRS; Human Resource Management
*Availability:* Talico, Inc., 2320 S. Third St., Ste. 5, Jacksonville Beach, FL 32250.
*Notes:* See team building and group process instruments (16362 to 16373). Time, 45 approx. Items, 50.

This instrument measures employees' opinions and attitudes about those aspects of the job and work environment that impact on morale, performance, and productivity. Employee perceptions are gathered in 10 categories which include communications, cost and performance, consciousness, nondiscrimination (EEO), growth and advancement, relationships, management and supervisory effectiveness, policies and work rules, pay and benefits, and safety and work conditions. The instument includes a write-in comment section as well. The instrument may be used in morale and motivation studies, climate studies, organizational analysis, and human resource management audits.

**16368**
**Organization Change Inventory.** Talico, Inc., Jacksonville Beach, FL 1988.
*Descriptors:* *Change Strategies; *Managerial Occupations; *Organizational Change; *Organizational Climate; *Organizational Development; Adults; Management Development
*Identifiers:* OCI; Schein (Edgar H)
*Availability:* Talico, Inc., 2320 S. Third St., Ste. 5, Jacksonville Beach, FL 32250.
*Notes:* See team building and group process instruments (16362 to 16373). Time, 20 approx. Items, 24.

This 24-question inventory administered to senior and middle-management represents major components of the organization process as perceived by Edgar H. Schein. This model assesses the organizational climate for unfreezing and pattern breaking, experimenting, changing, identifying and internalizing, refreezing, and attainment. The tool is specifically designed to help management evaluate an organization's readiness for change and renewal. It can be used for organizational analysis, strategic planning, organizational renewal, and team building.

**16369**
**Participative Climate Diagnosis.** Talico, Inc., Jacksonville Beach, FL 1988.
*Descriptors:* *Attitude Measures; *Change Strategies; *Employee Attitudes; *Organizational Climate; *Organizational Development; *Organizational Effectiveness; *Organizational Objectives; *Participative Decision Making; Adults; Informal Organization; Quality Circles; Self Evaluation (Groups)
*Availability:* Talico, Inc., 2320 S. Third St., Ste. 5, Jacksonville Beach, FL 32250.
*Notes:* See team building and group process instruments (16362 to 16373). Time, 20 approx. Items, 50.

This diagnostic instrument helps to assess the readiness of organizational climates for participative or employee involvement programs. Employees' perceptions about working conditions and the organizational environment which impact on their performance and productivity are categorized into 10 participative and performance categories. These categories include: creative climate, communications, productivity consciousness, participative climate, interpersonal climate, goals and stands, motivation change, problem solving, and union relations. The test may be self- or facilitator-administered. This instrument may be used for quality circle programs, productivity teams, attitude and climate studies, participative management training.

**16370**
**Survey of Organizational Effectiveness.** Talico, Inc., Jacksonville Beach, FL 1988.
*Descriptors:* *Attitude Measures; *Creativity; *Employee Attitudes; *Organizational Development; *Organizational Effectiveness; *Organizational Objectives; *Participative Decision Making; *Teamwork; Adults; Rating Scales; Self Evaluation (Groups)
*Identifiers:* Organizational Competence Theory; SOE
*Availability:* Talico, Inc., 2320 S. Third St., Ste. 5, Jacksonville Beach, FL 32250.
*Notes:* See team building and group process instruments (16362 to 16373). Time, 20 approx. Items, 24.

This diagnostic tool, based on the organizational competency theory, helps management evaluate the effectiveness and performance competence at all levels of the organization by measuring current levels of collaboaration, commitment, and creativity. Specifically, it measures the commitment of the workers to the organization's goals and objectives, as well as the workers' sense of their individual contributions. It also measures how the employees work together as a team and use their full creative capability to solve problems and make decisions. The survey is administered by a facilitator. The survey may be used for climate studies, organization change and renewal, performance and productivity improvement, and organizational competence studies.

**16371**
**Team Task Analysis.** Talico, Inc., Jacksonville Beach, FL 1988.
*Descriptors:* *Creativity; *Group Dynamics; *Organizational Development; *Problem Solving; *Task Analysis; *Teamwork; Adults; Brainstorming; Decision Making; Staff Development
*Identifiers:* Creative Problem Solving; CPS; TTA
*Availability:* Talico, Inc., 2320 S. Third St., Ste. 5, Jacksonville Beach, FL 32250.
*Notes:* See team building and group process instruments (16362 to 16373).

TTA is a 6-step task analysis and problem-solving model, rather than a measurement instrument. The 6 steps include describing the problem, gathering additional facts, setting an objective, determining problem causes, developing alternative solutions, and evaluating alternatives. The TTA is based upon recognized creative problem-solving (CPS) principles. The time required to use this tool is a function of the problem assigned or selected. The tool may be used at any level in the organization for team building, problem solving/decision making training, productivity improvement, and management/supervisory training.

**16372**
**Team Climate Survey.** Talico, Inc., Jacksonville Beach, FL 1988.
*Descriptors:* *Group Dynamics; *Organizational Climate; *Organizational Communication; *Organizational Development; *Participative Decision Making; *Teamwork; Adults; Quality Circles; Rating Scales; Self Evaluation (Groups); Self Evaluation (Individuals)
*Identifiers:* TCS; Work Groups
*Availability:* Talico, Inc., 2320 S. Third St., Ste. 5, Jacksonville Beach, FL 32250.
*Notes:* See team building and group process instruments (16362 to 16373). Time, 20 approx. Items, 25.

The TCS consists of 25 items/statements, each dealing with an issue related to the potential success of a participative management activity. Employees use an assigned or unassigned group task as a basis for using this tool. The instrument measures such issues as knowledge skills, information sharing, management and supervisory support, participation motivation, instrumentality and valence, and outcomes. The perceptions of 3 hierarchical levels, the team, the immediate supervisors of the team, and senior management, can be measured by using this multilevel format. This survey can be used by participative problem-solving teams, productivity task teams, and quality circles for team building.

**16373**
**Team Communication Analysis.** Talico, Inc., Jacksonville Beach, FL 1988.
*Descriptors:* *Group Dynamics; *Interpersonal Communication; *Organizational Communication; *Organizational Development; Adults; Feedback; Formative Evaluation; Staff Development
*Identifiers:* TCA
*Availability:* Talico, Inc., 2320 S. Third St., Ste. 5, Jacksonville Beach, FL 32250.
*Notes:* See team building and group process instruments (16362 to 16373). Time, 20 approx. Items, 2.

The TCA is a form or aid by which group process facilitators or individual members of a team can construct 2 diagrams depicting the flow or direction, frequency, and duration (long vs. short) of communication among team members. This form assists in visually depicting the above aspects of communication. Team members receive feedback on the collected TCA data and diagram for the purpose of team critique and assessment of the extent to which group members are participating in the group task. A sample TCA form is provided for the users to study and construct simulated or practice TCA diagrams before creating their own. This aid may be used in team building, management and supervisory training, communication analysis, and conference leadership training.

**16376**
**Leadership Contingency Wheel.** Talico, Inc., Jacksonville Beach, FL 1987.
*Descriptors:* *Leadership Styles; *Management Development; *Managerial Occupations; Adults; Leadership Training
*Identifiers:* LCW
*Availability:* Talico, Inc., 2320 S. Third St., Ste. 5, Jacksonville Beach, FL 32250.
*Notes:* See management and supervisory development instruments (16374 to 16386), especially the Leadership Effectiveness Profile (16377). Time, 10 approx.

Purpose is to help managers and supervisors determine which leadership style and behavior are appropriate for each employee's job and psychological maturity. Indicates best choice among alternative leadership styles for important leadership practices, such as communication, decision making, and control. Is effective when used with the Leadership Effectiveness Profile (16377). Content validity has been established through literature research. Can be used with all levels of employees and for management and supervisory training, coaching and counseling, employee performance improvement.

**16377**
**Leadership Effectiveness Profile.** Talico, Inc., Jacksonville Beach, FL 1987.
*Descriptors:* *Leadership Styles; *Management Development; *Managerial Occupations; Adults; Leadership Training
*Identifiers:* LEP
*Availability:* Talico, Inc., 2320 S. Third St., Ste. 5, Jacksonville Beach, FL 32250.
*Notes:* See management and supervisory development instruments (16374 to 16386), especially the Leadership Contingency Wheel (16376). Time, 40 approx. Items, 15.

Used to identify managers' and supervisors' leadership style preferences, evaluate their diagnostic skills and adaptability regarding leadership situations, and assess their overall potential leadership effectiveness. Based upon contemporary contingency and situational leadership theories. Construct validity was established using the "known groups" method. Can be used for training, needs analysis, development coaching, career pathing, self development, and leadership-training.

**16378**
**Management Effectiveness Profile.** Talico, Inc., Jacksonville Beach, FL 1987.
*Descriptors:* *Management Development; *Managerial Occupations; *Supervisory Methods; Adults; Rating Scales
*Identifiers:* MEP
*Availability:* Talico, Inc., 2320 S. Third St., Ste. 5, Jacksonville Beach, FL 32250.
*Notes:* See management and supervisory development instruments (16374 to 16386). Time, 30 approx. Items, 24.

Developed to help assess the perceived effectiveness of management and supervisory practices and to facilitate performance coaching and counseling. Can be completed by the managers themself, supervisors, subordinates, or peers. Measures perceptions about how well managers or supervisors perform key management functions: planning, organizing, directing or implementing, and controlling. Covers 24 important management cycle issues such as goal setting, delegating, training, assigning work, decision making, communicating, and other areas. Useful with middle through upper management staff. Can be used for development coaching, analysis of training needs, performance appraisal, career counseling, or communication improvement.

**16379**
**Management Practices Audit.** Talico, Inc., Jacksonville Beach, FL 1987.
*Descriptors:* *Leadership Styles; *Management Development; *Managerial Occupations; *Supervisory Methods; Adults; Rating Scales
*Identifiers:* MPA
*Availability:* Talico, Inc., 2320 S. Third St., Ste. 5, Jacksonville Beach, FL 32250.
*Notes:* See management and supervisory development instruments (16374 to 16386). Time, 35 approx. Items, 44.

May be completed by managers, their supervisors, peers, or subordinates to assess the effectiveness of demonstrated management practices and skills in various management cycle activities, such as planning, organizing, implementing, and controlling. Also used to help identify leadership styles and preferences. Specific issues covered in the questionnaire include conceptual thinking, analytical and diagnostic skills, goal setting, interviewing and counseling skills, work distribution and problem solving, setting performance standards, recognizing employee performance, using control systems, handling constructive criticism, and improving productivity. May be used for management and supervisory training, performance appraisal, coaching and counseling, career development, leadership training, and analysis of training needs.

**16380**
**Management Practices Inventory.** Talico, Inc., Jacksonville Beach, FL 1987.
*Descriptors:* *Management Development; *Managerial Occupations; *Supervisory Methods; Adults; Rating Scales
*Identifiers:* MPI
*Availability:* Talico, Inc., 2320 S. Third St., Ste. 5, Jacksonville Beach, FL 32250.
*Notes:* See management and supervisory development instruments (16374 to 16386). Items, 50.

Multilevel diagnostic instrument to measure managerial effectiveness in 25 management practices, behaviors, and applications of skill. The 25 dimensions (with 2 items per dimension) follow the traditional management cycle of planning, organizing, directing, and controlling. Other skills assessed include motivation, communication skills and practices, and technical expertise. Can be completed by managers themselves, their supervisors, and subordinates. May be used for training needs analysis, performance appraisal, development coaching, career pathing, self-development, communication improvement, or performance improvement.

**16381**
**Management Training Needs Analysis.** Talico, Inc., Jacksonville Beach, FL 1987.
*Descriptors:* *Management Development; *Managerial Occupations; *Supervisory Training; Adults; Rating Scales
*Identifiers:* MTNA
*Availability:* Talico, Inc., 2320 S. Third St., Ste. 5, Jacksonville Beach, FL 32250.
*Notes:* See management and supervisory development instruments (16374 to 16386). Time, 40 approx. Items, 48.

Used to help identify training and development needs for managers, supervisors, or candidates for supervisory positions. Covers 12 skill areas necessary for successful supervisory and managerial performance. Areas include leadership, communications, human relations, time management, counseling, discipline, and others. To be used with first- and second-level managers and supervisors or candidates for those positions.

**16382**
**Supervisory Practices Survey.** Talico, Inc., Jacksonville Beach, FL 1987.
*Descriptors:* *Management Development; *Managerial Occupations; *Supervisory Methods; *Supervisory Training; Adults; Questionnaires; Rating Scales
*Identifiers:* SPS
*Availability:* Talico, Inc., 2320 S. Third St., Ste. 5, Jacksonville Beach, FL 32250.
*Notes:* See management and supervisory development instruments (16374 to 16386). Time, 30 approx. Items, 39.

Used to measure those supervisory practices and attitudes that influence supervisory effectiveness and to provide a basis for supervisory development. The survey is a 4-part instrument that focuses on current practices and attitudes of supervisors. Among dimensions assessed are time management, motivation, communication, employee discipline, and performance management. Suitable for use with first-level supervisors and lower-level middle management. Can be used for supervisory practices and skills assessment, development counseling, training needs analysis, and training evaluation.

**16383**
**Supervisory Skills Aptitude Test.** Talico, Inc., Jacksonville Beach, FL 1987.
*Descriptors:* *Knowledge Level; *Management Development; *Managerial Occupations; *Supervisory Training; Adults; Questionnaires
*Identifiers:* SSAT
*Availability:* Talico, Inc., 2320 S. Third St., Ste. 5, Jacksonville Beach, FL 32250.
*Notes:* See management and supervisory development instruments (16374 to 16386). Time, 35 approx. Items, 50.

Developed to measure knowledge of the functions, skills and practices required of a successful supervisor. Also used to help identify training needs and to help in evaluating the effectiveness of supervisory and management training courses. Categories measured include responsibilities of a supervisor, leadership, planning and organizing, time management, human relations, communication, employee motivation, counseling and discipline, improving work performance, and teamwork. To be used with first- and second-level supervisors, middle-level managers, and candidates for supervisory positions. May be used in training needs analysis, supervisory skills development, supervisory and management assessment, career development, and selection and advancement assessment.

**16384**
**Supervisory Styles Inventory.** Talico, Inc., Jacksonville Beach, FL 1987.
*Descriptors:* *Leadership Styles; *Management Development; *Managerial Occupations; *Supervisory Methods; Adults; Forced Choice Technique; Questionnaires
*Identifiers:* SSI
*Availability:* Talico, Inc., 2320 S. Third St., Ste. 5, Jacksonville Beach, FL 32250.
*Notes:* See management and supervisory development instruments (16374 to 16386). Time, 30 approx. Items, 20.

Developed to help managers and supervisors assess and critique their leadership style and to evaluate whether a manager or supervisor prefers people-centered or task-centered leadership. The following supervisory skills are assessed: communication, leadership, motivation, problem solving, and organizational skills. Used with first- and second-level supervisors and middle-level managers. May be used for leadership development, self/professional/career development, human relations training, performance appraisal, coaching and counseling, management and supervisory training.

**16386**
**Management and Supervisory Development Profile.** Talico, Inc., Jacksonville Beach, FL 1987.
*Descriptors:* *Management Development; *Profiles; Adults; Managerial Occupations; Questionnaires
*Availability:* Talico, Inc., 2320 S. Third St., Ste. 5, Jacksonville Beach, FL 32250.
*Notes:* See management and supervisory development instruments (16374 to 16386).

Shows how to evaluate current effectiveness of managers and supervisors, how to assess their readiness for advancement, and how to prepare them for increased leadership responsibilities. Instruments focus on management practices, motive acquisition, leadership effectiveness, career values, position preference, and growth ambition.

**16387**
**Career Development Profile.** Talico, Inc., Jacksonville Beach, FL 1987.
*Descriptors:* *Career Counseling; *Management Development; *Managerial Occupations; *Supervisors; *Vocational Interests; Adults; Check Lists; Rating Scales
*Identifiers:* CDP
*Availability:* Talico, Inc., 2320 S. Third St., Ste. 5, Jacksonville Beach, FL 32250.
*Notes:* See career development and HRD instruments (16387 to 16396). Time, 45 approx. Items, 60.

Used to aid managers, supervisors, and human resource personnel design career development programs and facilitate career counseling and coaching. Used to obtain a variety of career development information from management level or potential managers. A semi-structured instrument that focuses on employees' career interests, ambitions, motivations, and goals. Determines the applicability of 30 key work practices to employees' jobs and helps to assess their interests and current skill level regarding those practices. Is work-behavior oriented. There is no predictive index. Administered and interpreted by a facilitator. Can be used for career coaching and counseling or for training needs analysis.

**16388**
**Career Values Scale.** Talico, Inc., Jacksonville Beach, FL 1987.
*Descriptors:* *Attitude Measures; *Management Development; *Managerial Occupations; *Occupational Aspiration; *Vocational Interests; Adults; Values
*Identifiers:* CVS
*Availability:* Talico, Inc., 2320 S. Third St., Ste. 5, Jacksonville Beach, FL 32250.
*Notes:* See career development and HRD instruments (16387 to 16396).

Developed to help managerial staff gain a clearer understanding about the values they assign to various career-related factors and to aid in career planning and counseling activites. Helps to measure career interests, goals, needs, and aspirations in 4 major dimensions: work environment, position preference, growth/ambition, and career introspection. Self- or facilitator-administered. Normative and reliability data are under development. Can be used for career planning, self/professional/career development, coaching and counseling, and selection and advancement.

**16389**
**Clerical Productivity Analysis.** Talico, Inc., Jacksonville Beach, FL 1987.
*Descriptors:* *Clerical Workers; *Work Environment; Adults; Attitude Measures; Productivity; Rating Scales
*Identifiers:* CPA
*Availability:* Talico, Inc., 2320 S. Third St., Ste. 5, Jacksonville Beach, FL 32250.
*Notes:* See career development and HRD instruments (16387 to 16396). Time, 25 approx. Items, 40.

Developed to help office managers and supervisors evaluate those elements that influence clerical work force productivity most significantly. Included are elements relating to physical environment and human resources, such as training, staffing, and morale/motivation. May be self- or administrator-administered. Useful for office supervision training and development, aiding clerical worker productivity and improvement, and coaching and counseling. Clerical staff rates each item twice: its importance in helping employee do the job and the employee's agreement or disagreement with the content of each item.

**16390**
**Employee Orientation Checklist.** Talico, Inc., Jacksonville Beach, FL 1987.
*Descriptors:* *Entry Workers; *Orientation; Adults; Check Lists; Employees
*Identifiers:* EOC
*Availability:* Talico, Inc., 2320 S. Third St., Ste. 5, Jacksonville Beach, FL 32250.
*Notes:* See career development and HRD instruments (16387 to 16396).

Checklist to assist personnel and line managers or supervisors in insuring that newly hired or transferred employees receive proper orientation into the organization and into their particular work unit.

**16391**
**Employee/Supervisor Expectation Agreement.** Talico, Inc., Jacksonville Beach, FL 1987.
*Descriptors:* *Employee Responsibility; *Employees; *Employer Employee Relationship; *Expectation; *Supervisors; Adults; Check Lists
*Identifiers:* ESEA
*Availability:* Talico, Inc., 2320 S. Third St., Ste. 5, Jacksonville Beach, FL 32250.
*Notes:* See career development and HRD instruments (16387 to 16396). Time, 15 approx.

Can serve as an aid for improving communication and understanding between supervisors and subordinates regarding their basic responsibilities toward each other. Designed to help employees and supervisors understand what the other expects. Aids supervisors in analyzing their effectiveness.

**16392**
**Employee Training Needs Analysis.** Talico, Inc., Jacksonville Beach, FL 1988.
*Descriptors:* *Clerical Workers; *Needs Assessment; *Training Objectives; Adults; Questionnaires
*Identifiers:* ETNA
*Availability:* Talico, Inc., 2320 S. Third St., Ste. 5, Jacksonville Beach, FL 32250.
*Notes:* See career development and HRD instruments (16387 to 16396).

Developed to help training specialists identify training and development needs for clerical employees. Divided into 3 parts. Part 1 is used to list important department training-related information. Part 2 summarizes training needs in 14 clerical skill and function areas plus basic supervisory functions. Part 3 is used to help assess training goals and objectives. To be completed by training specialists. Content validity has been established through literature research. Clerical skills assessed include those requiring manual dexterity, numerical and verbal comprehension, interpersonal competence, and data manipulation.

**16393**
**Employment Interview Checklist.** Talico, Inc., Jacksonville Beach, FL 1987.
*Descriptors:* *Employment Interviews; *Personnel Selection; Adults; Check Lists
*Identifiers:* EIC
*Availability:* Talico, Inc., 2320 S. Third St., Ste. 5, Jacksonville Beach, FL 32250.
*Notes:* See career development and HRD instruments (16387 to 16396). Items, 25.

Used to help managers, supervisors, or personnel staff improve their employment interviewing skills and effectiveness. Guides the interviewer through work history, performance evaluation, education, personal characteristics, and career goals. Can be used as a checklist that guides the interview sequence and serves as a record of the discussion.

**16394**
**Performance Development Inventory.** Talico, Inc., Jacksonville Beach, FL 1987.
*Descriptors:* *Job Performance; *Managerial Occupations; *Personnel Evaluation; Adults; Questionnaires; Rating Scales
*Identifiers:* PDI
*Availability:* Talico, Inc., 2320 S. Third St., Ste. 5, Jacksonville Beach, FL 32250.
*Notes:* See career development and HRD instruments (16387 to 16396). Time, 45 approx.

A form used to facilitate objective performance appraisals and appraisal interviews of managerial or near-managerial staff. Can aid in facilitating performance and career counseling or coaching. Focuses on objectively developed work behaviors, performance objectives, indicators, and results. Bilevel format. Self- and/or supervisor-administered. After filling out form, requires 1 to 2 hours for appraisal interview.

**16395**
**Safety Practices Audit.** Talico, Inc., Jacksonville Beach, FL 1987.
*Descriptors:* *Employees; *Safety; *Work Environment; Adults; Attitude Measures; Knowledge Level; Questionnaires; Rating Scales
*Identifiers:* SPA
*Availability:* Talico, Inc., 2320 S. Third St., Ste. 5, Jacksonville Beach, FL 32250.
*Notes:* See career development and HRD instruments (16387 to 16396). Time, 45 approx. Items, 40.

Used to measure awareness and attitudes regarding personal and organizational safety and to improve and develop employee safety consciousness. Measures employees' knowledge and awareness of such issues as safety and emergency care procedures, safety practices, facilities, safety training, accident rates, causes, and related issues. Also aids in the identification of safety problems and elicits suggestions for improvement. Experimental instrument for which reliability and normative data are being collected. Can be used for safety program evaluation, organization analysis, or safety training and needs analysis.

**16396**
**Termination Interview Guide.** Talico, Inc., Jacksonville Beach, FL 1987.
*Descriptors:* *Dismissal (Personnel); Adults; Guidelines; Questionnaires
*Identifiers:* Exit Interviews; TIG
*Availability:* Talico, Inc., 2320 S. Third St., Ste. 5, Jacksonville Beach, FL 32250.
*Notes:* See career development and HRD instruments (16387 to 16396).

Designed to help managers, supervisors, and supervisory personnel prepare and conduct employee termination interviews. Contains a set of termination interview guidelines and suggests a format to follow when meeting with the employee.

**16400**
**Sales Management Inventory.** Talico, Inc., Jacksonville Beach, FL 1987.
*Descriptors:* *Managerial Occupations; *Sales Occupations; *Supervisory Methods; Adults; Management Development; Questionnaires; Rating Scales
*Identifiers:* SMI
*Availability:* Talico, Inc., 2320 S. Third St., Ste. 5, Jacksonville Beach, FL 32250.
*Notes:* See sales training and development instruments (16397 to 16402). Time, 30 approx. Items, 25.

Used to help sales managers and supervisors improve their skills in planning, organizing, motivating, and directing salespeople and in insuring that sales objectives or quotas are met. Questionnaire covers such issues as goal setting, communication, training, counseling, and problem solving. Provides feedback to sales managers at all levels. Has content and construct validity and reliability. Can be used for development coaching, training needs analysis, performance appraisal, career pathing, or communication improvement.

**16401**
**Sales Motivation Survey.** Talico, Inc., Jacksonville Beach, FL 1987.
*Descriptors:* *Managerial Occupations; *Motivation; *Salesmanship; *Sales Workers; Adults; Questionnaires; Rating Scales
*Identifiers:* SMS
*Availability:* Talico, Inc., 2320 S. Third St., Ste. 5, Jacksonville Beach, FL 32250.
*Notes:* See sales training and development instruments (16397 to 16402). Time, 25 approx. Items, 40.

Designed to help sales managers and supervisors determine how motivated their sales force is to meet or exceed sales objectives and quotas. Also provides salespersons with feedback on their current motivational need or goals. Multilevel format helps sales managers and supervisors compare their own assessment of employees' motivational levels with employees' self perceptions. Can be self- or facilitator-administered. Can be used in employees sales motivation studies, sales management and supervisory training, self-development, and coaching and counseling.

**16402**
**Salesperson Performance Questionnaire.** Talico, Inc., Jacksonville Beach, FL 1987.
*Descriptors:* *Evaluation Criteria; *Job Performance; *Managerial Occupations; *Personnel Evaluation; *Sales Workers; Adults; Questionnaires; Rating Scales
*Identifiers:* SPQ
*Availability:* Talico, Inc., 2320 S. Third St., Ste. 5, Jacksonville Beach, FL 32250.
*Notes:* See sales training and development instruments (16397 to 16402). Time, 45 approx.

Helps sales managers and supervisors to improve overall performance and effectiveness of their sales force by developing specific performance objectives for salespeople, establishing performance indicators, and measuring results. Serves as a performance appraisal instrument that focuses on objective work behaviors required for effective sales performance. A 3-part questionnaire consisting of sales behaviors, objectives and results, and career development. Bilevel format can be self- or supervisor-administered. Followed by an appraisal interview. Can be used for performance appraisal or coaching and counseling.

**16403**
**Supervisory Proficiency Tests, Series 1.** Talico, Inc., Jacksonville Beach, FL 1986.
*Descriptors:* *Knowledge Level; *Management Development; *Managerial Occupations; *Supervisory Training; Adults; Discipline; Grievance Procedures; Human Relations; Interpersonal Relationship; Job Training; Leadership Styles; Motivation; Organizational Communication; Time Management
*Availability:* Talico, Inc., 2320 S. Third St., Ste. 5, Jacksonville Beach, FL 32250.

Designed to measure knowledge and skills in key areas of supervisory management. There are 10 tests, 9 measuring specific supervisory skills plus a general test. Each test consists of 25 true-false items and requires about 15 minutes to complete. Series 1 deals primarily with human skills required of a supervisor. These tests are most suitable for first- and second-level supervisors. They are said to be bias-free, as well as industry bias-free and union status bias-free. Can be used in formal supervisory or management training courses either as pre- and posttests or as learning instruments during the course of the training program. The 9 specific skills covered are communications, complaints and grievances, counseling and discipline, employee motivation, employee training, human relations, interpersonal relations, leadership, and time management.

**16404**
**Superior Management Practices Questionnaire.** Kinlaw, Dennis C. 1987.
*Descriptors:* *Administrators; *Job Performance; *Middle Management; *Supervisors; *Supervisory Methods; Adults; Employer Employee Relationship; Interpersonal Communication; Leadership Styles; Motivation Techniques; Problem Solving; Productivity
*Identifiers:* SMPQ
*Availability:* Talico, Inc., 2320 S. Third St., Ste. 5, Jacksonville Beach, FL 32250.
*Notes:* See Kinlaw management and organizational development instruments (16404 to 16410). Items, 49.

This questionnaire is designed to differentiate superior middle managers and supervisors from others. It will assist management in assessing the degree to which they use superior practices, and to obtain feedback about their practices from subordinates, peers, and supervisors. This instrument has 7 clusters to describe management practices. They include action/innovation and problem solving; performance and productivity; contact and interaction; personnel communication and relationships; subordinate motivation and development; team orientation; and leadership style and personal characteristics.

**16405**
**Problem Solving Skills Questionnaire.** Kinlaw, Dennis C. 1983.
*Descriptors:* *Interpersonal Communication; *Interpersonal Competence; *Managerial Occupations; *Problem Solving; Adults; Questionnaires; Supervisors
*Identifiers:* PSSQ
*Availability:* Talico, Inc., 2320 S. Third St., Ste. 5, Jacksonville Beach, FL 32250.
*Notes:* See Kinlaw management and organizational development instruments (16404 to 16410). Items, 20.

Designed to help managers, supervisors and other key personnel measure their perception of communication behaviors that contribute to successful interpersonal transactions. This questionnaire provides feedback concerning an individual's ability to discriminate between interpersonal communication responses that facilitate the development of a problem-solving conversation and those who hinder the development of such a conversation. Positive and negative responses are required with this tool. Projections and interpretations can be made based on an analysis of scores.

**16406**
**Performance Appraisal Inventory.** Kinlaw, Dennis C. 1985.
*Descriptors:* *Administrator Role; *Administrators; *Personnel Evaluation; *Professional Development; *Supervisors; Adults
*Identifiers:* PAI
*Availability:* Talico, Inc., 2320 S. Third St., Ste. 5, Jacksonville Beach, FL 32250.
*Notes:* See Kinlaw management and organizational development instruments (16404 to 16410). Items, 20.

This feedback instrument is designed for individual growth and organizational development. Its purpose is to provide managers and supervisors with an understanding of the characteristics of effective performance appraisal systems, the questions that must be resolved to make a performance appraisal work, and the performance appraisal cycle; practical assistance in developing performance plans; and practical guidance for conducting the performance assessment interviews. Effective systems are systems in which managers can use and value ways of maintaining and improving the performance of the organization, themselves, and their employees.

**16407**
**Motivation Assessment Inventory.** Kinlaw, Dennis C. 1984.
*Descriptors:* *Administrators; *Job Performance; *Managerial Occupations; *Motivation; *Personnel Evaluation; *Productivity; *Supervisors; *Supervisory Methods; Adults; Rating Scales; Work Environment
*Identifiers:* Herzberg (Frederick); MAI; Maslow (Abraham)
*Availability:* Talico, Inc., 2320 S. Third St., Ste. 5, Jacksonville Beach, FL 32250.
*Notes:* See Kinlaw management and organizational development instruments (16404 to 16410). Items, 60.

This assessment inventory is designed to provide managers and supervisors with a tool for managing productivity by managing motivation and performance. This instrument provides practical guidelines for improving productivity by improving management and supervisory practices. It includes factors that contribute to successful performance, clear expectations, competency, and facilitating work environment. Need theories of Abraham Maslow and Frederick Herzberg are provided and diagramed. References are available.

**16408**
**Interaction and Involvement Questionnaire.** Kinlaw, Dennis C. 1987.
*Descriptors:* *Administrators; *Employer Employee Relationship; *Job Enrichment; *Supervisors; *Supervisory Methods; Administrator Effectiveness; Adults; Rating Scales
*Identifiers:* IIQ
*Availability:* Talico, Inc., 2320 S. Third St., Ste. 5, Jacksonville Beach, FL 32250.
*Notes:* See Kinlaw management and organizational development instruments (16404 to 16410). Items, 45.

Designed to assist managers to assess their own interaction and involvement practices and to obtain feedback about their practices from subordinates, peers, and supervisors. This instrument measures the degree to which managers and supervisors initiate opportunities for employee involvement. Involvement includes 3 areas of activities: innovation, which entails supervisors encouraging subordinates and coworkers to present new ideas; planning, which extends opportunities of subordinates and coworkers to participate in the various planning processes; and problem solving, where subordinates and coworkers can be given the chance to use team decision making to solve problems.

**16409**
**Environment Assessment Questionnaire.** Kinlaw, Dennis C. 1986.
*Descriptors:* *Administrators; *Attitude Measures; *Employee Attitudes; *Managerial Occupations; *Supervisors; *Work Environment; Adults; Job Enrichment; Job Performance; Job Satisfaction; Motivation; Problem Solving
*Identifiers:* EAQ
*Availability:* Talico, Inc., 2320 S. Third St., Ste. 5, Jacksonville Beach, FL 32250.
*Notes:* See Kinlaw management and organizational development instruments (16404 to 16410). Items, 75.

Designed to assist managers and supervisors assess employees' perception of a specific work group's environment and to provide organizations with a tool for conducting a large-scale analysis of employee perceptions. This questionnaire measures how positive members of organizations and work groups are about 5 variables that influence performance. These are: clarity, fairness, appreciation, responsiveness, and involvement. Tests were performed on employees of work groups that were classified as high performing and compared with those classified as average or below average.

**16411**
**Inter Group Feedback Questionnaire.** Kinlaw, Dennis C. 1988.
*Descriptors:* *Feedback; *Interprofessional Relationship; *Organizational Development; *Organizational Effectiveness; *Professional Development; *Teamwork; Adults; Rating Scales
*Identifiers:* IFQ
*Availability:* Talico, Inc., 2320 S. Third St., Ste. 5, Jacksonville Beach, FL 32250.
*Notes:* For instruments in the work group improvement and team development series, see 16411 through 16414. Items, 40.

Measures 8 perceived characteristics that predict the level of effective team performance between 2 or more work groups. The more positive one work group is about members of the other work group, the higher the level of team performance between the two groups will be. The 8 characteristics are direction, support, systems, resources, cooperation, sensitivity, structure, and conflict resolution. Can be used for intergroup team development, work group performance improvement, manager and supervisor training. A feedback instrument for individual growth and organizational development.

**16412**
**Work Group Development Questionnaire.** Kinlaw, Dennis C. 1988.
*Descriptors:* *Feedback; *Interprofessional Relationship; *Organizational Development; *Organizational Effectiveness; *Professional Development; *Teamwork; Adults; Rating Scales
*Identifiers:* WDQ
*Availability:* Talico, Inc., 2320 S. Third St., Ste. 5, Jacksonville Beach, FL 32250.
*Notes:* For instruments in the work group improvement and team development series, see 16411 through 16414. Time, 20 approx. Items, 50.

A feedback instrument for individual growth and organizational development. Measures 5 perceived characteristics that predict the level of team development in a work group. The more positive the group members are about the characteristics, the higher the level of team development will be. The 5 characteristics are inclusion, commitment, loyalty, pride, and trust. Is self-administered. May be self-scored or scored by trainer. Can be used for team development, work group performance improvement, manager and supervisor training, or productivity and quality improvement training.

**16413**
**Work Group Effectiveness Questionnaire.** Kinlaw, Dennis C. 1988.
*Descriptors:* *Feedback; *Interprofessional Relationship; *Organizational Development; *Organizational Effectiveness; *Professional Development; *Teamwork; Adults; Questionnaires; Rating Scales
*Identifiers:* WEQ
*Availability:* Talico, Inc., 2320 S. Third St., Ste. 5, Jacksonville Beach, FL 32250.
*Notes:* For instruments in the work group improvement and team development series, see 16411 through 16414. Time, 20 approx. Items, 54.

A feedback instrument for individual growth and organizational development. Measures 9 perceived conditions that predict the performance of a work group. The more positive group members are about these conditions, the higher the performance of the group will be. The conditions are clarity, fairness, appreciation, responsiveness, involvement, resources, systems, competencies, and improvement focus. Can be used for team development, work group performance improvement, manager and supervisor training, and productivity and quality improvement training.

**16414**
**Work Group Leadership Questionnaire.** Kinlaw, Dennis C. 1988.
*Descriptors:* *Feedback; *Leadership Styles; *Managerial Occupations; *Supervisory Methods; *Teamwork; Adults; Rating Scales; Self Evaluation (Individuals)
*Identifiers:* WLQ
*Availability:* Talico, Inc., 2320 S. Third St., Ste. 5, Jacksonville Beach, FL 32250.
*Notes:* For instruments in the work group improvement and team development series, see 16411 through 16414. Time, 20 approx. Items, 48.

Designed for work group leaders' personal assessment and for obtaining feedback from subordinates, peers, and supervisors. Measures 8 sets of practices that indicate superior work group leaders. The 8 practices are action focus, performance focus, improvement focus, contact focus, relationship focus, development focus, team focus, and character focus. Has face validity. Is self-administered and may be self-scored or scored by the trainer. Can be used for manager and supervisor assessment, career planning and development, or manager and supervisor training.

**16416**
**WorkStyle Preference Inventory.** McFletcher Corp., Scottsdale, AZ 1984.
*Descriptors:* *Attitude Measures; *Employee Attitudes; *Work Attitudes; Adults; Rating Scales; Self Evaluation (Individuals)
*Identifiers:* WSPI
*Availability:* McFletcher Corp., 8075 E. Morgan Trail, Ste. 1, Scottsdale, AZ 85258.
*Notes:* Items, 18.

The Work Style Preference Inventory (WSPI) is based on a comparison of actual work activities and the way in which workers prefer to carry out any work-related activities. The WSPI has 3 purposes. It helps the worker to understand and identify his or her needs and preferences in regard to organizing and taking part in work experiences. It helps the organization and the worker to learn what activities the job actually requires. It also "compares the congruency" of the workers preference and job requirements. Roles include: (1) worker—performs specific tasks; (2) supervisor—coordinates others' activities; (3) manager—organizes, directs, plans, and controls the operation.

**16417**
**Listening Practices Feedback Report.** Brandt Management Group, Richmond, VA 1982.
*Descriptors:* *Feedback; *Listening Habits; *Listening Skills; *Work Environment; Adults; Self Evaluation (Individuals)
*Identifiers:* LPFR
*Availability:* Brandt Management Group, 8423 Freestone Ave., P.O. Box 29384, Richmond, VA 23229.
*Notes:* Items, 28.

This instrument is designed to assist people in understanding how they are perceived as listening and responding to others in the day-to-day business environment. It is intended to help with work relationships. This report is organized into 2 parts. Part 1 gives a comparison of self-perception to perception of others. It also indicates an overall listening practice quotient. Part 2 consists of listening practices reported in descending order of importance and is grouped in 3 categories—major, intermediate, and minor. This tool does not measure listening ability or comprehension. It is not a performance evaluation or a personality profile. It indicates how an individual is perceived as a listener.

16419
**Clerical Abilities Battery.** Psychological Corp., San Antonio, TX
*Descriptors:* *Clerical Workers; *Occupational Tests; *Personnel Selection; *Promotion (Occupational); Adults; Filing; Mathematical Applications; Proofreading; Timed Tests
*Identifiers:* CAB
*Availability:* Psychological Corp., 555 Academic Ct., San Antonio, TX 78204.
*Notes:* Time, 70. Items, 384.

The Clerical Abilities Battery (CAB) consists of 7 short tests to be used in hiring and promoting clerical personnel. Each test measures a clerical task normally found in the workplace. The full battery includes: (1) filing test; (2) comparing information test; (3) copying information test; (4) using tables test; (5) proofreading test; (6) addition and subtraction test; and (7) reasoning with numbers test. The test directions and test items should not be difficult for anyone who reads at or above the sixth grade level.

16422
**Exploring Career Options.** National Computer Systems, Minneapolis, MN 1987.
*Descriptors:* *Interest Inventories; *Vocational Interests; Adolescents; Adults; Career Choice; Older Adults; Self Evaluation (Individuals)
*Identifiers:* ECO
*Availability:* National Computer Systems, Professional Assessment Services, P.O. Box 1416, Minneapolis, MN 55440.
*Notes:* Items, 632.

This report will help to identify work values, interests, and current skills and can be used to match particular characteristics to a variety of career options. This instrument is categorized into five parts: Part 1 contains 132 self-descriptive adjectives; Part 2 contains 91 items dealing with work attitudes and values; Part 3 contains 220 items showing interests in activities and school subjects; Part 4 contains 104 items concerning likes and dislikes in various occupations; Part 5 contains 51 vocabulary items and 30 number problems to be solved. This word and number section is designed to help one understand how one's skills with words and numbers compare and relate to those of other persons of various ages and occupations. There is also a section containing 6 items on one's self and background.

16425
**Climate Impact Profile System.** Performax Systems International, Inc., Minneapolis, MN 1986.
*Descriptors:* *Leadership Styles; *Managerial Occupations; *Work Environment; *Work Ethic; Adults; Management Development; Performance Factors; Questionnaires; Self Evaluation (Individuals)
*Availability:* Carlson Learning Co., P.O. Box 59159, 12805 State Hwy. 55, Minneapolis, MN 55451.
*Notes:* Items, 40.

Self-administered instrument that allows respondents to gather, process, and interpret information about how people attempt to influence others in an identified environment or situation. Allows subjects to develop more self-understanding and to understand others and their organizations in terms of the influencing styles and methods they use. Provides the user with a model for dealing with all aspects of personal and organizational performance. Is effective in such areas as management development, executive consulting, task analysis, coaching and counseling, team building, conflict management and resolution, strategic planning, organizational development, and leadership effectiveness. Is a global social or work climate analysis used to develop understanding of personal and organizational modes of impacting.

16428
**Activity Perception System, Revised.** Geier, John G. 1987.
*Descriptors:* *Activities; *Expectation; *Role Perception; *Social Cognition; Adults; Peer Relationship; Rating Scales; Self Evaluation (Individuals); Work Environment
*Availability:* Carlson Learning Co., Carlson Parkway, P.O. Box 59159, Minneapolis, MN 55459-8247.
*Notes:* See also the Personal Profile System (16427). Items, 32.

This instrument is designed for opening the lines of communication. Created for people who work together or share common activities. This tool allows people to identify expectations, such as role, task, or project expectations, and provides a specific organized interpretation of behaviors that define how one views one's approach to accomplishing identified expectations or objectives. It can be applied to social or work settings, and provides descriptions of the similarities and differences in human perception in a nonthreatening manner. It is recommended that this assessment tool be used in conjunction with the Personal Profile System.

16453
**Pro Care.** Professional Training Systems, Atlanta, GA 1989.
*Descriptors:* *Certification; *Health Occupations; *Nurses Aides; *Nursing; *Nursing Education; *Occupational Tests; Adults; Competency Based Education; Interactive Video; Nursing Homes; Situational Tests; State Programs; Work Sample Tests
*Availability:* Program Director, Center for Occupational and Professional Assessment, Educational Testing Service, Princeton, NJ 08541.
*Notes:* See also Nurse Aide (Assistant) Program (16495).

This health care training and assessment program is designed for use with nurse assistants working in nursing homes and long-term care facilities. The nurse aide's skill is evaluated via interactive videodisc showing scenes involving patient care followed by questions about proper procedures. Scores are computed electronically. When used for certification, scores are sent to individual participating states. The states maintain files on the performance of nurse assistants. A paper and pencil test is also available. See Nurse Aide (Assistant) Program (16495).

16457
**Management Skills Profile/MSP.** Personnel Decisions, Minneapolis, MN 1989.
*Descriptors:* *Administrators; *Feedback; *Job Performance; *Management Development; *Profiles; *Supervisory Methods; Adults; Questionnaires; Rating Scales; Staff Development
*Identifiers:* MSP
*Availability:* Personnel Decisions, Inc., 2000 Plaza VII Tower, 45 S. Seventh St., Minneapolis, MN 55402.
*Notes:* Time, 30. Items, 140.

This 140-item questionnaire gathers information about an individual's managerial performance of specific job-related skills, e.g., human relations, motivating, coaching, and developing, as perceived by the manager's co-workers, as well as the manager's. The developmental feedback report created from this information forms the basis for the individual development plan created by the manager and geared for self-improvement on the job.

16474
**Comprehensive Nursing Achievement for Practical Nursing Students, Form 3135.** NLN Test Service, New York, NY
*Descriptors:* *Licensing Examinations (Professions); *Nursing Education; *Practical Nursing; Adults; Nurses
*Identifiers:* National Council Licensure Examination; National League of Nursing; NCLEX(PN); Nursing Process
*Availability:* NLN Test Service, 10 Columbus Circle, New York, NY 10019.
*Notes:* Time, 180 approx. Items, 166.

This prelicensure readiness test assists students in practical nursing programs to prepare for the National Council Licensure Examination (NCLEX-PN). It is designed to be administered at the end of the student's formal education program to assess readiness for the practical nurse licensure examination and to provide practice in taking a nationally standardized test of nursing knowledge. The broad areas of clinical content and nursing process are measured. More specific questions on the exam pertain to representative case situations and conditions commonly encountered by the beginning health care practitioner. These situations include care of adult and elderly patients, as well as nursing care during childbearing and nursing care of children.

16475
**Fundamentals for Practical Nursing Students, Form 4616.** NLN Test Service, New York, NY
*Descriptors:* *Achievement Tests; *Anatomy; *Nursing Education; *Nutrition; *Physiology; *Practical Nursing; Adults
*Identifiers:* National League of Nursing; Nursing Practice; Nursing Process
*Availability:* NLN Test Service, 10 Columbus Circle, New York, NY 10019.
*Notes:* Time, 90 approx. Items, 94.

This test focuses on measuring the knowledge of practical nursing students in the areas of anatomy and physiology, normal nutrition, and nursing practice. It is designed to be administered early in the student's program, after completion of basic learning experiences. The following areas are assessed: identifying basic bodily structures and functions, selecting appropriate measures for giving care to patients, and identifying both nutritional requirements and elements of foods. Items dealing with nursing practice include: principles of therapeutic communication, the nursing process, vital signs, body mechanics, and aseptic technique.

16476
**Maternity Nursing for Practical Nursing Students, Form 1182.** NLN Test Service, New York, NY
*Descriptors:* *Achievement Tests; *Birth; *Neonates; *Nursing Education; *Practical Nursing; *Pregnancy; Adults; Nutrition
*Identifiers:* *Maternity Nursing; National Nursing League
*Availability:* NLN Test Service, 10 Columbus Circle, New York, NY 10019.
*Notes:* Time, 120 approx. Items, 113.

This test measures the achievement of objectives related to maternal nursing. It is administered to practical nursing students after completion of a course in nursing care during the childbearing cycle. The areas measured are: antepartum, intrapartum and postpartum, and neonate. Special questions focus on nursing process related to medications and their application to care during pregnancy, delivery, postpartum and newborn care. Patient situations presenting both normal and unexpected findings are presented. Items testing nutrition and therapeutic communication are integrated throughout the test.

16477
**Medical-Surgical Nursing for Practical Nursing Students, Form 4218.** NLN Test Service, New York, NY
*Descriptors:* *Achievement Tests; *Nursing Education; *Practical Nursing; *Surgery; Adults
*Identifiers:* Medical Nursing; National Nursing League; Nursing Process; Surgical Nursing
*Availability:* NLN Test Service, 10 Columbus Circle, New York, NY 10019.
*Notes:* Time, 120 approx. Items, 115.

This test, designed to be administered to practical nursing students after completion of a course on the care of adults with medical or surgical conditions, measures knowledge and facts related to the care of these patients. The questions relate to patient situations a practical nurse might encounter when caring for adult clients with medical/surgical conditions at various stages of the adult life cycle. Integrated throughout the test are questions related to pharmacology, communication, patient teaching, and diet therapy.

**16478**
**Mental Health Concepts for Practical Nursing Students, Form 4415.** NLN Test Service, New York, NY
*Descriptors:* *Achievement Tests; *Mental Health; *Nursing Education; *Practical Nursing; *Psychological Patterns; *Stress Variables; *Well Being; Adults; Nurses; Stress Management
*Identifiers:* National Nursing League; Nursing Process
*Availability:* NLN Test Service, 10 Columbus Circle, New York, NY 10019.
*Notes:* Time, 120 approx. Items, 102.

This test measures the practical nursing student's understanding of basic behaviors/concepts and nursing interventions based on the principles of mental health. The questions test nursing knowledge of behavior manifestations of well-being or stress characteristic throughout the life cycle. The test further assesses students' abilities to select appropriate nursing goals and interventions for clients and their families based on recognizing the rationale for nursing interventions and client behaviors evoked by illness and stress.

**16479**
**Nursing Mobility Profile I, Forms 5213, 5223.** NLN Test Service, New York, NY
*Descriptors:* *Achievement Tests; *Advanced Placement; *Birth; *Licensing Examinations (Professions); *Neonates; *Nurses; *Nursing Education; *Practical Nursing; *Pregnancy; Adults; Profiles
*Identifiers:* *Licensed Practical Nurse (LPN); *Licensed Visiting Nurse (LVN); Maternity Nursing; National Nursing League; National Validation Exam for Educational Mobility; Nursing Process; Pediatric Nursing
*Availability:* NLN Test Service, 10 Columbus Circle, New York, NY 10019.
*Notes:* Time, 420. Items, 402.

This test battery, consisting of forms 5213 and 5223, evaluates the previous learning and experience of Licensed Practical Nurses (LPNs)/Licensed Visiting Nurses (LVNs) in 3 areas. These areas are: nursing foundations, nursing care during childbearing, and the nursing care of the child. These content areas are printed in 2 books. The results assist schools in granting advanced placement and/or credit in programs preparing students for RN licensure. Questions in Book One focus on assessing beginning skills in meeting the physiological and psychosocial needs of clients with stable conditions. The 2 sections in Book Two focus on nursing care during antepartal, postpartal, and neonatal periods, as well as nursing care of hospitalized children of all ages at various stages on the wellness continuum.

**16480**
**Nursing of Children for Practical Nursing Students, Form 4113.** NLN Test Service, New York, NY
*Descriptors:* *Achievement Tests; *Nursing Education; *Practical Nursing; Adults; Nurses
*Identifiers:* National League of Nurses; Nursing Process; *Pediatric Nursing
*Availability:* NLN Test Service, 10 Columbus Circle, New York, NY 10019.
*Notes:* Time, 120 approx. Items, 116.

This test measures the practical nursing student's knowledge of pediatric nursing. Areas measured include knowledge of growth and development of children and application of nursing interventions. Specifically this tool measures skills associated with prevention based on age-related needs, the care of sick children, medications, therapeutic communication, nutrition, and the teaching and emotional support of family members.

**16481**
**Pharmacology for Practical Nurses, Form 1782.** NLN Test Service, New York, NY
*Descriptors:* *Achievement Tests; *Nursing Education; *Pharmacology; *Practical Nursing; Adults; Drug Therapy
*Identifiers:* National Nursing League
*Availability:* NLN Test Service, 10 Columbus Circle, New York, NY 10019.
*Notes:* Time, 90 approx. Items, 99.

This test measures practical nursing students' knowledge of pharmacology. It includes questions dealing with drug administration and calculations, as well as the effects and therapeutics of commonly used drugs. Interpretation of medical orders and observation techniques to detect side effects or adverse reactions from these drugs is also tested. A correction-for-guessing formula is used in scoring.

**16508**
**The MbM Questionnaire, Second Edition.** Sashkin, Marshall 1990.
*Descriptors:* *Administrators; *Motivation; *Work Environment; Adults; Safety; Security (Psychology); Social Cognition; Interpersonal Relationship; Self Esteem; Self Actualization
*Availability:* Organization Design and Development, Inc., 2002 Renaissance Blvd., Ste. 100, King of Prussia, PA 19406-2746.

This is a 20-item questionnaire to measure one's internal motivations, in terms of the concept of human motivation as developed by Abraham Maslow. It is designed to help managers make effective use of the motivation that everyone has. By using this tool, managers can learn what employees want and what motivates them in return for effective job performance. The results can be used to better understand one's own needs and motivators. There are no correct answers. Each of the 4 scales of the questionnaire, including safety and security (SS), social and belongingness (SB), self-esteem (SE), and self-actualization (SA), has a minimum of 5 points and a maximum of 25 points. (TJS)

**16509**
**Leadership Dynamics Inventory.** Talico, Inc., Jacksonville Beach, FL 1988.
*Descriptors:* *Administrators; *Leadership Qualities; *Leadership Styles; *Management Development; Adults; Forced Choice Technique; Managerial Occupations; Supervisors
*Identifiers:* LDI
*Availability:* Talico, Inc., 2320 S. Third St., Ste. 5, Jacksonville Beach, FL 32250.
*Notes:* Time, 20 approx. Items, 15.

Instrument used to determine individuals' leadership effectiveness by assessing their leadership strategies. Best results are obtained when instrument is administered to the individuals, their supervisors, and their subordinates and peers. Items are arranged in pairs, and respondents indicate which statement of the pair best describes the leadership style of the person being assessed. Focuses on 6 leadership strategies: coercive, reward, legitimate, referent, expert, and rational. May be used to assist in career and professional development, management training needs analysis, and management training.

**16517**
**Participative Management Inventory.** Talico, Inc., Jacksonville Beach, FL 1988.
*Descriptors:* *Administrators; *Managerial Occupations; *Participative Decision Making; *Supervisors; Adults; Forced Choice Technique; Likert Scales; Management Development; Rating Scales
*Identifiers:* PMI
*Availability:* Talico, Inc., 2320 S. Third St., Ste. 5, Jacksonville Beach, FL 32250.
*Notes:* Time, 20 approx. Items, 35.

Designed to measure the amount of participative management that managers or supervisors engage in as both they and their subordinates perceive it. Instrument consists of 2 sections: participative behaviors and practice, which makes use of a 5-point Likert-type scale to rate the extent to which managers engage in participative management and participative climate control, which makes use of paired statements to rate participative management practices. May be used for management and supervisory training, career and professional development, counseling and coaching, and management assessment.

**16518**
**Superior Leadership Skills Inventory.** Kinlaw, Dennis C.; Talico, Inc., Jacksonville Beach, FL 1988.
*Descriptors:* *Leadership; *Leadership Qualities; *Management Development; *Skills; Adults; Career Planning; Likert Scales; Rating Scales; Self Evaluation (Individuals)
*Identifiers:* SLSI
*Availability:* Talico, Inc., 2320 S. Third St., Ste. 5, Jacksonville Beach, FL 32250.
*Notes:* Time, 15 approx. Items, 30.

Instrument for use by individuals to assess their leadership skills. Items focus on skills usually associated with superior leaders. Individuals indicate the extent to which each skill applies to them. Divided into 6 sections: establishing vision; stimulating people to gain new competencies; helping people overcome obstacles; helping people overcome failure; leading by example; and including others in their success. Results may be used to help improve leadership skills. May also be useful for career planning and training. May be used by individuals to rate their supervisors and/or subordinates.

**16522**
**Performance Based Teacher Evaluation.** Missouri Department of Elementary and Secondary Education, Jefferson City, MO 1984.
*Descriptors:* *Classroom Techniques; *Teacher Effectiveness; *Teacher Evaluation; *Teacher Improvement; *Teaching Skills; Adults; Classroom Observation Techniques; Educational Assessment; Educational Improvement; Formative Evaluation; Interpersonal Relationship; Summative Evaluation; Teacher Responsibility
*Availability:* Missouri Dept. of Elementary and Secondary Education, P.O. Box 480, Jefferson City, MO 65102.
*Notes:* For related performance based evaluation instruments, see 16523 through 16524. Items, 19.

The purpose of this evaluation is to facilitate and improve classroom instruction and enhance student learning. This tool is designed to identify teacher's strengths and weaknesses and provide direction for maintaining and improving teacher skills through professional development activities. It should include a formative evaluation phase, both scheduled and unscheduled classroom observations that are designed to help teachers improve their performance; and a summative phase, which is a composite of information obtained through the formative observation.

**16523**
**Performance Based Evaluation of School Superintendents.** Missouri Department of Elementary and Secondary Education, Jefferson City, MO 1986.
*Descriptors:* *Administrator Effectiveness; *Administrator Evaluation; *Leadership Qualities; *Observation; *Superintendents; Adults; Formative Evaluation; Interprofessional Relationship; Leadership Responsibility; School Administration; Summative Evaluation
*Identifiers:* Missouri Legislation 1985 (Section 168 410); The Excellence in Education Act of 1985
*Availability:* Missouri Dept. of Elementary and Secondary Education, P.O. Box 480, Jefferson City, MO 65102.
*Notes:* For related performance based evaluation instruments, see 16522 and 16524. Items, 24.

The primary purpose of this tool is to facilitate and improve the educational process through administrative leadership. The key elements in the development of performance-based evaluation for superintendents are identified as job-related expectations; documentation of skills; feedback regarding skills, opportunity for improvement, goals for district, and decision making. An outline of the recommended procedure is provided, which entails a 3-part process for evaluation. They include preparatory, formative, and summative phases. Key terms are provided.

**16524**
**Performance Based Principal Evaluation in Missouri Schools.** Missouri Department of Elementary and Secondary Education, Jefferson City, MO 1987.

*Descriptors:* *Administrator Effectiveness; *Administrator Evaluation; *Principals; Adults; Educational Assessment; Educational Improvement; Formative Evaluation; Instructional Leadership; Interpersonal Relationship; Leadership Responsibility; Observation; School Administration; Summative Evaluation; Teacher Administrator Relationship
*Availability:* Missouri Dept. of Elementary and Secondary Education, P.O. Box 480, Jefferson City, MO 65102.
*Notes:* For related performance based evaluation instruments, see 16522 through 16523. Items, 23.

The primary purpose of this evaluation is to facilitate and improve instruction through administrative leadership. It involves regular observation and supervision of school principals. Strengths and weaknesses are identified and job targets are defined. Formative and summative phases are included as a guide to assist local school personnel and provide a basis for administrative decision making.

**16525**
**Self-Assessment Exam: Body Cavity Fluids.** American Society of Clinical Pathologists, Chicago, IL 1988.
*Descriptors:* *Allied Health Occupations; *Knowledge Level; *Self Evaluation (Individuals); Adults; Cytology; Health Personnel; Pathology
*Availability:* American Society of Clinical Pathologists, P.O. Box 12075, Chicago, IL 60612-0075.
*Notes:* Items, 48.

Self-assessment exam that helps individuals measure their strengths and potential weaknesses in specific laboratory specialties. Self-assessment programs are available to meet the needs of all clinical laboratory personnel - pathologists, residents, clinical scientists, and technologists. There are 48 35-mm slide-related questions used to assess knowledge of all types of body fluids, including spinal, pleural, and cerebrospinal fluid. Helps to improve the skills of specimen analysis and patient diagnosis.

**16526**
**Administrative Management-by-Objectives Appraisal System.** McGrail, Janet; And Others 1987.
*Descriptors:* *Administrative Policy; *Administrator Effectiveness; *Administrator Evaluation; *Administrators; *Job Performance; *School Administration; Administrator Responsibility; Administrator Role; Adults; Management by Objectives; Questionnaires; Self Evaluation (Individuals)
*Identifiers:* AMOAS
*Availability:* I.E. Banreb Associates, 541 Woodview Dr., Longwood, FL 32779.

Designed to evaluate school administrators on the basis of a set of objectives established jointly with the administrator's immediate supervisor and on daily job performance. Each objective is weighted, and each category of the position description, in which everyday job performance is measured, carries a specific rating. The combined rating from both areas determines the administrator's salary increases for the year. Specific job descriptions and sets of objectives must be developed locally. The system requires a minimum of 2 performance reviews a year and a final evaluation.

**16528**
**Skillscope for Managers.** Kaplan, Robert E.
*Descriptors:* *Job Skills; *Managerial Occupations; Adults; Check Lists; Self Evaluation (Individuals); Skill Analysis
*Availability:* Center for Creative Leadership, One Leadership Pl., P.O. Box 26300, Greensboro, NC 27438-6300.
*Notes:* Formerly titled Skills Assessment Form. Items, 98.

Skillscope is an instrument for assessing one's own managerial weaknesses and strengths. It is a checklist of 98 managerial skills broken down into 15 clusters. Managers get feedback on how they rate themselves in comparison to how their workers rate them. It can be used in manager development programs, assessment for development, and organizational needs analysis.

**16539**
**Situational Interview.** Life Insurance Marketing and Research Association, Inc., Hartford, CT 1983.
*Descriptors:* *Employment Interviews; *Insurance Occupations; *Job Applicants; *Sales Occupations; *Situational Tests; Adults; Rating Scales
*Availability:* Life Insurance Marketing and Research Association, Inc., P.O. Box 208, Hartford, CT 06141-0208.
*Notes:* Items, 9.

Provides a look at the candidate's reactions to various situations that could be encountered in insurance sales. Candidate's response to each situation is rated. There is not a prescribed response to each situation. Candidate's abilities are evaluated by these job-related responses.

**16558**
**Teamness Index.** Hall, Jay 1988.
*Descriptors:* *Teamwork; *Work Environment; Adults; Measures (Individuals); Rating Scales
*Availability:* Pfeiffer and Co., formerly University Associates, 8517 Production Ave., San Diego, CA 92121-2280.
*Notes:* Items, 24.

A survey about the conditions of work and the array of feelings that might exist among 2 or more people as they work together. Designed to be filled out by each group member. Items survey the characteristics of these team work relationships. Each member of the team, using a 9-point scale states how true each statement is for him- or herself.

**16559**
**Management of Motives Index.** Hall, Jay 1986.
*Descriptors:* *Incentives; *Managerial Occupations; *Motivation Techniques; Adults; Questionnaires; Self Evaluation (Individuals)
*Availability:* Pfeiffer and Co., formerly University Associates, 8517 Production Ave., San Diego, CA 92121-2280.
*Notes:* Items, 60.

The purpose of this instrument is to make a person's motivational assumptions and theories more explicit. It provides information about personal practices, and allows one to speculate systematically and meaningfully about the consequences of these acts. This tool assesses the strengths of 5 different need systems - self actualization, ego-status, belonging, safety, and basic - in terms of their relative importance to self and the effect they have on the work situation.

**16560**
**Management Practices Update.** University Associates, San Diego, CA 1987.
*Descriptors:* *Interpersonal Relationship; *Managerial Occupations; *Self Evaluation (Individuals); *Supervisory Methods; Adults; Surveys
*Identifiers:* MPU
*Availability:* Pfeiffer and Co., formerly University Associates, 8517 Production Ave., San Diego, CA 92121-2280.
*Notes:* Items, 24.

Designed to provide information about an individual's managerial behavior in 3 skill areas. The area of interpersonal relationships measures communication and sharing of information when dealing with subordinates or those whose activities are directed by the individual manager. The motivation management of organizational members area concerns productivity, job satisfaction and quality of work life. Personal management style, the third area, deals with an analysis of management, planning and goal setting, implementation, and performance evaluation. There are no wrong or right answers to this survey.

**16561**
**Participative Management Survey.** Hall, Jay 1988.
*Descriptors:* *Administrators; *Behavior Rating Scales; *Employer Employee Relationship; *Participative Decision Making; Adults; Surveys
*Identifiers:* PMS
*Availability:* Pfeiffer and Co., formerly University Associates, 8517 Production Ave., San Diego, CA 92121-2280.
*Notes:* Items, 50.

A survey for managers to determine how often they provide opportunities for the people that they supervise to experience personal involvement and influence at work. The test items are expressed in behavioral terms as actual practices which the manager may or may not use. Response to each item shows actual frequency of use by using a rating scale.

**16562**
**Employee Involvement Survey.** Hall, Jay 1988.
*Descriptors:* *Employer Employee Relationship; *Participative Decision Making; Adults; Rating Scales
*Identifiers:* EIS
*Availability:* Pfeiffer and Co., formerly University Associates, 8517 Production Ave., San Diego, CA 92121-2280.
*Notes:* Items, 50.

Two-part survey about how often a person is provided opportunities by management for personal involvement and influence at work and how often a person would like to have such opportunities provided. Staff members can rate, on a 9-point scale, their manager's actual practices as well as how frequently they would desire such practices.

**16563**
**Team Process Diagnostic, Revised.** Hall, Jay 1989.
*Descriptors:* *Diagnostic Tests; *Formative Evaluation; *Teamwork; Adults; Self Evaluation (Groups)
*Availability:* Pfeiffer and Co., formerly University Associates, 8517 Production Ave., San Diego, CA 92121-2280.
*Notes:* Items, 32.

A behavior-based assessment of members' contributions to team functioning. Deigned to break down barriers to team effectiveness.

**16564**
**Social Styles Analysis/Other.** Wilson Learning Corp., Eden Prairie, MN 1989.
*Descriptors:* *Behavior Patterns; *Interpersonal Relationship; *Peer Evaluation; *Work Environment; Adults; Assertiveness; Computer Assisted Testing; Interpersonal Competence; Occupational Tests; Personality Traits; Rating Scales; Social Behavior
*Availability:* Pfeiffer and Co., formerly University Associates, 8517 Production Ave., San Diego, CA 92121-2280.
*Notes:* See also Social Styles Analysis/Self (16565). Time, 10. Items, 31.

This analysis of interpersonal behavior in work relationships assists people to recognize, appreciate, and accommodate individual differences by adapting their own style to that of others. Scoring identifies the driven, expressive, amiable or analytical type. Identifies assertiveness and responsiveness as "tell" or "ask" assertive and "control" or "emote" responsive. An additional instrument performs a self-analysis. Others rate the person on 30 characteristics via a 7-point high/low scale for each characteristic. A computer-administered version is available in addition to a paper and pencil version. May also be rated by friends or family members.

**16565**
**Social Styles Analysis/Self.** Wilson Learning Corp., Eden Prairie, MN 1989.

*Descriptors:* *Behavior Patterns; *Interpersonal Relationship; *Self Evaluation (Individuals); *Work Environment; Adults; Assertiveness; Computer Assisted Testing; Interpersonal Competence; Occupational Tests; Personality Traits; Rating Scales; Social Behavior
*Availability:* Pfeiffer and Co., formerly University Associates, 8517 Production Ave., San Diego, CA 92121-2280.
*Notes:* See also Social Styles Analysis/Other (16564). Time, 10. Items, 31.

This analysis of interpersonal behavior in work relationships assists people to recognize, appreciate, and accommodate individual differences by adapting their own style to that of others. Subjects rate a person of their choosing on 30 characteristics via a 7-point high-low scale for each. Subjects rate themself as "less" or "more" so. Scoring identifies subject as driven, expressive, amiable, or analytical with "tell" or "ask" assertiveness and "control" or "emote" responsiveness. An additional instrument is a peer rating scale. A computer-administered version is available in addition to a paper and pencil version.

**16567**
**Firefighter Entry Level Examinations: Alpha Examination.** Wollack and Associates, Greenwood, CA 1989.
*Descriptors:* *Fire Fighters; *Occupational Tests; *Personnel Selection; Adults; Mathematics; Mechanical Skills; Reading Comprehension; Tables (Data)
*Availability:* Wollack and Associates, 2550 Hoboken Creek Rd., P.O. Box 72, Greenwood, CA 95635.
*Notes:* Time, 120. Items, 100.

This pre-employment test for entry-level firefighter applicants is based on a comprehensive study guide and workbook that can be used as a training tool for applicants who may need to improve their job-related basic skills. Useful with educationally disadvantaged candidates. All questions are multiple choice.

**16603**
**Normative Needs Inventory, N2.** Smith, August William 1985.
*Descriptors:* *Managerial Occupations; *Motivation; *Needs; *Occupational Tests; *Supervisors; *Supervisory Methods; Achievement Need; Administrators; Adults; Affiliation Need; Psychological Needs; Safety; Security (Psychology)
*Availability:* Development Dynamics, P.O. Box 4747, Bryan, TX 77805.

This inventory is designed to measure how individuals relate to needs and motivation at work. An individual's emphasis on particular needs and motives is said to explain behaviors and performance as a manager and leader and to have impact on his or her effectiveness. The respondent divides 5 points between 2 possible answer choices according to how important each point is to him or her. Scores are plotted on a graph of needs, motives, and trade-offs related to management styles.

**16605**
**QUEST.** Life Insurance Marketing and Research Association, Inc., Hartford, CT 1987.
*Descriptors:* *Computer Assisted Testing; *Insurance Occupations; *Personnel Selection; Adults; French; Job Satisfaction; Occupational Tests; Predictive Measurement; Sales Occupations; Work Attitudes
*Identifiers:* Career Profile
*Availability:* Life Insurance Marketing and Research Association, Inc., P.O. Box 208, Hartford, CT 06141-0208.
*Notes:* Time, 150 approx.

This computer-administered form of the Career Profile (12114) is designed to determine which of a series of job candidates has the potential for success as an insurance agent. Two separate profiles are available for individuals who have experience in insurance, and for those who have none. Covers attitudes toward present job, skills and abilities, goals, opinions, and career expectations for new agents. Covers satisfaction with sales career, clients, sales activity, income, and managerial background for current agents. Computerized reports predict production level (top 25%), probability of surviving 1 year on the job, and inconsistent test responses. Available in English and French.

**16613**
**MEAS Police Officer Examination.** Merit Employment Assessment, Flossmoor, IL 1981.
*Descriptors:* *Aptitude Tests; *Occupational Tests; *Personnel Selection; *Police; Adults; Arithmetic; Knowledge Level; Mathematics; Memory; Problem Solving; Verbal Ability; Visual Perception
*Identifiers:* Deductive Reasoning; Inductive Reasoning
*Availability:* Merit Employment Assessment Services, Inc., 2630 Flossmoor Rd., Ste. 202, Flossmoor, IL 60422.
*Notes:* Time, 150. Items, 94.

The MEAS Policy Officer Examination is based on a job analysis of 266 police agencies and 2,610 incumbent police officers. It measures knowledge, skills, and abilities required of an entry-level police officer, including verbal ability, numerical ability, deductive reasoning, inductive reasoning, information appraisal, problem sensitivity, problem solving, perceptual skills, rote memory, concept memory. Validation studies have been performed. May be handscored locally or computer-scored by publisher.

**16614**
**MEAS Firefighter Examination.** Merit Employment Assessment, Flossmoor, IL 1981.
*Descriptors:* *Aptitude Tests; *Fire Fighters; *Occupational Tests; *Personnel Selection; Adults; Arithmetic; Knowledge Level; Mechanical Skills; Memory; Reading; Spatial Ability
*Availability:* Merit Employment Assessment Services, Inc., 2630 Flossmoor Rd., Ste. 202, Flossmoor, IL 60422.
*Notes:* Time, 150. Items, 90.

This examination is based on a job analysis of the firefighter position. It measures knowledge, skills, and abilities needed to perform the tasks identified in the analysis. May be handscored locally or computerized scoring can be provided. Reading level for the actual test is grade 7. A study guide is available and training materials can be purchased. These are designed to assist with affirmative action by giving practice with test-taking skills.

**16617**
**Law Enforcement Candidate Record.** Richardson, Bellows, Henry and Co., Inc., Washington, DC 1989.
*Descriptors:* *Aptitude Tests; *Occupational Tests; *Personnel Selection; *Police; Adults; Arithmetic; Biographical Inventories; Memory; Spatial Ability; Verbal Ability; Visual Discrimination
*Identifiers:* Clerical Checking
*Availability:* Richardson, Bellows, Henry and Co., Inc., 1140 Connecticut Ave., N.W., Ste. 610, Washington, DC 20036.
*Notes:* Time, 180. Items, 589.

This selection procedure for entry-level law enforcement personnel was designed to maximize job relatedness and minimize score differences for female and minority subgroups. Uses high school reading level. Sexually biased wording has been removed. Said to be unaffected by user organizaton's location, size and type. Based on a job analysis including 90 work-task and 46 ability-behavior elements. The autobiographical questionnaire covers academic history/orientation, physical health/activity, work history/orientation, self-esteem, social orientation/skills, and application history and influences. This test reduces the typical full standard deviation difference between some subgroups' scores on aptitude/cognitive tests by 38.5 percent.

**16623**
**SBS Teacher Observation Code.** Walker, Hill M.; And Others
*Descriptors:* *Instruction; *Teacher Behavior; *Teacher Effectiveness; *Teaching Methods; Adults; Elementary Secondary Education; Teachers
*Identifiers:* SBS
*Availability:* CHD Publications, Center on Human Development, University of Oregon, Eugene, OR 97403.

A coding system designed to provide a comprehensive assessment of the teacher's instructional and management behavior that is verbalized during the process of teaching. The 3 major sections used for assessing are structure, which describes the teacher's organizational and monitoring behaviors; instructional, used to record the teacher's verbal behavior in the classroom; and management, used to record the teacher's attention and verbal behavior when focused on student social behavior, discipline and/or classroom control. This tool should be used only during academic periods and will accommodate both group and individual instructional procedures.

**16626**
**Principals in Community Education Programs.** Drake, Jackson M.; Miller, Brian P. 1982.
*Descriptors:* *Community Education; *Community Leaders; *Leadership; *Principals; Adults; Community Coordination; Elementary Secondary Education; Leadership Responsibility
*Availability:* *NASSP Bulletin,* v66 p18-26, Oct 1982.
*Notes:* Items, 25.

Checklist of 25 competency statements is used to describe 8 task areas essential for the minimal functions of the principal in relationship to education in the community. Under each task area the minimal competencies needed are listed. These statements help determine what competencies the principal must fill for community education to function.

**16627**
**Leadership Functions and Instructional Effectiveness.** Duke, Daniel L. 1982.
*Descriptors:* *Instructional Effectiveness; *Instructional Leadership; *Leadership Responsibility; *Principals; Adults; Elementary Secondary Education
*Availability:* *NASSP Bulletin,* v66 p1-12, Oct 1982.
*Notes:* Items, 42.

Assesses the functions of instructional leadership. Checklist presents specific things to look for to determine whether the leader is adequately fulfilling a function.

**16628**
**Taking Your Leadership Temperature.** Ernest, Bill 1982.
*Descriptors:* *Leadership Styles; *Principals; Adults; Elementary Secondary Education
*Availability:* *NASSP Bulletin,* v66 p13-17, Oct 1982.
*Notes:* Items, 4.

Assesses a principal's leadership style using the managerial grid model. By answering the questions, a principal describes his or her approach to planning, operations, wrap-up, and overall leadership philosophy. Responses are coded for each of the managerial styles.

**16638**
**Work Stress Inventory.** Barone, David F. 1982.
*Descriptors:* *Risk; *Stress Variables; *Work Environment; Adults; Clerical Workers; Employer Employee Relationship; Females; Fire Fighters; Interpersonal Relationship; Likert Scales; Males; Nurses; Occupational Tests; Police; Professional Occupations; Role Conflict; Teachers
*Identifiers:* TIM(P)
*Availability:* Tests in Microfiche, Test Collection, Educational Testing Service, Princeton, NJ 08541.
*Notes:* Items, 40.

This scale is a general measure of work stress. Norms are included for 12 white collar occupations and also for males and females as groups. Stress is defined as "a misfit between environmental demands and individual capabilities." Items cover job stressors of work overload and underload, role conflict, role ambiguity, nonparticipation and problems with supervisors and others. Uses 5-point Likert-type scales in a paper-and-pencil format for group or individual administration.

**16670**
**Leader Adaptability and Style Inventory.** Hersey, Paul; Blanchard, Kenneth H. 1981.
*Descriptors:* *Leadership; *Leadership Styles; *Questionnaires; Adults
*Identifiers:* LASI
*Availability:* *Training and Development Journal,* p34-54, Jun 1981.
*Notes:* Items, 12.

Questionnaire assesses a person's leadership in many situations (job, volunteer organizations, parenting). Leadership behavior is measured on a 3-dimensional grid: style (task or people orientation); style range (how many styles a person uses); and style adaptability (appropriate use of leadership style taking into account maturity of subordinates).

**16673**
**It's All in What You Ask: Questions for Search Committees.** Project on the Status and Education of Women, Association of American Colleges, Washington, DC 1988.
*Descriptors:* *Administrators; *Attitude Measures; *Employment Interviews; *Faculty; *Females; *Personnel Selection; *Search Committees (Personnel); Adults; Educational Environment; Higher Education; Questionnaires
*Identifiers:* Womens Issues
*Availability:* Project on the Status and Education of Women, Association of American Colleges, 1818 R St., N.W., Washington, DC 20009.

An interview guide for the use of members of search committees at colleges or universities when screening prospective administrators and/or faculty. Used to gauge candidates' concerns about issues concerning women. Divided into 3 sections: general questions, questions for prospective administrators, and questions for prospective faculty. May also be used to raise search committee's awareness of women's issues, help the search committee develop their own questions, and allow other administrators to examine the present status of women. No technical data included.

**16676**
**Comprehensive Personality Profile.** Craft, Larry L. 1989.
*Descriptors:* *Occupational Tests; *Personality Measures; *Personnel Selection; *Sales Occupations; Adults; Questionnaires
*Identifiers:* CPP
*Availability:* E.F. Wonderlic Personnel Test, Inc., 820 Frontage Rd., Northfield, IL 60093.
*Notes:* Time, 20 approx. Items, 88.

Assesses personality in terms of sales potential. Used for employee selection and employee development, to improve management skills, communications and team building. Can be administered as a paper-and-pencil test or by computer. Scored using your in-house computer. Provides 4 computer-generated reports: selection report relates the applicant's personality to 24 different job factors; manager's supervisory report gives you specific directives on managing the employee to peak performance; addendum report for sales managers relates candidate's personality to each step of the sales process; individual's self report highlights the candidate's basic approach to life and work situations.

**16677**
**Differential Aptitude Tests for Personnel and Career Assessment.** Bennett, George K.; And Others 1989.
*Descriptors:* *Aptitude Tests; *Career Guidance; *Job Placement; *Personnel Evaluation; Abstract Reasoning; Adults; Job Training; Language Usage; Mathematical Applications; Mechanical Skills; Spatial Ability; Spelling; Verbal Ability
*Identifiers:* Clerical Aptitude; DAT
*Availability:* Psychological Corp., 555 Academic Ct., San Antonio, TX 78204.
*Notes:* Time, 114. Items, 450.

Integrated battery of aptitude tests designed to assist human resource managers, industrial personnel specialists, and vocational counselors in personnel guidance, hiring, training, assessment, and assignment. Consists of 8 components that may be administered singly or in any combination. Yields 9 scores. Multiple test booklets contain 2 to 3 tests that measure skills in related areas. This instrument is a shortened version of Differential Aptitude Tests, Form V (11437), which is for use with junior and senior high school students. Contains information on norms, validities, and score equivalencies.

**16688**
**Entrepreneurial Style and Success Indicator.** Shenson, Howard L.; Anderson, Terry D. 1988.
*Descriptors:* *Entrepreneurship; Adults; Likert Scales; Rating Scales; Self Evaluation (Individuals); Success
*Identifiers:* ESSI
*Availability:* Career Research and Testing, 2005 Hamilton Ave., Ste. 250, San Jose, CA 95125.

Three-part instrument designed to assist individuals in understanding their entrepreneurial style and potential. The first part assesses entrepreneurial style. Individuals rank themselves according to words that describe them. The second part assesses foundations of entrepreneurship. On a 10-point, Likert-type scale individuals indicate how well 28 statements apply to them. The third part is an in-depth evaluation of the answers given in the first 2 parts. This evaluation allows individuals to work on developing their entrepreneurial strength according to areas in which they may be weak.

**16689**
**Managerial Competence Review.** Hall, Jay 1989.
*Descriptors:* *Administrator Characteristics; *Administrator Effectiveness; *Administrator Evaluation; *Situational Tests; Administrator Attitudes; Adults; Employee Attitudes; Participative Decision Making; Rating Scales
*Identifiers:* Administrator Involvement; Employee Participation; Management Skills; Management Styles; Managerial Grid
*Availability:* Teleometrics International, 1755 Woodstead Ct., The Woodlands, TX 77380.
*Notes:* Items, 60.

A rating scale designed to help managers determine the impact of their management on others. Employees indicate what they believe their managers' responses would be to 12 management situations. Each situation has 5 alternative responses. On a 10-point scale, employees rank how characteristic each response would be of their managers. Measures managers' managerial beliefs, involvement practices, management of motives, and interpersonal competence. Resulting scores are plotted on a managerial grid which yields 5 levels of managerial competence. Should be used in conjunction with the Managerial Competence Index (16690) in which managers rate themselves according to the same management situations.

**16690**
**Managerial Competence Index.** Hall, Jay 1989.
*Descriptors:* *Administrator Effectiveness; *Administrator Characteristics; *Managerial Occupations; *Situational Tests; *Supervisory Methods; Administrator Attitudes; Adults; Participative Decision Making; Rating Scales; Self Evaluation (Individuals)
*Identifiers:* Administrator Involvement; Employee Participation; Management Skills; Management Styles; Managerial Grid
*Availability:* Teleometrics International, 1755 Woodstead Ct., The Woodlands, TX 77380.
*Notes:* Items, 60.

A rating scale designed to help managers gain information about their styles of management. Managers indicate what their responses would be to 12 management situations. Each situation has 5 alternative responses. On a 10-point scale, managers indicate how characteristic each response would be of them. Measures managerial beliefs, involvement practices, management of motives, and interpersonal competence. Resulting scores are plotted on a managerial grid which yields 5 levels of managerial competence. Should be used in conjunction with Managerial Competence Review (16689) in which employees rate their managers according to the same management situations.

**16691**
**Management Transactions Audit: Other.** Hall, Jay; Griffith, C. Leo 1989.
*Descriptors:* *Administrator Characteristics; *Administrators; *Employer Employee Relationship; *Interaction; *Managerial Occupations; *Situational Tests; *Supervisory Methods; Administrator Attitudes; Adults; Rating Scales; Administrator Effectiveness
*Identifiers:* Management Skills; Managerial Styles; MTAO
*Availability:* Teleometrics International, 1755 Woodstead Ct., The Woodlands, TX 77380.
*Notes:* Items, 108.

A questionnaire to be completed by individuals working for particular managers. Respondents indicate the way in which they believe their managers would respond to 18 statements. Then, they indicate what their own responses would be to the same statements. Each statement has 3 responses to which 5 points may be distributed to show the degree of likelihood of each response. Results are interpreted as a function of the individuals' parent, adult, and child subsystems, in terms of how transactions between 2 individuals are affected by the subsystem in use by both. Should be used in conjunction with the Management Transactions Audit (7556), which is completed by the managers. Includes data and charts on norms.

**16708**
**Chartered Financial Analyst Program.** Institute of Chartered Financial Analysts, Charlottesville, VA
*Descriptors:* *Certification; *Finance Occupations; *Financial Services; *Knowledge Level; Accounting; Adults; Investment; Occupational Tests; Professional Occupations
*Identifiers:* Chartered Financial Analysts
*Availability:* Institute of Chartered Financial Analysts, P.O. Box 3668, Charlottesville, VA 22903.

The Chartered Financial Analyst Examination is a program of self-study and testing for investment professionals who have completed a bachelor's degree program. It is administered once a year in June at 100 examination centers worldwide. Measures knowledge of the investment profession. A study guide is available for preparation. There are 3 examinations: Level 1, Level 2, Level 3. Covers over 40 topic areas for Level 3, fewer for other levels, including laws and regulations, ethical standards, basic accounting, equity analysis, macroeconomics, etc.

**16733**
**HRD Climate Survey.** Rao, T. Venkateswara; Abraham, E.
*Descriptors:* *Labor Force Development; *Organizational Climate; Adults; Likert Scales
*Availability:* Pfeiffer, J. William, ed., *The 1990 Annual: Developing Human Resources.* San Diego: University Associates, 1990. Pfeiffer and Co., formerly University Associates, 8517 Production Ave., San Diego, CA 92121-2280.
*Notes:* Items, 38.

The Human Resources Development (HRD) Climate Survey is based on the theory that a basic level of development climate is necessary for the success of the organization's HRD mechanisms. The survey measures the development climate. Its 38 items can be classified into 3 categories: 1) general climate; 2) OCTAPAV cultures; and 3) HRD. General climate items deal with the importance given to HRD by the organization. OCTA-PAC items deal with the extent to which the following characteristics are valued and promoted: openness, confrontation, trust, autonomy, proactivity, authenticity, and collaboration. HRD items reflect the extent to which HRD mechanisms are seriously implemented. The survey was planned to collect data and provide feedback to organizations about their HRD climates. The survey was given to 1,614 respondents from 41 different organizations. Trends observed in HRD climates are listed.

**16734**
**Networking Skills Inventory.** Byrum-Robinson, Beverly; Womeldorff, J. David
*Descriptors:* *Network Analysis; *Social Networks; Adults; Likert Scales
*Availability:* Pfeiffer, J. William, ed., *The 1990 Annual: Developing Human Resources.* San Diego: University Associates, 1990. Pfeiffer and Co., formerly University Associates, 8517 Production Ave., San Diego, CA 92121-2280.
*Notes:* Items, 24.

The inventory measures the degree to which an individual's behavior is conducive to networking. Networking is defined as "the ability to create and maintain an effective, widely based system of resources that works to the mutual benefit of oneself and others." The instrument's development involved structured interviews with HRD professionals who were seen as expert networkers and further research with local professionals in the field. The behavioral items in the survey were derived from those interviews. The 24 items ask participants to respond to statements in terms of how often they engage in the behavior. It can be used with individuals, in groups, at the organizational level, at the managerial level, and in training. Normative data are given.

**16768**
**Executive Success Profile.** Personnel Decisions, Minneapolis, MN
*Descriptors:* *Management Development; *Managerial Occupations; Administrators; Adults; Questionnaires
*Identifiers:* ESP
*Availability:* Personnel Decisions, Inc., 2000 Plaza VII Tower, 45 S. Seventh St., Minneapolis, MN 55402-1608.
*Notes:* Items, 188.

Provides feedback to general managers and executives about their performance from their peers, subordinates, and superiors. Useful to established and new executives seeking to improve their performance and skills and to organizations wishing to assess executive skills and identify succession planning needs.

**16769**
**Individual Development Profile.** Personnel Decisions, Minneapolis, MN
*Descriptors:* *Administrators; *Management Development; *Professional Personnel; Administrator Qualifications; Adults; Questionnaires
*Identifiers:* IDP
*Availability:* Personnel Decisions, Inc., 2000 Plaza VII Tower, 45 S. Seventh St., Minneapolis, MN 55402-1608.
*Notes:* Items, 140.

Assesses strengths and development needs of professionals, key contributors, and aspiring managers within an organization. Identifies high potential and managerial readiness. Pinpoints development needs. Individuals receive assessments from 3 perspectives: self, peers, and superiors. Covers 18 skill areas.

**16770**
**Consulting Skills Profile.** Personnel Decisions, Minneapolis, MN
*Descriptors:* *Consultants; Adults; Business; Communication Skills; Questionnaires
*Identifiers:* CSP
*Availability:* Personnel Decisions, Inc., 2000 Plaza VII Tower, 45 S. Seventh St., Minneapolis, MN 55402-1608.
*Notes:* Items, 110.

Designed to give feedback to staff experts who operate as internal consultants. Designed for people in any function whose responsibility is to consult with other functions. Receive feedback from 4 perspectives: self, boss, peers, and organizational clients. Provides specific development suggestions for on-the-job improvement.

**16819**
**Motivational Patterns Inventory.** Byrd, Richard E.; Neher, William R.
*Descriptors:* *Behavior Patterns; *Motivation; Adults; Organizational Climate; Self Evaluation (Individuals)
*Availability:* Pfeiffer and Co., formerly University Associates, 8517 Production Ave., San Diego, CA 92121-2280.
*Notes:* Items, 20.

Self-assessment instrument designed to assist individuals in determining their styles of motivation. Each question has 3 choices from which the individuals choose the response that best fits them. They may also make a second choice if they find 2 responses that are close. Works on assumption that individuals fall into 1 of 3 behavior patterns: farmers, hunters, or shepherds. Results may help individuals determine areas within their organizations for which they would be best suited. May also help individuals understand the reasons for which people have different motivational values and that all types are necessary within a functioning organization. May help them to deal with conflicts among various subcultures in an organization. Instrument is self-scored. No technical data included.

**16825**
**Time Management Profile.** Douglas, Merrill; Baker, Larry 1984.
*Descriptors:* *Behavior Rating Scales; *Efficiency; *Self Concept; *Self Evaluation (Individuals); *Time Management; *Work Environment; Adults; Profiles
*Availability:* Carlson Learning Co., Carlson Parkway, P.O. Box 59159, Minneapolis, MN 55459-8247.
*Notes:* Items, 60.

One primary objective for this time management profile is to help assess one's time management behaviors, and to serve as a guide to becoming a better manager of time. The other objective is to help a person to be more successful in performance, as he or she learns to differentiate between good and bad time behavior. This self-report instrument can help one discover present strengths and improvement opportunities in managing time and will also improve the opportunities for future growth. This tool contains 2 levels of assessment: basic, which is applicable to any job; and managerial, which is applicable to supervisory or management positions.

**16826**
**Sales Pathfinder System.** Performax Systems International, Inc., Minneapolis, MN 1987.
*Descriptors:* *Occupational Tests; *Salesmanship; *Sales Occupations; *Sales Workers; *Self Evaluation (Individuals); Adults; Behavior Rating Scales; Feedback; Job Performance
*Availability:* Carlson Learning Co., Carlson Parkway, P.O. Box 59159, Minneapolis, MN 55459-8247.
*Notes:* Items, 50.

This instrument provides a proficiency-based measure of sales performance. It supplies objective, measurable information on the sales knowledge and skills of staff members. This tool can be utilized to describe individual, department, and group sales staff and diagnose specific performance issues. Some factors measured in this survey are knowledge of self, others, communication, selling, product, procedures, and the market. This instrument helps to tailor sales education to the needs of sales personnel and is designed to increase sales effectiveness by providing specific actions for future success.

**16860**
**Examination in Expanded Functions for Dental Assisting and Dental Hygiene.** Dental Assisting National Board, Chicago, IL 1988.
*Descriptors:* *Certification; *Dental Assistants; *Knowledge Level; *Licensing Examinations (Professions); *Occupational Tests; Adults
*Identifiers:* New Jersey
*Availability:* Dental Assisting National Board, Inc., 216 E. Ontario St., Chicago, IL 60611.
*Notes:* Items, 235.

This examination is designed to be taken by dental assistants applying to be registered dental assistants or dental hygienists applying for licensure in dental hygiene expanded functions in the state of New Jersey. State dental associations and dentistry boards determine standards and requirements. Test taker must be board certified. Both multiple-choice and matching questions are used. The exam covers morphology, histology, physiology, pharmacology, pathology, general anatomy, dental anatomy, microbiology, chemistry, psychology, and embryology.

**16861**
**Dental Radiation Health and Safety Examination.** Dental Assisting National Board, Chicago, IL 1988.
*Descriptors:* *Dental Assistants; *Knowledge Level; *Licensing Examinations (Professions); *Occupational Tests; *Radiology; Adults; Certification; Personnel Selection
*Availability:* Dental Assisting National Board, Inc., 216 E. Ontario St., Chicago, IL 60611.
*Notes:* Time, 180. Items, 100.

This licensing examination may be used by government bodies, employers, or other organizations who have a need to measure employee competence in dental radiation health and safety for persons performing dental radiography procedures. Examination dates, deadlines, and testing locations are specified by the publisher. Items are multiple choice and matching format. Areas covered are radiographic exposure and processing, mounting and labeling, and radiation health and safety.

**16874**
**Career Profile Inventory.** Nowack, Kenneth M. 1990.
*Descriptors:* *Career Choice; *Career Development; Adults; Occupational Aspiration; Occupational Mobility; Occupational Tests; Political Socialization; Questionnaires; Vocational Maturity; Work Environment
*Availability:* Organization Design and Development, Inc., 2002 Renaissance Blvd., King of Prussia, PA 19406-2746.
*Notes:* Time, 30. Items, 10.

Designed to assist in determining at which stage an individual is in career development, career path preference, and political style orientation. Identifies possible positions of respondent in each category. Respondent indicates which of 4 possible choices of statements relative to each area is typical of the way his or her career is now and the way he or she would prefer it to be.

**16875**
**My Timestyle.** Brewer, James H. 1990.
*Descriptors:* *Attitude Measures; *Corporate Education; *Employee Attitudes; *Interpersonal Relationship; *Time Management; *Work Attitudes; Adults; Behavior Patterns; Occupational Tests; Self Evaluation (Individuals); Trainers
*Availability:* Organization Design and Development, Inc., 2002 Renaissance Blvd., Ste. 100, King of Prussia, PA 19406-2746.
*Notes:* Time, 5. Items, 16.

A self-scoring and interpreting instrument designed to assist the respondents in determining their work style as it relates to use of time and handling of deadlines. Forced choice and multiple-choice items cover stress, interpersonal relations, motivation, etc. A profile is developed that designates respondent as a road runner, race horse, tom cat, or new pup, depending on task completion behaviors and interpersonal relationships.

**16876**
**My BEST Communication Style.** Brewer, James H. 1989.

*Descriptors:* *Communication Skills; *Corporate Education; *Interpersonal Communication; *Work Environment; Adults; Behavior Patterns; Occupational Tests
*Availability:* Organization Design and Development, Inc., 2002 Renaissance Blvd., Ste. 100, King of Prussia, PA 19406-2746.
*Notes:* Items, 18.

Designed to assist adults in a work environment in determining which of 4 communication styles they use. Styles are bold, sympathetic, expressive, and technical. Respondents select from 4 choices of behavior patterns, the one they would most often use in a given situation. The inventory is self-scored. Interpretations are provided for each style.

**16877**
**Personal Stress Assessment Inventory.** Kindler, Herbert S. 1989.
*Descriptors:* *Burnout; *Employees; *Stress Management; *Stress Variables; Adults; Behavior Problems; Psychological Patterns; Psychosomatic Disorders; Rating Scales; Recreational Activities; Self Evaluation (Individuals); Social Desirability
*Identifiers:* PSAI; Relaxation; Rustout
*Availability:* Organization Design and Development, Inc., 2002 Renaissance Blvd., King of Prussia, PA 19406-2746.
*Notes:* Time, 30. Items, 160.

Designed to assist employees in identifying factors that may be contributing to their stress. Said to be useful in assisting employees in making lifestyle changes that would be beneficial to them, their associates, and the organization. Covers respondent's ways of looking at events, resilience, stress sources, personal attitudes, health symptoms. High scores are said to be indicative of approaching burnout. Low scores are indicative of rustout. A social desirability scale is included to avoid tendency of respondents to "fake good."

**16878**
**My BEST Leadership Style.** Brewer, James H. 1989.
*Descriptors:* *Administrators; *Corporate Education; *Leadership Styles; *Supervisors; *Work Environment; Adults; Behavior Patterns; Occupational Tests
*Availability:* Organization Design and Development, Inc., 2002 Renaissance Blvd., Ste. 100, King of Prussia, PA 19406-2746.
*Notes:* Items, 32.

Designed to assist individuals in the corporate setting to determine their leadership style and how personality affects leadership behaviors. Styles include bold, expressive, sympathetic, and technical. Suggestions are given for modifying behavior. No technical information is included.

**16879**
**Pre-Evaluation Profile.** Brewer, James H. 1989.
*Descriptors:* *Administrators; *Occupational Tests; *Personality Traits; *Personnel Evaluation; *Supervisors; Adults; Employees; Self Evaluation (Individuals)
*Identifiers:* PEP; *Performance Appraisal
*Availability:* Organization Design and Development, Inc., 2002 Renaissance Blvd., Ste. 100, King of Prussia, PA 19406-2746.
*Notes:* Items, 18.

Designed for use by supervisors prior to evaluation of employee performance. The supervisor selects, from a list of personality traits, those descriptive of her- or himself and the employee. Said to assist the supervisor in recognizing personality and personal style differences so that ratings can be based on employee results and products rather than methods and processes. No technical information is provided.

**16880**
**Project Description Questionnaire.** de Jaager, Gerald 1988.
*Descriptors:* *Problem Solving; *Leadership Styles; *Employees; Adults; Questionnaires; Program Development; Teamwork; Rating Scales; Labor; Supervisors; Feedback
*Identifiers:* Project Management; PD; Administrators Force
*Availability:* Organization Design and Development, Inc., 2002 Renaissance Blvd., Ste. 100, King of Prussia, PA 19406-2746.

This instrument is a guide to successful project execution in the work force. It can be used at the beginning of a project to help anticipate specific problems and take early preventative action; during a project when a problem is encountered so corrective action can be taken; or at the end of a project so those involved can learn from their successes and disappointments. Ten dimensions of project management are covered: skill of project members; clarity of project leader role; quality of project plans and schedules; management support; communication; control; stability of plans and specifications; client relations; organizational support; and commitment/leadership. Dimensions receiving higher scores are relative strengths and lower scores indicate potential areas for improvement. Also included in this tool is a team member questionnaire requesting feedback from the project staff about the way the project has been managed. It is also based on a 0 to 6 rating scale. (TJS)

**16881**
**Group Perceptions Inventory.** Kovach, Barbara 1989.
*Descriptors:* *Attitude Measures; *Corporate Education; *Employees; *Group Behavior; *Interpersonal Relationship; *Supervisors; Administrators; Adults; Occupational Tests; Social Cognition
*Identifiers:* GPI
*Availability:* Human Systems Analysis, 95 Cuyler Rd., Princeton, NJ 08540.
*Notes:* Items, 72.

This self-evaluation is designed to assess a supervisor or manager's perceptions of the general personal style of a work group in terms of the group's response to people, ideas, and situations. Three types of groups are described: producers, integrators, and processors. Six components make up the rating system: openness to people, openness to ideas, analysis, synthesis, decision making, and performance. No technical information is provided.

**16883**
**Learning Diagnostic Questionnaire.** Honey, Peter; Mumford, Alan 1990.
*Descriptors:* *Cognitive Style; *Corporate Education; *Diagnostic Tests; *Learning Processes; Adults; Employee Attitudes; Employees; Forced Choice Technique; Occupational Tests; Trainers
*Identifiers:* LDQ
*Availability:* Organization Design and Development, Inc., 2002 Renaissance Blvd., Ste. 100, King of Prussia, PA 19406-2746.
*Notes:* Time, 20. Items, 120.

Helps to assess individual's ability and willingness to make and take learning opportunities. Designed to provide information about the respondent's knowledge of and skills in learning; oportunities for learning in his or her work situation; and his or her attitudes and emotions about learning. Used by trainers in an industrial setting. Self-scored by the test taker. Norms are provided for comparison. An accompanying workbook contains structured learning activities.

**16884**
**Learning Styles Questionnaire.** Honey, Peter; Mumford, Alan 1989.
*Descriptors:* *Cognitive Style; *Corporate Education; *Learning Processes; *Work Environment; Adults; Employees; Occupational Tests; Trainers
*Identifiers:* LSQ
*Availability:* Organization Design and Development, Inc., 2002 Renaissance Blvd., Ste. 100, King of Prussia, PA 19406-2746.
*Notes:* Items, 80.

Designed to assist adults in the corporate environment in discovering their preferred learning style, which is based on habits acquired over the years. Respondent compares self to behaviors described in 80 statements. Uses an agree-disagree format. Learners are described as activists, reflectors, theorists, and pragmatists. No technical data are included.

**16887**
**Risk Taking in Organizations.** Moore, Maggie; Gergen, Paul 1985.
*Descriptors:* *Organizations (Groups); *Risk; Adults; Cultural Influences; Decision Making; Individual Power; Norms; Questionnaires; Rating Scales
*Availability:* Organization Design and Development, Inc., 2002 Renaissance Blvd., Ste. 100, King of Prussia, PA 19406-2746.
*Notes:* Items, 44.

One of 2 instruments that addresses risk taking in organizations. It includes a model that shows that both the individuals and the organizations influence how individuals take risks. Organization norms are the informal rules that have developed over time, and have greatly influenced the behavior of employees. The Organization Norms Questionnaire will identify the norms in the respondents' organization that relate to the risk taking of its employees. It includes 24 items and measures the impact of the structural/cultural factors. The Individual Tendency Scale, which includes 20 items, will help the respondents focus on some of the factors that determine their actions when the outcomes are unknown or uncertain when some risks are involved. This scale measures the impact of the individual tendency factors, which include past experiences with risk taking; decision-making skills; and a general inclination (or disinclination) to take risks. There are no wrong or right answers to this instrument.

**16888**
**PAVE: Indicators of Excellent Organizations.** Stoner-Zemel, Jesse 1989.
*Descriptors:* *Attitude Measures; *Employee Attitudes; *Employees; *Organizational Climate; *Organizational Effectiveness; Adults; Organizational Objectives; Rating Scales
*Identifiers:* PAVE
*Availability:* Organization Design and Development, Inc., 2002 Renaissance Blvd., King of Prussia, PA 19406-2746.
*Notes:* Items, 36.

Allows employees to rate their company or work unit on 6 identified areas of organizational excellence. Scores can be benchmarked against other companies to determine areas of strengths and/or weaknesses. No technical data supplied.

**16894**
**Uniform Certified Public Accountant Examination.** American Institute of Certified Public Accountants, New York, NY
*Descriptors:* *Accounting; *Certified Public Accountants; *Finance Occupations; *Knowledge Level; *Licensing Examinations (Professions); *Occupational Tests; Adults; Business Administration; College Graduates; State Licensing Boards
*Availability:* American Institute of Certified Public Accountants, Inc., 1211 Ave. of the Americas, New York, NY 10036.
*Notes:* Time, 1140.

This examination was designed for use as part of the licensing procedure for accountants. Assesses candidates' technical and professional competence in accounting. A 4-year college degree with a major in accounting is required before the candidate can sit for the exam. Potential test takers should contact their state board of accountancy. A list of locations of state boards can be had by contacting the National Association of State Boards of Accountancy, 545 Fifth Avenue, New York, NY 10017.

**16924**
**Career Commitment.** Blau, Gary J. 1988.

*Descriptors:* *Attitude Measures; *Careers; *Employee Attitudes; *Employees; Adults; Career Change; Likert Scales; Rating Scales
*Identifiers:* Career Commitment; Job Involvement; Organizational Commitment
*Availability:* *Journal of Vocational Behavior,* v32 n3 p284-97, Jun 1988.
*Notes:* Items, 25.

Designed to measure individuals' commitment to their careers by measuring their attitudes toward their professions or vocations. Includes items that measure job involvement, organizational commitment, and withdrawal cognitions to determine if these 3 factors are operationally distinct from career commitment. Items are answered on a 5-point, Likert-type scale. Contains basic technical information and concludes that additional research is necessary, especially using varying populations, to determine the reliability and validity of this instrument.

**16930**
**HuTec Corporation: In-Basket Exercise.** Organizational Performance Dimensions, Los Angeles, CA 1988.
*Descriptors:* *Administrator Effectiveness; *Administrator Responsibility; *Administrator Role; *Administrators; *Leadership Qualities; *Managerial Occupations; *Manufacturing Industry; *Situational Tests; Adults; Decision Making; Planning; Simulation; Supervisory Methods
*Identifiers:* *In Basket Simulation
*Availability:* Organization Design and Development, Inc., 2002 Renaissance Blvd., Ste. 100, King of Prussia, PA 19406-2746.
*Notes:* Time, 90 approx. Items, 23.

Designed to train managers in administrative responsibilities. Appropriate for manufacturing and production-oriented companies. Participants are to act on each of the 23 administrative items by delegating, making decisions, planning meetings, directing discussions with their superiors or employees, asking for information, making plans, and exercising control. This tool can be administered individually or in a group. Norms, validity, and reliability data have been established. Large-scale users of this instrument may purchase the software to administer, score, and create narrative reports on their own.

**16931**
**Our Best Team.** Brewer, James H. 1989.
*Descriptors:* *Cooperation; *Interprofessional Relationship; *Organizational Effectiveness; *Self Evaluation (Individuals); *Teamwork; Adults; Measures (Individuals); Work Environment
*Availability:* Organization Design and Development, Inc., 2002 Renaissance Blvd., Ste. 100, King of Prussia, PA 19406-2746.
*Notes:* Items, 32.

This instrument is designed to help explore the personal aspects of working together on team projects, committees, or a task force. It will point out the strengths and weaknesses in teams in relationship to tasks and provide the user with an understanding of the importance of a team's composition: how the dynamics of a team will play out if one personality type is overrepresented; how the tasks may need to dictate the profile of the teams; and how individuals can make a greater contribution to the team. This tool does not answer all of the questions about human behavior but should be used as an exercise to begin improving personal and organizational performance.

**16932**
**Change State Indicator: Profiling Global People.** Organization Design and Development, King of Prussia, PA 1989.
*Descriptors:* *Attitude Measures; *Change Strategies; *Organizational Change; Adults; Attitude Change; Rating Scales; Self Evaluation (Individuals); Values
*Availability:* Organization Design and Development, Inc., 2002 Renaissance Blvd., Ste. 100, King of Prussia, PA 19406-2746.
*Notes:* Time, 25 approx. Items, 31.

Designed to help put values in a new perspective and assist the process of organizational change and transformation. This scale identifies 5 stages of change: Alpha, beta, gamma, delta, and new alpha. This tool is useful to practitioners for change management in understanding and explaining how value systems develop in people, organizations, and entire cultures.

**16944**
**Maxi Management: A System for Management Effectiveness.** Albrecht, Karl 1987.
*Descriptors:* *Administrator Effectiveness; *Administrators; *Feedback; *Leadership Qualities; *Role Perception; Adults; Employer Employee Relationship; Interprofessional Relationship; Leadership Styles; Peer Evaluation; Self Evaluation (Groups); Self Evaluation (Individuals); Supervisory Methods
*Availability:* Shamrock Press, 1277 Garnet Ave., P.O. Box 90699, San Diego, CA 92109.
*Notes:* Items, 41.

A feedback system that helps gather and analyze feedback from employees about the skills of their managers. This organizational tool is useful in helping managers maximize their effectiveness by increasing their self-awareness and self-understanding. It works on the principle of multidirectional feedback, giving useful information about the way one manages. Managers get a printed report that shows how their boss, employees, and peers perceive them on critical dimensions of behavior related to the 4 managerial roles of strategist, leader, problem solver, and administrator. The report compares the managers' own perceptions with those of others who interact with them on a daily basis.

**16967**
**The CFA Study Guide.** Institute of Chartered Financial Analysts, Charlottesville, VA 1990.
*Descriptors:* *Certification; *Finance Occupations; *Financial Services; *Knowledge Level; *Money Management; *Occupational Tests; Accounting; Adults; Economics
*Availability:* The Institute of Chartered Financial Analysts, P.O. Box 3668, Charlottesville, VA 22903.
*Notes:* Time, 180. Items, 148.

This guide is intended to help the Chartered Financial Analysis (CFA) candidate learn the concepts and techniques of the Institute of Chartered Financial Analysis (ICFA) Body of Knowlege and to prepare for the current CFA examination. The Level 1 test covers 7 subject areas: ethical and professional standards; financial accounting; quantitative analysis; economics; fixed income securities analysis; equity securities analysis; and portfolio management. Mastery of the CFA curriculum is the major purpose of the CFA program.

**16990**
**Group Styles Inventory.** Human Synergistics, Plymouth, MI 1990.
*Descriptors:* *Group Dynamics; *Group Experience; *Work Environment; Adults; Problem Solving; Rating Scales; Self Directed Groups
*Identifiers:* GSI
*Availability:* Human Synergistics, 39819 Plymouth Rd., Plymouth, MI 48170.
*Notes:* Items, 72.

This inventory enables the assessment of a particular style or styles of the work group following a simulated or real problem-solving session. When an individual's results are combined with those of the other members of the group, a group perception is obtained. Upon completion of this program, a person is able to describe the 12 constructive or defensive styles that can emerge in groups; identify the particular style or styles characterizing one's own group; describe ways in which the personal styles of members and/or cultures of their organization can influence the style of a group; explain the productive or counterproductive impact that group styles can have on group effectiveness; describe a model for effective group processes; and identify, initiate, and implement changes in how an individual works with others to improve group process skills.

**17020**
**Leader Authenticity Scale.** Henderson, James E.; Hoy, Wayne K. 1982.
*Descriptors:* *Leaders; *Leadership Qualities; *Principals; *Teacher Administrator Relationship; Adults; Behavior Rating Scales; Behavior Standards; Leadership Responsibility
*Identifiers:* LAS
*Availability:* ERIC Document Reproduction Service, 7420 Fullerton Rd., Ste. 110, Springfield, VA 22153-2852 ED221130, 78 pages).
*Notes:* Items, 32.

Measures leader authenticity as defined by the extent to which 3 aspects of behavior are demonstrated: acceptance of organizational and personal responsibility for actions, outcomes, and mistakes; nonmanipulation of subordinates; and salience of self over role. Research focused only on teacher-principal relations. Information on validity included.

**17021**
**Management Opinionnaire.** Sistrunk, Walter E.; Jenkins, Elton R. 1980.
*Descriptors:* *Leadership Styles; *Superintendents; Administrator Attitudes; Administrator Role; Adults; Elementary Secondary Education; Questionnaires
*Availability:* ERIC Document Reproduction Service, 7420 Fullerton Rd., Ste. 110, Springfield, VA 22153-2852 ED197430, 46 pages).
*Notes:* Items, 27.

Surveys preferred style of leadership of superintendents of schools. Based on 5 management styles: management-by-agreement; management-by-balance; management-by-noninvolvement; management-by-support; and management-by-authority.

**17022**
**Principal Leadership and Self Appraisal of Effectiveness.** Miserandino, Anthony 1986.
*Descriptors:* *Administrator Effectiveness; *Principals; *School Effectiveness; *Self Evaluation (Individuals); Administrator Role; Adults; Leadership; Models; Questionnaires; Secondary Education
*Availability:* ERIC Document Reproduction Service, 7420 Fullerton Rd., Ste. 110, Springfield, VA 22153-2852 ED275027, 14 pages).
*Notes:* Items, 15.

A self-appraisal form for school principals to elicit an evaluation and understanding of the factors that impact their personal effectiveness as principals. Can help determine their strengths and weaknesses.

**17041**
**Matching Your Special Skills to the Marketplace.** Moore, Donna J. 1981.
*Descriptors:* *Career Exploration; *Employment Potential; *Job Skills; *Vocational Evaluation; Adults; Employment Opportunities; Higher Education; Job Banks; Job Placement; Occupational Information; Older Adults; Secondary Education; Vocational Aptitude
*Identifiers:* SDS
*Availability:* JIST Works, Inc., 720 N. Park Ave., Indianapolis, IN 46202-3431.

This instrument is designed to be used as a career exploration tool to discover a large number of career options. It incorporates a complete version of the Self-Directed Search (SDS) which is a career exploration tool that includes over 1,100 occupations and has been normed for use with all persons who read and are aged 15 to 70, junior high school through post-graduate. This instrument features a separate table cross-referencing recommended SDS occupations to federal job titles and information sources. It can be used by government employees wanting to move up or make a change; individuals exploring government employment opportunity and advancement programs for minorities, women and other target groups; retiring military personnel considering government employment; and anyone considering a career in government.

**17045**
**Healthcare Financial Management Association Certification Programs.** Healthcare Financial Management Association, Westchester, IL 1989.
*Descriptors:* *Certification; *Finance Occupations; *Health Facilities; *Knowledge Level; *Managerial Occupations; *Medical Services; *Money Management; *Occupational Tests; Adults; Professional Personnel
*Identifiers:* CMPA; FHFMA
*Availability:* Healthcare Financial Management Association, 2 Westbrook Corporate Center, Ste. 700, Westchester, IL 60154.

These examinations are designed to assess the mastery in the fields of healthcare, financial management, and patient accounts management. They offer qualified members an opportunity to upgrade their professional status within the fields. Included in the certification process is the Fellowship Examination (FHFMA), which measures the candidate's knowledge of healthcare financial theory and practice, as well as gauge capacity for leadership in the field. The other examination is the Certified Manager of Patient Accounts (CMPA), which measures the candidate's knowledge of accounts receivable management, departmental management, accounting, healthcare industry, and data processing/information systems. These exams are offered annually and applicants must pass certain eligibility requirements for certification.

**17062**
**Initial Career Profile.** Life Insurance Marketing and Research Association, Inc., Hartford, CT 1983.
*Descriptors:* *Insurance Companies; *Insurance Occupations; *Salesmanship; *Job Applicants; Adults; Self Evaluation (Individuals); Rating Scales; Occupations
*Identifiers:* LIMRA
*Availability:* Life Insurance Marketing and Research Association, Inc., P.O. Box 208, Hartford, CT 06141-0208.

Designed to give companies an idea of an applicant's potential for success in insurance sales. This questionnaire allows companies to realize more high-producing, new agents per investment dollar; higher production of new agents in their first 12 months per investment dollar; and savings in financing subsidies. Some of the items in this tool describe concerns or worries that some applicants may have about becoming an insurance sales representative. Questions are based on a rating scale. (TJS)

**17064**
**Training Needs Assessment Test.** Tagliaferri, Louis E. 1989.
*Descriptors:* *Leadership Styles; *Managerial Occupations; *Needs Assessment; *Supervisory Methods; Adjustment (to Environment); Adults; Counseling Techniques; Decision Making; Human Relations; Job Performance; Leadership Training; Motivation; Problem Solving; Productivity; Teamwork; Time Management; Verbal Communication
*Identifiers:* TNAT
*Availability:* Talico, Inc., 2320 S. Third St., Ste. 5, Jacksonville Beach, FL 32250.
*Notes:* Time, 45 approx. Items, 105.

This instrument is used to evaluate the cognitive skills and leadership qualities of managers, supervisors and/or candidates for these positions. It is made up of 2 parts. Part 1 consists of objective items that measure the respondent's understanding of management and supervisory principles, practices, and behaviors. It evaluates a person's understanding in the skill dimensions of coaching and counseling, communication, human relations, motivation, team building, leadership, employee discipline, performance management, problem solving/decision making, training, work assignments, planning and organizing, finance and cost control, productivity/quality improvement, and time management. Part 2 identifies leadership style orientation which includes adaptability.

**17125**
**The Teacher Evaluation Scale.** McCarney, Stephen B. 1986.
*Descriptors:* *Instruction; *Teacher Behavior; *Teacher Evaluation; *Teacher Improvement; *Teachers; Adults; Rating Scales; Teaching Methods
*Identifiers:* PIM; TES
*Availability:* Hawthorne Educational Services, P.O. Box 7570, Columbia, MO 65205.
*Notes:* Items, 35.

This evaluative instrument was designed to be used to identify desirable teacher behavior, document teacher performance, identify strengths and areas for improvement, compare the individual teacher to a nationwide standard, provide a comparison within a school system, develop goals for professional improvement, document individual teacher improvement over time, and identify in-service needs. This tool can be used in conjunction with the *Professional Improvement Manual* (PIM) which was designed to offer administrators and teachers suggestions for specific areas of professional improvement. Together, they provide evaluation, feedback, direction, and specific strategies for improvement with reevaluation as a means of documenting improvement.

**17133**
**Personalysis.** Noland, James R. 1984.
*Descriptors:* *Managerial Occupations; *Occupational Tests; *Personality Measures; *Personality Traits; Administrators; Adults; Behavior Patterns; Employees; Family Counseling; Group Behavior; Job Placement; Management Teams; Promotion (Occupational); Stress Variables; Supervisors
*Identifiers:* Berne (Eric); Freud (Sigmund); Jung (Carl G)
*Availability:* Management Technologies, Inc., 1200 Post Oak Blvd., Ste. 520, Houston, TX 77056.
*Notes:* Time, 15.

This personality measure is designed for use in industry to describe personal characteristics of individuals in work groups and management teams to show how individuals should be placed, motivated, and managed. The inventory is self-administered, and uses forced-choice item format. It is returned to the publisher for computer scoring. A profile is generated and a graph can be produced that depicts the individual's personal characteristics using 4 colors. May be used when making decisions about placement, promotion, conflict resolution, team building, etc. Developed based on constructs derived from theories of Freud, Jung, and Berne. Analysis reveals personal style under stress conditions. A technical manual is provided that discusses split-half and test-retest reliability and content, concurrent, construct, and predictive validities. Industrial norms are used. Also suggested for use in studying family member relationships.

**17143**
**Listening Climate Indicator.** Performax Systems International, Inc., Minneapolis, MN
*Descriptors:* *Job Performance; *Listening Skills; *Work Environment; Adults; Communication Problems; Employee Attitudes; Employees
*Availability:* Carlson Learning Co., Carlson Parkway, P.O. Box 59159, Minneapolis, MN 55459-8247.
*Notes:* See also: Attitudinal Listening Profile (16426). Items, 12.

This assessment instrument was designed to increase listening effectiveness on the job. The focus is on how a person's listening skills contribute to productivity and performance. The use of this tool can illustrate how some communication misunderstandings can occur at work by comparing similarities and differences in listening skills. It can clarify the listening climate of an organization and help individuals focus on objectives. This instrument can be used in conjunction with the Attitudinal Listening Profile (16426).

**17145**
**The Personal Development Profile.** O'Connor, Michael 1990.
*Descriptors:* *Behavior Rating Scales; *Consciousness Raising; *Employees; *Personality Traits; *Social Cognition; Adults; Groups; Individual Characteristics; Interests; Work Environment
*Availability:* Carlson Learning Co., Carlson Parkway, P.O. Box 59159, Minneapolis, MN 55459-8247.
*Notes:* Items, 24.

This behavioral assessment instrument is designed specifically for groups and individuals who are interested in improving their people knowledge. It is a tool for teaching front-line employees how to understand their behavioral style, and applying the results to developing higher self-esteem and self-confidence in their personal and professional lives. Includes the 4 basic behavior tendencies: dominance, influencing, cautiousness, and steadiness. It provides response phrases and brief descriptions of 15 classical behavior patterns.

**17159**
**Instrument for Assessing Attitudes about Merit Pay.** Weber, Larry 1988.
*Descriptors:* *Attitude Measures; *Merit Pay; *Teachers; Administrator Attitudes; Adults; Likert Scales; Rating Scales; Teacher Attitudes
*Availability:* *Educational Research Quarterly*, v12 n2 p2-7, 1988.
*Notes:* Items, 16.

A questionnaire designed to measure educators' attitudes toward merit pay for teachers. On a 4-point Likert-type scale, respondents indicate the degree to which they agree or disagree with each of 16 statements. Includes information on reliability.

**17163**
**Certified Public Accountant Examination for the State of New Jersey.** American Institute of Certified Public Accountants, New York, NY
*Descriptors:* *Accounting; *Certified Public Accountants; *Licensing Examinations (Professions); Adults; Financial Audits
*Identifiers:* CPA
*Availability:* State Board of Accountancy, State of New Jersey, Div. of Community Affairs, 1100 Raymond Blvd., Newark, NJ 07102.
*Notes:* See also Uniform Certified Public Accountant Examination (16894).

This examination for licensing as a certified public accountant in the state of New Jersey covers public accounting and auditing practices. Applicants for the examination must meet an experience requirement of 2 years work at the firm or office of a licensed certified public accountant. A baccalaureate degree is required. New versions are developed periodically.

**17168**
**Working with My Boss.** Brewer, James H. 1989.
*Descriptors:* *Employer Employee Relationship; *Personality Traits; *Work Environment; Adults; Employees; Questionnaires; Supervisory Methods
*Availability:* Career Research and Testing, 2005 Hamilton Ave., Ste. 250, San Jose, CA 95125.
*Notes:* Items, 32.

This instrument is designed to aid in understanding that most people have a mixture of different personality types. The purpose of this assessment tool is to identify these personality patterns in one's boss through word association and situation analysis selections. Identifying these personalities allow communication and working relations to be more productive. The 4 personality types to choose from in this instrument include: bold boss, expressive boss, sympathetic boss, and technical boss. There are no right or wrong answers.

**17171**
**Situational Leadership II: Leadership Skills Assessment.** Blanchard, Kenneth H.; And Others 1990.

*Descriptors:* *Administrator Evaluation; *Leadership Styles; *Supervisors; *Supervisory Methods; Adults; Behavior; Feedback; Rating Scales
*Availability:* Blanchard Training and Development, 125 State Pl., Escondido, CA 92025.
*Notes:* Time, 20 approx. Items, 24.

The purpose of this assessment instrument is to provide feedback to one's immediate supervisor or manager. It offers situations in which users describe their manager's recent behavior and leadership skills. This tool is rated on a scale ranging from 1, indicating never, to 6, indicating always.

**17181**
**Management Action Planner.** Performax Systems International, Inc., Minneapolis, MN 1987.
*Descriptors:* *Behavior Patterns; *Change Strategies; *Employees; Administrators; Adults; Behavior Change; Profiles; Supervisors
*Availability:* Carlson Learning Co., Carlson Parkway, P.O. Box 59159, Minneapolis, MN 55459-8247.

This planning instrument allows supervisors or managers, at any level, to identify another person's behavioral style and then to develop and implement a behavioral management action strategy. It includes multiple applications for managers and supervisors, which include an employee reading profile, pattern tendencies, management strategies, and supervision planner. A behavioral intensity chart identifies several descriptive behaviors to determine tendencies.

**17186**
**Group Development Stage Analysis.** Carew, Don; And Others 1990.
*Descriptors:* *Group Dynamics; *Leadership Styles; *Morale; *Productivity; *Work Environment; Adults; Behavioral Objectives; Interpersonal Communication; Teamwork
*Availability:* Blanchard Training and Development, 125 State Pl., Escondido, CA 92025.
*Notes:* Items, 28.

This instrument will enable team leaders and group members to diagnose a group's stage of development. It will also pinpoint the appropriate leadership behaviors needed to develop the group into a high-performing team. There are 7 characteristics to assess the group's productivity and morale in order to diagnose development. They are: purpose, empowerment, relationships and communication, flexibility, optimal performance, recognition and appreciation, and morale. Scoring is based on group developmental stage.

**17220**
**Automated Manufacturing Systems Technician Test Item Bank I: Industrial Automation Assessment.** National Occupational Competency Testing Institute, Big Rapids, MI 1988.
*Descriptors:* *Automation; *Industrial Personnel; *Item Banks; *Occupational Tests; *Robotics; *Technical Education; *Technical Occupations; *Trade and Industrial Education; Adults; Apprenticeships; Competency Based Education; Diagnostic Tests; Employees; Knowledge Level; Mechanical Skills; On the Job Training; Skilled Workers; Trainees
*Identifiers:* NOCTI
*Availability:* National Occupational Competency Testing Institute, 409 Bishop Hall, Ferris State University, Big Rapids, MI 49307.
*Notes:* See 17221 for a description of the Automated Manufacturing Systems Technician Item Bank II: Automation/Robotics. Items, 310.

This computer-generated item bank is part of a series of 2 item banks concerned with automation and designed for training in the service and maintenance of industrial automated/robotic systems. Development was assisted by experts in labor, management, education, user companies and manufacturers, including the Robotic Industries Association. This portion of the computer-generated item bank is diagnostic in nature and evaluates the level of knowledge and competency needed for a trainee or student to advance in the field of service and maintenance of industrial automated/robotic systems. Areas of measurement include: engineering graphics (36 items); statics and dynamics (81 items); design of machine elements (69 items); industrial manufacturing (80 items); safety in the modern facility (44 items). Available on disc in IBM compatible format. Technical drawings are included as camera-ready copy.

**17221**
**Automated Manufacturing Systems Technician Test Item Bank II: Automation/Robotics.** National Occupational Competency Testing Institute, Big Rapids, MI 1988.
*Descriptors:* *Industrial Personnel; *Item Banks; *Occupational Tests; *Robotics; *Technical Education; *Technical Occupations; *Trade and Industrial Education; Adults; Apprenticeships; Automation; Competency Based Education; Employees; Knowledge Level; Mechanical Skills; On the Job Training; Skilled Workers; Trainees
*Identifiers:* NOCTI
*Availability:* National Occupational Competency Testing Institute, 409 Bishop Hall, Ferris State University, Big Rapids, MI 49307.
*Notes:* See 17220 for a description of the Automated Manufacturing Systems Technician Item Bank I: Industrial Automation. Items, 250.

This computer-generated item bank is part of a series of 2 item banks concerned with automation and designed for training in the service and maintenance of industrial automated/robotic systems. Development was assisted by experts in labor, management, education, user companies and manufacturers, including the Robotic Industries Association. Questions presented in this item bank are at the journeyman level of apprenticeship. Areas covered are: integration and testing of assemblies of integrated system unit (ISU) (49 items); operation and preproduction implementation of ISU (52 items); preventive maintenance of ISU (39 items); scheduled maintenance for ISU (26 items); immediate/emergency service for ISU (34 items); modification of ISU's service application (20 items); maintain and store documentation (6 items); and continuing education (8 items). Available on disc in IBM compatible format. Technical drawings are included as camera-ready copy.

**17225**
**Administrative Careers with America: Careers in Health, Safety, and Environmental Occupations.** U.S. Office of Personnel Management, Washington, DC
*Descriptors:* *Conservation (Environment); *Federal Government; *Health Occupations; *Personnel Selection; *Professional Occupations; *Public Administration; *Safety; Adults; Arithmetic; Competitive Selection; Managerial Occupations; Mathematics; Multiple Choice Tests; Occupational Tests; Problem Solving; Reading Comprehension; Tables (Data); Thinking Skills; Vocabulary
*Availability:* Testing Research and Applications Div., Career Entry and Employee Development Group, U.S. States Office of Personnel Management, Washington, DC 20415.
*Notes:* See also other Administrative Careers with America Tests in the areas of Careers in Writing and Public Information Occupations (17226); Careers in Business, Finance, and Management Occupations (17227); Careers in Personnel, Administration, and Computer Occupations (17228); Careers in Benefits Review, Tax, and Legal Occupations (17229); and Careers in Law Enforcement and Investigation Occupations (17230). Time, 210.

This examination is 1 of 6 designed for use in hiring employees to work for the federal government in 6 occupational groupings in the professional and administrative sector. It is a competitive examination. This particular test is used in filling entry-level jobs in the health, safety, and environmental occupation area. Applicants are selected according to merit system principles. This exam consists of a written test of job-related abilities. An additional questionnaire, the Individual Achievement Record (17231), a biographical inventory, is also given. The written test is designed to measure the ability to understand language and the ability to use reasoning in the context of language, as well as to solve quantitative problems and problems presented in tabular form.

**17226**
**Administrative Careers with America: Careers in Writing and Public Information Occupations.** U.S. Office of Personnel Management, Washington, DC 1988.
*Descriptors:* *Competitive Selection; *Entry Workers; *Federal Government; *Information Services; *Personnel Selection; *Writing Skills; Adults; Arithmetic; Information Scientists; Mathematics; Multiple Choice Tests; Occupational Tests; Problem Solving; Professional Occupations; Reading Comprehension; Tables (Data); Thinking Skills; Vocabulary
*Availability:* Testing Research and Applications Div., Career Entry and Employee Development Group, U.S. Office of Personnel Management, Washington, DC 20415.
*Notes:* See also other Administrative Careers with America Tests in the areas of Careers in Health, Safety, and Environmental Occupations (17225); Careers in Business, Finance, and Management Occupations (17227); Careers in Personnel, Administration, and Computer Occupations (17228); Careers in Benefits Review, Tax, and Legal Occupations (17229); and Careers in Law Enforcement and Investigation Occupations (17230). Time, 100.

This examination is 1 of 6 designed for use in hiring employees to work for the federal government in 6 occupational groupings in the professional and administrative sector. It is a competitive examination. This particular test is used in filling entry-level jobs that pertain to giving or preparing information. Applicants are selected according to merit system principles. This exam consists of a written test of job-related abilities. An additional questionnaire, the Individual Achievement Record (17231), a biographical inventory, is also given. The written test is designed to measure the ability to understand language and the ability to use reasoning in the context of language, as well as to solve quantitative problems and problems presented in tabular form.

**17227**
**Administrative Careers with America: Careers in Business, Finance, and Management Occupations.** U.S. Office of Personnel Management, Washington, DC 1988.
*Descriptors:* *Business Administration; *Competitive Selection; *Entry Workers; *Federal Government; *Finance Occupations; *Managerial Occupations; *Personnel Selection; Adults; Arithmetic; Mathematics; Multiple Choice Tests; Occupational Tests; Problem Solving; Professional Occupations; Public Administration; Reading Comprehension; Tables (Data); Thinking Skills; Vocabulary
*Availability:* Testing Research and Applications Div., Career Entry and Employee Development Group, U.S. Office of Personnel Management, Washington, DC 20415.
*Notes:* See also other Administrative Careers with America Tests in the areas of Careers in Health, Safety, and Environmental Occupations (17225); Careers in Writing and Public Information Occupations (17226); Careers in Personnel, Administration, and Computer Occupations (17228); Careers in Benefits Review, Tax, and Legal Occupations (17229); and Careers in Law Enforcement and Investigation Occupations (17230). Time, 100.

This examination is 1 of 6 designed for use in hiring employees to work for the federal government in 6 occupational groupings in the professional and administrative sector. It is a competitive examination. This particular test is used in filling entry-level jobs in the business, finance, and management occupations area. Applicants are selected according to merit system principles. This exam consists of a written test of job-related abilities.

An additional questionnaire, the Individual Achievement Record (17231), a biographical inventory is also given. The written test is designed to measure the ability to understand language and the ability to use reasoning in the context of language, as well as to solve quantitative problems and problems presented in tabular form.

**17228**
**Administrative Careers with America: Careers in Personnel, Administration, and Computer Occupations.** U.S. Office of Personnel Management, Washington, DC 1988.
*Descriptors:* *Competitive Selection; *Data Processing Occupations; *Entry Workers; *Federal Government; *Human Services; *Managerial Occupations; *Personnel Selection; *Public Administration; Adults; Arithmetic; Mathematics; Multiple Choice Tests; Occupational Tests; Problem Solving; Professional Occupations; Reading Comprehension; Tables (Data); Thinking Skills; Vocabulary
*Availability:* Testing Research and Applications Div., Career Entry and Employee Development Group, U.S. Office of Personnel Management, Washington, DC 20415.
*Notes:* See also other Administrative Careers with America Tests in the areas of Careers in Health, Safety, and Environmental Occupations (17225); Careers in Writing and Public Information Occupations (17226); Careers in Business, Finance, and Management Occupations (17227); Careers in Benefits Review, Tax, and Legal Occupations (17229); and Careers in Law Enforcement and Investigation Occupations (17230). Time, 100.

This examination is 1 of 6 six designed for use in hiring employees to work for the federal government in 6 occupational groupings in the professional and administrative sector. It is a competitive examination. This particular test is used in filling entry-level jobs that pertain to personnel matters, administration, and computer-related occupations. Applicants are selected according to merit system principles. This exam consists of a written test of job-related abilities. An additional questionnaire, the Individual Achievement Record (17231), a biographical inventory is also given. The written test is designed to measure the ability to understand language and the ability to use reasoning in the context of language, as well as to solve quantitative problems and problems presented in tabular form.

**17229**
**Administrative Careers with America: Careers in Benefits Review, Tax, and Legal Occupations.** U.S. Office of Personnel Management, Washington, DC 1988.
*Descriptors:* *Competitive Selection; *Entry Workers; *Federal Government; *Fringe Benefits; *Human Services; *Laws; *Personnel Selection; *Taxes; Adults; Arithmetic; Mathematics; Multiple Choice Tests; Occupational Tests; Problem Solving; Professional Occupations; Reading Comprehension; Tables (Data); Thinking Skills; Vocabulary
*Availability:* Testing Research and Applications Div., Career Entry and Employee Development Group, U.S. Office of Personnel Management, Washington, DC 20415.
*Notes:* See also other Administrative Careers with America Tests in the areas of Careers in Health, Safety, and Environmental Occupations (17225); Careers in Writing and Public Information Occupations (17226); Careers in Business, Finance, and Management Occupations (17227); Careers in Personnel, Administration, and Computer Occupations (17228); and Careers in Law Enforcement and Investigation Occupations (17230). Time, 100.

This examination is 1 of 6 designed for use in hiring employees to work for the federal government in 6 occupational groupings in the professional and administrative sector. It is a competitive examination. This particular test is used in filling entry-level jobs that pertain to employee benefits review, and tax-related and law-related occupations. Applicants are selected according to merit system principles. This exam consists of a written test of job-related abilities. An additional questionnaire, the Individual Achievement Record (17231), a biographical inventory is also given. The written test is designed to measure the ability to understand language and the ability to use reasoning in the context of language, as well as to solve quantitative problems and problems presented in tabular form.

**17230**
**Administrative Careers with America: Careers in Law Enforcement and Investigation Occupations.** U.S. Office of Personnel Management, Washington, DC 1988.
*Descriptors:* *Personnel Selection; *Law Enforcement; *Federal Government; Adults; Occupational Tests; Professional Occupations; Competitive Selection; Multiple Choice Tests; Vocabulary; Reading Comprehension; Thinking Skills; Mathematics; Problem Solving; Arithmetic; Tables (Data)
*Availability:* Testing Research and Applications Div., Career Entry and Employee Development Group, U.S. Office of Personnel Management, Washington, DC 20415.
*Notes:* See also other Administrative Careers with America Tests in the areas of Careers in Health, Safety, and Environmental Occupations (17225); Careers in Writing and Public Information Occupations (17226); Careers in Business, Finance, and Management Occupations (17227); Careers in Personnel, Administration, and Computer Occupations (17228); and Careers in Benefits Review, Tax, and Legal Occupations (17229). Time, 100.

This examination is 1 of 6 designed for use in hiring employees to work for the federal government in 6 occupational groupings in the professional and administrative sector. It is a competitive examination. This particular test is used in filling entry-level jobs that pertain to law enforcement occupations and investigative occupations. Applicants are selected according to merit system principles. This exam consists of a written test of job-related abilities. An additional questionnaire, the Individual Achievement Record (17231), a biographical inventory is also given. The written test is designed to measure the ability to understand language and the ability to use reasoning in the context of language, as well as to solve quantitative problems and problems presented in tabular form.

**17231**
**Individual Achievement Record.** U.S. Office of Personnel Management, Washington, DC 1988.
*Descriptors:* *Biographical Inventories; *Competitive Selection; *Entry Workers; *Federal Government; *Personnel Selection; Adults; Individual Characteristics; Multiple Choice Tests; Occupational Tests; Professional Occupations; Profiles; Questionnaires
*Identifiers:* IAR
*Availability:* Testing Research and Applications Div., Career Entry and Employee Development Group, U.S. Office of Personnel Management, Washington, DC 20415.
*Notes:* Time, 20.

This multiple-choice questionnaire is designed to assess a job applicant's experiences, skills, and achievements in school, employment, and other activities. The questionnaire is based on research concerning the characteristics and experiences of successful people in professional and administrative occupations. Provides a broad picture of the test taker's qualification for a wide range of jobs.

**17234**
**Canadian Observation Model for French Teachers.** LeBlanc, Doris; London, Dalton 1989.
*Descriptors:* *Beginning Teachers; *Classroom Observation Techniques; *French; *Language Teachers; *Teacher Evaluation; Competence; Foreign Countries; Likert Scales; Rating Scales
*Identifiers:* Canada
*Availability:* *Canadian Modern Language Review,* v45 n4 p675-82, May 1989.

An instrument designed as a guideline for classroom observation of beginning teachers, or teachers in training, of French as a second language. The instrument is written in French. There are 2 versions, the first in which the observer indicates the competence of the teachers on a Likert-type scale and another in which the observer records the teachers' competence in a free format. Instrument assesses teachers' lesson plans, methods of instruction, use of French, relations with students, and overall rating. Results help teachers recognize weak points, indicate where they are professionally, give them an overall indication of how well they are doing, and give suggestions for improvement.

**17255**
**SkilRater Office Skills Assessment System.** Wonderlic, E.F.
*Descriptors:* *Keyboarding (Data Entry); *Knowledge Level; *Occupational Tests; *Office Machines; *Office Occupations; *Personnel Selection; *Typewriting; *Word Processing; Adults; Job Placement; Proofreading; Staff Development
*Availability:* E.F. Wonderlic Personnel Test, Inc., 820 Frontage Rd., Northfield, IL 60093.
*Notes:* Time, 85 approx.

This instrument is an automated typing, data entry, and word processing skills assessment system. It measures the candidate's knowledge of the keyboard; typing speed and accuracy; the ability to produce perfect documents from source material; proofreading skills; finding and correcting errors and making modifications; the ability to enter data into fixed-field formatted screens; word processing knowledge and skills; and competence in using word processing functions. This tool is used to make better hiring decisions, to improve employee placement decisions, and to measure employee development. It conforms to existing laws, standards, and regulations relevant to pre-employment testing procedures.

**17332**
**AEQUITAS.** Educational Testing Service, Princeton, NJ; KEE Systems, Columbia, MD; Olsten Temporary Services, Princeton, NJ 1989.
*Descriptors:* *Clerical Occupations; *Industrial Training; *Occupational Tests; *Personnel Selection; *Word Processing; Adults; Computer Assisted Testing; Filing; Keyboarding (Data Entry)
*Identifiers:* IBM DisplayWrite; Microsoft Word; WordPerfect
*Availability:* KEE, Inc., 9135 Guilford Rd., Columbia, MD 21046.

This instrument was designed for use in the training and placement of employees in clerical positions requiring word processing. Areas tested include: filing, word processing of letters, invoices, and columnar reports. Word processing software packages used are IBM Displaywrite, Microsoft Word, and WordPerfect.

**17371**
**Miner Sentence Completion Scale, Form T.** Organizational Measurement Systems Press, Atlanta, GA 1984.
*Descriptors:* *Employee Attitudes; *Motivation; *Projective Measures; Adults; College Faculty; Counseling; Employees; Organizational Development; Professional Occupations; Questionnaires; Work Attitudes
*Availability:* Organizational Measurement Systems Press, P.O. Box 1656, Buffalo, NY 14221.
*Notes:* See also Miner Sentence Completion Scale, Form P (14073). Items, 40.

A measure of an individual's motivation for use in employee counseling and organizational development. Normative data derive from a sample of professors in business schools involved in teaching, writing, and consulting.

**17391**
**Machinist Test, Form A.** Ramsay Corp., Pittsburgh, PA 1989.

*Descriptors:* *Achievement Tests; *Machinists; *Multiple Choice Tests; *Occupational Tests; Adults; Knowledge Level; Skilled Workers
*Availability:* Ramsay Corp., 1050 Boyce Rd., Pittsburgh, PA 15241-3907.
*Notes:* Time, 120 approx. Items, 120.

This multiple-choice test measures knowledge and skills in machining areas. It covers the areas of: heat treating; layout, cutting and assembly; print reading; steels, metals and materials; mechanical principles and repair; machine tools; rigging; and tools, material, and equipment. This test of knowledge and skill is suitable for group use. Machine scoring is available. The test is untimed with a suggested time limit of 2 hours.

**17392**
**Assessment Exercises, Self-Inventories, Tests, and Survey Instruments.** Training House, Inc., Princeton, NJ 1990.
*Descriptors:* *Employees; *Job Performance; *Managerial Occupations; *Needs Assessment; *Resource Materials; *Self Evaluation (Individuals); Adults; Professional Development; Skill Development; Surveys; Training
*Availability:* Training House, Inc., 100 Bear Brook Rd., P.O. Box 3090, Princeton, NJ 08543-3090.
*Notes:* See also 16131, 16133 through 16137, 16140, 16142 through 16143, 16145, 17403 through 17412 for related instruments. Items, 20.

Designed for in-company use to produce measurably improved performance among employees at every organizational level. This series contains 20 assessment exercises, self-inventories, tests, and surveys for use as a resource and a needs assessment. Each exercise includes instructions for self-scoring and interpreting the results.

**17393**
**Welding Test, Form A.** Ramsay Corp., Pittsburgh, PA 1987.
*Descriptors:* *Achievement Tests; *Multiple Choice Tests; *Occupational Tests; *Welding; Adults; Knowledge Level; Skilled Occupations
*Availability:* Ramsay Corp., 1050 Boyce Rd., Pittsburgh, PA 15241-3907.
*Notes:* Time, 120 approx. Items, 100.

This instrument is a multiple-choice test that measures knowledge and skills in welding areas. It covers the areas of print reading; welding; welder maintenance and operation; tools, machines, materials, and equipment; rigging; and production welding and calculations. This tool is suitable for group use. A machine scoring service is available. This test is untimed with a suggested limit of 2 hours.

**17395**
**Society of Cost Estimating and Analysis Professional Certification Program.** Society of Cost Estimating and Analysis, Alexandria, VA
*Descriptors:* *Business Skills; *Certification; *Cost Effectiveness; *Cost Estimates; *Finance Occupations; *Occupational Tests; Adults; Economics
*Availability:* Society of Cost Estimating and Analysis, 101 S. Whiting St., Ste. 201, Alexandria, VA 22304.

This examination is used in conjunction with an education requirement and a job experience requirement for applicants to the society's certification program. It measures knowledge and skills required of a person who prepares cost estimates and analyses. The examination is administered twice per year. Requires knowledge of business related subjects generally acquired in undergraduate courses leading to degrees in business administration, industrial management or industrial engineering, such as cost accounting and managerial economics. Also requires knowledge of cost concepts, cost theory, data and measurement, estimation and testing statistical theory, and analysis techniques.

**17403**
**Managerial/Supervisory Pre-Training Planning Sheet.** Training House, Inc., Princeton, NJ 1988.
*Descriptors:* *Administrators; *Management Development; *Managerial Occupations; *Needs Assessment; *Supervisors; Adults; Planning; Rating Scales; Supervisory Methods; Training Methods
*Availability:* Training House, Inc., 100 Bear Brook Rd., P.O. Box 3090, Princeton, NJ 08543.
*Notes:* See Assessment Exercises, Self Inventories, Tests, and Survey Instruments (17392) for related tests. Items, 24.

Designed for in-company use to produce measurably improved performance among employees at every organizational level, these assessment exercises, self-inventories, tests, and surveys are contained in a kit. Useful as a resource and a needs assessment instrument and includes instructions for self-scoring and interpreting the results. Managerial/Supervisory Pre-Training Planning Sheet assesses the views, expectations, and needs of managers/supervisors prior to launching a management development program. Three aspects of training and evaluating, with respondents (future participants and their managers) assigning ratings to needs on 25 skills.

**17404**
**Personal Development Options.** Training House, Inc., Princeton, NJ
*Descriptors:* *Administrators; *Career Development; *Individual Development; *Management Development; Adults; Occupational Aspiration; Planning
*Availability:* Training House, Inc., 100 Bear Brook Rd., P.O. Box 3090, Princeton, NJ 08543.
*Notes:* See Assessment Exercises, Self Inventories, Tests, and Survey Instruments (17392) for related tests.

Designed for in-company use to produce measurably improved performance among employees at every organizational level, these assessment exercises, self-inventories, tests, and surveys are contained in a kit. Useful as a resource and a needs assessment instrument and includes instructions for self-scoring and interpreting the results. Personal Development Options provides an outline of 25 options for personal growth and development. Participants select the options that apply to them, then draw up a personal development plan to be discussed with their manager. Some options include assignment to task force or team, training (as learner or instructor), and job rotation.

**17405**
**What Do You Say?** Training House, Inc., Princeton, NJ 1986.
*Descriptors:* *Employees; *Interpersonal Communication; Adults; Self Evaluation (Individuals); Social Cognition
*Availability:* Training House, Inc., 100 Bear Brook Rd., P.O. Box 3090, Princeton, NJ 08543.
*Notes:* See Assessment Exercises, Self Inventories, Tests, and Survey Instruments (17392) for related tests. Items, 12.

Designed for in-company use to produce measurably improved performance among employees at every organizational level, these assessment exercises, self-inventories, tests, and surveys are contained in a kit. Useful as a resource and a needs assessment instrument and includes instructions for self-scoring and interpreting the results. What Do You Say? is a self-assessment instrument designed to give respondents insight into ways in which they respond to people in interpersonal communications. There are 12 episodes, or situations to which the respondent will answer, selecting the responses that seem most appropriate. Raw scores on 4 response styles include: empathic, critical, searching, and advising. These styles are tied to patterns of communication and the 3 ego states: parent, adult, and child. This exercise is based on a 3-point system.

**17406**
**Job Satisfaction and Dissatisfaction.** Training House, Inc., Princeton, NJ 1989.
*Descriptors:* *Employees; *Job Satisfaction; *Quality of Working Life; *Work Attitudes; Adults; Behavior Rating Scales; Occupational Aspiration; Self Evaluation (Individuals)
*Identifiers:* Maslow (Abraham)
*Availability:* Training House, Inc., 100 Bear Brook Rd., P.O. Box 3090, Princeton, NJ 08543.
*Notes:* See Assessment Exercises, Self Inventories, Tests, and Survey Instruments (17392) for related tests. Items, 10.

Designed for in-company use to produce measurably improved performance among employees at every organizational level, these assessment exercises, self-inventories, tests, and surveys are contained in a kit. Useful as a resource and a needs assessment instrument and includes instructions for self-scoring and interpreting the results. Job Satisfaction and Dissatisfaction is a self-assessment exercise consisting of 10 items, each followed by 3 statements. The respondent is to choose the statement most agreed with. This exercise is based on Dr. Abraham Maslow's hierarchy of human needs. Scores on each of the 5 levels indicate the relative importance of these needs of the respondent.

**17407**
**Dealing with Groups.** Training House, Inc., Princeton, NJ 1988.
*Descriptors:* *Group Behavior; *Leadership Qualities; Adults; Behavior Rating Scales; Employees; Self Evaluation (Individuals)
*Availability:* Training House, Inc., 100 Bear Brook Rd., P.O. Box 3090, Princeton, NJ 08543.
*Notes:* See Assessment Exercises, Self Inventories, Tests, and Survey Instruments (17392) for related tests. Items, 10.

Designed for in-company use to produce measurably improved performance among employees at every organizational level, these assessment exercises, self-inventories, tests, and surveys are contained in a kit. Useful as a resource and a needs assessment instrument and includes instructions for self-scoring and interpreting the result. Dealing With Groups is an exercise that measures behaviors in dealing with groups. These behaviors can be viewed as judgmental, nurturing, or accepting. The roles filled and the responses received reflect effectiveness in influencing others. By ranking 10 sets of 4 statements, the scores will show the behavior toward which the respondent tends to lean.

**17408**
**Self-Assessment in Writing Skills.** Training House, Inc., Princeton, NJ 1990.
*Descriptors:* *Employees; *Self Evaluation (Individuals); *Writing Skills; *Writing Tests; Adults
*Availability:* Training House, Inc., 100 Bear Brook Rd., P.O. Box 3090, Princeton, NJ 08543.
*Notes:* See Assessment Exercises, Self-Inventories, Tests, and Survey Instruments (17392) for related tests. Time, 120 approx.

Designed for in-company use to produce measurably improved performance among employees at every organizational level, these assessment exercises, self-inventories, tests, and surveys are contained in a kit. Useful as a resource and a needs assessment instrument and includes instructions for self-scoring and interpreting the results. Self-Assessment In Writing Skills is divided into 2 parts. Part 1 measures the respondent's ability to edit a 2-page proposal, line by line, to improve its content and style. Part 2 asks the respondent to rewrite the proposal to improve its organization and format. Each part is scored separately with a total point possibility of 100.

**17409**
**Analytical Thinking Test.** Training House, Inc., Princeton, NJ 1990.

*Descriptors:* *Cognitive Ability; *Critical Thinking; *Employees; *Induction; *Logical Thinking; *Thinking Skills; Adults; Self Evaluation (Individuals)
*Availability:* Training House, Inc., 100 Bear Brook Rd., P.O. Box 3090, Princeton, NJ 08543.
*Notes:* See Assessment Exercises, Self-Inventories, Tests, and Survey Instruments (17392) for related tests.

Designed for in-company use to produce measurably improved performance among employees at every organizational level, these assessment exercises, self-inventories, tests, and surveys are contained in a kit. Useful as a resource and a needs assessment instrument and includes instructions for self-scoring and interpreting the results. Analytical Thinking Test is an assessment in which the respondent analyzes 5 situations and evaluates the correctness of statements describing each. Then, an argument on the pros and cons of a new law is developed and the reasoning is scored.

**17410**
**The Time of Your Life.** Training House, Inc., Princeton, NJ 1988.
*Descriptors:* *Employees; *Quality of Life; *Time Management; Adults; Life Satisfaction; Self Evaluation (Individuals)
*Availability:* Training House, Inc., 100 Bear Brook Rd., P.O. Box 3090, Princeton, NJ 08543.
*Notes:* See Assessment Exercises, Self-Inventories, Tests, and Survey Instruments (17392) for related tests. Items, 25.

Designed for in-company use to produce measurably improved performance among employees at every organizational level, these assessment exercises, self-inventories, tests, and surveys are contained in a kit. Useful as a resource and a needs assessment instrument, and includes instructions for self-scoring and interpreting the results. The Time Of Your Life is an exercise that gives insights into how time is being utilized. Statements describe different aspects of time management. The individual has 3 responses from which to choose to best describe feelings or experiences. The results of this instrument places the individual into 1 of 4 categories: slave, balanced, master, and obsessed.

**17411**
**Coping with Stress.** Training House, Inc., Princeton, NJ 1989.
*Descriptors:* *Coping; *Employees; *Stress Management; Adjustment (to Environment); Adults; Life Events; Rating Scales; Self Evaluation (Individuals)
*Availability:* Training House, Inc., 100 Bear Brook Rd., P.O. Box 3090, Princeton, NJ 08543.
*Notes:* See Assessment Exercises, Self-Inventories, Tests, and Survey Instruments (17392) for related tests. Items, 60.

Designed for in-company use to produce measurably improved performance among employees at every organizational level, these assessment exercises, self-inventories, tests, and surveys are contained in a kit. Useful as a resource and a needs assessment instrument, and includes instructions for self-scoring and interpreting the results. Coping With Stress is a 3-part assessment tool. Part 1 measures reaction to stress by rating 30 statements using a 4-point rating scale. These scores indicate one's responses to stress on 4 scales: obsession, hysteria, anxiety, and phobia. Part 2 is also a 4-point rating scale that describes in 10 statements how to deal with stress. This shows how healthy one's adjustment has been. Part 3 lists 20 common sources of stress, some of which include divorce, employment termination, pregnancy, and arrest. The subject indicates which of these events he or she has experienced in the past year.

**17412**
**Putting You in the Picture.** Training House, Inc., Princeton, NJ 1989.
*Descriptors:* *Employees; *Photographs; *Projective Measures; *Values; Achievement Need; Adults; Affiliation Need; Dependency (Personality); Failure; Long Range Planning; Prediction; Security (Psychology); Self Evaluation (Individuals); Success
*Availability:* Training House, Inc., 100 Bear Brook Rd., P.O. Box 3090, Princeton, NJ 08543.
*Notes:* See Assessment Exercises, Self-Inventories, Tests, and Survey Instruments (17392) for related tests. Items, 4.

Designed for in-company use to produce measurably improved performance among employees at every organizational level, these assessment exercises, self-inventories, tests, and surveys are contained in a kit. Useful as a resource and a needs assessment instrument, and includes instructions for self-scoring and interpreting the result. Putting You In The Picture is a self-assessment tool in which the respondent is given 4 photos and then writes a brief story about each. Stories are then analyzed against 6 factors or orientations, success/failure, past/future, achiever/affiliator, long-range/short-range, security/challenge, and task/people. Participants work in pairs, analyzing each other's stories.

**17418**
**Development Officers Screening Instrument.** Cook, Diana L.; And Others 1990.
*Descriptors:* *Administrator Selection; *Educational Administration; *Employment Interviews; *Occupational Information; *Screening Tests; Adults; Rating Scales
*Identifiers:* *Development Officers (College)
*Availability:* *Currents,* v16 n4 p44-46, Apr 1990.
*Notes:* Items, 60.

An instrument designed to assist managers in hiring the best candidate for the position of development officer in a university. Consists of 2 parts. Part 1 is a review of the job description, in which managers indicate the knowledge and training, skills, and values necessary for a person to be successful in the position. This information should be used as criteria for revising job descriptions and for writing job advertisements. Part 2 uses the same scale as a basis for interviewing prospective candidates. Managers then match the candidate's knowledge, training, skills, and values with those determined as necessary for the position. Instrument offers managers a way to clarify the objectives and expectations of a position and to select the person whose background best matches that necessary for the job.

**17443**
**Leadex.** Albrecht, Karl 1990.
*Descriptors:* *Administrators; *Leadership Qualities; *Self Concept; Administrator Effectiveness; Adults; Profiles; Rating Scales; Self Evaluation (Individuals)
*Identifiers:* *Leadership Effectiveness
*Availability:* Karl Albrecht & Associates, 910 Grand Ave., Ste. 206, San Diego, CA 92109.

For use as a multilevel evaluation tool. Can also be used for self-perception purposes to identify special strengths, as well as developmental needs. This tool can help managers at all levels become more effective by increasing their self-awareness and self-understanding. Based on a rating scale with numbers ranging from 1 to 5, this instrument offers 6 leadership components. These components are: vision and values, direction, persuasion, support, development, and appreciation.

**17451**
**Faculty Satisfaction Questionnaire.** Serafin, Ana Gil 1991.
*Descriptors:* *College Faculty; *College Instruction; *Job Satisfaction; *Noninstructional Responsibility; *Research; *Spanish; *Staff Role; *Teacher Role; Biographical Inventories; College Environment; Higher Education; Likert Scales; Rating Scales; Research Problems; Spanish Speaking; Teacher Background; Teaching Conditions
*Identifiers:* TIM(Q); Venezuela
*Availability:* Tests in Microfiche, Test Collection, Educational Testing Service, Princeton, NJ 08541.
*Notes:* Items, 37.

This instrument is designed to measure faculty satisfaction with the role functions of teaching, research, and service. It was created to help identify elements in the level of faculty satisfaction with their position functions. Items are grouped into 3 dimensions, teaching statements, research statements, and service statements. English and Spanish versions are available. A separate biographical section requests gender, age, academic rank, teaching experience, and other related information. Uses 5-point, Likert-type items. Respondents indicate whether they are very satisfied, satisfied, neutral, dissatisfied, or very dissatisfied with the roles they perform as described by each of the statements. A satisfaction score is produced. Technical information on reliability for each variable was determined by use of Cronbach's alpha coefficient.

**17510**
**Perceptions of Organizational Politics Scale.** Kacmar, K. Michele; Ferris, Gerald R. 1991.
*Descriptors:* *Employee Attitudes; *Organizational Climate; *Work Environment; Adults; Employees; Likert Scales; Rating Scales
*Identifiers:* Organizational Culture; Political Culture; POPS
*Availability:* *Educational and Psychological Measurement,* v51 n1 p193-205, Spr 1991.
*Notes:* Items, 12.

A questionnaire designed to measure how employees perceive political aspects of their work environments. On a 5-point, Likert-type scale, employees indicate how strongly they agree or disagree with 12 statements. The statements cover 3 factors: general political behavior; going along to get ahead; and pay and promotion. Extensive information on statistical analysis is included.

**17524**
**Individual Beliefs about Organizational Ethics.** Froelich, Kristina S.; Kottke, Janet L. 1991.
*Descriptors:* *Attitude Measures; *Employee Attitudes; *Moral Values; *Organizational Climate; Adults; Conflict of Interest; Likert Scales; Rating Scales
*Identifiers:* *Business Ethics
*Availability:* *Educational and Psychological Measurement,* v51 n2 p377-83, Sum 1991.
*Notes:* Items, 10.

A scale designed to assess employees' attitudes about ethical behavior in a business section. On a 7-point, Likert-type scale, employees indicate how strongly they agree or disagree with statements concerning ethical dilemmas in the workplace. Statements reflect the extent to which individuals believe the company should be supported in the face of an ethical conflict and the extent to which employees should lie to protect the company. Scale may be used to identify and explore potential ethical conflicts in business settings. Technical data are included.

**17534**
**Empowerment Profile.** Jones, John E.; Bearley, William L. 1988.
*Descriptors:* *Administrative Organization; *Leadership Qualities; *Power Structure; *Professional Autonomy; Administration; Adults; Decision Making; Rating Scales; Work Environment
*Availability:* Organization Design and Development, Inc., 2002 Renaissance Blvd., Ste. 100, King of Prussia, PA 19406-2746.
*Notes:* Items, 99.

Intended to give an understanding of the respondent's work realities. This tool provides an opportunity to consider strategies and tactics to increase personal power and to empower employees. A 7-point rating scale is used. Items are rated twice, once for the respondent and a second time for the respondent's employees collectively. Scores are plotted on a profile that represents a general level of influence over work situations. The dimensions that are characterized by the scores include: strengths, autonomy, centrality, involvement, control, influence, resources, and organizational climate.

**17535**

**Leadership Strategies Inventory.** Sims, Henry P. Jr.; Manz, Charles C. 1990.

*Descriptors:* *Leadership Qualities; *Leadership Styles; Adults; Collegiality; Employer Employee Relationship; Employers; Interpersonal Relationship; Interprofessional Relationship; Rating Scales

*Availability:* Organization Design and Development, Inc., 2002 Renaissance Blvd., Ste. 100, King of Prussia, PA 19406-2746.

*Notes:* Items, 48.

This inventory is designed to help respondents gain some useful information about their leadership behavior. It provides an opportunity to examine the impact of that behavior on others, as well as on the organization as a whole. The tool measures 4 different leadership strategies: the strong man, the transactor, the visionary hero, and the superleader. Three of these styles are oriented to the past or present time, while the fourth style looks to the future. Also included in this instrument is a Leadership Strategies Inventory - Other, which provides objective feedback from employees concerning leadership behavior of their employer/respondent, and the impact of this person's behavior on others and on the organization as a whole.

**17538**

**The Name of the Game: Team Strategies for Effective Organizations.** Sashkin, Marshall 1990.

*Descriptors:* *Interprofessional Relationship; *Management Teams; *Teamwork; Administrator Effectiveness; Adults; Organizational Effectiveness; Questionnaires; Self Evaluation (Groups)

*Identifiers:* Organizing Strategies

*Availability:* Organization Design and Development, Inc., 2002 Renaissance Blvd., Ste. 100, King of Prussia, PA 19406-2746.

*Notes:* Items, 36.

Team Strategies for Effective Organizations was developed to help members of a management or work team examine the strategy and nature of the assumptions they make about how they should work together. It is intended to aid team members in examining and analyzing their assumptions, which may lead to improved team effectiveness.

**17539**

**Self-Management Assessment.** Fulmer, Robert M. 1991.

*Descriptors:* *Administrators; *Individual Power; *Managerial Occupations; *Self Evaluation (Individuals); Adults; Decision Making; Interpersonal Competence; Interprofessional Relationship; Rating Scales; Self Actualization

*Identifiers:* SMA

*Availability:* Organization Design and Development, Inc., 2002 Renaissance Blvd., Ste. 100, King of Prussia, PA 19406-2746.

*Notes:* Items, 80.

Assists in self-analysis and evaluation on 10 different dimensions that characterize excellence in self-management, as well as demonstrating how effectively professional and personal interests and pursuits are directed. The intention of this tool is to reflect a representative array of attitudes, behaviors, and values in life in order to effectively determine their usefulness and give options for desired changes.

**17540**

**Management Practices Questionnaire.** Nowack, Kenneth M. 1988.

*Descriptors:* *Management Development; *Managerial Occupations; *Supervisors; *Supervisory Methods; Administrators; Adults; Communication Skills; Decision Making; Interpersonal Competence; Planning; Questionnaires; Rating Scales; Self Evaluation (Individuals)

*Identifiers:* Management Styles

*Availability:* Organizational Performance Dimensions, 20950-38 Oxnard St., Woodland Hills, CA 91367.

*Notes:* Items, 100.

A questionnaire that provides a summary of critical skills and competencies needed for supervision and management. It is based on job analyses of supervisory and management positions in organizations. This tool is also based on extensive norms and summarizes perceptions from 5 persons who will also complete the questionnaire about the program participant. It will provide a computerized feedback report that is useful for developmental planning purposes. Major categories of supervisory and managerial activities are: communications, interpersonal, administrative, and decision making. A response scale ranges from 1 to 7. Raw scores and standard scores, with a mean of 50 and standard deviation of 10, are presented for each scale.

**17628**

**Communication Competencies of Women Managers Scale.** Berryman-Fink, Cynthia 1982.

*Descriptors:* *Attitude Measures; *Business Communication; *Communication Skills; *Employee Attitudes; *Interpersonal Competence; *Interprofessional Relationship; *Women Administrators; Adults; Employer Attitudes; Employer Employee Relationship

*Identifiers:* CCWMS

*Availability:* *Communication Quarterly,* v33 n2 p137-48, Spr 1985.

*Notes:* Time, 15 approx. Items, 30.

A summated rating scale consisting of 30 statements measuring perceived communication competencies of women managers. Some items pertain to the ability to communicate to other persons, and some items pertain to the ability to understand and accept communications from other persons. Some items are positive statements, while others are of a negative nature. Based on the responses from 178 persons employed in a variety of organizations, the internal consistency of the scale was 0.90.

**17643**

**Comprehensive Personnel System.** Anderson, Terry D.; Zeiner, Brian 1989.

*Descriptors:* *Employees; *Personnel Management; Adults; Career Planning; Job Placement; Job Training; Personnel Evaluation; Personnel Selection; Questionnaires; Staff Development

*Identifiers:* CPS

*Availability:* Career Research and Testing, 2005 Hamilton Ave., Ste. 250, San Jose, CA 95125.

Personnel assessment, development, and planning system, most appropriately used by small- to medium-sized organizations. Encompasses all phases of the staffing process, including screening, selection, planning for training, and career path planning and research. Designed to be used in conjunction with the Personal Style Indicator (15718), Entrepreneurial Style and Success Indicator (16688), and the Job Style Indicator (16686).

**17648**

**Hilson Career Satisfaction Index.** Inwald, Robin E. 1989.

*Descriptors:* *Job Satisfaction; *Stress Variables; Adults; Anger; Behavior Problems; Hostility; Work Environment

*Identifiers:* HCSI

*Availability:* Hilson Research, Inc., P.O. Box 239, 82-28 Abingdon Rd., Kew Gardens, NY 11415.

*Notes:* Time, 30 approx. Items, 161.

Developed to aid in the identification of employee stress symptoms, performance difficulties, negative attitudes towards work, antisocial attitudes, and/or substance abuse difficulties. Designed to identify job dissatisfaction and stress patterns. Normative data are provided for various occupations.

**17666**

**Trust Orientation Profile.** Chartier, Myron R.

*Descriptors:* *Teamwork; *Employees; *Trust (Psychology); *Credibility; Adults; Behavior Rating Scales; Interpersonal Relationship; Team Training

*Availability:* Pfeiffer, J. William, ed., *The 1991 Annual: Developing Human Resources.* San Diego: University Associates, 1991. Pfeiffer and Co., formerly University Associates, 8517 Production Ave., San Diego, CA 92121-2280.

Useful for intact work groups or teams with trust being an integral part of teamwork. This instrument measures the context of interpersonal and team relationships and is useful as a trust climate survey in interpersonal relationships; as a survey within a team or an organization; and as a tool for team-building and team-development sessions with coworkers. Respondents choose between 2 alternatives based on how they actually behave or feel or how a situation is perceived. Respondents then calculate trust/mistrust ratios for themselves on each of the 12 dimensions and for trust as a whole. There are no reliability or validity data available. Used by trainers, consultants, or facilitators in training groups; for demonstration purposes; to generate data for training or organizational development sessions; and for other group applications. Instrument is not intended for in-depth personal growth, psychodiagnostic, or therapeutic work. Intended for use in training groups; for demonstration purposes; to generate data for training or organization development sessions; and for other group applications in which the trainer, consultant, or facilitator helps respondents use the data for achieving some form of progress. (TJS)

**17667**

**Managerial Work Values Scale.** Rao, T. Venkateswara

*Descriptors:* *Work Ethic; *Administrators; *Work Attitudes; *Managerial Occupations; Adults; Occupational Aspiration; Leadership; Job Satisfaction; Creativity; Economics; Status; Interpersonal Relationship; Collegiality; Work Environment; Behavior Rating Scales; Values Clarification; Career Development

*Identifiers:* Paired Comparisons

*Availability:* Pfeiffer, J. William, ed., *The 1991 Annual: Developing Human Resources.* San Diego: University Associates, 1991. Pfeiffer and Co., formerly University Associates, 8517 Production Ave., San Diego, CA 92121-2280.

Developed to focus specifically on 9 work values of managers, using the paired-comparison method to measure their relative strengths. The values/work dimensions include: creativity, economics, independence, status, service, academics, security, collegiality, and work conditions. Each item in a pair represents 1 of the 9 work dimensions. Since values influence managers' choices, which are important in determining managerial effectiveness because they influence outcomes, managers are likely to make better decisions in all situations if they act with an awareness of their reasons and with the knowledge of the extent to which their values direct their decisions. Useful as a values clarification activity and can be used in conjunction with any career development program. An action plan can be created for helping respondents to bring their careers more closely in line with their work values. Instrument is not intended for in-depth personal growth, psychodiagnostic, or therapeutic work. Intended for use in training groups; for demonstration purposes; to generate data for training or organization development sessions; and for other group applications in which the trainer, consultant, or facilitator helps respondents use the data for achieving some form of progress. (TJS)

**17668**

**Management Styles Spectrum.** Murrell, Kenneth

*Descriptors:* *Employees; *Supervisory Methods; *Organizational Climate; Adults; Leadership Styles; Interpersonal Relationship; Organizations (Groups); Behavior Rating Scales

*Identifiers:* *Management Styles

*Availability:* Pfeiffer, J. William, ed., *The 1991 Annual: Developing Human Resources.* San Diego: University Associates, 1991. Pfeiffer and Co., formerly University Associates, 8517 Production Ave., San Diego, CA 92121-2280.

Designed to help form a view of an organization's culture as directly affected by the prevailing management style. This tool assists employees in assessing the degree to which the climate in their organization supports empowerment. With the use of this instrument, practioners can determine the existing organizational-empowerment culture before beginning to examine and implement processes that enhance empowerment. There are no right or wrong answers. Responses to each item are based on the behavior and actions of the managers. The best response is the one that most accurately describes the organization. Letter codes are used in scoring. There are 2 endpoints on each continuum and three midpoints which indicate varying degrees between the end points. Respondent is to try to determine where the organization fits between the end points. Instrument is not intended for in-depth personal growth, psychodiagnostic, or therapeutic work. Intended for use in training groups; for demonstration purposes; to generate data for training or organization development sessions; and for other group applications in which the trainer, consultant, or facilitator helps respondents use the data for achieving some form of progress. Subtests include: Management-Information and Communication-System Skills; Decision-Making and Action-Taking Skills; Project-Planning, Organizing, and System-Integration Skills; Systems-Evaluation and Internal-Control Skills; Leadership, Motivation, and Reward-Systems Skills; Selection Placement, and Human Resource Development Skills. (TJS)

**17669**
**Total Quality Management Inventory.** Reagan, Gaylord
*Descriptors:* *Employees; *Quality Control; Adults; Leadership Qualities; Planning; Administrators; Teamwork; Rating Scales; Administration; Questionnaires
*Identifiers:* TQ
*Availability:* Pfeiffer, J. William, ed., *The 1992 Annual: Developing Human Resources.* San Diego: University Associates, 1992. Pfeiffer and Co., formerly University Associates, 8517 Production Ave., San Diego, CA 92121-2280.

A strategic, integrated management philosophy that is based on the concept of achieving ever-higher levels of customer satisfaction. Designed for use as an action-research tool, based on 8 categories: top-management leadership and support; strategic planning; focus on the customer; employee training and recognition; employee empowerment and teamwork; quality measurement and analysis; quality assurance; and quality and productivity improvement results. Respondents choose the statement that best describes the present situation in the organization. Scores identify the categories that are more significant than others. Used with audiences ranging from executive managers to nonmanagement personnel. Instrument is not intended for in-depth personal growth, psychodiagnostic, or therapeutic work. Intended for use in training groups; for demonstration purposes; to generate data for training or organization development sessions; and for other group applications in which the trainer, consultant, or facilitator helps respondents use the data for achieving some form of progress. (TJS)

**17672**
**Maintenance Engineering Test.** Ramsay, Roland T. 1991.
*Descriptors:* *Occupational Tests; *Mechanical Skills; *Equipment Maintenance; *Knowledge Level; Adults; Electrical Systems; Machine Repairers; Mechanics (Process); Multiple Choice Tests
*Identifiers:* MAINTEST
*Availability:* Ramsay Corp., 1050 Boyce Rd., Pittsburgh, PA 15241-3907.
*Notes:* Time, 120. Items, 155.

Measures practical mechanical and electrical knowledge of maintenance employees. Measures 21 mechanical and electrical areas. Paper and pencil multiple-choice format.

**17676**
**Law Enforcement Personal History Questionnaire.** Hilson Research, Inc., Kew Gardens, NY 1983.
*Descriptors:* *Biographical Inventories; *Job Applicants; *Law Enforcement; *Psychological Evaluation; *Security Personnel; Adults; Questionnaires
*Identifiers:* PHQ
*Availability:* Hilson Research, Inc., P.O. Box 239, 82-28 Abingdon Rd., Kew Gardens, NY 11415.
*Notes:* Items, 34.

Five-page comprehensive psychological questionnaire designed for law enforcement/security officer applicants. Provides information for follow-up with job candidates and for verification of other psychological test results.

**17682**
**Teamwork.** Talico, Inc., Jacksonville Beach, FL 1986.
*Descriptors:* *Group Behavior; *Problem Solving; *Program Development; *Simulation; *Teamwork; *Training Methods; Adjustment (to Environment); Administrators; Adults; Communication Skills; Employees; Group Dynamics; Interpersonal Competence; Leadership; Management Games; Management Teams; Motivation; Participation; Productivity; Supervisors
*Availability:* Talico, Inc., 2320 S. Third St., Ste. 5, Jacksonville Beach, FL 32250.
*Notes:* See management exercises (17683 through 17691) for related instruments. Time, 45 approx.

A series of simulations, management games, role plays, and exercises that are useful for assessment, training, and development. These instruments will assist in assessing the skills and proficiency of managers, supervisors, and candidates for those positions. Each set of material contains facilitator administration guidelines, instructions, discussion notes, and copies of participant materials. Teamwork is a simulation exercise that focuses on group behavior and problem solving and emphasizes the need for collaboration and open, candid, and honest communication. Factors that should be observed and discussed as a result of this exercise are: productivity, leadership, participation, communication, motivation, group-mindedness, and atmosphere.

**17683**
**Counseling.** Talico, Inc., Jacksonville Beach, FL 1986.
*Descriptors:* *Career Counseling; *Management Games; *Managerial Occupations; *Program Development; *Simulation; *Supervisors; *Training Methods; Administrators; Adults; Check Lists; Communication Skills; Creativity; Employees; Interpersonal Competence; Interviews; Management Teams
*Availability:* Talico, Inc., 2320 S. Third St., Ste. 5, Jacksonville Beach, FL 32250.
*Notes:* See management exercises (17682 through 17691) for related instruments. Time, 120 approx.

A series of simulations, management games, role plays, and exercises that are useful for assessment, training and development. These instruments will assist in assessing the skills and proficiency of managers, supervisors, and candidates for those positions. Each set of materials contains facilitator administration guidelines, instructions, discussion notes, and copies of participant materials. Counseling is a simulation exercise that dramatizes, instructs, and evaluates career counseling practices and principles. It offers a process by which current career counseling skills can be evaluated, sharpened, and refined. This tool demonstrates to supervisors and managers how to improve interviewing skills; how to assess employee abilities and motivation for advancement and growth. Included is a checklist of issues that should be incorporated in every interview. They are: communicative skills, creativity, drive, analytical ability, foresight, judgment, responsibility, technical proficiency, resourcefulness, and sociability. Designed for all levels of management.

**17684**
**Conflict Resolution.** Talico, Inc., Jacksonville Beach, FL 1986.
*Descriptors:* *Conflict Resolution; *Employees; *Intergroup Relations; *Management Games; *Program Development; *Training Methods; Adults; Group Dynamics; Interpersonal Communication; Interpersonal Competence; Management Teams; Problem Solving
*Availability:* Talico, Inc., 2320 S. Third St., Ste. 5, Jacksonville Beach, FL 32250.
*Notes:* See management exercises (17682 through 17691) for related instruments. Time, 150 approx.

A series of simulations, management games, role plays, and exercises that are useful for assessment, training and development. These instruments will assist in assessing the skills and proficiency of managers, supervisors, and candidates for those positions. Each set of materials contains facilitator administration guidelines, instructions, discussion notes, and copies of participant materials. Conflict Resolution is an exercise that assists participants in developing skills for handling conflict in interpersonal and intergroup situations. It also provides a process to measure the effectiveness of various conflict resolution techniques in relation to individual and organizational goals. Some of the basic causes of conflict that are examined in this exercise are: value differences, divergent goals, role pressure, perceptual differences, and status. Designed for all levels in the work force.

**17685**
**Complaint Handling.** Talico, Inc., Jacksonville Beach, FL 1986.
*Descriptors:* *Listening Skills; *Management Games; *Managerial Occupations; *Program Development; *Supervisors; *Training Methods; Administrators; Adults; Communication Skills; Counseling; Employer Employee Relationship; Interpersonal Competence
*Availability:* Talico, Inc., 2320 S. Third St., Ste. 5, Jacksonville Beach, FL 32250.
*Notes:* See management exercises (17682 through 17691) for related instruments. Time, 90 approx.

A series of simulations, management games, role plays, and exercises that are useful for assessment, training and development. These instruments will assist in assessing the skills and proficiency of managers, supervisors, and candidates for those positions. Each set of materials contains facilitator administration guidelines, instructions, discussion notes, and copies of participant materials. Complaint Handling is an exercise that assists managers and supervisors in improving their skills in handling employee complaints with sensitivity by training them to listen to subordinates' concerns and problems. The exercise demonstrates to administrators how to gather and analyze facts, then impartially counsel employees regarding the role that effective communication plays in complaint resolution.

**17686**
**Performance Appraisal.** Talico, Inc., Jacksonville Beach, FL 1986.
*Descriptors:* *Evaluation Methods; *Management Games; *Managerial Occupations; *Personnel Evaluation; *Program Development; *Questioning Techniques; *Role Playing; *Supervisors; *Training Methods; Administrators; Adults; Employees; Interviews
*Availability:* Talico, Inc., 2320 S. Third St., Ste. 5, Jacksonville Beach, FL 32250.
*Notes:* See management exercises (17682 through 17691) for related instruments.

A series of simulations, management games, role plays, and exercises that are useful for assessment, training and development. These instruments will assist in assessing the skills and proficiency of managers, supervisors, and candidates for those positions. Each set of materials contains facilitator administration guidelines, instructions, discussion notes, and copies of participant materials. Performance Appraisal is a role play exercise that focuses on a critical management skill, which is conducting effective performance appraisal interviews. This tool will help managers and supervisors in better understanding the developmental and evaluative objectives of performance appraisal and develop skill in preparing appraisals and conducting the appraisal discussion objectively to increase effectiveness. Being descriptive and specific, and focusing attention on controllable behavior rather than on personality traits are some factors appraised in this simulated exercise.

**17687**
**Managing Stress.** Talico, Inc., Jacksonville Beach, FL
*Descriptors:* *Management Games; *Managerial Occupations; *Program Development; *Stress Management; *Supervisors; *Training Methods; Adjustment (to Environment); Administrators; Adults; Coping; Employees; Job Performance; Management Teams; Personality Traits; Stress Variables
*Availability:* Talico, Inc., 2320 S. Third St., Ste. 5, Jacksonville Beach, FL 32250.
*Notes:* See management exercises (17682 through 17691) for related instruments.

A series of simulations, management games, role plays, and exercises that are useful for assessment, training and development. These instruments will assist in assessing the skills and proficiency of managers, supervisors, and candidates for those positions. Each set of materials contains facilitator administration guidelines, instructions, discussion notes, and copies of participant materials. Managing Stress is an exercise to help develop stress management, consciousness, and awareness. It also assists in developing skills in identifying stress sources, and explores the direct relationship between personality factors and stress tolerance, which affects job performance. Several coexisting job factors that affect levels of stress tolerance are addressed. They include: overload of work, conflict, uncertainty, change, and delegation. Accountability, sociability, temperament, self-esteem, flexibility, and risk-acceptance are the personality characteristics also included in the list of stress sources. This exercise should be a requisite for all supervisory and management development programs.

**17688**
**Decision Making.** Talico, Inc., Jacksonville Beach, FL 1986.
*Descriptors:* *Decision Making Skills; *Management Games; *Managerial Occupations; *Middle Management; *Program Development; *Supervisors; *Training Methods; *Verbal Communication; Adults; Employees; Group Dynamics; Problem Solving
*Availability:* Talico, Inc., 2320 S. Third St., Ste. 5, Jacksonville Beach, FL 32250.
*Notes:* See management exercises (17682 through 17691) for related instruments. Time, 90 approx.

A series of simulations, management games, role plays, and exercises that are useful for assessment, training, and development. These instruments will assist in assessing the skills and proficiency of managers, supervisors, and candidates for those positions. Each set of materials contains facilitator administration guidelines, instructions, discussion notes, and copies of participant materials. Decision Making is an exercise to improve effectiveness in task attainment, verbal communication, and decision-making skills in relation to individual performance in a group atmosphere. It also aids in problem solving and examines the participant's current level of data collection. The steps include: prioritizing issues, defining and diagnosing the issue, setting objectives, developing courses of action, selecting a course of action, executing, and follow-up. Useful for middle-management and first-line supervisors with 1 to 3 years of experience.

**17689**
**Creative Problem Solving.** Talico, Inc., Jacksonville Beach, FL 1986.
*Descriptors:* *Employees; *Management Games; *Problem Solving; *Program Development; *Training Methods; Adults; Brainstorming; Information Utilization; Work Environment
*Identifiers:* CPS
*Availability:* Talico, Inc., 2320 S. Third St., Ste. 5, Jacksonville Beach, FL 32250.
*Notes:* See management exercises (17682 through 17691) for related instruments.

A series of simulations, management games, role plays, and exercises that are useful for assessment, training and development. These instruments will assist in assessing the skills and proficiency of managers, supervisors, and candidates for those positions. Each set of materials contains facilitator administration guidelines, instructions, discussion notes, and copies of participant materials. Problem Solving is an exercise which aids in assessing current skill levels of resource utilization and information processing. Its purpose is to strengthen creative problem-solving skills by teaching techniques for identifying, analyzing, and solving problems that impact the work environment. This tool is good for all levels in the work force.

**17690**
**Time Management.** Talico, Inc., Jacksonville Beach, FL 1986.
*Descriptors:* *Administrator Effectiveness; *Decision Making Skills; *Management Games; *Managerial Occupations; *Program Development; *Supervisors; *Time Management; *Training Methods; Administrators; Adults; Leadership Qualities; Management Teams; Performance Factors; Problem Solving; Timed Tests
*Identifiers:* In Basket Simulation
*Availability:* Talico, Inc., 2320 S. Third St., Ste. 5, Jacksonville Beach, FL 32250.
*Notes:* See management exercises (17682 through 17691) for related instruments. Time, 60 approx.

A series of simulations, management games, role plays, and exercises that are useful for assessment, training, and development. These instruments will assist in assessing the skills and proficiency of managers, supervisors, and candidates for those positions. Each set of materials contains facilitator administration guidelines, instructions, discussion notes, and copies of participant materials. Time Management is an in-basket exercise that focuses on decision-making skills and task performance. It evaluates organizational skills of managers and supervisors, and will train them in time management principles. This is a timed exercise where the participant must demonstrate skills in the areas of problem analysis, self-organization, delegation, and other skills that impact on leadership and managerial effectiveness.

**17691**
**Work Assignments.** Talico, Inc., Jacksonville Beach, FL 1986.
*Descriptors:* *Communication Skills; *Management Games; *Managerial Occupations; *Motivation; *Program Development; *Role Playing; *Supervisors; *Task Analysis; *Training Methods; Administrators; Adults; Decision Making; Employees; Interpersonal Competence; Job Satisfaction; Management Teams
*Availability:* Talico, Inc., 2320 S. Third St., Ste. 5, Jacksonville Beach, FL 32250.
*Notes:* See management exercises (17682 through 17690) for related instruments. Time, 30 approx.

A series of simulations, management games, role plays, and exercises that are useful for assessment, training, and development. These instruments will assist in assessing the skills and proficiency of managers, supervisors, and candidates for those positions. Each set of materials contains facilitator administration guidelines, instructions, discussion notes, and copies of participant materials. Work Assignments is an exercise designed to lend assistance to managers and supervisors to develop skills in areas of communication, task analysis, and motivation in issuing work assignments to subordinates. This will help improve the clarity and appropriateness of work assignments made in order to avoid misunderstandings that can lead to poor work performance, employee dissatisfaction, and disciplinary problems. This role-play exercise focuses on certain steps in making successful work assignments: constructing the work assignment, being decisive, verifying employee's understanding, and follow-up. Designed for first- and second-level supervisors.

**17692**
**Five Star Supervisor Leadership Skills Inventory.** Tagliaferri, Louis E. 1990.
*Descriptors:* *Leadership Styles; *Management Development; *Managerial Occupations; *Supervisors; Administrator Characteristics; Administrators; Adults; Behavior Rating Scales; Social Cognition; Supervisory Methods; Work Ethic
*Identifiers:* LSI
*Availability:* Talico, Inc., 2320 S. Third St., Ste. 5, Jacksonville Beach, FL 32250.
*Notes:* Time, 20 approx. Items, 28.

Provides feedback to supervisors and managers so they can compare their personal leadership behavior, skills, and practices to those of superior supervisors and managers. Using a rating scale, the test measures the respondent's perceptions about certain aspects of personal leadership behavior, skills and practices. These aspects relate to the primary qualities that include pride and confidence, work ethics, work standards, teamwork, values, creativity, and leadership. Designed for developmental purposes only. Is ideal for first- and second-level managers and supervisors.

**17693**
**Five Star Supervisor Communication Skills Inventory.** Tagliaferri, Louis E. 1990.
*Descriptors:* *Communication Skills; *Managerial Occupations; *Supervisors; Administrators; Adults; Expressive Language; Management Development; Rating Scales
*Identifiers:* CSI
*Availability:* Talico, Inc., 2320 S. Third St., Ste. 5, Jacksonville Beach, FL 32250.
*Notes:* Time, 20 approx. Items, 30.

Provides feedback to managers and supervisors in order for them to compare their personal communication skills with those that are characteristic of superior managers and supervisors. This multilevel learning resource tool consists of items that are grouped into 10 sets. Three sets relate to communication roles, while the remaining sets are steps that supervisors and managers can take to assist in achieving effective communication. This tool can be facilator-scored and interpreted.

**17694**
**Communication Effectiveness Scale.** Talico, Inc., Jacksonville Beach, FL 1990.
*Descriptors:* *Management Development; *Managerial Occupations; *Organizational Communication; Adults; Rating Scales
*Identifiers:* CES
*Availability:* Talico, Inc., 2320 S. Third St., Ste. 5, Jacksonville Beach, FL 32250.
*Notes:* Time, 25 approx. Items, 48.

The purposes of Communication Effectiveness Scale (CES) are to evaluate the quality of communication practices among managers and supervisors, to provide feedback, and to facilitate coaching with respect to perceived communication effectiveness. This scale measures perceptions about communication practice effectiveness in 6 key communication skill dimensions. These dimensions include verbal, written, performance, intergroup (with peers and superiors), listening skills, and coaching and counseling. Is applicable for communication skills development, organization improvement, human relations training, self-/professional/career development, coaching and counseling, and performance improvement. Designed in multilevel format to obtain assessment perceptions from line and staff managers, supervisors, nonsupervisory management level employees, and employees at other levels on a selected basis.

**17695**
**Time Management Inventory.** Talico, Inc., Jacksonville Beach, FL 1990.

*Descriptors:* *Time Management; Adults; Management Development; Rating Scales
*Identifiers:* TMI
*Availability:* Talico, Inc., 2320 S. Third St., Ste. 5, Jacksonville Beach, FL 32250.
*Notes:* Time, 30 approx. Items, 25.

The purpose of Time Management Inventory (TMI) is to develop consciousness and awareness about the importance of time utilization, and teach key time management principles. A learning instrument that will help managers, supervisors, and employees at all levels to improve their self- and time management practices. It emphasizes planning, scheduling, work organization, prioritization, and delegation. Designed to facilitate learning rather than measure knowledge, skill, or behavior per se. Applicable for time management training and performance coaching and counseling. A time management planning guide helps respondents to develop strategies that will overcome major time management barriers that may be affecting their work.

**17696**
**Leadership Influence Strategies Questionnaires.** Kinlaw, Dennis C. 1986.
*Descriptors:* *Communication Audits; *Communication Skills; *Employees; *Leadership Styles; Administrator Effectiveness; Adults; Rating Scales; Self Evaluation (Individuals); Supervisors
*Identifiers:* Communication Strategies; LISQ; Management Styles
*Availability:* Talico, Inc., 2320 S. Third St., Ste. 5, Jacksonville Beach, FL 32250.
*Notes:* Time, 20 approx. Items, 60.

The purposes of this instrument are to give individuals information about the strategies that they typically use to influence others, and to help individuals identify opportunities to strengthen their strategies for influencing others. This self-administered instrument should be completed by the subject and by at least 4 persons who know the subject well enough to give feedback. Applicable for employee development programs, individual career planning, and manager and supervisor training. Suitable for all professions and work levels. Rating scale response ranges from 1 to 5.

**17697**
**Effective Listening Skills Questionnaire.** Kinlaw, Dennis C. 1989.
*Descriptors:* *Listening Skills; *Managerial Occupations; Administrators; Adults; Communication (Thought Transfer); Interpersonal Relationship; Problem Solving; Questionnaires; Rating Scales
*Identifiers:* ELSQ
*Availability:* Talico, Inc., 2320 S. Third St., Ste. 5, Jacksonville Beach, FL 32250.
*Notes:* Items, 10.

Measures an individual's ability to listen effectively by providing feedback on ability to discriminate between evaluative and nonevaluative responses to a series of statements. This instrument is designed to help supervisors, managers, and other key people measure their perception of listening behaviors. It offers 2 alternate responses to 10 different statements and asks the respondents to weigh their selections according to the degree of certainty that they had about the response by entering a number from 1 to 5 in the appropriate blank.

**17711**
**Locus of Control Inventory.** Pareek, Udai 1992.
*Descriptors:* *Locus of Control; *Employees; *Employee Attitudes; *Personal Autonomy; Adults; Self Evaluation (Groups); Rating Scales; Organizational Development; Job Satisfaction; Individual Power; Self Concept
*Availability:* Pfeiffer, J. William, ed., *The 1992 Annual: Developing Human Resources.* San Diego: University Associates, 1992. Pfeiffer and Co., formerly University Associates, 8517 Production Ave., San Diego, CA 92121-2280.

Designed to measure internality and externality in the organizational context. Based on 3 subscales with a 5-point rating scale consisting of 10 statements each for internality (I), externality-others (EO), and externality-chance (EC). This assessment tool reflects the way a person views what happens in an organization in relation to how much control the person believes he or she has in important organizational matters; how much control is held by others; and to what degree the person believes events are a matter of luck. General, success or effectiveness, influence, acceptability, career, advancement, and rewards are 7 areas linked to the locus of control. Can be used for both research and training purposes in human development, organization development, or training packages. Norms, reliability, and validity data are available. Instrument is not intended for in-depth personal growth, psychodiagnostic, or therapeutic work. Intended for use in training groups; for demonstration purposes; to generate data for training or organization development sessions; and for other group applications in which the trainer, consultant, or facilitator helps respondents use the data for achieving some form of progress. Subtests include: Internal; External-Others; External-Chance. (TJS)

**17712**
**Burnout Inventory.** Warley, William Randolph 1992.
*Descriptors:* *Burnout; *Teamwork; *Quality of Working Life; *Job Satisfaction; *Employees; *Alienation; *Organizational Climate; Adults; Group Testing; Self Evaluation (Individuals); Rating Scales; Job Performance; Planning
*Availability:* Pfeiffer, J. William, ed., *The 1992 Annual: Developing Human Resources.* San Diego: University Associates, 1992. Pfeiffer and Co., formerly University Associates, 8517 Production Ave., San Diego, CA 92121-2280.

To be used as a tool for examining burnout potential so that follow-up action planning can be done. Can also be used to establish a group burnout assessment of a department or a work team. This instrument is individually evaluated on a 6-point rating scale, ranging from strongly agree to strongly disagree. The 73 inventory statements incorporate the work context, organizational, and alienation factors. Responses reflect the individual's total response to work and its environment. Work context factors linked to burnout are: boredom, upward communication, decision influence, growth opportunities, personal control, salary, task identity, task responsibility, task significance, skill variety, specialized skills, supervisor support, and workload. No reliability or validity data are available. Instrument is not intended for in-depth personal growth, psychodiagnostic, or therapeutic work. Intended for use in training groups; for demonstration purposes; to generate data for training or organization development sessions; and for other group applications in which the trainer, consultant, or facilitator helps respondents use the data for achieving some form of progress. Subtests include: Perception of Job Content; Perception of Immediate Supervisor; Perception of the Organization. (TJS)

**17714**
**NTE Specialty Area Tests: Biology.** Educational Testing Service, Princeton, NJ 1990.
*Descriptors:* *Achievement Tests; *Beginning Teachers; *Biology; *Certification; *Professional Occupations; *Secondary School Teachers; *Teacher Education Programs; College Students; Cytology; Ecology; Evolution; Higher Education; Knowledge Level; Molecular Structure; Philosophy; Science and Society; Scientific Methodology; Student Evaluation
*Availability:* NTE Programs, Educational Testing Service, CN 6051, Princeton, NJ 08541-6051.
*Notes:* Time, 120. Items, 150.

The NTE Program tests are standardized, secure, examinations that are measures of academic achievement for college students in teacher education programs and for advanced candidates who have received additional training in specific fields. This test is designed to assess the preparation of prospective teachers of secondary school biology. Approximately 90 percent of the questions are taken from the content areas of molecular and cellular biology; biology of plants, animals, fungi and protists; evolution; and ecology. Other questions deal with the history, philosophy and methodology of science, technology and social issues.

**17715**
**NTE Specialty Area Tests: Chemistry.** Educational Testing Service, Princeton, NJ 1990.
*Descriptors:* *Achievement Tests; *Beginning Teachers; *Certification; *Chemistry; *Professional Occupations; *Secondary School Teachers; *Teacher Education Programs; Atomic Structure; Chemical Equilibrium; Chemical Reactions; Ecology; Higher Education; Kinetics; Knowledge Level; Laboratory Experiments; Molecular Structure; Oxidation; Student Evaluation; Thermodynamics
*Availability:* NTE Programs, Educational Testing Service, CN 6051, Princeton, NJ 08541-6051.
*Notes:* Time, 120. Items, 120.

The NTE Program tests are standardized, secure, examinations that are measures of academic achievement for college students in teacher education programs and for advanced candidates who have received additional training in specific fields. This test is designed to assess the preparation of prospective teachers of secondary school chemistry. The content focuses on the structure of matter (nuclear, atomic, and molecular); the states of matter; the reactions of matter (stoichiometry and equations, oxidation-reduction, acid-base reactions, thermodynamics, kinetics, and equilibrium); examples of matter (periodic relations, important elements and compounds); significant laboratory experiences; and environmental issues related to chemistry.

**17716**
**NTE Specialty Area Tests: Educational Leadership: Administration and Supervision.** Educational Testing Service, Princeton, NJ 1990.
*Descriptors:* *Achievement Tests; *Administrator Education; *Administrators; *Certification; *Educational Administration; *Leadership; *Masters Programs; *Professional Occupations; *Supervisors; Data Interpretation; Decision Making; Educational Principles; Educational Theories; Educational Trends; Evaluative Thinking; Groups; Higher Education; Instructional Leadership; Knowledge Level; Needs Assessment; Principals; Problem Solving; School Administration; School Supervision; Student Evaluation
*Availability:* NTE Programs, Educational Testing Service, CN 6051, Princeton, NJ 08541-6051.
*Notes:* Time, 120. Items, 145.

The NTE Program tests are standardized, secure, examinations that are measures of academic achievement for college students in teacher education programs and for advanced candidates who have received additional training in specific fields. This test is designed to assess the professional knowledge and functions of an educational administrator or supervisor. The examination is intended primarily for those who are candidates for master's degrees or who already possess master's degrees and are seeking first appointments as administrators or supervisors. Three major content categories covered are instructional leadership, administrative leadership, and individual and group leadership skills. Some questions cover knowledge of trends, principles, and theories, data interpretation, identification of implications or consequences. Others cover the ability to generalize, determine priorities and relationships, integrate knowledge or theory to produce new information or patterns, and judge the value of a process or product on the basis of logical consistency.

**17717**
**NTE Specialty Area Tests: Physics.** Educational Testing Service, Princeton, NJ

*Descriptors:* *Achievement Tests; *Beginning Teachers; *Certification; *Physical Sciences; *Physics; *Professional Occupations; *Secondary School Teachers; *Teacher Education Programs; Electricity; Energy; Higher Education; Knowledge Level; Magnets; Matter; Mechanics (Physics); Nuclear Physics; Student Evaluation
*Availability:* NTE Programs, Educational Testing Service, CN 6051, Princeton, NJ 08541-6051.
*Notes:* Time, 120. Items, 100.

The NTE Program tests are standardized, secure, examinations that are measures of academic achievement for college students in teacher education programs and for advanced candidates who have received additional training in specific fields. This test is designed to assess the preparation of prospective teachers of secondary school physics. Questions are specific to the field of physics and also deal with topics common to physical science in general. The test questions cover the topics of mechanics, heat, wave motion, electricity and magnetism, atomic and nuclear physics, the nature of matter, and the interaction of matter and energy.

**17718**
**NTE Specialty Area Tests: Teaching English as a Second Language.** Educational Testing Service, Princeton, NJ 1990.
*Descriptors:* *Achievement Tests; *Beginning Teachers; *Certification; *English (Second Language); *Professional Occupations; *Teacher Education Programs; *Teachers; Cultural Awareness; Curriculum; Elementary School Students; Evaluation Methods; Higher Education; Instructional Materials; Knowledge Level; Linguistics; Oral Language; Secondary School Students; Student Evaluation; Teaching Methods; Teaching Models
*Availability:* NTE Programs, Educational Testing Service, CN 6051, Princeton, NJ 08541-6051.
*Notes:* Time, 120. Items, 115.

The NTE Program tests are standardized, secure, examinations that are measures of academic achievement for college students in teacher education programs and for advanced candidates who have received additional training in specific fields. This test is designed to assess the preparation of prospective teachers of English as a Second Language (ESL). Assesses the examinees' pedagogical knowledge of teaching ESL to students across a range from kindergarten through grade 12. In the first section of the test examinees evaluate the oral production of ESL students via taped recordings. The second section of the test is multiple choice. It covers linguistics, including phonology, morphology, syntax, psycholinguistics, and sociolinguistics. Also covered are pedagogical methods and techniques, evaluation and assessment, cultural awareness, the ESL profession, curriculum and materials, and programs and models.

**17719**
**NTE Specialty Area Tests: Technology Education.** Educational Testing Service, Princeton, NJ 1990.
*Descriptors:* *Achievement Tests; *Beginning Teachers; *Certification; *Elementary School Teachers; *Professional Occupations; *Secondary School Teachers; *Teacher Education Programs; *Technology; Building Trades; Communications; Higher Education; Knowledge Level; Manufacturing; Program Development; Transportation
*Identifiers:* Professionalism; Societal Impact
*Availability:* NTE Programs, Educational Testing Service, CN 6051, Princeton, NJ 08541-6051.
*Notes:* Time, 120. Items, 150.

The NTE Program tests are standardized, secure, examinations that are measures of academic achievement for college students in teacher education programs and for advanced candidates who have received additional training in specific fields. This test is designed to assess the preparation of prospective teachers of technology in middle school, junior high, and senior high school. Assesses examinees' understanding of concepts, knowledge, and principles. Emphasizes knowledge of communication, construction, manufacture, and transportation technologies and industries and the impact of these areas on individuals and society. Includes a professional component that emphasizes program development, management, and professionalism.

**17720**
**NTE Specialty Area Tests: School Social Worker.** Educational Testing Service, Princeton, NJ 1992.
*Descriptors:* *Achievement Tests; *Certification; *Masters Programs; *Professional Occupations; *School Social Workers; Agency Cooperation; Child Advocacy; Elementary School Students; Helping Relationship; Higher Education; Knowledge Level; Parents; Prevention; School Personnel; Secondary School Students; Student Evaluation; Teachers
*Availability:* NTE Programs, Educational Testing Service, CN 6051, Princeton, NJ 08541-6051.
*Notes:* Time, 120. Items, 120.

The NTE Program tests are standardized, secure, examinations that are measures of academic achievement for college students in teacher education programs and for advanced candidates who have received additional training in specific fields. This test is designed to assess the preparation of persons who have completed master's level programs in social work, who have taken courses in school social work, and who expect to become school social workers in the public schools. The test measures knowledge and skills required of school social workers in the context of 5 job dimensions that were derived from a job analysis of school social workers. These are relationship and services to children and families; relationship with and services to teachers and school staff; services to other school personnel; administrative and professional tasks; and interagency collaboration, prevention, and advocacy.

**17722**
**Industrial Occupational Competency Tests, Journeyworker Level Two: Welding (021).** National Occupational Competency Testing Institute, Big Rapids, MI 1989.
*Descriptors:* *Occupational Tests; *Personnel Evaluation; *Personnel Selection; *Welding; Adults; Industrial Training; Job Skills; Knowledge Level; Multiple Choice Tests; Performance Tests; Promotion (Occupational); Skilled Workers; Work Sample Tests
*Identifiers:* IOCT; National Occupational Competency Testing Institute; NOCTI
*Availability:* National Occupational Competency Testing Institute, 409 Bishop Hall, Ferris State University, Big Rapids, MI 49307.
*Notes:* For the complete series of Industrial Occupational Competency Tests, Entry Level One, see 17778 through 17845. For the Industrial Occupational Competency Tests, Journeyworker Level Two, see 17721 through 17777. Time, 420. Items, 174.

Level Two assessments measure worker competency at the journeyworker level. These were designed for use in industry to measure journeyworker-level skills in prospective and current employees. Both written and performance components are included in the tests and separate scores are reported. May be used for employee selection, upgrading or advancement, and in planning training or retraining programs. The written assessment is multiple choice and covers factual knowledge, technical information, understanding of principles, and problem-solving skills related to the occupation or skill. The performance component is administered in a shop and consists of manipulative tasks related to a particular occupation. The written test covers shielded metal arc welding, gas tungsten arc welding, oxyfuel welding, brazing, gas metal arc welding, basic metallurgy, testing, welding defects and causes, welding symbols, hard surfacing, electricity, joint design, general welder qualifications, and other processes. The performance test covers gas metal arc welding, shielded metal arc welding, oxyfuel welding, and gas tungsten arc welding.

**17723**
**Industrial Occupational Competency Tests, Journeyworker Level Two: Tool and Die Making (040).** National Occupational Competency Testing Institute, Big Rapids, MI 1989.
*Descriptors:* *Occupational Tests; *Personnel Evaluation; *Personnel Selection; *Tool and Die Makers; Adults; Industrial Training; Job Skills; Knowledge Level; Multiple Choice Tests; Performance Tests; Promotion (Occupational); Skilled Workers; Work Sample Tests
*Identifiers:* IOCT; National Occupational Competency Testing Institute; NOCTI
*Availability:* National Occupational Competency Testing Institute, 409 Bishop Hall, Ferris State University, Big Rapids, MI 49307.
*Notes:* For the complete series of Industrial Occupational Competency Tests, Entry Level One, see 17778 through 17845. For the Industrial Occupational Competency Tests, Journeyworker Level Two, see 17721 through 17777. Time, 450. Items, 180.

Level Two assessments measure worker competency at the journeyworker level. These were designed for use in industry to measure journeyworker-level skills in prospective and current employees. Both written and performance components are included in the tests and separate scores are reported. May be used for employee selection, upgrading or advancement, and in planning training or retraining programs. The written assessment is multiple choice and covers factual knowledge, technical information, understanding of principles, and problem-solving skills related to the occupation or skill. The performance component is administered in a shop and consists of manipulative tasks related to a particular occupation. The written test covers inspection, shop math, metallurgy/heat treating, machining, drill press, milling machine, grinding, numerical control, benchwork, and die making. The performance test covers surface grinder, jig borer, vertical mill with digital readout and drill press, punch press operation, and identifying stamping irregularities.

**17724**
**Industrial Occupational Competency Tests, Journeyworker Level Two: Textile Production/Fabrication (038).** National Occupational Competency Testing Institute, Big Rapids, MI 1989.
*Descriptors:* *Occupational Tests; *Personnel Evaluation; *Personnel Selection; Adults; Industrial Training; Job Skills; Knowledge Level; Multiple Choice Tests; Performance Tests; Promotion (Occupational); Skilled Workers; Work Sample Tests
*Identifiers:* IOCT; National Occupational Competency Testing Institute; NOCTI; *Textiles
*Availability:* National Occupational Competency Testing Institute, 409 Bishop Hall, Ferris State University, Big Rapids, MI 49307.
*Notes:* For the complete series of Industrial Occupational Competency Tests, Entry Level One, see 17778 through 17845. For the Industrial Occupational Competency Tests, Journeyworker Level Two, see 17721 through 17777. Time, 420. Items, 200.

Level Two assessments measure worker competency at the journeyworker level. These were designed for use in industry to measure journeyworker-level skills in prospective and current employees. Both written and performance components are included in the tests and separate scores are reported. May be used for employee selection, upgrading or advancement, and in planning training or retraining programs. The written assessment is multiple choice and covers factual knowledge, technical information, understanding of principles, and problem-solving skills related to the occupation or skill. The performance component is administered in a shop and consists of manipulative tasks related to a particular occupation. The written test covers apparel assembly, power machine operations, textile terms, fabric finishes, fiber content, fabric structure, fiber content handling, alterations, and pattern making. The performance test covers apparel assembly, power machine operations, textiles, alterations, and pattern making.

**17725**
**Industrial Occupational Competency Tests, Journeyworker Level Two: Small Engine Repair (056).** National Occupational Competency Testing Institute, Big Rapids, MI 1989.
*Descriptors:* *Machine Repairers; *Occupational Tests; *Personnel Evaluation; *Personnel Selection; *Small Engine Mechanics; Adults; Industrial Training; Job Skills; Knowledge Level; Multiple Choice Tests; Performance Tests; Promotion (Occupational); Skilled Workers; Work Sample Tests
*Identifiers:* IOCT; National Occupational Competency Testing Institute; NOCTI
*Availability:* National Occupational Competency Testing Institute, 409 Bishop Hall, Ferris State University, Big Rapids, MI 49307.
*Notes:* For the complete series of Industrial Occupational Competency Tests, Entry Level One, see 17778 through 17845. For the Industrial Occupational Competency Tests, Journeyworker Level Two, see 17721 through 17777. Time, 420. Items, 180.

Level Two assessments measure worker competency at the journeyworker level. These were designed for use in industry to measure journeyworker-level skills in prospective and current employees. Both written and performance components are included in the tests and separate scores are reported. May be used for employee selection, upgrading or advancement, and in planning training or retraining programs. The written assessment is multiple choice and covers factual knowledge, technical information, understanding of principles, and problem-solving skills related to the occupation or skill. The performance component is given in a shop and consists of manipulative tasks related to a particular occupation. The written test covers engine servicing, knowledge of safety and safe use of tools, equipment, and measuring devices of the trade; theory of two-cycle and four-cycle engines; electrical system; fuel system; and parts and inventory. The performance test covers electrical systems, engine service and repair, fuel systems, and peripherals.

**17726**
**Industrial Occupational Competency Tests, Journeyworker Level Two: Small Engine Repair (005).** National Occupational Competency Testing Institute, Big Rapids, MI 1989.
*Descriptors:* *Machine Repairers; *Occupational Tests; *Personnel Evaluation; *Personnel Selection; *Small Engine Mechanics; Adults; Industrial Training; Job Skills; Knowledge Level; Multiple Choice Tests; Performance Tests; Promotion (Occupational); Skilled Workers; Work Sample Tests
*Identifiers:* IOCT; National Occupational Competency Testing Institute; NOCTI
*Availability:* National Occupational Competency Testing Institute, 409 Bishop Hall, Ferris State University, Big Rapids, MI 49307.
*Notes:* For the complete series of Industrial Occupational Competency Tests, Entry Level One, see 17778 through 17845. For the Industrial Occupational Competency Tests, Journeyworker Level Two, see 17721 through 17777. Time, 480. Items, 165.

Level Two assessments measure worker competency at the journeyworker level. These were designed for use in industry to measure journeyworker-level skills in prospective and current employees. Both written and performance components are included in the tests and separate scores are reported. May be used for employee selection, upgrading or advancement, and in planning training or retraining programs. The written assessment is multiple choice and covers factual knowledge, technical information, understanding of principles, and problem-solving skills related to the occupation or skill. The performance component is administered in a shop and consists of manipulative tasks related to a particular occupation. The written test covers fuel systems and carburetion, ignition and starting systems, troubleshooting, engine operation, cylinder block servicing and overhaul, benchwork, testing and inspection, trade applications of science, trade-related information, preventive maintenance, lubricating systems and lubrication, transmissions of power and drive units, trade computations, and cooling and exhaust systems. The performance test covers engine analysis, cylinder block servicing and overhaul, fuel systems and carburetion, ignition and starting systems, troubleshooting, lubricating systems and lubrication, cooling and exhaust systems, preventive maintenance, benchwork, and testing and inspection.

**17727**
**Industrial Occupational Competency Tests, Journeyworker Level Two: Sheet Metal (011).** National Occupational Competency Testing Institute, Big Rapids, MI 1989.
*Descriptors:* *Metal Working; *Occupational Tests; *Personnel Evaluation; *Personnel Selection; *Sheet Metal Work; Adults; Industrial Training; Job Skills; Knowledge Level; Multiple Choice Tests; Performance Tests; Promotion (Occupational); Skilled Workers; Work Sample Tests
*Identifiers:* IOCT; National Occupational Competency Testing Institute; NOCTI
*Availability:* National Occupational Competency Testing Institute, 409 Bishop Hall, Ferris State University, Big Rapids, MI 49307.
*Notes:* For the complete series of Industrial Occupational Competency Tests, Entry Level One, see 17778 through 17845. For the Industrial Occupational Competency Tests, Journeyworker Level Two, see 17721 through 17777. Time, 520. Items, 169.

Level Two assessments measure worker competency at the journeyworker level. These were designed for use in industry to measure journeyworker-level skills in prospective and current employees. Both written and performance components are included in the tests and separate scores are reported. May be used for employee selection, upgrading or advancement, and in planning training or retraining programs. The written assessment is multiple choice and covers factual knowledge, technical information, understanding of principles, and problem-solving skills related to the occupation or skill. The performance component is administered in a shop and consists of manipulative tasks related to a particular occupation. The written test covers layout and drafting, sheet metal machinery, bench and hand tools—processing, materials, welding, fluxes, sheet metal fabrication, application of trade science, computations, and hazards. The performance test covers fabrication and assembly and pattern layout (stretchout).

**17729**
**Industrial Occupational Competency Tests, Journeyworker Level Two: Refrigeration (043).** National Occupational Competency Testing Institute, Big Rapids, MI 1989.
*Descriptors:* *Occupational Tests; *Personnel Evaluation; *Personnel Selection; *Refrigeration; Adults; Industrial Training; Job Skills; Knowledge Level; Multiple Choice Tests; Performance Tests; Promotion (Occupational); Skilled Workers; Work Sample Tests
*Identifiers:* IOCT; National Occupational Competency Testing Institute; NOCTI
*Availability:* National Occupational Competency Testing Institute, 409 Bishop Hall, Ferris State University, Big Rapids, MI 49307.
*Notes:* For the complete series of Industrial Occupational Competency Tests, Entry Level One, see 17778 through 17845. For the Industrial Occupational Competency Tests, Journeyworker Level Two, see 17721 through 17777. Time, 420. Items, 180.

Level Two assessments measure worker competency at the journeyworker level. These were designed for use in industry to measure journeyworker-level skills in prospective and current employees. Both written and performance components are included in the tests and separate scores are reported. May be used for employee selection, upgrading or advancement, and in planning training or retraining programs. The written assessment is multiple choice and covers factual knowledge, technical information, understanding of principles, and problem-solving skills related to the occupation or skill. The performance component is administered in a shop and consists of manipulative tasks related to a particular occupation. The written test covers commercial service and installation, domestic service, and industrial service and installation. The performance test requires the test taker to assemble a refrigeration system; cut, flare, swedge, solder tubing; wire components; charge system, set controls, troubleshoot and correct faults; and operate system to specifications.

**17730**
**Industrial Occupational Competency Tests, Journeyworker Level Two: Radio/TV Repair (048).** National Occupational Competency Testing Institute, Big Rapids, MI 1989.
*Descriptors:* *Occupational Tests; *Personnel Evaluation; *Personnel Selection; *Television Radio Repairers; Adults; Industrial Training; Job Skills; Knowledge Level; Multiple Choice Tests; Performance Tests; Promotion (Occupational); Skilled Workers; Work Sample Tests
*Identifiers:* IOCT; National Occupational Competency Testing Institute; NOCTI
*Availability:* National Occupational Competency Testing Institute, 409 Bishop Hall, Ferris State University, Big Rapids, MI 49307.
*Notes:* For the complete series of Industrial Occupational Competency Tests, Entry Level One, see 17778 through 17845. For the Industrial Occupational Competency Tests, Journeyworker Level Two, see 17721 through 17777. Time, 430. Items, 193.

Level Two assessments measure worker competency at the journeyworker level. These were designed for use in industry to measure journeyworker-level skills in prospective and current employees. Both written and performance components are included in the tests and separate scores are reported. May be used for employee selection, upgrading or advancement, and in planning training or retraining programs. The written assessment is multiple choice and covers factual knowledge, technical information, understanding of principles, and problem-solving skills related to the occupation or skill. The performance component is administered in a shop and consists of manipulative tasks related to a particular occupation. The written test covers color and black and white receivers, solid state and tube circuitry, fundamental electronic theory, signal characteristics, TV & FM transmissions and reception, antenna and transmission lines, test equipment, servicing. The performance test covers television service and repair, radio equipment service and repair, recording equipment service and repair.

**17731**
**Industrial Occupational Competency Tests, Journeyworker Level Two: Quantity Food Preparation (017).** National Occupational Competency Testing Institute, Big Rapids, MI 1989.
*Descriptors:* *Food Service; *Occupational Tests; *Personnel Evaluation; *Personnel Selection; Adults; Industrial Training; Job Skills; Knowledge Level; Multiple Choice Tests; Performance Tests; Promotion (Occupational); Skilled Workers; Work Sample Tests
*Identifiers:* IOCT; National Occupational Competency Testing Institute; NOCTI
*Availability:* National Occupational Competency Testing Institute, 409 Bishop Hall, Ferris State University, Big Rapids, MI 49307.
*Notes:* For the complete series of Industrial Occupational Competency Tests, Entry Level One, see 17778 through 17845. For the Industrial Occupational Competency Tests, Journeyworker Level Two, see 17721 through 17777. Time, 360. Items, 195.

Level Two assessments measure worker competency at the journeyworker level. These were designed for use in industry to measure journeyworker-level skills in prospective and current employees. Both written and performance components are included in the tests and separate scores are reported. May be used for employee selection, upgrading or advancement, and in planning training or retraining programs. The written assessment is multiple choice and covers factual knowledge, technical information, understanding of principles, and problem-solving skills related to the occupation or skill. The performance component is given in a shop and consists of manipulative tasks related to a particular occupation.

The written test covers food groups; sanitation; purchasing; guest service; cost control; proper use, selection and cleaning of equipment and tools; receiving/storage; menu planning; safety. The performance test covers methods of food preparation; assembling and portioning ingredients; use of equipment; general knowledge, including organization and timing of preparation; interpretation of recipes; cleaning procedures; use of utensils and hand tools; use of preparation areas; recipes, and menus.

**17732**
**Industrial Occupational Competency Tests, Journeyworker Level Two: Quantity Food Preparation (055).** National Occupational Competency Testing Institute, Big Rapids, MI 1989.
*Descriptors:* *Food Service; *Occupational Tests; *Personnel Evaluation; *Personnel Selection; Adults; Industrial Training; Job Skills; Knowledge Level; Multiple Choice Tests; Performance Tests; Promotion (Occupational); Skilled Workers; Work Sample Tests
*Identifiers:* IOCT; National Occupational Competency Testing Institute; NOCTI
*Availability:* National Occupational Competency Testing Institute, 409 Bishop Hall, Ferris State University, Big Rapids, MI 49307.
*Notes:* For the complete series of Industrial Occupational Competency Tests, Entry Level One, see 17778 through 17845. For the Industrial Occupational Competency Tests, Journeyworker Level Two, see 17721 through 17777. Time, 520. Items, 200.

Level Two assessments measure worker competency at the journeyworker level. These were designed for use in industry to measure journeyworker-level skills in prospective and current employees. Both written and performance components are included in the tests and separate scores are reported. May be used for employee selection, upgrading or advancement, and in planning training or retraining programs. The written assessment is multiple choice and covers factual knowledge, technical information, understanding of principles, and problem-solving skills related to the occupation or skill. The performance component is administered in a shop and consists of manipulative tasks related to a particular occupation. The written test covers cost control and menu planning, safety and cleanliness, waitressing and customer service, nutrition, food purchasing, food receiving/storage, food preparation, safety, and cleanliness. The performance test covers organization of work area; selection of proper tools, utensils and ingredients; cleanliness; safety practices; correct weights and measurements; and food preparation.

**17733**
**Industrial Occupational Competency Tests, Journeyworker Level Two: Printing (Offset) (019).** National Occupational Competency Testing Institute, Big Rapids, MI 1989.
*Descriptors:* *Occupational Tests; *Personnel Evaluation; *Personnel Selection; *Printing; Adults; Industrial Training; Job Skills; Knowledge Level; Multiple Choice Tests; Performance Tests; Promotion (Occupational); Skilled Workers; Work Sample Tests
*Identifiers:* IOCT; National Occupational Competency Testing Institute; NOCTI
*Availability:* National Occupational Competency Testing Institute, 409 Bishop Hall, Ferris State University, Big Rapids, MI 49307.
*Notes:* For the complete series of Industrial Occupational Competency Tests, Entry Level One, see 17778 through 17845. For the Industrial Occupational Competency Tests, Journeyworker Level Two, see 17721 through 17777. Time, 480. Items, 200.

Level Two assessments measure worker competency at the journeyworker level. These were designed for use in industry to measure journeyworker-level skills in prospective and current employees. Both written and performance components are included in the tests and separate scores are reported. May be used for employee selection, upgrading or advancement, and in planning training or retraining programs. The written assessment is multiple choice and covers factual knowledge, technical information, understanding of principles, and problem-solving skills related to the occupation or skill. The performance component is administered in a shop and consists of manipulative tasks related to a particular occupation. The written test covers typography, layout and composition, camera photo mechanical, presswork, stripping and platemaking, binding and finishing, trade information, and job safety. The performance test covers design and composition, bindery/finishing, photo preparatory - image carriers, and image transfer (presswork).

**17734**
**Industrial Occupational Competency Tests, Journeyworker Level Two: Printing (Letterpress) (073).** National Occupational Competency Testing Institute, Big Rapids, MI 1989.
*Descriptors:* *Occupational Tests; *Personnel Evaluation; *Personnel Selection; *Printing; Adults; Industrial Training; Job Skills; Knowledge Level; Multiple Choice Tests; Performance Tests; Promotion (Occupational); Skilled Workers; Work Sample Tests
*Identifiers:* IOCT; National Occupational Competency Testing Institute; NOCTI
*Availability:* National Occupational Competency Testing Institute, 409 Bishop Hall, Ferris State University, Big Rapids, MI 49307.
*Notes:* For the complete series of Industrial Occupational Competency Tests, Entry Level One, see 17778 through 17845. For the Industrial Occupational Competency Tests, Journeyworker Level Two, see 17721 through 17777. Time, 480. Items, 200.

Level Two assessments measure worker competency at the journeyworker level. These were designed for use in industry to measure journeyworker-level skills in prospective and current employees. Both written and performance components are included in the tests and separate scores are reported. May be used for employee selection, upgrading or advancement, and in planning training or retraining programs. The written assessment is multiple choice and covers factual knowledge, technical information, understanding of principles, and problem-solving skills related to the occupation or skill. The performance component is administered in a shop and consists of manipulative tasks related to a particular occupation. The written test covers typography, layout and composition, camera photo mechanical, presswork, stripping and platemaking, binding and finishing, trade information, and job safety. The performance test covers design and composition, presswork, and bindery.

**17735**
**Industrial Occupational Competency Tests, Journeyworker Level Two: Power Sewing (036).** National Occupational Competency Testing Institute, Big Rapids, MI 1989.
*Descriptors:* *Occupational Tests; *Personnel Evaluation; *Personnel Selection; *Sewing Machine Operators; Adults; Industrial Training; Job Skills; Knowledge Level; Multiple Choice Tests; Performance Tests; Promotion (Occupational); Skilled Workers; Work Sample Tests
*Identifiers:* IOCT; National Occupational Competency Testing Institute; NOCTI
*Availability:* National Occupational Competency Testing Institute, 409 Bishop Hall, Ferris State University, Big Rapids, MI 49307.
*Notes:* For the complete series of Industrial Occupational Competency Tests, Entry Level One, see 17778 through 17845. For the Industrial Occupational Competency Tests, Journeyworker Level Two, see 17721 through 17777. Time, 480. Items, 200.

Level Two assessments measure worker competency at the journeyworker level. These were designed for use in industry to measure journeyworker-level skills in prospective and current employees. Both written and performance components are included in the tests and separate scores are reported. May be used for employee selection, upgrading or advancement, and in planning training or retraining programs. The written assessment is multiple choice and covers factual knowledge, technical information, understanding of principles, and problem-solving skills related to the occupation or skill. The performance component is administered in a shop and consists of manipulative tasks related to a particular occupation. The written test covers power machine operation, apparel assembly, general knowledge of the needle trade, general knowledge of terminology in apparel assembly, and trade tools and attachments. The performance test covers assembling techniques, sewing machines, tools and attachments, finishing techniques, materials, and safety and cleanup.

**17737**
**Industrial Occupational Competency Tests, Journeyworker Level Two: Painting and Decorating (035).** National Occupational Competency Testing Institute, Big Rapids, MI 1989.
*Descriptors:* *Occupational Tests; *Painting (Industrial Arts); *Personnel Evaluation; *Personnel Selection; Adults; Industrial Training; Job Skills; Knowledge Level; Multiple Choice Tests; Performance Tests; Promotion (Occupational); Skilled Workers; Work Sample Tests
*Identifiers:* IOCT; National Occupational Competency Testing Institute; NOCTI
*Availability:* National Occupational Competency Testing Institute, 409 Bishop Hall, Ferris State University, Big Rapids, MI 49307.
*Notes:* For the complete series of Industrial Occupational Competency Tests, Entry Level One, see 17778 through 17845. For the Industrial Occupational Competency Tests, Journeyworker Level Two, see 17721 through 17777. Time, 420. Items, 190.

Level Two assessments measure worker competency at the journeyworker level. These were designed for use in industry to measure journeyworker-level skills in prospective and current employees. Both written and performance components are included in the tests and separate scores are reported. May be used for employee selection, upgrading or advancement, and in planning training or retraining programs. The written assessment is multiple choice and covers factual knowledge, technical information, understanding of principles, and problem-solving skills related to the occupation or skill. The performance component is administered in a shop and consists of manipulative tasks related to a particular occupation. The written test covers exterior and interior painting, wall covering, wood finishing, color and color harmony, estimating, safety and first aid, spray painting, stenciling, and general information. The performance test covers wood finishing, wall covering, exterior and interior painting, color and color harmony, and cleanup.

**17738**
**Industrial Occupational Competency Tests, Journeyworker Level Two: Microcomputer Repair (085).** National Occupational Competency Testing Institute, Big Rapids, MI 1989.
*Descriptors:* *Machine Repairers; *Microcomputers; *Occupational Tests; *Personnel Evaluation; *Personnel Selection; Adults; Industrial Training; Job Skills; Knowledge Level; Multiple Choice Tests; Performance Tests; Promotion (Occupational); Skilled Workers; Work Sample Tests
*Identifiers:* IOCT; National Occupational Competency Testing Institute; NOCTI
*Availability:* National Occupational Competency Testing Institute, 409 Bishop Hall, Ferris State University, Big Rapids, MI 49307.
*Notes:* For the complete series of Industrial Occupational Competency Tests, Entry Level One, see 17778 through 17845. For the Industrial Occupational Competency Tests, Journeyworker Level Two, see 17721 through 17777. Time, 390. Items, 200.

Level Two assessments measure worker competency at the journeyworker level. These were designed for use in industry to measure journeyworker-level skills in prospective and current employees. Both written and performance components are included in the tests and separate scores are reported. May be used for employee selection, upgrading or advancement, and in planning training or retraining programs. The written assessment is multiple choice and covers factual knowledge, technical information, understanding of principles, and problem-solving skills related to the occupation or skill. The performance component is administered in a shop and consists of manipulative tasks related to a particular occupation. The written test covers safety, hand tools, D.C. theory, A.C. theory, semiconductors, digital, flip flops and registers, encoders and decoders, counters, multiplexer and demultiplexer, A/D and D/A converters, computer maintenance fundamentals and peripherals, and microprocessors. The performance test covers troubleshooting solid state circuit devices, computer malfunctions and peripherals, constructing/analyzing digital circuits, constructing full-wave bridge rectifier, and analyzing the power supply.

**17739**
**Industrial Occupational Competency Tests, Journeyworker Level Two: Mechanical Technology (023).** National Occupational Competency Testing Institute, Big Rapids, MI 1989.
*Descriptors:* *Mechanics (Physics); *Mechanics (Process); *Occupational Tests; *Personnel Evaluation; *Personnel Selection; Adults; Electricity; Engineering Drawing; Fluid Mechanics; Industrial Training; Job Skills; Knowledge Level; Machine Tools; Mathematics; Multiple Choice Tests; Performance Tests; Programming; Promotion (Occupational); Skilled Workers; Work Sample Tests
*Identifiers:* IOCT; National Occupational Competency Testing Institute; NOCTI
*Availability:* National Occupational Competency Testing Institute, 409 Bishop Hall, Ferris State University, Big Rapids, MI 49307.
*Notes:* For the complete series of Industrial Occupational Competency Tests, Entry Level One, see 17778 through 17845. For the Industrial Occupational Competency Tests, Journeyworker Level Two, see 17721 through 17777. Time, 480. Items, 180.

Level Two assessments measure worker competency at the journeyworker level. These were designed for use in industry to measure journeyworker-level skills in prospective and current employees. Both written and performance components are included in the tests and separate scores are reported. May be used for employee selection, upgrading or advancement, and in planning training or retraining programs. The written assessment is multiple choice and covers factual knowledge, technical information, understanding of principles, and problem-solving skills related to the occupation or skill. The performance component is administered in a shop and consists of manipulative tasks related to a particular occupation. The written test covers statics, strength of materials, mathematics, metallurgy, electricity, physics, fluid mechanics, thermodynamics, applications of basic computer programming to engineering, and machine shop. The performance test covers hydraulics, writing a computer program for a mathematical formula, electricity, designing a V-pully, strength of materials, machine tool operations, and metallurgy.

**17740**
**Industrial Occupational Competency Tests, Journeyworker Level Two: Materials Handling (033).** National Occupational Competency Testing Institute, Big Rapids, MI 1989.
*Descriptors:* *Facility Inventory; *Occupational Tests; *Personnel Evaluation; *Personnel Selection; Adults; Industrial Training; Job Skills; Knowledge Level; Multiple Choice Tests; Performance Tests; Promotion (Occupational); Skilled Workers; Warehouses; Work Sample Tests
*Identifiers:* IOCT; National Occupational Competency Testing Institute; NOCTI
*Availability:* National Occupational Competency Testing Institute, 409 Bishop Hall, Ferris State University, Big Rapids, MI 49307.
*Notes:* For the complete series of Industrial Occupational Competency Tests, Entry Level One, see 17778 through 17845. For the Industrial Occupational Competency Tests, Journeyworker Level Two, see 17721 through 17777. Time, 445. Items, 199.

Level Two assessments measure worker competency at the journeyworker level. These were designed for use in industry to measure journeyworker-level skills in prospective and current employees. Both written and performance components are included in the tests and separate scores are reported. May be used for employee selection, upgrading or advancement, and in planning training or retraining programs. The written assessment is multiple choice and covers factual knowledge, technical information, understanding of principles, and problem-solving skills related to the occupation or skill. The performance component is administered in a shop and consists of manipulative tasks related to a particular occupation. The written test covers receiving, inventory controls, warehousing, shipping and distribution, equipment for materials handling, transportation, purchasing, and storage of material. The performance test covers equipment use and operation, shipping procedures, receiving procedures, warehouse proposal, inventory, storage, and purchasing.

**17745**
**Industrial Occupational Competency Tests, Journeyworker Level Two: Industrial Electronics (016).** National Occupational Competency Testing Institute, Big Rapids, MI 1989.
*Descriptors:* *Electronics; *Occupational Tests; *Personnel Evaluation; *Personnel Selection; Adults; Industrial Training; Job Skills; Knowledge Level; Multiple Choice Tests; Performance Tests; Promotion (Occupational); Skilled Workers; Work Sample Tests
*Identifiers:* IOCT; National Occupational Competency Testing Institute; NOCTI
*Availability:* National Occupational Competency Testing Institute, 409 Bishop Hall, Ferris State University, Big Rapids, MI 49307.
*Notes:* For the complete series of Industrial Occupational Competency Tests, Entry Level One, see 17778 through 17845. For the Industrial Occupational Competency Tests, Journeyworker Level Two, see 17721 through 17777. Time, 420. Items, 150.

Level Two assessments measure worker competency at the journeyworker level. These were designed for use in industry to measure journeyworker-level skills in prospective and current employees. Both written and performance components are included in the tests and separate scores are reported. May be used for employee selection, upgrading or advancement, and in planning training or retraining programs. The written assessment is multiple choice and covers factual knowledge, technical information, understanding of principles, and problem-solving skills related to the occupation or skill. The performance component is administered in a shop and consists of manipulative tasks related to a particular occupation. The written test covers D.C. circuits/basic electronics, A.C. circuits, semiconductors, electronic circuits, digital, electronic control devices/circuitry, analysis/instrumentation, symbols, and microprocessors/systems. The performance test requires use of measuring instruments, troubleshooting and repair, assembly and determination of circuit characteristics, and analysis.

**17748**
**Industrial Occupational Competency Tests, Journeyworker Level Two: Heating (044).** National Occupational Competency Testing Institute, Big Rapids, MI 1989.
*Descriptors:* *Heating; *Occupational Tests; *Personnel Evaluation; *Personnel Selection; Adults; Industrial Training; Job Skills; Knowledge Level; Multiple Choice Tests; Performance Tests; Promotion (Occupational); Skilled Workers; Work Sample Tests
*Identifiers:* IOCT; National Occupational Competency Testing Institute; NOCTI
*Availability:* National Occupational Competency Testing Institute, 409 Bishop Hall, Ferris State University, Big Rapids, MI 49307.
*Notes:* For the complete series of Industrial Occupational Competency Tests, Entry Level One, see 17778 through 17845. For the Industrial Occupational Competency Tests, Journeyworker Level Two, see 17721 through 17777. Time, 420. Items, 178.

Level Two assessments measure worker competency at the journeyworker level. These were designed for use in industry to measure journeyworker-level skills in prospective and current employees. Both written and performance components are included in the tests and separate scores are reported. May be used for employee selection, upgrading or advancement, and in planning training or retraining programs. The written assessment is multiple choice and covers factual knowledge, technical information, understanding of principles, and problem-solving skills related to the occupation or skill. The performance component is administered in a shop and consists of manipulative tasks related to a particular occupation. The written test covers hot water, hot air, steam, gravity, forced air, and loop systems, different types of controls, service and testing of heating systems, heating plants. The performance test covers hot water, hot air, gravity, forced air, and loop systems; measurements, calculations, primary controls, and thermostats; fan, limit, and safety switches; stack controls; zone controls; circulators; ignition; heating plants; and layout and testing; service and testing, including inspection, disassembly, repair and troubleshooting.

**17757**
**Industrial Occupational Competency Tests, Journeyworker Level Two: Computer Technology (026).** National Occupational Competency Testing Institute, Big Rapids, MI 1989.
*Descriptors:* *Computer Science; *Occupational Tests; *Personnel Evaluation; *Personnel Selection; Adults; Industrial Training; Job Skills; Knowledge Level; Multiple Choice Tests; Performance Tests; Programming; Promotion (Occupational); Skilled Workers; Work Sample Tests
*Identifiers:* IOCT; National Occupational Competency Testing Institute; NOCTI
*Availability:* National Occupational Competency Testing Institute, 409 Bishop Hall, Ferris State University, Big Rapids, MI 49307.
*Notes:* For the complete series of Industrial Occupational Competency Tests, Entry Level One, see 17778 through 17845. For the Industrial Occupational Competency Tests, Journeyworker Level Two, see 17721 through 17777. Time, 480. Items, 180.

Level Two assessments measure worker competency at the journeyworker level. These were designed for use in industry to measure journeyworker-level skills in prospective and current employees. Both written and performance components are included in the tests and separate scores are reported. May be used for employee selection, upgrading or advancement, and in planning training or retraining programs. The written assessment is multiple choice and covers factual knowledge, technical information, understanding of principles, and problem-solving skills related to the occupation or skill. The performance component is administered in a shop and consists of manipulative tasks related to a particular occupation. The written test covers general information mass storage devices, data entry, micros, system architecture, COBOL, BASIC, flowcharting, operating systems and application software, and I/O devices. The performance test requires the test taker to demonstrate file preparation, flowcharting, source listing, and output.

**17758**
**Industrial Occupational Competency Tests, Journeyworker Level Two: Computer Science for Secondary Teachers (080).** National Occupational Competency Testing Institute, Big Rapids, MI 1989.
*Descriptors:* *Computer Science; *Occupational Tests; *Personnel Evaluation; *Personnel Selection; *Programming Languages; *Secondary School Teachers; Adults; Industrial Training; Job Skills; Knowledge Level; Multiple Choice Tests; Performance Tests; Promotion (Occupational); Skilled Workers; Work Sample Tests
*Identifiers:* IOCT; National Occupational Competency Testing Institute; NOCTI
*Availability:* National Occupational Competency Testing Institute, 409 Bishop Hall, Ferris State University, Big Rapids, MI 49307.

*Notes:* For the complete series of Industrial Occupational Competency Tests, Entry Level One, see 17778 through 17845. For the Industrial Occupational Competency Tests, Journeyworker Level Two, see 17721 through 17777. Time, 540. Items, 158.

Level Two assessments measure worker competency at the journeyworker level. These were designed for use in industry to measure journeyworker-level skills in prospective and current employees. Both written and performance components are included in the tests and separate scores are reported. May be used for employee selection, upgrading or advancement, and in planning training or retraining programs. The written assessment is multiple choice and covers factual knowledge, technical information, understanding of principles, and problem-solving skills related to the occupation or skill. The performance component is administered in a shop and consists of manipulative tasks related to a particular occupation. The written test covers general concepts, program design, microcomputers, and on-line communications, including magnetic files and data communications. The performance test covers use of microcomputers for word processing and spreadsheets, systems analysis, program design, BASIC programming, PASCAL programming, FORTRAN programming, and COBOL programming.

**17759**
**Industrial Occupational Competency Tests, Journeyworker Level Two: Commercial Photography (070).** National Occupational Competency Testing Institute, Big Rapids, MI 1989.
*Descriptors:* *Occupational Tests; *Personnel Evaluation; *Personnel Selection; *Photography; Adults; Industrial Training; Job Skills; Knowledge Level; Multiple Choice Tests; Performance Tests; Promotion (Occupational); Skilled Workers; Work Sample Tests
*Identifiers:* IOCT; National Occupational Competency Testing Institute; NOCTI
*Availability:* National Occupational Competency Testing Institute, 409 Bishop Hall, Ferris State University, Big Rapids, MI 49307.
*Notes:* For the complete series of Industrial Occupational Competency Tests, Entry Level One, see 17778 through 17845. For the Industrial Occupational Competency Tests, Journeyworker Level Two, see 17721 through 17777. Time, 480. Items, 150.

Level Two assessments measure worker competency at the journeyworker level. These were designed for use in industry to measure journeyworker-level skills in prospective and current employees. Both written and performance components are included in the tests and separate scores are reported. May be used for employee selection, upgrading or advancement, and in planning training or retraining programs. The written assessment is multiple choice and covers factual knowledge, technical information, understanding of principles, and problem-solving skills related to the occupation or skill. The performance component is administered in a shop and consists of manipulative tasks related to a particular occupation. The written test covers 35mm camera operation, photo printing, film processing, film characteristics, lighting, print finishing, composition, filters, light meters, and light and color. The performance test covers 35mm camera operation, film processing, printing/enlarging, and lighting.

**17760**
**Industrial Occupational Competency Tests, Journeyworker Level Two: Commercial Art (029).** National Occupational Competency Testing Institute, Big Rapids, MI 1989.
*Descriptors:* *Commercial Art; *Occupational Tests; *Personnel Evaluation; *Personnel Selection; Adults; Industrial Training; Job Skills; Knowledge Level; Multiple Choice Tests; Performance Tests; Promotion (Occupational); Skilled Workers; Work Sample Tests
*Identifiers:* IOCT; National Occupational Competency Testing Institute; NOCTI
*Availability:* National Occupational Competency Testing Institute, 409 Bishop Hall, Ferris State University, Big Rapids, MI 49307.
*Notes:* For the complete series of Industrial Occupational Competency Tests, Entry Level One, see 17778 through 17845. For the Industrial Occupational Competency Tests, Journeyworker Level Two, see 17721 through 17777. Time, 480. Items, 125.

Level Two assessments measure worker competency at the journeyworker level. These were designed for use in industry to measure journeyworker-level skills in prospective and current employees. Both written and performance components are included in the tests and separate scores are reported. May be used for employee selection, upgrading or advancement, and in planning training or retraining programs. The written assessment is multiple choice and covers factual knowledge, technical information, understanding of principles, and problem-solving skills related to the occupation or skill. The performance component is administered in a shop and consists of manipulative tasks related to a particular occupation. The written test covers design and typography, drawing and rendering, production, printing, and general fundamentals. The performance test covers black and white rendering, keyline/mechanical, and magazine ad layout.

**17761**
**Industrial Occupational Competency Tests, Journeyworker Level Two: Civil Technology (018).** National Occupational Competency Testing Institute, Big Rapids, MI 1989.
*Descriptors:* *Civil Engineering; *Drafting; *Occupational Tests; *Personnel Evaluation; *Personnel Selection; Adults; Industrial Training; Job Skills; Knowledge Level; Multiple Choice Tests; Performance Tests; Promotion (Occupational); Skilled Workers; Work Sample Tests
*Identifiers:* IOCT; National Occupational Competency Testing Institute; NOCTI
*Availability:* National Occupational Competency Testing Institute, 409 Bishop Hall, Ferris State University, Big Rapids, MI 49307.
*Notes:* For the complete series of Industrial Occupational Competency Tests, Entry Level One, see 17778 through 17845. For the Industrial Occupational Competency Tests, Journeyworker Level Two, see 17721 through 17777. Time, 480. Items, 152.

Level Two assessments measure worker competency at the journeyworker level. These were designed for use in industry to measure journeyworker-level skills in prospective and current employees. Both written and performance components are included in the tests and separate scores are reported. May be used for employee selection, upgrading or advancement, and in planning training or retraining programs. The written assessment is multiple choice and covers factual knowledge, technical information, understanding of principles, and problem-solving skills related to the occupation or skill. The performance component is administered in a shop and consists of manipulative tasks related to a particular occupation. The written test covers surveying steel structures, drafting, soil, asphalt, concrete, instrumentation, and general engineering information. The performance test covers surveying, drafting, concrete, soils, and asphalt.

**17762**
**Industrial Occupational Competency Tests, Journeyworker Level Two: Child Care and Guidance (081).** National Occupational Competency Testing Institute, Big Rapids, MI 1989.
*Descriptors:* *Child Care Occupations; *Day Care; *Occupational Tests; *Personnel Evaluation; *Personnel Selection; Adults; Child Development; Classroom Techniques; Industrial Training; Job Skills; Knowledge Level; Multiple Choice Tests; Parent Teacher Cooperation; Performance Tests; Promotion (Occupational); Skilled Workers; Work Sample Tests
*Identifiers:* IOCT; National Occupational Competency Testing Institute; NOCTI
*Availability:* National Occupational Competency Testing Institute, 409 Bishop Hall, Ferris State University, Big Rapids, MI 49307.
*Notes:* For the complete series of Industrial Occupational Competency Tests, Entry Level One, see 17778 through 17845. For the Industrial Occupational Competency Tests, Journeyworker Level Two, see 17721 through 17777. Time, 420. Items, 200.

Level Two assessments measure worker competency at the journeyworker level. These were designed for use in industry to measure journeyworker-level skills in prospective and current employees. Both written and performance components are included in the tests and separate scores are reported. May be used for employee selection, upgrading or advancement, and in planning training or retraining programs. The written assessment is multiple choice and covers factual knowledge, technical information, understanding of principles, and problem-solving skills related to the occupation or skill. The performance component is administered in a shop and consists of manipulative tasks related to a particular occupation. The written portion of the test covers infant-toddler development and learning, preschool and young child development and learning, guiding behavior, health and safety, center management, and special needs children. The performance test covers infant diapering, toddler observation, large group teaching, small group teaching, daily program plans, role play (parent/staff interaction), and role play (child discipline situation).

**17763**
**Industrial Occupational Competency Tests, Journeyworker Level Two: Carpentry (007).** National Occupational Competency Testing Institute, Big Rapids, MI 1989.
*Descriptors:* *Carpentry; *Occupational Tests; *Personnel Evaluation; *Personnel Selection; Adults; Industrial Training; Job Skills; Knowledge Level; Multiple Choice Tests; Performance Tests; Promotion (Occupational); Skilled Workers; Work Sample Tests
*Identifiers:* IOCT; National Occupational Competency Testing Institute; NOCTI
*Availability:* National Occupational Competency Testing Institute, 409 Bishop Hall, Ferris State University, Big Rapids, MI 49307.
*Notes:* For the complete series of Industrial Occupational Competency Tests, Entry Level One, see 17778 through 17845. For the Industrial Occupational Competency Tests, Journeyworker Level Two, see 17721 through 17777. Time, 480. Items, 200.

Level Two assessments measure worker competency at the journeyworker level. These were designed for use in industry to measure journeyworker-level skills in prospective and current employees. Both written and performance components are included in the tests and separate scores are reported. May be used for employee selection, upgrading or advancement, and in planning training or retraining programs. The written assessment is multiple choice and covers factual knowledge, technical information, understanding of principles, and problem-solving skills related to the occupation or skill. The performance component is administered in a shop and consists of manipulative tasks related to a particular occupation. The written test covers exterior finish, interior finish, roof framing and roofing, rough framing, floors, walls, energy conservation, estimating, tools and equipment, layout, footings, foundation, stair construction, and general knowledge. The performance test covers wall layout from plan, story pole layout, roof layout and framing, exterior finish, interior finish/baseboard and crown molding, interior finish/inside door hardware, and layout stair stringer.

**17764**
**Industrial Occupational Competency Tests, Journeyworker Level Two: Cabinet Making and Millwork (024).** National Occupational Competency Testing Institute, Big Rapids, MI 1989.
*Descriptors:* *Cabinetmaking; *Carpentry; *Occupational Tests; *Personnel Evaluation; *Personnel Selection; Adults; Industrial Training; Job Skills; Knowledge Level; Multiple Choice Tests; Performance Tests; Promotion (Occupational); Skilled Workers; Work Sample Tests

*Identifiers:* IOCT; National Occupational Competency Testing Institute; NOCTI
*Availability:* National Occupational Competency Testing Institute, 409 Bishop Hall, Ferris State University, Big Rapids, MI 49307.
*Notes:* For the complete series of Industrial Occupational Competency Tests, Entry Level One, see 17778 through 17845. For the Industrial Occupational Competency Tests, Journeyworker Level Two, see 17721 through 17777. Time, 420. Items, 183.

Level Two assessments measure worker competency at the journeyworker level. These were designed for use in industry to measure journeyworker-level skills in prospective and current employees. Both written and performance components are included in the tests and separate scores are reported. May be used for employee selection, upgrading or advancement, and in planning training or retraining programs. The written assessment is multiple choice and covers factual knowledge, technical information, understanding of principles, and problem-solving skills related to the occupation or skill. The performance component is administered in a shop and consists of manipulative tasks related to a particular occupation. The written test covers machines, hand tools, finishing, joinery, assembly, planning, wood/stock selection, and safety. The performance test covers machines, hand tools, planning and layout, assembly, joinery, finish, safety, and wood/stock selection.

**17765**
**Industrial Occupational Competency Tests, Journeyworker Level Two: Building Trades Maintenance (025).** National Occupational Competency Testing Institute, Big Rapids, MI 1989.
*Descriptors:* *Building Trades; *Occupational Tests; *Personnel Evaluation; *Personnel Selection; Adults; Industrial Training; Job Skills; Knowledge Level; Maintenance; Multiple Choice Tests; Performance Tests; Promotion (Occupational); Skilled Workers; Work Sample Tests
*Identifiers:* IOCT; National Occupational Competency Testing Institute; NOCTI
*Availability:* National Occupational Competency Testing Institute, 409 Bishop Hall, Ferris State University, Big Rapids, MI 49307.
*Notes:* For the complete series of Industrial Occupational Competency Tests, Entry Level One, see 17778 through 17845. For the Industrial Occupational Competency Tests, Journeyworker Level Two, see 17721 through 17777. Time, 515. Items, 200.

Level Two assessments measure worker competency at the journeyworker level. These were designed for use in industry to measure journeyworker-level skills in prospective and current employees. Both written and performance components are included in the tests and separate scores are reported. May be used for employee selection, upgrading or advancement, and in planning training or retraining programs. The written assessment is multiple choice and covers factual knowledge, technical information, understanding of principles, and problem-solving skills related to the occupation or skill. The performance component is administered in a shop and consists of manipulative tasks related to a particular occupation. The written test covers electrical installation, carpentry, painting and wall applications, plumbing, masonry, metal processes, and related knowledge of basic principles. The performance test covers plumbing, masonry, welding, electrical installation, carpentry, glass installation, lockset installation, and painting and wall applications.

**17766**
**Industrial Occupational Competency Tests, Journeyworker Level Two: Building and Home Maintenance Services (067).** National Occupational Competency Testing Institute, Big Rapids, MI 1989.
*Descriptors:* *Construction Industry; *Maintenance; *Occupational Tests; *Personnel Evaluation; *Personnel Selection; Adults; Building Trades; Industrial Training; Job Skills; Knowledge Level; Multiple Choice Tests; Performance Tests; Promotion (Occupational); Skilled Workers; Work Sample Tests
*Identifiers:* IOCT; National Occupational Competency Testing Institute; NOCTI
*Availability:* National Occupational Competency Testing Institute, 409 Bishop Hall, Ferris State University, Big Rapids, MI 49307.
*Notes:* For the complete series of Industrial Occupational Competency Tests, Entry Level One, see 17778 through 17845. For the Industrial Occupational Competency Tests, Journeyworker Level Two, see 17721 through 17777. Time, 480. Items, 162.

Level Two assessments measure worker competency at the journeyworker level. These were designed for use in industry to measure journeyworker-level skills in prospective and current employees. Both written and performance components are included in the tests and separate scores are reported. May be used for employee selection, upgrading or advancement, and in planning training or retraining programs. The written assessment is multiple choice and covers factual knowledge, technical information, understanding of principles, and problem-solving skills related to the occupation or skill. The performance component is administered in a shop and consists of manipulative tasks related to a particular occupation. The written test covers floor stripping, refinishing and buffing, carpet care, general electricity and repair, building security, fire prevention, records, general cleaning, plumbing, employee/staff relations, heating, and painting. The performance test covers general cleaning of office or classroom and a restroom or shower/locker room area; floor stripping, refinishing, and buffing; carpet care; welding or soldering; electrical repair; small hand/power tools; and interior/exterior painting.

**17768**
**Industrial Occupational Competency Tests, Journeyworker Level Two: Brick Masonry (051).** National Occupational Competency Testing Institute, Big Rapids, MI 1989.
*Descriptors:* *Construction Industry; *Masonry; *Occupational Tests; *Personnel Evaluation; *Personnel Selection; Adults; Building Trades; Industrial Training; Job Skills; Knowledge Level; Multiple Choice Tests; Performance Tests; Promotion (Occupational); Skilled Workers; Work Sample Tests
*Identifiers:* IOCT; National Occupational Competency Testing Institute; NOCTI
*Availability:* National Occupational Competency Testing Institute, 409 Bishop Hall, Ferris State University, Big Rapids, MI 49307.
*Notes:* For the complete series of Industrial Occupational Competency Tests, Entry Level One, see 17778 through 17845. For the Industrial Occupational Competency Tests, Journeyworker Level Two, see 17721 through 17777. Time, 520. Items, 200.

Level Two assessments measure worker competency at the journeyworker level. These were designed for use in industry to measure journeyworker-level skills in prospective and current employees. Both written and performance components are included in the tests and separate scores are reported. May be used for employee selection, upgrading or advancement, and in planning training or retraining programs. The written assessment is multiple choice and covers factual knowledge, technical information, understanding of principles, and problem-solving skills related to the occupation or skill. The performance component is administered in a shop and consists of manipulative tasks related to a particular occupation. The written test covers brick, block, fireplace, building layout, stone, tile, glass block, pave brick, and general knowledge. The performance test covers brick and block wall, brick 4-inch return corner, brick chimney construction, glass block window construction, brick and block parapet wall, segmental arch, and blueprint reading.

**17769**
**Industrial Occupational Competency Tests, Journeyworker Level Two: Baking (059).** National Occupational Competency Testing Institute, Big Rapids, MI 1989.
*Descriptors:* *Bakery Industry; *Occupational Tests; *Personnel Evaluation; *Personnel Selection; Adults; Food Service; Industrial Training; Job Skills; Knowledge Level; Multiple Choice Tests; Performance Tests; Promotion (Occupational); Skilled Workers; Work Sample Tests
*Identifiers:* IOCT; National Occupational Competency Testing Institute; NOCTI
*Availability:* National Occupational Competency Testing Institute, 409 Bishop Hall, Ferris State University, Big Rapids, MI 49307.
*Notes:* For the complete series of Industrial Occupational Competency Tests, Entry Level One, see 17778 through 17845. For the Industrial Occupational Competency Tests, Journeyworker Level Two, see 17721 through 17777. Time, 420. Items, 200.

Level Two assessments measure worker competency at the journeyworker level. These were designed for use in industry to measure journeyworker-level skills in prospective and current employees. Both written and performance components are included in the tests and separate scores are reported. May be used for employee selection, upgrading or advancement, and in planning training or retraining programs. The written assessment is multiple choice and covers factual knowledge, technical information, understanding of principles, and problem-solving skills related to the occupation or skill. The performance component is administered in a shop and consists of manipulative tasks related to a particular occupation. The written test covers general baking knowledge, classification and properties of ingredients, bread and rolls, cake doughnuts, yeast-raised dough, cookies, cakes, danish-puff pastry, pies, safety and sanitation, handling and storage of ingredients, weights and measures, and general baking math. The performance test covers dough preparation, bread, rolls, cakes, and pastries.

**17770**
**Industrial Occupational Competency Tests, Journeyworker Level Two: Auto Mechanic (003).** National Occupational Competency Testing Institute, Big Rapids, MI 1989.
*Descriptors:* *Auto Mechanics; *Occupational Tests; *Personnel Evaluation; *Personnel Selection; Adults; Industrial Training; Job Skills; Knowledge Level; Multiple Choice Tests; Performance Tests; Promotion (Occupational); Skilled Workers; Work Sample Tests
*Identifiers:* IOCT; National Occupational Competency Testing Institute; NOCTI
*Availability:* National Occupational Competency Testing Institute, 409 Bishop Hall, Ferris State University, Big Rapids, MI 49307.
*Notes:* For the complete series of Industrial Occupational Competency Tests, Entry Level One, see 17778 through 17845. For the Industrial Occupational Competency Tests, Journeyworker Level Two, see 17721 through 17777. Time, 480. Items, 190.

Level Two assessments measure worker competency at the journeyworker level. These were designed for use in industry to measure journeyworker-level skills in prospective and current employees. Both written and performance components are included in the tests and separate scores are reported. May be used for employee selection, upgrading or advancement, and in planning training or retraining programs. The written assessment is multiple choice and covers factual knowledge, technical information, understanding of principles, and problem-solving skills related to the occupation or skill. The performance component is administered in a shop and consists of manipulative tasks related to a particular occupation. The written test covers welding, filling operations and plastics, repairing sheet metal, refinishing, panel replacement, frame (unitized body repair), front end alignment, electrical and accessory systems, and brakes. The performance test covers engines, engine analysis and repair, air conditioning, fuel systems, electrical, charging system, emission systems, drive lines and components, suspension and steering, batteries, and basic automotive practices.

**17771**
**Industrial Occupational Competency Tests, Journeyworker Level Two: Auto Body Repair.** National Occupational Competency Testing Institute, Big Rapids, MI 1989.
*Descriptors:* *Auto Body Repairers; *Occupational Tests; *Personnel Evaluation; *Personnel Selection; Adults; Industrial Training; Job Skills; Knowledge Level; Multiple Choice Tests; Performance Tests; Promotion (Occupational); Skilled Workers; Work Sample Tests
*Identifiers:* IOCT; National Occupational Competency Testing Institute; NOCTI
*Availability:* National Occupational Competency Testing Institute, 409 Bishop Hall, Ferris State University, Big Rapids, MI 49307.
*Notes:* For the complete series of Industrial Occupational Competency Tests, Entry Level One, see 17778 through 17845. For the Industrial Occupational Competency Tests, Journeyworker Level Two, see 17721 through 17777. Time, 455. Items, 190.

Level Two assessments measure worker competency at the journeyworker level. These were designed for use in industry to measure journeyworker-level skills in prospective and current employees. Both written and performance components are included in the tests and separate scores are reported. May be used for employee selection, upgrading or advancement, and in planning training or retraining programs. The written assessment is multiple choice and covers factual knowledge, technical information, understanding of principles, and problem-solving skills related to the occupation or skill. The performance component is administered in a shop and consists of manipulative tasks related to a particular occupation. The written test covers welding, filling operations and plastics; repairing sheet metal; refinishing; panel replacement; frame (unitized body repair); front-end alignment; electrical and accessory systems; and brakes. The performance test covers metal forming, welding, diagnosing structural damage, refinishing, and electrical troubleshooting.

**17772**
**Industrial Occupational Competency Tests, Journeyworker Level Two: Auto Body Repair (002).** National Occupational Competency Testing Institute, Big Rapids, MI 1989.
*Descriptors:* *Auto Body Repairers; *Occupational Tests; *Personnel Evaluation; *Personnel Selection; Adults; Industrial Training; Job Skills; Knowledge Level; Multiple Choice Tests; Performance Tests; Promotion (Occupational); Skilled Workers; Work Sample Tests
*Identifiers:* IOCT; National Occupational Competency Testing Institute; NOCTI
*Availability:* National Occupational Competency Testing Institute, 409 Bishop Hall, Ferris State University, Big Rapids, MI 49307.
*Notes:* For the complete series of Industrial Occupational Competency Tests, Entry Level One, see 17778 through 17845. For the Industrial Occupational Competency Tests, Journeyworker Level Two, see 17721 through 17777. Time, 520. Items, 190.

Level Two assessments measure worker competency at the journeyworker level. These were designed for use in industry to measure journeyworker-level skills in prospective and current employees. Both written and performance components are included in the tests and separate scores are reported. May be used for employee selection, upgrading or advancement, and in planning training or retraining programs. The written assessment is multiple choice and covers factual knowledge, technical information, understanding of principles, and problem-solving skills related to the occupation or skill. The performance component is administered in a shop and consists of manipulative tasks related to a particular occupation. The written test covers welding and brazing; filling operations and plastics; repairing sheet metal; refinishing; panel replacement; frame (unitized body repair); front end alignment; electrical and accessory systems; glass, trim and hardware; estimating; tools and equipment; and safety. The performance test covers sheet metal repair, refinishing, glass trim repair, diagnosing structural damage, and electrical work.

**17773**
**Industrial Occupational Competency Tests, Journeyworker Level Two: Audio-Visual Communications.** National Occupational Competency Testing Institute, Big Rapids, MI 1989.
*Descriptors:* *Audiovisual Communications; *Occupational Tests; *Personnel Evaluation; *Personnel Selection; Adults; Audiovisual Aids; Industrial Training; Job Skills; Knowledge Level; Multiple Choice Tests; Performance Tests; Photography; Promotion (Occupational); Skilled Workers; Work Sample Tests
*Identifiers:* IOCT; National Occupational Competency Testing Institute; NOCTI
*Availability:* National Occupational Competency Testing Institute, 409 Bishop Hall, Ferris State University, Big Rapids, MI 49307.
*Notes:* For the complete series of Industrial Occupational Competency Tests, Entry Level One, see 17778 through 17845. For the Industrial Occupational Competency Tests, Journeyworker Level Two, see 17721 through 17777. Time, 530. Items, 180.

Level Two assessments measure worker competency at the journeyworker level. These were designed for use in industry to measure journeyworker-level skills in prospective and current employees. Both written and performance components are included in the tests and separate scores are reported. May be used for employee selection, upgrading or advancement, and in planning training or retraining programs. The written assessment is multiple choice and covers factual knowledge, technical information, understanding of principles, and problem-solving skills related to the occupation or skill. The performance component is administered in a shop and consists of manipulative tasks related to a particular occupation. The written test covers general information and theory, broadcasting, lighting, multi-image, graphics/visuals, photography, audio/radio, television, and film. The performance test covers still photography camera operation and negative development, still photo printing, audio production studio, editing and splicing audiotape, television shooting and editing, transparency design, motion picture operation and splicing, and tape recorder operation.

**17774**
**Industrial Occupational Competency Tests, Journeyworker Level Two: Architectural Drafting.** National Occupational Competency Testing Institute, Big Rapids, MI 1989.
*Descriptors:* *Architectural Education; *Drafting; *Occupational Tests; *Personnel Evaluation; *Personnel Selection; Adults; Industrial Training; Job Skills; Knowledge Level; Multiple Choice Tests; Performance Tests; Promotion (Occupational); Skilled Workers; Work Sample Tests
*Identifiers:* IOCT; National Occupational Competency Testing Institute; NOCTI
*Availability:* National Occupational Competency Testing Institute, 409 Bishop Hall, Ferris State University, Big Rapids, MI 49307.
*Notes:* For the complete series of Industrial Occupational Competency Tests, Entry Level One, see 17778 through 17845. For the Industrial Occupational Competency Tests, Journeyworker Level Two, see 17721 through 17777. Time, 540. Items, 200.

Level Two assessments measure worker competency at the journeyworker level. These were designed for use in industry to measure journeyworker-level skills in prospective and current employees. Both written and performance components are included in the tests and separate scores are reported. May be used for employee selection, upgrading or advancement, and in planning training or retraining programs. The written assessment is multiple choice and covers factual knowledge, technical information, understanding of principles, and problem-solving skills related to the occupation or skill. The performance component is administered in a shop and consists of manipulative tasks related to a particular occupation. The written test covers basic architectural graphic communication, environmental and safety considerations, planning and design, materials and methods of construction, construction specifications, project administration, print reading and cost estimating, and engineering systems. The performance test covers lettering and line quality, dimensions and notes, scale use and conversions, application of standards, analysis, synthesis, and development of graphic data.

**17775**
**Industrial Occupational Competency Tests, Journeyworker Level Two: Appliance Repair (027).** National Occupational Competency Testing Institute, Big Rapids, MI 1989.
*Descriptors:* *Appliance Repair; *Occupational Tests; *Personnel Evaluation; *Personnel Selection; Adults; Industrial Training; Job Skills; Knowledge Level; Multiple Choice Tests; Performance Tests; Promotion (Occupational); Refrigeration; Skilled Workers; Work Sample Tests
*Identifiers:* IOCT; National Occupational Competency Testing Institute; NOCTI
*Availability:* National Occupational Competency Testing Institute, 409 Bishop Hall, Ferris State University, Big Rapids, MI 49307.
*Notes:* For the complete series of Industrial Occupational Competency Tests, Entry Level One, see 17778 through 17845. For the Industrial Occupational Competency Tests, Journeyworker Level Two, see 17721 through 17777. Time, 500. Items, 200.

Level Two assessments measure worker competency at the journeyworker level. These were designed for use in industry to measure journeyworker-level skills in prospective and current employees. Both written and performance components are included in the tests and separate scores are reported. May be used for employee selection, upgrading or advancement and in planning, training, or retraining programs. The written assessment is multiple choice and covers factual knowledge, technical information, understanding of principles, and problem-solving skills related to the occupation or skill. The performance component is administered in a shop and consists of manipulative tasks related to a particular occupation. The written test covers refrigeration, fundamentals of electricity, kitchen equipment, major heating devices, laundry equipment, power tools, and small appliances. The performance test covers use of wattmeter/ohmmeter, electric wiring, laundry equipment, refrigeration, microwave repair, and solid state diagnosing.

**17776**
**Industrial Occupational Competency Tests, Journeyworker Level Two: Airframe and Powerplant Mechanic (001).** National Occupational Competency Testing Institute, Big Rapids, MI 1989.
*Descriptors:* *Aviation Mechanics; *Occupational Tests; *Personnel Evaluation; *Personnel Selection; Adults; Electricity; Industrial Training; Job Skills; Knowledge Level; Multiple Choice Tests; Performance Tests; Promotion (Occupational); Skilled Workers; Work Sample Tests
*Identifiers:* IOCT; National Occupational Competency Testing Institute; NOCTI
*Availability:* National Occupational Competency Testing Institute, 409 Bishop Hall, Ferris State University, Big Rapids, MI 49307.
*Notes:* For the complete series of Industrial Occupational Competency Tests, Entry Level One, see 17778 through 17845. For the Industrial Occupational Competency Tests, Journeyworker Level Two, see 17721 through 17777. Time, 540. Items, 200.

Level Two assessments measure worker competency at the journeyworker level. These were designed for use in industry to measure journeyworker-level skills in prospective and current employees. Both written and performance components are included in the tests and separate scores are reported. May be used for employee selection, upgrading or advancement, and in planning training or retraining programs. The written assessment is multiple choice and covers factual knowledge, technical information, understanding of principles, and problem-solving skills related to the occupation or skill. The performance component is administered in a shop and consists of manipulative tasks related to a particular occupation. The written test covers aircraft science, aircraft materials, aviation regulations, aircraft structures, aircraft theory of flight, aircraft propellers, aircraft electrical and instrument systems, aircraft fluid and environmental systems, reciprocating engine systems, and turbine engine systems. The performance test covers sheet metal work, servicing landing gear, non-destructive test techniques, completion of maintenance documents, use of airworthiness directives, carburetor service, and engine tune-up.

**17848**
**Word Processing Test.** Psychological Corp., San Antonio, TX 1985.
*Descriptors:* *High School Students; *Employees; *Word Processing; *Occupational Tests; *Job Applicants; Trainees; Secondary Education; Vocational Education; Input Output; Editing; Office Occupations Education; Adults
*Identifiers:* WP
*Availability:* The Psychological Corp., 555 Academic Ct., San Antonio, TX 78204.

Designed to measure 2 operating abilities: inputting and editing material. Individual subtests were constructed to provide standardized measures of important aspects of operating word processors. Included are two forms, A and B, each available for use with Wang OIS and VS Systems, the Wang PC, and selected IBM systems. Form A is to be used by personnel departments of business and industrial firms for testing applicants and employees. Form B is available to schools, vocational training programs, and employment agencies, as well as business and industrial firms. Users of this instrument are urged to collect normative information for their own population of applicants, employees, trainees, or students. Subtests include: Input Test; Edit Test; Text Edit; and Table Edit. (TJS)

**17851**
**NTE Specialty Area Tests: Education of Students with Mental Retardation.** Educational Testing Service, Princeton, NJ 1991.
*Descriptors:* *Achievement Tests; *Beginning Teachers; *Certification; *Mild Mental Retardation; *Moderate Mental Retardation; *Professional Occupations; *Severe Mental Retardation; *Special Education Teachers; *Teacher Education Programs; Child Development; Disabilities; Educational Diagnosis; Elementary School Students; Higher Education; Knowledge Level; Learning; Preschool Children; Secondary School Students
*Availability:* NTE Programs, Educational Testing Service, CN 6051, Princeton, NJ 08541-6051.
*Notes:* Time, 120. Items, 150.

The NTE Program tests are standardized, secure examinations that are measures of academic achievement for college students in teacher education programs and for advanced candidates who have received additional training in specific fields. This test is designed to assess the preparation of prospective teachers of students with mental retardation. Topics assessed include general principles of child development and learning and developmental characteristics of students with mental retardation. Some questions require knowledge of secondary handicapping conditions, but the test questions cover primarily the identification and instruction of students of preschool through secondary age with mild, moderate, severe, and profound retardation.

**17859**
**Supervisory Skills Test.** Talico, Inc., Jacksonville Beach, FL 1989.
*Descriptors:* *Administrators; *Supervisors; *Supervisory Methods; *Administrator Effectiveness; *Middle Management; Employees; Adults; Thinking Skills; Computer Assisted Testing; Objective Tests; Supervision; Leadership Styles; Job Applicants
*Identifiers:* SS
*Availability:* Talico, Inc., 2320 S. Third St., Ste. 5, Jacksonville Beach, FL 32250.

The purpose of this instrument is to evaluate the cognitive skills of managers, supervisors and/or candidates for those positions. Measures respondent's understanding of management and supervisory principles, practices, and behaviors. Twelve management and supervisory skill dimensions are evaluated. Useful for training needs analysis, management and supervisory training, and career counseling and development. Suitable for first-level supervision through middle management. Available as a paper and pencil exercise and on an IBM compatible computer. Subtests include: Planning and Organizing; Communication; Complaint Handling; Coaching and Counseling; Employee Discipline; Motivation; Training; Human Behavior; Teamwork; Leadership; Time Management; and Problem Solving. (TJS)

**17860**
**Profile of Personal Development Needs.** Tagliaferri, Louis E. 1990.
*Descriptors:* *Individual Development; *Administrator Effectiveness; *Managerial Occupations; Adults; Employees; Administrators; Rating Scales; Peer Evaluation; Interprofessional Relationship; Interpersonal Competence; Skilled Occupations; Job Skills; Feedback; Supervision
*Identifiers:* PDN
*Availability:* Talico, Inc., 2320 S. Third St., Ste. 5, Jacksonville Beach, FL 32250.

Designed to assess the technical application, conceptual skills, and human skills that are required for any management level employee to perform their job effectively. Also provides developmental feedback to these employees, including accountants, buyers, engineers, market researchers, wage and salary analysts, auditors, and planners. Categorized into 12 skill dimensions that have been found to impact on the work effectiveness of nonsupervisory management level employees. Instrument is based on a 5-point rating scale that allows respondents to indicate whether each behavior or practice is applicable to the employee's job. Useful as a training needs analysis tool and as an aid for professional or career development. Subtests include: Setting Goals and Objectives; Listening and Responding; Leading Through Influence; Interacting with Others; Achieving Superior Work Results; Managing Time; Communicating with Others; Making Correct Decisions; Developing Synergistic Teamwork; Demonstrating Job Expertise; Demonstrating Creative Ability; and Focusing on Total Quality Management (TJS)

**17862**
**Total Quality Management Survey.** Tagliaferri, Louis E. 1991.
*Descriptors:* *Employees; *Quality of Working Life; *Organizational Climate; *Organizations (Groups); *Total Quality Management; Adults; Job Satisfaction; Likert Scales
*Identifiers:* TQM
*Availability:* Talico, Inc., 2320 S. Third St., Ste. 5, Jacksonville Beach, FL 32250.
*Notes:* See also customer service and sales instruments (17861 through 17868) for related instruments.

A questionnaire that will help senior management evaluate the total quality management climate of its organization with respect to the criteria. Consists of eight sets of six items each with a Likert-type response scale. Categories measured include quality processes, quality results, human resource utilization, teamwork, communication and information, customer focus, continuous improvement, and management and leadership. This tool can be self-administered and self-scored by the organization. Suitable for all levels of employees within any business, industrial or governmental organization.(TJS)

**17863**
**Problem Solving** Talico, Inc., Jacksonville Beach, FL 1986.
*Descriptors:* *Employees; *Creative Thinking; *Problem Solving; *Brainstorming; *Decision Making Skills; Adults; Group Testing; Individual Testing; Teamwork; Organizations (Groups)
*Availability:* Talico, Inc., 2320 S. Third St., Ste. 5, Jacksonville Beach, FL 32250.

Designed for in-company use to produce measurably improved performance among employees at every organizational level, these assessment exercises, self-inventories, tests, and surveys are contained in a kit. Useful as a resource and a needs assessment instrument and includes instructions for self-scoring and interpreting the results. Problem Solving is an exercise to measure creative problem-solving and decision-making skills of employees at any level of an organization. Useful for developing the creative capability of employees, and, when administered to groups or teams, it can be used for team-building purposes. A flow chart is used for introducing participants to the creative problem-solving process. The objectives are to introduce employees to the principles and methods of solving problems creatively and to develop the group problem-solving and decision-making skills of employees. (TJS)

**17864**
**Customer Service Listening Skills Exercise.** Talico, Inc., Jacksonville Beach, FL 1991.
*Descriptors:* *Employees; *Listening Skills; *Sales Occupations; Adults; Sensitivity Training
*Availability:* Talico, Inc., 2320 S. Third St., Ste. 5, Jacksonville Beach, FL 32250.

Exercise is designed to help customer service and sales personnel achieve better results through a careful understanding and clarification of customer needs. Provides an experiential learning opportunity by which customer service employees can develop active listening skills. Consists of an audio cassette tape exercise focusing on 5 types of statements commonly made by customers to customer service and sales employees. The statements require that employees identify customer needs, defuse emotion, respond to a challenge, sell a product or service, and solve a problem. Useful for customer service and sales skill development, listening skills development, and sensitivity and awareness training. (TJS)

**17865**
**Customer Service Climate Survey.** Talico, Inc., Jacksonville Beach, FL 1991.
*Descriptors:* *Employees; *Sales Occupations; *Organizational Climate; Adults; Organizations (Groups); Rating Scales; Job Satisfaction; Employer Employee Relationship; Likert Scales
*Availability:* Talico, Inc., 2320 S. Third St., Ste. 5, Jacksonville Beach, FL 32250.

Questionnaire is designed to be administered to all members of an organization's customer service and sales staff to measure how effectively an organization's work climate supports and facilitates success among customer service and sales personnel. Contains 8 sets of 5 items, and is based on a Likert-type scale. Key climate dimensions measured in the item sets include job challenge and variety, job importance, task conflict, role overload, leadership consideration, organizational identification, management concern, and customer focus. Useful for morale and motivation studies, climate assessment, and customer service improvement studies. Can be self-administered and is suitable for all levels of customer service and sales employees. (TJS)

**17866**
**Quality Customer Service Test.** Talico, Inc., Jacksonville Beach, FL 1991.
*Descriptors:* *Objective Tests; *Thinking Skills; *Sales Occupations; Adults; Employees; Job Training; Listening; Responses; Rating Scales; Pretests Posttests; Feedback
*Identifiers:* QCS
*Availability:* Talico, Inc., 2320 S. Third St., Ste. 5, Jacksonville Beach, FL 32250.

Objective test was designed to be used primarily as a learning instrument to improve the skills of customer service and sales employees. Its purpose is to help managers measure cognitive skills with respect to performance oriented customer service and sales behaviors, practices and techniques. Assesses 6 specific skill dimensions that include customer focus, listening and responding, problem solving, selling, interacting, and closing. Each set is comprised of 4 interrelated items. Useful for customer service and sales training, career development, training needs analysis, providing feedback about current levels of customer service skills, reinforcing key customer service principles, and serving as a pretest or posttest that measures how well learned principles are understood. Suitable for all levels of sales and customer service employees. As a learning instrument, this tool was designed to be used only as a developmental aid. (TJS)

**17867**
**Customer Service Skills Assessment.** Talico, Inc., Jacksonville Beach, FL 1991.
*Descriptors:* *Employees; *Sales Occupations; *Salesmanship; Adults; Organizations (Groups); Behavior Rating Scales; Problem Solving; Leadership Styles; Peer Evaluation; Quality of Working Life
*Identifiers:* CSS
*Availability:* Talico, Inc., 2320 S. Third St., Ste. 5, Jacksonville Beach, FL 32250.

Designed to be used primarily as a learning instrument to help management collect data about the extent to which customer service and sales employees engage in behaviors and practices that research suggests are crucial to providing quality customer service. This is a multilevel instrument that obtains respondent's perceptions about the assessed person's behaviors and practices in crucial customer service skill dimensions (self, superior, peers, or subordinates). Four items each comprise the 6 skill dimension sets. Skill dimensions measured are customer focus, listening and responding, problem solving, selling, interacting, and closing. Useful for customer service and sales training, career development, and training needs analysis. Suitable for all levels of customer service and sales employees. A Likert-type response scale is used.(TJS)

**17874**
**Survey of Work Styles.** Jackson, Douglas N.; Gray, Anna Mavrogiannis 1990.
*Descriptors:* *Type A Behavior; *Employees; Adults; Work Environment; Questionnaires; Work Ethic; Behavior Patterns
*Identifiers:* SWS; TABP
*Availability:* Sigma Assessment Systems, Inc., 1110 Military St., P.O. Box 610984, Port Huron, MI 48061-0984.

Designed to yield a profile measure of the Type A behavior pattern (TABP). Useful in a number of research settings, such as studies of employee selection and placement, investigations of the personological bases for job satisfaction, employee turnover and absenteeism; research on work-related stress; studies of individual differences in the physiological concomitants of stress; and investigations of interpersonal behavior in the workplace, including group performance, conflict and cooperation, negotiation, and supervisory styles. Also useful in studies of the behavioral bases for coronary heart disease and other medical disorders; the investigation of health maintenance behaviors; psychological studies relating to retirement, quality of marital relations, maintenance of self-esteem, and responses to environmental stress. Lastly, this survey can be used in studies of job performance and satisfaction, including goal achievement, responses to task failure, and promotability. Subscales include: impatience; anger; time urgency; work involvement; job dissatisfaction; competitiveness. (TJS)

**17901**
**Entry-Level Police Service Tests, Specialized Examination: Radio Police Dispatcher, 47B.** International Personnel Management Association, Alexandria, VA
*Descriptors:* *Entry Workers; *Occupational Tests; *Personnel Selection; *Police; Abstract Reasoning; Adults; Computation; Filing; Map Skills; Pronunciation; Reading Comprehension; Tables (Data); Vocabulary
*Identifiers:* *Radio Dispatchers
*Availability:* International Personnel Management Association, 1617 Duke St., Alexandria, VA 22314.
*Notes:* Time, 105. Items, 105.

Tests developed for the International Personnel Management Association (IPMA) are used in a variety of jurisdictions and represent generalized public service requirements. The tests are used for the purpose of selecting and promoting police officers and firefighters and clerical workers in public service positions. Validity studies have shown validity of the tests for selection and promotion; however, tests cannot be assumed to be valid for all purposes. Test users are responsible for demonstrating validity for their particular jurisdictions. Reading lists are available for many promotional examinations offered through IPMA's test rental service. Study guides are available for some entry-level tests. Portions of this examination contain questions that require previous experience and/or exposure to materials on the reading list. Content covers reading comprehension, abstract reasoning, arithmetic calculations, filing skill, tabular interpretation, pronunciation, vocabulary, map reading, judgment, radio dispatching, radio operations, and radio logs.

**17902**
**Promotional Police Service Tests: Command Level, Police Administrator (Lieutenant), 564.** International Personnel Management Association, Alexandria, VA
*Descriptors:* *Occupational Tests; *Police; *Promotion (Occupational); Administrator Role; Adults; Investigations; Police Action; Police Community Relationship; Supervision
*Identifiers:* *Police Lieutenants
*Availability:* International Personnel Management Association, 1617 Duke St., Alexandria, VA 22314.
*Notes:* Time, 150. Items, 145.

Tests developed for the International Personnel Management Association (IPMA) are used in a variety of jurisdictions and represent generalized public service requirements. The tests are used for the purpose of selecting and promoting police officers and firefighters and clerical workers in public service positions. Validity studies have shown validity of the tests for selection and promotion; however, tests cannot be assumed to be valid for all purposes. Test users are responsible for demonstrating validity for their particular jurisdictions. Reading lists are available for many promotional examinations offered through IPMA's test rental service. Study guides are available for some entry-level tests. Useful with several job titles depending on local job requirements and job analysis. Covers patrol, investigative, legal, administrative, supervisory, and police role in the community. Command level tests may be suitable for jobs of lieutenant, captain, assistant chief, chief, etc.

**17903**
**Promotional Police Service Tests: Command Level, Police Administrator (Captain), 565.** International Personnel Management Association, Alexandria, VA
*Descriptors:* *Occupational Tests; *Police; *Promotion (Occupational); Administrator Role; Adults; Investigations; Police Action; Police Community Relationship; Supervision
*Identifiers:* *Police Captains
*Availability:* International Personnel Management Association, 1617 Duke St., Alexandria, VA 22314.
*Notes:* Time, 180. Items, 170.

Tests developed for the International Personnel Management Association (IPMA) are used in a variety of jurisdictions and represent generalized public service requirements. The tests are used for the purpose of selecting and promoting police officers and firefighters and clerical workers in public service positions. Validity studies have shown validity of the tests for selection and promotion; however, tests cannot be assumed to be valid for all purposes. Test users are responsible for demonstrating validity for their particular jurisdictions. Reading lists are available for many promotional examinations offered through IPMA's test rental service. Study guides are available for some entry-level tests. May be useful with other job titles, such as lieutenant, captain, assistant chief, and chief, depending on local job requirements and job analysis. Content covers patrol, investigation, legal, administration, supervisory, and police role in the community.

**17904**
**Promotional Police Service Tests: Command Level, Police Administrator (Assistant Chief), 566.** International Personnel Management Association, Alexandria, VA
*Descriptors:* *Occupational Tests; *Police; *Promotion (Occupational); Administrator Role; Adults; Investigations; Police Action; Police Community Relationship; Supervision
*Identifiers:* Police Chiefs; *Police Chiefs (Assistants)
*Availability:* International Personnel Management Association, 1617 Duke St., Alexandria, VA 22314.
*Notes:* Time, 180. Items, 170.

Tests developed for the International Personnel Management Association (IPMA) are used in a variety of jurisdictions and represent generalized public service requirements. The tests are used for the purpose of selecting and promoting police officers and firefighters and clerical workers in public service positions. Validity studies have shown validity of the tests for selection and promotion; however, tests cannot be assumed to be valid for all purposes. Test users are responsible for demonstrating validity for their particular jurisdictions. Reading lists are available for many promotional examinations offered through IPMA's test rental service. Study guides are available for some entry-level tests. May be useful with other job titles, such as lieutenant, captain, assistant chief, and chief, depending on local job requirements and job analysis. Content covers patrol, investigative, administrative, supervisory, and police role in the community.

**17906**
**Promotional Police Service Tests: Command Level, Police Administrator (Chief), 568.** International Personnel Management Association, Alexandria, VA
*Descriptors:* *Occupational Tests; *Police; *Promotion (Occupational); Administrator Role; Adults; Interprofessional Relationship; Public Relations; Supervision
*Identifiers:* *Police Lieutenants
*Availability:* International Personnel Management Association, 1617 Duke St., Alexandria, VA 22314.
*Notes:* Time, 180. Items, 180.

Tests developed for the International Personnel Management Association (IPMA) are used in a variety of jurisdictions and represent generalized public service requirements. The tests are used for the purpose of selecting and promoting police officers and firefighters and clerical workers in public service positions. Validity studies have shown validity of the tests for selection and promotion; however, tests cannot be assumed to be valid for all purposes. Test users are responsible for demonstrating validity for their particular jurisdictions. Reading lists are available for many promotional examinations offered through IPMA's test rental service. Study guides are available for some entry-level tests. May be useful with other job titles, such as lieutenant, captain, assistant chief, and chief, depending on local job requirements and job analysis. Content covers operational field activities, internal management, public relations, interaction with agencies in the criminal justice system, and interaction with local officials.

**17907**
**Entry-Level Fire Service Tests: Firefighter Examinations, 275.1 and 275.2.** International Personnel Management Association, Alexandria, VA
*Descriptors:* *Entry Workers; *Occupational Tests; *Personnel Selection; *Fire Fighters; Adults; Observation; Evaluative Thinking; Memory; Computation; Spatial Ability; Reading Comprehension; Vocabulary; Mechanical Skills
*Availability:* International Personnel Management Association, 1617 Duke St., Alexandria, VA 22314.

Tests developed for the International Personnel Management Association (IPMA) are used in a variety of jurisdictions and represent generalized public service requirements. The tests are used for the purpose of selecting and promoting police officers, firefighters, and clerical workers in public service positions. Validity studies have shown validity of the tests for selection and promotion; however, tests cannot be assumed to be valid for all purposes. Test users are responsible for demonstrating validity for their particular jurisdictions. Reading lists are available for many promotional examinations offered through IPMA's test rental service. Study guides are available for some entry-level tests. Using job analysis, data, items were constructed to assess abilities important to satisfactory performance in the following job dimensions: responding to alarms, firefighting and extinguishing operations, postfire operations, emergency operations, rescue operations, fire prevention, equipment maintenance, fire investigation, training and drills, firehouse duties, public relations, and routing apparatus. Content covers observational judgment, spatial scanning, association memory, mathematical computation, spatial orientation, reading comprehension, vocabulary, memory for ideas, and mechanical aptitude.

**17908**
**Entry-Level Correctional Officer Examination.** International Personnel Management Association, Alexandria, VA
*Descriptors:* *Correctional Institutions; *Entry Workers; *Institutional Personnel; *Occupational Tests; *Personnel Selection; Adults; Computation; Memory; Observation; Reading Comprehension; Thinking Skills
*Availability:* International Personnel Management Association, 1617 Duke St., Alexandria, VA 22314.

Tests developed for the International Personnel Management Association (IPMA) are used in a variety of jurisdictions and represent generalized public service requirements. The tests are used for the purpose of selecting and promoting police officers, firefighters, and clerical workers in public service positions. Validity studies have shown validity of the tests for selection and promotion; however, tests cannot be assumed to be valid for all purposes. Test users are responsible for demonstrating validity for their particular jurisdictions. Reading lists are available for many promotional examinations offered through IPMA's test rental service. Study guides are available for some entry-level tests. Using job analysis data, items were constructed to assess abilities important to satisfactory performance in the following job dimensions: inmate supervision, coordination of inmate activities, supervision of visiting rooms, use of force, conducting rounds, shift changes, bookings, inmate release, situational emergencies, medical treatments, inmate transport, report writing, mail/package delivery, general security measures, and general administrative duties. Content covers reading comprehension, counting, observation, memory, general reasoning, inductive reasoning, and deductive reasoning.

**17920**
**Meeting Effectiveness Questionnaire.** Pyle, Laura 1991.
*Descriptors:* *Meetings; *Self Evaluation (Groups); *Work Environment; Administrators; Adults; Employees; Program Effectiveness; Questionnaires
*Identifiers:* MEQ
*Availability:* Organizational Design and Development, Inc., 2002 Renaissance Blvd., Ste. 100, King of Prussia, PA 19406-2746.
*Notes:* Items, 22.

A tool to assess and improve meetings. Measures 5 areas that can make or break a meeting: purpose, appropriate attendees, effective time utilization, quality discussion, and desired outcomes. Designed primarily for action-oriented meetings (where interactive discussion takes place, ideas are exchanged, and decisions are made) rather than information meetings (where data are disseminated or presentations given to a passive audience). Included are 2 essential tools: the coordinator's guide which contains instructions for conducting the process and scoring the results; and the participant's guide which contains the materials that meeting attendees need to record their impressions of meeting effectiveness. Useful for line managers, human resource professionals, trainers/consultants, meeting facilitators, or meeting attendees.

**17950**
**Consultant Effectiveness Survey.** Knoff, Howard M.; And Others 1991.
*Descriptors:* *School Psychologists; *School Counselors; *Counselor Performance; *Counselor Characteristics; *Counseling Effectiveness; *Counselor Evaluation; *Consultants; Adults; Likert Scales; Interpersonal Competence; Elementary Secondary Education
*Availability:* *School Psychology Review,* v20 n1 p81-96, 1991.

This is an experimental survey administered to practitioners and experts in school psychological consulting to determine the characteristics and skills that are necessary for an effective school psychological counselor. The focus is on counselors whose clients are teachers and parents. On a 7-point Likert scale, respondents indicate how important each of 75 skills or characteristics is for an effective counselor. The scale is organized into 5 factors, with different factor solutions for experts and practitioners. The factors for the expert group are: consultation process skills, expert skills, personal characteristics, interpersonal skills, and professional respect. Factors are the same for the practitioner group, except for the fifth factor which is called consultant directiveness. Items within each factor differ between the expert and practitioner factor solutions. The instrument is still in the developmental stages, but goals for its use are to help consultants to use effective behaviors with parents and teachers; to identify areas for training in school psychology and consultation; to recommend prerequisite skills needed for school psychology practice; to provide inservice and continuing education training; and to provide the basis of evaluative or output measures of consultation success. Technical data on factor analyses are included. (KMC)

**17990**
**General Clerical Test.** Psychological Corp., San Antonio, TX 1988.
*Descriptors:* *Clerical Occupations; *Cognitive Ability; *Job Applicants; *Performance Tests; *Personnel Selection; Adults; Arithmetic; Grammar; Reading Comprehension; Spelling; Vocabulary
*Identifiers:* GCT
*Availability:* The Psychological Corp., 555 Academic Ct., San Antonio, TX 78204.
*Notes:* Time, 46.

A comprehensive ability test made up of 9 parts and employed primarily for the selection or classification of applicants. The parts in this instrument consist of checking, alphabetizing, arithmetic computation, error location, arithmetic reasoning, spelling, reading comprehension, vocabulary, and grammar. Basic human abilities are measured by the subtests and are related to performance in a wide range of jobs and learning environments. The clerical subtest score is based on speed and accuracy in perceptual tasks involving attention to detail. The numerical subtest score reflects performance on 3 kinds of numerical tasks which are essential in many positions. The verbal subtest score is based on the measurement of 4 language-related skills which are extremely important in many positions. Performance on all parts of the test is influenced to some extent by speed. The total score may be considered an estimate of general cognitive ability. Each part of the test is timed.

**17992**
**The Manager Profile Record.** Richardson, Bellows, Henry and Co., Inc., Washington, DC 1985.
*Descriptors:* *Biographical Inventories; *Managerial Occupations; *Self Evaluation (Individuals); Adults; Professional Occupations; Questionnaires
*Identifiers:* MPR
*Availability:* Richardson, Bellows, Henry and Co., Inc., 1140 Connecticut Ave., N.W., Ste. 610, Washington, DC 20036.
*Notes:* Items, 242.

A standardized autobiographical and judgment questionnaire system designed to be used along with other job-related information to identify candidates with a high potential for success in managerial and professional classifications. It can achieve a substantial improvement in the quality of managerial and professional workforce. Designed to ensure that uniform procedures are followed in administering the system so that all candidates are afforded an equal opportunity to demonstrate the competencies and characteristics it measures. Divided into 2 parts. Part 1 consists of questions about one's self, interests and experiences. Part 2 consists of statements and descriptions of situations in which the respondent is to make judgments or decisions about each of them. Essentially self-administering with no time limits for completion. For purposes of standardization and confidence in the reliability of results, the detailed directions that are included in the guide should be followed to the letter in all situations.

**17994**
**Employability Development Plan.** Ludden, LaVerne; And Others 1985.
*Descriptors:* *Career Planning; *Employment Potential; Adults; Labor Market; Needs Assessment; Records (Forms)
*Availability:* JIST Works, Inc., 720 N. Park Ave., Indianapolis, IN 46202-3431.

This instrument can be used to provide a method for completing an administrative task required by many employment and training programs and as a guide for identifying the participant's employment weaknesses and strengths and assisting them in becoming more competitive in the job market. Developed as a tool to assist program staff in recording and analyzing the needs of participants. Designed to record basic information and test/assessment data about a client; identify and analyze the barriers that impede employability; provide a standard set of considerations for each participant who is reviewed; provide criteria to assess the potential for enhancing a participant's employability within the structure of an employment and training program; summarize and record participant information on a single form; determine the priorities that must be addressed to move a participant toward employment; provide the structure to outline a plan that will develop competencies within the employment and training program; and provide a system for prescribing a training program and monitoring the participant's progress.

**18006**
**Employee Aptitude Survey: Test 1—Verbal Comprehension, Form A, Revised.** Grimsley, G.; And Others 1984.
*Descriptors:* *Aptitude Tests; *Employees; *Occupational Tests; *Personnel Selection; *Verbal Communication; Career Counseling; Cognitive Ability; Job Applicants; Perception Tests; Psychomotor Skills
*Identifiers:* EAS
*Availability:* Psychological Corp., 555 Academic Ct., San Antonio, TX 78204.
*Notes:* Time, 55 approx.

A battery of employment tests designed to meet the practical requirements of a personnel office. Consists of 10 cognitive, perceptual, and psychomotor ability tests. Nine of the 10 tests have 5-minute time limits. The remaining test requires 2 to 10 minutes of testing time. Is a tool for personnel selection and a useful diagnostic tool for vocational guidance and career counseling. For situations in which it is desirable to retest an individual on an alternate form, special retest norms are provided for interpreting retest scores. Test 1 - Verbal Comprehension measures the ability to use words in oral and written communication and in planning.

**18012**
**Tacit Knowledge Inventory for Managers.** Wagner, Richard K.; Sternberg, Robert J. 1991.
*Descriptors:* *Administrators; *Experiential Learning; *Learning Experience; *Managerial Occupations; *Prior Learning; Knowledge Level; Leadership Styles; Personnel Selection; Promotion (Occupational); Rating Scales
*Identifiers:* TKIM
*Availability:* The Psychological Corp., 555 Academic Ct., San Antonio, TX 78204.
*Notes:* Items, 91.

Designed to identify individuals whose "street smarts," "learning the ropes ability," "common sense," and "practical know-how rarely expressed openly or taught directly," indicate the potential for excellent performance in managerial and executive careers. Tacit knowledge can be categorized on the basis of its content, context, and orientation. This inventory can be used to guide organizations in the selection of entry-level managers, promotion of lower- and middle-level managers to higher ranks, and as a diagnostic tool for training and development. It samples managerial tacit knowledge by presenting examinees with descriptions of managerial work-related scenarios and asking them to judge the quality of a variety of response alternatives. Performance is evaluated by comparing an individual's responses to those of an expert group of managers.

**18016**
**Typing Test for Business, Revised.** Doppelt, Jerome E.; And Others 1991.
*Descriptors:* *Work Sample Tests; *Job Applicants; *Typewriting; *Occupational Tests; Adults; Norm Referenced Tests; Clerical Workers
*Identifiers:* TT
*Availability:* Psychological Corp., 555 Academic Ct., San Antonio, TX 78204.

The typing test is designed to assess applicants' skills in 5 kinds of typing required for business. It consists of 5 forms that independently assess applicants' skills in typing straight copy, letters, revised manuscripts, numbers, and tables. Each skill area has 2 equivalent forms, AR and BR, allowing examinees to be retested after completion of training. There are also 2 unscored practice copies for warm-up in each testing situation. As each form is scored separately, applicants may be administered only the forms for the areas in which proficiency is required. The test has been revised to eliminate sex stereotypic language found in the original typing test (3649). The test contains norms for applicants applying for jobs in industrial and service organizations, hospital, utility company, and university settings. Other technical data are also included. (KMC)

**18026**
**Measures of Ingratiatory Behaviors in Organizational Settings.** Kumar, Kamalesh; Beyerlein, Michael 1991.
*Descriptors:* *Employer Employee Relationship; *Social Behavior; Adults; Self Evaluation (Individuals); Behavior Rating Scales; Likert Scales; Organizational Climate
*Identifiers:* MIBOS; Ingratiation Tactics; Impression Management
*Availability:* *Journal of Applied Psychology,* v76 n5 p619-27, Oct 1991.

This self-report instrument is designed to assess employees' uses of ingratiatory tactics in their relationships with supervisors. Ingratiatory tactics are defined as assertive behaviors organizational members may use to enhance their images and to gain commendation or praise from their supervisors. The instrument measures 4 tactics: other enhancement, opinion conformity, self-presentation, and favor rendering. On a 5-point Likert-type scale, employees indicate how often they engage in these behaviors. The instrument may be used by researchers to study ingratiatory behaviors in organizations and relate these behaviors to major social issues within the organizations. Information on the instrument's reliability and validity is included. (KMC)

**18035**
**Coaching Process Questionnaire.** McBer and Co., Boston, MA 1992.
*Descriptors:* *Administrators; *Leadership Qualities; *Management by Objectives; *Rating Scales; *Supervisory Methods; Adults; Questionnaires; Work Environment
*Identifiers:* Coaching; CPQ
*Availability:* McBer and Co., 137 Newbury St., Boston, MA 02116.
*Notes:* Items, 40.

Focuses on the coaching style of management and provides managers with an assessment of their coaching skills. These skills are based on 4 key elements: diagnostic skills, coaching techniques, coaching qualities, and coaching model. The goal is to help employees establish objectives that will enable them to work more effectively with increased autonomy and satisfaction. The profile and interpretive notes equip the participant with scoring and interpretation guides along with helpful suggestions for conducting coaching sessions. The employee version provides feedback from employees on how they experience their manager's coaching efforts. Useful in managerial training, career development, succession planning, monitoring performance, day-to-day problem solving, and performance appraisals.

**18036**
**Influence Strategies Exercise.** McBer and Co., Boston, MA 1991.
*Descriptors:* *Influences; *Managerial Occupations; *Supervisory Methods; Administration; Adults; Perception; Questionnaires; Rating Scales; Self Evaluation (Individuals); Work Environment
*Identifiers:* ISE
*Availability:* McBer and Co., 137 Newbury St., Boston, MA 02116.
*Notes:* Time, 20 approx. Items, 54.

A tool for understanding how people influence others. It is self-scoring and provides feedback on 9 commonly used strategies in management. Participants receive feedback from their own self-perceptions and from how others perceive them. Included are interpretive notes that provide thorough explanations of each influencing strategy, with helpful hints on how to increase each of them. Useful for participants in understanding how effective management requires a variety of influence strategies, learning about those styles that are frequently used by managers today, receiving feedback on how they influence others, receiving feedback on how others see them using influence, and learning helpful ways in which they can enhance their influence strategies. Suggested applications for supervisory and managerial development, leadership development, negotiation skills, and coaching and counseling.

**18037**
**Supervisory Behavior Description Questionnaire.** Fleishman, Edwin A. 1989.
*Descriptors:* *Administrators; *Behavior Patterns; *Employer Employee Relationship; *Leadership Styles; *Managerial Occupations; *Supervisors; Adults; Behavior Rating Scales; Questionnaires; Supervisory Methods
*Identifiers:* SBD
*Availability:* London House, SRA Product Group, 9701 W. Higgins Rd., Rosemont, IL 60018.
*Notes:* See Thurstone Test of Mental Alertness (18035); SRA Verbal (18036); CRT Skills Test (18038); and Common Business Oriented Language Test (18039) for related instruments. Time, 20 approx. Items, 48.

Designed to measure the behavior patterns of supervisory and management personnel on 2 major dimensions of leadership: consideration and structure. Provides a measure of the leadership patterns exhibited by supervisors, managers, and administrators in their on-the-job performance. This instrument can also be used by colleagues, supervisors, or as a self-description. Useful as an instructional aid in management training programs and in training evaluation.

**18038**
**CRT Skills Test.** Science Research Associates, Inc., Rosemont, IL 1990.
*Descriptors:* *Computer Assisted Testing; *Data Processing; *Microcomputers; *Occupational Tests; *Personnel Selection; Adults
*Identifiers:* CRT
*Availability:* London House, SRA Product Group, 9701 W. Higgins Rd., Rosemont, IL 60018.
*Notes:* See Thurstone Test of Mental Alertness (18035); SRA Verbal (18036); Supervisory Behavior Description Questionnaire (18037); and Common Business Oriented Language Test (18039) for related instruments. Time, 25.

Developed to assist managers in identifying and selecting persons with the skills required to perform successfully on jobs that require operating CRT equipment. This is a hands-on test which can be administered on an IBM or compatible PC. Presented in 3 separately timed sections which can be administered independently or in combination. Part 1 is a 10-minute timed test measuring speed and accuracy in entering both alpha and numeric data. Part 2 is a 5-minute timed test that assesses speed and accuracy in entering numeric data only. Part 3 is a 10-minute timed test that measures the ability to retrieve customer files and to identify the correct answers to customers' questions.

**18039**
**Common Business Oriented Language Test.** Science Research Associates, Inc., Rosemont, IL 1989.
*Descriptors:* *Computer Assisted Testing; *Knowledge Level; *Occupational Tests; *Personnel Selection; *Programming Languages; *Screening Tests; Adults; Computers
*Identifiers:* *COBOL Programming Language
*Availability:* London House, SRA Product Group, 9701 W. Higgins Rd., Rosemont, IL 60018.
*Notes:* See Thurstone Test of Mental Alertness (81035); SRA Verbal (18036); Supervisory Behavior Description Questionnaire (18037); and CRT Skills Test (1838) for related instruments. Time, 45. Items, 44.

A technical knowledge exam designed to measure the extent to which individuals are knowledgeable about Common Business Oriented Language (COBOL). Used as a preemployment screening device for COBOL programmers. Can also be used as a placement tool or to assess training needs by organizations. In some situations, applicants may request retesting. The test was developed according to equal employment opportunity and affirmative action guidelines. This is not a timed test.

**18081**
**The Career Exploration Inventory.** Liptak, John J. 1992.
*Descriptors:* *Career Exploration; *Interest Inventories; Adults; Career Planning; Economically Disadvantaged; Older Adults; Secondary School Students; Youth
*Identifiers:* CEI
*Availability:* JIST Works, Inc., 720 N. Park Ave., Indianapolis, IN 46202-3431.
*Notes:* Items, 120.

A self-scoring, self-interpreting interest instrument designed to help explore and plan 3 major areas of one's life: work, leisure activities, and education or learning. Responses are scored in relation to 15 major clusters of interest, which will help identify which career, leisure, and educational goals best relate to interests. It provides a developmental approach that measures interests from the past, present, and those anticipated in the future. This instrument will also help locate additional sources of information on occupations, leisure activities and related educational programs that one may want to consider more carefully. Does not measure ability or motivation. Useful for a wide range of individual and group counseling situations, such as with employed and unemployed adults, students, youth, and special groups—economically disadvantaged, corrections, substance abusing, and other populations. Easy to read and simple to interpret with minimal counselor intervention. Can be used by career development researchers, career counselors, job search specialists, and leisure counselors.

**18082**
**The Team Leadership Practices Inventory: Measuring Leadership of Teams.** Kouzes, James M.; Posner, Barry Z. 1992.
*Descriptors:* *Behavior Rating Scales; *Leaders; *Leadership; *Teamwork; Adults; Group Behavior; Group Dynamics; Self Evaluation (Individuals)
*Identifiers:* TEAM LPI
*Availability:* Pfeiffer and Co., 8517 Production Ave., San Diego, CA 92121-2280.
*Notes:* Items, 30.

Focuses on the key behaviors and actions of high-performing teams and self-directed work groups. Useful as a guide in beginning team-development activities and as feedback in ongoing improvement efforts. Used by a manager or leader with a work team to explore and discuss how well the fundamental leadership functions are being fulfilled within the team. One of the formal leader's fundamental tasks is to liberate the leader in each team member and to turn each member into a leader. Team members can identify leadership practices and behaviors that need development and support. Five key leadership practices are offered to assist in development and support where needed. These practices are challenging the process, inspiring a shared vision, enabling others to act, modeling the way, and encouraging the heart. Designed to be self-scored by the team members. The scoring system allows maximum flexibility and offers team members the chance to develop ownership of the inventory data, as well as a firsthand sense of the range of differences and similarities in their common experiences.

**18090**
**IDEAS: Interest Determination, Exploration and Assessment System.** Johansson, Charles B. 1990.
*Descriptors:* *Career Exploration; *Interest Inventories; *Secondary School Students; *Vocational Interests; Adolescents; Adults; Secondary Education
*Availability:* National Computer Systems, Professional Assessment Services, P.O. Box 1416, Minneapolis, MN 55440.
*Notes:* See Self-Directed Search (14041) for related instrument. Time, 40 approx. Items, 128.

An interest inventory to help provide information about people's current career preferences. Some of the activities measured include science, writing, sales, public speaking, nature/outdoors, mechanical/fixing, business, medical, and child care. The 16 scoring scales in this instrument are designed only to differentiate among these broader categories. Each homogeneous scale is composed of 8 items that are internally consistent, with each having high item intercorrelations within each scale. The goals and strategies for this instrument are to construct a short, easy-to-administer measure; develop a modest number of scales that are valid, reliable, easy-to-interpret, and comprehensive in coverage; develop an inventory that is useful for either gender and is not racially biased; make the inventory as simple and easy to understand as possible while still retaining a valid psychometric instrument; and provide a linkage with resource materials that are organized or codified according to Holland's 6-sided R-I-A-S-E-C model (realistic, investigative, artistic, social, enterprising, and conventional). Contains a 5-choice response option.

**18096**
**Staff Orientation in Early Childhood Programs.** O'Sullivan, Barbara 1987.
*Descriptors:* *Early Childhood Education; *Resource Materials; *Skill Development; *Staff Orientation; *Teachers; *Training Methods; Planning
*Availability:* Kaplan School Supply Corp., 1310 Lewisville-Clemmons Rd., P.O. Box 609, Lewisville, NC 27023-0609.

Manual is an overview of the expectations of the position as a teacher of young children. It provides an opportunity to work with the supervisor to identify areas where additional training is needed. The purpose of this manual is twofold: to provide ideas and skill building tools, and to be a resource tool. It can be used in new staff orientation or as a refresher for personnel already on staff. Opportunities are provided to set goals and to design a training plan for further professional development. Contents of the manual are based on the criteria of the accreditation system of the National Academy of Early Childhood Programs which is a division of the National Association for the Education of Young Children (NAEYC).

**18099**
**Employee Empowerment Survey.** Talico, Inc., Jacksonville Beach, FL 1991.
*Descriptors:* *Employees; *Work Environment; *Leadership Training; *Organizational Climate; *Administrator Effectiveness; Adults; Rating Scales; Leadership Styles; Supervisors; Power Structure; Group Behavior; Self Evaluation (Groups); Teamwork
*Identifiers:* *Empowerment
*Availability:* Talico, Inc., 2320 S. Third St., Ste. 5, Jacksonville Beach, FL 32250.

Used to help managers, supervisors, training professionals, and other human resource professionals determine the extent to which their organization is enhancing the value of employee contribution, by creating an empowered work climate. This tool can be used to determine whether an empowered work climate exists within individual work groups or within the entire organization. The tool is made up of 8 sets of 6 items each, which focus on the following empowerment dimensions: leadership, team focus, shared responsibility, open communications system, the job itself, total quality management focus, work conditions, and the work environment.(TJS)

**18106**
**Legendary Service Leader Assessment.** Ryan, Sean; And Others 1991.
*Descriptors:* *Administrators; *Leadership Styles; *Supervisory Methods; Adults; Employees; Rating Scales; Work Environment
*Identifiers:* LSLA
*Availability:* Blanchard Training and Development, 125 State Pl., Escondido, CA 92025.
*Notes:* Items, 65.

To provide feedback needed to continuously improve leadership and results. Useful to managers to assist them in making significant changes in the way they lead their people. Service skills of managers can be evaluated by their subordinates. Instrument consists of a self-assessment to be filled out by the manager, and an other-assessment to be filled out by the people who report to the manager. Also included is a custom profile of results from the self- and other-assessments and a feedback guide that directs managers to develop action plans based on their feedback. Designed to be repeated at regular intervals (every 6 to 12 months is recommended).

**18117**
**Commercial Refrigeration Examination.** Air-Conditioning and Refrigeration Institute, Arlington, VA 1992.
*Descriptors:* *Air Conditioning Equipment; *Basic Skills; *Certification; *Entry Workers; *Knowledge Level; *Occupational Tests; *Refrigeration Mechanics; *Technical Occupations; Multiple Choice Tests; Questionnaires; Skilled Occupations
*Identifiers:* ARI; GAMA; PES
*Availability:* Air-Conditioning and Refrigeration Institute, 1501 Wilson Blvd., 6th Floor, Arlington, VA 22209.
*Notes:* See Light Commercial Air-Conditioning and Heating Examination (18119) and Residential Air-Conditioning and Heating Examination (18120) for related instruments. Items, 100.

Designed to test for knowledge of the fundamentals and basic skills necessary for entry-level technicians. Candidates who graduate from the Air-Conditioning and Refrigeration Institute (ARI) program, will design, install, service, and repair the heating, air-conditioning, and refrigeration equipment that ARI and Gas Appliance Manufacturers Association (GAMA) manufacturers produce. Examinations are prepared and administered in conjunction with the Professional Examination Service (PES). PES is a not-for-profit testing organization that has been designing and administering national testing programs since 1941. There are 3 examinations included in this series: Residential Air-Conditioning and Heating, Light Commercial Air- Conditioning and Heating, and Commercial Refrigeration. Each exam consists of 100 multiple-choice questions and is scored on the basis of correct answers only. The Commercial Refrigeration Examination content area covers system design and component application, installation and start-up, preventive maintenance, and service and repair.

**18119**
**Light Commercial Air-Conditioning and Heating Examination.** Air-Conditioning and Refrigeration Institute, Arlington, VA 1992.
*Descriptors:* *Air Conditioning Equipment; *Basic Skills; *Certification; *Entry Workers; *Knowledge Level; *Occupational Tests; *Refrigeration Mechanics; *Technical Occupations; Adults; Multiple Choice Tests; Questionnaires; Skilled Occupations
*Identifiers:* ARI; GAMA
*Availability:* Air-Conditioning and Refrigeration Institute, 1501 Wilson Blvd., 6th Floor, Arlington, VA 22209.
*Notes:* See Residential Air-Conditioning and Heating (18120) and Commercial Refrigeration (18117) for related instruments. Items, 100.

Designed to test for knowledge of the fundamentals and basic skills necessary for entry-level technicians. Candidates who graduate from the Air-Conditioning and Refrigeration Institute (ARI) program, will design, install, service, and repair the heating, air-conditioning, and refrigeration equipment that ARI and Gas Appliance Manufacturers Association (GAMA) manufacturers produce. Examinations are prepared and administered in conjunction with the Professional Examination Service (PES). PES is a not-for-profit testing organization that has been designing and administering national testing programs since 1941. There are 3 examinations included in this series: Residential Air-Conditioning and Heating, Light Commercial Air-Conditioning and Heating, and Commercial Refrigeration. Each exam consists of 100 multiple-choice questions and is scored on the basis of correct answers only. The Light Commercial Air Conditioning and Heating Examination content area covers start-up and preventive maintenance, service and repair, and installation.

**18120**
**Residential Air-Conditioning and Heating Examination.** Air-Conditioning and Refrigeration Institute, Arlington, VA 1992.
*Descriptors:* *Air Conditioning Equipment; *Basic Skills; *Certification; *Entry Workers; *Knowledge Level; *Occupational Tests; *Refrigeration Mechanics; *Technical Occupations; Adults; Multiple Choice Tests; Questionnaires; Skilled Occupations
*Identifiers:* ARI; GAMA; PES
*Availability:* Air-Conditioning and Refrigeration Institute, 1501 Wilson Blvd., 6th Floor, Arlington, VA 22209.
*Notes:* See Light Commercial Air-Conditioning and Heating Examination (18119) and Commercial Refrigeration (18117) for related instruments. Items, 100.

Designed to test for knowledge of the fundamentals and basic skills necessary for entry-level technicians. Candidates who graduate from the Air-Conditioning and Refrigeration Institute (ARI) program, will design, install, service, and repair the heating, air conditioning, and refrigeration equipment that ARI and Gas Appliance Manufacturers Association (GAMA) manufacturers produce. Examinations are prepared and administered in conjunction with the Professional Examination Service (PES). PES is a not-for-profit testing organization that has been designing and administering national testing programs since 1941. There are 3 examinations included in this series: Residential Air-Conditioning and Heating, Light Commercial Air-Conditioning and Heating, and Commercial Refrigeration. Each exam consists of 100 multiple-choice questions and is scored on the basis of correct answers only. The Residential Air-Conditioning and Heating Examination content area covers start-up and preventive maintenance, service and repair, and installation.

**18125**
**Organizational Climate Exercise II.** McBer and Co., Boston, MA 1991.
*Descriptors:* *Job Satisfaction; *Organizational Climate; *Quality of Working Life; Adults; Employees; Rating Scales; Work Environment
*Identifiers:* OCE II

*Availability:* McBer and Co., 137 Newbury St., Boston, MA 02116.

A self-scoring, statistical instrument designed to evaluate the internal environment of an organization. Measures 6 dimensions which include flexibility, responsibility, standards, rewards, clarity, and team commitment. It includes a 2-part exercise that asks participants to describe the actual climate and the ideal climate. The identification of any significant gaps between the actual and the ideal climate enables the company to prioritize and facilitate organizational change where needed. It focuses on assessing those climate elements critical to performance and productivity, which include an organization's structure, policies, procedures, norms, and management practices. The profile and interpretive notes that accompany the exercise provide the facilitator with directions for scoring, profiling, and interpretating, along with suggestions on how to conduct a feedback session.

**18129**
**Career Assessment Battery.** Piney Mountain Press, Inc., Cleveland, GA 1991.
*Descriptors:* *Career Counseling; *Career Planning; *High School Students; *Interest Inventories; *School Guidance; *Vocational Interests; Career Choice; High Schools; Rating Scales; School Counselors; Videotape Recordings
*Identifiers:* CAB
*Availability:* Piney Mountain Press, Inc., P.O. Box 333, Cleveland, GA 30528.
*Notes:* Items, 49.

An instrument designed to assess the career interests, abilities, and needs of high school students to assist counselors in providing career guidance. Instrument is administered via a videotape. Students watch the video which explains how to complete the assessment. Responses to questions or statements are made on a student worksheet. Test administrators collect the worksheets and, using software provided for the instrument, enter the data into a computer for analysis. The computer generates a list of career clusters and specific occupations for individual students. Software also may group students of like interests together so that they may be counseled as a group. The instrument contains 12 dimensions for career assessment, uses a standardized occupational classification system, covers approximately 12,000 occupational titles, and is compatible with state and national career information data, such as the *Dictionary of Occupational Titles.* Instrument gives attention to minority and gender issues and may be useful in equity programs. Includes sample output from student data. No technical information included.

**18130**
**Vocational Inventory Video.** Piney Mountain Press, Inc., Cleveland, GA 1991.
*Descriptors:* *Career Counseling; *High School Students; *Interest Inventories; *School Guidance; *Vocational Education; *Vocational Interests; Career Choice; Disabilities; High Schools; Job Training; Rating Scales; School Counselors; Videotape Recordings
*Identifiers:* VIV
*Availability:* Piney Mountain Press, Inc., P.O. Box 333, Cleveland, GA 30528.
*Notes:* Time, 30 approx. Items, 15.

A video administered interest inventory designed to assess high school students' interests in school-based training programs. Video overviews 15 training programs offered in high schools and familiarizes students with the vocational criteria to make decisions about entering the programs, the training requirements, and examples of jobs for which the students may be qualified at the end of each of the programs. After viewing the video for each program, students indicate whether or not they would be interested in the program, or whether they would like to learn more about it. Students showing high levels of interest in particular programs may be assessed further to determine potential for success. Students interested in more information about programs may be given the opportunity to explore them through vocational counseling, work sampling, or vocational shadowing. Students not interested in any programs may be administered a more comprehensive vocational evaluation. Instruments may be administered to groups or individually. It may be administered to handicapped and disadvantaged students and may be adapted to students who are blind or deaf.

**18134**
**Employee Aptitude Survey: Test 2—Numerical Ability, Form A.** Grimsley, G.; And Others 1980.
*Descriptors:* *Aptitude Tests; *Arithmetic; *Employees; *Mathematics Tests; *Occupational Tests; *Personnel Selection; Career Counseling; Cognitive Ability; Job Applicants; Perception Tests; Psychomotor Skills
*Identifiers:* EAS
*Availability:* Psychological Corp., 555 Academic Ct., San Antonio, TX 78204.
*Notes:* Time, 55 approx.

A battery of employment tests designed to meet the practical requirements of a personnel office. Consists of 10 cognitive, perceptual, and psychomotor ability tests. Nine of the 10 tests have 5-minute time limits. The remaining test requires 2 to 10 minutes of testing time. Is a tool for personnel selection and a useful diagnostic tool for vocational guidance and career counseling. For situations in which it is desirable to retest an individual on an alternate form, special retest norms are provided for interpreting retest scores. Test 2 - Numerical Ability measures skill in the 4 fundamental operations of addition, subtraction, multiplication, and division. Integers, decimal fractions, and common fractions were included in separate tests that are separately timed.

**18135**
**Parker Team Player Survey: Styles of Another Person.** Parker, Glenn M. 1991.
*Descriptors:* *Employees; *Teamwork; Adults; Group Behavior; Rating Scales; Surveys; Work Environment
*Availability:* XICOM, Inc., Sterling Forest, Woods Rd., Tuxedo, NY 10987.
*Notes:* See Parker Team Player Survey (18146) for related instrument. Items, 18.

Assists participants in identifying the styles of other members of their team. Results lead to an assessment of current strengths and provide a basis for a plan for increasing their effectiveness as team players. Based on the concepts of the Parker Team Player Survey (PTPS), this exercise allows individuals to extend their profiles to incorporate colleagues' feedback based on observations of the individual as a team player. Team members learn about themselves, and gain insight into the styles of fellow team members.

**18136**
**Employee Aptitude Survey: Test 4—Visual Speed and Accuracy, Form A.** Grimsley, G.; And Others 1980.
*Descriptors:* *Aptitude Tests; *Employees; *Nonverbal Tests; *Occupational Tests; *Personnel Selection; *Timed Tests; *Visual Measures; Career Counseling; Cognitive Ability; Job Applicants; Perception Tests; Psychomotor Skills
*Identifiers:* EAS
*Availability:* Psychological Corp., 555 Academic Ct., San Antonio, TX 78204.
*Notes:* Time, 55 approx.

A battery of employment tests designed to meet the practical requirements of a personnel office. Consists of 10 cognitive, perceptual, and psychomotor ability tests. Nine of the 10 tests have 5-minute time limits. The remaining test requires 2 to 10 minutes of testing time. Is a tool for personnel selection and a useful diagnostic tool for vocational guidance and career counseling. For situations in which it is desirable to retest an individual on an alternate form, special retest norms are provided for interpreting retest scores. Test 4 - Visual Speed and Accuracy has items that were selected using a table of random numbers and hence require no item analysis.

**18137**
**Employee Aptitude Survey: Test 5—Space Visualization, Form A, Revised.** Grimsley, G.; And Others 1985.
*Descriptors:* *Aptitude Tests; *Employees; *Occupational Tests; *Personnel Selection; *Spatial Ability; *Visualization; Career Counseling; Cognitive Ability; Job Applicants; Perception Tests; Psychomotor Skills
*Identifiers:* EAS
*Availability:* Psychological Corp., 555 Academic Ct., San Antonio, TX 78204.
*Notes:* Time, 55 approx.

A battery of employment tests designed to meet the practical requirements of a personnel office. Consists of 10 cognitive, perceptual, and psychomotor ability tests. Nine of the 10 tests have 5-minute time limits. The remaining test requires 2 to 10 minutes of testing time. Is a tool for personnel selection and a useful diagnostic tool for vocational guidance and career counseling. For situations in which it is desirable to retest an individual on an alternate form, special retest norms are provided for interpreting retest scores. Test 5 - Space Visualization uses the block format which offers factorial purity and known predictive validity, for a wide variety of mechanical tasks, and item analysis, arranging the problems in increasing order of difficulty.

**18138**
**Employee Aptitude Survey: Test 6—Numerical Reasoning, Form A, Revised.** Grimsley, G.; And Others 1985.
*Descriptors:* *Abstract Reasoning; *Aptitude Tests; *Employees; *Numbers; *Occupational Tests; *Personnel Selection; Arithmetic; Career Counseling; Cognitive Ability; Job Applicants; Perception Tests; Psychomotor Skills
*Identifiers:* EAS
*Availability:* Psychological Coιp., 555 Academic Ct., San Antonio, TX 78204.

A battery of employment tests designed to meet the practical requirements of a personnel office. Consists of 10 cognitive, perceptual, and psychomotor ability tests. Nine of the 10 tests have 5-minute time limits. The remaining test requires 2 to 10 minutes of testing time. Is a tool for personnel selection and a useful diagnostic tool for vocational guidance and career counseling. For situations in which it is desirable to retest an individual on an alternate form, special retest norms are provided for interpreting retest scores. Test 6 - Numerical Reasoning is based on number series. It uses a multiple-choice format.

**18139**
**Employee Aptitude Survey: Test 7—Verbal Reasoning, Form A, Revised.** Grimsley, G.; And Others 1985.
*Descriptors:* *Abstract Reasoning; *Aptitude Tests; *Employees; *Occupational Tests; *Personnel Selection; *Thinking Skills; *Verbal Tests; Career Counseling; Cognitive Ability; Job Applicants; Perception Tests; Psychomotor Skills
*Identifiers:* EAS
*Availability:* Psychological Corp., 555 Academic Ct., San Antonio, TX 78204.
*Notes:* Time, 55 approx.

A battery of employment tests designed to meet the practical requirements of a personnel office. Consists of 10 cognitive, perceptual, and psychomotor ability tests. Nine of the 10 tests have 5-minute time limits. The remaining test requires 2 to 10 minutes of testing time. Is a tool for personnel selection and a useful diagnostic tool for vocational guidance and career counseling. For situations in which it is desirable to retest an individual on an alternate form, special retest norms are provided for interpreting retest scores. Test 7 - Verbal Reasoning is based on the ability to recognize that available facts do not always support a conclusion, which is an element in arriving at business and other practical decisions, and that formal logic is not the only tool in everyday thinking.

**18140**
**Employee Aptitude Survey: Test 8—Word Fluency.** Grimsley, G.; And Others 1981.

*Descriptors:* *Aptitude Tests; *Employees; *Letters (Alphabet); *Occupational Tests; *Personnel Selection; *Word Recognition; Career Counseling; Cognitive Ability; Job Applicants; Perception Tests; Psychomotor Skills
*Identifiers:* EAS
*Availability:* Psychological Corp., 555 Academic Ct., San Antonio, TX 78204.
*Notes:* Time, 55 approx.

A battery of employment tests designed to meet the practical requirements of a personnel office. Consists of 10 cognitive, perceptual, and psychomotor ability tests. Nine of the 10 tests have 5-minute time limits. The remaining test requires 2 to 10 minutes of testing time. Is a tool for personnel selection and a useful diagnostic tool for vocational guidance and career counseling. For situations in which it is desirable to retest an individual on an alternate form, special retest norms are provided for interpreting retest scores. Test 8 - Word Fluency is a test that is standardized for 3 letters: C, M, and S. These multiple forms demonstrate that "the word gets around", and some highly motivated applicants will practice in advance. The use of the 3 standardized letters in random fashion cuts down on this effect.

**18141**
**Employee Aptitude Survey: Test 9—Manual Speed and Accuracy.** Psychological Corp., San Antonio, TX 1984.
*Descriptors:* *Aptitude Tests; *Assembly (Manufacturing); *Employees; *Mechanical Skills; *Occupational Tests; *Personnel Selection; *Timed Tests; Career Counseling; Cognitive Ability; Job Applicants; Perception Tests; Psychomotor Skills
*Identifiers:* EAS
*Availability:* Psychological Corp., 555 Academic Ct., San Antonio, TX 78204.
*Notes:* Time, 55 approx.

A battery of employment tests designed to meet the practical requirements of a personnel office. Consists of 10 cognitive, perceptual, and psychomotor ability tests. Nine of the 10 tests have 5-minute time limits. The remaining test requires 2 to 10 minutes of testing time. Is a tool for personnel selection and a useful diagnostic tool for vocational guidance and career counseling. For situations in which it is desirable to retest an individual on an alternate form, special retest norms are provided for interpreting retest scores. Test 9 - Manual Speed and Accuracy is useful in selecting applicants for precision assembly jobs. It also measures the ability to withstand monotony.

**18142**
**Employee Aptitude Survey: Test 10—Symbolic Reasoning, Form A.** Ruch, F.L.; Ford, J.S. 1985.
*Descriptors:* *Aptitude Tests; *Employees; *Mathematical Logic; *Occupational Tests; *Personnel Selection; *Symbols (Mathematics); *Thinking Skills; Career Counseling; Cognitive Ability; Job Applicants; Perception Tests; Psychomotor Skills
*Identifiers:* EAS
*Availability:* Psychological Corp., 555 Academic Ct., San Antonio, TX 78204.
*Notes:* Time, 55 approx.

A battery of employment tests designed to meet the practical requirements of a personnel office. Consists of 10 cognitive, perceptual, and psychomotor ability tests. Nine of the 10 tests have 5-minute time limits. The remaining test requires 2 to 10 minutes of testing time. Is a tool for personnel selection and a useful diagnostic tool for vocational guidance and career counseling. For situations in which it is desirable to retest an individual on an alternate form, special retest norms are provided for interpreting retest scores. Test 10 - Symbolic Reasoning measures ability to evaluate symbolic relations. Arranged in order of difficulty. It offers an "uncertain" response category.

**18146**
**Parker Team Player Survey.** Parker, Glenn M. 1991.
*Descriptors:* *Employees; *Teamwork; Adults; Surveys; Rating Scales; Work Environment; Group Behavior
*Identifiers:* Style
*Availability:* XICOM, Inc., Sterling Forest, Woods Rd., Tuxedo, NY 10987.
*Notes:* See Parker Team Player: Styles of Another Player (18135) for related instrument.

A short, self-scoring survey that assists individuals' in identifying their primary team player styles. It provides the user with immediate feedback regarding their primary and less active styles. Four major styles are identified. They are: contributor, collaborator, communicator, and challenger. The feedback materials describe each style in detail, including the strengths and weaknesses associated with each. Also offers suggestions on how to appropriately use one's style and how to develop a plan to achieve overall team effectiveness. (TJS)

**18168**
**Entry-Level Police Service Tests: Police Officer Examination, A-3.** International Personnel Management Association, Alexandria, VA
*Descriptors:* *Entry Workers; *Occupational Tests; *Personnel Selection; *Police; *Public Service Occupations; Evaluative Thinking; Logical Thinking; Memory; Police Action; Promotion (Occupational); Tests; Verbal Ability
*Identifiers:* POE
*Availability:* International Personnel Management Association, 1617 Duke St., Alexandria, VA 22314.
*Notes:* See Entry-Level Police Service Tests: Police Officer Examination, 175.1 and 175.2 (15678) and 375.1 and 375.2 (18169), and Entry-Level Police Officer Background Data Questionnaire (18170) for related instruments. Time, 130. Items, 100.

Tests were developed for the International Personnel Management Association (IPMA) and are used in a variety of jurisdictions and represent generalized public service requirements. The tests are used for the purpose of selecting and promoting police officers, firefighters, and clerical workers in public service positions. They cannot be assumed to be valid for all purposes. Test users are responsible for demonstrating validity for their particular jurisdictions. Study guides are available for some entry-level tests. Reading lists are available for many promotional examinations offered through IPMA's test rental service. Items in the Entry-Level Police Officer, A-3 test assess abilities that are important to satisfy performance in the following job dimensions: ability to learn and apply police information; ability to remember details; verbal ability; ability to follow directions; and ability to use judgment and logic. Included in this instrument is a study guide designed to be used immediately prior to the test. No prior training or experience in the job of police officer is assumed of candidates taking these tests. The A-3 police officer test is supported by criterion-related validity and psychometric analysis.

**18169**
**Entry-Level Police Service Tests: Police Officer Examination, 375.1 and 375.2.** International Personnel Management Association, Alexandria, VA
*Descriptors:* *Communication Skills; *Entry Workers; *Evaluative Thinking; *Logical Thinking; *Map Skills; *Memory; *Occupational Tests; *Personnel Selection; *Police; *Police Action; Promotion (Occupational); Public Service Occupations; Records (Forms)
*Identifiers:* POE
*Availability:* International Personnel Management Association, 1617 Duke St., Alexandria, VA 22314.
*Notes:* See Entry-Level Police Service Tests: Police Officer Examination, 175.1 and 175.2 (15678) and A-3 (18168), and Entry-Level Police Officer Background Data Questionnaire (18170) for related instruments. Time, 130. Items, 100.

Tests were developed for the International Personnel Management Association (IPMA) and are used in a variety of jurisdictions and represent generalized public service requirements. The tests are used for the purpose of selecting and promoting police officers, firefighters, and clerical workers in public service positions. They cannot be assumed to be valid for all purposes. Test users are responsible for demonstrating validity for their particular jurisdictions. Study guides are available for some entry-level tests. Reading lists are available for many promotional examinations offered through IPMA's test rental service. The Entry-Level Police Officer Exams (POE) 375.1 and 375.2 are revised versions of the POE 175.1 and 175.2 examinations. These tests are alternate forms and can be used interchangeably for retesting or security purposes. Test items were constructed to assess abilities that are important to satisfy performance in the following job dimensions: ability to learn and apply police information; ability to remember details; communication skills; ability to acurately complete report forms; ability to interpret maps and accident diagrams; and ability to use judgement and logic. Included is a study guide designed to be used immediately prior to the test. No prior training or experience in the job of police officer is assumed of candidates taking these tests. These tests are supported by criterion-related validity and psychometric analysis.

**18170**
**Entry-Level Police Officer Background Data Questionnaire.** International Personnel Management Association, Alexandria, VA
*Descriptors:* *Background; *Biographical Inventories; *Entry Workers; *Interpersonal Competence; *Occupational Tests; *Personnel Selection; *Physical Fitness; *Police; *Self Esteem; *Work Attitudes; Interaction; Public Service Occupations; Questionnaires
*Identifiers:* BDQ; POE
*Availability:* International Personnel Management Association, 1617 Duke St., Alexandria, VA 22314.
*Notes:* See Entry-Level Police Service Tests: Police Officer Examination, 175.1 and 175.2 (15678), and 375.1 and 375.2 (18169), and Entry-Level Police Officer Service Tests: Police Officer Examination, A-3 (18168) for related instruments. Time, 40. Items, 106.

Tests were developed for the International Personnel Management Association (IPMA) and are used in a variety of jurisdictions and represent generalized public service requirements. The tests are used for the purpose of selecting and promoting police officers, firefighters, and clerical workers in public service positions. They cannot be assumed to be valid for all purposes. Test users are responsible for demonstrating validity for their particular jurisdictions. Study guides are available for some entry-level tests. Reading lists are available for many promotional examinations offered through IPMA's test rental service. Background Data Questionnaire (BDQ) assesses certain background and personal characteristics that traditional police ability tests are not designed to assess. Measures qualities that differ from a standard ability test. Examples of such characteristics include: work history and habits; physical preparation; dealing with people; and self-confidence. It is recommended that this test be given along with one of IPMA's other entry-level police officer tests. All BDQ's will be scored by IPMA.

**18182**
**NLN Diagnostic Readiness Test for RN Licensure.** National League for Nursing, New York, NY
*Descriptors:* *Knowledge Level; *Achievement Tests; *Nursing; *College Seniors; *Undergraduate Study; *Licensing Examinations (Professions); Entry Workers; Standardized Tests; Higher Education
*Identifiers:* Practice Tests; Nursing Students; DR
*Availability:* National League for Nursing, 350 Hudson St., New York, NY 10014

National League for Nursing (NLN) achievement tests for baccalaureate nursing students are standardized tests designed to measure individual achievement in nursing content areas included in the baccalaureate curriculum. Designed to help graduating seniors prepare for the National Council Licensure Examination for Registered Nurses (NCLEX-RN). Assesses the knowledge and skills needed for entry-level practice as measured by the licensure examination. Provides valuable practice, which helps to reduce the anxiety associated with taking NCLEX-RN. Subtests include: Human Functioning; Nursing Process; Clinical Content; and Client Needs.

**18215**
**Five Star Supervisor Motivation Skills Inventory.** Tagliaferri, Louis E. 1990.
*Descriptors:* *Motivation Techniques; *Administrators; *Supervisors; *Managerial Occupations; Adults; Behavior Rating Scales; Employer Employee Relationship; Likert Scales; Work Environment
*Identifiers:* MSI
*Availability:* Talico, Inc., 2320 S. Third St., Ste. 5, Jacksonville Beach, FL 32250.

Useful in evaluating the motivation skills and practices of managers and supervisors. It also provides feedback about the effectiveness of supervisory motivational practices and behaviors. Consists of 28 items in 7 sets of 4 items each with a Likert-type response scale. Dimensions measured are related to basic, yet crucial practices or behaviors, which impact significantly on employee motivation. This multilevel instrument assesses the extent to which managers and supervisors know their employees, show that they care, treat employees fairly, train and coach, make performance count, reward for performance, and set an example. (TJS)

**18216**
**Five Star Supervisor Team Builder Skills Inventory.** Tagliaferri, Louis E. 1990.
*Descriptors:* *Administrators; *Teamwork; *Managerial Occupations; *Forced Choice Technique; Adults; Leadership Styles; Feedback; Management Teams; Self Evaluation (Individuals); Interprofessional Relationship; Management Development; Skill Development
*Availability:* Talico, Inc., 2320 S. Third St., Ste. 5, Jacksonville Beach, FL 32250.

A self-assessment instrument that measures the extent to which the respondent may engage in 8 sets of practices that research has shown are focus issues of superior team builders. These practices are action, performance, improvement, contact, relationships, development, team interaction, and personal character. Inventory consists of 16 forced choice pairs of practices. Respondents are required to select the specific practice that is most applicable to them. Provides managers, supervisors, and team leaders with feedback about the extent to which they may use practices characteristic of those used by superior team builders. It also provides these administrators with self- assessment information that will help them improve their team building skills. Applicable for team leaders skill development, team building, management development, career development, and performance coaching. (TJS)

**18217**
**Insight Inventory.** Handley, Patrick 1990.
*Descriptors:* *Personality Measures; *Personality Traits; *Work Environment; *Family Environment; *Behavior Rating Scales; Adults; Teamwork; Profiles; Self Evaluation (Individuals); Leadership Training; Stress Management; Career Planning; Interviews
*Availability:* Human Resource Development Press, 22 Amherst Rd., Amherst, MA 01002

A self-scoring instrument that provides information on 4 ways people use their personalities. It measures styles of getting one's way (direct or indirect), responding to people (outgoing or reserved), pacing activity (urgent or steady), and dealing with details (unstructured or precise). Provides 2 profiles based on 2 environments. One profile describes how a person behaves at work, and the other profile describes how the person behaves at home. This instrument points out awareness of these characteristics and helps people understand themselves and others, and guides them in making temporary changes (flex their style) to work better with others. Also included in this instrument is a companion piece, the Style Feedback Set, which provides ratings from 5 coworkers. Useful for team building, leadership training, customer service, stress management, career planning, sales training, job interviewing, and performance coaching. Subtests include: Personal Style; Work Style. (TJS)

**18221**
**National Certification Examinations for Addiction Counselors, Level I.** Professional Testing Corp., New York, NY
*Descriptors:* *Counselor Certification; *Alcoholism; *Drug Abuse; *Knowledge Level; *Occupational Tests; Adults
*Identifiers:* NCAC; NCC
*Availability:* Professional Testing Corp., 1211 Ave. of the Americas, 15th Floor, New York, NY 10036.
*Notes:* See National Certification Examinations for Addiction Counselors, Level II (18222) for related instrument.

The objectives of this certification program are to promote competency in alcoholism and drug abuse counseling by promoting the formal recognition of the professionalism of addiction counselors; to recognize formally those individuals who meet the standards established by the National Association of Alcoholism and Drug Abuse Counselors (NAADAC) Certification Commission (NCC). Additional objectives are to encourage continued professional growth in alcoholism and drug abuse counseling for the purpose of improving the quality of care to addicted persons; to establish, measure, and monitor the level of knowledge required for certification in alcoholism and drug abuse counseling; and to assist employers, labor unions, health care providers, educators, and other practitioners, as well as the public, in identifying qualified addiction counselors. Level I counselors must have 3 years of supervised experience in alcoholism and/or drug abuse counseling, and documentation of 270 contact hours of education and training in alcoholism and/or drug abuse or related counseling subjects. Level I counselors may upgrade to Level II. The certification program is sponsored by NAADAC. Candidates must meet current state certification requirements. Certification is awarded for a 2-year period. It may be revoked for falsifying information, misrepresentation of status, revocaton or suspension of state licensure, or violation of NAADAC code of ethics. (TJS)

**18222**
**National Certification Examinations for Addiction Counselors, Level II.** Professional Testing Corp., New York, NY
*Descriptors:* *Counselor Certification; *Alcoholism; *Drug Abuse; *Knowledge Level; *Occupational Tests; Adults
*Identifiers:* NCAC
*Availability:* Professional Testing Corp., 1211 Ave. of the Americas, 15th Floor, New York, NY 10036.
*Notes:* See National Certification Examinations for Addiction Counselors, Level I (18221) for related instrument.

The objectives of this certification are to promote competency in alcoholism and drug abuse counseling by promoting the formal recognition of the professionalism of addiction counselors; to recognize formally those individuals who meet the standards established by the National Association of Alcoholism and Drug Abuse Counselors (NAADAC) Certification Commission (NCC). Additional objectives are to encourage continued professional growth in alcoholism and drug abuse counseling for the purpose of improving the quality of care to addicted persons; to establish, measure, and monitor the level of knowledge required for certification in alcoholism and drug abuse counseling; and to assist employers, labor unions, health care providers, educators, and other practitioners, as well as the public, in identifying qualified addiction counselors. Level II counselors must have 5 years of full-time supervised experience in alcoholism and/or drug abuse counseling, and documentation of 450 contact hours of education and training in alcoholism and/or drug abuse or related counseling subjects to meet eligibility requirements. The certification program is sponsosred by NAADAC. Candidates must meet current state certification requirments. Certification is awarded for a 2-year period. It may be revoked for falsifying information, misrepresentation of status, revocation or suspension of state licensure or violation of NAADAC code of ethics. (TJS)

**18223**
**Supervisory Aptitude Test.** Talico, Inc., Jacksonville Beach, FL 1991.
*Descriptors:* *Supervisors; *Employer Employee Relationship; *Occupational Tests; *Interpersonal Competence; Adults; Timed Tests; Middle Management; Aptitude Tests
*Identifiers:* SA
*Availability:* Talico, Inc., 2320 S. Third St., Ste. 5, Jacksonville Beach, FL 32250.

To help assess a candidate's potential to perform the interaction skills characteristic of successful supervisors. Consists of 15 situations describing a particular interaction between a supervisor and a subordinate. Respondents are to choose which of 2 communication alternatives would be more effective for a supervisor in dealing with the situation. This is a timed test that must be administered under proctored conditions. Applicable for career development and assessment and training needs analysis. Suitable for first- and second-level supervisory positions. (TJS)

**18224**
**Supervisor's Performance Inventory.** Kinlaw, Dennis C. 1991.
*Descriptors:* *Supervisors; *Supervisory Methods; *Job Performance; *Leadership Styles; *Administrator Evaluation; Adults; Rating Scales; Employer Employee Relationship; Teamwork
*Identifiers:* SP
*Availability:* Talico, Inc., 2320 S. Third St., Ste. 5, Jacksonville Beach, FL 32250.

Designed for personal assessment and for obtaining feedback from subordinates, peers, and superiors. It measures 8 sets of practices that distinguish superior supervisors from average and below average group leaders. The purpose of this instrument is to assess the degree to which supervisors use superior practices and identify specific targets to improve supervisor performance. Subtests include: Action Focus; Performance Focus; Improvement Focus; Contact Focus; Relationship Focus; Development Focus; Team Focus; and Character Focus.(TJS)

**18225**
**Supervisory Training Assessment.** Talico, Inc., Jacksonville Beach, FL 1991.
*Descriptors:* *Supervisory Training; *Skill Development; *Problem Solving; *Work Attitudes; Adults; Behavior Rating Scales; Supervisory Methods; Time Management
*Identifiers:* ST
*Availability:* Talico, Inc., 2320 S. Third St., Ste. 5, Jacksonville Beach, FL 32250.

Assists in assessing training and development needs for first- and second-level supervisors. This multidimensional instrument focuses on both supervisory work behavior and on attitudes that can affect supervisory behaviors. It assesses the respondent's time management practices, evaluates perceptions about various supervisory situations, tests problem-solving ability, and identifies opportunities to improve supervisory skill. Applicable for training needs analysis, and coaching and counseling. Subtests include: Time Management; Job Situation; Problem Analysis; and Work Practices. (TJS)

**18229**
**Leadership Practices Inventory—Delta.** Kouzes, James M.; Posner, Barry Z. 1992.
*Descriptors:* *Behavior Rating Scales; *Leadership Styles; *Supervisors; *Supervisory Methods; Adults; Self Evaluation (Individuals)
*Identifiers:* LP
*Availability:* Pfeiffer and Co., formerly University Associates, 8517 Production Ave., San Diego, CA 92121-2280.
*Notes:* See Leadership Practices Inventory (15559) for related instrument.

A behavior rating scale that makes it possible for training participants to assess changes in their leadership practices - conscious and conspicuous changes that have or have not occurred since taking the original Leadership Practice Inventory (LPI) assessment. With this tool, leaders can recognize improvements and areas that need more attention, analyze self perceptions, and create firm action plans for improving skills. Also included is LPI - Delta: Observer, which is completed by subordinates, supervisors, and colleagues of the leaders who are taking the self-evaluation instrument. It gives feedback on noticeable changes that have occurred over a period of time, and whether more change is desired. Each instrument contains 30 items. (TJS)

**18231**
**Instructional Leadership Inventory.** Maehr, Martin L.; Ames, Russell 1988.
*Descriptors:* *Instructional Leadership; *Principals; Adults; Questionnaires; Self Evaluation (Individuals)
*Identifiers:* ILEAD; ILI
*Availability:* MeriTech, Inc., 111 N. Market St., Champaign, IL 61820.
*Notes:* See also School Administrator Assessment Survey (18230) and Instructional Climate Inventory (18232). Items, 110.

Designed to study a principal's activities during a work day. Assesses 5 instructional leadership areas: defines mission, manages curriculum, supervises teaching, monitors student progress, and promotes instructional climate. Completed by the principal as a self-report measure. One of three leadership and school climate assessment instruments in the Instructional Leadership Evaluation and Development Program (ILEAD). Reports of results are obtained through mail-in processing or by using purchased software.

**18238**
**Coaching Skills Inventory.** Kinlaw, Dennis C. 1991.
*Descriptors:* *Change Agents; *Employer Employee Relationship; *Managerial Occupations; Adults; Rating Scales
*Identifiers:* Coaching; CSI
*Availability:* Pfeiffer and Co., formerly University Associates, 8517 Production Ave., San Diego, CA 92121-2280.
*Notes:* Time, 15 approx. Items, 50.

Designed to help managers, supervisors, and other administrators evaluate their success in performing coaching functions and to help them take steps to improve their coaching skills. There is a form for self-evaluation and one for subordinates to rate the supervisor. The categories on which managers are rated include contact and core skills, counseling, mentoring, tutoring, and confronting/challenging.

**18239**
**Management Inventory on Leadership, Motivation and Decision-Making.** Kirkpatrick, Donald L. 1991.
*Descriptors:* *Decision Making; *Leadership Styles; *Managerial Occupations; *Motivation; Adults; Questionnaires; Supervisory Training
*Identifiers:* MILMD
*Availability:* Dr. Donald L. Kirkpatrick, 1920 Hawthorne Dr., Elm Grove, WI 53122.
*Notes:* Time, 20 approx. Items, 55.

Agree-disagree format to elicit opinions or managers' leadership, motivation, and decision-making strategies. Can be used to determine training needs, to stimulate discussion in a training session, to evaluate the effectiveness of a training program, to assist in the selection of managers.

**18240**
**Management Inventory of Performance Appraisal and Coaching.** Kirkpatrick, Donald L. 1990.
*Descriptors:* *Change Agents; *Managerial Occupations; *Personnel Evaluation; Adults
*Identifiers:* Coaching; MIPAC
*Availability:* Dr. Donald L. Kirkpatrick, 1920 Hawthorne Dr., Elm Grove, WI 53122.
*Notes:* Time, 20 approx.

Agree/disagree format to elicit opinions on managers' performance appraisal and coaching strategies. Can be used to determine the need for coaching, as a tool for discussion, to evaluate the effectiveness of a training course, and to provide information for on-the-job coaching.

**18246**
**Oetting/Michaels Anchored Ratings for Therapists.** Oetting, E.R.; Michaels, Laurie 1982.
*Descriptors:* *Professional Training; *Psychologists; *Therapists; *Trainees; Adults; Behavior Rating Scales; Graduate Students; Higher Education
*Identifiers:* OMART
*Availability:* Rocky Mountain Behavioral Science Institute, P.O. Box 1066, Fort Collins, CO 80522.
*Notes:* Items, 34.

Behavior-anchored assessment of a therapist trainee's skills as a professional psychologist. Designed for use in evaluating a trainee as part of a professional training program. A supervisor briefly describes and then rates the trainee's behaviors on each of the 34 scales. Behavioral anchors provide points of reference that help a supervisor assess a trainee's skills.

**18247**
**How Independent Is Our Team?—The Gulowsen Autonomy Scales.** Glaser, Rollin 1991.
*Descriptors:* *Management Teams; *Professional Autonomy; *Teamwork; Adults; Decision Making; Interpersonal Relationship; Rating Scales
*Identifiers:* Gulowsen Autonomy Scales
*Availability:* Organization Design and Development, Inc., 2002 Renaissance Blvd., Ste. 100, King of Prussia, PA 19406-2746.
*Notes:* Time, 55 approx. Items, 35.

Used to help work groups clarify the degree of decision-making independence they presently possess. Used with newly formed self-managing teams or groups that are unsure of their current status. John Gulowsen (1971) formulated 7 criteria for autonomy. These criteria include goal formulation, performance, production method, assigning tasks, membership, leadership, and individual jobs. These criteria have been converted to 7 scales with 5 items each for this inventory.

**18248**
**Risk-Taking Assessment Guide.** Kindler, Herbert S. 1991.
*Descriptors:* *Decision Making; *Risk; Adults; Careers; Job Training; Managerial Occupations
*Availability:* Organization Design and Development, Inc., 2002 Renaissance Blvd., Ste. 100, King of Prussia, PA 19406-2746.
*Notes:* Time, 45 approx.

Provides a framework for an individual to systematically decide how to handle personal, career, and organizational risks. Consists of an exercise in which the respondent identifies a problem situation involving risk. Individual must determine options, other people involved, and additional concerns. Data are pulled together in a decision assessment matrix that is then rated for outcome and probability. Useful for career and management training.

**18250**
**ASTD Trainer's Toolkit: California State University, Fresno.** American Society for Training and Development, Alexandria, VA 1990.
*Descriptors:* *Employees; *Job Skills; *Vocational Evaluation; *Needs Assessment; Adults; Data Collection; Multiple Choice Tests; Skill Analysis
*Availability:* Pfeiffer and Co., 8517 Production Ave., San Diego, CA 92121-2280.
*Notes:* For the instruments contained in the American Society for Training and Development (ASTD) Trainer's Toolkit, see 18250 through 18265.

The American Society for Training and Development (ASTD) Trainer's Toolkit series is designed to provide practitioners with working documents developed and used by other HRD practitioners. These needs assessment instruments can serve as a springboard for any professional new to the process, as well as provide seasoned veterans with innovative approaches. Each toolkit includes journal articles for background information. The California State University, Fresno tool is a generalized data collection form used on a large, diverse population. The structure of this tool is a combination of open-ended responses with multiple-choice and fill-in-the-blank options. Focus is on general skill areas rather than on specific tasks or skills for specific jobs. Respondents are to rank in order of importance the training topic in which they are most interested. Useful for identifying perceived needs and interests or specific skill or knowledge needs for individual job positions. It also surveys the use and effectiveness of previous training programs. The employee population receives feedback after the results are tabulated. (TJS)

**18251**
**ASTD Trainer's Toolkit: Chase Manhattan Bank, N.A.** American Society for Training and Development, Alexandria, VA 1990.
*Descriptors:* *Administrators; *Needs Assessment; *Adjustment (to Environment); *Banking; *Supervisory Training; Adults; Questionnaires; Middle Management; Leadership Qualities; Multiple Choice Tests
*Availability:* Pfeiffer and Co., 8517 Production Ave., San Diego, CA 92121-2280.
*Notes:* For the instruments contained in the American Society for Training and Development (ASTD) Trainer's Toolkit, see 18250 through 18265.

The American Society for Training and Development (ASTD) Trainer's Toolkit series is designed to provide practitioners with working documents developed and used by other HRD practitioners. These needs assessment instruments can serve as a springboard for any professional new to the process, as well as provide seasoned veterans with innovative approaches. Each toolkit includes journal articles for background information. The Chase Manhattan Bank, N.A. is a needs analysis process designed for a multinational assessment in response to significant environmental changes that affect the banking business. Useful in formulating training and development strategies on the managerial level. Managers are asked to respond to questions regarding their business strategy, their people resources, and their development priorities. Focus is on skills, knowledge, and attributes needed to be successful in the business. Respondents rank the order of delivery strategies for each category. This instrument uses fill-in-the-blank, multiple-choice, and open-ended responses. (TJS)

**18252**
**ASTD Trainer's Toolkit: Comerica, Inc.** American Society for Training and Development, Alexandria, VA 1992.
*Descriptors:* *Online Systems; *Employees; *Needs Assessment; Adults; Rating Scales; Task Analysis; Self Evaluation (Individuals); Likert Scales
*Availability:* Pfeiffer and Co., 8517 Production Ave., San Diego, CA 92121-2280.
*Notes:* For the instruments contained in the American Society for Training and Development (ASTD) Trainer's Toolkit, see 18250 through 18265.

The American Society for Training and Development (ASTD) Trainer's Toolkit series is designed to provide practitioners with working documents developed and used by other HRD practitioners. These needs assessment instruments can serve as a springboard for any professional new to the process, as well as provide seasoned veterans with innovative approaches. Each toolkit includes journal articles for background information. The form for Comerica, Inc. is a Likert-type response scale used to determine training needs for skills at the task level within a department. This self-assessment measures current proficiency levels in both procedures and online technical needs and is designed for a population of approximately 75 mainframe systems users in an organization employing more than 5,000 people. It is useful for identifying tasks that are required by staff in each area of the organization, and for identifying the skill level (1-4) that is required for each task. Desired skill levels are set for each staff grade level. It does not measure current levels of proficiency against needed levels of proficiency. The instrument may be effective for specific technical skills. (TJS)

**18253**
**ASTD Trainer's Toolkit: EG and G, Inc.** American Society for Training and Development, Alexandria, VA 1990.
*Descriptors:* *Organizational Effectiveness; *Administrators; *Leadership Qualities; *Needs Assessment; Adults; Rating Scales; Supervisors; Work Environment; Likert Scales
*Availability:* Pfeiffer and Co., 8517 Production Ave., San Diego, CA 92121-2280.
*Notes:* For the instruments contained in the American Society for Training and Development (ASTD) Trainer's Toolkit, see 18250 through 18265.

The American Society for Training and Development (ASTD) Trainer's Toolkit series is designed to provide practitioners with working documents developed and used by other HRD practitioners. These needs assessment instruments can serve as a springboard for any professional new to the process, as well as provide seasoned veterans with innovative approaches. Each toolkit includes journal articles for background information. The form for EG and G, Inc. is an internal needs survey used to involve upper-level management in assuming responsibility for training decisions. A Likert-type response scale is used in which respondents are urged to differentiate between wants and needs. The object is to tie the training needs to the corporate strategy, thus improving organizational effectiveness. Some of the needs assessed include time management, interviewing skills, effective communications, problem solving, business writing, motivation, employee recognition/feedback, disciplining, and basics of supervision. (TJS)

**18254**
**ASTD Trainer's Toolkit: Eli Lilly and Co.** American Society for Training and Development, Alexandria, VA 1990.
*Descriptors:* *Trainees; *Needs Assessment; *Occupational Information; *Engineers; Adults; Likert Scales; Profiles; Employees; Work Attitudes; Ability Identification; Work Environment
*Identifiers:* *Mechanical Engineers
*Availability:* Pfeiffer and Co., 8517 Production Ave., San Diego, CA 92121-2280.
*Notes:* For the instruments contained in the American Society for Training and Development (ASTD) Trainer's Toolkit, see 18250 through 18265.

The American Society for Training and Development (ASTD) Trainer's Toolkit series is designed to provide practitioners with working documents developed and used by other HRD practitioners. These needs assessment instruments can serve as a springboard for any professional new to the process, as well as provide seasoned veterans with innovative approaches. Each toolkit includes journal articles for background information. The form for Eli Lilly and Co. is an assessment instrument developed as a pilot study for the company's mechanical engineers. It was designed to pinpoint how mechanical engineer trainees spend their time, what is important in their job, and what competencies they feel they have. Information gathered is used to determine the optimal level of proficiency, the current level of proficiency, and the difference between the 2 levels. This difference comprises the training needs. The form includes sections for providing demographic information, identifying contacts and interactions, a skills usage profile, a competency profile, and a set of open-ended questions. A fill-in-the-blanks format is used, as well as a Likert-scale format in obtaining information. (TJS)

**18255**
**ASTD Trainer's Toolkit: Honeywell, Inc.** American Society for Training and Development, Alexandria, VA 1990.
*Descriptors:* *Knowledge Level; *Employees; *Job Skills; *Ability Identification; *Needs Assessment; Adults; Likert Scales; Questionnaires; Work Environment; Multiple Choice Tests
*Availability:* Pfeiffer and Co., 8517 Production Ave., San Diego, CA 92121-2280.
*Notes:* For the instruments contained in the American Society for Training and Development (ASTD) Trainer's Toolkit, see 18250 through 18265.

The American Society for Training and Development (ASTD) Trainer's Toolkit series is designed to provide practitioners with working documents developed and used by other HRD practitioners. These needs assessment instruments can serve as a springboard for any professional new to the process, as well as provide seasoned veterans with innovative approaches. Each toolkit includes journal articles for background information. The form for Honeywell, Inc. is a self-assessment designed for a department within a large organization. The form was used with the Materials Acquisition Department of Honeywell. This instrument involves the program director, instructors, the "audience", and subject matter experts. The format is comprised of Likert-scale questions and multiple-choice questions. Questions concern a specific training topic, the respondent's current level of skills and knowledge, and needed level of skills and knowledge for specific jobs. Results are tabulated and the audience is asked to help define the training objectives. The overall process includes collaboration and clarification of training needs from various sources. (TJS)

**18256**
**ASTD Trainer's Toolkit: Kris Schaeffer and Associates.** American Society for Training and Development, Alexandria, VA 1990.
*Descriptors:* *Salesmanship; *Sales Workers; *Needs Assessment; Adults; Employees; Job Skills; Work Environment; Questionnaires; Knowledge Level
*Availability:* Pfeiffer and Co., 8517 Production Ave., San Diego, CA 92121-2280.
*Notes:* For the instruments contained in the American Society for Training and Development (ASTD) Trainer's Toolkit, see 18250 through 18265.

The American Society for Training and Development (ASTD) Trainer's Toolkit series is designed to provide practitioners with working documents developed and used by other HRD practitioners. These needs assessment instruments can serve as a springboard for any professional new to the process, as well as provide seasoned veterans with innovative approaches. Each toolkit includes journal articles for background information. The form for Kris Schaeffer and Associates Selling Skills Questionnaire is part of a consultant's needs analysis for sales staff. It has several parts for collecting information from various sources. This tool collects data from the immediate supervisors of sales representatives (reps), from sales reps' colleagues and customers, and allows input from the sales reps themselves. A portion of this instrument asks supervisors to assess both the level of proficiency needed by each rep and the proficiency demonstrated by that rep. This allows the scorer to determine the difference between optimal and actual levels of proficiency. Background information about the sales environment, the activity of the organization, and the particular sales rep's contributions to the organization are collected using multiple-choice questions. The sales reps' knowledge and skills as perceived by the sales reps, by their manager, and by coworkers are identified in each selling skills profile. Also included in the profile are key sales steps as the customers perceive them.(TJS)

**18257**
**ASTD Trainer's Toolkit: Mayo Foundation.** American Society for Training and Development, Alexandria, VA 1990.
*Descriptors:* *Needs Assessment; *Job Skills; *Interpersonal Competence; *Management Development; *Administrators; *Supervisory Training; Adults; Rating Scales; Data Collection; Likert Scales
*Availability:* Pfeiffer and Co., 8517 Production Ave., San Diego, CA 92121-2280.
*Notes:* For the instruments contained in the American Society for Training and Development (ASTD) Trainer's Toolkit, see 18250 through 18265.

The American Society for Training and Development (ASTD) Trainer's Toolkit series is designed to provide practitioners with working documents developed and used by other HRD practitioners. These needs assessment instruments can serve as a springboard for any professional new to the process, as well as provide seasoned veterans with innovative approaches. Each toolkit includes journal articles for background information. The form for Mayo Foundation is a needs assessment used to collect data for the management development needs of managers. It allows the respondents to rate themselves, their supervisors, and their subordinates. The form covers a variety of topics, some of which include specific job skills and interpersonal skills required by managers. A Likert-scale format is used to rate each knowledge and skill. This tool also uses multiple-choice and fill-in-the-blank responses and open-ended questions to collect demographic information.(TJS)

**18258**
**ASTD Trainer's Toolkit: Noxell Corporation.** American Society for Training and Development, Alexandria, VA 1990.
*Descriptors:* *Needs Assessment; *Administrators; *Interpersonal Competence; *Supervisory Training; Adults; Likert Scales; Supervisors; Work Environment; Decision Making
*Availability:* Pfeiffer and Co., 8517 Production Ave., San Diego, CA 92121-2280.
*Notes:* For the instruments contained in the American Society for Training and Development (ASTD) Trainer's Toolkit, see 18250 through 18265.

The American Society for Training and Development (ASTD) Trainer's Toolkit series is designed to provide practitioners with working documents developed and used by other HRD practitioners. These needs assessment instruments can serve as a springboard for any professional new to the process, as well as provide seasoned veterans with innovative approaches. Each toolkit includes journal articles for background information. The form for the Noxell Corp. is a self-assessment instrument that uses a Likert scale to rate the importance of a skill to respondents' current jobs and how much improvement they would like to gain. Respondents are asked to assess their needs to perform better on the current job. The skills assessed in this form are general management and interpersonal skills. The form could also be used to assess their specific tasks. After results are tabulated on the computer, report sheets list topics in order of respondents' need for training. Used to assess a large group of staff members, most of whom are managers and supervisors.(TJS)

**18259**
**ASTD Trainer's Toolkit: Organizational Performance Dimensions.** American Society for Training and Development, Alexandria, VA
*Descriptors:* *Needs Assessment; *Data Collection; *Attitude Measures; *Job Satisfaction; *Job Performance; *Organizational Development; Adults; Training Objectives; Self Evaluation (Individuals); Likert Scales; Work Environment
*Availability:* Pfeiffer and Co., 8517 Production Ave., San Diego, CA 92121-2280.
*Notes:* For the instruments contained in the American Society for Training and Development (ASTD) Trainer's Toolkit, see 18250 through 18265.

The American Society for Training and Development (ASTD) Trainer's Toolkit series is designed to provide practitioners with working documents developed and used by other HRD practitioners. These needs assessment instruments can serve as a springboard for any professional new to the process, as well as provide seasoned veterans with innovative approaches. Each toolkit includes journal articles for background information. An Organizational and Training Needs Assessment Survey for the consulting company, Organizational Performance Dimensions, was designed to collect data for both organizational development and individual training needs, which can be tailored to an organization's specific needs. This instrument could serve as a generic skills assessment for most organizations. It is a self-assessment tool divided into two parts, with both sections using Likert-scale responses. The job/worklife dimensions section is an attitude survey that rates the employee's satisfaction with the current level of some aspect or characteristic of job/worklife (for example, opportunity for growth and development, commitment, and enthusiasm). The second section examines the skills, knowledge, and attributes dimensions. Respondents are asked to rate the importance of each dimension to their jobs and their current levels of proficiency in each dimension. The survey is administered by an external consultant. (TJS)

**18260**
**ASTD Trainer's Toolkit: Southern Company Services.** American Society for Training and Development, Alexandria, VA 1990.
*Descriptors:* *Needs Assessment; *Data Collection; *Training Objectives; Adults; Employees; Work Environment
*Availability:* Pfeiffer and Co., 8517 Production Ave., San Diego, CA 92121-2280.
*Notes:* For the instruments contained in the American Society for Training and Development (ASTD) Trainer's Toolkit, see 18250 through 18265.

The American Society for Training and Development (ASTD) Trainer's Toolkit series is designed to provide practitioners with working documents developed and used by other HRD practitioners. These needs assessment instruments can serve as a springboard for any professional new to the process, as well as provide seasoned veterans with innovative approaches. Each toolkit includes journal articles for background information. The Southern Company Services form is a needs analysis system that involves a unique method of data collection that allows employees, managers, and executives to indicate what they perceive are actual training needs. The information obtained is helpful in allocating training funds. Employees collect information based on 2 forms - Questions for Consideration, and Training Needs Documentation. The data collected enables employee representatives to prioritize training needs. Information collected that does not pertain to training needs is also compiled. This tool is useful in large companies with diverse employees. Process involves all levels of employees and encourages interactions between the levels. (TJS)

**18261**
**ASTD Trainer's Toolkit: Stromberg-Carlson.** American Society for Training and Development, Alexandria, VA 1990.
*Descriptors:* *Needs Assessment; *Job Performance; Adults; Training Methods; Employees; Students; Task Analysis; Questionnaires; Surveys
*Identifiers:* Customer
*Availability:* Pfeiffer and Co., 8517 Production Ave., San Diego, CA 92121-2280.
*Notes:* For the instruments contained in the American Society for Training and Development (ASTD) Trainer's Toolkit, see 18250 through 18265.

The American Society for Training and Development (ASTD) Trainer's Toolkit series is designed to provide practitioners with working documents developed and used by other HRD practitioners. These needs assessment instruments can serve as a springboard for any professional new to the process, as well as provide seasoned veterans with innovative approaches. Each toolkit includes journal articles for background information. The Stromberg-Carlson instrument identifies the job performance needs of customers to enhance the company's current training programs and to help identify potential needs of future customers. Three training surveys are included. The Student Training Survey, which asks the students who have completed the training program, to evaluate their performance on specific tasks they do every day on the job. The Training Survey, similar to the Student Training Survey, is sent to the supervisors of all employees who received training. In this survey, the supervisors can judge only whether training was adequate, instead of identifying which elements of training were inadequate. The Customer Training Questionnaire is used if customers cannot meet for a follow-up interview to discuss training programs and exchange ideas. Each survey uses a combination of Likert-scale and alternate-response questions, with an open-ended section for additional comments. Surveys are written in a task analysis format. (TJS)

**18262**
**ASTD Trainer's Toolkit: Tennessee Valley Authority.** American Society for Training and Development, Alexandria, VA 1990.
*Descriptors:* *Needs Assessment; *Data Collection; *Supervisors; Adults; Employees; Administrators; Organization; Administrator Evaluation; Likert Scales
*Identifiers:* TV
*Availability:* Pfeiffer and Co., 8517 Production Ave., San Diego, CA 92121-2280.
*Notes:* For the instruments contained in the American Society for Training and Development (ASTD) Trainer's Toolkit, see 18250 through 18265. This Tennessee Valley Authority instrument is a federal document and cannot be copyrighted. The material may be reproduced.

The American Society for Training and Development (ASTD) Trainer's Toolkit series is designed to provide practitioners with working documents developed and used by other HRD practitioners. These needs assessment instruments can serve as a springboard for any professional new to the process, as well as provide seasoned veterans with innovative approaches. Each toolkit includes journal articles for background information. The Tennessee Valley Authority instrument assesses the proficiency levels of supervisors and managers. The subordinate assessment of supervisors survey combines a series of questions with open-ended questions. A Likert-scale format rates the importance of each skill, the current level of proficiency, and the required level of proficiency. The open-ended questions are used to evaluate the questionnaire itself and to allow respondents to evaluate their own responses. Other sources used for data collection include administrative performance ratings, employee development plans, and information on human resource development practices in other organizations within the industry. (TJS)

**18263**
**ASTD Trainer's Toolkit: Training House, Inc.** American Society for Training and Development, Alexandria, VA 1990.
*Descriptors:* *Needs Assessment; *Communication Skills; *Competence; Adults; Employees; Administrators; Organization; Likert Scales; Supervisory Methods; Self Evaluation (Individuals); Questionnaires
*Availability:* Pfeiffer and Co., 8517 Production Ave., San Diego, CA 92121-2280.
*Notes:* For the instruments contained in the American Society for Training and Development (ASTD) Trainer's Toolkit, see 18250 through 18265.

The American Society for Training and Development (ASTD) Trainer's Toolkit series is designed to provide practitioners with working documents developed and used by other HRD practitioners. These needs assessment instruments can serve as a springboard for any professional new to the process, as well as provide seasoned veterans with innovative approaches. Each toolkit includes journal articles for background information. There are 2 forms from the Training House, Inc.: the Communication Audit and the Proficiency Assessment Report (PAR). The Communication Audit shows how to use a set of questions to assess one topic area. Respondents are asked to rate top management, their supervisors,and themselves on different communication skills. Then respondents score the section and reflect on what the scores indicate about the organization and the process and channels of communication. The format is a set of open-ended questions asking to summarize the respondent's responses to the previous sections of the survey and to outline a course of action. The PAR assesses managerial and supervisory competencies, using a Likert-scale format with the intended audience being the supervisors and managers. Each proficiency is enclosed in a box containing a definition of the concept and two Likert scales. One scale rates the relevance of the skill to the respondent's job. The second scale rates the respondent's level of proficiency. PAR can be used as a self-assessment tool for supervisors, an assessment tool for the manager above the supervisor, or for employees rating their supervisors. (TJS)

**18264**
**ASTD Trainer's Toolkit: Valley Bank of Nevada.** American Society for Training and Development, Alexandria, VA 1990.
*Descriptors:* *Needs Assessment; *Skill Development; Adults; Employees; Supervisors; Administrators; Surveys
*Availability:* Pfeiffer and Co., 8517 Production Ave., San Diego, CA 92121-2280.
*Notes:* For the instruments contained in the American Society for Training and Development (ASTD) Trainer's Toolkit, see 18250 through 18265.

The American Society for Training and Development (ASTD) Trainer's Toolkit series is designed to provide practitioners with working documents developed and used by other HRD practitioners. These needs assessment instruments can serve as a springboard for any professional new to the process, as well as provide seasoned veterans with innovative approaches. Each toolkit includes journal articles for background information. The Valley Bank of Nevada needs analysis survey covers a wide range of skills, including customer service, planning, performance management, technical and personnel development skills. It asks respondents to rate themselves and their subordinates on current training needs and on future development needs. By surveying for both self and subordinate needs, 2 views are collected. This instrument is known as a communications starter rather than a decision-making tool. (TJS)

**18265**
**ASTD Trainer's Toolkit: West Virginia University.** American Society for Training and Development, Alexandria, VA 1990.
*Descriptors:* *Needs Assessment; *Clerical Workers; Adults; Employees; Work Environment; Likert Scales; Multiple Choice Tests; Training; Computers; Computer Software; Data Collection; Organizational Effectiveness; Individual Development; Attitude Measures
*Availability:* Pfeiffer and Co., 8517 Production Ave., San Diego, CA 92121-2280.
*Notes:* For the instruments contained in the American Society for Training and Development (ASTD) Trainer's Toolkit, see 18250 through 18264.

The American Society for Training and Development (ASTD) Trainer's Toolkit series is designed to provide practitioners with working documents developed and used by other HRD practitioners. These needs assessment instruments can serve as a springboard for any professional new to the process, as well as provide seasoned veterans with innovative approaches. Each toolkit includes journal articles for background information. The West Virginia University instrument surveys the secretarial and clerical staff of West Virginia University. The format combines fill-in-the-blank, multiple-choice, and open-ended responses to collect information on demographics and topics ranging from computer hardware and software applications to personal development areas. The survey also collects data on how much each department uses the existing training programs, the extent and effectiveness of on-the-job training within each department, whether individual departments offer formal training programs, and whether departments support requests for training. The questions are written to survey the respondents' actual interest in the topics, instead of their perceived or actual levels of proficiency. The form serves as an overview of the training situation for the secretarial and clerical staff. It assesses the overall environment and attitudes surrounding training for this staff level. Instrument is useful in developing a training strategy for the clerical classification. (TJS)

**18277**
**Manager Style Appraisal, Revised.** Hall, Jay; And Others 1990.
*Descriptors:* *Attitude Measures; *Employee Attitudes; *Managerial Occupations; *Supervisory Methods; Adults; Rating Scales
*Availability:* Teleometrics International, 1755 Woodstead Ct., The Woodlands, TX 77380.

The survey is used to obtain staff assessment of their manager's supervisory and management practices. Results can be used to provide feedback to the manager. Sixty management alternatives are presented 5 at a time under each of 12 different situations. The objective is to select the alternatives most characteristic and least characteristic of the manager, and then to place the remaining 3 alternatives on the scale that ranges from completely characteristic to completely uncharacteristic.(MH)

**18279**
**Organizational Beliefs Questionnaire: Pillars of Excellence, Revised.** Sashkin, Marshall 1991.
*Descriptors:* *Organizational Climate; *Work Attitudes; Adults; Questionnaires; Values; Rating Scales
*Identifiers:* OB
*Availability:* Organization Design and Development, Inc., 2002 Renaissance Blvd., Ste. 100, King of Prussia, PA 19406-2746.

Designed to help respondents and associates in an organization develop some useful insights into the culture of their organization. An organization's culture consists of the set of beliefs or values with which most of its members would agree. By understanding the effects of the organization's culture, a positive and healthy influence may occur with the use of this instrument. Included are statements that refer to possible viewpoints or beliefs of people in an organization. The respondent is to rate, as an objective observer, the degree to which people agree or disagree with each statement, and not report on their own personal feelings. (TJS)

**18281**
**The Managerial Mirror.** Sashkin, Marshall 1990.
*Descriptors:* *Work Environment; *Administrators; *Organizational Climate; *Managerial Occupations; Behavior Patterns; Adults
*Availability:* Organization Design and Development, Inc., 2002 Renaissance Blvd., Ste. 100, King of Prussia, PA 19406-2746.

Developed to help managers see clearly the effects of their own actions that define the climate in their organizations. It is important that this instrument be used with reflective feedback from others (colleagues, employees, or supervisors). Inventory contains 50 statements. Each item concerns a specific type of behavior that may or may not be characteristic of the respondent. The objectives of this instrument are to understand the importance of creating a positive management climate in the workplace; to understand how perceptions are formed and how they can affect behavior; to understand how employees' perception of management fairness can affect behavior; to understand the 10 dimensions of management fairness (trust, consistency, truthfulness, integrity, expectations, equity, influence, justice, respect, and procedures); to understand what manager behaviors impact the 10 climate dimensions; and to understand the benefits of creating a positive management climate that is perceived by employees as fair. (TJS)

**18283**
**Intergroup Diagnostic Survey.** Jones, John E.; Bearley, William L. 1992.
*Descriptors:* *Work Environment; *Group Dynamics; *Intergroup Relations; *Employees; *Organizational Climate; Adults; Interpersonal Communication
*Identifiers:* ID
*Availability:* Organization Design and Development, Inc., 2002 Renaissance Blvd., Ste. 100, King of Prussia, PA 19406-2746.

Designed to diagnose important aspects of how groups relate to each other inside organizations. Its major use is in improvement efforts in which 2 or more work groups are attempting to bridge gaps among each other. Other uses are to assess the intergroup climate (vertical, horizontal, informal, and external) within an organization; to conduct research on intergroup relations; to compare perceptions within a group regarding intergroup relations; and to study the effects of improvement efforts (reorganizations and interventions) on intergroup relations. (TJS)

**18285**
**Facilitator Behavior Questionnaire: Helping Teams Become Self-Managing.** Glaser, Rollin 1991.
*Descriptors:* *Teamwork; *Self Efficacy; *Self Management; Adults; Work Environment; Leadership Qualities; Questionnaires
*Identifiers:* Facilitator Styles; FB
*Availability:* Organization Design and Development, Inc., 2002 Renaissance Blvd., Ste. 100, King of Prussia, PA 19406-2746.

To assist in learning about one's style of facilitation. Facilitation is defined in this instrument as one's approach to helping others, as, for example, work groups attempting to become self-managing or self-directing. The instrument is designed to bring together 3 areas of research. These include models of effective leadership; a group development model; and the learning needs of workers who are becoming self-managing teams. Included are 24 common situations faced by self-managing teams and their facilitators. Respondents are to assume the facilitator role and choose the alternative that represents how one would actually act if offered 4 alternatives. (TJS)

**18338**
**Fleishman Job Analysis Survey.** Fleishman, Edwin A.; Reilly, Maureen E. 1992.
*Descriptors:* *Job Analysis; *Ability Identification; Adults; Rating Scales; Surveys; Cognitive Ability; Psychomotor Skills; Perceptual Motor Coordination; Physical Mobility; Interpersonal Relationship
*Identifiers:* FJA
*Availability:* Consulting Psychologists Press, Inc., 3803 E. Bayshore Rd., Palo Alto, CA 94303.
*Notes:* This was formerly called the Manual for the Ability Requirement Scales (MARS).

The survey provides a linkage between the tasks performed on the job and the personal capacities that are necessary for their performance. It provides a quantitative description of the knowledge, skills, and abilities (KSAs) required on jobs. It is useful for identifying characteristics of jobs and tasks that are related to the abilities people need to perform these jobs and tasks. The survey includes 52 abilities grouped into the cognitive, psychomotor, physical, and sensory-perceptual domains. Abilities are organized into a rating-scale booklet according to these domains.(TJS)

**18340**
**Job Descriptive Index, Revised.** Balzer, William K.; And Others 1990.
*Descriptors:* *Job Satisfaction; *Quality of Working Life; Administrators; Adults; Occupational Information; Questionnaires; Rating Scales; Supervisors; Work Environment
*Identifiers:* JDI
*Availability:* Dept. of Psychology, Bowling Green State University, Bowling Green, OH 43403-0228.
*Notes:* Time, 5 approx. Items, 90.

The Job Description Index (JDI) is a useful tool for spotting different problem areas in organizations. It measures 5 principal facets of job satisfaction that have been identified as important across numerous organizations and employee groups. These 5 areas include the work itself, pay, promotion, supervision, and people on your present job. The Job in General (JIG) scale included in this instrument reflects individual's general feelings toward their jobs. It permits an overall evaluation of satisfaction with the job as a whole. Practitioners and researchers with humanitarian, economic, and theoretical concerns will find this tool useful. Managers, supervisors, human resource administrators, work psychologists, and management consultants, as well as vocational guidance, management training, economics, and government personnel can utilize this measure to assess job satisfaction.

**18344**
**Quality Potential Assessment.** Hall, Jay 1992.
*Descriptors:* *Organizational Climate; *Attitude Measures; *Employee Attitudes; *Job Performance; Adults; Rating Scales
*Identifiers:* QP
*Availability:* Teleometrics International, 1755 Woodstead Ct., The Woodlands, TX 77380.

The instrument is designed to provide important information about an organization, such as data on the organization's policies, practices, and logistics and the degree to which this information encourages staff to give their best to the organization. The evaluation of the organizational functioning is based on the theory called Competence Theory which supports the belief that people will do what has to be done. This survey reflects individuals' views of how their organization supports, or fails to support, the organizational conditions necessary for the expression of competence. The individual rates each item twice: once for actual conditions and once for desired conditions. (MH)

**18345**
**Reality Check Survey.** Hall, Jay 1989.
*Descriptors:* *Managerial Occupations; *Supervisory Methods; *Attitude Measures; *Employee Attitudes; Adults; Objective Tests; Rating Scales
*Identifiers:* RC
*Availability:* Teleometrics International, 1755 Woodstead Ct., The Woodlands, TX 77380.

The survey is designed to allow staff to provide managers with the opportunity to reflect on their managerial practices, which reflect certain beliefs managers have regarding the capabilities, motives, and intentions of staff they supervise. There are 2 parts to the survey. Part 1, consisting of 20 items, allows the respondents to describe the circumstances under which they feel they do, or would do, their best work. Part 2 consists of the same 20 items and asks staff to consider their manager's actions toward them. (MH)

**18346**
**The Career Profile, Second Edition.** Life Insurance Marketing and Research Association, Inc., Hartford, CT 1992.
*Descriptors:* *Insurance Companies; *Personnel Selection; *Profiles; *Sales Occupations; Adults; Questionnaires; Work Experience
*Availability:* Life Insurance Marketing and Research Association, Inc., P.O. Box 208, Hartford, CT 06141-0208.

A selection questionnaire that provides an assessment of a candidate's probability of success in insurance sales. Designed to be one of the first steps in the selection process. Each candidate receives a Career Profile rating that helps to identify which candidates have the greatest probability of success in an insurance or financial services sales career before the company makes a substantial investment of time and money. Career Profile result consists of the candidate profile report, which is an indication of the candidate's overall probability of success; and the candidate self-assessment, which will help in conducting a formal, structured, follow-up interview with the candidate. Included in this instrument are 2 versions: the Advanced Career Profile questionnaire which is used if the candidate has had any amount of full-time insurance sales experience. The other version is the Initial Career Profile questionnaire which is used for everyone else. A student edition will soon be available.

**18347**
**Assessment Inventory for Management.** Life Insurance Marketing and Research Association, Inc., Hartford, CT 1991.
*Descriptors:* *Cognitive Ability; *Individual Characteristics; *Managerial Occupations; *Sales Occupations; *Screening Tests; Administrators; Adults; Behavior Rating Scales; Check Lists; Job Skills
*Identifiers:* AIM
*Availability:* Life Insurance Marketing and Research Association, Inc., P.O. Box 208, Hartford, CT 06141-0208.
*Notes:* Items, 343.

Designed to measure cognitive abilities and personal characteristics needed to perform the job tasks and job behaviors necessary for success in field management. It is a paper-and-pencil test battery suitable for screening candidates for field sales management positions. Test is divided into 4 parts consisting of multiple-choice questions, and an adjective checklist. It enables identification of candidates with opportunity for success in field sales management, provides a solid foundation on which to develop managers and general agents, and save companies money and time. Seven job task areas are looked at to determine a successful manager. These include staffing, training, performance management, administration, sales assistance and support, business management, and agency development. Twelve job behaviors are also identified and rated. These include communicating, counseling, supporting, delegating, motivating, rewarding, teambuilding, networking, coordinating, monitoring, planning, and problem solving and decision making.

**18350**
**Management Styles Inventory, Revised.** Hall, Jay; And Others 1990.
*Descriptors:* *Managerial Occupations; *Self Evaluation (Individuals); *Supervisory Methods; Adults; Rating Scales
*Availability:* Teleometrics International, 1755 Woodstead Ct., The Woodlands, TX 77380.

The inventory is a self-evaluation used to provide managers with information about the way they manage, or would manage, under a variety of conditions. Contains 60 management alternatives presented 5 at a time under 12 different situations. The managers are to select the characteristic for each situation that is most like themselves and least like themselves. The remaining three alternatives are placed on the scale that ranges from completely characteristic to completely uncharacteristic.

**18382**
**The Gulowsen Autonomy Scales (Experimental Version).** Glaser, Rollin 1991.
*Descriptors:* *Decision Making; *Organizational Development; *Professional Autonomy; *Work Environment; Adults; Rating Scales; Teamwork
*Availability:* Organization Design and Development, Inc., 2002 Renaissance Blvd., Ste. 100, King of Prussia, PA 19406-2746.
*Notes:* Items, 35.

This inventory offers an individual and an individual's work group a way to assess its degree of independence in decision making. Seven criteria are used in this tool as a way of introducing some order to facilitate communication about how self-managing teams should operate and how they can be effective. This tool is useful for work groups and organizations as a way of clarifying the various labels used to describe autonomous workgroups. Results of this inventory should be used to promote a discussion in the group that is aimed at clarifying the group's decision-making authority and identifying changes that could help the group to become more effective in its work, its relationships with each other, and its relationship with other teams.

**18393**
**Organizational Commitment Questionnaire.** Mowday, Richard T.; Steers, Richard M. 1979.
*Descriptors:* *Attitude Measures; *Employee Attitudes; *Employees; *Organizations (Groups); Adults; Likert Scales; Questionnaires; Work Environment
*Identifiers:* Commitment; OCQ
*Availability:* *Journal of Vocational Behavior,* v14 n2 p224-47, Apr 1979.
*Notes:* Items, 15.

Designed to measure employee commitment. Instrument consists of a series of statements that represent possible feelings that individuals might have about the company or organization for which they work. Based on a 7-point Likert rating scale, respondents are to indicate the degree of their agreement or disagreement with each statement. Organization commitment is defined by the authors as the relative strength of an individual's identification with and involvement in a particular organization, characterized by 3 related factors. These factors include a strong belief in and acceptance of the organization's goals and values; a willingness to exert considerable effort on behalf of the organization; and a strong desire to maintain membership in the organization.

**18429**
**Access Management Survey.** Hall, Jay 1989.
*Descriptors:* *Administrator Effectiveness; *Managerial Occupations; *Self Evaluation (Individuals); *Work Environment; Adults; Rating Scales
*Identifiers:* AMS
*Availability:* Teleometrics International, 1755 Woodstead Ct., The Woodlands, TX 77380.
*Notes:* Items, 25.

The survey is a self-evaluation by managers of how they proceed to manage such tasks as problem-solving processes, information flow, budgets, work design, technical resource allocation, and employee morale. This survey gives managers the information on their effectiveness in managing the sociotechnical aspects of work and provides them with insights as to what they might do differently.

**18430**
**Survey of Employee Access.** Hall, Jay 1989.
*Descriptors:* *Administrator Effectiveness; *Employee Attitudes; *Managerial Occupations; *Work Environment; Adults; Rating Scales
*Identifiers:* SEA
*Availability:* Teleometrics International, 1755 Woodstead Ct., The Woodlands, TX 77380.
*Notes:* Items, 25.

The survey is designed to give employees the opportunity to evaluate how effectively their managers handle problem-solving processes, information flow, budgets, work design, technical resource allocations, and employee morale. These are the equipment, designs, and technical resources to which the employees must have access and that the manager is responsible for providing.

**18431**
**Organizational Goal-Setting Questionnaire, Second Edition.** Latham, Gary P.; Locke, Edwin A. 1991.
*Descriptors:* *Administrator Evaluation; *Employee Attitudes; *Managerial Occupations; *Organizational Objectives; Adults; Rating Scales
*Identifiers:* OGSQ
*Availability:* Organization Design and Development, Inc., 2002 Renaissance Blvd., Ste. 100, King of Prussia, PA 19406-2746.
*Notes:* Items, 50.

The purpose of the questionnaire is to help managers and/or their organizations obtain feedback on the effectiveness of managers' goal-setting practices on their associates. This rating scale consists of 50 items and covers 10 dimensions: goal clarity and specificity; supervisor supportiveness; goal efficacy; goal rationale; rewards; performance appraisal; organizational support; goal stress; goal conflict; and dysfunctional side effects. Managers do not complete the questionnaires on their own goal-setting practices. At least 4 associates should complete the questionnaire.

**18432**
**Negotiating Style Profile.** Glaser, Rollin; Glaser, Christine 1991.
*Descriptors:* *Employee Attitudes; *Managerial Occupations; *Self Evaluation (Individuals); *Supervisors; Adults; Rating Scales
*Identifiers:* *Negotiation Processes
*Availability:* Organization Design and Development, Inc., 2002 Renaissance Blvd., Ste. 100, King of Prussia, PA 19406-2746.
*Notes:* Items, 30.

This profile is a rating scale designed to help managers gain an understanding of their negotiating style. There are two forms: one to be filled out by associates and one that is a self-assessment. There are 5 characteristic negotiating styles: defeat the other party at any cost; work to build a win-win outcome; accommodate the other party's needs; withdraw and remove oneself; and find an acceptable agreement.

**18433**
**The Visionary Leader: Leader Behavior Questionnaire, Third Edition.** Sashkin, Marshall 1990.
*Descriptors:* *Leadership Styles; *Managerial Occupations; *Supervisors; Adults; Rating Scales
*Identifiers:* LBQ
*Availability:* Organization Design and Development, Inc., 2002 Renaissance Blvd., Ste. 100, King of Prussia, PA 19406-2746.
*Notes:* Items, 50.

The questionnaire is used to help managers assess their visionary and managerial leadership skills and to discover insights into their personal approach to the leadership process and how it contributes to the organization's general level of excellence. There are 2 forms: a self-evaluation form and a form to be filled in by an associate. Scoring and interpretation show what kind of leader the manager is: charismatic individual, visionary thinker, organizational thinker, visionary charismatic, organizational architect, organizational planner, underdeveloped manager, aspiring leader, or self-actualizing leader.

**18435**
**Important Components of a Career Scale.** Galbraith, Michael 1987.
*Descriptors:* *Males; *Nurses; *Nontraditional Occupations; *Career Choice; Adults; Likert Scales
*Identifiers:* ICC; TIM(S)
*Availability:* Tests in Microfiche, Test Collection, Educational Testing Service, Princeton, NJ 08541.

The ICC was developed as part of a study to begin examining and describing males who choose nontraditional careers, such as nursing, and to explore the factors that influence males to work in predominately female occupations. The ICC has 44 items and 6 scales: power (PW), money (MN), prestige (PS), relationships with clients (RC), relationships with peers (RP), and relationships in general (RG). In addition to the ICC, the study also uses demographic data and the Bem Sex Role Inventory (BSRI), published by Consulting Psychologists Press. Subjects respond to the ICC, using a 5-point Likert scale. Each item in the ICC is answered on a 5-point scale with 5 being very important and 1 not at all important. Items can be categorized by subscales.

**18457**
**Total Quality Management Assessment Inventory.** Sashkin, Marshall; Kiser, Kenneth J. 1992.
*Descriptors:* *Organizational Climate; *Self Evaluation (Groups); *Total Quality Management; Adults; Rating Scales; Supervisory Methods; Values
*Identifiers:* TQM
*Availability:* Organization Design and Development, Inc., 2002 Renaissance Blvd., Ste. 100, King of Prussia, PA 19406-2746

The inventory is used to help staff assess how well the organization works in terms of the principles of total quality management (TQM). There are 2 parts to the inventory. The first examines the extent to which the various TQM techniquess are practiced in the organization. The second part examines the organizational culture, management styles, shared values and beliefs of staff, and the practices based on these values. There are 49 items in the inventoy. (mh)

**18492**
**Perceived Environmental Uncertainty Questionnaire.** Jerrell, Jeanette M. 1984.
*Descriptors:* *Job Satisfaction; *Administrators; *Superintendents; *Educational Environment; School Psychologists; Counselor Role; Rating Scales; Perception; Questionnaires; Adults
*Identifiers:* PEU; Boundary Spanning
*Availability:* Jeanette M. Jerrell, Cognos Associates, 111 Main St., Ste. 5, Los Altos, CA 94022

The questionnaire assesses the extent to which superintendents in rural school systems perceive the environment as uncertain or turbulent. It also measures the extent to which superintendents involve other school personnel, namely psychologists, in boundary-spanning functions. Divided into 3 sections, sections 1 and 2 ask superintendents to assess the extent to which alternative actions, their probabilities of occurrence, and outcomes could be specified. Responses are based on a 5-point rating scale with options ranging from complete disagreement to complete agreement. Section 3 is scaled on a 7-point rating scale using descriptive anchors representing opposite extremes of a continuum. In this section, respondents are to characterize the perceived external context of the school system as predictable, volatile, complex, and manageable. (TJS)

**18502**
**Team Communication Effectiveness Assessment.** Talico, Inc., Jacksonville Beach, FL 1992.
*Descriptors:* *Teamwork; *Organizational Communication; *Communication Skills; *Employees; Adults; Likert Scales; Self Evaluation (Groups)
*Identifiers:* TCE
*Availability:* Talico, Inc., 2320 S. Third St., Ste. 5, Jacksonville Beach, FL 32250.

The purpose of the 25-item scale is to help members of work teams assess and improve the quality and effectiveness of their task-related communication skills. The Likert-type rating scale is self-administered and can be completed in 15-20 minutes. It is useful at any organizational level for team building, communication training, work team development, and management and supervisory training. There are 5 areas of team communication quality assessed: relevancy, utility, trust, openness, and inclusion. (mh)

**18503**
**Team Empowerment Practices Test.** Talico, Inc., Jacksonville Beach, FL 1992.
*Descriptors:* *Organizational Climate; *Employer Employee Relationship; *Employees; Adults; Objective Tests; Questionnaires
*Identifiers:* TEPT; *Empowerment
*Availability:* Talico, Inc., 2320 S. Third St., Ste. 5, Jacksonville Beach, FL 32250.

The purpose of this 25-item true-false test is to help employees at all levels increase their knowledge and awareness of empowerment concepts and practics. The instrument is designed as a learning aid rather than an assessment instrument and should be administered by a facilitator. The instrument can be completed in about 15 minutes. It can be used at all organizational levels for empowerment training, total quality management programs, self-directed work teams, team building, and supervisory and management training. (mh)

**18505**
**Team Member Behavior Analysis.** Talico, Inc., Jacksonville Beach, FL 1992.
*Descriptors:* *Employees; *Teamwork; *Behavior Patterns; Adults; Likert Scales; Self Evaluation (Individuals)
*Identifiers:* TMB
*Availability:* Talico, Inc., 2320 S. Third St., Ste. 5, Jacksonville Beach, FL 32250.

The purpose of this 40-item rating scale is to familiarize work team members with constructive and dysfunctional team behaviors and to provide individual team members with feedback about how their personal behaviors are perceived by and affect other team members. The items are categorized into 10 areas, 5 of which measure construcive behavior and 5 of which measure dysfuncional behavior. The 10 areas are initiator, facilitator, motivator, harmonizer, analyzer, playboy, aggressor, monopolizer, resistor, and nonparticipator. The scale can be either self-administered or facilitator-administered in approximately 20-25 minutes. It can be used at all organizational levels for team building, work team development, management and supervisory training, and continuous improvement in team development. (mh)

**18506**
**Team Problem Solving Skills Inventory.** Talico, Inc., Jacksonville Beach, FL 1992.
*Descriptors:* *Adults; *Employees; *Teamwork; *Problem Solving; Self Evaluation (Individuals); Likert Scales
*Identifiers:* TPSS
*Availability:* Talico, Inc., 2320 S. Third St., Ste. 5, Jacksonville Beach, FL 32250.

The purpose of the 30-item Likert-type scale is to provide work team members with feedback on their problem-solving processes and to help improve their problem-solving skills. The items fall into 5 categories: systematic methods, statistical processes, creativity and innovation, information processing, and work team interaction. The scale can be completed in 15-20 minutes and can either be self-administered or facilitator-administered. It can be used at all organizational levels to help develop problem-solving and decision-making skills or for team building and work team development. (mh)

**18507**
**Total Quality Team Effectiveness Inventory.** Talico, Inc., Jacksonville Beach, FL 1992.
*Descriptors:* *Employees; *Teamwork; *Organizational Effectiveness; *Total Quality Management; Adults; Likert Scales; Self Evaluation (Individuals)
*Identifiers:* TQTEI; TQM
*Availability:* Talico, Inc., 2320 S. Third St., Ste. 5, Jacksonville Beach, FL 32250.

The 30-item, 5-point rating scale is designed to help work teams learn and apply behaviors and practices that will facilitate total quality team performance. The inventory assesses team performance in 6 areas: active listening, inclusion, processing information, sharing responsibility, solving problems, and focusing on continual improvement. The inventory takes 15-20 minutes to complete and can either be self-administered or facilitator-administered. It is suitable for use at all organizational levels for continuous improvement teams, total quality action teams, self-directed work teams, empowerment training, general team building, and management and supervisory training. (mh)

**18511**
**AccuVision Systems: Teller and Financial Services System.** Psychological Corp., San Antonio, TX
*Descriptors:* *Personnel Selection; *Professional Development; *Simulation; *Financial Services; *Banking; Adults; Videotape Recordings; Computer Assisted Testing; Finance Occupations
*Availability:* Psychological Corp., 555 Academic Ct., San Antonio, TX 78204.
*Notes:* For other instruments in the AccuVision Systems, see 18512 through 18514.

AccuVision Systems are job-related evaluation systems that combine video, computers, and simulations. The system uses video vignettes to depict typical situations that are likely to occur in a given job. This can be used for personnel selection or for diagnosing staff developmental and training needs. The computer-generated feedback can be used as an aid in personnel selection by providing a probability of success statement, as well as information on applicants' performance in the skills measured by the system. For current staff, the report provides only development information based on the person's performance in the skills measured by the system. A concurrent validation was conducted for each of the 4 systems. The Teller and Financial Services System consists of 13 video simulations and measures such skills as judgment, customer relations, soliciting new or additional business, identifying customer dissatisfaction, attention to detail, and an optional section on math ability. It includes both face-to-face and telephone interactions. The test can be administered in 60 minutes. (mh)

**18512**
**AccuVision Systems: Secretarial and Clerical Skills System.** Psychological Corp., San Antonio, TX
*Descriptors:* *Personnel Selection; *Professional Development; *Simulation; *Secretaries; *Clerical Workers; Adults; Videotape Recordings; Computer Assisted Testing
*Availability:* Psychological Corp., 555 Academic Ct., San Antonio, TX 78204.
*Notes:* For other instruments in the AccuVision Systems, see 18511 through 18514.

AccuVision Systems are job-related evaluation systems that combine video, computers, and simulations. The system uses video vignettes to depict typical situations that are likely to occur in a given job. This can be used for personnel selection or for diagnosing staff developmental and training needs. The computer-generated feedback can be used as an aid in personnel selection by providing a probability of success statement, as well as information on applicants' performance in the skills measured by the system. For current staff, the report provides only development information based on the person's performance in the skills measured by the system. A concurrent validation was conducted for each of the 4 systems. The Secretarial and Clerical Skills System consists of 12 video simulations and measures such skills as customer relations, organizing and prioritizing, problem solving, proofreading, and attention to detail. It includes both face-to-face and telephone interactions. The test can be administered in 60 minutes. (mh)

**18513**
**AccuVision Systems: Customer Service System.** Psychological Corp., San Antonio, TX
*Descriptors:* *Personnel Selection; *Professional Development; *Simulation; Adults; Videotape Recordings; Computer Assisted Testing
*Identifiers:* *Customer Services
*Availability:* Psychological Corp., 555 Academic Ct., San Antonio, TX 78204.
*Notes:* For other instruments in the AccuVision Systems, see 18511 through 18514.

AccuVision Systems are job-related evaluation systems that combine video, computers, and simulations. The system uses video vignettes to depict typical situations that are likely to occur in a given job. This can be used for personnel selection or for diagnosing staff developmental and training needs. The computer-generated feedback can be used as an aid in personnel selection by providing a probability of success statement, as well as information on applicants' performance in the skills measured by the system. For current staff, the report provides only development information based on the person's performance in the skills measured by the system. A concurrent validation was conducted for each of the 4 systems. The Customer Service System consists of 20 video simulations and measures such skills as customer relations, judgment, and soliciting new or additional business. It includes both face-to-face and telephone interactions. The test can be administered in 60 minutes. (mh)

**18514**
**AccuVision Systems: Supervisory and Managerial System.** Psychological Corp., San Antonio, TX
*Descriptors:* *Managerial Occupations; *Personnel Selection; *Professional Development; *Simulation; Adults; Videotape Recordings; Computer Assisted Testing
*Availability:* Psychological Corp., 555 Academic Ct., San Antonio, TX 78204.
*Notes:* For other instruments in the AccuVision Systems, see 18511 through 18513.

AccuVision Systems are job-related evaluation systems that combine video, computers, and simulations. The system uses video vignettes to depict typical situations that are likely to occur in a given job. This can be used for personnel selection or for diagnosing staff developmental and training needs. The computer-generated feedback can be used as an aid in personnel selection by providing a probability of success statement, as well as information on applicants' performance in the skills measured by the system. For current staff, the report provides only development information based on the person's performance in the skills measured by the system. A concurrent validation was conducted for each of the 4 systems. The Supervisory and Managerial System consists of 14 video simulations and measures such skills as team building, situational style of interacting, influence, initiative, and analysis and problem solving. The test can be administered in 105 minutes. (mh)

**18521**
**Diagnostic Assessment of Lending Skills and Knowledge.** Educational Testing Service, Princeton, NJ 1993.
*Descriptors:* *Occupational Tests; *Diagnostic Tests; *Industrial Training; *Banking; *Finance Occupations; Adults; Knowledge Level; Accounting; Credit (Finance)

*Availability:* Robert Morris Associates, 1 Liberty Pl., 1650 Market St., Ste. 2300, Philadelphia, PA 19103.

This diagnostic assessment was developed for use by financial institutions in determining how much training and in what areas their loan and credit officers need in order to achieve competence. Testees will have from 3 to 5 years experience in the loan and credit field. The instrument was designed only for training purposes. Four hours are required for administration of the 165 multiple-choice questions covering financial accounting, financial statement analysis, cash flow analysis, loan structuring and pricing, legal documentation, environmental issues and lender liability, and early detection of potential problem loans. Bank training officers administering the test receive test results that indicate whether test performance in each content area was acceptable or if more in-depth training is needed. (ADM)

**18523**
**Clinical Specialist in Gerontological Nursing.** American Nurses Credentialing Center, Washington, DC 1993.
*Descriptors:* *Nurses; *Occupational Tests; *Knowledge Level; *Adults; *Clinical Experience
*Identifiers:* Certification MN Nursing
*Availability:* American Nurses Credentialing Center, 600 Maryland Ave., S.W., Ste. 100 West, Washington, DC 20024-2571.

This is one of a series of American Nurses Association certification exams which assesses the knowledge, understanding, and application of professional nursing theory and practice in defined functional or clinical areas in nursing. Clinical specialists in gerontological nursing are experts in providing, directing, and influencing the care of older adults and their families and significant others in a variety of settings. They provide comprehensive gerontological nursing services independently or collaboratively with a multidisciplinary team. Specialists demonstrate an in-depth understanding of the dynamics of aging, as well as the interventions necessary for health promotion and management of health status alterations. Examination topics include practice, education, consultation, research, and administration. The eligibility requirements for applicants are to currently hold an active RN license in the United States; hold a master's or higher degree in nursing, preferably in gerontological nursing; have practiced a minimum of 12 months following completion of the master's degree; and have provided a minimum of 800 hours (post-master's) of direct patient care or clinical management in gerontological nursing within the past 24 months.(TJS)

**18524**
**Clinical Specialist in Community Health Nursing.** American Nurses Credentialing Center, Washington, DC 1993.
*Descriptors:* *Nurses; *Occupational Tests; *Certification; *Clinical Experience; *Public Health; Adults; Knowledge Level; Nursing
*Availability:* American Nurses Credentialing Center, 600 Maryland Ave., S.W., Ste. 100 West, Washington, DC 20024-2571.
*Notes:* This program is offered in collaboration with the American Public Health Association, Public Health Nursing Section.

This is one of a series of American Nurses Association certification exams that assesses the knowledge, understanding, and application of professional nursing theory and practice in defined functional or clinical areas in nursing. The community health nurse specialist can perform all functions of the community health nurse generalist. The specialist possesses substantial clinical experience in the assessment of the health of a community and proficiency in planning, implementation, and evaluation of population-focused programs. The skills of this specialist are based on knowledge of epidemiology, demography, biometrics, environmental health, community structure and organization, community development, management, program evaluation, and policy development. Examination topics covered are public health sciences, community assessment process, program administration, trends and issues, theory, research, and health care delivery systems. The eligibility requirements for applicants are to currently hold an active RN license in the United States; hold a master's or higher degree in nursing with a specialization in community/public health nursing practice; currently practice an average of 12 hours weekly in community/public health nursing; and have practiced, post-master's, a minimum of 1,400 hours in community/public health nursing with 800 of the 1,400 hours having occurred within the past 24 months. (TJS)

**18525**
**Home Health Nurse.** American Nurses Credentialing Center, Washington, DC 1993.
*Descriptors:* *Nurses; *Occupational Tests; *Certification; Adults; Knowledge Level; Holistic Approach; Nursing
*Identifiers:* Home Health Care
*Availability:* American Nurses Credentialing Center, 600 Maryland Ave., S.W., Ste. 100 West, Washington, DC 20024-2571.

This is one of a series of American Nurses Association certification exams that assesses the knowledge, understanding, and application of professional nursing theory and practice in defined functional or clinical areas in nursing. Home health nurses incorporate a broad spectrum of knowledge in the application of nursing to provide client care in the home, place of residence, or appropriate community site. It is holistic and is focused on the individual client, integrating family/caregiver, environmental and community resources to promote an optimal level of client well-being. The framework of practice is care management which includes the use of the nursing process to assess, diagnose, plan and evaluate care; performing nursing interventions, including teaching; coordinating and using referrals and resources; providing and monitoring all levels of technical care; collaborating with other disciplines and providers; identifying clinical problems and using research knowledge; supervising ancillary personnel; and advocating for the client's rights to self-determination. Examination topics include program management, concepts and models, and clinical management, as well as trends, issues, and research. Eligibility requirements for applicants are to currently hold an active RN license in the United States, hold a baccalaureate or higher degree in nursing, have practiced as a licensed registered nurse for a minimum of 2 years, have practiced as a licensed registered nurse in home health nursing a minimum of 2,000 hours within the past 48 months, and currently practice home health nursing a minimum of 8 hours per week. (TJS)

**18526**
**Nursing Continuing Education/Staff Development.** American Nurses Credentialing Center, Washington, DC 1993.
*Descriptors:* *Nurses; *Occupational Tests; *Certification; *Continuing Education; *Staff Development; Adults; Knowledge Level; Nursing
*Availability:* American Nurses Credentialing Center, 600 Maryland Ave., S.W., Ste. 100 West, Washington, DC 20024-2571.
*Notes:* The program is offered in collaboration with the National Nursing Staff Development Organization and the ANA Council on Continuing Education and Staff Development.

This is one of a series of American Nurses Association certification exams that assesses the knowledge, understanding, and application of professional nursing theory and practice in defined functional or clinical areas in nursing. The nurse in continuing education/staff development practice is engaged in providing non-academic learning activities intended to build upon the educational and experiential bases of professional nurses and other personnel who assist in providing nursing care. These learning activities are designed for the enhancement of nursing practice, education, administration, research, or theory development to improve the health of the public. The purposes of these learning activities include supporting learner attitudes on the value of lifelong learning; contributing to the development, maintenance, and enhancement of competent nursing practice; promoting professional development; and advancing career goals. Examination topics in this instrument include foundations of practice, educational process, management of offerings and programs, and roles. Eligibility requirements for applicants are to currently hold an active RN license in the United States, hold a baccalaureate or higher degree in nursing, have practiced as an actively licensed registered nurse in nursing continuing education and/or staff development for a minimum of 4,000 hours during the past 5 years, and currently practice as an actively licensed registered nurse in nursing continuing education and/or staff development an average of 20 hours or more per week. (TJS)

**18527**
**College Health Nurse.** American Nurses Credentialing Center, Washington, DC 1993.
*Descriptors:* *Nurses; *Occupational Tests; *Certification; *School Nurses; *Higher Education; Adults; Knowledge Level; Nursing
*Availability:* American Nurses Credentialing Center, 600 Maryland Ave., S.W., Ste. 100 West, Washington, DC 20024-2571.

This is one of a series of American Nurses Association certification exams that assesses the knowledge, understanding, and application of professional nursing theory and practice in defined functional or clinical areas in nursing. The framework for college health nursing practice includes health promotion, specific disease protection, early diagnosis, prompt treatment to limit or prevent disability, and rehabilitation. Its mission is to enhance the educational process by modifying or removing health-related barriers to learning, to promote an optimal level of wellness, to enable the individual to make informed decisions about health-related concerns and to empower clients to be self-directed and well-informed consumers of health care services. Examination topics include foundations of college health, environment, client care, roles, and issues and trends. Eligibility requirements for applicants are to currently hold an active RN license in the United States, hold a baccalaureate or higher degree in nursing, have a minimum of 1,500 hours of practice as a licensed registered nurse in college health nursing practice, and currently practice college health nursing an average of 8 hours per week. Technical data are not provided. (TJS)

**18528**
**Perinatal Nurse.** American Nurses Credentialing Center, Washington, DC 1993.
*Descriptors:* *Nurses; *Occupational Tests; *Certification; *Perinatal Influences; Adults; Knowledge Level; Nursing
*Availability:* American Nurses Credentialing Center, 600 Maryland Ave., S.W., Ste. 100 West, Washington, DC 20024-2571.

This is one of a series of American Nurses Association certification exams that assesses the knowledge, understanding and application of professional nursing theory and practice in defined functional or clinical areas in nursing. The exam for perinatal nurses contains a core of knowledge and skills essential to implement the American Nurses Association standards of Maternal and Child Health Nursing Practice. These skills may be applied in hospitals, clinics, and community settings where perinatal nurses may focus on a given aspect of maternal-child care delivery in roles that may have been traditionally defined as maternity nursing and neonatal nursing. Examination topics covered in this instrument are issues and trends, antepartum, intrapartum, postpartum, and neonatal. Eligibility requirements for applicants are to currently hold an active RN license in the United States, and have practiced as a licensed registered nurse in perinatal nursing a minimun of 2,100 hours, 600 hours of which must have been within the past 3 years. (TJS)

**18548**
**Group Behavior Inventory.** Friedlander, Frank 1985.
*Descriptors:* *Group Behavior; *Attitude Measures; *Group Dynamics; *Teamwork; Likert Scales; Questionnaires; Organizations (Groups); Adults; Interprofessional Relationship
*Identifiers:* GB
*Availability:* *Management Communication Quarterly,* v2 n3 p424-48, Feb 1989.
*Notes:* For related instruments, see Team Interaction Profile (18549) and Job Reaction Questionnaire (18550).

The instrument is used to measure the attitudes toward work group meetings, performance and interactional dimensions of organizational work within groups. It does not measure performance that occurs outside of meetings. The instrument consists of 71 items which are divided into 9 dimensions: group effectiveness, approach to versus withdrawal from leader, mutual influence, personal involvement and participation, intragroup trust versus intragroup competitiveness, general evaluation of group meetings, submission to versus rebellion against leader, leader control, and role and idea conformity. The instrument is based on a Likert-type rating scale in which group members select a response to most items from 5 alternatives ranging from strongly agree to strongly disagree. A few of the items use a 7-point scale or call for a number to be inserted in a blank. Technical data are provided. (TJS)

**18549**
**Team Interaction Profile.** Wilson Learning Corp., Eden Prairie, MN 1998.
*Descriptors:* *Teamwork; *Group Behavior; *Group Dynamics; *Middle Management; Interpersonal Relationship; Job Performance; Participant Satisfaction; Likert Scales; Rating Scales; Adults; Work Environment; Supervisors
*Identifiers:* TI
*Availability:* Wilson Learning Corp., 7500 Flying Cloud Dr., Eden Prairie, MN 55344-3975
*Notes:* For related instruments, see Group Behavior Inventory (18548) and Job Reaction Questionnaire (18550).

The instrument is designed to assess the performance of group members who need to cooperate and work together closely as a team. It measures 8 dimensions of work group behavior and 2 dimensions of satisfaction: personal and group. The tool consists of 10 dimensions: rapid response, shared responsibliity, focus on task, communication norms, future focus, alignment on purpose, participative leadership (encompases 2 dimensions), open communication, and satisfactions. Group members are asked to respond to items on a 6-point rating scale that ranges from almost never to almost always. There are some items that ask about personal or general group member satisfaction for which the 6-point scale ranges from not satisfied to very satisfied. Scores on each dimension are interpreted with reference to 3 stages of group development: low scores indicate that the work unit is functioning as a collection of individuals; intermediate scores indicate that the work unit is functioning as a group; and high scores indicate that the work unit has reached the level of a high-performance team. The scale is appropriate for use with middle managers or supervisors in the production/manufacturing area. Technical data are available. (TJS)

**18550**
**Job Reaction Questionnaire.** Donovan, M. 1967.
*Descriptors:* *Job Satisfaction; *Teamwork; *Work Environment; Questionnaires; Likert Scales; Employees; Attitude Measures; Group Unity; Adults; Interpersonal Relationship
*Identifiers:* JR
*Availability:* *Management Communication Quarterly,* v2 n3 p424-48, Feb 1989.
*Notes:* For related instruments, see Group Behavior Inventory (18548) and Team Interaction Profile (18549).

The instrument is designed to assess the impact of employee involvement programs on employee attitudes and toward perceptions about their work life. It consists of 44 items and is based on a 5-point Likert rating scale with response options ranging from strongly disagree to strongly agree. The instrument is divided into 9 subscales with 2 illustrative items given for each scale: work planning and efficiency, cooperation among work groups, management communication, personal influence, use of job knowledge, task significance, recognition/interpersonal feedback, overall job satisfaction, and room for improvement. It can also be used to diagnose problem areas and provide focus for change in the organization. It is appropriate for use with factory workers and takes about 20 minutes to complete. Technical data are available. (TJS)

**18561**
**Developmental Inventory of Sources of Stress.** Higbee, Jeanne L.; Dwinell, Patricia L. 1992.
*Descriptors:* *College Freshmen; *Stress Variables; *Stress Management; *Anxiety; *Student Behavior; *Student Attitudes; Rating Scales; Likert Scales; Time Management; Interpersonal Relationship; Drug Use; Drinking; Eating Habits; Sleep; High Risk Students
*Identifiers:* Academic Stress
*Availability:* *Research and Teaching in Developmental Education,* v8 n2 p27-40, Spr 1992.

This 65-item inventory was created to help college freshmen identify the sources of stress over which they have control so that they may take responsibility for the direction of their lives and reduce stress. The inventory uses 5 scales to identify the attitudes and behaviors that may be stress producing: time management; physical lifestyle; chemical stressors; academics; and interaction. On a 5-point, Likert-type scale, students indicate the frequency of each stress-producing attitude or behavior. The inventory may be used by counselors, advisors or faculty in the classroom or in individual or group counseling sessions to identify students who need to reduce stress. It may be very useful in helping high-risk students. The individual scales may be used for sessions on time management, health and wellness issues, alcohol awareness, academic anxiety, communication skills, and assertiveness training. Technical data are included. (klm)

**18563**
**Inwald Survey 5.** Inwald, Robin E. 1991.
*Descriptors:* *Attitude Measures; *Screening Tests; *Employees; *Personnel Selection; *Job Applicants; Adults; Objective Tests; Personality Measures; Behavior Patterns; Self Evaluation (Individuals); Personnel Evaluation
*Identifiers:* IS5
*Availability:* Hilson Research, Inc., 82-28 Abingdon Rd., P.O. Box 239, Kew Gardens, NY 11415.

The true-false inventory identifies a variety of personality and behavioral characteristics in job applicants or current employees. It is designed specifically to aid organizations in selecting and/or placing employees who will be able to satisfy job requirements. The instrument consists of 162 questions and contains 3 main scales (composed of 11 content areas) to measure an individual's behaviors, attitudes, and characteristics. The 3 scales are: lack of conscientiousness/reliability; lack of work ethic; and lack of social initiative. Scoring is done by Hilson Research, with test results in the form of a computer-generated report. This report includes a narrative report, critical items for follow-up evaluation, psychologist's rating prediction, predictions of termination, profile graph, and item print-out for each person tested. The instrument is in compliance with the Americans with Disabilities Acts (ADA) for use as a screening test. Technical data are provided. (TJS)

**18568**
**Medical Career Development Inventory.** Savickas, Mark L.; And Others 1984.
*Descriptors:* *Career Development; *Physicians; *Coping; Adults
*Identifiers:* MDC
*Availability:* *Journal of Vocational Behavior,* v25 n1 p106-23, Aug 1984.

The instrument measures both degree of vocational development and readiness to cope with the developmental tasks encountered in a physician's career. It consists of 35 items that address coping behaviors germane to dealing with the vocational tasks constituting the career development continuum of physicians. Technical data are provided. (TJS)

**18569**
**Diagnosing Organizational Culture.** Harrison, Roger; Stokes, Herb 1992.
*Descriptors:* *Organizational Climate; *Employees; *Cultural Context; *Organizational Development; Work Environment; Adults; Role Perception; Services; Power Structure; Achievement; Identification
*Availability:* Pfeiffer and Co., 8517 Production Ave., San Diego, CA 92121-2280.

The instrument is designed to help members of organizations identify aspects of organizations' culture. The purpose is to get people talking and sharing their insights about the cultures of their own organizations. It assesses how people treat one another, what values they live by, how people are motivated to produce, and how people use power in the organization. Four basic organizational cultures are measured: power-oriented, role, achievement, and support. The instrument contains 15 "beginnings" of sentences that describe some aspect of organizational functioning and design. Following each of the beginnings are 4 possible "endings". Respondents are to rank the phrases following each sentence beginning that come closest to describing the way things are in their organization. Response options range from the first that least describes the way things are to the fourth that comes closest to describing the way things are. Technical data are not provided. (TJS)

**18580**
**Team-Review Survey.** Francis, Dave; Young, Don 1992.
*Descriptors:* *Teamwork; *Self Evaluation (Groups); *Organizational Effectiveness; Adults; Rating Scales
*Availability:* Pfeiffer and Co., 8517 Production Ave., San Diego, CA 92121-2280.

This survey contains 108 statements that relate to team effectiveness. It assesses a team's strengths and weaknesses. By completing the survey, team members give a picture of what works and what does not in the functioning of a team. This instrument takes about 2 hours to complete with the help of a facilitator.(BAE)

**18581**
**Team Communication Inventory.** Glaser, Rollin 1993.
*Descriptors:* *Teamwork; *Communication Skills; *Meetings; *Behavior Patterns; *Self Evaluation (Groups); *Work Environment; Adults; Group Discussion; Questionnaires; Rating Scales
*Availability:* Organization Design and Development, Inc., 2002 Renaissance Blvd., Ste. 100, King of Prussia, PA 19406-2746.

This measure helps team members understand more clearly how various role behaviors are being used by team members during meetings. This information will enable team members to work toward more productive team discussions. The instrument consists of 3 different activities: evaluating the team discussion, developing a team consensus, and giving and receiving feedback. There are a total of 56 questions to be answered using a 5-point rating scale.(BAE)

**18596**
**Spectrum: An Organizational Development Tool.** Braskamp, Larry A.; Maehr, Martin L. 1985.
*Descriptors:* *Employees; *Organizational Climate; *Organizational Development; *Individual Development; *Quality of Working Life; *Incentives; Adults; Organizations (Groups); Job Satisfaction; Work Environment; Surveys
*Availability:* MeriTech, Inc., 111 N. Market St., Champaign, IL 61820.

The tool is used for organizational and individual development and measures the personal incentives that motivate individual workers; the opportunities the workers see for fulfillment in their present jobs; and the culture of the organization as a whole. Each element (job, organization, and worker) is assessed in terms of the same 4 characteristics: accomplishment, recognition, power, and affiliation. The instrument contains 200 items that require sixth-grade reading level. Three different computer reports are included to analyze information from the survey. Type 1 Report provides feedback to employees about their personal incentives/values, and opportunities in their present job for satisfying these values. Type 2 Report parallels the Type 1 Report by providing feedback on personal incentives and available opportunities. The Group Report generates a detailed statistical analysis of survey responses and provides management with feedback on employee perceptions of organization culture, degree of commitment, and areas of job satisfaction. The survey takes less than one hour to complete. Technical data are provided.(TJS) Materials:

**18614**
**Behaviorally Anchored Rating Scale for Nursing Assistant Performance.** Stoskopf, Carleen H.; And Others 1992.
*Descriptors:* *Nurses Aides; *Nursing Homes; *Long Term Care; *Job Performance; *Personnel Evaluation; Adults; Naturalistic Observation; Rating Scales
*Identifiers:* Behaviorally Anchored Rating Scales; Performance Based Evaluation; Service Delivery Assessment
*Availability:* *Evaluation Review,* v16 n3 p333-45, Jun 1992

This instrument is a behaviorally anchored rating scale used to rate the job performance of nursing assistants in long-term care facilities. It is designed to measure the behavioral dimensions of the nursing assistants' job performance rather than outcomes. Independent observers rate nursing assistants' behavior in 27 care-giving situations as being either correct or incorrect. Ratings may also be made by supervisors. The instrument may be used to reveal skill deficiencies, thus suggesting points of improvement or topics for training courses. It has been shown to reduce subjectivity and personal bias. Technical data are included. (klm)

**18668**
**WorkStyle Patterns Inventory.** McIntosh-Fletcher, W. Thomas; McIntosh-Fletcher, Donna 1993.
*Descriptors:* *Work Environment; Adults; Self Evaluation (Individuals)
*Identifiers:* WSP
*Availability:* The McFletcher Corp., 10617 Hayden Rd., Ste. 103, Scottsdale, AZ 85260.

This measure indicates the work style that best suits an individual's preferences and work requirements. This assessment is used to identify how an individual prefers to approach work, and the approach the individual's position or current assignment requires. It contains 20 statements with 4 choices in each being ranked on a scale of 1 to 4.(BAE)

**18676**
**A Survey of Leadership Practices, Form H.** Wilson, Clark L.; O'Hare, Donal 1989.
*Descriptors:* *Leadership Qualities; *Administrators; *Managerial Occupations; Questionnaires; Rating Scales; Leadership Styles; Feedback; Adults; Middle Management
*Identifiers:* SLP(H)
*Availability:* Consulting Psychologists Press, Inc., 3803 E. Bayshore Rd., Palo Alto, CA 94303.

The instrument is designed to evaluate leadership skills and provide guidance to executives. It is geared toward the person in a management position who also has responsibilities that require leadership skills. The multilevel assessment consists of 85 questions and is based on a 7-point rating scale with response options ranging from very limited extent, never, or not at all to very great extent, always or without fail. It is appropriate for use with middle and senior managers, senior project leaders, and technical and professional people who must build support for their innovations. The questionnaire provides feedback on leadership skills. Technical data are not provided. (TJS)

**18684**
**A Survey of My Team Mates, Form MTM-C.** Wilson, Clark L. 1992.
*Descriptors:* *Teamwork; *Work Environment; *Interprofessional Relationship; Surveys; Questionnaires; Rating Scales; Adults; Employees; Group Dynamics; Collegiality; Feedback
*Identifiers:* MT
*Availability:* Consulting Psychologists Press, Inc., 3803 E. Bayshore Rd., Palo Alto, CA 94303.
*Notes:* For a related instrument, see A Survey of Our Team, Form OT-C (18703).

The survey assesses the operational and group process skills of the individual members as seen by their colleagues. It gives feedback on the team and its members. The survey centers around the way people work together in teams or work groups. It consists of 72 questions and offers 7 response options ranging from extremely small extent, never, or not at all to extremely high degree, always, or without fail. Respondents are to rate on the basis of how well they feel about the person named on the survey. They are to compare that person to other people they have worked with. No technical data are provided. (TJS)

**18690**
**The Judd Tests.** Psychological Corp., San Antonio, TX 1992.
*Descriptors:* *Computer Software; *Computer Assisted Testing; *Job Skills; *Occupational Tests; *Job Applicants; Screening Tests; Diagnostic Tests; Adults
*Availability:* The Psychological Corp., 555 Academic Ct., San Antonio, TX 78204.

The automated tests of software skills measure proficiency in DOS, WordPerfect, Microsoft Word, Lotus 1-2-3, or Paradox. The tests are used for employment screening, employee training and development, and posttraining evaluation to measure the effectiveness of the training program. They help instructors diagnose the skill level of trainees and determine appropriate levels of training curriculum. The tests diagnose errors in keystroke-by-keystroke detail, relating those errors both to instructional treatment and to specific prescriptions for remediation. Accuracy and efficiency scores are calculated immediately upon task completion. Three levels of reporting are given. The summary is a one screen/page report showing an examinee's accuracy and efficiency scores for each software feature tested; condensed reporting details keystrokes, seconds used, accuracy scores, and efficiency scores for each task; and the detailed report diagnoses each task, indicating keystrokes used and where mistakes were made. The tests can be administered individually or in groups, and time requirements can range from minutes to one and one-half hours, depending on time limits set by test administrator. The tests can be used on an IBM PC/XT/AT, PS/2, or fully compatible system operating with DOS 2.1 or higher. Technical data are not provided. (TJS)

**18695**
**Benchmarks: Developmental Reference Points for Managers and Executives.** Lombardo, Michael M.; McCauley, Cynthia D. 1990.
*Descriptors:* *Feedback; *Managerial Occupations; Adults; Peer Evaluation; Self Evaluation (Individuals); Administrators; Questionnaires; Behavior Rating Scales
*Availability:* Center for Creative Leadership, P.O. Box 26300, One Leadership Pl., Greensboro, NC 27438-6300.

The questionnaire is a feedback instrument that measures the lessons of experience and problems that can stall the careers of managers and executives. It is used in one-on-one consultations and in workshops with managers and executives who wish to examine their strengths and weaknesses. The tool consists of 164 items and is based on 5-point rating scales with response options ranging from not at all to to a very great extent, strongly disagree to strongly agree, and among the worst to among the best. Included in the instrument is a survey, with 1 titled Self to be filled out by the manager, and 11 titled Rater, to be filled out by a combination of peers, direct reports, and bosses. Each survey takes about 30 minutes to complete and provides the rater with the opportunity to evaluate the manager on 16 skills that are critical to the work of an effective leader and 6 factors that, if left unchecked, often predict derailment. No technical data are provided. (TJS)

**18696**
**The Insight Survey.** Values Technology, Kettering, OH 1991.
*Descriptors:* *Values; *Needs Assessment; *Leadership Styles; Adults; Surveys; Self Evaluation (Groups)
*Availability:* Values Technology, 532 Stonehaven Rd., Kettering, OH 45429

The survey is designed to give guidance to people regarding the relationship of value priorities to one's skills and leadership styles. It identifies the skills needed to make those values come alive in one's work and relationships. The tool covers the entire range of human values, although not all of the items will be appropriate for everyone's situation. It consists of 125 statement stems and offers 5 response options. Included in this tool is a workbook that is designed for use with the profile to give specific information on what a person values most in life. A composite report is compiled based on the results from the survey. Individuals within a group can also provide quality information about the group's culture and leadership development opportunities with the use of this tool. Technical data are not provided. (TJS)

**18703**
**A Survey of Our Team, Form OT-C.** Wilson, Clark L. 1992.
*Descriptors:* *Employees; *Teamwork; *Work Environment; *Interprofessional Relationship; Surveys; Questionnaires; Behavior Rating Scales; Adults; Feedback; Group Dynamics; Collegiality
*Availability:* Consulting Psychologists Press, Inc., 3803 E. Bayshore Rd., Palo Alto, CA 94303.
*Notes:* For a related instrument, see A Survey of My Team Mates, Form MTM-C (18674).

The survey assesses the self-management processes of the team as a unit. Team members see how closely their individual evaluation of the team processes agrees with the average of the other members. The instrument consists of 71 items and is based on a 7-point rating scale with response options ranging from extremely small extent, never, or not at all to extremely high degree, always, or without fail. Respondents are to rate each item on the basis of how well they feel the team functions as it goes about its assigned duties. No technical data are provided. (TJS)

**18707**
**Course Planning Exploration for Program Self-Study.** National Center for Research to Improve Postsecondary Teaching and Learning, Ann Arbor, MI 1991.
*Descriptors:* *College Faculty; *Course Organization; Colleges; Higher Education; Administrators; Decision Making; Behavior Rating Scales
*Identifiers:* CPE; NCRIPTAL
*Availability:* National Center for Research to Improve Postsecondary Teaching and Learning, 2400 School of Education Bldg., University of Michigan, Ann Arbor, MI 48109-1259.

The self-report instrument is designed to help college faculty examine and discuss the assumptions they bring to course planning, an important role requiring expertise and effective decision making. College administrators may find the program useful as a way of understanding influences on course planning. The instrument explores issues of course planning among college faculty who teach in various undergraduate fields by focusing questions on a specific course that an instructor currently teaches. It is divided into 11 parts: your course; your program; your beliefs about education; your teaching field; influences on your course planning; sources of teaching assistance; selecting course content; establishing course goals and objectives; arranging course content; selecting learning activities; and personal data. The answer format varies; some parts are rating scales and some are answered yes or no. The tool is appropriate for use by program or department faculty, college administrators, or basic researhers. It takes about 45 to 60 minutes to complete. There are no norms since there are no right planning behaviors for college teachers. (TJS)

**18719**
**Profile of Aptitude for Leadership.** Training House, Inc., Princeton, NJ 1991.
*Descriptors:* *Profiles; *Leadership Styles; *Behavior Rating Scales; *Self Evaluation (Individuals); Adults; Work Environment; Organizational Climate; Employees
*Identifiers:* PAL
*Availability:* Training House, Inc., 100 Bear Brook Rd., P.O. Box 3090, Princeton, NJ 08543-3090.

The instrument identifies 4 styles of leadership and the ways in which leaders influence others and achieve goals, both in personal and organizational settings. The 4 styles are manager, supervisor, entrepreneur, and technician. Respondents have 6 points to assign to each set of statements that describe the behavior (values, perceptions, and actions) of leaders. These statements are presented in groups of 4. By rating statements about leadership behavior compared to one's own views, individuals will determine the degree to which each type of leadership contributes to their own style. Technical data are not provided. (TJS)

**18721**
**Empowerment Management Inventory.** Talico, Inc., Jacksonville Beach, FL 1992.
*Descriptors:* *Employer Employee Relationship; *Managerial Occupations; Adults; Questionnaires; Rating Scales
*Identifiers:* *Empowerment
*Availability:* Talico, Inc., 2320 S. Third St., Ste. 5, Jacksonville Beach, FL 32250.

This instrument measures the extent to which managers and supervisors are perceived to engage in meaningful empowerment related behavior with subordinates. Also, it evaluates whether or not these behaviors and practices occur under conditions that are supportive of empowerment programs. This is a bilevel instrument (manager or supervisor and subordinates). It contains 45 items and requires 20 to 30 minutes to complete.(BAE)

**18725**
**Role Conflict and Role Ambiguity Inventory.** Olk, Mary E.; Friedlander, Myrna L. 1992.
*Descriptors:* *Counselor Training; *Trainees; *Role Conflict; *Graduate Students; Rating Scales; Likert Scales; Expectation; Supervisors; Graduate Study; Higher Education
*Identifiers:* RCRAI; *Role Ambiguity
*Availability:* *Journal of Counseling Psychology*, v39 n3 p389-97, Jul 1992.

This scale was developed to assess the role conflict and role ambiguity experienced by counselor trainees who, in this capacity, are called on to perform multiple roles of student, trainee, counselor, client, and colleague. It contains a 19-item Role Ambiguity Scale which assesses trainees' uncertainty about supervisory expectations and how they will be evaluated by their supervisors, and a 10-item Role Conflict Scale which assesses experiences in which expectations associated with the role of student oppose those associated with the role of counselor and colleague. Students respond to items on a 5-point, Likert-type scale. Instrument may help supervisors become aware of trainees' experiences of role conflict and ambiguity so that they may teach trainees about the various roles and role expectations and alert them to problems that may result. Technical data are included. (klm)

**18733**
**Faculty at Work: A Survey of Motivations, Expectations, and Satisfactions.** Blackburn, Robert T.; Lawrence, Janet H. 1991.
*Descriptors:* *College Faculty; *Work Environment; *Motivation; *Teacher Attitudes; Postsecondary Education; Universities; Surveys; Questionnaires; Rating Scales; Self Concept; Self Efficacy; Job Satisfaction; Teaching Conditions; Performance Factors; Self Evaluation (Individuals); Adults
*Identifiers:* NCRIPTAL
*Availability:* National Center for Research to Improve Postsecondary Teaching and Learning, 2400 School of Education Bldg., University of Michigan, Ann Arbor, MI 48109-1259.

The questionnaire was designed to gather data to measure college or university faculty members' motivation process. The goals are to better understand why faculty members vary in their commitment to and involvement in teaching and to consider ways their knowledge can be used to improve post-secondary education. The instrument is divided into 6 sections: work environment on the respondents' campus; faculty members' self-image and professional activities; demographics and work satisfaction; teaching assumptions and performance evaluation; descriptions of a valued professor on their campus and comparison of themselves against that prototype; and work environment and its effects on respondents. The instrument enables groups or individuals to evaluate their personal fit within an organization and to consider how that fit affects faculty role performance. It can also be used to assess institutional progress toward long-term goals, such as creating a supportive climate for teaching. The format of the survey is a rating scale with a variety of response options. Technical data are provided. (TJS)

**18755**
**Manufacturing Engineering Certification Exam.** Society of Manufacturing Engineers, Dearborn, MI
*Descriptors:* *Certification; *Engineers; *Manufacturing; *Study Guides; *Occupational Tests; *Knowledge Level; Adults; Multiple Choice Tests; Computer Oriented Programs; Technology; Mathematics; Administration; Design Requirements; Quality Control; Economics
*Identifiers:* CMfgT; CMfgE
*Availability:* Society of Manufacturing Engineers, One SME Dr., P.O. Box 930, Dearborn, MI 48121-0930.
*Notes:* For a related instrument, see Fundamentals of Manufacturing Certification Exam (18756).

The instrument is a study guide designed to familiarize the candidate with topics that are included on the Manufacturing Engineering Certification Exam. The Manufacturing Certification program offers 2 different certifications. The first certification, which results in the designation of Certified Manufacturing Technologist (CMfgT), involves a 3-hour multiple-choice examination covering the fundamentals of manufacturing. Topics on this exam include mathematics/applied science; design; materials; manufacturing processes; management/economics; quality control; and computer applications/automation. The second certification confers the designation of Certified Manufacturing Engineer (CMfgE), and requires the passage of both the Fundamentals of Manufacturing Exam and the Manufacturing Engineering Certification exam. The Manufacturing Engineering Certification exam is divided into 2 sections. Section 1 consists of approximately 110 questions. Section 2 has 3 options, and each candidate is to select only 1. Each option has approximately 40 process-based questions covering integration and control, processes, and support operations. All candidates must pass both sections, in addition to the Fundamentals of Manufacturing Exam, to become certified. The Fundamentals Exam is waived for individuals who have a Professional Engineer's (PE) license. No technical data are provided. (TJS)

**18756**
**Fundamentals of Manufacturing Certification Exam.** Society of Manufacturing Engineers, Dearborn, MI
*Descriptors:* *Certification; *Engineers; *Manufacturing; *Study Guides; Adults; Multiple Choice Tests; Computer Oriented Programs; Quality Control; Design Requirements; Marketing; Safety; Drafting; Economics; Mathematics; Technology; Operating Engineering
*Identifiers:* CMfgE; CMfgT
*Availability:* Society of Manufacturing Engineers, One SME Dr., P.O. Box 930, Dearborn, MI 48121-0930.
*Notes:* For a related instrument, see Manufacturing Engineering Certification Exam (18755).

The instrument is a study guide designed to familiarize the candidate with topics that are included on the Manufacturing Engineering Certification Exam. The Manufacturing Certification program offers 2 different certifications. To obtain the status of Certified Manufacturing Technologist (CMfgT), a person must pass a 3-hour, multiple-choice examination covering the fundamentals of manufacturing. Topics on this exam include: mathematics/applied science; materials; drafting and engineering drawing; manufacturing processes; management/economics; quality control/quality assurance; and computer application/automation. To obtain the status of Certified Manufacturing Engineer (CmfgE), a person must pass the Fundamentals of Manufacturing exam and another multiple-choice examination covering the following topics: design and planning of tool and equipment; R&D of manufacturing processes; tools and equipment; design of systems; safety; design of facilities; management; methods functions; and marketing and distribution. The exam is designed for individuals with a minimum of 4 years of manufacturing-related education or 4 years of manufacturing-related work experience. Students with 2 years of manufacturing-related education are allowed to take the exam, but are expected to have more difficulty. No technical data are provided. (TJS)

**18759**
**The Small Business Test.** Ingram, Colin 1990.
*Descriptors:* *Entrepreneurship; *Business Administration; *Small Businesses; Rating Scales; Adults; Success
*Availability:* Guidance Centre, Ontario Institute for Studies in Education, 712 Gordon Baker Rd., Toronto, Ontario M2H 3R7, Canada.

The instrument is an assessment of entrepreneurial abilities. In the assessment, the reader takes on the role of the small business owner. Reactions to situations affecting the success of a business provide an honest appraisal of entrepreneurial skills. It brings together descriptions of many factors that are often overlooked—factors that contribute strongly to chances for success. The test is divided into 7 categories: personal characteristics, planning and organization, knowledge and experience, marketing, financial factors, location (wholesale & manufacturing only), and special skills for mail-order (for mail-order business only). The test describes the prime factors that will affect business. Some factors are about personality, habits, and skills. These factors require making judgments about oneself which may be highly subjective. The test is based on a 10-point rating scale with response options ranging from excellent to very poor. The respondent reads the description for each factor then assigns a grade from 0 to 10 for each. The score is related to results from real-life small businesses. No technical data are provided. (TJS)

**18801**
**Survey of Executive Leadership, Form C.** Connolly, Paul M.; And Others 1991.
*Descriptors:* *Rating Scales; *Leadership Qualities; *Work Environment
*Identifiers:* EXEC(C)
*Availability:* Consulting Psychologists Press, Inc., 3803 E. Bayshore Rd., Palo Alto, CA 94303.

**18810**
**My Leadership Practices.** George Truell Associates, Williamsville, NY 1992.
*Descriptors:* *Managerial Occupations; *Self Evaluation (Individuals); *Leadership Styles; Adults; Likert Scales
*Availability:* PAT Publications, P.O. Box 681, Buffalo, NY 14221.
*Notes:* See also My Manager's Leadership Practices (18811).

One of 2 instruments designed to help managers assess how effectively they help their staff lead themselves. The 5-point rating scale is for managers' self-evaluation and contains 30 items that cover 10 leadership practices: modeling, goal setting, positive thinking, fine tuning, positive reinforcement, supportive climate, self-analysis, self-administered rewards, innovation, and self-direction.(MH)

**18811**
**My Manager's Leadership Practices.** George Truell Associates, Williamsville, NY 1992.
*Descriptors:* *Managerial Occupations; *Leadership Styles; Adults; Likert Scales
*Availability:* PAT Publications, P.O. Box 681, Buffalo, NY 14221.
*Notes:* See also My Leadership Practices (18810)

One of 2 learning instruments designed to help managers assess how effectively they help their staff lead themselves. This 5-point rating scale is used by employees to rate their managers on 30 items that cover 10 leadership practices: modeling, goal setting, positive thinking, fine tuning, positive reinforcement, supportive climate, self-analysis, self-administered rewards, innovation, and self-direction. (MH)

**18816**
**Here's How I See Our Organization.** George Truell Associates, Williamsville, NY
*Descriptors:* *Employees; *Attitude Measures; *Organizational Climate; Likert Scales; Adults
*Availability:* PAT Publications, P.O. Box 681, Buffalo, NY 14221.

The instrument is designed to help staff identify management's current operating style. The description of the working environment reflects the way an organization is being managed. There are 16 questions and the instrument is based on the the work of Rensis Likert who identified 4 kinds of managerial style: autocratic, benevolent authoritative, consultative, and fully participative. (MH)

**18821**
**Co-worker Involvement Index, Revised.** Rusch, Frank R.; McNair, Jeff 1989.
*Descriptors:* *Employees; *Peer Relationship; Adults; Job Performance
*Availability:* Frank R. Rusch, University of Illinois at Urbana-Champaign, Transition Research Institute, 61 Children's Research Center, 51 Gerty Dr., Champaign, IL 61820.
*Notes:* An earlier version, entitled Co-worker Involvement Instrument, can be found in *Career Development for Exceptional Individuals;* v5 n1 p23-36, Spr 1992.

The index assesses the extent to which coworkers are involved with supported employees at specific job placements. The index allows employment training specialists and job supervisors to estimate coworker involvement with employees after job placement. It is based on research that assumes coworker involvement enhances job performance as a result of social interactions between supported employees and their coworkers. The 9 areas assessed are: physical integration, social integration, training, associating (frequency), associating (appropriateness), befriending, advocating, evaluating, and giving information. Technical data are available. (MH)

**19068**
**Campbell-Hallam Team Development Survey.** Hallam, Glenn; Campbell, David 1992.
*Descriptors:* *Rating Scales; *Teamwork; *Organizational Development; Adults
*Identifiers:* TD
*Availability:* NCS Assessments, P.O. Box 1416, Minneapolis, MN 55440.

The survey contains 93 items on a 6-point rating scale and is designed for use by teams of 3 to 10 people to assess the perceptions of the team members regarding the strengths and weaknesses of the team. The survey serves the following purposes: to stimulate a focused discussion about the team's strengths and weaknesses; to help the team identify, acknowledge, and address its problems; to give team members an opportunity to share their ideas; to help team leaders compare their perceptions with those of the team members; to help the team see how it is perceived by outside observers, such as clients; to pinpoint areas to be addressed in future team development activities; and to collect benchmark data to track future team progress. (MH)

**19127**
**Campbell Organizational Survey.** Campbell, David 1990.
*Descriptors:* *Job Satisfaction; *Attitude Measures; *Work Attitudes; Work Environment; Adults
*Identifiers:* COS; Campbell Work Orientations; CW
*Availability:* National Computer Systems, Inc., P.O. Box 1416, Minneapolis, MN 55440.
*Notes:* See also Campbell Leadership Index (19128).

This short survey is designed to collect information about an individual's feelings of satisfaction or frustration with various aspects of work, such as supervision, pay, coworkers, or support for innovation. It is a component of the Campbell Work Orientations (CWO), a collection of surveys focusing on the psychological aspects of the working environment. The survey is intended for use in educational institutions, human resource departments, training and development programs, and individual counseling and therapy. It is an attitude survey and a job satisfaction questionnaire that provides a personal profile for each respondent, as well as summary statistics. Thirteen scales are included: The Work Itself; Working Conditions; Freedom from Stress; Co-Workers; Supervision; Top Leadership; Pay; Benefits; Job Security; Promotional Opportunities; Feedback/Communications; Organizational Planning; and Support for Innovation. Reliability and validity data are provided. (JW)

**19128**
**Campbell Leadership Index.** Campbell, David 1991.
*Descriptors:* *Leadership Qualities; Self Evaluation (Individuals); Adults; Rating Scales
*Identifiers:* CLI; Campbell Work Orientations; CW
*Availability:* National Computer Systems, Inc., P.O. Box 1416, Minneapolis, MN 55440.
*Notes:* See also Campbell Organizational Survey (19127).

This is an adjective checklist designed to be used in the assessment of leadership characteristics. It has 100 adjectives listed in alphabetical order, each with a definition ranging from "Active—In motion, on the go," to "Witty—Clever and amusing with words". Respondents are asked to indicate on a 6-point scale ranging from Always to Never how descriptive each adjective is of them. Three to 5 observers also are asked to rate each respondent using the same 100 adjectives and the same scale. The resulting profile shows the comparison on 5 orientations: leadership, energy, affability, dependability, and resilience. It is a component of the Campbell Work Orientations (CWO), a collection of surveys focusing on the psychological aspects of the working environment. Reliability and validity data are provided. (JW)

**19132**
**Career Preference Scale.** Tagliaferri, Louis E. 1987.
*Descriptors:* *Forced Choice Technique; *Employees; *Career Choice; Adults; Career Counseling; Job Applicants; Self Evaluation (Individuals)
*Identifiers:* CP
*Availability:* Talico, Inc., 2320 S. Third St., Ste. 5, Jacksonville Beach, FL 32250.

The scale helps employees to assess career interests, goals, needs, and values in 4 major areas: work environment preference, position preference, growth aspiration, and career introspection. It consists of 4 sets of 10 paired comparisons, a total of 80 single items, in which the respondent must make a career values preference choice, and then rank order the top 5 choices in each set. The instrument may be self-administered or administered by a facilitator. It takes approximately 20 minutes to complete. There is also a semistructured section in which employees give additional information about career goals, development needs, and career planning strategies. The scale is designed to help both employers and employees, including job applicants, achieve the best possible person-job match and respect an individual's preference for a variety of job-related conditions. (MH)

**19135**
**Employee Assistance Program Inventory.** Anton, William D.; Reed, James R. 1994.
*Descriptors:* *Screening Tests; *Employees; *Adult Counseling; *Psychological Patterns; *Employee Assistance Programs; Adults; Norm Referenced Tests
*Identifiers:* EAP
*Availability:* Psychological Assessment Resources, Inc., P.O. Box 998, Odessa, FL 33556.

The inventory was designed as an intake or screening tool for use by professionals in employee assistance programs who provide counseling and other services to adult workers. Use of the inventory makes it possible to identify employees' psychological problems and can be used as a basis for appropriate referrals or short-term interventions. The inventory covers 10 problem domains: anxiety, depression, self-esteem problems, marital problems, family problems, external stressors, interpersonal conflict, work adjustment, problem minimization, and effects of substance abuse. There are 120 items in the 4-point scale, which takes approximately 20 minutes to complete. The test was standardized and validated for use with employed adults aged 18 and over. (MH)

**800222**
**ACER Higher Test WL-WQ.** Australian Council for Educational Research, Victoria, Australia 1982.
*Descriptors:* *Adults; *Career Guidance; *College Students; *Intelligence Tests; *Secondary School Students; Abstract Reasoning; Academic Ability; Adolescents; Cognitive Ability; Cognitive Measurement; Foreign Countries; Higher Education; Intelligence; Secondary Education; Vocational Aptitude
*Identifiers:* Australia
*Availability:* Australian Council for Educational Research, P.O. Box 210, Hawthorn, Victoria 3122, Australia.
*Notes:* See also ACER Higher Test ML-MQ (Second Edition) (800198). Time, 60 approx. Items, 72.

Designed to measure general intellectual ability for use in vocational guidance of adolescents and adults. The linguistic section consists of items, such as analogies, classifications, proverbs, and logical reasoning. The quantitative section consists of items concerning number series, number matrices, and arithmetical reasoning questions. Form W was produced as a parallel form of Form M (800198).

**800244**
**Work Aspect Preference Scale.** Pryor, Robert G.L. 1983.
*Descriptors:* *Adults; *College Students; *High School Students; *Interest Inventories; *Vocational Interests; *Work Attitudes; Career Guidance; Foreign Countries; Higher Education; High Schools; Work Environment
*Identifiers:* Australia; WAPS
*Availability:* Australian Council for Educational Research, P.O. Box 210, Hawthorn, Victoria 3122, Australia.
*Notes:* Time, 15 approx. Items, 52.

Designed to assess respondent's degree of preference for 13 qualities of work. Developed for use in vocational counseling to stimulate the exploration of preferences in relation to work and to provide relevant data for vocational counselor. May be used with high school and college students, adults, and with individual with disabilities as an aid in rehabilitating them for work.

**800259**
**Career Development Inventory—Australia.** Lokan, Jan 1984.
*Descriptors:* *Career Development; *Career Education; *Career Exploration; *Secondary Education; *Self Evaluation (Individuals); Attitude Measures; Career Guidance; Decision Making; Foreign Countries; Knowledge Level; Questionnaires; Secondary School Students
*Identifiers:* Australia; CDI(A)
*Availability:* Australian Council for Educational Research, P.O. Box 210, Hawthorn, Victoria 3122, Australia.
*Notes:* Time, 40 approx. Items, 92.

The Career Development Inventory—Australia (CDI-A) is a questionnaire designed to assess a range of behaviors that are relevant to the process of making appropriate career decisions, including both attitudes and cognitive skills. It is most appropriately used with secondary students in grades 8-11, but in particular circumstances, it may be used with younger or older students, and with adolescents who have left school. The instrument is intended primarily as an aid to career teachers, advisors, and counselors. It assesses students' career planning progress, readiness for exploratory experiences, and decision-making skills in the following 4 areas: Career Planning (CP), Career Exploration (CE), World of Work Information (WW), and Career Decision Making (DM). An Occupational Group Preference Form is on the back of the answer sheet. It has a list of 100 jobs arranged in 20 groups and asks the students to check jobs they might like when they go to work. Most students can complete both the CDI-A and Occupational Group Preference Form in the typical 40-minute class period.

**800290**
**Personnel Selection Testing Program.** Australian Council for Educational Research, Victoria, Australia 1987.
*Descriptors:* *Aptitude Tests; *Clerical Occupations; *Personnel Selection; *Semiskilled Occupations; *Vocational Aptitude; Adults; Apprenticeships; Foreign Countries
*Identifiers:* Australia; GATB; General Aptitude Test Battery; PSTP; Test Batteries
*Availability:* Australian Council for Educational Research, P.O. Box 210, Hawthorn, Victoria 3122, Australia.

Secure testing program offered by the Australian Council for Educational Research. Australian adaptation of the paper-and-pencil tests from the U.S. Department of Labor's General Aptitude Test Battery (GATB). There are 4 tests used for the selection of clerical personnel: vocabulary, arithmetic, arithmetic reasoning, and name comparison. The following 5 tests are a battery used to select trade apprentices: 3-dimensional space, figure matching, shape matching, mark making, and ACER Mathematics Test E (which is a non-GATB test and is being revised). This testing program is still in the developmental stages and will be subject to continuing revision.

**800292**
**Self-Directed Search, Australian Edition.** Holland, John L. 1988.
*Descriptors:* *Career Counseling; *Interest Inventories; *Vocational Interests; Adolescents; Adults; Foreign Countries; Older Adults; Self Evaluation (Individuals)
*Identifiers:* Australia; Holland (John L); RIASEC; SDS
*Availability:* Australian Council for Educational Research Ltd., P.O. Box 210, Hawthorn, Victoria 3122, Australia.
*Notes:* Time, 50. Items, 228.

This Australian version has been amended to alter spellings and language to conform to Australian usage. Scores are matched to occupations listed in the *Australian Standard Classification of Occupations Dictionary (ASCO).* The test itself is a self-administered, self-scoring, self-interpreted vocational counseling tool. The respondent indicates interest in activities encountered in a variety of occupations. Based on John L. Holland's RIASEC theory categorizing jobs as realistic, investigative, artistic, social, enterprising, and conventional.

**800319**
**Occupational English Test.** McNamara, T.F. 1990.
*Descriptors:* *English; *Health Occupations; *Health Personnel; *Language Proficiency; *Language Tests; *Occupational Tests; *Reading Comprehension; *Writing Ability; Adults; Foreign Countries; Listening Comprehension Tests
*Identifiers:* Australia; COPQ; DEET; NOOSR
*Availability:* T.F. McNamara, Applied Linguistics, University of Melbourne, Parkville, Victoria 3052, Australia.

An English language proficiency test taken by overseas-trained health professionals who are currently entering Australia. This measure is part of a 3-stage process of registration for practice in Australia, after an initial verification of documentation. Its development and administration are handled by the Council for Overseas Professional Qualifications (COPQ), which is an expanded version of the National Office for Overseas Skills Recognition (NOOSR), part of the Commonwealth Government's Department of Employment, Education and Training. The remaining 2 stages of registration are: profession-specific pencil-and-paper tests of professional clinical knowledge; and practical clinical tests of professional competence. Time allowed for each test varies.

**800324**
**ACER Test of Employment Entry Mathematics.** Izard, John; And Others 1992.
*Descriptors:* *Mathematics Tests; *Trainees; *Apprenticeships; *Personnel Selection; Adults; Foreign Countries; Mathematics Skills; Occupational Tests; Employment Qualifications
*Identifiers:* TEEM; Australia
*Availability:* Australian Council for Educational Research, P.O. Box 210, Hawthorn, Victoria 3122, Australia.

This is a group test of basic mathematical ability. This test contains 32 multiple-choice items and has a 25-minute time limit. It is designed for use in the selection of apprentices, trainees, and any other technical and trades personnel who need to use basic mathematics to perform their work. Technical data are included.(BAE)

**800326**
**ACER Short Clerical Test, Form D.** Australian Council for Educational Research, Victoria, Australia 1982.
*Descriptors:* *Clerical Occupations; *Occupational Tests; *Aptitude Tests; *Personnel Selection; Adults; Arithmetic; Visual Acuity; Foreign Countries
*Identifiers:* Australia
*Availability:* Australian Council for Educational Research Ltd., Radford House, Frederick St., Hawthorn, Victoria 3211, Australia.
*Notes:* See ACER Short Clerical Test, Form C (800325) and ACER Short Clerical Test, Form E (800327) for related tests. Time, 10. Items, 165.

Designed to measure 2 aspects of aptitude for routine clerical work, verbal and numerical. Test 1 consists of 105 item pairs containing copy and original. Candidates are required to check the copy against the original for accuracy in a 5-minute checking test. Speed and accuracy in perception of similarities in verbal and numerical material are important in most routine clerical positions that require the maintenance of accurate records. In Test 2, a 5-minute arithmetic test is given to measure competence in routine calculations. Consists of 60 items requiring addition and subtraction of 2- and 3-digit numbers; addition and subtraction of sums of money; and addition, subtraction, multiplication, and division of numbers and money. Test is found most useful in the selection of staff for routine clerical positions. May be useful as an aid in vocational counseling to assess aptitude for clerical work. May be administered individually or in groups. Two parallel forms of the test, Form A and Form B (800062), were originally developed. With the introduction of decimal currency in Australia in 1966, this made it necessary to rewrite several test items. As a result, Form C replaced the 2 original forms. In 1979, a *Revised Manual* was published that included norms based on data collected from the years 1977 to 1979 from results of a variety of occupational groups and job applicants. Two new alternative forms, Form D and Form E, were developed to replicate Form C in content and presentation.

**800327**
**ACER Short Clerical Test, Form E.** Australian Council for Educational Research, Victoria, Australia 1982.
*Descriptors:* *Clerical Occupations; *Occupational Tests; *Aptitude Tests; *Personnel Selection; Adults; Visual Acuity; Foreign Countries; Arithmetic
*Identifiers:* Australia
*Availability:* Australian Council for Educational Research Ltd., Radford House, Frederick St., Hawthorn, Victoria 3122, Australia.
*Notes:* See ACER Short Clerical Test, Form C (800325) and ACER Short Clerical Test, Form D (800326) for related tests.

Designed to measure 2 aspects of aptitude for routine clerical work, verbal and numerical. Test 1 consists of 105 item pairs containing copy and original. Candidates are required to check the copy against the original for accuracy in a 5-minute checking test. Speed and accuracy in perception of similarities in verbal and numerical material are important in most routine clerical positions that require the maintenance of accurate records. In Test 2, a 5-minute arithmetic test is given to measure competence in routine calculations. Consists of 60 items requiring addition and subtraction of 2- and 3-digit numbers; addition and subtraction of sums of money; addition, subtraction, multiplication, and division of numbers and money. Test is found most useful in the selection of staff for routine clerical positions. May be useful as an aid in vocational counseling to assess aptitude for clerical work. May be administered individually or in groups. Two parallel forms of the test, Form A and Form B (800062), were originally developed. With the introduction of decimal currrency in Australia in 1966, this made it necessary to rewrite several test items. As a result, Form C replaced the 2 original forms. In 1979, a *Revised Manual* was published that included norms based on data collected from the years 1977 to 1979 from results of a variety of occupational group and job applicants. Two new alternative forms, Form D and Form E were developed to replicate Form C in content and presentation. (TJS)

**810508**
**The Career Problem Check List.** Crowley, A.D. 1983.
*Descriptors:* *Adolescents; *Career Counseling; *Career Planning; Check Lists; College Students; Foreign Countries; Secondary School Students
*Identifiers:* CPCL; England
*Availability:* NFER-Nelson Publishing Co., Darville House, 2 Oxford Rd. East, Windsor, Berkshire SL4 1DF, England.
*Notes:* Time, 15 approx. Items, 100.

Developed to help career counselors rapidly identify the problems that secondary school or college students are experiencing in making career plans. The checklist covers 7 general areas of concern: problems at school or college, making decisions, concerns at home, obtaining specific occupational information, applying for a job or course, starting work, and facing problems outside work. May be used to identify student needs prior to a guidance interview, in the planning stages of a career program, as a discussion aid on career-related topics, or to monitor the impact of a career program.

**810528**
**General Occupational Interest Inventory.** Holdsworth, Ruth; Cramp, Lisa 1982.
*Descriptors:* *Interest Inventories; *Semiskilled Occupations; *Supervisors; *Vocational Interests; Adolescents; Adults; Career Counseling; Dropouts; Foreign Countries; Personnel Selection
*Identifiers:* England; Great Britain
*Availability:* Saville and Holdsworth, Ltd., Test Sales Department, Management Centre, Woodstock Lane North, Long Ditton, Surrey KT6 5HN, England.
*Notes:* Time, 40 approx. Items, 216.

Designed as an interest inventory for school dropouts and those with average educational attainment. Includes activities suitable for semiskilled to supervisory level occupations. Untimed inventory that should take between 20 to 40 minutes to complete. Suitable for use in business, industry, and education and also for such purposes as vocational guidance, career counseling and planning, job relocation, retirement counseling, and for organizational decision making in employee selection and placement.

**810529**
**Advanced Occupational Interest Inventory.** Holdsworth, Ruth; Cramp, Lisa 1982.
*Descriptors:* *Interest Inventories; *Managerial Occupations; *Professional Occupations; *Skilled Occupations; *Vocational Interests; Adolescents; Adults; Career Counseling; Dropouts; Foreign Countries; Personnel Selection; Supervisors
*Identifiers:* England; Great Britain
*Availability:* Saville and Holdsworth, Ltd., Test Sales Department, Management Centre, Woodstock Lane North, Long Ditton, Surrey KT6 5HN, England.
*Notes:* Time, 40 approx. Items, 228.

Designed as a vocational interest inventory for adults and school leavers (dropouts) with higher educational attainments. Includes activities in 19 job categories ranging from skilled and supervisory jobs up to professional and managerial levels. Inventory is untimed but should take between 20 to 40 minutes to complete. Suitable for use in business, industry, and education and for such purposes as vocational guidance, career planning, job relocation, retirement counseling, and for organizational decision making in employee selection and placement.

**810530**
**Critical Reasoning Test Battery.** Nyfield, Gill; And Others 1983.
*Descriptors:* *Abstract Reasoning; *Cognitive Tests; *Logical Thinking; *Problem Solving; Administrator Selection; Adolescents; Adults; Career Choice; Foreign Countries; Student Evaluation; Student Placement
*Identifiers:* CRTB; England; Great Britain; Test Batteries
*Availability:* Saville and Holdsworth, Ltd., Test Sales Department, Management Centre, Woodstock Lane North, Long Ditton, Surrey KT6 5HN, England.
*Notes:* Time, 80. Items, 140.

Contains 3 reasoning tests that may be used in education, commerce and industry, and development of students and employees over the age of 15. Appropriate for use with a range of individuals from school dropouts to academic students to junior managers or supervisors in industry. May be used to help students decide on courses of study, to assist them in reaching career decisions, or for employee selection in companies where higher reasoning skills are necessary for certain jobs. May also be used for assessment and guidance within a company. The verbal evaluation section measures the ability to understand and evaluate the logic of various kinds of arguments. The interpreting data section measures the ability to make correct decisions or inferences from numerical or statistical data presented as tables or diagrams. The diagrammatic series assesses reasoning with diagrams and requires subject to discover logical rules governing sequences occurring in rows of symbols and diagrams. Each subtest may be administered alone or the entire test may be given.

**810585**
**Graduate and Managerial Assessment.** The Hatfield Polytechnic, England Psychometric Research Unit, Hertfordshire, England 1985.
*Descriptors:* *Aptitude Tests; *Managerial Occupations; *Personnel Selection; *Professional Personnel; *Promotion (Occupational); Adults; Foreign Countries; Multiple Choice Tests
*Identifiers:* England; GMA; Great Britain
*Availability:* NFER-Nelson Publishing Co., Darville House, 2 Oxford Rd. East, Windsor, Berkshire SL4 1DF, England.

Intended for use in the recruitment, selection, and assessment of college graduates; the identification of management and promotion potential; and the recruitment of individuals who may be capable of entering higher education. There are 3 test areas: numerical, verbal, and abstract. Each of the tests has been designed on the basis of a separate set of specific objectives. The numerical section can be used to assess graduates in general disciplines for finance-related occupations. The verbal section is applicable in selecting and assessing candidates for occupations that involve the critical appraisal of verbal material. The abstract section was designed to deemphasize educational attainment and to assess skills, such as fluid intelligence, divergent thinking, induction, and other cognitive skills. The tests come in 2 forms.

**810602**
**Tests in Arithmetic.** Associated Examining Board, Surrey, England 1986.
*Descriptors:* *Achievement Tests; *Adolescents; *Arithmetic; *Job Applicants; Adults; Foreign Countries; Mathematics Tests; Personnel Selection
*Identifiers:* England; Great Britain
*Availability:* Associated Examining Board, Stag Hill House, Guildford, Surrey GU2 5XJ, England.

Developed to give specific evidence of the numerical ability of young people seeking employment. Provides a measure of attainment for young people in a form that prospective employers find useful. There are 2 tests. The basic arithmetic test provides a basic qualification in arithmetic for those about to leave school. It may also be used to measure achievement of the less able in schools and for those adolescents and adults studying basic arithmetic in education colleges. The proficiency in arithmetic test is a more challenging test than the basic arithmetic test and is used for students in schools and colleges who want this type of qualification.

**810603**
**Tests in Basic English, Revised.** Associated Examining Board, Surrey, England 1985.
*Descriptors:* *Achievement Tests; *Adolescents; *English; *Job Applicants; Adults; Foreign Countries; Listening Comprehension; Personnel Selection; Reading Comprehension; Writing Skills
*Identifiers:* England; Great Britain
*Availability:* Associated Examining Board, Stag Hill House, Guildford, Surrey GU2 5XJ, England.
*Notes:* Time, 85.

Tests are designed to assess transferable skills that enable individuals to get the most out of further training or education or to be more successful in their early years of employment. Can also be used as a measure of achievement for students in schools and for adolescents and adults studying basic English in other courses of training. The test assesses the ability to communicate in written form; to read, understand, and make use of data in a wide variety of forms; and to listen to and understand information and requests presented orally. There is a 25-minute listening exercise and a 60-minute written paper.

**810604**
**Test in Basic Graphicacy.** Associated Examining Board, Surrey, England 1985.
*Descriptors:* *Achievement Tests; *Adolescents; *Graphs; *Job Applicants; Adults; Foreign Countries; Personnel Selection; Visual Aids
*Identifiers:* England; Great Britain
*Availability:* Associated Examining Board, Stag Hill House, Guildford, Surrey GU2 5XJ, England.
*Notes:* Time, 90.

Designed to assess transferable skills that allow individuals to get the most out of further training or education or to be more successful in their early years of employment. Test covers a number of subject areas and assesses the ability to communicate in graphic form. Covers knowledge and understanding of signs and symbols, information and numerical data represented in graphical form, diagrammatic forms commonly used to represent planned sequences, and methods of representing 3-dimensional objects in 2 dimensions.

**810605**
**Tests in Life Skills.** Associated Examining Board, Surrey, England 1985.
*Descriptors:* *Achievement Tests; *Adolescents; *Daily Living Skills; *Job Applicants; Adults; Foreign Countries; Personnel Selection
*Identifiers:* England; Great Britain
*Availability:* Associated Examining Board, Stag Hill House, Guildford, Surrey GU2 5XJ, England.
*Notes:* Time, 90.

Designed to assess transferable skills that enable individuals to get the most out of further training or education and to be more successful in their early years of employment. This test has been developed to enable teachers to design their own social and life skills teaching around a core content. Topics covered on the test include life-style, money management, looking after oneself, and rights and responsibilites. The test assesses individuals' knowledge and ability to apply that knowledge, understand information, and make informed decisions.

**810606**
**Basic Test in Computer Awareness.** Associated Examining Board, Surrey, England 1985.
*Descriptors:* *Achievement Tests; *Adolescents; *Computer Literacy; *Job Applicants; Adults; Foreign Countries; Personnel Selection
*Identifiers:* England; Great Britain
*Availability:* Associated Examining Board, Stag Hill House, Guildford, Surrey GU2 5XJ, England.
*Notes:* Time, 90.

Designed to assess transferable skills that will enable individuals to get the most out of further education or training and to be more successful in the early years of employment. Some practical work with computers is necessary in order to take the test which covers the ability to demonstrate knowledge of the uses and limitations of computers; to understand current trends in information technology and its economic and social implications; to understand what computer systems are; and to understand what a simple program is and why it works.

**810630**
**Management Interest Inventory.** Saville and Holdsworth, Surrey, England 1987.
*Descriptors:* *Administrators; *Interest Inventories; *Managerial Occupations; *Vocational Interests; Adults; Foreign Countries; Occupational Tests; Professional Occupations; Self Evaluation (Individuals)
*Identifiers:* England; Great Britain
*Availability:* Saville and Holdsworth, Ltd., Test Sales Department, Management Centre, Woodstock Lane North, Long Ditton, Surrey KT6 5HN, England.
*Notes:* Time, 40 approx. Items, 144.

A rating scale designed to assist both organizations and individuals in making decisions relating to selection, placement, and career development at the management level. Also suitable for individuals just moving into management, such as supervisors or graduate trainees. Questions in the inventory have been compiled from an analysis of some 250 management job descriptions obtained from 19 companies. They are designed to provide a structured approach to establishing preferences for a series of 12 management functions (such as sales, finance, and personnel), and 12 management skills (such as organizing and directing). In addition, the inventory produces a summary of self-reported experience across various functions and skills.

**810676**
**Edinburgh Questionnaires.** Raven, John 1982.
*Descriptors:* *Job Satisfaction; *Motivation; *Organizational Climate; Adults; Behavior Patterns; Foreign Countries; Interpersonal Relationship; Occupational Information; Occupational Tests; Problems; Values; Work Environment
*Identifiers:* Great Britain; Scotland
*Availability:* H.K. Lewis, 136 Gower St., London WC1E 6BS, England.

This measure of personal interest and organizational climate uses the Value-Expectancy-Instrumentality Theory to measure motivation. Said to identify a problem or behavior important to an employee, determine the consequences the employee anticipates in tackling the problem or engaging in the behavior, and the value attached to each consequence. Thus, it measures the motivation to engage in the behavior. Respondents write sentences concerned with their specific work problems or behaviors.

**810677**
**Basic Skills Tests.** Smith, Pauline; Whetton, Chris 1988.
*Descriptors:* *Achievement Tests; *Basic Skills; *Literacy; *Mathematics Skills; *Personnel Evaluation; *Personnel Selection; *Screening Tests; Adults; Arithmetic; Estimation (Mathematics); Foreign Countries; Mathematical Applications; Reading Comprehension; Writing Skills
*Identifiers:* England; Great Britain
*Availability:* NFER-Nelson Publishing Co., Darville House, 2 Oxford Rd. East, Windsor, Berkshire SL4 1DF, England.

Developed mainly for use in the initial screening of new trainees or employees, in situations where academic qualifications may not be available or may be absent. Can be used for employee selection for lower-level positions or for screening individuals who need remedial help or training. Consists of 2 tests: literacy and numeracy. The literacy test measures reading comprehension and information-seeking and writing ability (optional). The numeracy test covers calculating, approximating, and problem solving. Some of the major uses of the test are screening applications for a job or course, identifying individuals' training needs, doing pre- and postevaluations, and providing background information for individuals in the process of self-assessment.

**810678**
**Occupational Stress Indicator.** Cooper, Cary; And Others 1988.
*Descriptors:* *Administrators; *Managerial Occupations; *Occupational Tests; *Organizational Climate; *Stress Variables; *Supervisors; Adults; Behavior Patterns; Coping; Employees; Foreign Countries; Job Satisfaction; Physical Health; Questionnaires; Type A Behavior
*Identifiers:* England; Great Britain; OSI
*Availability:* NFER-Nelson Publishing Co., Darville House, 2 Oxford Rd. East, Windsor, Berkshire SL4 1DF, England.
*Notes:* Time, 40.

This 7-part series of questionnaires is designed to assist an organization in measuring sources of stress within the organization and quantifying stress-related factors, such as lack of employee commitment, poor company culture, and poor interpersonal relations. Can be taken by managers at all levels in any department. Points out the need for corporate training, company restructuring, and/or stress management programs. Scoring reveals individual characteristics leading to stress, including Type A and other behavior; coping styles and methods; job satisfaction; and physical and mental ill health. A group profile is prepared to quantify results.

**810679**
**Computer Commands.** Nfer Nelson Publishing Co., Windsor, England 1987.
*Descriptors:* *Aptitude Tests; *Computers; *Data Processing; *Data Processing Occupations; *Occupational Tests; *Personnel Selection; *Word Processing; Adults; Clerical Occupations; Foreign Countries; Simulation
*Identifiers:* England; Great Britain
*Availability:* NFER-Nelson Publishing Co., Darville House, 2 Oxford Rd. East, Windsor, Berkshire SL4 1DF, England.
*Notes:* See also Computer Rules (810680). Time, 20. Items, 34.

Designed to measure aptitude for learning word processing software or general aptitude for learning to work with computers. Test taker must understand a given set of commands that will be used to alter a table consisting of 2 grids divided into cells that contain letters. Test taker determines how the grids differ, then chooses commands from a given set that would make the change. Norms are provided on a sample of 580 college students in Great Britain. Reliability and validity are discussed. Users are encouraged to develop their own norms.

**810680**
**Computer Rules.** Nfer Nelson Publishing Co., Windsor, England 1987.
*Descriptors:* *Aptitude Tests; *Data Processing; *Data Processing Occupations; *Occupational Tests; *Personnel Selection; Adults; Clerical Occupations; Computers; Foreign Countries; Simulation; Word Processing
*Identifiers:* England; Great Britain
*Availability:* NFER-Nelson Publishing Co., Darville House, 2 Oxford Rd. East, Windsor, Berkshire SL4 1DF, England.
*Notes:* See also Computer Commands (810679).

Designed to measure aptitude for those entering employment or training in occupations where computers are used as basic operational tools. For use in selection of employees who will use computers or word processing equipment. Involves items that require the test taker to follow or infer rules of use. Normed on a sample of university students in computer science classes or interacting with computers. Publisher advises the user to develop local norms.

**810683**
**Modern Occupational Skills Tests: Decision Making.** Blinkhorn, Steve 1989.
*Descriptors:* *Clerical Occupations; *Critical Thinking; *Decision Making Skills; *Occupational Tests; *Office Occupations; *Office Practice; *Personnel Selection; *Problem Solving; *Recruitment; Adults; Foreign Countries; Office Management
*Identifiers:* England; Great Britain; MOS
*Availability:* NFER-Nelson Publishing Co., Darville House, 2 Oxford Rd. East, Windsor, Berkshire SL4 1DF, England.
*Notes:* See also Modern Occupational Skills Tests (810684 through 810691). Time, 15. Items, 24.

The MOS Tests offer a wide range of assessments designed to help human resource professionals recruit and develop staff in clerical, secretarial, and administrative posts, and junior management. Flexibility is a key feature to this series, so a wide range of assessments covering different types of job content at varying levels of difficulty is provided. The tests should help employers to identify individuals who will make the most effective use of their knowledge. There are 9 tests in the series: verbal checking, numerical checking, technical checking, numerical awareness, numerical estimation, spelling and grammar, word meanings, filing, and decision making. The MOS Tests are speed tests. The most difficult of all MOS Tests is the Decision Making Test, which is designed to assess the ability to understand and apply rules, regulations, and criteria in choosing between options. Subjects must be able to understand instructions, make categorization and coding decisions, and do simple calculations. Useful in occupations that require planning, scheduling and dealing with client claims, such as insurance and claim clerks, office supervisors, junior officers managers, and higher level secretaries.

**810684**
**Modern Occupational Skills Tests: Filing.** Blinkhorn, Steve 1989.
*Descriptors:* *Clerical Occupations; *Filing; *Occupational Tests; *Office Occupations; *Office Practice; *Personnel Selection; *Recruitment; Adults; File Clerks; Foreign Countries; Office Management
*Identifiers:* England; Great Britain; MOS
*Availability:* NFER-Nelson Publishing Co., Darville House, 2 Oxford Rd. East, Windsor, Berkshire SL4 1DF, England.
*Notes:* See also Modern Occupational Skills Tests (810683 through 810691). Time, 12. Items, 100.

The MOS Tests offer a wide range of assessments designed to help human resource professionals recruit and develop staff in clerical, secretarial, and administrative posts, and junior management. Flexibility is a key feature to this series, so a wide range of assessments covering different types of job content at varying levels of difficulty is provided. The tests should help employers to identify individuals who will make the most effective use of their knowledge. There are 9 tests in the series: verbal checking, numerical checking, technical checking, numerical awareness, numerical estimation, spelling and grammar, word meanings, filing, and decision making. The MOS Tests are speed tests. Filing measures the ability to put records in the correct place in files that are organized using a variety of systems. Alphabetical and numerical are the 2 basic filing methods used, and all follow the normal rules of filing. This is an attainment test and is most applicable in the recruitment of inexperienced staff for occupations involving filing and recording tasks.

**810685**
**Modern Occupational Skills Tests: Numerical Awareness.** Blinkhorn, Steve 1989.
*Descriptors:* *Arithmetic; *Clerical Occupations; *Computation; *Occupational Tests; *Office Occupations; *Office Practice; *Personnel Selection; *Recruitment; Adults; Foreign Countries; Office Management
*Identifiers:* England; Great Britain; MOS
*Availability:* NFER-Nelson Publishing Co., Darville House, 2 Oxford Rd. East, Windsor, Berkshire SL4 1DF, England.
*Notes:* See also Modern Occupational Skills Tests (810683 through 810691). Time, 8. Items, 18.

The MOS Tests offer a wide range of assessments designed to help human resource professionals recruit and develop staff in clerical, secretarial, and administrative posts, and junior management. Flexibility is a key feature to this series, so a wide range of assessments covering different types of job content at varying levels of difficulty is provided. The tests should help employers to identify individuals who will make the most effective use of their knowledge. There are 9 tests in the series: verbal checking, numerical checking, technical checking, numerical awareness, numerical estimation, spelling and grammar, word meanings, filing, and decision making. The MOS Tests are speed tests. Numerical Awareness is designed for the detection of computational errors and their correction. It is designed to test arithmetic skills in various work settings, and requires skill in addition, subtraction, multiplication, division, an understanding of percentage, and the ability to work with fractions and the concept of time. Useful in occupations such as accounts clerks, bank clerks, stock controllers, and cashiers.

**810686**
**Modern Occupational Skills Tests: Numerical Checking.** Blinkhorn, Steve 1989.
*Descriptors:* *Clerical Occupations; *Numbers; *Occupational Tests; *Office Occupations; *Office Practice; *Personnel Selection; *Recruitment; Adults; Foreign Countries; Office Management; Error Patterns
*Identifiers:* England; Great Britain; MOS; Numerical Checking
*Availability:* NFER-Nelson Publishing Co., Darville House, 2 Oxford Rd. East, Windsor, Berkshire SL4 1DF, England.
*Notes:* See also Modern Occupational Skills Tests (810683 through 810691). Time, 8.

The MOS Tests offer a wide range of assessments designed to help human resource professionals recruit and develop staff in clerical, secretarial, and administrative posts, and junior management. Flexibility is a key feature to this series, so a wide range of assessments covering different types of job content at varying levels of difficulty is provided. The tests should help employers to identify individuals who will make the most effective use of their knowledge. There are 9 tests in the series: verbal checking, numerical checking, technical checking, numerical awareness, numerical estimation, spelling and grammar, word meanings, filing, and decision making. The MOS Tests are speed tests. Numerical checking is designed to measure the ability to detect quickly and accurately, errors in various sorts of numerical data. The task does not require any arithmetical or mathematical ability and is not intellectually demanding. Useful in occupations where care has to be taken to ensure the numerical content of documents or files is accurate, such as data processors, clerks in the financial sector, some word processor operators and typists, and proofreaders.

**810687**
**Modern Occupational Skills Tests: Numerical Estimation.** Blinkhorn, Steve 1989.
*Descriptors:* *Clerical Occupations; *Computation; *Estimation (Mathematics); *Occupational Tests; *Office Occupations; *Office Practice; *Personnel Selection; *Recruitment; Adults; Foreign Countries; Office Management
*Identifiers:* England; Great Britain; MOS
*Availability:* NFER-Nelson Publishing Co., Darville House, 2 Oxford Rd. East, Windsor, Berkshire SL4 1DF, England.
*Notes:* See also Modern Occupational Skills Tests (810683 through 810691). Time, 12. Items, 20.

The MOS Tests offer a wide range of assessments designed to help human resource professionals recruit and develop staff in clerical, secretarial, and administrative posts, and junior management. Flexibility is a key feature to this series, so a wide range of assessments covering different types of job content at varying levels of difficulty is provided. The tests should help employers to identify individuals who will make the most effective use of their knowledge. There are 9 tests in the series: verbal checking, numerical checking, technical checking, numerical awareness, numerical estimation, spelling and grammar, word meanings, filing, and decision making. The MOS Tests are speed tests. Numerical Estimation is designed to measure the ability to make quick and rough approximations to complex calculations. The content of the items in this text is varied and involves numeric reasoning skills and decisions about best and quick estimates where planning of quantities is necessary. Useful in occupations such as salespersons, insurance clerks, secretaries, office managers, and many craftpersons.

**810688**
**Modern Occupational Skills Tests: Spelling and Grammar.** Blinkhorn, Steve 1989.
*Descriptors:* *Clerical Occupations; *Grammar; *Occupational Tests; *Office Occupations; *Office Practice; *Personnel Selection; *Recruitment; *Spelling; Adults; Foreign Countries; Office Management
*Identifiers:* England; Great Britain; MOS
*Availability:* NFER-Nelson Publishing Co., Darville House, 2 Oxford Rd. East, Windsor, Berkshire SL4 1DF, England.
*Notes:* See also Modern Occupational Skills Tests (810683 through 810691). Time, 8. Items, 4.

The MOS Tests offer a wide range of assessments designed to help human resource professionals recruit and develop staff in clerical, secretarial, and administrative posts, and junior management. Flexibility is a key feature to this series, so a wide range of assessments covering different types of job content at varying levels of difficulty is provided. The tests should help employers to identify individuals who will make the most effective use of their knowledge. There are 9 tests in the series: verbal checking, numerical checking, technical checking, numerical awareness, numerical estimation, spelling and grammar, word meanings, filing, and decision making. The MOS Tests are speed tests. Spelling and Grammar is designed to measure the ability to detect errors of spelling and grammar embedded in text. Prior knowledge of the correct answer facilitates recognition of the error. The spelling errors fall into the categories of letter omissions; addition of extra letters; transposition of letters; substitution of one letter for another; and misspelled words. The grammatical errors fall into the categories of verb errors; noun and pronoun errors; punctuation errors that affect meaning; preposition usage; correspondence between adjectives and adverbs; and their respective nouns and verbs. Useful in occupations that involve the production and checking of documents, such as secretaries, typists, proofreaders, word processor operators, and many types of clerks.

**810689**
**Modern Occupational Skills Tests: Technical Checking.** Blinkhorn, Steve 1989.
*Descriptors:* *Clerical Occupations; *Error Correction; *Occupational Tests; *Office Occupations; *Office Practice; *Personnel Selection; *Recruitment; Adults; Foreign Countries; Office Management
*Identifiers:* England; Great Britain; MOS; *Technical Checking
*Availability:* NFER-Nelson Publishing Co., Darville House, 2 Oxford Rd. East, Windsor, Berkshire SL4 1DF, England.
*Notes:* See also Modern Occupational Skills Tests (810683 through 810691). Time, 12. Items, 28.

The MOS Tests offer a wide range of assessments designed to help human resource professionals recruit and develop staff in clerical, secretarial, and administrative posts, and junior management. Flexibility is a key feature to this series, so a wide range of assessments covering different types of job content at varying levels of difficulty is provided. The tests should help employers to identify individuals who will make the most effective use of their knowledge. There are 9 tests in the series: verbal checking, numerical checking, technical checking, numerical awareness, numerical estimation, spelling and grammar, word meanings, filing, and decision making. The MOS Tests are speed tests. Technical checking is designed to measure the ability to detect errors when information has been changed from one form into another, for example verbal into numerical. Subjects must also be able to translate this information from one form to another. Useful in occupations where consistency of information presented in different forms is necessary, such as bank clerks, research assistants, and proofreaders of technical reports and instructional materials.

**810690**
**Modern Occupational Skills Tests: Verbal Checking.** Blinkhorn, Steve 1989.
*Descriptors:* *Clerical Occupations; *Error Correction; *Occupational Tests; *Office Occupations; *Office Practice; *Personnel Selection; *Proofreading; *Recruitment; Adults; Foreign Countries; Office Management
*Identifiers:* England; Great Britain; MOS; *Verbal Checking
*Availability:* NFER-Nelson Publishing Co., Darville House, 2 Oxford Rd. East, Windsor, Berkshire SL4 1DF, England.
*Notes:* See also Modern Occupational Skills Tests (810683 through 810691). Time, 8.

The MOS Tests offer a wide range of assessments designed to help human resource professionals recruit and develop staff in clerical, secretarial, and administrative posts, and junior management. Flexibility is a key feature to this series, so a wide range of assessments covering different types of job content at varying levels of difficulty is provided. The tests should help employers to identify individuals who will make the most effective use of their knowledge. There are 9 tests in the series: verbal checking, numerical checking, technical checking, numerical awareness, numerical estimation, spelling and grammar, word meanings, filing, and decision making. The MOS Tests are speed tests. Verbal checking is designed to give a measure of the ability to accurately and quickly detect errors in texts of various sorts. Task does not require skill in spelling or grammar. The content and layout is similar to materials found in the workplace. Useful in occupations where documents must be checked and corrected, such as secretaries, typists, clerks, data entry staff, library assistants, proofreaders, research assistants, and warehouse personnel.

**810691**
**Modern Occupational Skills Tests: Word Meanings.** Blinkhorn, Steve 1989.
*Descriptors:* *Clerical Occupations; *Occupational Tests; *Office Occupations; *Office Practice; *Personnel Selection; *Recruitment; *Semantics; *Verbal Ability; Adults; Foreign Countries; Office Management
*Identifiers:* England; Great Britain; MOS
*Availability:* NFER-Nelson Publishing Co., Darville House, 2 Oxford Rd. East, Windsor, Berkshire SL4 1DF, England.
*Notes:* See also Modern Occupational Skills Tests (810683 through 810690). Time, 12.

The MOS Tests offer a wide range of assessments designed to help human resource professionals recruit and develop staff in clerical, secretarial, and administrative posts, and junior management. Flexibility is a key feature to this series, so a wide range of assessments covering different types of job content at varying levels of difficulty is provided. The tests should help employers to identify individuals who will make the most effective use of their knowledge. There are 9 tests in the series: verbal checking, numerical checking, technical checking, numerical awareness, numerical estimation, spelling and grammar, word meanings, filing, and decision making. The MOS Tests are speed tests. Word Meanings is designed as a measure of language comprehension and word choice. This task is used to identify words used incorrectly and replace them with sensible words. Useful in occupations where staff must read and understand documents or write documents themselves. Occupations include word processor operators, secretaries, typists, office supervisors, office managers, salespersons, and many types of clerks.

**810697**
**Skillscan: Assessment in Youth Training.** Nfer Nelson Publishing Co., Windsor, England 1986.
*Descriptors:* *Communication Skills; *Problem Solving; *Trainees; Adults; Check Lists; Foreign Countries; Identification; Thinking Skills; Training Methods
*Identifiers:* England; Great Britain
*Availability:* NFER-Nelson Publishing Co., Darville House, 2 Oxford Rd. East, Windsor, Berkshire SL4 1DF, England.
*Notes:* Items, 40.

A client-centered program devised to carry out the initial assessment of trainees. It provides early recognition of individual trainees' strengths and weaknesses, and preferences. Useful in shaping decisions about initial placement and planning training programs. Consists of 2 basic components: an assignment pact for the trainee, which presents the trainee with a situation that has to be dealt with and a solution arrived at; and a user guide for the managing agent or supervisor, which interprets the answers. Numerical skills, communication (literacy skills), problem-solving skills, overall impression, and ideas for the training program, are the core skill areas assessed.

**810701**
**General Ability Tests: Non-Verbal.** Smith, Pauline; Whetton, Chris 1988.
*Descriptors:* *Aptitude Tests; *Cognitive Processes; *Nonverbal Tests; *Occupational Tests; *Personnel Selection; *Vocational Aptitude; Adults; Foreign Countries; Industrial Training
*Identifiers:* England; Great Britain; Occupational Test Series
*Availability:* NFER-Nelson Publishing Co., Darville House, 2 Oxford Rd. East, Windsor, Berkshire SL4 1DF, England.
*Notes:* Time, 15. Items, 36.

One of 4 tests in a series designed to measure reasoning and other cognitive processes for the selection and placement of employees in training courses in industry. The test measures symbolic reasoning using clasification of shapes and analogies, and series and patterns. Norms are for white male apprentices and trainees in England and Scotland. Validity and reliability data are reported. In addition, other General Ability Tests are available for the following aptitudes: spatial (810703), verbal (810704), and numerical (810702).

**810702**
**General Ability Tests: Numerical.** Smith, Pauline; Whetton, Chris 1988.
*Descriptors:* *Aptitude Tests; *Cognitive Processes; *Induction; *Mathematics Skills; *Occupational Tests; *Personnel Selection; *Vocational Aptitude; Adults; Convergent Thinking; Foreign Countries; Industrial Training
*Identifiers:* England; Great Britain; Occupational Test Series
*Availability:* NFER-Nelson Publishing Co., Darville House, 2 Oxford Rd. East, Windsor, Berkshire SL4 1DF, England.
*Notes:* Time, 15. Items, 36.

One of 4 tests in a series designed to measure reasoning and other cognitive processes for the selection and placement of employees in training courses in industry. Uses verbal analogies as a measure of inductive reasoning. Norms are for white male apprentices and trainees in England and Scotland. Validity and reliabilty data are reported. Measures the ability to understand relationships between numbers in a series and find missing numbers. Other tests cover spatial ability (810703), nonverbal ability (810701), and verbal ability (810704).

**810703**
**General Ability Tests: Spatial.** Smith, Pauline; Whetton, Chris 1988.
*Descriptors:* *Aptitude Tests; *Occupational Tests; *Personnel Selection; *Spatial Ability; *Vocational Aptitude; Adults; Cognitive Processes; Foreign Countries; Industrial Training
*Identifiers:* England; Great Britain; Occupational Test Series
*Availability:* NFER-Nelson Publishing Co., Darville House, 2 Oxford Rd. East, Windsor, Berkshire SL4 1DF, England.

*Notes:* Time, 15. Items, 80.

One of 4 tests in a series designed to measure reasoning and other cognitive processes for the selection and placement of employees in training courses in industry. Uses "surface development" tasks that involve imagining the result of folding up a flat pattern into a 3-dimensional object. Useful in occupations in the engineering, craft, design, or construction industry. Norms are for white male apprentices and trainees in England and Scotland. Validity and reliability data are reported. Other tests in the series measure the following aptitudes: numerical (810702), nonverbal (810701), and verbal (810704).

**810704**
**General Ability Tests: Verbal.** Smith, Pauline; Whetton, Chris 1988.
*Descriptors:* *Aptitude Tests; *Cognitive Processes; *Occupational Tests; *Personnel Selection; *Verbal Tests; *Vocational Aptitude; Adults; Convergent Thinking; Foreign Countries; Induction; Industrial Training
*Identifiers:* England; Great Britain; Occupational Test Series
*Availability:* NFER-Nelson Publishing Co., Darville House, 2 Oxford Rd. East, Windsor, Berkshire SL4 1DF, England.
*Notes:* Time, 15. Items, 36.

One of 4 tests in a series designed to measure reasoning and other cognitive processes for the selection and placement of employees in training courses in industry. Uses verbal analogies as a measure of inductive reasoning. Norms are for white male apprentices and trainees in England and Scotland. Validity and reliability data are reported. In addition, other General Ability Tests are available for the following aptitudes: spatial (810703); nonverbal (810701); and numerical (810702).

**810710**
**Attitude to Industry Scale.** Phillips, C.A.; And Others 1988.
*Descriptors:* *Attitude Measures; *College Students; *High School Students; *Industrial Education; *Industry; *Science Education; *Student Attitudes; Foreign Countries; Higher Education; High Schools; Likert Scales; Rating Scales; Technical Education
*Identifiers:* England; Great Britain
*Availability: Research in Science and Technological Education,* v6 n2 p145-57, 1988.
*Notes:* Items, 40.

Developed to assess the attitudes that students taking science courses containing industrial and technical materials have toward industry. Students indicate how strongly they agree or disagree with 40 statements about industry. Statements cover the social and interpersonal aspects, the cognitive and intellectual aspects, and the creative and problem-solving aspects of industry. Includes an interview schedule that assesses students' background in and general feelings about industry. Technical information is included.

**810780**
**Basic Test in World of Work.** Associated Examining Board, Surrey, England 1992.
*Descriptors:* *Achievement Tests; *Basic Skills; *Employment Potential; Foreign Countries; Secondary Education; Adults
*Identifiers:* England; Great Britain; AE
*Availability:* Associated Examining Board, Stag Hill House, Guildford, Surrey GU2 5XJ, England.
*Notes:* For other tests in the Basic Tests series, see 810781 through 810784.

The basic tests have been designed with the assistance of employers and teachers to assess the kinds of skills and knowledge required by employers in a wide range of industries. There are 2 kinds of tests: basic tests and basic tests (special). The basic tests represent a core of skills that students might study as part of a general education. Special tests meet the needs of trainees entering specific industries. There are two parts to the Basic Test in World of Work. There is a 90-minute written paper that tests students' ability to show they understand how businesses work and the role of the employer and employee within a business structure. Candidates are also assessed on a range of practical skills, including communicating orally and in writing, carrying out simple calculations, and performing simple work-related tasks. (MH)

**810781**
**Basic Test in Geography.** Associated Examining Board, Surrey, England 1992.
*Descriptors:* *Achievement Tests; *Geography; *Employment Potential; Foreign Countries; Secondary Education; Adults
*Identifiers:* England; Great Britain; AE
*Availability:* Associated Examining Board, Stag Hill House, Guildford, Surrey GU2 5XJ, England.
*Notes:* For other tests in the Basic Tests series, see 810780 through 810784.

The basic tests have been designed with the assistance of employers and teachers to assess the kinds of skills and knowledge required by employers in a wide range of industries. There are 2 kinds of tests: basic tests and basic tests (special). The basic tests represent a core of skills that students might study as part of a general education. Special tests meet the needs of trainees entering specific industries. The geography test takes 90 minutes to complete and consists of a written paper assessing a working knowledge of specified geographical locations. Test takers use a variety of maps in simulated practical situations. The final section of the test includes a number of everyday geographical locations. (MH)

**810782**
**Basic Test in Science.** Associated Examining Board, Surrey, England 1992.
*Descriptors:* *Achievement Tests; *Sciences; *Employment Potential; Foreign Countries; Secondary Education; Adults
*Identifiers:* England; Great Britain; AE
*Availability:* Associated Examining Board, Stag Hill House, Guildford, Surrey GU2 5XJ, England.
*Notes:* For other tests in the Basic Tests series, see 810780 through 810784.

The basic tests have been designed with the assistance of employers and teachers to assess the kinds of skills and knowledge required by employers in a wide range of industries. There are 2 kinds of tests: basic tests and basic tests (special). The basic tests represent a core of skills that students might study as part of a general education. Special tests meet the needs of trainees entering specific industries. The science test takes 90 minutes and covers the basic minimum knowledge and understanding required of school leavers. It is concerned with the applications of science. The written paper covers keeping fit, keeping warm, keeping mobile, keeping fed, keeping sheltered, and keeping in touch.(MH)

**810783**
**Basic Test (Special) in Geography for Tourism and Leisure.** Associated Examining Board, Surrey, England 1992.
*Descriptors:* *Achievement Tests; *Geography; *Tourism; *Employment Potential; Foreign Countries; Secondary Education; Adults
*Identifiers:* England; Great Britain; AE
*Availability:* Associated Examining Board, Stag Hill House, Guildford, Surrey GU2 5XJ, England.
*Notes:* For other tests in the Basic Tests series, see 810780 through 810784.

The basic tests have been designed with the assistance of employers and teachers to assess the kinds of skills and knowledge required by employers in a wide range of industries. There are 2 kinds of tests: basic tests and basic tests (special). The basic tests represent a core of skills that students might study as part of a general education. Special tests meet the needs of trainees entering specific industries. The test assesses locational knowledge, mapwork, and problem-solving skills appropriate to the needs of the travel, tourism, and leisure industry. The test is in 2 parts: short questions testing knowledge of special places of major tourist importance and 4 long questions based on real travel situations.(MH)

**810796**
**Fox Critical Reasoning Test—Verbal.** Fox, Glen 1992.
*Descriptors:* *Norm Referenced Tests; *Cognitive Ability; *Personnel Selection; *Managerial Occupations; *Verbal Ability; *Thinking Skills; Foreign Countries; Adults
*Identifiers:* England; Great Britain
*Availability:* Morrisby Organization, 83 High St., Hemel Hempstead, Hertfordshire, HP1 3AH, England

The Fox test is a norm-referenced test of general ability that can be used to make selection decisions on groups of applicants for managerial positions. The test consists of 20 items and takes 30 minutes to complete. It is said to be appropriate for both sexes and for all ethnic groups. Since it is a measure of verbal critical reasoning, it does require a degree of verbal educational attainment, so that those who speak English as a second language might be at a disadvantage.

**810808**
**Critical Reasoning Tests (CRT).** Smith, Pauline; Whetton, Chris 1992.
*Descriptors:* *Managerial Occupations; *Personnel Selection; *Critical Thinking; Information Processing; Adults
*Availability:* NFER-Nelson Publishing Co., Darville House, 2 Oxford Rd. East, Windsor, Berkshire SL4 1DF, England.

The Critical Reasoning Tests (CRT) are designed for use in the selection of entry-level or middle managers or executives. The tests assess key intellectual skills that are needed for success in any managerial occupation. There are 2 assessments, verbal and numerical, related by a common scenario which provides the context for the questions that deal with the activities of a fictitious commercial company. The verbal test measures information processing situations. The numerical test measures the interpretation of numerical information. Both tests use questions that require the test taker to recognize that insufficient data has been provided for a definitive answer to be reached. Norms are provided. (JW)

**830366**
**L'Orientation Par Soi-Meme.** Holland, John L. 1980.
*Descriptors:* *Career Guidance; *French; *Interest Inventories; *Self Evaluation (Individuals); *Vocational Interests; Adolescents; Adults; Foreign Countries; High School Students
*Identifiers:* Canada; Holland (John L); Self Directed Search
*Availability:* Guidance Centre, Faculty of Education, University of Toronto, 252 Bloor St. West, Toronto, Ontario M5S 2Y3, Canada.
*Notes:* Time, 60 approx. Items, 192.

French language version of the Self-Directed Search, a self-administered counseling aid based on Holland's theory of vocational choice. Determines a person's resemblance to 6 occupational types.

**830399**
**Canadian Occupational Interest Inventory.** Begin, Luc; Lavallee, Luc 1982.
*Descriptors:* *Career Counseling; *Interest Inventories; *Vocational Interests; Adults; Forced Choice Technique; Foreign Countries
*Identifiers:* Canada; COII
*Availability:* Nelson Canada, 1120 Birchmount Rd., Scarborough, Ontario M1K 5G4, Canada.
*Notes:* Time, 40 approx. Items, 70.

Designed for use in career counseling to assist individuals in determining occupations from which they would derive the greatest satisfaction. May be administered to groups or individuals. There are 14 items related to each of 5 interest factors: things-people, business contact-scientific, routine-creative, social-solitary, and prestige-production.

# SUBJECT INDEX

**Employer Attitudes**



**Employer Employee Relationship**



**Employment Interviews**



**Employment Potential**



**Employment Qualifications**



**Empowerment**



**Energy**



**Energy Audits**



**Energy Occupations**



**Engineering**



**Engineering Education**



**Engineering Technicians**



**Engineers**



**English**



**English Literature**



**English (Second Language)**



**Entrepreneurship**



**Entry Workers**

**Occupational Therapists**



**Office Machines**



**Office Management**



**Office Occupations**



**Office Practice**



**Oncology**



**Online Systems**



**Optometry**



**Oral Tests**



**Organizational Change**



**Organizational Climate**

**Pharmaceutical Education**



**Pharmacists**



**Pharmacology**



**Pharmacy**



**Philosophy**



**Photographs**

# AUTHOR INDEX

# TITLE INDEX